36: *British Novelists, 1890-1929: Modernists,* edited by Thomas F. Staley (1985)

37: *American Writers of the Early Republic,* edited by Emory Elliott (1985)

38: *Afro-American Writers After 1955: Dramatists and Prose Writers,* edited by Thadious M. Davis and Trudier Harris (1985)

39: *British Novelists, 1660-1800,* 2 parts, edited by Martin C. Battestin (1985)

40: *Poets of Great Britain and Ireland Since 1960,* 2 parts, edited by Vincent B. Sherry, Jr. (1985)

41: *Afro-American Poets Since 1955,* edited by Trudier Harris and Thadious M. Davis (1985)

42: *American Writers for Children Before 1900,* edited by Glenn E. Estes (1985)

43: *American Newspaper Journalists, 1690-1872,* edited by Perry J. Ashley (1986)

44: *American Screenwriters,* Second Series, edited by Randall Clark, Robert E. Morsberger, and Stephen O. Lesser (1986)

45: *American Poets, 1880-1945,* First Series, edited by Peter Quartermain (1986)

46: *American Literary Publishing Houses, 1900-1980: Trade and Paperback,* edited by Peter Dzwonkoski (1986)

47: *American Historians, 1866-1912,* edited by Clyde N. Wilson (1986)

48: *American Poets, 1880-1945,* Second Series, edited by Peter Quartermain (1986)

49: *American Literary Publishing Houses, 1638-1899,* 2 parts, edited by Peter Dzwonkoski (1986)

50: *Afro-American Writers Before the Harlem Renaissance,* edited by Trudier Harris (1986)

51: *Afro-American Writers from the Harlem Renaissance to 1940,* edited by Trudier Harris (1987)

52: *American Writers for Children Since 1960: Fiction,* edited by Glenn E. Estes (1986)

53: *Canadian Writers Since 1960,* First Series, edited by W. H. New (1986)

54: *American Poets, 1880-1945,* Third Series, 2 parts, edited by Peter Quartermain (1987)

55: *Victorian Prose Writers Before 1867,* edited by William B. Thesing (1987)

56: *German Fiction Writers, 1914-1945,* edited by James Hardin (1987)

57: *Victorian Prose Writers After 1867,* edited by William B. Thesing (1987)

58: *Jacobean and Caroline Dramatists,* edited by Fredson Bowers (1987)

59: *American Literary Critics and Scholars, 1800-1850,* edited by John W. Rathbun and Monica M. Grecu (1987)

60: *Canadian Writers Since 1960,* Second Series, edited by W. H. New (1987)

61: *American Writers for Children Since 1960: Poets, Illustrators, and Nonfiction Authors,* edited by Glenn E. Estes (1987)

62: *Elizabethan Dramatists,* edited by Fredson Bowers (1987)

63: *Modern American Critics, 1920-1955,* edited by Gregory S. Jay (1988)

64: *American Literary Critics and Scholars, 1850-1880,* edited by John W. Rathbun and Monica M. Grecu (1988)

65: *French Novelists, 1900-1930,* edited by Catharine Savage Brosman (1988)

66: *German Fiction Writers, 1885-1913,* 2 parts, edited by James Hardin (1988)

67: *Modern American Critics Since 1955,* edited by Gregory S. Jay (1988)

68: *Canadian Writers, 1920-1959,* First Series, edited by W. H. New (1988)

69: *Contemporary German Fiction Writers,* First Series, edited by Wolfgang D. Elfe and James Hardin (1988)

70: *British Mystery Writers, 1860-1919,* edited by Bernard Benstock and Thomas F. Staley (1988)

(Continued on back endsheets)

Canadian Writers, 1890-1920

Dictionary of Literary Biography • Volume Ninety-two

Canadian Writers, 1890-1920

Edited by
W. H. New
University of British Columbia

8232

A Bruccoli Clark Layman Book
Gale Research Inc.
Detroit, New York, London

Manufactured by Edward Brothers, Inc.
Ann Arbor, Michigan
Printed in the United States of America

Library of Congress Cataloging-in-Publication Data

Canadian writers, 1890-1920/edited by W. H. New.
    p. cm.–(Dictionary of literary biography; v. 92)
    "A Bruccoli Clark Layman book."
    ISBN 0-8103-4572-2
    1. Canadian literature–Dictionaries. 2. Canadian
literature–Bio-bibliography. 3. French-Canadian literature–
Dictionaries. 4. French-Canadian literature–Bio-bibliog-
raphy. 5. Authors, Canadian–Biography–Dictionaries.
I. New, William H. II. Series.
PR9180.2.C37 1990
810.9'003–dc20
[B]
                                                        89-48355
                                                        CIP

Contents

Plan of the Series...ix

Foreword xi

Acknowledgments...xv

Grant Allen (1848-1899) 3
   Paul Matthew St. Pierre

Olivar Asselin (1874-1937) 10
   Michel Gaulin

Marius Barbeau (1883-1969) 13
   Edith Fowke

Robert Barr (1850-1912).................................17
   John Parr

Nérée Beauchemin (1850-1931) 24
   Jack Warwick

Harry Bernard (1898-1979)..............................26
   Rosanna Furgiuele

Adèle Bibaud (1854-1941) 29
   Mary Jean Green

Georges Bugnet (1879-1981) 30
   E. D. Blodgett

Arthur de Bussières (1877-1913)......................33
   Maurice Lebel

William Wilfred Campbell (1858-1918) 35
   Carl F. Klinck

Bliss Carman (1861-1929) 38
   Donald Stephens

Jean Charbonneau (1875-1960) 45
   Peyton Brien

René Chopin (1885-1953) 48
   Kathleen L. Kellett

Ralph Connor (Charles William Gordon)
(1860-1937)...50
   Michael Hurley

Maurice Constantin-Weyer (1881-1964) 56
   John J. O'Connor

Isabella Valancy Crawford (1850-1887) 63
   Carole Gerson

Louis Dantin (Eugène Seers) (1865-1945)..........69
   Hans R. Runte

Frank Parker Day (1881-1950) 72
   Eric Thompson

Guy Delahaye (Guillaume Lahaise)
(1888-1969)..75
   Alexandre L. Amprimoz

Merrill Denison (1893-1975)............................77
   Chris Johnson

Gonzalve Desaulniers (1863-1934)....................82
   Jean-Guy Hudon

Lily Dougall (1858-1923) 85
   Lorraine McMullen

William Henry Drummond (1854-1907)...........88
   Paul Matthew St. Pierre

Marcel Dugas (1883-1947) 91
   Alexandre L. Amprimoz

Norman Duncan (1871-1916) 94
   Janet Giltrow

Sara Jeannette Duncan (1861-1922)...................97
   Thomas E. Tausky

Wilfrid Eggleston (1901-1986).........................105
   David Ingham

Hubert Evans (1892-1986) 108
   Catherine McLay

Albert Ferland (1872-1943)..............................111
   Maurice Lebel

Françoise (Robertine Barry) (1863-1910).........115
   Mary Jean Green

John Murray Gibbon (1875-1952) 117
   Terrence Craig

Rodolphe Girard (1879-1956)..........................120
   Valerie Raoul

Martin Allerdale Grainger (1874-1941) 124
   Carole Gerson

Alain Grandbois (1900-1975)...........................127
   David F. Rogers

Wilfred Thomason Grenfell (1865-1940) 132
   Neil K. Besner

Grey Owl (Archibald Stansfeld Belaney)
(1888-1938)..137
   Stanley E. McMullin

Frederick Philip Grove (Felix Paul Greve)
(1879-1948)..143
   Walter Pache

Contents

Louis Hémon (1880-1913) 156
  Larry Shouldice

William Albert Hickman (1877-1957) 159
  Paul Matthew St. Pierre

Pauline Johnson (1861-1913) 162
  Donald A. Precosky

Alice C. Jones (1853-1933) 165
  Gwendolyn Davies

Marian Keith (Mary Esther MacGregor)
  (1874?-1961) 169
  Misao Dean

Archibald Lampman (1861-1899) 172
  Bruce Nesbitt

Napoléon-P. Landry (1884-1956) 179
  Hans R. Runte

Agnes Christina Laut (1871-1936) 181
  Carole Gerson

Stephen Leacock (1869-1944) 184
  Louis K. MacKendrick

James Le Rossignol (1866-1969) 196
  John Stockdale

William Dawson LeSueur (1840-1917) 198
  Clifford G. Holland

William Douw Lighthall (1857-1954) 201
  Paul Matthew St. Pierre

Florence Randal Livesay (1874-1953) 205
  Carole Gerson

Jean-Aubert Loranger (1896-1942) 208
  Maurice Lebel

Albert Lozeau (1878-1924) 211
  Jacqueline Viswanathan

Madge Macbeth (1880-1965) 213
  Carole Gerson

Wilson MacDonald (1880-1967) 216
  Richard Duprey

Agnes Maule Machar (1837-1927) 220
  Carole Gerson

Isabel Ecclestone MacKay (1875-1928) 222
  Diana M. A. Relke

Andrew Macphail (1864-1938) 225
  Paul Matthew St. Pierre

Frère Marie-Victorin (Conrad Kirouac)
  (1885-1944) 228
  Michel Gaulin

Peter McArthur (1866-1924) 232
  John Lennox

Nellie Letitia McClung (1873-1951) 234
  Hilda L. Thomas

John McCrae (1872-1918) 237
  Carole Gerson

Jean Newton McIlwraith (1859-1938) 239
  Misao Dean

William McLennan (1856-1904) 242
  Neil K. Besner

Lucy Maud Montgomery (1874-1942) 246
  Frances Frazer

Louvigny de Montigny (1876-1955) 254
  David F. Rogers

Dora Mavor Moore (1888-1979) 257
  Paul Leonard

Paul Morin (1889-1963) 259
  Evelyne Voldeng

Jean Narrache (Emile Coderre)
  (1893-1970) 261
  Alexandre L. Amprimoz

Emile Nelligan (1879-1941) 265
  Kathy Mezei

Frederick John Niven (1878-1944) 271
  W. H. New

Robert Norwood (1874-1932) 276
  R. Alex Kizuk

Martha Ostenso (1900-1963) 279
  Anthony John Harding

Marjorie Pickthall (1883-1922) 285
  Donald A. Precosky

E. J. Pratt (1882-1964) 287
  Michael Darling

Adjutor Rivard (1868-1945) 298
  Margot Northey

Charles G. D. Roberts (1860-1943) 301
  Patricia Morley

Theodore Goodridge Roberts
  (1877-1953) 309
  Neil K. Besner

Camille Roy (1870-1943) 314
  Susan Jackel

Laura Goodman Salverson (1890-1970) 316
  Paul Hjartarson

B. K. Sandwell (1876-1954) 319
  John Lennox

Edward Sapir (1884-1939) 322
  Regna Darnell

Margaret Marshall Saunders (1861-1947)........327
Carole Gerson

Duncan Campbell Scott (1862-1947)..............331
Leon Slonim

Frederick George Scott (1861-1944)..............337
Sandra A. Djwa

Eva Senécal (1905-   )........................340
Mary Jean Green

Robert Service (1874-1958)....................342
Carl F. Klinck and W. H. New

Ernest Thompson Seton (1860-1946)..............349
Patricia Morley

Francis Sherman (1871-1926)...................355
Robert Gibbs

Jessie Georgina Sime (1868-1958) 356
W. H. New

Bertrand William Sinclair (1881-1972) 362
Laurie Ricou

Constance Lindsay Skinner (1877-1939)..........366
Diana M. A. Relke

Robert J. C. Stead (1880-1959).................370
Margery Fee

Arthur Stringer (1874-1950)...................374
Dick Harrison

Alan Sullivan (1868-1947).....................378
W. H. New

Edward William Thomson (1849-1924)..........385
Eric Thompson

Joanna Ellen Wood (1867-1927)................388
Carole Gerson

Supplementary Reading List....................391

Contributors................................401

Cumulative Index............................405

Plan of the Series

. . . Almost the most prodigious asset of a country, and perhaps its most precious possession, is its native literary product—when that product is fine and noble and enduring.

Mark Twain*

The advisory board, the editors, and the publisher of the *Dictionary of Literary Biography* are joined in endorsing Mark Twain's declaration. The literature of a nation provides an inexhaustible resource of permanent worth. We intend to make literature and its creators better understood and more accessible to students and the reading public, while satisfying the standards of teachers and scholars.

To meet these requirements, *literary biography* has been construed in terms of the author's achievement. The most important thing about a writer is his writing. Accordingly, the entries in *DLB* are career biographies, tracing the development of the author's canon and the evolution of his reputation.

The purpose of *DLB* is not only to provide reliable information in a convenient format but also to place the figures in the larger perspective of literary history and to offer appraisals of their accomplishments by qualified scholars.

The publication plan for *DLB* resulted from two years of preparation. The project was proposed to Bruccoli Clark by Frederick G. Ruffner, president of the Gale Research Company, in November 1975. After specimen entries were prepared and typeset, an advisory board was formed to refine the entry format and develop the series rationale. In meetings held during 1976, the publisher, series editors, and advisory board approved the scheme for a comprehensive biographical dictionary of persons who contributed to North American literature. Editorial work on the first volume began in January 1977, and it was published in 1978. In order to make *DLB* more than a reference tool and to compile volumes that individually have claim to status as literary history, it was decided to organize volumes by topic, period, or genre. Each of these freestanding volumes provides a biographical-bibliographical guide and overview for a particular area of literature. We are convinced that this organization—as opposed to a single alphabet method—constitutes a valuable innovation in the presentation of reference material. The volume plan necessarily requires many decisions for the placement and treatment of authors who might properly be included in two or three volumes. In some instances a major figure will be included in separate volumes, but with different entries emphasizing the aspect of his career appropriate to each volume. Ernest Hemingway, for example, is represented in *American Writers in Paris, 1920-1939* by an entry focusing on his expatriate apprenticeship; he is also in *American Novelists, 1910-1945* with an entry surveying his entire career. Each volume includes a cumulative index of subject authors and articles. Comprehensive indexes to the entire series are planned.

With volume ten in 1982 it was decided to enlarge the scope of *DLB*. By the end of 1986 twenty-one volumes treating British literature had been published, and volumes for Commonwealth and Modern European literature were in progress. The series has been further augmented by the *DLB Yearbooks* (since 1981) which update published entries and add new entries to keep the *DLB* current with contemporary activity. There have also been *DLB Documentary Series* volumes which provide biographical and critical source materials for figures whose work is judged to have particular interest for students. One of these companion volumes is entirely devoted to Tennessee Williams.

We define literature as the *intellectual commerce of a nation*: not merely as belles lettres but as that ample and complex process by which ideas are generated, shaped, and transmitted. *DLB* entries are not limited to "creative writers" but extend to other figures who in their time and in their way influenced the mind of a people. Thus the series encompasses historians, journalists, publishers, and screenwriters. By this means readers of *DLB* may be aided to perceive litera-

*From an unpublished section of Mark Twain's autobiography, copyright © by the Mark Twain Company.

ture not as cult scripture in the keeping of intellectual high priests but firmly positioned at the center of a nation's life.

DLB includes the major writers appropriate to each volume and those standing in the ranks immediately behind them. Scholarly and critical counsel has been sought in deciding which minor figures to include and how full their entries should be. Wherever possible, useful references are made to figures who do not warrant separate entries.

Each *DLB* volume has a volume editor responsible for planning the volume, selecting the figures for inclusion, and assigning the entries. Volume editors are also responsible for preparing, where appropriate, appendices surveying the major periodicals and literary and intellectual movements for their volumes, as well as lists of further readings. Work on the series as a whole is coordinated at the Bruccoli Clark Layman editorial center in Columbia, South Carolina, where the editorial staff is responsible for accuracy of the published volumes.

One feature that distinguishes *DLB* is the illustration policy—its concern with the iconography of literature. Just as an author is influenced by his surroundings, so is the reader's understanding of the author enhanced by a knowledge of his environment. Therefore *DLB* volumes include not only drawings, paintings, and photographs of authors, often depicting them at various stages in their careers, but also illustrations of their families and places where they lived. Title pages are regularly reproduced in facsimile along with dust jackets for modern authors. The dust jackets are a special feature of *DLB* because they often document better than anything else the way in which an author's work was perceived in its own time. Specimens of the writers' manuscripts are included when feasible.

Samuel Johnson rightly decreed that "The chief glory of every people arises from its authors." The purpose of the *Dictionary of Literary Biography* is to compile literary history in the surest way available to us—by accurate and comprehensive treatment of the lives and work of those who contributed to it.

The *DLB* Advisory Board

Foreword

This volume is the fifth in a series devoted to Canadian writers whose primary language is English or French. (For the others see volumes 53, 60, 68, and 88.) Concentrating on the period 1890-1920, this volume focuses on writers who came to prominence at this time, and on several additional writers whose careers were substantially shaped by the events of the three decades, events such as immigration, political demonstration, and war. Overall, the volume concerns itself with the effects of a new literary nationalism on literary endeavor in Canada, and with the politics of criticism and resistance. For this was a period when masculine, English, and European values shaped what was thought of as the "national tradition"—and when feminist, regional, and francophone causes were beginning to declare their opposition. It was a period when urban realities opposed wilderness romances; when the social proprieties of literary convention (expressed in both style and subject) ran up against the blunt experience of war, poverty, and social unrest; when nation began to question empire; and when satire tried to unseat sentimentality. But it was also a period when wilderness convention and historical romance still constituted the literary vogue.

By 1890 the new nation of Canada was establishing itself as a separate continental society. It had acquired independence from Britain in 1867 and was expanding west to the prairies and the Pacific coast. The Canada First Movement had been founded in 1868 and by the end of the century was developing into the Imperial Federation Movement (a political ideal espoused by Sara Jeannette Duncan). Indirectly, Canada First values—Protestant and Ontario-centered as they were—would also lend strength to the Nationaliste Movement in Quebec, a francophone separatist movement led by Henri Bourassa. Other developments confirmed the image of national self-possession. The Royal Northwest Mounted Police had been founded in 1873 and sent to the prairie territories by the federal government to guarantee social stability as the new railway encouraged settlement westward. The telephone had been invented by Brantford's Alexander Graham Bell in 1876, revolutionizing communications techniques. Calixa Lavallée had composed the new national anthem, "O Canada," in 1880 (though it would be almost a century before English words were officially adopted). The Canadian Pacific Railway was completed in 1885, becoming a symbol of national unity, though in the same year the millenarian Métis leader Louis Riel was hanged, becoming a symbol of francophone martyrdom. In many ways the nation appeared to be turning from a frontier past to a "civilized," "ordered" conventionality. "Development" was a social ideal, and many urban dwellers were learning to take Victorian and Edwardian comforts for granted. Yet there remained sources of unrest, which World War I would soon intensify.

Women's organizations in the 1890s, for example—from the Women's Christian Temperance Union, to the Toronto Women's Literary Club (founded in 1876 by Dr. Emily Stowe), to the Halifax societies founded by Anna Leonowens, to the campaigns led by Cora Hind, Nellie McClung, and the francophone journalist Robertine Barry (Françoise)—actively espoused such causes as suffrage reform. Yet when women did get the vote federally, during World War I, it was granted at the outset as a strategy to serve a different aim: the first women to acquire voting privileges were those with husbands and sons in the armed forces. On military involvements, as on other issues, Canada divided on linguistic and cultural grounds. Quebeckers largely opposed participation in the "English" war and actively resisted conscription. Hence the political opposition to "les anglais"—articulated by Jules-Paul Tardivel in his 1895 novel *Pour la patrie*—intensified during the war in *Nationaliste* calls for separation. The early works of Harry Bernard and later conservative political works, such as those of Jean Narrache, derive directly from this position.

Ethnic divisiveness surfaced in other ways as well, most violently during the 1914 *Komagata Maru* incident, when the government refused to let a boatload of Sikh immigrants land in Vancouver; Asian-Canadians were disenfranchised; and native Canadians had little except exotic status, as when the poet Pauline Johnson achieved fame as an Iroquois "princess." The strong biases in favor of Europe took many forms. But when Prime Minister Wilfrid Laurier's minister of the interior, Sir Clifford Sifton, managed to attract numerous East European and Ukrainian settlers to the prairies, he was complicating rather than simplifying the national cultural mix. Personally, he favored the absorption of minorities into what he accepted as the cultural mainstream (he considered the Ukrainians "peasants" and the prairies "empty"), but his actions had other consequences. They led to the further alienation of native groups from their ancestral lands, and they would lead over the course of many years to a questioning of the validity of the received mainstream itself. By the 1920s writers such as Martha Ostenso and Laura Goodman Salverson (both with a Scandinavian background) and Evelyn Eaton and Winnifred Reeve (sisters with part-Japanese backgrounds) were emerging to claim the distinctiveness that a non-Anglo-Celtic (and non-francophone) heritage could provide.

One of the many English-speaking immigrant writers at this time, Martin Allerdale Grainger, produced *Woodsmen of the West* (1908), one of the first effective fictions from British Columbia. A tale of the logging industry, the book portrayed experience realistically. On the east coast, works by Norman Duncan and Wilfred Grenfell demonstrated that the exigencies of Newfoundland and outport life could also be represented accurately, and that artistry and "realism" were not mutually exclusive terms. Such books were early attempts to counter the national cultural norms that were being shaped primarily within Ontario and Quebec, and also the conventions of romance that had become the staples of cultural distortion. Popular literature most obviously reveals the stereotypes. William Henry Drummond's *The Habitant* (1897) typifies anglophone suspicions of Quebec Catholicism, and they dismiss what they perceive to be rural simplicity, just as Tardivel's novel exaggerated the threat and the wickedness of Ontario Protestantism. Robert Service's ebullient Yukon rhymes sketched a cardboard North. Ralph Connor's stock Presbyterians earned guaranteed success, in such novels as *The Man from Glengarry* (1901), because of their Christian manliness (terms that are forceful reminders of two hierarchies of social value). Fiction by the French writer Louis Hémon (and later by Georges Bugnet, a 1905 immigrant, and

Maurice Constantin-Weyer, who immigrated in 1907) also sentimentalized francophone custom; for that very reason, Hémon's *Maria Chapdelaine* (1916) became an instant classic: to a francophone readership it was a testament to faith and martyrdom, to an anglophone readership a tale of backwardness and bucolic romance. Frederick John Niven's early potboilers (though his later novels analyzed more credibly the social pressures of immigrant communities in Canada and mercantile philistinism in Scotland) drew heavily on American wild-west conventions. Another writer, Arthur Stringer–best remembered, perhaps, as the author behind the "Perils of Pauline" serial films–extended stereotypes to portraits of women and the lives of settlers. Against all such images, serious writers were trying variously to contend.

One response involved humor. Stephen Leacock is only the most familiar name among a group of writers who were satirizing the pretentiousness of a colonial society aspiring to cosmopolitanism, as in his *Sunshine Sketches of a Little Town* (1912). Other humorists include Sara Jeannette Duncan, E. W. Thomson, Grant Allen, Albert Hickman, Peter McArthur (who contributed frequently to *Punch*), Robert Barr (who collaborated with Jerome K. Jerome in the *Idler*), and (of more consequence because his direct satiric target was the Catholic clergy) Rodolphe Girard in *Marie Calumet* (1908).

On another front Duncan Campbell Scott, author of *In the Village of Viger* (1896), exposed the limitations of sentimental representations of Quebec; Frère Marie-Victorian made his name both as realist and botanical linguist; Adjutor Rivard (in *Chez Nous*, 1914) confronted the specificities of town life. In poetry the "Groupe-des-six-éponges," which became "L'école littéraire de Montréal" in 1895 and involved Arthur de Bussières, Gonzalve Desaulniers, Albert Ferland, Nérée Beauchemin, and Emile Nelligan, sought to adapt symbolist techniques to Quebec landscapes; indeed the gifted and thwarted mad youth Nelligan became over the course of time a cultural symbol himself, an evocation of a creative identity martyred by the forces that held him captive, a nationalist symbol for an *indépendantiste* Quebec. The distinguished critic Olivar Asselin, moreover, demonstrated the complexities of Quebec's cultural history.

Third, against the distorted portraits of women, women themselves were to rebel, as in the work of Sara Jeannette Duncan (possibly the most accomplished prose stylist of the period, noted for her trans-Atlantic comedies and her studies of the manners and mores of the Anglo-Indian civil service). There were others: among them, Agnes Maule Machar (Fidelis: a Salvation Army apologist), Alice Jones, Adèle Bibaud, Nellie McClung, as well as Marjorie Pickthall and later Eva Sénécal in poetry, Dora Mavor Moore in drama, and Agnes Christina Laut in criticism.

Yet the literary practice of Pickthall and McClung—and of two leading children's writers, Margaret Marshall Saunders and Lucy Maud Montgomery—raises at the same time questions about the function of sentimentality as a literary technique. Many critics either dismissed it altogether or praised it selectively as a sign of "feeling" in the work of women writers. McClung, however, was to use it as a deliberate ploy; her *Sowing Seeds in Danny* (1908) sold one hundred thousand copies to a public eager for tender romance—hence the novel served the author's main purpose, for its narrative reached its intended audience, carefully urging female readers to be dissatisfied with the social status quo. Montgomery's *Anne of Green Gables* (1908) and other works—although the most realistic of Montgomery's writings were her extraordinary letters, published posthumously—likewise argued for opportunities for women and asserted women's ability to manage their own lives with intelligence and wit.

In many respects the forces such writers were resisting are exemplified best by the writings most celebrated during these years, the poems and tales of the so-called "Confederation Group." The central members of this loose assembly included Sir Charles G. D. Roberts, whose first volume of poetry (published in 1880) encouraged others to write; his cousin Bliss Carman, a devotee of rhythmic chant and open-road enthusiasm, later imitated by Wilson MacDonald; D. C. Scott; Archibald Lampman; and Wilfred Campbell. Sometimes Isabella Valancy Crawford is critically associated with them. Of their poems, those that are generally most celebrated focus on the natural world, discovering in a local landscape a symbolic counterpart for a state of mind, a resonance with the human condition. Influenced as much by American transcendentalism (Emerson was a distant relative of Carman) as by Victorian romanticism, these writers represented a shift away from the artifice of elevated diction that had characterized many Canadian writings of the earlier nineteenth century, yet they were by no means radical. An obvious but much less re-

marked feature of their work is its reliance on classical allusions. And socially the writers tended to be conservative. Scott, working in the federal Department of Indian Affairs, rejected the appeals of nativism; he presumed the inevitability and the value of the total assimilation of the native peoples into a European system of values. Moreover, though most of the Confederation Group disputed established church practices, they did not spurn some form of religious belief; and while they sought to legitimize in art the local scene, they remained faithful to such ideal absolutes as beauty. Theirs was a frame of reference that conservative critics could appreciate, a set of familiar values that would govern much Canadian criticism well past 1920, as in the influential reviews and editorial judgments of John Murray Gibbon, and B. K. Sandwell.

The Confederation writers' prose reconfirms this position. Roberts's work particularly (in the novels and the animal stories, such as *Kindred of the Wild*, 1902) portrays a "nature red in tooth and claw" with which human beings could identify and yet to which they could feel morally and intellectually superior. Parallel works include the stories by Roberts's brother Theodore and those by Ernest Thompson Seton, all of them influencing such later writers as Alan Sullivan, Hubert Evans, and Grey Owl (A. S. Belaney), the last of whom had immigrated to Canada in 1906 to assume his identity as an "Indian" naturalist. The term "human beings," however, has to be understood as the Confederation writers' generalization for "men"; theirs was fundamentally a hierarchical scheme in which women played only a contributory role. "Nature," the wilderness, was deemed a territory for men to know. Because these writers also equated the wilderness with the new nation, made it out to be the distinctive feature of Canada, this version of Canadian social character came to function politically in more ways than one. Those writers such as S. J. Duncan, who had a shrewd eye for urban realities, might dispute the Confederation writers' wilderness norms, and the socialist poet Dorothy Livesay would actively oppose them in the 1920s and 1930s; but for the general public, the wilderness proved an appealing image of identity. Romantic versions of nature long influenced the terms of Canadian critical assessment, and an idealized version of nature long continued (even after 1920: as in the "agricultural ideology" of Harry Bernard or in the Acadian writings of

Napoléon-P. Landry) to feature as a literary setting.

The careers of two apparently more modern writers—Frederick Philip Grove and E. J. Pratt—testify to this continuing appeal. While both continued their careers well into mid century, they both became established before 1920 and remained deeply affected by late-nineteenth-century values. The Newfoundlander Pratt, long perceived as the foremost national poet and a writer of epics, is more readily recognized after the fact as a lyrical romance writer, shaped by Darwinian science, Methodist theology, and Newfoundland tall-tale traditions. The German-born Grove (who suppressed his real identity as Felix Paul Greve when he disappeared from Europe and resurfaced with a new name in Manitoba) appeared on the surface to celebrate naturalism and knowledge and to reject social conventions, yet at heart he remained the European romantic, in love at once with a heroic version of wilderness America and with the opportunity to establish himself in the new land as landed gentry. Political contradictions abound.

Despite these glimpses of a controllable wilderness and a secure paradigm of ownership, the world was changing, and Canada with it. Canada entered World War I automatically, as part of the empire, but left it as a separate signatory to the Treaty of Paris. The nation was asking to be internationally recognized. Imperial values continued to be expressed—Leacock continued to write, as did Mazo de la Roche, and numerous novelists sentimental about the past, including Wilfred Eggleston, and Frank Parker Day, but the Imperial Round Table Movement, to which Leacock belonged, did not long survive. One of Leacock's friends, John McCrae, author of "In Flanders Fields," died during the war. Another, Andrew Macphail, closed down the *University Magazine* in 1920 because a readership keen on imperial values had disappeared. Georgina Sime, in *Sister Woman* (1919), was portraying a different kind of urban reality: one that for women was marked by stillbirths, abortion, penury, failed marriage, and lies.

By the end of the war Edward Sapir and Marius Barbeau were beginning to analyze the nature of language, native culture, and folk customs, extending the range of what was conventionally understood by the word "literature." Merrill Denison and Madge Macbeth were experimenting with satire. The 1917 revolution in Russia gave prominence to ideas that Communist writers such as Joe Wallace would later espouse and conservatives such as Robert Service would oppose. In 1918 Alain Grandbois set off on the travels that would result in his influential poetry. The 1919 general strike in Winnipeg, moreover, signaled that society was as volatile at home as abroad, and that civil disparities bred social unrest. In such contexts a new generation of writers was about to turn Canadian writing in several different directions.

—W. H. New

Acknowledgments

This book was produced by Bruccoli Clark Layman, Inc. Karen L. Rood is senior editor for the *Dictionary of Literary Biography* series. Jack Turner and Margaret A. Van Antwerp were the in-house editors.

Production coordinator is James W. Hipp. Systems manager is Charles D. Brower. Photography editor is Susan Todd. Jean W. Ross is permissions editor. Layout and graphics supervisor is Penney L. Haughton. Copyediting supervisor is Bill Adams. Typesetting supervisor is Kathleen M. Flanagan. Typography coordinator is Sheri Beckett Neal. Information Systems Analyst is George F. Dodge. Charles Lee Egleston and Laura Ingram are editorial associates. The production staff includes Rowena Betts, Anne L. M. Bowman, Teresa Chaney, Patricia Coate, Sarah A. Estes, Mary L. Goodwin, Willie M. Gore, Cynthia Hallman, Susan C. Heath, David Marshall James, Kathy S. Merlette, Laura Garren Moore, John Myrick, Laurrè Sinckler, Jennifer Toth, Pascale Thiery, and Betsy L. Weinberg.

Walter W. Ross and Parris Boyd did the library research with the assistance of the reference staff at the Thomas Cooper Library of the University of South Carolina: Gwen Baxter, Daniel Boice, Faye Chadwell, Cathy Eckman, Gary Geer, Cathie Gottlieb, David L. Haggard, Jens Holley, Jackie Kinder, Marcia Martin, Laurie Preston, Jean Rhyne, Carol Tobin, and Virginia Weathers.

John Stockdale, author of the entry on James Le Rossignol, expresses his gratitude to Helen Dvoraceh, Gabrielle Slotsue, and Violet L. Matte, relatives of Le Rossignol, and to Dean Gary Schwendiman, College of Business Administration, University of Nebraska.

The editor expresses special thanks to the Harry Ransom Humanities Research Center, University of Texas at Austin, to Joe Jones of the University of British Columbia Library (Humanities Division), and to Robin Van Heck, Leslie Gentes, Eva-Marie Kröller, Eric Thompson, Carole Gerson, Jane Watt, and Beverly Westbrook. Nicky Drumbolis of Letters, Steven Temple of Steven Temple Books, and Kenneth Landry of the *Dictionnaire des œuvres littéraires du Québec* have provided valuable assistance in securing illustrative materials.

Dictionary of Literary Biography • Volume Ninety-two

Canadian Writers, 1890-1920

Dictionary of Literary Biography

Grant Allen
(24 February 1848-28 October 1899)

Paul Matthew St. Pierre
Simon Fraser University

See also the Allen entry in *DLB 70: British Mystery Writers, 1860-1919.*

BOOKS: *Physiological Aesthetics* (London: King, 1877; New York: Appleton, 1877);

The Colour-Sense: Its Origin and Development (Boston: Houghton, Osgood, 1879; London: Trübner, 1879);

Anglo-Saxon Britain (London: Society for Promoting Christian Knowledge, 1881; New York: Young, 1881);

The Evolutionist at Large (London: Chatto & Windus, 1881; New York: Fitzgerald, 1881; revised, London: Chatto & Windus, 1884);

Vignettes from Nature (London: Chatto & Windus, 1881; New York: Fitzgerald, 1882);

The Colours of Flowers as Illustrated in the British Flora (London: Macmillan, 1882; London & New York: Macmillan, 1891);

Colin Clout's Calendar: The Record of a Summer, April-October (London: Chatto & Windus, 1883; New York: Funk & Wagnalls, 1883);

Flowers and Their Pedigrees (London: Longmans, 1883; New York: Appleton, 1884);

Biographies of Working Men (London: Society for Promoting Christian Knowledge, 1884; London: Society for Promoting Christian Knowledge/New York: Young, 1885);

Philistia, as Cecil Power (London: Chatto & Windus, 1884; New York: Munro, 1884);

Strange Stories (London: Chatto & Windus, 1884);

Babylon, as Power (3 volumes, London: Chatto & Windus, 1885; 1 volume, New York: Appleton, 1885); as Allen (London: Chatto & Windus, 1893);

Charles Darwin (London: Longmans, Green, 1885; New York: Appleton, 1885);

Charles Darwin: His Life and Work, by Allen and A. R. Wallace (New York: Humboldt, 1886);

In All Shades (3 volumes, London: Chatto & Windus, 1886; 1 volume, Chicago: Rand, McNally, 18-?);

Common Sense Science (Boston: Lothrop, 1886);

Kalee's Shrine, by Allen and May Cotes (Bristol: Arrowsmith/London: Simpkin, Marshall, 1886; New York: New Amsterdam Book Company, 1897); republished as *The Indian Mystery; or, Kalee's Shrine* (New York: New Amsterdam Book Company, 1902);

For Maimie's Sake: A Tale of Love and Dynamite (London: Chatto & Windus, 1886; New York: Appleton, 1886);

The Beckoning Hand and Other Stories (London: Chatto & Windus, 1887);

A Terrible Inheritance (London: S.P.C.K., 1887; New York: Crowell, 18-?);

The Devil's Die (3 volumes, London: Chatto & Windus, 1888; 1 volume, New York: Lovell, 1888);

Force and Energy: A Theory of Dynamics (London & New York: Longmans, Green, 1888);

A Half-Century of Science, by Allen and T. H. Huxley (New York: Humboldt, 1888);

This Mortal Coil (3 volumes, London: Chatto & Windus, 1888; 1 volume, New York: Appleton, 1889);

The White Man's Foot (London: Hatchards, 1888);

Falling in Love, with Other Essays on More Exact Branches of Science (London: Smith, Elder, 1889; New York: Appleton, 1890);

Individualism and Socialism. Reprinted from "Contemporary Review" of May 1889 (Glasgow: Scottish Land Restoration League, 1889);

Dr. Palliser's Patient (London: Mullen, 1889);

The Jaws of Death (London: Simpkin, Marshall, 1889; New York: New Amsterdam Book Company, 1897);

The Tents of Shem (3 volumes, London: Chatto & Windus, 1889; 1 volume, Chicago: Rand, Mc-Nally, 1889);

A Living Apparition (London: S.P.C.K., 1889);

The Great Taboo (London: Chatto & Windus, 1890; New York: Harper, 1891);

The Sole Trustee (London: S.P.C.K., 1890);

Wednesday the Tenth; a Tale of the South Pacific (Boston: Lothrop, 1890); republished as *The Cruise of the Albatross, or When Was Wednesday the Tenth? A Story of the South Pacific* (Boston: Lothrop, 1898);

The Duchess of Powysland (1 volume, New York: United States Book Company, 1891; 3 volumes, London: Chatto & Windus, 1892);

Dumaresq's Daughter (3 volumes, London: Chatto & Windus, 1891; 1 volume, New York: Harper, 1891);

Recalled to Life (Bristol: Arrowsmith, 1891; New York: Holt, 1891);

What's Bred in the Bone (London: Tit-bits Offices, 1891; Boston: Tucker, 1891);

Blood Royal (Toronto: National, 1892; New York: Cassell, 1892; London: Chatto & Windus, 1893);

Science in Arcady (London: Lawrence & Bullen, 1892);

An Army Doctor's Romance (New York: Tuck, 1893; London & New York: Tuck, 1894);

Ivan Greet's Masterpiece (London: Chatto & Windus, 1893);

Michael's Crag (Chicago & New York: Rand, McNally, 1893; London: Leadenhall, 1893);

The Scallywag (3 volumes, London: Chatto & Windus, 1893; 1 volume, New York: Cassell, 1893);

The Lower Slopes (London: Elkin Mathews & John Lane/Chicago: Stone & Kimball, 1894);

At Market Value (2 volumes, London: Chatto & Windus, 1894; 1 volume, Chicago & New York: Neely, 1894);

Post-Prandial Philosophy (London: Chatto & Windus, 1894);

Under Sealed Orders (1 volume, New York: Collier, 1894; 3 volumes, London: Chatto & Windus, 1895);

The Woman Who Did (Boston: Roberts/London: John Lane, 1895);

The British Barbarians: A Hill-top Novel (London: John Lane, 1895; New York & London: Putnam's, 1895);

The Desire of the Eyes and Other Stories (New York: Fenno, 1895);

In Memoriam: George Paul Macdonell (London: Lund, 1895);

The Story of the Plants (London: Newnes, 1895; New York: Appleton, 1895); revised by Marcus Woodward (London: Hodder & Stoughton, 1926);

A Bride from the Desert (New York: Fenno, 1896);

Moorland Idylls (London: Chatto & Windus, 1896);

A Splendid Sin (London: White, 1896; New York: Buckles, 1899);

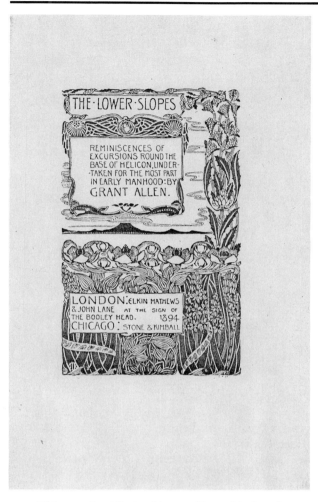

Title page for Allen's 1894 autobiographical work

An African Millionaire: Episodes in the Life of the Illustrious Colonel Clay (London: Richards, 1897; New York: Arnold, 1897);

Tom, Unlimited: A Story for Children, as Martin Leach Warborough (London: Richards, 1897);

The Evolution of the Idea of God: An Inquiry into the Origins of Religions (London: Richards, 1897; New York: Holt, 1897);

The Type-writer Girl, as Olive Pratt Rayner (London: Pearson, 1897; New York: Street & Smith, 1900);

Grant Allen's Historical Guides, 12 volumes (London: Richards, 1897-1912);

The Incidental Bishop (London: Pearson, 1898; New York: Appleton, 1898);

Flashlights on Nature (New York: Doubleday & McClure, 1898; London: Newnes, 1899);

Linnet: A Romance (London: Richards, 1898; New York: New Amsterdam Book Company, 1900);

The European Tour: A Handbook for Americans and Colonists (London: Richards, 1899; New York: Dodd, Mead, 1899);

Miss Cayley's Adventures (London: Richards, 1899; New York: Putnam's, 1899);

Rosalba: The Story of Her Development, as Rayner (New York & London: Putnam's, 1899);

Twelve Tales (London: Richards, 1899);

Hilda Wade: A Woman with Tenacity of Purpose, by Allen and Arthur Conan Doyle (London: Richards, 1900; New York & London: Putnam's, 1900);

Plain Words on the Woman Question (Chicago: Harman, 1900);

The Backslider (New York & London: Lewis, Scribner, 1901);

County and Town in England (London: Richards, 1901; New York: Dutton, 1901);

In Nature's Workshop (London: Newnes, 1901);

Sir Theodore's Guest and Other Stories (Bristol: Arrowsmith, 1902);

Evolution in Italian Art, edited by J. W. Cruickshank (London: Richards, 1903; New York: Wessels/London: Richards, 1908);

The Hand of God and Other Posthumous Essays, edited by Edward Clodd (London: Watts, 1909);

The Reluctant Hangman and Other Stories of Crime, edited by Tom and Enid Schantz (Boulder, Colo.: Aspen, 1973).

OTHER: Richard A. Proctor, ed., *Nature Studies,* comprises studies by Allen, Thomas Foster, Andrew Wilson, Edward Clodd, and Proctor (New York: Funk & Wagnalls, 1883);

The Attis of Caius Valerius Catullus translated into English verse, with dissertations on the myth of Attis, on the origin of tree-worship, and on the Galliambic metre by Grant Allen (London: Nutt, 1892);

Gilbert White, *The Natural History of Selborne,* edited, with notes, by Allen (London: John Lane, 1902).

Prolific, versatile, original, even profound, Grant Allen dedicated his life to the quest for incontrovertible knowledge through the written word. Celebrated not only as a writer of literature and criticism but as a historian, naturalist, anthropologist, biographer, and physicist, Allen made lasting contributions to Victorian and twentieth-century thought. He was at once a man of his age and a man who helped to give his age the shape of modernism.

He was born Charles Grant Blairfindie Allen on 24 February 1848 at Alwington, near Kingston, Ontario. His father, J. Antisell Allen, a graduate of Trinity College, Dublin, was an Irish church minister who immigrated to Canada in 1840. His mother, Charlotte Catherine Ann Grant, was the only daughter of Charles William, fifth Baron de Longueuil, whose family had come to Canada in 1746. Grant Allen spent most of his youth in Canada, in and around Wolfe Island and Howe Island in the Thousand Islands archipelago of the St. Lawrence River. His early upbringing was informal: his father acted as his tutor, and Allen was left free to explore nature, becoming a naturalist naturally, one could say, from early on. He was a sickly child, however; a delicate constitution bothered him throughout his life and contributed to his early death.

When Allen was thirteen, his family moved to New Haven, Connecticut, where he received instruction from a Yale tutor. In 1862 Allen was sent to school at the Collège Impériale in Dieppe, France. He completed his secondary education at King Edward's School in Birmingham, England. In 1867 he matriculated at Oxford, where he won a Senior Classical Postmastership to become a Merton College Scholar. As a university student, he began to consolidate his long-standing interest in writing. His first publication was a poem entitled "Two Portraits" in the short-lived *Oxford University Magazine and Review* (December 1869). He would later republish it as "Forecast and Fulfilment" in *The Lower Slopes* (1894). Receiving first-class honors in his Moderations (1869) and second class in his Greats (1870), Allen was awarded a B.A. in 1871.

For the next year he earned money by tutoring at Oxford and teaching at Brighton College, Cheltenham College, and Reading Grammar School. As tutor to the sons of Lord Huntly, he met Ellen Jerrard, whom he married in the spring of 1873. They traveled to Jamaica in June 1873, where Allen took up a position as professor of mental and moral philosophy at Government College, Spanish Town. The experience was not entirely a happy one. The college had been only recently founded when Allen arrived, and, like postrevolution Jamaica itself, was on unstable ground. He became principal shortly before the college's abolition in 1876.

Illustration by Gordon Browne for Miss Cayley's Adventures *(1899), which features a female detective*

He found his three years in Jamaica quite productive. In reading the *Attis* of Catullus with his students, for example, he opened himself up to a poem he would later translate into English (1892). He also gathered material he would incorporate into some of the scientific essays collected in *The Evolutionist at Large* (1881), *Vignettes from Nature* (1881), and *Colin Clout's Calendar* (1883), and into fiction such as his short stories "The Reverend John Creedy" and "Ivan Greet's Masterpiece" and his novels *In All Shades* (1886) and *The Devil's Die* (1888).

Allen came to write short stories by accident. Around 1880 he submitted to *Belgravia* a scientific article in which he attempted to prove man's incapacity to perceive ghosts; because of the fanciful nature of his subject, he decided to cast the article in the form of a story and to use a pseudonym, J. Arbuthnot Wilson. To his surprise, he was encouraged to submit more work of the same kind, so he wrote the short stories "Our Scientific Observations on a Ghost" and "My New Year's Eve Among the Mummies." He went on to submit "The Reverend John Creedy" and "The Curate of Churnside" to *Cornhill*, and submissions to *Graphic*, the *Contemporary Review*, *Sketch*, *Illustrated London News*, *Pall Mall Magazine*, *Speaker*, and *Longman's Magazine* followed. The bulk of Allen's short fiction is collected in four volumes:

Strange Stories (1884), *The Beckoning Hand* (1887), *Ivan Greet's Masterpiece* (1893), and *Twelve Tales* (1899).

"Ivan Greet's Masterpiece" is one of the most startling of Allen's stories. It is a parable with a simple premise. Greet sails to the West Indies to write his masterpiece. In Jamaica he finds the perfect conditions for writing; he also finds a native lover, Clemmy, and they have a child, Vanna. Within ten months Greet completes his manuscript, but before he can send it to England for publication, he dies of fever (a not uncommon death in Allen's stories). Clemmy is all too familiar with the manuscript. (At one point she laments, "Him mind on him book. Him doan't tink ob dem ting. Him mind too full. Him doan't tink to lub me.") She dedicates her life to raising enough money to get the manuscript published, but while she is away at work her hut burns to the ground; Clemmy huddles overnight in the ashes of the hut, comforting the baby. In the morning "Little Vanna just breathed in her dead mother's arms," and the reader comes to recognize what Greet could not: the ephemerality of literary creation and the human creature. The phrase *just breathed* is typical of Allen's calculated concern with the ironic, the ambiguous, and the cynical.

After returning to England from Jamaica in 1876, Allen supported himself and his wife by tutoring again at Oxford, but he soon began to establish himself as a scientific writer. His first book, *Physiological Aesthetics* (1877), draws heavily on the aesthetic and biological principles of John Ruskin and Charles Darwin (who, along with Herbert Spencer, was one of Allen's mentors and lifelong friends). In his striking personal thesis, a celebration of the central nervous system as the filter of man's essentially sensual experience, Allen might be seen as a mediator between Aristotle and Marshall McLuhan. In his second book, *The Colour-Sense* (1879), like so many of his scientific treatises a paean of praise to Darwinism, Allen argues that we derive our ability in color differentiation from fruit-eating progenitors, who had to develop a very sensitive nervous system capable of distinguishing subtle color gradations just to survive. Allen exploits this kind of anthropologist's view throughout his scientific writing.

In 1879 he began writing for the *Daily News* (London), but with the onset of the brisk English winter he had to quit because of respiratory problems. He stayed in Hyéres, France, until May 1880. After settling in Dorking, Surrey, in 1881

Allen continued to spend his winters abroad: his ongoing search for salubrious climates took him to Algeria, Austria, Italy, and Egypt. But professionally the 1880s were healthy years for Allen. His travel provided him with the raw material for his *European Tour* (1899) and his (incomplete) *Historical Guides* series on Florence (1897), Paris (1897), Venice (1898), and the cities of Belgium (1897). In addition to launching his career as a short-story writer in the 1880s, Allen published (under the pen name Cecil Power) the first of his many novels: *Philistia* (1884) and *Babylon* (1885).

Like virtually all his fiction to follow, *Philistia* examines the theme of ethical nonconformity and freedom from convention. At the start of the novel Ernest proposes formulaically to Miss Oswald: " 'Edie,' he said, beginning again more boldly, and taking her little gloved hand almost unresistingly in his; 'Edie, you know my secret. I love you. Can you love me?' " Her response is equally predictable: "Consider the difference in our positions." But in Grant Allen's fictional world, the predictable response is deadly. In the course of the novel, Ernest embraces nonconformity in socialism, whereas Edie comes to recognize the potential of all organization to enslave. At the end of the novel Ernest appears to see his own predicament, as he tells Herr Max: "As things are constituted now, there seems only one life that's really worth living for an honest man, and that's a martyr's. A martyr's or else a worker's. And I, I greatly fear, have managed somehow to miss being either." But Edie can see *through* his predicament, chiding him: "Now don't be a silly, there's a dear, or say that you can't drive away from the office of the 'Social Reformer' in Lady Hilda's brougham." Throughout Allen's fiction such pragmatism is usually the prerogative of women, and the novelist openly celebrates it, albeit from a male point of view.

Among his other early popular novels are the romantic *In All Shades, For Maimie's Sake* (1886), *The Devil's Die*, and *The Tents of Shem* (1889), which feature exotic settings and improbable adventures; the didactic *A Splendid Sin* (1896) and *The Type-writer Girl* (1897), both espousing socialist principles and exposing the injustices of the workplace; and the entertaining *An African Millionaire* (1897), *Miss Cayley's Adventures* (1899), and *Hilda Wade* (1900), good examples of the Victorian mystery genre. Allen's greatest popular success was *What's Bred in the Bone* (1891), anticipating Robertson Davies's work of the same name

Manuscript reproduced as the epigraph for Edward Clodd's book Grant Allen *(1900)* by about a century. It won Allen a prize of a thousand pounds from the novel's publisher, Tit-bits.

His most controversial novel is *The Woman Who Did* (1895), which Allen wrote in Perugia in the spring of 1893. The story begins conventionally enough. At the Surrey home of Mrs. Dewsbury, Alan Merrick is introduced to Miss Hermina Barton and immediately falls in love with her: "But it was her face particularly that struck Alan Merrick at first sight. That face was above all things the face of a free woman. Something so frank and fearless shone in Hermina's glance, as her eye met his, that Alan, who respected human freedom above all other qualities in man or woman, was taken on the spot by its perfect air of untrammelled liberty." As it happens, Hermina is "free" in more than the philosophical sense: she objects to marriage on principle and insists on pursuing her reciprocal love for Alan in a de facto relationship. As she tells her host at the beginning: "I don't think you quite understand my plans in life, Mrs. Dewsbury. It isn't my present intention to *go in* for anybody." Alan and Hermina travel to Europe as friends and lovers, registering in hotels as "Mr. and Mrs. Alan Merrick" only in a nod to common sense. After Alan contracts typhoid fever and dies at Perugia (once again, a typical death in Allen's fiction), the novel goes on to address the main issue of this common-law relationship, a daughter, Dolores. Now a young woman, Dolores is in love with Walter Brydges, stepson of the local vicar, Mr. Hawkshaw, who objects to his marriage into a family of questionable morality. Walter broaches the subject to Dolores, who, it turns out, suspects nothing of her illegitimacy. Many complications arise, and in the end Walter stands by Dolores, against convention, but Dolores cannot in conscience marry in the dim light of her mother's nonconformity. When Hermina commits suicide to free her daughter, Allen endorses her right to do so: "Not for nothing does blind fate vouchsafe such martyrs to humanity. From their graves shall spring glorious the church of the future." Allen's closing words are typical of his open-ended conclusions: "Hermina Barton's stainless soul has ceased to exist forever."

Allen had great difficulty getting *The Woman Who Did* published, until the London publisher John Lane took a chance on it. Critical and public reactions were hostile. When a condensed version of the novel was serialized in the *Review of Reviews* (March 1895), Irish booksellers refused to carry it, seeing it as an attack on the Christian sacrament of marriage. This kind of notoriety cost Allen sales during the last four years of his life. Ironically, *The Woman Who Did* did not propose a very heterodox morality. Allen always saw the emancipation of women through some kind of marriage and through childbirth. Never one to cave in to public opinion, Allen went on to publish the even more strident *The British Barbarians* (1895), a dystopian satire on British culture, set six centuries in the future.

Allen delineates his socialist, nonconformist, naturalist philosophy most clearly in two works: *The Evolution of the Idea of God: An Inquiry into the Origins of Religions* (1897) and its sequel, *The Hand of God and Other Posthumous Essays* (1909).

While traveling in Venice in early 1899, Allen contracted a malarial disease that, upon his return to London, confounded his specialists. His condition gradually deteriorated, and he died on 28 October 1899.

Allen's writing has been durable: most of his work went through numerous republishings, and recently some of his fiction and scientific writing has been reissued in library reprint series and in scholarly editions. The work of this Canadian expatriate will be remembered not only for its unquestionable entertainment value but for its substantial contribution to the transitional questioning and reevaluating that marked the beginning of the modern age in Canada and throughout the world.

References:

G. H. Clarke, "Grant Allen," *Queen's Quarterly*, 45 (1938): 487-496;

Edward Clodd, *Grant Allen: A Memoir, with a Bibliography* (London: Richards, 1900);

Malcolm Elwin, *Old Gods Falling* (New York: Essay Index Reprint Series, 1939), pp. 315-319;

F. Harrison, *Grant Allen* (N.p., 1899);

Richard Le Gallienne, *Grant Allen* (New York: Tucker, 1900).

Olivar Asselin

(8 November 1874-18 April 1937)

Michel Gaulin

Carleton University

BOOKS: *A Quebec View of Canadian Nationalism: An Essay by a Dyed-in-the-Wool French-Canadian on the Best Means of Ensuring the Greatness of the Canadian Fatherland* (Montreal, 1909);

La Défense navale de l'empire britannique (Montreal, 1909);

L'Emigration belge et française au Canada: Rapport sur une enquête faite au Canada durant l'hiver de 1911-12 par M. Olivar Asselin, à la demande du ministère de l'intérieur (Ottawa, 1913); translated as *Emigration from Belgium and France to Canada: Report on an Enquiry Made During the Winter 1911-12 by Mr. Oliver Asselin, at the Request of the Department of the Interior* (Ottawa, 1913);

Le Sou de la pensée française (Montreal, 1913);

"L'Action catholique," les évêques et la guerre: Petit Plaidoyer pour la liberté de pensée du bas clergé et des laïques (Montreal, 1915);

Les Evêques et la propagande de "L'Action catholique" (Montreal, 1915);

Pourquoi je m'enrôle: Discours prononcé au Monument National, à Montréal, le 21 janvier 1916 . . . (Montreal, 1916);

Les Volontaires canadiens-français (Paris, 1917);

L'Œuvre de l'abbé Groulx: Conférence faite à la salle Saint-Suplice à Montréal le 15 février 1923 sous les auspices du Cercle d'Action française des étudiants à l'Université de Montréal (Montreal: Bibliothèque de l'Action Française, 1923);

Pensée française, edited by Gérard Dagenais (Montreal: Editions de l'Action Canadienne-Française, 1937);

Trois textes sur la liberté, edited by J.-L. Gagnon (Montreal: HMH, 1970)—comprises *"L'Action catholique," les évêques et la guerre; Les Evêques et la propagande de "L'Action catholique,"* and *Pourquoi je m'enrôle;*

Olivar Asselin toujours vivant, edited by M.-A. Gagnon (Montreal: Presses de l'Université du Québec, 1974).

Olivar Asselin (charcoal sketch by J.-Arthur Le May, from his Mille Têtes, *1929)*

OTHER: Jules Fournier, *Souvenirs de prison,* preface by Asselin (Montreal, 1910);

Fournier, ed., *Anthologie des poètes canadiens,* preface by Asselin (Montreal: Granger, 1920; revised, 1933);

Fournier, *Mon Encrier,* 2 volumes, preface by Asselin (Montreal: Privately printed, 1922).

Olivar Asselin is remembered as one of the most forceful and articulate journalists French Canada has had. A leader, with Henri Bourassa, of the nationalist movement of the early years of the twentieth century, and an energetic defender of the French intellectual tradition in Canada, he founded three newspapers in the course of his career. But he also underwent periods during which he seemed to be at loose ends, anxiously in search of some ever-elusive principle of unity. Many of his initiatives appeared to contradict some of his most fervently held beliefs, and these inconsistencies mystified his friends and admirers.

Jean-François-Olivar Asselin was born in Saint-Hilarion, Quebec, on 8 November 1874, the son of Rieul Asselin, a tanner, and Adèle-Cédulie Tremblay Asselin. After six years of junior seminary in Rimouski, in summer 1892 he joined his parents in Fall River, Massachusetts, where they had immigrated. He worked first in the textile industry and, from 1894, having opted for journalism, served a four-year apprenticeship with several short-lived Franco-American newspapers in Massachusetts and Rhode Island. When the Spanish-American War began in 1898, he joined the U.S. Army, thereby taking American citizenship. He rose to the rank of corporal but did not see action.

Asselin returned to Canada permanently in 1900, although he did not regain his Canadian citizenship until 1911. He worked briefly for several newspapers in Montreal and was, for a short period of time, literary editor of *Les Débats,* an elegantly written nationalistic weekly. From 1901 to 1903 he worked as secretary to Lomer Gouin, a minister in the government of Quebec, who later became premier. He married Alice Le Boutillier on 3 August 1902, and their union produced four sons.

In March of 1903 Asselin organized the Ligue Nationaliste to bring together the mounting forces of opposition to British imperialism in Canada. French-Canadian nationalism was experiencing one of its cyclical revivals, in the wake of the controversial decision by the government of Wilfrid Laurier to send Canadian troops to fight for Britain in South Africa. Never an accomplished public speaker, Asselin joined forces with Henri Bourassa, the great public orator, who had split with Laurier over this issue in 1899. Without calling for an end to the colonial link or putting into question the federal system of government, the Ligue advocated the greatest possible measure of autonomy for Canada in relation to Great Britain and, within the country itself, for the provinces vis-à-vis the federal govern-

ment. It called for the adoption of economic and other policies which favored a sense of Canadian nationhood.

In March of 1904 Asselin launched his first paper, a weekly, *Le Nationaliste,* to pursue the ideals of the Ligue. There, he honed the incisive journalistic style that would make him famous, by excoriating all instances of perceived political stupidity and cowardice. But he also pushed for reforms—a better husbandry of natural resources, the establishment of a network of industrial education, an end to Canadian appeals to the Judicial Committee of British Privy Council—which successive governments would slowly implement over the course of the next half century or so.

Asselin's years at *Le Nationaliste* were among the best of his life, marked as they were by tireless activity, suits and countersuits, which resulted in his being twice imprisoned for short periods, and an unsuccessful bid for election as a nationalist candidate in the provincial election of 1905. He left the editorship unexpectedly in early 1908 and the following year published *A Quebec View of Canadian Nationalism,* a clear and elegantly written statement meant for the English-Canadian public.

When Bourassa founded his own paper, *Le Devoir,* in January 1910, Asselin was briefly at his side, but the relationship between the two men had soured. There ensued, for Asselin, a relatively fallow period, during which he ran, unsuccessfully again, in the federal election of 1911, that of Laurier's downfall. During 1911 and 1912 he also conducted a study for the Canadian government into conditions for francophone immigration, which was published in 1913. He served a controversial term as president of the Société Saint-Jean-Baptiste, during which he organized the "Sou de la pensée française" (Pennies in support of French thought), a grass-roots fund-raising initiative designed to assist the French schools of Ontario in their struggle against a government they considered hostile to their aspirations.

It was World War I that once more propelled Asselin into the thick of action. He became embroiled in a long-drawn-out controversy over what he considered to be the French-Canadian bishops' ill-advised injunction to their flock regarding their duty to participate in the war at Britain's side, writing two books on the issue in 1915. He then totally baffled his supporters, in late 1915, not only by enlisting himself but also by organizing a battalion entirely composed of, and led by, French Canadians. Asselin himself saw no contradiction in his gesture, in that this was something that he was doing voluntarily—as against yielding to any pressure from either Church or State. Furthermore, in his mind, he was going to war not so much in defense of the British Empire as to come to the rescue of France (*Pourquoi je m'enrôle* [Why I've Enlisted], 1916, covers this controversy). He saw action in early 1917 and was awarded the French Légion d'Honneur for military achievement. He was demobilized in June 1919, after serving on the staff of the Canadian delegation to the Paris Peace Conference.

The 1920s were largely devoted to Asselin's lifelong concern for the poor and the underprivileged. He became volunteer secretary and fundraiser for the Œuvre de la Merci and was instrumental in bringing to Canada from France the Brothers Hospitaliers of Saint-Jean-de-Dieu to assume responsibility for the organization.

In 1930, after twenty years of absence, Asselin returned to active journalism. He became editor of *Le Canada*, the paper of the Quebec Liberal party. This act was seen as another about-face on the part of the staunch nationalist of the early years of the century who was now going to work for the party which the nationalists had traditionally distrusted. Asselin countered that his freedom of expression had been preserved in the agreement he had made with the party. He surrounded himself with a young and dynamic team whose members looked upon him as their mentor. Many of them later became prominent in French-Canadian journalism, thus extending Asselin's influence into the 1960s and 1970s.

Asselin left *Le Canada* at the end of February 1934 and the following month launched his own daily, *L'Ordre*. By then his nationalism had moved away from its original political expression in favor of an emphasis on cultural and intellectual development, calling for opening up to international influences. But the Church continued to be wary of Asselin, and the combined influence of a highly publicized warning against the paper by the powerful Cardinal-Archbishop of Quebec, J.-M.-Rodrigue Villeneuve, and of financial difficulties forced the paper to close in May 1935. A month later Asselin launched his last paper, *La Renaissance*, a weekly which folded in December.

By then a man broken in both health and spirit, Asselin became a public servant once more, serving as chairman of the Quebec Old-Age Pensions Commission, but was forced by ill health to resign his position a few months before his death, which occurred on 18 April 1937. In the last months of his life, he had become an "associate" of the Brothers Hospitaliers of Saint-Jean-de-Dieu, and at his request, he was buried in the cowl of the order, thus bringing to a surprising close a life which, throughout, had been fraught with controversy.

Biography:
Marcel-A. Gagnon, *La Vie orageuse d'Olivar Asselin*, 2 volumes (Montreal: L'Homme, 1962).

References:
Hermas Bastien, *Olivar Asselin* (Montreal: Valiquette, 1938);
Pierre Berthiaume, "La Pensée paradoxale d'Olivar Asselin," in *L'Essai et la prose d'idées au Québec*, edited by F. Gallays, S. Simard, and P. Wyczynski (Montreal: Fides, 1985), pp. 379-395.

Papers:
Asselin's correspondence, personal papers, and notes, classified in chronological and alphabetical order, together with his articles from the daily *Le Canada* (1930-1952), are on deposit at the Bibliothèque Municipale de Montréal.

Marius Barbeau
(5 March 1883-27 March 1969)

Edith Fowke
York University

BOOKS: *Huron and Wyandot Mythology* (Ottawa: Government Printing Bureau, 1915);

Indian Days in the Canadian Rockies (Toronto: Macmillan, 1923);

The Downfall of Temlaham (Toronto: Macmillan, 1928);

The Church of Saint Pierre, Island of Orleans, Quebec, by Barbeau and Ramsay Traquair (Toronto: Bridgens, 1929);

Totem Poles of the Gitksan, Upper Skeena River, British Columbia (Ottawa: F. A. Acland, 1929);

Au Coeur de Québec (Montreal: Zodiaque, 1934);

Cornelius Krieghoff, Pioneer Painter of North America (Toronto: Macmillan, 1934);

La Merveilleuse Aventure de Jacques Cartier (Montreal: Lévesque, 1934);

Grand'mère raconte (Montreal: Beauchemin, 1935);

Il était une fois (Montreal: Beauchemin, 1935);

The Kingdom of Saguenay (Toronto: Macmillan, 1936);

Quebec, Where Ancient France Lingers (Toronto: Macmillan, 1936); French edition published as *Quebec ou survit l'ancienne France* (Quebec: Librairie Garneau, 1937);

Romancero du Canada (Toronto: Macmillan, 1937);

Assomption Sash (Ottawa: National Museum, 1939); French edition published as *Ceinture fléchée* (Montreal: Paysana, 1945);

Aux armes, Canadiens! (Ottawa: Hutte Canadienne des Chevaliers de Colomb, 1941);

Henri Julien (Toronto: Ryerson, 1941);

Les Rêves des chasseurs (Montreal: Beauchemin, 1942);

Maîtres artisans de chez-nous (Montreal: Zodiaque, 1942);

Côté, the Wood Carver (Toronto: Ryerson, 1943);

Les Enfants disent (Montreal: Paysana, 1943);

Mountain Cloud (Toronto: Macmillan, 1944; London: Quality, 1948);

Saintes Artisanes: I. Les Brodeuses (Montreal: Fides, 1944);

Allouette! Nouveau recueil de chansons populaires avec mélodies, choisies dans le répertoire du Mu-

Marius Barbeau (photograph by André Larose)

sée National du Canada (Montreal: Lumen, 1946);

Painters of Quebec (Toronto: Ryerson, 1946);

Saintes Artisanes: II. Mille Petites Adresses (Montreal: Fides, 1946);

Alaska Beckons (Toronto: Macmillan, 1947);

L'Arbre des rêves (Montreal: Lumen, 1948); English edition published as *The Tree of Dreams* (Toronto: Oxford, 1955);

Le Rêve de Kamalmouk (Montreal: Fides, 1948);

Totem Poles, 2 volumes (Ottawa: E. Cloutier, 1950-1951);

Les Contes du Grand-Père Sept-Heures, 12 volumes (Montreal: Chantecler, 1950-1953);

The Tsimshian, Their Arts and Music, by Barbeau, V. E. Garfield, and P. S. Wingert (New York: Augustin, 1951);

Haida Myths Illustrated in Argillite Carvings (Ottawa: National Museum, 1953);

Haida Carvers in Argillite (Ottawa: National Museum, 1957);

I Have Seen Quebec (Toronto: Macmillan, 1957); French edition published as *J'ai vu Québec* (Quebec: Garneau, 1957);

Trésor des anciens Jésuites (Ottawa: National Museum, 1957);

Medicine-men on the North Pacific Coast (Ottawa: National Museum, 1958);

Pathfinders in the North Pacific (Caldwell, Idaho: Caxton, 1958);

Roundelays; Folk Dances and Games Collected in Canada and New England (Ottawa: National Museum, 1958):

Huron-Wyandot Traditional Narratives (Ottawa: National Museum, 1960);

Tsimsyan Myths (Ottawa: National Museum, 1961);

Jongleur Songs of Old Quebec (New Brunswick, N.J.: Rutgers University Press, 1962);

Le Rossignol y chante (Ottawa: National Museum, 1962);

Folklore (Montreal: Académie Canadienne-Française, 1965);

Indian Days on the Western Prairies (Ottawa: National Museum, 1965);

Peaux-Rouges d'Amérique: leurs moeurs, leurs coutumes (Montreal: Beauchemin, 1965);

Comment on découvrit l'Amérique (Montreal: Beauchemin, 1966);

Fameaux peaux-rouges d'Amérique du nord-est au nord-ouest (Montreal: Beauchemin, 1966);

La Saguenay légendaire (Montreal: Beauchemin, 1967);

Louis Jobin, statuaire (Montreal: Beauchemin, 1968);

En Roulant ma boule (Ottawa: National Museum, 1982);

Art of the Totem (Surrey, B.C. & Washington, D.C.: Hancock House, 1984);

Pantagruel in Canada (Ottawa: National Museum, 1984);

Le Roi Boit (Ottawa: National Museum, 1987).

OTHER: *Folk Songs of French Canada*, edited by Barbeau and Edward Sapir (New Haven: Yale University Press, 1925);

Chansons canadiennes: French Canadian Folk Songs, compiled by Barbeau and Paul England (London: Harris/Boston: Boston Music, 1929);

Chansons populaires du Vieux Québec, edited by Barbeau (Ottawa: National Museum, 1935);

translated by Regina Lenore Shoolman as *Folk-songs of Old Quebec* (Ottawa: National Museum, 1935);

The Indian Speaks, edited by Barbeau and Grace Melvin (Toronto: Macmillan, 1943);

Come A Singing! Canadian Folk Songs, edited by Barbeau, Arthur Lismer, and Arthur Bourinot (Ottawa: Cloutier, 1947);

The Golden Phoenix, and other French-Canadian Fairy Tales, edited by Barbeau and Michael Hornyansky (Toronto: Oxford, 1958; New York: Walck, 1958).

SELECTED PERIODICAL PUBLICATIONS
UNCOLLECTED: "Contes populaires canadiens," *Journal of American Folklore*, 29 (1916): 1-54; 30 (1917): 1-140;

"Chants populaires du Canada," *Journal of American Folklore*, 32 (1919): 1-89;

"Anecdotes de Gaspé de la Beauce, et de Temiscouata," *Journal of American Folklore*, 33 (1920): 173-258;

"Trois Beaux Canards; 92 versions canadiennes," *Archives de Folklore*, 2 (1947): 191-292;

"The Ermatinger Collection of Voyageur Songs (ca. 1830)," *Journal of American Folklore*, 67 (1954): 147-161;

"La Complainte de Cadieux, coureur de bois (ca. 1709)," *Journal of American Folklore*, 67 (1954): 163-183.

Frédéric Charles Joseph Marius Barbeau was Canada's pioneer anthropologist and folklorist. In an age of increasing specialization he ranged over the whole field of anthropology and folklore, collecting, studying, and describing Indian myths, ceremonials, language, music, arts, and culture; French-Canadian folktales, songs, art, games, handicrafts, and architecture; and even some Anglo-Canadian songs. A prolific writer and completely bilingual, he published some fifty major books, as many more pamphlets and monographs, and some seven hundred articles in over a hundred different periodicals ranging from scientific journals to popular magazines and daily papers.

The son of Charles Barbeau, a horse dealer, and Marie Virginie Morency, Barbeau was born in Sainte-Marie-de-la-Beauce, Quebec, where he received his early education. He went on to earn a B.A. at the College of Sainte-Anne-de-la-Pocatière in 1903, then studied law at Laval University. He was admitted to the bar in 1907 but won a Rhodes scholarship and spent three years at

Frontispiece and title page for Barbeau's 1944 novel about Canadian fur traders and their relationships with Indian women

Oriel College, Oxford, where he studied anthropology, archaeology, and ethnology. He also attended the Sorbonne in Paris. In 1910 he received a Bachelor of Science degree and diploma in anthropology from Oxford, writing his thesis on "The Totemic System of the North-Western Tribes of North America," and then spent another semester studying the ethnology of Indian songs.

When Barbeau returned to Canada in 1911 he joined the staff of the National Museum of Canada as anthropologist and ethnologist. He began his fieldwork at a Huron Indian reserve in the small village of Notre-Dame-de-Lorette near Quebec City. Recording on Edison wax cylinders, he collected some seventy songs and many tales from an old Huron, Prosper Vincent. He continued his research among the Hurons for three years and used this knowledge in his first book, *Huron and Wyandot Mythology* (1915). In 1912 he made an expedition to British Columbia, where he recorded songs from the Salish Indians and went on to record tales from tribes of the Northeast Woodlands. The fact that some of the Indian tales contained elements borrowed from French tales stimulated his interest in French-Canadian traditions, and the distinguished anthropologist Franz Boas, whom he met in 1913, encouraged him to pursue this interest.

Some thought that Ernest Gagnon had noted the full repertoire of French-Canadian songs in his *Chansons populaires du Canada* (1865), but Barbeau decided to investigate. In 1916 he set out on a recording expedition down the St. Lawrence and soon found enough folk songs and folktales to prove there was a rich French-

Canadian heritage waiting to be illuminated. In the years that followed he carried out many field trips, collecting Indian lore in the Rockies and along the Pacific coast, and French lore throughout his native province, then published his findings in books and articles.

Many of his most important books document the traditions of the Huron and Wyandot tribes of eastern Canada, and the Gitksan, Haida, and Tsimshian tribes of the Northwest. His other major books include the three massive volumes of the "Repertoire de la chanson folklorique française au Canada": *Le Rossignol y chante* (1962), *En Roulant ma boule* (1982), and *Le Roi Boit* (1987), the last two of which were published long after Barbeau's death.

Although most of his books present folklore directly, he also used his knowledge of Indian legends and tribal rituals in two novels. *The Downfall of Temlaham* (1928) tells of a disturbance among the Indians of the Upper Skeena River in 1886 that shows the Indians' ambivalence toward the white man's civilization. *Mountain Cloud* (1944) reflects the custom of fur traders mating with Indian women, contrasting a Scotsman who deserts his Indian wife with a French-Canadian who shares his life with an Indian girl.

Barbeau was also greatly interested in folk art: he collected many examples and wrote extensively of Quebec artists, notably the painter Cornelius Krieghoff, the sculptor Louis Jobin, and the wood-carver Jean-Baptiste Côté. He also encouraged Emily Carr and helped to promote her work.

Barbeau was active in professional societies. He joined the American Folklore Society in 1911 and served a term as president in 1918. In 1916 he became an associate editor of the *Journal of American Folklore*, a position he held until 1950. During that time he prepared ten special issues containing valuable material on Canadian folklore, including eight series of "Contes populaires canadiens" that presented 197 French-Canadian tales, many of which he had collected himself. Also in 1916 he was invited to join the Royal Society of Canada, and in 1933 he became president of its French-language division. He was also a devoted member of the International Folk Music Council, and in 1956 he organized the Canadian

Folk Music Society, serving as its president until 1963. Through his efforts Canada hosted the fourteenth annual conference of the International Folk Music Council in Quebec City in 1961. He was also instrumental in establishing Laval University's renowned folklore archives. Barbeau retired from the National Museum in 1948 but retained his office and continued to work there until his death, transcribing the texts and melodies he had gathered in the field.

Barbeau's contribution to Canadian folklore can hardly be overestimated. In 1947 the second volume of *Les Archives de Folklore* was entitled "Hommage à Marius Barbeau," and the April-June 1950 issue of the *Journal of American Folklore* was dedicated to "Dr. Marius Barbeau, dean of Canadian folklorists," saluting "his high standards of scholarship as a collector and interpreter of the folklore and the folk art and folk culture of his Canadian homeland." When he died in 1969 the Canadian press noted:

> He gave the National Museum a collection of 195 Eskimo songs, more than 3,000 Indian, close to 7,000 French-Canadian, and 1,500 old English songs. Many of them are still on the old tube-like records that came off his Edison recorder. . . . "I would need two lives to process all my research," he once said.

His long list of honors includes the Gold Medal of the Royal Society of Canada; honorary degrees from the universities of Montreal, Laval, and Oxford; and being named "Companion of the Order of Canada."

Far from being an ivory-tower scholar, he spared no effort to preserve and promote folklore in as many ways as he could. He lectured at universities, spoke before numerous organizations, and appeared frequently on radio and television. In addition to his scientific works he also wrote books designed for the general public, encouraged other writers to use his material, and prepared several recordings on Canadian folk music, in one of which he describes "My Life in Recording Canadian Indian Folk-Lore."

Papers:
Barbeau's papers are in the Archives of the National Museum of Civilization in Ottawa.

Robert Barr

(16 September 1850-21 October 1912)

John Parr

See also the Barr entry in *DLB 70: British Mystery Writers, 1860-1919.*

BOOKS: *Strange Happenings,* as Luke Sharp (London: Dunkerley, 1883);

One Day's Courtship, as Luke Sharp, in *The Record of Badalia Herodsfoot,* by Rudyard Kipling. *One Day's Courtship,* by Luke Sharp (London: Detroit Free Press, 1890);

In a Steamer Chair and Other Shipboard Stories (New York: Stokes, 1892; London: Chatto & Windus, 1892);

From Whose Bourne (London: Chatto & Windus, 1893; New York: Stokes, 1896);

In the Midst of Alarms (Philadelphia: Lippincott, 1894; London: Methuen, 1894);

The Face and The Mask (London: Hutchinson, 1894; New York: Stokes, 1895);

One Day's Courtship, and The Heralds of Fame (New York & London: Stokes, 1896);

The Mutable Many (New York & London: Stokes, 1896; London: Methuen, 1897);

Revenge! (New York: Stokes, 1896; London: Chatto & Windus, 1896);

A Woman Intervenes. Or, The Mistress of the Mine (New York & London: Stokes, 1896; London: Chatto & Windus, 1896);

Tekla: A Romance of Love and War (Toronto: Morang, 1898; New York: Stokes, 1898); republished as *The Countess Tekla* (London: Methuen, 1899);

Jennie Baxter, Journalist (New York: Stokes, 1899; London: Methuen, 1899);

The Strong Arm (Toronto: Briggs, 1899; New York: Stokes, 1899; London: Methuen, 1900); revised and abridged as *Gentlemen: The King!* (New York: Stokes, 1899);

The Unchanging East (2 volumes, Boston: Page, 1900; 1 volume, London: Chatto & Windus, 1900);

The King Dines (London: McClure, 1901); republished as *A Prince of Good Fellows* (New York: McClure, Phillips, 1902; London: Chatto & Windus, 1902);

Robert Barr

The Victors: A Romance of Yesterday Morning & This Afternoon (New York: Stokes, 1901; London: Methuen, 1902);

The O'Ruddy: A Romance, by Barr and Stephen Crane (New York: Stokes, 1903; London: Methuen, 1904);

Over the Border: A Romance (New York: Stokes, 1903; London: Isbister, 1903);

A Chicago Princess (New York: Stokes, 1904); republished as *The Tempestuous Petticoat* (London: Methuen, 1905);

The Woman Wins (New York: Stokes, 1904); republished as *The Lady Electra* (London: Methuen, 1904);

The Speculations of John Steele (New York: Stokes, 1905; London: Chatto & Windus, 1905);

A Rock in the Baltic (Toronto: McLeod & Allen, 1906; New York & London: Authors and Newspapers Association, 1906; London: Hurst & Blackett, 1907);

The Triumphs of Eugène Valmont (New York: Appleton, 1906; London: Hurst & Blackett, 1906);

The Watermead Affair (Philadelphia: Altemus, 1906);

The Measure of the Rule (London: Constable, 1907; New York: Appleton, 1908);

Young Lord Stranleigh (New York: Appleton, 1908; London, Melbourne & Toronto: Ward, Lock, 1908);

Cardillac (New York: Stokes, 1909; London: Mills & Boon, 1909);

Stranleigh's Millions (London: Nash, 1909);

The Girl in the Case. Being the Manoeuvres of the Inadvertent Mr. Pepperton (London: Nash, 1910);

The Sword Maker (New York: Stokes, 1910; London: Mills & Boon, 1910);

Lady Eleanor, Lawbreaker (Chicago & New York: Rand, McNally, 1911);

Lord Stranleigh, Philanthropist (London: Ward, Lock, 1911);

The Palace of Logs (London: Mills & Boon, 1912);

Lord Stranleigh Abroad (London: Ward, Lock, 1913);

My Enemy Jones: An Extravaganza (London: Nash, 1913); republished as *Unsentimental Journey* (London: Hodder & Stoughton, 1915);

A Woman in a Thousand (London: Hodder & Stoughton, 1913);

The Helping Hand and Other Stories (London: Mills & Boon, 1920);

Tales of Two Continents (London: Mills & Boon, 1920);

Selected Stories of Robert Barr, edited by John Parr (Ottawa: University of Ottawa Press, 1977).

PLAY PRODUCTIONS: *An Emperor's Romance,* adapted by Barr and Cosmo Hamilton from *Tekla,* Hartlepool, Grand Theatre, 1 January 1901;

The Conspiracy, by Barr and S. Lewis Ransom, Dublin, 8 November 1907; London, Adelphi Theatre, 9 September 1908;

The Hanging Outlook, by Barr and John Savile Judd, London, Court Theatre, 11 July 1912;

Lady Eleanor, Lawbreaker, Liverpool, Repertory, 14 December 1912;

OTHER: "A. Conan Doyle and Robert Barr; Real Conversation Between Them," in *Human Documents: Portraits and Biographies of Great Men of To-Day* (New York: McClure, 1896), pp. 188-199;

The Conspiracy, by Barr and S. Lewis Ransom, in *Short Modern Plays,* second series, edited by S. R. Littlewood (London: Macmillan, 1939).

SELECTED PERIODICAL PUBLICATIONS
UNCOLLECTED:
FICTION
"A Dangerous Journey" (serial), as Luke Sharp, *Detroit Free Press,* 10 October-12 December 1875;

"A Conglomerate Interview with Mark Twain, Personally Conducted by Luke Sharp," *Idler Magazine,* 1 (February 1892): 79-84;

"Francis Bret Harte . . . The Ideal Interview," as Luke Sharp, *Idler Magazine,* 1 (May 1892): 301-306;

"Two of a Kind," *Idler Magazine,* 5 (February 1894): 147-152;

"An Electrical Slip," *English Illustrated Magazine,* 11 (April 1894): 711-718;

"The Revolt of the _____ ," *Idler Magazine,* 4 (April 1894): 357-369;

"The Vengeance of the Dead," *English Illustrated Magazine,* 9 (May 1894): 835-843;

"The Woman of Stone," *Idler Magazine,* 5 (May 1894): 459-466;

"The Driver With His Back to the Horses," *English Illustrated Magazine,* 11 (July 1894): 1013-1021;

"The Hour and the Man," *English Illustrated Magazine,* 11 (August 1894): 1139-1145;

"The Christmas Picture," *Idler Magazine,* 6 (January 1895): 521-534;

"A Man Fights Best in His Own Township," *McClure's Magazine,* 9 (September 1897): 928-939;

"An Unjust Accusation," *McClure's Magazine,* 10 (November 1897): 47-53;

"How Nelson Lost His Eye," *Strand Magazine,* 15 (June 1898): 681-687;

"The Gift of Abner Grice," *McClure's Magazine,* 11 (September 1898): 433-442;

"Three Expert Cyclists," *Canadian Magazine,* 13 (May 1899): 64-69;

"The Making of Howard Carruth," *Strand Magazine,* 18 (August 1899): 208-217;

"Arrival of the Unexpected," *Strand Magazine,* 18 (December 1899): 648-656;

Barr at his Idler *desk, circa 1894 (photograph by Fradelle & Young)*

"The Lady Gwendolyn Episode," *Canadian Magazine*, 14 (April 1900): 513-518;

"Within An Ace of the End of the World," *McClure's Magazine*, 14 (April 1900): 545-554;

"The Pasha's Prisoner: A Story of Modern Turkey," *McClure's Magazine*, 15 (May 1900): 35-44;

"On the Housetop," *Canadian Magazine*, 15 (August 1900): 363-368;

"The Typewriter Girl," *Strand Magazine*, 20 (August 1900): 161-169;

"Wizard of Wall Street," *Everybody's Magazine*, 3 (October 1900): 397-405;

"Mystery of the Expert," *Strand Magazine*, 21 (May 1901): 578-583;

"The Island Man-Trap," *Strand Magazine*, 22 (September 1901): 289-302;

"A Sweet Thing in Trusts," *Strand Magazine*, 22 (October 1901): 409-415;

"A Deputation to the King," *McClure's Magazine*, 18 (January 1902): 232-240;

"Try Not That Pass," *Strand Magazine*, 23 (February 1902): 209-215;

"The Probation of Buckles' Ghost," *Saturday Evening Post*, 175 (19 July 1902): 3-4;

"The Kidnapping of Rochervelt," *Saturday Evening Post*, 175 (4 April 1903): 1-3, 21-23;

"Famous Test," *Strand Magazine*, 26 (December 1903): 642-656;

"The Mystery of the Five Hundred Diamonds," *Saturday Evening Post*, 176 (4 June 1904): 1-3; (11 June 1904): 6-7, 21-23;

"Lady Beatie's Spanish Investment," *Strand Magazine*, 28 (December 1904): 639-648;

"The Mutual Dilemma," *Strand Magazine*, 30 (December 1905): 727-737;

"The Windfall," *Windsor Magazine*, 25 (February 1907): 351-360;

"An Extra Turn," *American Magazine*, 68 (October 1909): 604-610;

"The Case of the Bronson Patent," *Canadian Magazine*, 34 (April 1910): 507-514;

"The Bombshell," *Canadian Magazine*, 35 (December 1910): 106-112;

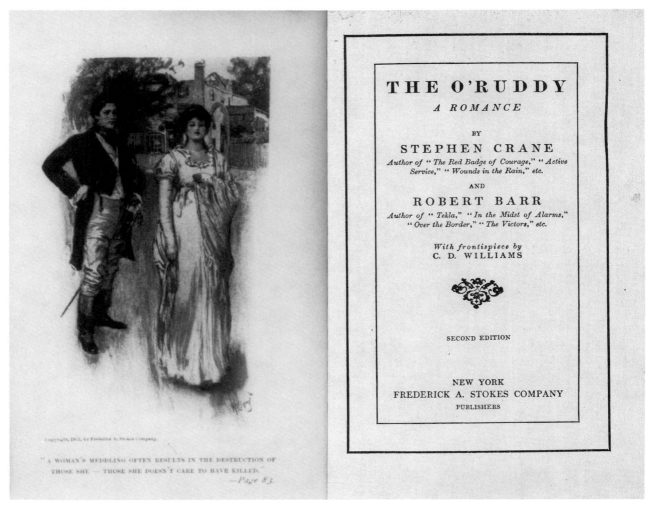

Frontispiece and title page for the 1903 novel started by Crane and completed by Barr following Crane's death in 1900

"Née Corrigan," *Canadian Magazine,* 40 (April 1913): 533-538.

NONFICTION

"Famous Idling Places–Hyeres," *Idler Magazine,* 1 (April 1892): 329-333;

"Fighting With Four Fists," *Idler Magazine,* 2 (August 1892): 115-126;

"Mont St. Michel," *Idler Magazine,* 4 (September 1893): 201-209;

"The Folks Play in the Tyrol," *Idler Magazine,* 4 (January 1894): 581-596;

"Shall and Will," *Bookman* (New York), 2 (December 1895): 287-288;

"Harold Frederic, The Author of *The Market Place,*" *Saturday Evening Post,* 171 (17 December 1898): 396-397;

"A Scrap of History," *Canadian Magazine,* 15 (June 1900): 160-163;

"An American Sculptor," *Outlook,* 79 (4 March 1905): 557-562;

"The Future of Great Britain and Canada" and "What Came of It at Last?" *Canadian Magazine,* 25 (October 1905): 490-493;

"When Welsh and Irish Rule," *Technical World Magazine,* 17 (April 1912): 147-153;

"Me and the Militia," *Canadian Magazine,* 42 (December 1913): 159-163;

"How Finley McGillis Held the Pier," *Canadian Magazine,* 42 (January 1914): 267-272.

Of considerable popular appeal at the turn of the century, the London-based novelist and short-story writer Robert Barr was part of a literary fraternity that included Stephen Crane, Arthur Conan Doyle, and Rudyard Kipling. Now, however, Barr is scarcely remembered other than for occasional contributions to the crime-fiction genre, such as the first Sherlock Holmes parody, "The Great Pegram Mystery" (1892; collected in *The Face and the Mask*, 1894), and a series featuring his own master sleuth, *The Triumphs of Eugène Valmont* (1906). As far as Barr's contributions to the development of Canadian literature are concerned, the standard critical response has been to dismiss his writings as the commercial productions of a bygone era, lowly ephemera undeserving of any scholarly attention. However, the truth of the matter is that Barr is a major Canadian humorist, as worthy of remembrance as, say, Stephen Leacock.

Robert Barr was born in Glasgow, Scotland, on 16 September 1850, but four years later the family emigrated and settled in rural Ontario. In 1862 Barr's brother James was born, and he, too, went on to achieve distinction as a comic writer, under the pen name of Angus Evan Abbott. In 1866 Barr joined the St. Thomas Volunteers to help fight against the invading Fenians, an experience–largely composed of comic mishaps, according to the essays "Me and the Militia" (*Canadian Magazine*, December 1913) and "How Finley McGillis Held the Pier" (*Canadian Magazine*, January 1914)–that provided the factual background for his first novel, *In the Midst of Alarms* (1894).

A later satiric novel, *The Measure of the Rule* (1907), was based upon the author's appalled reaction to the Toronto Normal School, which he entered in 1873 after several years of teaching on a temporary certificate. In 1876, though, the same year as his marriage to Eva Bennett of Raleigh, Ontario, Barr abandoned his teaching career– and Canada as well–to join the *Detroit Free Press*, contributing humorous articles under the pseudonym Luke Sharp. The essay "Literature in Canada" (1899; included in the 1973 edition of *The Measure of the Rule*) indicates, with characteristic Barr sprightliness, just why he departed:

I never expected to get pay for anything published in Canada, but was always glad when the editors did not send me a bill for publishing my contributions. . . .

My advice then to the Walter Scott tramping the streets of Toronto is: "Get over the border as soon as you can; come to London or go to New York; shake the dust of Canada from your feet. Get out of a land that is willing to pay money for whiskey, but wants its literature free in the shape of Ayer's Almanac, in my day the standard work of reference throughout the rural districts, because it cost nothing. Vamoose the ranch. Go

back when all the rest of the world is acquainted with you, and you may find that Canada has, perhaps, some knowledge of your existence. . . ."

In 1881 Barr moved to London to establish an English edition of the *Detroit Free Press;* then two years later he published his first book, *Strange Happenings* (1883), as Luke Sharp. It was not until the following decade, though, that Barr's literary career was fully launched. In 1892, as well as entering into partnership with humorist Jerome K. Jerome to found what was to become a leading periodical, the *Idler*, Barr brought out the first book to appear under his own name, a short-story collection, *In a Steamer Chair and Other Shipboard Stories*. From then on, until Barr's death in 1912, he wrote constantly and published some thirty books, including short-story collections, novels, and one travel book, *The Unchanging East* (1900).

Noted as a masterful raconteur and an inveterate lover of cigarettes (which he had specially imported from the United States), the burly and bearded Robert Barr is described by Arthur Conan Doyle as "a volcanic Anglo- or rather, Scot-American, with a violent manner, a wealth of strong adjectives, and one of the kindest natures underneath it all." Barr was a highly enterprising individual, as is illustrated by his literary output and various personal anecdotes. During his reporting days with the *Detroit Free Press*, Barr is said to have crossed a mile-wide river by leaping from ice floe to ice floe to supply his paper with an exclusive murder story. Later, during his London days, Barr, who had managed to become an honorary Iroquois chief, convinced an actual Iroquois chief to visit the House of Commons in full ceremonial regalia, thereby impressing Prime Minister William Gladstone and Sir William Harcourt sufficiently for them to promise a redressing of Indian grievances.

As is to be expected, the resourceful qualities that characterize Barr's life characterize his writing as well. In one of his articles, "An American Sculptor" (*Outlook*, 4 March 1905), Barr offers a comment that could serve as his own artistic credo: "There is no greater coward than Opposing Circumstance. If it sees you are determined on a fight, it will retreat; and if you advance, Opposing Circumstance will knuckle under altogether." Barr's protagonists, both male and female, customarily lived by this philosophy of life throughout the variety of fictional genres in which Barr wrote: historical and contemporary

Barr with Arthur Conan Doyle at Doyle's house just outside London,
circa 1894 (photograph by Fradelle & Young)

romantic-adventure stories, crime fiction, social satire, and farce. Still, a defeatist tale occasionally appears, such as the short story "The Reclamation of Joe Hollends" (collected in *The Face and The Mask*), a sardonic depiction of do-gooder social welfare policies; but the prevailing tone of Barr's work is one of buoyantly humorous optimism.

Of course, late-twentieth-century humor tends to be black humor, a circumstance that suggests a likely reason for the general indifference to Barr's writing. Then, too, there is another element that would distress a modern reader: the frequent reliance on late-Victorian, naively romantic melodrama–an element that weakens such an otherwise well-drawn novel as *The Measure of the Rule,* with its deft handling of satire (of the 1870s Toronto Normal School) and farcical misadventure. However, the modern reader can bypass these flaws by simply settling for nothing less than the best of Barr, which can be found in the short stories, the essays, and the delightful travel book, *The Unchanging East,* which offers this information:

Manchester . . . provides one tug for the stem and another for the stern of every steamship that leaves her port, and thus the trio go cautiously down the canal, the spirit of Manchester hovering over the craft all the way down the Mersey, murmuring "For Heaven's sake be careful!" The consequence is there are no shipwrecks on the Manchester Canal. Passengers on a liner are not distressed by picking up emaciated, starving sailors in an open boat. No one is ever marooned on its banks and mutinies rarely take place in its quiet waters, for the crews know if they raised a fuss the captain would simply call in the police.

Comic playfulness is clearly Barr's main strength, well displayed in "The Great Pegram Mystery": "I dropped in on my friend, Sherlaw Kombs. . . . I found him playing the violin with a look of sweet peace and serenity on his face, which I never noticed on the countenances of those within hearing distance."

In the essay "How To Write a Short Story" (1897; included in *Selected Stories,* 1977) Barr reveals both his wit and his artistic credo: "My model is Euclid, whose justly celebrated book of short stories, entitled *The Elements of Geometry,* will live when most of us who are scribbling today are forgotten. Euclid lays down his plot, sets instantly to work at its development, letting no incident creep in that does not bear relation to the climax, using no unnecessary word, always keeping his one end in view, and the moment he reaches the culmination he stops." Robert Barr deserves to be remembered, not for his romantic storytelling abilities–the sort of abilities that limit his contemporary Gilbert Parker (1860-1932) to being a mere specimen of his times–but for his comic inventiveness, a primary contribution to the Canadian humor tradition, carried on in the essays and sketches of Stephen Leacock and, more recently, the novels of Robertson Davies, W. O. Mitchell, and Mordecai Richler.

References:
C. Stan Allen, "A Glimpse of Robert Barr," *Canadian Magazine,* 4 (April 1895): 545-550;

Walter James Brown, "Robert Barr and Literature in Canada," *Canadian Magazine,* 15 (June 1900): 170-176;

John A. Cooper, "Canadian Celebrities. IX. Robert Barr," *Canadian Magazine,* 14 (December 1899): 181-182;

Arthur Conan Doyle, *Memories and Adventures* (Boston: Little, Brown, and Company, 1924), p. 113;

Francis W. Halsey, ed., *Authors of Our Day in Their Homes: Personal Descriptions and Interviews* (New York: Pott, 1902), pp. 247-254;

Louis K. MacKendrick, Introduction to *The Measure of the Rule* (Toronto: University of Toronto Press, 1973), pp. vii-xxi.

Papers:
Most of Barr's papers are in the Crane Collection at the Butler Library, Columbia University, and at the Regional History Department of the University of Western Ontario.

Nérée Beauchemin
(20 February 1850-29 June 1931)

Jack Warwick
York University

BOOKS: *Les Floraisons matutinales* (Trois-Rivières, Que.: Ayotte, 1897);
Patrie intime: Harmonies (Montreal: Librairie d'Action Canadienne-Française, 1928);
Choix de poésies, edited by Clément Marchand (Trois-Rivières, Que.: Bien Public, 1950);
Textes choisis et présentés par C. Marchand (Montreal: Fides, 1957);
Nérée Beauchemin: son œuvre, 3 volumes, edited by Armand Guilmette, critical edition (Montreal: Presses de l'Université du Québec, 1973-1974).

Nérée Beauchemin has been described as representing a decisive turning point in the development of French-Canadian poetry and as the most insipid poet of the nineteenth century. He was acclaimed, in his time, for bringing craftsmanship and refinement to a poetic tradition characterized by bombastic sloppiness. He lived in rural Quebec, which he celebrated without exaggeration or heavy didacticism, and is best remembered for delicate, precise vignettes of traditional French-Canadian country life.

Charles-Nérée Beauchemin was born 20 February 1850 in Yamachiche, a small town in the fertile belt near Three Rivers, Quebec. His father, Hyacinthe Beauchemin, was the local doctor, and Beauchemin was to follow in his footsteps. The poet's mother, Elzire Richer-Laflèche Beauchemin, was related to Louis-François Laflèche, the outspoken nationalist bishop of Three Rivers, and to Lomer Gouin, once premier of Quebec.

Beauchemin studied at the seminary in Nicolet; this does not imply a religious vocation, seminaries being then the regular place for a secondary education. From there he went on to study medicine at Laval University from 1870 to 1874. He returned to practice medicine in Yamachiche, where he remained for the rest of his life. The place was not without literary memories, being also the birthplace of Antoine Gérin-Lajoie, but Beauchemin was not closely associated with the main literary circles in Quebec and Montreal. He had apparently begun to write poetry while he was a student in Quebec City–his earliest known composition dates from that time–and he published verse from time to time in newspapers, though without any thought of making a literary career.

One of Beauchemin's early poems, "Rayons d'octobre" (October Sunbeams), attracted the attention of more established writers: Louis Fréchette sent congratulations. The poem is a visual and evocative depiction of traditional farm life, set in a mellow autumn scene, and ending with the image of a bird flying bravely into the advancing chill of nightfall. The moral message is only hinted at, and the versification is relatively free of padding and trite effects. Beauchemin continued modestly writing and publishing until, in 1888, the Royal Society of Canada awarded him a prize, based on about a hundred scattered poems. The same group of admirers elected him to membership in the Society in 1896, a circumstance that obliged him to publish a book. *Les Floraisons matutinales* (Morning Blossomings) appeared the following year; it was a collection of forty-five pieces, without any particular order or discernible principles of selection. The common underlying theme is fidelity: to nature, to religion, and to *la patrie*, which for Beauchemin means, above all, his own region. The collection also includes historical pieces that recall, thematically, the martial airs of Octave Crémazie and the Patriotic School. Stylistically, however, there is a distinct difference: "La cloche de Louisbourg" (The Bell of Louisbourg) is mainly devoted to a physical and artistic description of the bell saved from a fort that had seen important battles between French and English under the old regime. The poem won immediate praise because it avoided the rhetorical excesses of the older school.

The title of Beauchemin's second volume, *Patrie intime: Harmonies* (Intimate Homeland, Harmonies, 1928), more clearly defines his true nature. A preliminary poem declares that the poet

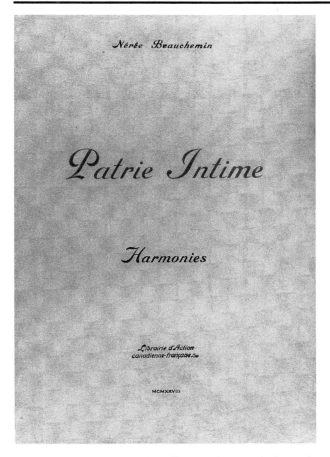

Cover for Beauchemin's 1928 collection of poems, the last published during his lifetime

has accepted life in the small circle lit by the blue sky under which he was born and where, as in a cloister, he has found complete inner peace. Meditation, nuance, and understatement, evident in his earliest work, take a decided upper hand, though there are still commemorative pieces that mark occasions great and small, public and personal. *Patrie intime* creates an enviably harmonious world in which art, truth, beauty, nature, and God form a serene family, perhaps like the author's own. (He had married Anna Lacerte, daughter of the local member of Parliament, and raised ten children in a large, old house.) Even when he speaks of the tantalizing goals of the artist, it is not as a *poète maudit* (cursed poet) driven mad by the unattainable: "Hantise" (Obsession) acknowledges the disappointment encountered by any poet at the inadequacy of his words, but more than that it expresses the ecstasy of playing with rhythms and phrases, the search that leads toward beauty, truth—even God. Death, a frequent theme, is always viewed with unshakable Christian faith.

Explicit religion plays a large part in Beauchemin's poetry; sometimes he literally describes the liturgy, the way one might paint a nativity. But his best-remembered compositions imbue ordinary life with a feeling some critics have described as mystical: the Sanctus enters the humble rural home, giving it spiritual value. The agricultural year and nature's cycle of death and renewal spread the same feeling into all Beauchemin's rural scenes, such as "La Glaneuse," his portrait of the gleaner in cheerful dialogue with a generous sun. Here, quite typically, nature participates in Christian charity without a hint of the dreaded ambiguity found in major telluric myths.

Beauchemin's is above all a visual art. It has been correctly observed that his tropology is rare but unadventurous; apart from his faith in Christian mysteries, he presents a literal, precise, material world. For this Gérard Bessette judges Beauchemin harshly; but others have hailed the evocative descriptions in Beauchemin's first book. Like the French Parnassians he is capable in his best work of painting a picture and relying on its suggestiveness.

Whereas writers' identifications with rural French-Canadians are often suspect, Beauchemin appears to write from inside the rural scene rather than about it. He proudly adopts the archaic diction of his neighbors and deftly adopts their conventional symbols, such as offering verbena as a sign of friendship. If ever the French-Canadian rural religious idyll (much decried since the Quiet Revolution) had a moment of truth, it is to be found in the verse of this modest country doctor, who died in 1931, only two years before his neighbor, Philippe Panneton (Ringuet, 1895-1960), started to write *30 Arpents* (1938; translated as *Thirty Acres*, 1940).

Biography:

Gonzalve Poulin, *Nérée Beauchemin* (Trois-Rivières, Que.: Editions du Bien Public, 1934).

References:

Gérard Bessette, *Les Images en poésie canadienne-française* (Montreal: Beauchemin, 1960), pp. 111-125;

Charles ab der Halden, *Etudes de littérature canadienne-française* (Paris: Rudeval, 1904);

Clément Marchand, Preface to *Choix de poésies* (Trois-Rivières, Que.: Bien Public, 1950).

Harry Bernard

(9 May 1898-16 May 1979)

Rosanna Furgiuele
York University

BOOKS: *L'Homme tombé* (Montreal: Albert Lévesque, 1924);

La Terre vivante (Montreal: Bibliothèque de l'Action Française, 1925);

La Maison vide (Montreal: Bibliothèque de l'Action Française, 1926);

La Dame blanche (Montreal: Bibliothèque de l'Action Française, 1927);

Essais critiques (Montreal: Librairie d'Action Canadienne-Française, 1929);

La Ferme des pins (Montreal: Librairie d'Action Canadienne-Française, 1930);

Juana, mon aimée (Montreal: Albert Lévesque, 1931);

Dolorès (Montreal: Albert Lévesque, 1932);

Montcalm se fâche (Montreal: Albert Lévesque, 1935);

Le Roman régionaliste aux Etats-Unis (1913-1940) (Montreal: Fides, 1949);

Les Jours sont longs (Montreal: Cercle du Livre de France, 1951);

Portages et routes d'eau en Haute-Mauricie (Trois-Rivières, Quebec: Editions du Bien Public, 1953).

SELECTED PERIODICAL PUBLICATIONS
UNCOLLECTED: "Roman de l'avarice," *Enseignement Secondaire au Canada,* 21 (February 1942): 376-389;

"Le Roman de la Nouvelle-Angleterre," *Mémoires de la Société Royale du Canada,* third series, 42, section 1 (1948): 9-27.

The son of Horace and Alexandra Boudreau Bernard, novelist and journalist Harry Bernard was born in London, England, in 1898. He studied in Paris and in Saint Albans, Vermont, and then at the *séminaire* in Saint-Hyacinthe, Quebec, where he received his B.A. in 1918. After one year of study in Lowell, Massachusetts, he enrolled at the University of Montreal, where he obtained his *licence ès lettres*. From 1919 to 1923 Bernard was parliamentary correspondent for *Le Droit* in Ottawa and eventually became director of *Le Courrier de Saint-Hyacinthe,* a newspaper with which he was associated from 1923 to 1970. From 1933 to 1934 he was also director of *L'Action Nationale* in Montreal. During a journalistic career spanning fifty years, Bernard contributed to several newspapers, often using the pseudonym L'Illettré to sign articles and literary reviews. He was married twice: to Louella Tobin and to Alice Sicotte. Three of his novels were awarded the Prix David: *L'Homme tombé* (The Fallen Man, 1924), *La Terre vivante* (The Living Earth, 1925), and *Juana, mon aimée* (1931). In 1959 the Royal Society of Canada honored him with its silver medal, and in 1961 he received the Prix Olivar Asselin. Bernard was six times the recipient of the Prix d'Action Intellectuelle. He died in Saint-Hyacinthe in 1979.

Although Bernard published articles, short stories, and critical essays, he is best remembered for his novels that belong to the regional literature of French Canada. His first novel, *L'Homme tombé,* depicts the negative influence of the city on the lives of a young couple. Despite his mother's objections, Dr. Etienne Normand marries a working-class girl, Alberte Dumont, only to discover that she yields to the frivolous temptations of urban life and neglects her duties as wife and mother. Unable to curb his wife's worldly aspirations, Dr. Normand comes to the sad realization that he has fallen into a state of indifference after only five years of marriage. This didactic novel presents an unflattering portrait of the social elite and illustrates how the illusory pleasures of city life, far from generating happiness, are instrumental in destroying family ties and in bringing about man's downfall.

La Terre vivante, La Maison vide (The Empty House, 1926), and *La Ferme des pins* (The Farm in the Pines, 1930) can be considered a triptych presenting three different aspects of the same theme. The author's aim is twofold: to awaken the national consciousness of French-Canadians in an attempt to encourage them to remain faithful to the traditional rural values that constitute their roots, and to portray urban life as an evil

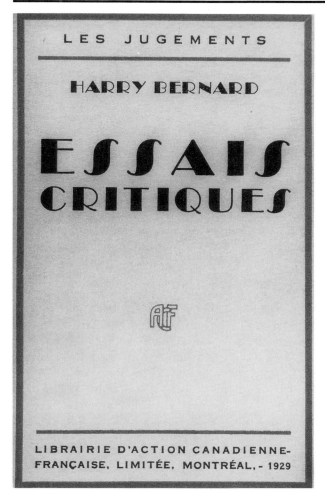

LES JUGEMENTS

HARRY BERNARD

ESSAIS CRITIQUES

LIBRAIRIE D'ACTION CANADIENNE-
FRANÇAISE, LIMITÉE, MONTRÉAL, - 1929

Cover for Bernard's influential 1929 book of literary criticism, in which he discusses the work of leading Quebec writers

that corrupts and ultimately leads to doom. The three novels preach the same moral: happiness is only possible insofar as one remains faithful to one's past and to the land inherited from one's ancestors. In *La Terre vivante* an elderly farmer longs to see his children inherit the land he has loved and cultivated. His dream is shattered when his son abandons the ancestral home and his daughters are lured away by the call of the city. By a strange turn of events, the youngest daughter, Marie, abandoned by the city doctor she loved, returns to her father's house and discovers that she has always loved the son of a neighboring farmer. By marrying him and settling on her father's farm, she assures the continuity of the agricultural tradition.

La Maison vide focuses on the disintegration of a French-Canadian family living in an urban environment, thus reiterating the viewpoint that the

city with its vices, passions, and frivolities, corrupts and destroys those who fall under its spell. The Dumontier family, who lives in a posh neighborhood in Ottawa, is completely taken up by the social whirl and slowly abandons all authentic values that characterize rural life. The secret marriage of one of the daughters to a Protestant anglophone clearly signals the break with the past.

The adverse effects of mixed marriages is the central theme of *La Ferme des pins*. Uncharacteristically, it is an anglophone, James Robertson, who feels threatened by assimilation and regrets having married a French-Canadian woman. Although he makes every effort to prevent his children from committing the same mistake, he fails with the two older sons, and in an attempt to save his youngest offspring, he buys a piece of land in Ontario where they can live among English-speaking people. In this novel Bernard demonstrates that the union of two nationalities produces disastrous consequences.

The themes presented in these three novels reiterate the agricultural ideology prevalent in French-Canadian regional literature of the time. The characters lack depth and can be reduced to stereotypes whose primary function is to illustrate a moral.

Juana, mon aimée differs from Bernard's previous works because of its innovative literary techniques and psychological analysis. The novel, set in the Canadian prairies, relates in the first person the memories of Raymond Chatel, a journalist in Ottawa and Montreal, who takes a health cure in Saskatchewan, where he meets Juana and falls in love with her. Believing him to be married, Juana puts an end to their romance and marries another. The love story of Chatel and Juana serves as a pretext to describe the natural beauties of the prairies and to depict the difficulties experienced by the colonists in the Canadian West.

The first-person narration is once again effectively used in *Dolorès* (1932). By means of flashbacks Jacques Forest relives a significant period in his life during which he meets Dolorès, with whom he shares a romantic adventure, putting aside for a time his professional and personal responsibilities. Their idyllic, make-believe existence comes to an end when Forest leaves the enchanted Laurentian region to return to Montreal and to reality. Although in many respects *Dolorès* is reminiscent of *Juana, mon aimée*, it offers a more penetrating psychological analysis of the characters.

Bernard's last novel, *Les Jours sont longs* (The Days Are Long, 1951), is undoubtedly his most polished and convincing work and shows a marked improvement in literary technique and psychological analysis. It is a retrospective account in which the narrator relives his years spent in the woods where he experienced both love and suffering. The plot and characters echo those of his previous works *Juana, mon aimée* and *Dolorès;* however, the original portrait of the Métis Amédée Cardinal and the elaborate description of the Canadian forest combine to contribute to the success of the novel.

Adapting material from French-Canadian legends and historical events, Bernard composed fourteen short stories published in 1927 under the title *La Dame blanche.* Unfortunately, the author concentrates more on the edification of his readers than on the description of the mores of another era. A modified version of this collection was published in 1935. The author omitted the last five stories and added "Montcalm se fâche," which became the title work of the new collection.

Published in 1929, *Essais critiques,* a collection of twelve essays, deals with various issues concerning a national literature, topics that range from Baudelaire's influence in Canada to regional literature to the problems of language in French-Canadian works. Bernard also comments on the works of Blanche Lamontagne-Beauregard, Louis Dantin (Eugène Seers), Jules Fournier, Robert de Roquebrune, Jean Chauvin, and Jean Narrache (Emile Coderre). Although this work was generally well received, Dantin in *Gloses critiques* (Critical Glosses, 1931, 1935) criticizes Bernard for attempting to thwart the freedom of expression of Canadian writers, and Claude-Henri Grignon in *Ombres et clameurs* (Shadows and Outcries, 1933) offered a scathing review.

In 1948 Bernard received his doctorate from the University of Montreal. *Le Roman régionaliste aux Etats-Unis (1913-1940)* (The Regional Novel in the United States), his thesis, published the following year, presents an inventory of more than three thousand American regional novels. By means of his historical analysis, the author intends to give Quebec writers a lesson in literary nationalism and thus serve the cause of regional literature in French Canada.

Harry Bernard has been criticized by some for his uniform writing style, his lack of originality, and his repetitiveness with regard to characters, plot, and themes. His primary concern appears to be not so much with refining his style as with delivering a message and voicing the agricultural ideology. Yet he was a prolific writer who enjoyed a certain reputation (as proven by the various awards he received), who left his mark on the regional literature of French Canada and played a role in the development of the French-Canadian psychological novel.

Adèle Bibaud

(3 March 1854-14 February 1941)

Mary Jean Green
Dartmouth College

BOOKS: *Trois Ans en Canada*, as Elèda Gonneville (Montreal: O. Bibaud, 1887); republished as *Avant la conquête: Episode de la guerre de 1757* (Montreal: Montreal Printing & Publishing, 1904);

Un Terrible Secret (Montreal: O. Bibaud, 1893);

Le Secret de la marquise et Un Homme d'honneur, published with *Poésies*, by Michel Bibaud (Montreal: Dalaire, 1906);

Les Fiancés de St-Eustache (Montreal, 1910);

Lionel Duvernoy (Montreal, 1912);

L'Homme qui pense: Contes de Noël (N.p., 1925).

OTHER: Maximilien Bibaud, *Le Panthéon canadien*, edited by Adèle and Victoria Bibaud (Montreal: Valois, 1891).

Adèle Bibaud was born on 3 March 1854 to Jean-Gaspard Bibaud, an eminent physician, and Virginie Pelletier Bibaud. The Bibaud family was known for its literary accomplishments. Adèle Bibaud's uncle Maximilien Bibaud (1824-1887) was the author of literary studies, including *Le Panthéon canadien,* of which Bibaud and her sister Victoria prepared an edition in 1891. She was the granddaughter of Michel Bibaud (1782-1857), who was a poet and one of Quebec's first historians.

Adèle Bibaud was one of only two francophone women to publish a novel in the nineteenth century (the other being Laure Conan). Her two novels carry on some of the interests of her grandfather, embellishing historical situations with melodramatic adventures and romantic *malentendus*. Both treat events of major importance in Quebec's history. Published under the pseudonym Elèda Gonneville, *Trois Ans en Canada* (Three Years in Canada, 1887) concerns the British attack on Quebec City in 1759, and *Les Fiancés de St-Eustache* (1910), which appeared under Bibaud's own name, is set during the Patriots' Rebellion of 1837. In each case the novel ends with a resounding defeat for the French Canadians, and all or most of the major characters

are killed. Thus, unlike Laure Conan, Bibaud did not focus on the heroic early years of the French settlement of Quebec but rather on the tragedy of French defeat.

In Bibaud's novels the historical events provide the backgrounds for conventional love plots. *Trois Ans en Canada* (republished as *Avant la conquête* [Before the Conquest], 1904), the more intricate of the novels, features two pairs of lovers, each relationship complicated by several jealous rivals. The most important authentic historical figure to appear in this novel is General Louis Joseph de Montcalm. In *Les Fiancés de St-Eustache* there is only one set of lovers, and there are fewer obstacles to their relationship. The central characters are the orphaned Lucienne and her fiancé, Pierre, a poor but industrious tutor who is killed, with other Patriots, in the church at Saint Eustache. Along with this thin plot line Bibaud includes an almost unrelated subplot and information on the historical background, including citations from speeches of the historical figure Louis-Joseph Papineau, who inspired the Patriots to rebel.

Bibaud's narratives are often interrupted by digressions that seem to betray some of her own concerns. In both novels historical events give way to debates about whether women should be writers. Not surprisingly, the author's viewpoint is supportive of literary women, who, she claims, make better and more sensitive wives–if they retain their feminine modesty and write only after domestic duties have been fulfilled. While Bibaud's heroines are often the helpless maidens of melodrama, they are also educated women who occasionally display literary and musical talents, capacities that are shown to be attractive to men.

In addition to her two novels Bibaud also published several shorter works, including *Le Secret de la marquise* (The Marquise's Secret, 1906) and the short stories, set in contemporary Quebec, that appeared under the title *Lionel Duvernoy* (1912). Her short pieces appeared in various periodicals, including *La Presse, Le Journal de Fran-çoise,* and *La Bonne Parole.* She died in Montreal on 14 February 1941. The interest of Bibaud's work lies neither in its literary form nor in its his-torical interpretations but rather in the light it sheds on the situation of the woman writer in Que-bec at the turn of the twentieth century.

Georges Bugnet

(23 February 1879-11 January 1981)

E. D. Blodgett
University of Alberta

BOOKS: *Le Lys de sang,* as Henri Doutremont (Montreal: Garand, 1923);

Nipsya, as Doutremont (Montreal: Edouard Ga-rand, 1924); translated by Constance Davies Woodrow (New York, London & Montreal: Louis Carrier, 1929);

Siraf (Montreal: Totem, 1934);

La Forêt (Montreal: Totem, 1935); translated by David Carpenter as *The Forest* (Montreal: Harvest House, 1976);

Voix de la solitude (Montreal: Totem, 1938);

Poèms, edited by Jean-Marcel Duciaume (Edmon-ton: Eglantier, 1978).

SELECTED PERIODICAL PUBLICATIONS

UNCOLLECTED: "Le Pin du Maskeg," *Le Ca-nada Français,* 12 (October 1924): 95-103; (November 1924): 176-185;

"Le Conte du Bouleau, de Mélèse et du Pic Rouge," *La Canada Français,* 19 (March 1932): 526-538;

La Défaite, Le Canada Français, 22 (September 1934): 40-58;

"Du Roman," *Le Canada Français,* 23 (November 1935): 217-225;

Ivan et Fedor, Le Canada Français, 26 (October 1938): 166-184;

"La Forêt," *Le Canada Français,* 27 (January 1940): 389-401.

Georges Bugnet holds a singular place in French-Canadian writing between the two wars. Although he is considered by many to be mar-ginal, others classify him as unique, the one writer of French origin published in the twenti-eth century whose career was fundamentally Cana-dian. He has frequently been compared to Louis Hémon, whose *Maria Chapdelaine* (1916) has played a more influential role in the history of French-Canadian literature, but Bugnet is at once more profound than Hémon and more re-sponsive to North American realities. He may fur-thermore be distinguished clearly from the tradi-tion within which Hémon is situated, that of the *roman du terroir* (novel of the soil), both by the vari-ety of his writing and by his somewhat ambigu-ous view of the natural world, which is at once clas-sical and Christian. In all things he was severely antimodern, intransigently Catholic, and yet a uni-versalist in the French neoclassical manner. It was perhaps this last trait, combined with the fact that his life was spent outside Quebec, that has pre-vented him from receiving the respect he is due as a major French-Canadian writer of the period between the two wars.

Georges-Charles-Jules Bugnet, son of Claude and Josephine Sebut Bugnet, was born 23 February 1879 in Chalon-sur-Saône, Bur-gundy, France. For a time he planned to become a priest but failed in his vocation. He then sought a career as a university professor but was unable to gain admittance because of his religion. He became the editor of the weekly journal *La Croix de la Haute Savoie* in 1904, but unwilling to compromise his religious views for the sake of the journal's publisher, Bugnet resigned by the end of the year. Early in 1905, with Julia Ley Bugnet, to whom he had been married for less than a year, he arrived in Canada, settling in northern Alberta. His Canadian plan was two-

Dust jacket for Bugnet's 1924 novel about a young Métisse who must choose among three suitors (written under the pseudonym Henri Doutremont)

fold: to become a financial success and return as soon as possible to his native France. He succeeded in neither part of his plan. Bugnet and his wife remained in Canada and eventually had nine children.

Bugnet's career as a writer of fiction did not begin until 1920, when in the spring he drafted his first novel, *Le Lys du sang* (The Blood Lily, 1923), a quest-romance set for the most part in the jungles of East Africa. Reminiscent of the fiction of Jules Verne and H. Rider Haggard, the object of the quest is a legendary lily that feeds on human blood. The quest is a vehicle for developing central themes: nature as mystery, the role of scientific knowledge versus religious faith, and the limits of human action. Bugnet, who published the novel under the pseudonym Henri Doutremont, hoped for at least a modest finan-

cial success, but his debut was inauspicious. He received neither financial reward nor critical accolades. Despite his sense of fantasy (unusual in writing of the period), his use of irony, and his handling of a romance configuration–the young hero between the fair and dark ladies of the spirit–the novel did not attract a readership.

Bugnet first attained critical success with a fable entitled "Le Pin du Maskeg" (The Pine in the Muskeg, 1924). He considered the tale his most characteristic and most Canadian piece. The central figure is a pine tree that symbolizes the superiority of nature over man. The human intrigue that occurs, significantly, at the foot of the tree, involves the murder of a woman's husband by the man who loves her. The murder is subsequently avenged by her son. Despite Bugnet's belief that the point of view of the tale was antisentimental, the narrator adores the pine to the point of pathetic fallacy. It was this work, however, that announced Bugnet's characteristic theme, nature's superb indifference to man unless man understands his own insufficiency and limitations. A minor masterpiece, it anticipates the tempered pastoral of *Nipsya* (1924; translated, 1929) and the tragedy of *La Forêt* (1935; translated as *The Forest*, 1976).

Both *Nipsya* (the Cree Indian word for willow) and *La Forêt* share the sense of nature as active participant that begins with "Le Pin du Maskeg." Part of Bugnet's response to nature may be attributed to the impact it made upon him in his solitude in Rich Valley, Alberta, and part may come from his religion, with its suggestions of Bonaventuran mysticism. But his interest in nature was also scientific, and he has been recognized by botanists for the hybrid roses he developed. The plant, whether flower or tree, and its transformation through seasonal change, is the model for how the human becomes part of his ontological place. It is the figure that marks Bugnet's notion of pastoral as religious.

The character who is closest to nature in his work is the Métisse, Nipsya, and she attains this stature by recognizing that love is a gift of self. This "don de soi" is the process by which nature's designs are realized. This theme, conjoined with Bugnet's theocentric sense of nature, led him to create characters that are abstractions rather than individuals. Hence, the three possible suitors that Nipsya considers appear primarily as incarnations of positions among which to choose. Only Nipsya has a psychological dimension, which changes according to her response to her suitors and becomes increasingly Jansenist in its self-renunciation as she commits herself to her choice.

The tragic response to nature is dramatized by the protagonists of *La Forêt*, the Bourgouins, whose name suggests "city dwellers." Their tragic flaw springs from the husband's belief that he can be the measure of nature and in his wife's belief that nature anthropomorphically reflects her moods. "Nature," however, as Bugnet remarked, "is not sad"; nature *is*, in all its ontological force. Failure to recognize this fact generates the tragic consequences symbolized by the apparently accidental drowning of the settlers' baby. *La Forêt* is considered Bugnet's most accomplished work.

Although he was not a great poet, nor received as such, Bugnet concluded his career with a collection entitled *Voix de la solitude* (Voices of Solitude, 1938) that includes philosophical verse, which was republished in 1978 under the title *Poèmes*. In 1934 he had produced *Siraf*, a scathing satire on the limitations of modernity, materialism, technology, and democracy, elaborating an attitude that, no matter how accurate, has been increasingly more out of key with French-Canadian ideologies. Bugnet also wrote two plays,

La Défaite (The Defeat) and *Ivan et Fedor*, both published in *Le Canada Français* during the 1930s. Despite the variety of his writings and his originality during the 1920s and 1930s, he now suffers the fate of being overlooked by most histories of French-Canadian literature. His virtual silence after the writing of *Voix de la solitude* no doubt contributed to his neglect.

References:

E. D. Blodgett, "Cold Pastorals," in *Configuration: Essays in the Canadian Literatures* (Downsview, Ont.: ECW, 1982);

E. K. Brown, "A Fine Novel in the West," in *Response and Evaluations—Essays on Canada*, edited by David Staines (Toronto: McClelland & Stewart, 1977), pp. 292-294;

Dave Carpenter, "A Canadian *Fête Mobile:* Interview with Georges Bugnet," *Journal of Canadian Fiction*, 2 (Spring 1973): 49-53;

Carpenter, "Georges Bugnet: An Introduction," *Journal of Canadian Fiction*, 1 (Fall 1972): 72-78;

Jean Papen, *Georges Bugnet: Homme de lettres canadien*, Saint-Boniface: Editions des Plaines, 1985.

Arthur de Bussières

(20 January 1877-7 May 1913)

Maurice Lebel
Laval University

BOOKS: *Les Bengalis: Poèmes épars,* edited by Casimir Hébert (Montreal: Garand, 1931);
Les Bengalis d'Arthur de Bussières, edited by Robert Giroux (Sherbrooke, Que.: Cosmos, 1975).

Arthur de Bussières was born on 20 January 1877 in Montreal, the same city where he died on 7 May 1913 at the age of thirty-six. His father, Fabien, and his mother, Rachel de Beriau Bussières, who were married in Montreal on 4 June 1873, had thirteen children altogether. Second in the family, Arthur could not (to his lifelong regret) pursue extended higher studies at a middle-class city college. Indeed, when de Bussières's primary education at Saint-Jean-Baptiste School on Rue Sanguinet (then run by the Clercs de Saint-Viateur) was finished, he was called to help his father with his work. Fabien de Bussières, like one of the characters drawn by the great French novelist and physician Georges Duhamel, was stricken every year by the urge to move his large family. He also moved from job to job, from cart driver to housepainter to store-window decorator. At the age of eighteen Arthur de Bussières left his father's house to lead his own life.

Born into poverty, he never escaped it. A Bohemian, a dreamer, and in due course an alcoholic, the young de Bussières was never assiduous in applying himself to the work of a painter or decorator. Completely lacking in any sense of practicality, living from day to day–solitary, taciturn, deprived, and destitute–he seemed destined to live solely for art, for poetry. Self-taught, he read widely, especially among the poets of the nineteenth century; his favorites included Victor Hugo, Alfred de Vigny, Théophile Gautier, José Maria de Heredia, Charles Baudelaire, Stéphane Mallarmé, and Leconte de Lisle. He held Heredia, to whom he dedicated a sonnet, to be his undisputed master, his model. Yet several of de Bussières's poems–including "Vers l'amour," "Celle que j'aimais," and "Mort d'une fleur" (Toward Love, The One I Loved, and

Death of a Flower)–reveal that, passionate admirer of the French Parnassian poets though he was, he also admired Lamartine and Alfred de Musset. Before all others, however, he was friends with other Quebec writers: first Emile Nelligan, then Jean Charbonneau, Albert Laberge, E. Z. Massicotte, and Charles Gill.

De Bussières is little known today. He would be known even less had not Casimir Hébert, Léon Paquin, and Robert Giroux collected, collated, and edited his seventy-six poems (of which fifty-seven are sonnets). Hébert, a librarian and poet in his own right, a member of the Royal Society of Canada and president of the Canadian Linguistics Society, has the distinction of having published most of de Bussières's work in 1931, eighteen years after the poet's death, thus rescuing it from oblivion. Of the sixty-one poems he brought together, nine had never before been printed, the others having appeared earlier in a variety of papers and journals such as *Le Monde Illustré, Le Passe-Temps, La Revue Populaire, Les Débats,* and *Les Soirées du Château de Ramezay.* Hébert's edition, despite its typographical errors, still remains a basic text. In addition to a note to the reader, it contains a preface by Charbonneau that provides precious information about the poet and his work. As for Paquin, in the course of his research for his doctorate (at the University of Ottawa in 1958) he found fifteen more unpublished poems by de Bussières, including nine sonnets. Eight of these works then appeared in the May-June 1965 issue of *La Barre du Jour.* Finally, in 1975, Robert Giroux edited and published a volume entitled *Les Bengalis d'Arthur de Bussières.* This book comprises both the poems from Hébert's edition and the discoveries made by Paquin. Giroux wrote an introduction and added a valuable chronology and a select bibliography. Such is the brief history of the sonnets, odes, madrigals, and rondeaux left behind by the poor poet of L'Ecole Littéraire de Montréal.

Though most of de Bussières's poems are sonnets, others vary in form. "Au Revoir" is a four-

ARTHUR de BUSSIÈRES

LES
BENGALIS

poèmes épars recueillis

par

CASIMIR HÉBERT

PRÉSIDENT DE LA SOCIÉTÉ DE LINGUISTIQUE
DU CANADA.

EDITIONS EDOUARD GARAND
1423-1425-1427, rue Ste-Elisabeth
MONTRÉAL
1931

Cover of the first collection of de Bussières's poetry, published eighteen years after his death

line work, "Automne et Choses Mortes" (Autumn and Dead Things) occupies seven lines, and "Vers l'amour" eleven. Several carry Latin titles, including "Nocturnae," "Vox temporum," "Requiescat in pace," and "Oceanus" (the last of these unfinished). He could have written them anywhere, for in them one finds scarcely any reference to his city or country. The poems that were written with Heredia as a model are cold, impassive, and chiseled like medals; they lack soul and warmth, though not brilliance, imagination, musicality, or rhythmic timbre. These poems portray exotic horizons, glorious mirages, and distant emirates. Their sonority of rhyme produces the effect of echo; their cumulative series of evocative words suggests incantation. Constantly the poems use metaphor and comparison; they draw on a rich, varied, and profuse vocabulary. Language itself

occupies pride of place in such works. Yet de Bussières was not only a Parnassian poet. He is linked also with the symbolists: to Baudelaire, for example, through his use of metonymy and synesthesia, and through the practice of *correspondances,* as can be heard in the way the voice of Baudelaire's *Les Fleurs du Mal* (1857) often sounds in his sonnets. Moreover, in about thirty of his poems–from "Ruines" to "Celles que j'aimais," from "Requiescat in pace" to "Mortuae" or "Orpha," from "Puisque" (Because) and "Mort d'une fleur" to "Chant de Noël," "Autrefois," and "Vers elle" (Christmas Song, In Former Times, and Toward Her)–de Bussières refuses to remain impersonal. The pronouns *je, me, mon, ma, moi* (I, me, my, mine) flow recurrently from his pen; and he clearly had an affection for the words *triste* and *tristesse* (sad and sadness). In these poems he is as romantic as Lamartine and de Musset, and truly one with Hugo.

Readers must remember to place these poems in their historical context. From 1896 to 1913 de Bussières was a member of L'Ecole Littéraire de Montréal—one might call it the School of Exoticism in Quebec poetry. It is important to recognize what this participation means, for the varied activities of this group of writers mark a critical stage of literary development. Partly as a result of their enterprise, writing in Quebec turned from cold Parnassian models to the manifold forms of the modern.

Reference:

Léon Paquin, "Arthur de Bussières, sa vie et son oeuvre," D. ès L. dissertation, University of Ottawa, 1958.

William Wilfred Campbell

(1 June 1858-1 January 1918)

Carl F. Klinck
University of Western Ontario

BOOKS: *Lake Lyrics and Other Poems* (St. John, N.B.: McMillan, 1889);

The Dread Voyage (Toronto: Briggs, 1893);

Mordred; and Hildebrand (Ottawa: Durie, 1895);

Beyond the Hills of Dream (Boston & New York: Houghton, Mifflin, 1899; Toronto: Morang, 1900);

The Collected Poems (New York & Chicago: Revell, 1905); republished as *The Poems of Wilfred Campbell* (Toronto: Briggs, 1905);

Ian of the Orcades; or, The Armourer of Girnigoe (New York: Revell, 1906; Edinburgh & London: Oliphant, Anderson & Ferrier, 1906);

Canada (London: Black, 1907);

Poetical Tragedies (Toronto: Briggs, 1908);

A Beautiful Rebel: A Romance of Upper Canada in Eighteen Hundred and Twelve (Toronto: Westminster, 1909; New York & London: Hodder & Stoughton, 1909);

The Beauty, History, Romance & Mystery of the Canadian Lake Region (Toronto: Musson, 1910; London: Hodder & Stoughton, 1911);

The Scotsman in Canada (London: Low, Marston, 1911);

Sagas of Vaster Britain: Poems of the Race, the Empire and the Divinity of Man (London: Hodder & Stoughton, 1914);

The Poetical Works, edited by W. J. Sykes (London: Hodder & Stoughton, 1922);

Snowflakes and Sunbeams (Ottawa: Golden Dog, 1974);

William Wilfred Campbell, as a student at the University of Toronto in the early 1880s (photograph courtesy of Queen's University)

Selected Poems, edited by Carl F. Klinck (Ottawa: Tecumseh, 1976).

OTHER: *Poems of Loyalty by British and Canadian Authors*, edited by Campbell (London & New York: Nelson, 1912);

The Oxford Book of Canadian Verse, edited by Campbell (Toronto & Oxford: Oxford University Press, 1913);

At the Mermaid Inn: Wilfred Campbell, Archibald Lampman, Duncan Campbell Scott in The Globe 1892-3, edited by Barrie Davies, includes essays by Campbell (Toronto & Buffalo: University of Toronto Press, 1979).

Wilfred Campbell was a late-Victorian and Edwardian Canadian poet who is frequently linked with Charles G. D. Roberts and Bliss Carman of New Brunswick, and with Archibald Lampman and Duncan Campbell Scott of Ontario. Like these two Ontario poets, he lived and wrote principally in Ottawa. His most distinctive contribution, however, was made in his first book, *Lake Lyrics and Other Poems* (1889), inspired by the scenery around his parents' home in Wiarton. His lyrics have more than local interest, for he created a mythology of the waters and shores of Georgian Bay and Lake Huron in terms of the Indians who lived long ago by "the lakes of the West." The poems can be read as Canadian or American—or as people of both nations read Henry Wadsworth Longfellow's *Song of Hiawatha* (1855).

William Wilfred Campbell was born in 1858 in Berlin (now Kitchener), Ontario, the second son of Matilda and Thomas Campbell, an Anglican clergyman. The family lived in various parts of the province before settling in the frontier mission of Wiarton in Campbell's fourteenth year. The cultural influence of his parents and home encouraged him to follow his father's calling. After several years of teaching school in the lake district, he studied at the University of Toronto and Wycliffe College. A significant exposure to American influences began when he continued his training for the ministry at the Episcopal Theological School, near Harvard. There, from 1883 until 1885, the young poet found what Phillips Brooks called "the most earnest piety with the most active intelligence."

Unprepared by poetry and theology to cope with evolutionary theories being introduced and adapted by John Fiske of Harvard in *Myths and Mythmakers*, Campbell responded emotionally to new concepts of life and its meaning. Fiske's "Old Tales and Superstitions Interpreted by Comparative Mythology" provided settings and images for the poetic dramatization of inner conflicts that would continue to unsettle Campbell while he served as an Anglican priest at West Claremont, New Hampshire, and St. Stephen, New Brunswick. Poems such as "The Were Wolves," "The Last Ride," and the title poem of *The Dread Voyage* (1893) show how he brooded with terrifying vividness over the physical grossness and spiritual barrenness of a merely material universe. Yet the potential for release from such tension was also in this book, for he took this opportunity to publish some of his finest poems, revealing a wholesome response to nature's beauty and strength.

In 1891 he had returned to the lakes at Southampton, Ontario, no longer feeling comfortable in the ministry. After a few months he had resigned to take a minor position in the civil service at Ottawa. Lampman and Scott joined him during 1892 and 1893 in writing a column of literary essays, "At the Mermaid Inn," for the Saturday *Globe* (Toronto). Each of the poets wrote noteworthy criticism and indulged in digressions. When Campbell wrote on "the false religious prejudice of a large extent in countries like Canada," the *Globe* publicly condemned his assertion that "the story of the Cross itself" was a myth "connected with the old phallic worship of some of our most remote ancestors." "Nature," he professed later, was his "greatest and best church." And his nature poems were his liturgy.

In the late nineteenth century, poems of nature and the spirit of man were welcomed by editors and readers of American journals. Campbell, Lampman, and other Canadians published dozens of poems in the United States: an American critic commented on "the songs of your Canadian minstrels, now so naturally incorporated with our own."

Campbell's *Beyond the Hills of Dream* (1899) contained his offerings to the American public. However, *The Collected Poems* (1905) revealed less careful selection, and less attention to the "exquisite" preferred by American editors. Campbell here showed openly that he valued thought above form and that he had chosen Britain as his home of song. He had begun promoting imperialism, and allegiance to "Vaster Britain . . . the mightiest race on earth." Jingoism was softened by emphasis upon the moral and spiritual traditions of "the race." Among the influences playing upon him at this time was his respect for Shakespeare's romantic, poetic dramas, which became models for his own tremendous efforts for success in writing "closet-dramas" in the neo-

Shakespearean robust style of romantic tragedy: he nearly succeeded with *Mordred; and Hildebrand* (1895). Lampman said that some of Campbell's plays had "enough fire and fury to blow up a theatre."

Imperial influences, strong in Ottawa at this time, reinforced Campbell's idealism, his theory of "race," his explorations in British history, his pride in his Scottish ancestry, and his passion for travel in the homeland. The personification of all this was his friend and the head of his clan, the ninth duke of Argyl, who had kept interest in Canada since he was governor-general as the marquess of Lorne (1878-1883). At Inveraray and elsewhere in Britain, the duke showed Campbell and his family extraordinary favors, encouraging the poet's idealism and then wisely encouraging responsibility to Canada.

Sagas of Vaster Britain (1914) became Campbell's final selection in his lifetime of his favorite poems. Preoccupation with evolutionary theories and materialism took the form of "the descent of man," countered, however, by "some godlike vision" and "the rare spirit of song." Patriotism was evident in a renewed emphasis upon the traditions inherited by Canada, and in "sagas" of heroic adventure. There was a refined historical approach, probably attributable to his employment in the Canadian Archives during the last ten years of his life.

During World War I Campbell rendered a full measure of patriotic service. He died early in 1918, before the war ended. *The Poetical Works* (1922) is a massive collection of his verse, which in company with all his other original books appears to be out of print. A recent booklet, *Selected Poems* (1976), is now available, however, and anthologies keep alive a dozen or more of his poems. Also, *Snowflakes and Sunbeams*, a small collection of poems that originally appeared in 1888 in the *St. Croix Courier* (St. Stephen, New Brunswick), was published in 1974.

Reference:
Carl F. Klinck, *Wilfred Campbell* (Toronto: Ryerson, 1942).

Bliss Carman
(15 April 1861-8 June 1929)

Donald Stephens
University of British Columbia

BOOKS: *Low Tide on Grand Pré: A Book of Lyrics* (London: Nutt, 1893; New York: Webster, 1893; Toronto: Copp, Clark, 1899);

Songs from Vagabondia, by Carman and Richard Hovey (Boston: Copeland & Day/London: Matthews & Lane, 1894);

Behind the Arras: A Book of the Unseen (Boston & New York: Lamson, Wolffe, 1895);

More Songs from Vagabondia, by Carman and Hovey (Boston: Copeland & Day, 1896);

Ballads of Lost Haven: A Book of the Sea (Boston & London: Lamson, Wolffe, 1897);

By the Aurelian Wall, and Other Elegies (Boston & New York: Lamson, Wolffe, 1898);

Last Songs from Vagabondia, by Carman and Hovey (Boston: Small, Maynard, 1900);

The Pipes of Pan, 5 volumes (Boston: Page, 1902-1905);

Ballads and Lyrics (London: Bullen, 1902; revised and enlarged edition, Toronto: McClelland & Stewart, 1923);

The Kinship of Nature (Boston: Page, 1903; London: Murray, 1904);

The Friendship of Art (Boston: Page, 1904);

Poems (New York: Scott-Thaw/London: Murray, 1904);

Sappho: One Hundred Lyrics (Boston: Page, 1904; Toronto: Copp, Clark, 1905; London: Moring, De La More, 1906);

The Poetry of Life (Boston: Page, 1905; London: Hodder & Stoughton, 1906);

The Making of Personality (Boston: Page, 1908);

The Rough Rider, and Other Poems (New York: Kennerley, 1909);

Address to the Graduating Class MCMXI of the Unitrinian School of Personal Harmonizing (New York: Privately printed at Tabard Press, 1911);

A Painter's Holiday, and Other Poems (New York: Privately printed by F. F. Sherman, 1911);

Echoes from Vagabondia (Boston: Small, Maynard, 1912);

Daughters of Dawn: A Lyrical Pageant or Series of Historic Scenes for Presentation with Music and Danc-

ing, by Carman and Mary Perry King (New York: Kennerley, 1913);

Earth Deities, and Other Rhythmic Masques, by Carman and King (New York: Kennerley, 1914);

April Airs: A Book of New England Lyrics (Boston: Small, Maynard, 1916);

James Whitcomb Riley: An Essay by Bliss Carman, and Some Letters to Him from James Whitcomb Ri-

ley (August 30, 1898-October 12, 1915) (New York: Privately printed for G. D. Smith, 1918);

Later Poems (Toronto: McClelland & Stewart, 1921; Boston: Small, Maynard, 1922);

Far Horizons (Boston: Small, Maynard, 1925);

Talks on Poetry and Life, edited by Blanche Hume (Toronto: Ryerson, 1926);

Sanctuary: Sunshine House Sonnets (Toronto: McClelland & Stewart, 1929; New York: Dodd, Mead, 1929);

Wild Garden (Toronto: McClelland & Stewart, 1929; New York: Dodd, Mead, 1929);

Bliss Carman's Poems (Toronto: McClelland & Stewart, 1931; New York: Dodd, Mead, 1931);

The Music of Earth, edited by Lorne Pierce (Toronto: Ryerson, 1931; New York: Privately printed [Sackett & Wilhelm], 1931);

Selected Poems, edited by Pierce (Toronto: McClelland & Stewart, 1954; New York: Dodd, Mead, 1954).

OTHER: *The World's Best Poetry*, edited by Carman, John Vance Cheney, Charles G. D. Roberts, Charles F. Richardson, and Francis H. Stoddard (Philadelphia: Morris, 1904);

Our Canadian Literature: Representative Verse, edited by Carman and Lorne Pierce (Toronto: Ryerson, 1925; revised, 1935); revised and enlarged as *Canadian Poetry in English*, edited by V. B. Rhodenizer (Toronto: Ryerson, 1954);

The Oxford Book of American Verse, edited by Carman (New York & London: Oxford University Press, 1927).

Bliss Carman was one of the Canadian Confederation poets–those born in the early 1860s, of whom Carman, Charles G. D. Roberts, Archibald Lampman, and Duncan Campbell Scott are the acknowledged leaders–who helped bring poetry to the attention of a Canadian public recovering from the problems attendant to an emerging country that celebrated its Confederation in 1867. Basically a romantic poet, Carman possessed an easy lyrical gift and created imagery at times startling and poignant. From 1895 to 1915 Carman was highly regarded among North American poets because he had become a hybrid Canadian-American in outlook, yet had retained that genuine, if uncertain, lyricism that played an important part in the development of Canadian poetry.

Carman, born 15 April 1861 in Fredericton, New Brunswick, came from a family that loved tradition, concerned with retaining a link with their English past. The son of John and Florence Carman, Bliss soon learned about this tradition: his father's family had settled in New York in 1631 and flourished there. But when the American Revolution took place, their love for England made the family move to the nearest English stronghold, New Brunswick, in 1783. This United Empire Loyalist strain was not only on Carman's father's side. His mother's family was descended from Rev. Daniel Bliss of Concord, Massachusetts, the great-grandfather of Ralph Waldo Emerson. In this environment Carman and his cousin–Charles G. D. Roberts–received a traditional, classical education. He studied in Fredericton from 1872 to 1878 under George R. Parkin, later chairman of the Rhodes Scholarship Trust, and graduated from the University of New Brunswick in 1881 with honors in Latin and Greek. He then went to Oxford for a short while, then to Edinburgh; but he was homesick and returned to Canada in 1883. From 1886 to 1888 he studied English literature at Harvard under Francis Child and took philosophy there from Josiah Royce. At Harvard he met the American poet Richard Hovey, with whom he was to collaborate later on the so-called Vagabondia series (1894-1900) to tell the "joys of the open road."

Having decided to become a professional poet, Carman worked for various publishing companies and magazines in New England. In 1896 he met Mary Perry King, the greatest and most sustained female influence on his life. For the rest of his life he lived either near Mrs. King and her husband or in a house on their grounds in New Canaan, Connecticut. Mrs. King was his patron, influencing him to accept the philosophy of unitrinianism, which offers serenity to the individual through a belief in the symmetry of all things: a person's life should be an equal balance of the physical, emotional, and mental aspects of his personality. This belief created a close personal relationship between Mrs. King and Carman but often alienated him from his family and his country. In the last ten years of his life he again became attached to his Canadian background, did a speaking tour of Canada, was presented with honorary degrees from various Canadian universities, and was buried in Fredericton, New Brunswick, where he was born.

Carman's first book, *Low Tide on Grand Pré: A Book of Lyrics* (1893), began to establish

Carman with his collaborator on the Vagabondia series (drawing by T. B. Meteyard; courtesy of Dartmouth College Library)

Carman's reputation and is his most outstanding collection of poems; he was thirty-two when it was published, and except for occasional bursts of imagination, his poetry remained the same in theme, mood, and intensity for the rest of his life. The title poem, as lyric, and as a representative poem of his time, Canadian and otherwise, is Carman at his best. The five-line stanzas are finely wrought, the rhythm well executed. The poem expresses the poet's longing for a lost love, for another time that can be no more; he compares his grief to the movement of the tide on the river. Though the images in this volume are at times forceful and clear, the underlying philosophy is too mystical to be lucid; he relies too heavily on suggestion to convey meaning. He is interested in the seasons in all their aspects—particularly spring—and equates this cycle with the high and low moments in the pulse of man. He takes the ordinary view, associating winter with death and cold, autumn with the ending of life and with nostalgia, summer with moments that show completion, and spring with awakening.

Three main images occur in this volume that were to recur throughout his work: the wind

as an ambiguous force, nature as seen in the growth of a flower, and April as a turning point in the year. The wind is more than just a presence, for it breathes an ambivalence, one of growth and of destruction: it reflects the conflicts and ambiguities of life. Carman here relies on his basic Christian upbringing—the Bible and the Book of Common Prayer were read daily in his parents' strongly Anglican home—in that the wind in its transcendent power is part of the generative force of God. It becomes, too, a symbol of the destructive powers and the fall of man from the state of innocence to a knowledge of good and evil. He aligns it with the discovery of the ultimate meaning of life. There is an elemental relationship with nature, a nature that cannot be completely understood. For Carman the world of nature and man depends for its existence upon a series of complex and interlocking cyclic actions. Though things change and die, there is a never-ending process of generic rebirth as steady as the sun's wheeling circuit through the sky, or the seasons' relentless progression. This cycle never loses its sense of mystery and awe.

This first volume was not a popular success—though it is now acknowledged as his best work—

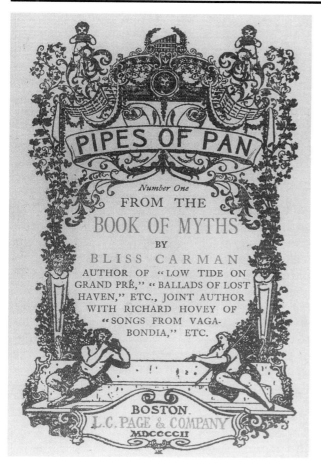

Title page for volume 1 of the series of poems in which Carman created his own mythology, drawing in part on ancient sources

and it was with the Vagabondia series (*Songs from Vagabondia*, 1894; *More Songs from Vagabondia*, 1896; and *Last Songs from Vagabondia*, 1900), written with Richard Hovey, that his fame became established with poems he wrote for a reading public who wanted light-and-easy verse. Carman and Hovey both felt that a new framework was needed for poetry written in North America in order to get the public's attention away from poets living in England. They wanted to create poetry that would captivate an audience. In order to do so they felt they should deal with lighter subjects, produce a lyrical pattern that would be easy to remember, and create themes that came from everyday experience. A bohemian quality is the trademark of the Vagabondia series, mingled with a little satire, a great deal of humor, happy love lyrics, and the occasional search for a higher plane through mystical symbolism. Carman's world of Vagabondia is one in which a person is freed of social restraints and then gains satisfac-

tion from the world around him in a return to nature; but though he condemns the hold the world has on the individual, there is no revolt in his voice. There is instead a touch of Walt Whitman in Carman's feeling that the values of the individual are submerged in the social world and that there are times to get away, to commune with nature. Carman and Hovey created in this series poetry of the good life, poetry marked by a youthful exuberance. There is an ease to the verse, a freedom in both content and style. But Hovey is the more exuberant one; Carman is more the quiet mystic, and the shadow of melancholy that marks all Carman's poetry also informs this series.

Melancholy becomes dominant in most of the work Carman composed between 1895 and 1905. He wrote elegies, a form that freed Carman from the vagaries of the mystical in his early verse. He took the classical elegy, touched it with strong pastoral images, and produced a poetry that is easy to understand while being very much in fashion at that time. Now he was writing poetry the public wanted and dealing with themes that were closer to his nature than the free Vagabondia quality or the transcendental flavor established in his earlier work. At this time, too, he wrote "The Grave-Tree," which includes these lines: "Let me have a scarlet maple / For the grave-tree at my head, / With the quiet sun behind it, / In the years when I am dead." The maple tree became one of the emblems associated with Carman's work. He saw the tree as a kind of haven at his last resting place, one that would be his "leafy cabin"; as autumn comes, "Leaf by leaf it will befriend me / As with comrades going home." The tree will turn scarlet, deeper scarlet, in the autumn "when the other world is near," his vision of the tree showing his love for nature and his awareness of a mystical presence there.

The Pipes of Pan (5 volumes, 1902-1905) shows Carman's whole imaginative vision. Up to this time his themes had been various; his best work had been sporadic. He could now see that he must look at his work with a more careful eye, and that he must have a framework to express his philosophy. He wanted to create a group of poems that would form a cohesive collection. He aimed for a dual achievement: to follow his essentially lyrical bent at which he knew he succeeded, yet also to aim for an epic quality. He achieved at times the lyrical intensity but never caught the extensive epic quality that he wanted. His purpose was to show that through many subjects, and

DAUGHTERS OF DAWN

A LYRICAL PAGEANT
OR SERIES OF HISTORIC SCENES
FOR PRESENTATION WITH
MUSIC AND DANCING

BY

BLISS CARMAN AND
MARY PERRY KING

WITH FIFTEEN ILLUSTRATIONS

*"What cannot be said can be sung,
What cannot be sung can be danced."*

NEW YORK
MITCHELL KENNERLEY
1913

*Title page for Carman's first collaboration with the woman
who was a profound influence on his religious beliefs*

with many forms, he could reveal his fundamental concept that there is present in the world a potential for harmony, and it is man's purpose to discover and maintain this harmony. For Carman this potential was material, spiritual, and mystical, and is present in all things; it has been present in all aspects of life, from the ancient times to the present. It is part of the myth and legend of man's thinking and desire. This transcendental vision is difficult to explain, let alone illustrate and define; only occasionally in the series does Carman succeed in doing so. His poetry, despite his intentions, remained diffuse and abstract.

His next major work of verse, *Sappho: One Hundred Lyrics* (1904), the undertaking of a restoration of the lyrics of Sappho (circa 610-580 B.C.), is Carman at his later best. With these lyrics he was able to use his classical education and his craft as a poet to create a series of poems that can sustain a reader's interest. Since her death Sappho has been alternately praised and damned. The Greeks considered her the greatest of the

lyric poets. For Plato, Sappho was the tenth muse. Though the Romans had condemned her and her poetry, the scholars of Carman's time took a new interest in her life and work. It was the ambiguity of Sappho's character and her lyrical gift that appealed to Carman. His method was to imagine each lost lyric as discovered, to translate it, yet to give to his own creations the fluidity and freedom associated with the original work. But there are obvious differences in the worldview and attitudes of the two poets. Where Sappho presents a radiant world, shining with gold, sunlight, and silver, Carman's world is soft and muted. Sappho loves the summer; Carman describes instead the autumn as it colors the earth when the sunlight sleeps in the vineyard; for Sappho an olive grove is full of brilliant light; for Carman the color is gray, the birds are brown where the shadows trail, and the sun is silver. But though Carman's lyrics lack the radiance of Sappho's landscapes, his world has a tender beauty of its own. Carman's landscapes are different, the sights and sounds are different, but Sappho's influence seems to have made Carman a more poignant, more haunting, and more successful poet. In form, too, the poets are not close. While Sappho was the true lyricist, delighting in fact and nature, Carman was more didactic, a believer in symbols in the world around him. For Sappho everything, including the gods, was simply real; for Carman there was always something within or beyond. However, thematically they are very close, as they marvel at the joy and wonder of life.

From 1904 onward, under the influence of Mary Perry King, Carman occasionally wrote books of essays (*The Friendship of Art*, 1904; *The Poetry of Life*, 1905; *The Making of Personality*, 1908; and *Talks on Poetry and Life*, 1926) to reveal his unitrinian philosophy. First of all, the essays defend his position as a poet. His aim, he tells the reader, is to create beauty, best done by bringing the natural world around him into focus. He attempts, also, to defend his conservative literary background, his attitudes about human behavior, his mysticism, and his transcendentalism. His optimism leads to a lavish language that is a weakness in these prose pieces. The successful essays are written in the easy, familiar style of Charles Lamb. The critical essays—concerning art and literature—are sterile in concept, style, and content, out of place in an age steeped in the tradition of the great Victorian prose stylists, such as

Carman, circa 1924

John Ruskin. Today they are simply a literary curiosity.

Most critics and biographers of Carman tend to divide his poetry into three distinct phases: an early and strongly romantic period, followed by one of excessive rationalism, which was in turn synthesized into his last phase, which included the best qualities of the first and second. These phases indicate the major limitation in Carman's work: there is little development or growth in Carman's poetry. For the most part it remained static through his entire career because of his tendency to follow the footpaths of others and to accept readily the traditions and statements of others.

Carman's poetry is permeated with strains of American and English literary heritage, and the strongest influence on his work was the romantic movement. Some of his work can be called imitation, for there are obvious echoes. Yet this style is what made him popular in Canada and the United States between 1895 and 1925; critics felt he was showing that the North American experience could be portrayed in the great tradition of William Wordsworth and John Keats. Carman, with the Confederation group, brought poetry to

a high state in Canada so that contemporary readers paid attention to poetry and to poets. It is this Confederation group that is now considered to be the first firm step in Canadian poetry, the foundation on which contemporary Canadian poetry is based. The strains of romanticism and the strong lyrical voice associated with the Confederation group were still evident in the poets writing in Canada in the 1980s.

Carman's whole attitude to poetry was that of a devotee rather than a true creator. There is no sign of growth as in Keats, no strongly conscious change as in William Butler Yeats. Even though his themes and craft are limited, he was able for the most part to give a spontaneous quality to his verse; and even when he is at his most original, there is an innate respect for the traditional standards and values of English poetry. Among several characteristics linking him with the nineteenth-century poets is his pervading melancholy—the sweet sadness of the transience of love and life that is akin to the sadness of Keats, Christina Rossetti, and Ernest Dowson. A counterquality is the optimism he derived in part from the unitrinianism of Mrs. King: the harmony of body, spirit, and mind within the universe comes when man respects himself and his environment, grasping the potential for strength and contentment by balancing all his mental and physical power. But in both the sad and the optimistic poetry, one quality pervades: a sentimental emotionalism that has a certain charm and poignancy characteristic of his age and at the same time is the result of his own personality, which centered on strong personal attachments.

The story of Bliss Carman—his poetry and his life—is incontestably Canadian. He had to go to the United States to achieve his reputation. He had to become seriously ill—in 1920—before Canadian critics and fellow poets began to praise him. His reputation reached a high point at the very beginning of his career, with *Low Tide on Grand Pré.* The next ten years sustained and somewhat extended the reputation that book had begun. Until his death in 1929, however, his reputation changed little, as though the critics were waiting for something to happen; they waited in vain. In the early twenties, because many credited him as the originator of a new school in Canadian poetry (along with Roberts), Carman retained a high position in recognition of his contribution to Canadian letters. He had wielded both a conscious and unconscious influence on poetry in Canada during his lifetime. He went out of fashion in the thirties but was never overly deprecated by critics, mainly because people did not want to level any criticism at a poet who had awakened the Canadian audience. He is now considered to be a minor poet, with occasional glows of brilliance, who once had a strong position in Canadian poetry and to whom a debt is due. Along with Robert Service and Pauline Johnson, he was, until 1967, the most widely anthologized poet in the history of Canadian letters. All Canadians acknowledge that the national literature is richer because of Carman.

There is nothing startling in the poetry of Carman; he belongs to his own time. His social thinking is very much in the mid nineteenth century, and to contemporary readers he appears naive. Though there is a slightness of content and a monotony of tone in Carman's work, there is a characteristic quality to his work, a tone showing a delicacy of expression, a haunting melancholy, and a musical lyricism. Within his limits, he displayed a consistency of expression; he was always able to capture the melody of a mood, the tone of an atmosphere, and the color of a setting. Carman was a sincere and simple author, whose poetry is subtle and takes time to appreciate; it, too, is sincere and without affectation. His work is a rich expression of common experience.

Letters:
Letters of Bliss Carman, edited by H. Pearson Gundy (Kingston, Ont.: McGill-Queen's University Press, 1981).

Bibliography:
William Inglis Morse, *Bliss Carman, Bibliography: Letters, Fugitive Verses and Other Data* (Windham, Conn.: Hawthorne, 1941).

Biographies:
James Cappon, *Bliss Carman* (Toronto: Ryerson, 1930);
Muriel Miller, *Bliss Carman: A Portrait* (Toronto: Ryerson, 1935);

References:
Desmond Pacey, "Bliss Carman," in his *Ten Canadian Poets* (Toronto: Ryerson, 1958), pp. 59-113;
Pacey, "Bliss Carman: A Reappraisal," *Northern Review* (February-March 1950): 2-10;
Donald Stephens, *Bliss Carman* (New York: Twayne, 1966).

Papers:
Most of Carman's correspondence and manuscripts are in the Hatheway Collection, Bonar Law-Bennett Library, University of New Brunswick. His letters to his mother, dated from 30 January 1883 to 27 August 1885, are in the Edith and Lorne Pierce Collection of Canadiana, Queen's University Library, Kingston, Ontario.

Jean Charbonneau
(3 September 1875-25 October 1960)

Peyton Brien

BOOKS: *Les Blessures* (Paris: Lemerre, 1912);
Des influences françaises au Canada, 3 volumes (Montreal: Beauchemin, 1916, 1918, 1920);
L'Age de sang (Paris: Lemerre, 1921);
Les Prédestinés (Montreal: Beauchemin, 1923);
L'Ombre dans le miroir (Montreal: Beauchemin, 1924);
La Flamme ardente (Montreal: Beauchemin, 1928);
L'Ecole littéraire de Montréal: Ses origines, ses animateurs, ses influences (Montreal: Levesque, 1935);
Tel qu'en sa solitude (Montreal: Valiquette/A.C.F., 1940);
Sur la borne pensive: L'Ecrin de Pandore (Paris: Lemerre, 1952).

Jean Charbonneau was well known as a poet, dramatist, literary critic, and historian. From 1893 to 1901 he also acted, with a troupe called Soirées de Famille, using the stage name Delagny. Under this same name he first published his poetry in literary journals between 1895 and 1900. Meanwhile he organized close to one hundred of his troupe's presentations. During 1894 and 1895 he was a member of the literary Groupe des Six Eponges (Group of Six Sponges). Charbonneau is remembered not so much for his own poetry, which was plentiful, but for his role in the development of literature in Quebec. He was cofounder (with Louvigny de Montigny) of the Ecole Littéraire de Montréal in 1895, serving a term as its president from 1907 to 1909. In 1935 he published the history of this school (which had provided Quebec with one of its greatest poets in Emile Nelligan). Charbonneau's will was a strong positive influence in Quebec's drive to develop a distinct, significant literature.

Born Joseph John Baptiste Charbonneau on 3 September 1875 in Montreal, he was the son of a carpenter, Charles Charbonneau, and his wife, Emma Laflamme Charbonneau. He attended the Collège Sainte Marie and then the Université de Montréal, achieving a law degree in 1903. The following year he married Marie-Anna Rheume.

Charbonneau's first published poetry appeared in issues of *La Samedi* beginning in 1895. Then some stories were featured in this same journal as well as in *Le Monde Illustré* until 1900. In 1900 the text of a conference on symbolism in which he participated and some poems were published in the Ecole Littéraire de Montréal's first collective volume, *Les Soirées du chateau de Ramezay*. Included in the group's second collective work, *Le terroir* (The Native, 1909), are other poems and informal talks on theater by Charbonneau.

Les Blessures (The Wounds, 1912), the poet's first solo collection, is a moral discourse denouncing materialism and human vanity. The "wounds" appear to result from the eternal necessity to confront the present. Charbonneau's denunciation is of a world that makes an absolute of childhood and refuses the flowering of life. Six more poetry collections appeared in the four decades that followed. Charbonneau's artistry increased, but the works are all similar in attitude and style.

In *L'Age de sang* (Age of Blood, 1921), his second collection, Charbonneau's classical literary roots are more fully expressed. Humans are portrayed as having turned from beauty and idealism to a thirst for domination. The poet endeavors to offer humankind a key to its salvation through depictions of interrogations of the world's great sages–particularly the Chaldean patriarchs, Zarathustra, and Christ. Charbonneau received his one poetry award, the Prix David, for his fourth collection, *L'Ombre dans le miroir* (The Shadow in the Mirror, 1924). Yet his greatest collection may be his final one, *Tel qu'en sa solitude* (This Is Solitude, 1940). Its outpouring, in alexandrines, was said to be a remarkably struck and closely woven impression of humanity's fervent, internal dream of perfection found beyond death. Even within this context Charbonneau remains true to his classical affiliations and shuns any poise of romanticism.

The publication of *Des influences françaises au Canada* (The Influence of French Literature on Canada, 1916-1920) constitutes a literary

Jean Charbonneau (right) with his friend Paul de Martigny, a journalist (photograph from Peintres et Ecrivains d'hier et d'aujourd'hui *by Albert Laberge, 1938)*

event: the first time a scholar had attempted to capture the role played by France with respect to Canada and Quebec. Published in three volumes over four years and created primarily as a work of literary history, it is notable also for its socio-historical approach to literary criticism. Although at first Charbonneau is critical of Quebec for a lack of originality and boldness in its few early literary efforts, his concluding position is that it is Quebecois literature that has perhaps best come to represent a tradition and vision with which France has lost touch. Historical documentation and philosophical arguments from Nietzsche and Schopenhauer, among others, bolster his assertions.

Des influences divided the critics. By many it was lauded for giving a sense of the past while indicating also a future direction. Other reviewers thought it "la prose sentimenteuse" (sentimental prose). Some insisted it was really a work of social philosophy and not, as Charbonneau presented it, a history. While the three volumes won for their author the Lauréat de l'Académie Française, no single major review ever treated the entire work.

Following his publication of *L'Ecole littéraire de Montréal* in 1935, Charbonneau was elected to the Société Royale du Canada. He became a translator for the Legislative Assembly of Quebec and remained so until his retirement in 1951. The next year he spent in France, also visiting Italy and Switzerland, before returning to dwell in Montreal in 1952. In 1956 he succumbed to a paralysis. After later spending a year in the Hôpital des deux Montagnes in Saint-Eustache, Charbonneau died in 1960.

Jean Charbonneau mostly lived the life of a solitary poet. His work constitutes principally a testimony for an era, of which the Ecole Littéraire de Montréal was a vital part. During his career he was awarded for his writing more than once, yet Charbonneau is not a chief figure in Quebec letters today. Supplements of the *Canadian Periodical Index* for every year since his death suggest that in that time none of his works has been retrospectively reviewed, nor has he been an essential figure of discussion. His laureate for *Des influences françaises au Canada* and his role as chief historian for the literary school he cofounded must have been among the deeper gratifications of Charbonneau's long and varied career. For in all his poetry, most directly perhaps in *L'Age de sang*, he explicitly portrays the poet as one who knows best the meaning of history because he has lived close to nature and the ideal.

Papers:

Charbonneau donated his unpublished works, many still in manuscript form, to the Center of Research in Canadian-French Civilization at the University of Ottawa. One hundred fifty sheets entitled "Voix disparues" (Missing Voices) comprise poetry written between 1893 and 1898. Another

178 sheets, "Les Enracinés" (Rooted), groups poems written between 1920 and 1925.

All of Charbonneau's dramatic works exist in manuscript state. The most important to him must have been "Zophyre," a prose drama in four acts written in 1904 but reshaped incessantly until 1956 (149 sheets). "Les Emmurés" (The Immured) is a prose drama of 71 sheets dated 1910. Undated is the fifty-sheet "La Mort de Tristan Isolde" (The Death of Tristan and Isolde). "Tentatives d'Evasion" (Escape Attempts) is an undated novel of 457 sheets, and "A l'ombre de l'oasis" (In the Shade of the Oasis) is a collection of thoughts gathered in 1925 (241 sheets).

Charbonneau's archives also contain the manuscript texts of several literary conferences and some roughly outlined critiques.

René Chopin
(21 April 1885-28 June 1953)

Kathleen L. Kellett
University of Toronto

BOOKS: *Le Coeur en exil* (Paris: Crès, 1913); *Dominantes* (Montreal: Lévesque, 1933).

René Chopin, along with Marcel Dugas, Paul Morin, and Guy Delahaye, is generally given a place in Quebec literary history as a "poète-artiste," preoccupied with the Parnassian ideal of form rather than with the contemporary regionalist dream of creating a "poésie du terroir" (poetry of the land). At the same time, Chopin's poetry expresses his profound affinity with the northern landscape.

Named after René de Chateaubriand (1768-1848), his mother's favorite author, René Chopin was the tenth child of Jules-Nestor Chopin, a French doctor, and Léocadie-Délia Brousseau Chopin, daughter of Antoine Brousseau, at one time the mayor of Sault-au-Recollet, Quebec, where Chopin was born on 21 April 1885. After a happy childhood in Sault-au-Recollet, on the Rivière des Prairies, Chopin was sent to Montreal at the age of fourteen to study at the Collège Sainte-Marie and stayed there to study law at Laval University. He qualified as a notary public in March 1910 but did not practice his profession until 1911, instead going to Paris for a year to study singing. During a trip to Rome he met Count Charles de Chozelles, thanks to whom he was to receive the Cross of the Chevalier de Latran, a pontifical order created by Pope Leo XIII. Upon his return to Canada in 1911, Chopin made a brief venture into journalism with fellow Quebec writer Jules Fournier but gave it up to devote himself to his work as a notary public in Montreal.

Encouraged by his friends to publish some of his poems, Chopin contributed to the journals *Le Nationaliste* and *L'Action*, but it was not until 1913 that he published the first collection of his poems, *Le Coeur en exil,* at the suggestion of his friend Dugas. He was not to publish another volume until 1933, when *Dominantes* appeared. His literary production also includes book reviews in the newspaper *Le Devoir,* to which he began to contribute in 1944.

Le Coeur en exil illustrates the considerable technique of this "poète-artiste" skilled in the art of formal verse, but it is the poet's intense identification with nature and his vague sense of pantheism that strike most readers. Chopin excelled in painting nature scenes onto which he inevitably projected his own feelings. In the opening poem, "Liminaire" (Introduction), Chopin expresses his sentiment of isolation by comparing the poet, whose "Rêve hautain" (lofty dream) is despised by his society, to a cherry tree, growing in poor soil at the foot of a cliff, menaced by the waters of the river and by harsh weather: "O Poète isolé! Comme ce pâle arbuste,/Dans ta fragilité,/ Prends racine au rocher orgueilleux et robuste/ De l'Idéalité" (O isolated poet! Like this pale bush,/ In your fragility,/Take root in the proud and sturdy rock/Of the ideal). Both the poet's feeling of ostracism and the use of the tree as a symbol of strength and isolation are recurrent themes in Chopin's poetry.

The title of the first series of poems in this volume, "Peintures canadiennes" (Canadian Paintings), suggests at first glance a regionalist aesthetic. However, the images within serve mainly to express the poet's emotions, and critics have questioned whether Chopin's landscapes are truly Canadian. Perhaps the most impressive poems in *Le Coeur en exil* are the winter scenes in the two sections "Ecrans de neige" and "Effets de neige" (Screens of Snow and Effects of Snow). In poems such as "Fleurs de gel" and "Ville de cristal" (Flowers of Frost and City of Crystal), winter is portrayed benignly as an artist who creates patterns of frost and ice, but other poems emphasize the harshness of this season. In particular the poem "Paysages polaires" (Polar Landscapes) describes the violence and majesty of the icy landscape that destroys its would-be conquerors. The section "Le Coeur vierge" (The Virgin Heart) contains poems about love, often with a sensual tone, most notably in the poem "Les Lèvres" (The

Lips). In certain poems the poet expresses a wistful desire for an ideal love; in "Le Sonnet de l'écolier" (The Sonnet of the Schoolboy), for example, the speaker yearns for "une Eve jeune et belle, plus que soeur" (a young and lovely Eve, who is more than a sister). The final section of *Le Coeur en exil* includes the "Poème du soleil" (Poem of the Sun), a trilogy that comprises "Laus solis," "Dementia solis," and "Vox solis" (Praise of the Sun, Madness of the Sun, and Voice of the Sun), which illustrate Chopin's tendency toward pantheism. In fact, Dugas felt himself obliged to counter the charge that Chopin was guilty of "adoring" the sun by insisting that all references to the sun's divinity were merely poetic license. In the same eulogistic study (*Apologies*, 1919) Dugas defends Chopin and, by implication, all of the "poètes-artistes," against the partisans of regionalist poetry. However, the generally positive reception of *Le Coeur en exil* suggests that the public was already attuned to this new aesthetic.

Chopin's second book, *Dominantes*, did not appear until twenty years after the first, but there is still a certain continuity between the two. Most of the poems in *Dominantes* are written in formal verse, though much has been made of Chopin's experimentation with free verse, a form not then popular in Quebec poetry, in the section "Echos et résonances," dedicated to Dugas, "prosateur lyrique" (lyrical prose writer). Chopin again begins the volume with a poem, "Comme ces fous . . ." (Like These Madmen . . .), that expresses the poet's alienation from his society, although here the tone is more bitter than in *Le Coeur en exil*. The poet's expression of his empathy with a sentient nature also recurs in *Dominantes*, receiving its most dramatic expression in "La Mort d'un Hêtre" (The Death of a Beech), which recounts the three-hundred-year history of a beech tree, ending with its tragic destruction by the city that has outgrown it. In Chopin's "Poèmes épigrammatiques," the theme of the poet's alienation is expressed with humor and self-mockery, notably in poems such as "Perplexité" and "Epigramme contre moi-même" (Epigram Against Myself). The final section, "Ce Diptyque à ma mère bien-aimée" (This Diptych for My Beloved Mother), seems by its religious tone to represent a departure from *Le Coeur en exil*. The diptych first speaks of the mystery of birth in "A un enfant qui vient de naître" (To a

Newly Born Child), and then of death in Chopin's "Invocation" for his deceased mother, whom he had dearly loved, having lived with her until her death in 1925.

Though literary history will, as Chopin feared in "Epigramme contre moi-même," remember him as a minor poet, his poetry deserves recognition not only because of his historical role as a "poète-artiste" breaking with the norms of the "poésie du terroir" but also because his poetry, whether anguished, sensuous, or sardonic, conveys an intensely personal message with which readers can empathize.

Biography:

Lucile Chopin, *Bio-bibliographie de M. René Chopin* (Montreal: Ecole de Bibliothécaires, University of Montréal, 1944).

References:

Samuel Baillargeon, "René Chopin (1885-1953)," in his *Littérature canadienne-française* (Montreal: Fides, 1957), pp. 224-228;

Berthelot Brunet, "René Chopin, habile homme et poète narquois," in his *Histoire de la littérature canadienne-française suivie de portraits d'écrivains* (Montreal: HMH, 1970), pp. 199-213;

Louis Dantin, "René Chopin," in his *Poètes de l'Amérique française: Etudes critiques,* second series (Montreal: Lévesque, 1934), pp. 57-72;

René Deguire, "René Chopin," *Cahiers de l'Académie Canadienne-Française*, 14 (1972): 91-97;

Marcel Dugas, "M. René Chopin," in his *Apologies* (Montreal: Paradis-Vincent, 1919), pp. 89-110;

André Major, "Les poètes artistes: l'école de l'exil," in *La Poésie Canadienne-française*, edited by Paul Wyczynski and others (Montreal: Fides, 1969), pp. 135-142;

Gilles Marcotte, "Poètes 'artistes': Paul Morin et René Chopin," in his *Une littérature qui se fait: Essais critiques sur la littérature canadienne-française* (Montreal: HMH, 1962), pp. 107-116;

Paul Morin, "René Chopin, poète magicien," *Qui?*, 4 (March 1953): 41-46;

Jeanne Paul-Crouzet, "René Chopin," in her *Poésie au Canada: De nouveaux classiques français* (Paris: Didier, 1946), pp. 232-248.

Ralph Connor
(Charles William Gordon)
(13 September 1860-31 October 1937)

Michael Hurley
Queen's University

BOOKS: *Black Rock: A Tale of the Selkirks* (Toronto: Westminster, 1898; New York: Revell, 1898; London: Hodder & Stoughton, 1899);

The Sky Pilot: A Tale of the Foothills (Toronto: Westminster, 1899; Chicago: Revell, 1899; London: Hodder & Stoughton, 1899); republished in part as *Gwen: An Idyll of the Canyon* (New York & Chicago: Revell, 1904);

The Man from Glengarry: A Tale of the Ottawa (Toronto: Westminster, 1901; Chicago & New York: Revell, 1901); republished as *The Man from Glengarry: A Tale of Western Canada* (London: Hodder & Stoughton, 1901);

The Cape and Its Story, or The Struggle for South Africa (London: Nelson, 1902);

Glengarry School Days: A Story of Early Days in Glengarry (Chicago & New York: Revell, 1902); republished as *Glengarry Days* (London: Hodder & Stoughton, 1902);

The Prospector: A Tale of Crow's Nest Pass (New York: Revell, 1904; London: Hodder & Stoughton, 1904);

The Pilot at Swan Creek (London: Hodder & Stoughton, 1905);

The Doctor: A Tale of the Rockies (Toronto: Westminster, 1906; New York & Chicago: Revell, 1906); republished as *The Doctor of the Crow's Nest* (London: Hodder & Stoughton, 1906);

The Settler (London & New York: Hodder & Stoughton, 1906);

The Life of James Robertson, Missionary Superintendent in the Northwest Territories (New York & Chicago: Revell, 1908; London: Hodder & Stoughton, 1908);

The Foreigner: A Tale of Saskatchewan (Toronto: Westminster, 1909; New York: Doran, 1909);

Corporal Cameron of the North West Mounted Police: A Tale of the Macleod Trail (Toronto: Westminster, 1912; New York: Doran, 1912); republished as *Corporal Cameron: A Tale of the*

© PIRIE MACDONALD

North West Mounted Police (London: Hodder & Stoughton, 1912);

The Patrol of the Sun Dance Trail (Toronto: Westminster, 1914; London: Hodder & Stoughton/ New York: Doran, 1914);

The Major (Toronto: McClelland, Goodchild & Stewart, 1917; New York: Doran, 1917; London: Hodder & Stoughton, 1917);

The Sky Pilot of No Man's Land (Toronto: McClelland & Stewart, 1919; New York: Doran, 1919; London: Hodder & Stoughton, 1919);

To Him That Hath: A Novel of the West Today (New York: Doran, 1921; London: Hodder & Stoughton, 1922; Toronto: McClelland & Stewart, 1928);

The Gaspards of Pine Croft (Toronto: McClelland & Stewart, 1923; New York: Doran, 1923); republished as *The Gaspards of Pine Croft: A Romance of the Wilderness* (London: Hodder & Stoughton, 1923);

Treading the Winepress: A Tale of Glengarry (New York: Doran, 1925; London: Hodder & Stoughton, 1925);

The Friendly Four and Other Stories (New York: Doran, 1926; London: Hodder & Stoughton, 1927);

The Runner: A Romance of the Niagaras (Toronto: Doubleday & Gundy, 1929; Garden City, N.Y.: Doubleday, Doran, 1927; London: Hodder & Stoughton, 1930);

The Rock and the River: A Romance of Quebec (Toronto: McClelland & Stewart, 1931; New York: Dodd, Mead, 1931; London: Lane, 1932);

The Arm of Gold (New York: Dodd, Mead, 1932); republished as *The Arm of Gold: Le Bras d'or* (London: Lane, 1933);

The Girl from Glengarry (Toronto: McClelland & Stewart, 1933; New York: Dodd, Mead, 1933); republished as *The Glengarry Girl* (London: Lane, 1934);

Torches Through the Bush: A Tale of Glengarry (Toronto: McClelland & Stewart, 1934; New York: Dodd, Mead, 1934); republished as *Torches Through the Bush* (London: Lane, 1935);

The Rebel Loyalist (Toronto: McClelland & Stewart, 1935; New York: Dodd, Mead, 1935; London: Lane, 1936);

The Gay Crusader (Toronto: McClelland & Stewart, 1936; New York: Dodd, Mead, 1936);

He Dwelt Among Us (New York & Chicago: Revell, 1936; London: Hodder & Stoughton, 1936);

Postscript to Adventure: The Autobiography of Ralph Connor (New York: Farrar & Rinehart, 1938; London: Hodder & Stoughton, 1938; Toronto: McClelland & Stewart, 1975).

Although Charles William Gordon considered himself primarily a Presbyterian minister, as the writer Ralph Connor he is one of the most popular and best-selling novelists Canada has ever had. His melodramatic, didactic romances of Christianity in action enjoyed a phenomenal vogue in Canada, the United States, and Great Britain. For over twenty years, from the late 1890s through the early 1920s, unrestrained enthusiasm from all segments of society made the prolific Connor Canada's most widely read writer. Wilfrid Laurier, Herbert Asquith, Theodore Roosevelt, and Woodrow Wilson cherished his friendship and counted themselves among his most avid readers. Ironically, Connor's extraordinary popularity was matched only by his equally extraordinary fall from favor.

Connor was born in the Indian Lands Presbyterian manse in Glengarry County, Canada West (which later became Ontario). His father, the Reverend Daniel Gordon, "a fiery Highlander," and especially his "saintly" mother, Mary Robertson Gordon, are repeatedly idealized in Connor's fiction. Besides his devoutly religious parents, he idolized his brothers, Gilbert and Robertson; they, too, are reflected in Connor's writing, in his always athletic fictional heroes of prodigious strength and religious ardor.

In 1883 Connor graduated from the University of Toronto and in 1887 he received a B.D. from Knox College in Toronto. In 1890 in Calgary he was ordained a minister of the Presbyterian Church. Stationed in Banff, Connor served as a missionary to the miners and lumbermen of the Northwest Territories whom he memorializes in his most enduring fiction. In 1894 he was called to Winnipeg's St. Stephen's Church, where he remained as pastor for the rest of his life. Connor kept in constant contact with the superintendent of the western missions, the Reverend James Robertson, and in 1908 he wrote the biography of this "rugged" missionary who inspired his activities as a minister and provided a model for the robust Christians of his novels.

Both Connor and Robertson were determined that the growing Canadian West would be shaped by the church and the law. It was, in fact, Connor's devotion to the western missions that transformed him, at the age of thirty-eight, into Ralph Connor. In 1896, as representative of the Western Home Missions, he was shocked by a movement to terminate further expansion. When he complained of the situation to the Reverend J. A. Macdonald, the editor of the Church-sponsored *Westminster Magazine*, Macdonald urged a reluctant Connor to write a short story

*Connor in 1917 in his Cameron Highlanders uniform
(photograph by Pirie MacDonald)*

had completed the manuscript for his first novel, *Black Rock: A Tale of the Selkirks,* published serially in *Westminster Magazine* in 1897. There was a strong didactic intent behind the first novel by "Ralph Connor," a pseudonym in part created through a telegrapher's misreading of "Cannor," from "Can.Nor.," an abbreviation of Canadian Northwest. As Connor wrote in his autobiography, *Postscript to Adventure* (1938): "My sole purpose was to awaken my church to the mighty religious adventure being attempted by the missionary pioneers in the Canada beyond the Great Lakes by writing a brief sketch of the things which as clerk of the biggest presbytery in the world I had come to know by personal experience."

Set in British Columbia in the 1880s, *Black Rock* tells of the successful campaign to start a western mission waged by a Presbyterian minister named Craig and the saintly widow Mrs. Mavor. Both are figures of refinement and culture from the East confronting the raw, turbulent world of the frontier. A first edition of five thousand copies was printed in 1898, an unheard-of figure for a small Canadian publisher and an unknown Canadian writer. According to George Doran, Connor's American publisher, the novel's "success was immediately so great that many pirated editions appeared; . . . the sale of millions of copies made Ralph Connor a household name in the United States and prepared a very large public for his later works." Connor's glowing picture of an idyllic West of infinite possibilities, Edward McCourt noted in his *The Canadian West in Fiction* (1949), proved better advertising material than anything dreamed up by railroad or government publicity men. Dick Harrison, in his *Unnamed Country* (1977), and Susan Wood, in an essay included in *The Westering Experience in American Literature* (1977), point to Connor's view of social mythology in development, the latter hailing him as "the most famous and influential of the Canadian mythmakers." Connor's Canadians pursue not freedom but a domestic haven of law and order patrolled by missionaries and Her Majesty's policemen.

Pleased at the attention his first novel had focused on the missions, Connor published *The Sky Pilot: A Tale of the Foothills* in 1899, the year he married Helen Skinner King, with whom he subsequently had seven children, one of whom (King Gordon) later became a political colleague of the poet F. R. Scott. With plenty of outdoor action and violence, Connor's second novel, like *Black*

based on his missionary experiences. He produced "Christmas Eve in a Lumber Camp." Hoping to impress fellow Presbyterians in the East with the urgent financial needs of the western missions, he wrote several more episodes until he

Rock, is the story of one strong man's influence on a primitive western community. A red-blooded "sky pilot," or missionary from eastern Canada, struggles to build a church and bring Christianity and temperance to Alberta's ranchers and farmers. As in *Black Rock,* the pattern exemplifies the dialectic between a civilized East and a mythic West, which W. H. New in *Articulating West* (1972) has identified in prairie literature. As pagan heroics give way to Christian refinement in this novel, Connor illustrates his persistent theme, the victory of civilization over unregenerate man and untamed nature. The heroes Connor subsequently portrays are churchmen and representatives of the established culture warring against the wilderness, unable to assimilate the prairie's dark, spontaneous, and irrational aspects. Their militant spiritual idealism often embodies what D. G. Jones in his *Butterfly on Rock* (1970) has termed "the arrogant and aggressive masculine logos, the God or father figure of Western culture."

The Sky Pilot had an immediate sale of 250,000 copies and sales later reached well over a million, a phenomenal event in Canadian publishing history. Readers responded to Connor's local color descriptions taken from personal experience. As he wrote in *Postscript to Adventure:* "I knew the country. I had ridden the ranges. I had pushed through the mountain passages. I had swum my bronco across the rivers. I had met the men–Hi Kendal and Bronco Bill and the rest were friends of mine." George Woodcock asserts, in *The Canadians* (1979), that it would be hard to find in the literature of the British Empire a more vigorous exposition of the doctrine of muscular Christianity. Connor felt, as he noted in *Postscript to Adventure,* that his sermons in fiction set forth "religion . . . in its true light as a synonym of all that is virile, straight, honourable and withal tender and gentle in true men and women."

What at the time seemed a convincing portrayal of the drama of the spiritual life now strikes most critics as naive and moralistic melodrama. For Elizabeth Waterston, in "The Lowland Tradition in Canadian Literature" (collected in *The Scottish Tradition in Canada,* edited by W. S. Reid, 1977), Connor's didactic writings partake of some "occupational hazards" of cleric-novelists: "blindness to ironies, vapid moralizing, and censorship of moral and psychological blasphemies." Desmond Pacey in *Creative Writing in Canada* (1967) argues that Connor's Christianity has no

theological or ethical subtlety and is simply "a hearty masculine backthumping do-goodism." Connor has also been faulted by critics for his sentimentality, structural inadequacies, and exaggerated characterization.

Connor's duties as minister of St. Stephen's led him to expand the church's social services to handle an increasing stream of immigrants. He worked out successful schemes of cooperation and joint missions between the various Protestant churches. To further "reap the spiritual harvest of these plains," he headed the movement for church union. The preface to his third novel, *The Man from Glengarry: A Tale of the Ottawa* (1901), highlights the pressing concerns of the church.

The book opens in the 1860s in the frontier settlements of Glengarry where dispossessed Highlanders, "as wild as the wild creatures of the forest," are engaged in a "heroic struggle with stern nature." The Presbyterian manse where Connor spent the first ten years of his life dominates the community. From it comes the civilizing influence of a minister named Murray (modeled on the author's father) and the courageous, uncomplaining Mrs. Murray (based on his mother). The latter inspires the moral growth of the hero, Ranald Macdonald. Like Gwen in *The Sky Pilot,* he is removed from the wilderness and learns rational self-control and obedience to God. Forsaking a violent passion for revenge, he renounces that personal self-assertion so characteristic of the hero of American romance in favor of the self-denial and self-discipline that mark all Connor's Christian heroes. Ranald becomes an eminent churchman, leading citizen, and successful businessman. Like many of Connor's protagonists, he leaves the corrupt urban East for the wholesome rural innocence of the West, there reforming a frontier operation. Transformations such as Ranald's, through the stuff of Connor's fiction, are attended with some regret; as he remarks in his autobiography, "The mighty sweeping of that religious upheaval tamed the fighting, drinking, lusting Glengarry men. . . . But the tales of the fierce old days survived down into my time, stirring my youthful heart with profound regret that deeds so heroically splendid should all be bad. For in spite of the Great Revival we were of the same race, with ancient lust of battle in our blood."

With the publication of *The Man from Glengarry,* Connor became the most widely read Canadian writer, a distinction he was to enjoy for the next twenty years. Within ten months, the novel

Photograph from Connor's posthumously published autobiography, Postscript to Adventure *(1938)*

sold twenty-five thousand copies in Canada. The first American edition ran to ninety-eight thousand copies, later editions to many hundreds of thousands. Within a few years, the combined sales of Connor's first three works exceeded five million. Still his most acclaimed novel, *The Man from Glengarry*, was published in a New Canadian Library edition in 1969.

Modern critics agree that the descriptions of varied phases of pioneer life represent Connor at his best. Ross Beharriell, in his introduction to the NCL edition, elevates it to the status of a "minor classic," an epic story of a heroic figure reaching manhood as the country reaches nationhood. In *The Man from Glengarry*, as Beharriell points out, Connor portrays Glengarry landscape meticulously; more than the picturesque, painted backdrop of his first two books, it is a setting in which the darker, indifferent side of the natural world sometimes emerges.

Internationally famous, Connor was in constant demand in Canada and abroad as a guest preacher and lecturer. In the spring of 1902, on the island of Birkencraig in the Lake of the Woods near Kenora, where he wrote most of his works, Connor began his fifth book, *Glengarry School Days: A Story of Early Days in Glengarry* (1902). It is a series of fifteen nostalgic fictional sketches, at once objective and dreamlike, based on memories of his boyhood experiences of pioneer life in Glengarry. The hero, Hughie Murphy, however, is not without a dark inner life. But like Lucy Maud Montgomery's Avonlea and Stephen Leacock's Mariposa, Connor's Glengarry reveals a Canadian longing for a vividly remembered world of childhood, home, family, and countryside remote from the new industrial cities. What Connor created out of the opening West he returned to the Ontario frontier of the past to discover in a purer form: a myth of national character. *Glengarry School Days* is his most enduring work because it fuses the dream of childhood and the dream of an untainted West and gives readers an ideal vision of themselves.

Connor wrote sketches so that they would be publishable as independent units in Canadian, American, and British periodicals. So great was the demand for Connor's material that the editor of the popular *Leslie's Monthly Magazine* accepted the pieces before seeing them. (The first Canadian edition of *Glengarry School Days*, ten thousand copies, was sold out before the day of publication.)

Connor became president of the Moral and Social Reform Council of Manitoba in 1907. While he was overseas during World War I, he was appointed senior chaplain of the Canadian forces in England, then senior chaplain of the 3rd Division in France. In 1916 Prime Minister Robert Borden asked him to present the Allies' cause to the United States, and in 1917 he was sent on a lecture tour to stimulate recruiting. Connor wrote three war books, *The Major* (1917), *The Sky Pilot of No Man's Land* (1919), and *Treading the Winepress: A Tale of Glengarry* (1925). The second, often considered his most powerful, has been described as "the epitome of a prevalent Anglo-Saxon Canadian view of the War–idealistic, Protestant evangelical, and British tribal" (*Literary History of Canada,* edited by Carl F. Klinck, 1973).

After the war Connor's popularity as a novelist went into eclipse. His genial faith in order, both spiritual and temporal, struck a disillusioned public as naive. Although he did continue writing, much of his postwar work, according to his grandson Charles Gordon, was primarily commercial. In 1921 Connor became moderator of the Presbyterian Church prior to its becoming part of the United Church of Canada. In the early 1920s he also served as chairman of the Joint Council of Industry for Manitoba, an experience that is reflected in his book about the 1919 Winnipeg strike, *To Him That Hath: A Novel of the West Today* (1921). His international activities on behalf of world peace led to his impassioned campaigning for the League of Nations. In 1938 his autobiography was published but received little attention.

Both Connor and his critics have agreed that his first four novels (of over twenty) constitute his best work. Although his books continued

to sell in scores of thousands for at least a decade after publication of *The Doctor: A Tale of the Rockies* (1906), with the exception of *The Foreigner: A Tale of Saskatchewan* (1909), they are excessively formulaic. Many explore themes of regeneration by the prairie, of Canadianization, and of social difficulties inherent in assimilation. Connor's novels remain of interest because of the powerful, if oversimplified, myth of a specific Anglo-Celtic Canadian identity which they embody; the West is the cradle of the new Canadian race, and his mythic Western heroes represent for him the best and most characteristic in Canadian civilization.

As George Woodcock has noted, an astonishing proportion of early Canadian fiction writers were clergymen of evangelical bent, but Ralph Connor is the only one who developed a fictional voice that still speaks "out of the Canadian nineteenth century with a degree of conviction."

References:
S. Ross Beharriell, Introduction to *Glengarry School Days* (Toronto: McClelland & Stewart, 1975);
Beharriell, Introduction to *The Man from Glengarry* (Toronto: McClelland & Stewart, 1969);
Dick Harrison, *Unnamed Country: The Struggle For a Canadian Prairie Fiction* (Edmonton: University of Alberta Press, 1977);
Edward McCourt, *The Canadian West in Fiction* (Toronto: Ryerson, 1949; revised edition, 1970), pp. 18-38;
Clara Thomas, *Our Nature–Our Voices* (Toronto: New Press, 1972), pp. 51-54;
J. Lee Thompson and John H. Thompson, "Ralph Connor and the Canadian Identity," *Queen's Quarterly,* 79 (Summer 1972): 159-170;
F. W. Watt, "Western Myth: The World of Ralph Connor," *Canadian Literature,* 1 (Summer 1959): 26-36;
Susan Wood, "Ralph Connor and the Tamed West," in *The Westering Experience in American Literature,* edited by Merrill Lewis and L. L. Lee (Bellingham: Western Washington University Press, 1977), pp. 199-205.

Papers:
The University of Manitoba library, Winnipeg, has manuscripts by Connor.

Maurice Constantin-Weyer

(24 April 1881-22 October 1964)

John J. O'Connor
University of Toronto

BOOKS: *Les Images*, as Maurice Constantin (Paris: Librairie Léon Vanier, 1902);

Vers l'ouest (Paris: Renaissance du Livre, 1921); translated by Edwin Granberry as *Towards the West* (New York: Macaulay, 1931);

Manitoba (Paris: Rieder, 1924);

La Bourrasque (Paris: Rieder, 1925); translated as *A Martyr's Folly* (Toronto: Macmillan, 1930); translated by Marie M. G. Jolas as *The Half-Breed* (New York: Macaulay, 1930);

Cavelier de La Salle (Paris: Rieder, 1927); translated by Lyle Frederickson as *The French Adventurer: The Life and Exploits of LaSalle* (New York: Macaulay, 1931);

Cinq Eclats de silex (Paris: Rieder, 1927);

Un Homme se penche sur son passé (Paris: Rieder, 1928); translated by Slater Brown as *A Man Scans His Past* (New York: Macaulay, 1929; Toronto: Macmillan, 1929);

Morvan (Paris: Rieder, 1929);

Shakespeare (Paris: Rieder, 1929);

Clairière: Récits du Canada (Paris: Stock/Delamain & Boutelleau, 1929); translated by Conrad Elphinstone as *Forest Wild* (London: Routledge, 1932);

P.C. de compagnie (Paris: Rieder, 1930);

La Salamandre (Paris: Etincelles, 1930);

La Vie du Général Yusuf (Paris: Gallimard, 1930);

Champlain (Paris: Plon, 1931);

Drapeau rouge (Paris: Editions des Portiques, 1931);

Du sang sur la neige (Paris: Cité des Livres, 1931);

Napoléon (Paris: Rieder, 1931);

L'Ame du vin (Paris: Rieder, 1932);

Les Secrets d'une maîtresse de maison, by Constantin-Weyer and Germaine Constantin-Weyer (Paris: Rieder, 1932);

Source de joie (Paris: Rieder, 1932);

Une Corde sur l'abîme (Paris: Rieder, 1933);

Mon Gai Royaume de Provence (Paris: Rieder, 1933);

Vichy, ville du charme (Clermont-Ferrand, Que., 1933); republished as *Vichy, la vie d'eau éternelle* (Vichy: Syndicat d'Initiatives, 1946);

Maurice Constantin-Weyer in 1952 (photograph courtesy of his daughter, Françoise Constantin-Weyer)

Un Sourire dans la tempête (Paris: Rieder, 1934);

Le Voyage de Leif L'Heureux (Paris: Le Masque, 1934);

La Croisière du jour sans fin (Paris: Rieder, 1935);

Le Flâneur sous la tente (Paris: Stock/Delamain & Boutelleau, 1935);

Les Compagnons de la houle (Paris: Fayard, 1936);

La Demoiselle de la mort (Paris: Librairie des Champs-Elysées, 1936);

Telle qu'elle était en son vivant (Paris: Librairie des Champs-Elysées, 1936); republished as *La Loi du nord; ou, Telle qu'elle était en son vivant* (Paris: Librairie des Champs-Elysées, 1947);

Aime une ombre (Paris: Librairie des Champs-Elysées, 1937);

La Marchande de mort (Paris: Librairie des Champs-Elysées, 1938);

Le Moulinet à tambour fixe: Pêche tous les poissons avec toutes les esches, avec tous les leurres (Paris: Librairie des Champs-Elysées, 1938);

La Nuit de Magdalena (Paris: Librairie des Champs-Elysées, 1938);

Les Tombes-d'amour (Paris: Librairie des Champs-Elysées, 1938);

Autour de l'épopée canadienne (Paris: Floury, 1940);

L'Equipe sans nom (Paris: Librairie des Champs-Elysées, 1940);

La Chasse au brochet (Paris: Librairie des Champs-Elysées, 1941);

Le Cheval de prise (Avignon: Aubanel, 1941);

Le Maître de la route (Geneva: Milieu du Monde, 1941);

La Vérendrye (Toulouse: Didier, 1941);

Canoes et kayaks, by Constantin-Weyer and Barbelay-Bertillot (Vichy: Commissariat Général à l'Education Générale et aux Sports, 1942);

L'Aventure vécue de Dumas père (Geneva: Milieu du Monde, 1944);

L'Ame allemande (Paris: Grasset, 1945);

Le Grand Will, by Constantin-Weyer and Clara Longworth-Chambrun (Paris: Editions de la Nouvelle France, 1945);

Le Bar de San Miguel (Paris: Simon, 1946);

La Chanson d'Ingrid (Paris: Grasset, 1946);

La Fille du soleil (Paris: Arts-France, 1946);

Sous le signe du vampire (Paris: L'Elan, 1947);

Vichy et son histoire (de ses origines à nos jours) (Vichy: Szabo, 1947);

Pronunciamiento (Paris: L'Elan, 1948);

Dans les Pas du naturaliste (Paris: Stock, Delamain & Boutelleau, 1950);

Naundorff ou Louis XVII? (Paris: SFELT, 1950);

La Vie privée des poissons (Paris: Stock, Delamain & Boutelleau, 1954); translated by Ray Turrell as *The Private Life of Fishes* (London: Bell, 1956);

Les Tragiques Amours de Bianca (Paris: Fayard, 1958);

Avec plus ou moins de rire (Saint-Boniface, Man.: Editions des Plaines, 1986).

SELECTED PERIODICAL PUBLICATIONS
UNCOLLECTED: "Au pays de Maria Chapdelaine," *L'Illustration* (Christmas 1931);
"L'Officier de troupe," *Les Œuvres Libres*, 224 (March 1940): 5-36;

"Rodéo," *Les Œuvres Libres*, new series 294 (January 1952): 25-110.

Although Maurice Constantin-Weyer's life and writing were divided between France and Canada, he is now remembered primarily as a novelist who drew upon Canadian prairie history and his own experiences in western Canada prior to World War I and presented them, greatly transformed, for readers in France. However, just a year before he won the Prix Goncourt, he lamented in the dedication to *Cavelier de La Salle* (1927; translated as *The French Adventurer: The Life and Exploits of LaSalle*, 1931) that "le Canada se souvient plus volontiers que la France" (Canada remembers more readily than France). It is true that very few histories of twentieth-century French literature mention him at all, and most of those that do merely acknowledge in passing his winning of the Goncourt prize in 1928. Nevertheless, though the praise was scanty, the literary output was not; the national libraries of France and Canada list some sixty volumes (including novels, biographies, literary criticism, local history, war memoirs, a play, and books on fishing and wine), record his translations into French (notably works by Shakespeare, Swift, and Thackeray), and indicate nearly two dozen prefaces and introductions written by Constantin-Weyer on a wide range of subjects. Although only six of his many books have been translated into English, these do include his most important works–novels dealing with western and northern Canada from the mid nineteenth century until World War I. Not surprisingly, it was one of these, *Un Homme se penche sur son passé* (1928; translated as *A Man Scans His Past*, 1929), that impressed the Académie Goncourt; it is certainly Constantin-Weyer's best work.

Inasmuch as Constantin-Weyer was a European confronting the western Canadian frontier and interpreting it in his works of history and fiction, his career follows lines remarkably parallel to those of Frederick Philip Grove (and, to a lesser extent, those of Archibald S. Belaney/Grey Owl). Born Maurice Constantin (Weyer, his second wife's maiden name, was added after his marriage) in Bourbonne-les-Bains (Haute-Marne), France, he was first educated in Coblence and Paris, then Langres and Avignon, a period in his life when he was much drawn to the classics (especially the *Odyssey*) and to narratives of adventure (in particular, *Don Quixote, Tom Jones, Les Trois Mousquetaires*, and the works of Rabelais). His

Constantin-Weyer and his dog, 1897 (photograph courtesy of Françoise Constantin-Weyer)

mother, Marie-Amélie Bompardt, came from Lorraine and was the granddaughter of a former mayor of Metz; and his father, Alphonse Marie Louis Xavier Constantin, a native of Provence, was a retired cavalry officer who had been wounded in the Franco-Prussian War and later became a journalist. After his father's death Maurice moved with his mother to Paris where, in 1898, he began science studies at the Sorbonne; these were abandoned in 1901 when his mother suffered financial loss. There followed two years of military service, after which Constantin-Weyer decided to emigrate. To this end, he sailed from Le Havre in July 1904, arriving in Saint-Claude, Manitoba, in September. Four years later he became a Canadian citizen.

Drawing upon the decade spent in western Canada, Constantin-Weyer offered French readers and critics a highly romanticized account of his life as a trapper, cowboy, farmer, lumberjack, and journalist—he was later to refer to this period as "ces années, où je jouais au sauvage" (those years when I played the savage). Most of the details of this game playing, however, have been vigorously challenged by Donatien Frémont in his exposé *Sur le ranch de Constantin-Weyer* (1932). Frémont claims that Constantin-Weyer's decade in Canada was, rather, a time of failure, deception, and indolence. Furthermore, in 1910, according to Frémont, Constantin-Weyer married a sixteen-year-old Métisse, Dina Proulx; and, by the time he sailed for France to fight in World War I, he had fathered three children and left mother, wife, and offspring destitute. But since most of his readers were an ocean away, he could easily invent his own heroic past and reconstruct that of western Canada, too. Nevertheless, a year after Frémont's denunciation, and no doubt in response to it, Constantin-Weyer did hint at some adjustments of fact in the Canadian books; in *Source de joie* (1932) he points out that his works constitute not a self-portrait but merely a study of a "*moi* complaisant à ma curiosité" (*self* conforming to my own interests) and adds: "Qu'importe, alors, si le modèle me ressemble ou ne me ressemble pas! ... Je voudrais que, sur ce moi ... le lecteur se gardât de mettre aucune figure définie" (What does it matter, then, if the model resembles me or not! ... I want the reader ... to beware of assigning any specific identity to this self).

Constantin-Weyer in 1910 with Dina-Proulx, who became his first wife later that year (photograph courtesy of Françoise Constantin-Weyer)

During the war Constantin-Weyer was several times decorated and was seriously wounded in 1917. While recuperating after the war, he met and married Germaine Weyer and decided to earn his living as a writer. In 1920, in recognition of his service during the war, he became a *chevalier* of the Légion d'Honneur, and in 1923 he was appointed editor of *Paris-Centre*, a newspaper in Nevers. During this period he published the first three of his books on western Canada: *Vers l'ouest* (1921; translated as *Towards the West*, 1931), *Manitoba* (1924), and *La Bourrasque* (1925; translated as *A Martyr's Folly* and as *The Half-Breed*, 1930). The first of these inaugurates Constantin-Weyer's revisionist history; it uses Louis Riel, Sr., father of the celebrated Métis leader, as the starting point for a highly improbable account of Indian wars, tragic death by freezing, and a melodramatic love triangle. At the same time, however, *Vers l'ouest* reveals Constantin-Weyer's skill in describing prairie landscape and flora and sounds

his first warning note about how civilization will destroy the prairie's native culture. This book also provided a formula to which Constantin-Weyer returned often in later works, even to the point of repeating several pages verbatim in *Manitoba* and *Un Homme se penche sur son passé*.

The general themes of *Vers l'ouest* recur in subsequent works. *Manitoba* is a very selective and distorted autobiographical memoir in which anticlericalism, the clash of white and Métis cultures, the mysteries of life and death, and the conflicting impulses of art and nature are all explored. Like his earlier Canadian works, *La Bourrasque* contains skillful landscape description but is often marred by poor plot construction, facile characterization, improbable dialogue, and egregious distortions of prairie history—in this instance, blatant inaccuracies in the treatment of Louis Riel, Jr.'s 1870 rebellion. These three early works were, in Constantin-Weyer's words, "fragments possibles d'une vaste fresque canadienne. Tantôt, c'est un tableau de moeurs sauvages: *Vers l'ouest*; tantôt, un épisode historique: *La Bourrasque*; tantôt quelques paysages qu'un soir berger a ramené comme un troupeau de souvenirs: *Manitoba*" (possible fragments of a vast Canadian fresco. Sometimes it's a tableau of savage customs: *Vers l'ouest*; sometimes it's a historical episode: *La Bourrasque*; sometimes some landscapes that an evening shepherd has brought home like a flock of memories: *Manitoba*). In these works, particularly in *La Bourrasque*, there is a pronounced anticlerical strain. All were promoted by the publisher under the general title of "Epopée canadienne."

From 1927 to 1930 Constantin-Weyer served as editor of a second newspaper, the *Journal de l'Ouest et du Centre* in Poitiers. Then he moved to Orléans where he remained until the beginning of World War II, when he took up residence with his family in Vichy. In 1932, in acknowledgment of his literary achievement, he was named *officier* in the Légion d'Honneur. Throughout the period between the two wars he continued to re-create western Canadian history and his own experiences in Manitoba, notably in *Cavelier de La Salle* (1927; translated as *The French Adventurer: The Life and Exploits of LaSalle*, 1931), *Cinq Eclats de silex* (Five Flakes of Flint, 1927), *Clairière* (1929; translated as *Forest Wild*, 1932), and especially in his prizewinning novel, *Un Homme se penche sur son passé*. His comment to Léon Côté on the plots of his novels seems particularly relevant to this much-praised work: "Ils ne

Constantin-Weyer and his second wife, Germaine, in 1928 and during World War II
(photographs courtesy of Françoise Constantin-Weyer)

sont pas compliqués: la trame romanesque tient en quelques mots. Elle sert de cadre à un poème de la volonté humaine affrontant une nature hostile" (They are not complicated: the novel's outline can be stated in a few words. It serves as the frame for a poem about the human will confronting hostile nature). No doubt such a thematic concern does explain part of the novel's extraordinary popularity and commercial success (in 1950, for example, Les Presses Universitaires de France published the 359th edition); but much of its appeal can be explained by its exceptional descriptive power and by the charm of its novelty for French readers. Constantin-Weyer's dedication to Emile Zavie notes that the novel is "aussi parfaitement étranger au goût du jour qu'un costume de cow-boy à l'Avenue de l'Opéra" (as perfectly strange to the taste of the day as would be a cowboy costume on the Avenue de l'Opéra). However, it should also be remembered that similar attention had recently been accorded another French novel about Canada: Marie Le Franc had

won the Prix Fémina the preceding year for *Grand-Louis l'innocent.*

In *Un Homme se penche sur son passé* Constantin-Weyer succeeds in fashioning an interesting story out of old materials. Although this narrative, concerning Monge, a cowboy turned fur trader and then farmer, resurrects most of his earlier themes and attitudes, the novelist succeeds here in rejuvenating his approach. The story of Monge's love for Hannah O'Molloy, his rivalry with Archer for her affection, and the long winter of fur trading in the high North with Paul Durand, the fiancé of Hannah's sister Magd, is told with economy and energy. As narrator, Monge is not given to excessive effusion on his life and circumstances but does manage to reflect his genuine anxiety about the impact of civilization on the prairie's traditions, the struggle for survival in a brutal and indifferent world, and the effects of alienation both in the North and on the western plain, where Monge's illusions about life with Hannah quickly give way to disappointment,

Constantin-Weyer in his study in Vichy after World War II
(photograph courtesy of Françoise Constantin-Weyer)

betrayal, and death. In both the fur-trading excursion and Monge's dramatic pursuit of his wife, daughter, and Archer, Constantin-Weyer's handling of plot and setting is skillful, and his treatment of character and theme is often original and compelling. These achievements not only make *Un Homme se penche sur son passé* his best work but also help to explain its winning of the Prix Goncourt in December 1928, though the success of the novel is qualified somewhat by unconvincing and unidiomatic English dialogue and especially by the deliberate repetition of descriptive passages the author had used in earlier books.

It is not surprising to learn that the Prix Goncourt had a considerable effect on Constantin-Weyer's career. Many books (several of them dedicated to members of the Académie Goncourt) were published in the four years that followed. In 1930 he gave up his newspaper work in Poitiers in order to write and paint. Along with these artistic pursuits, in the decade before World War II he traveled in Europe (Scandinavia, Germany, and Russia). At the same time,

Constantin-Weyer published four more "Canadian" works: *Napoléon* (1931), which borrows heavily from the themes and plot of *Un Homme se penche sur son passé* to demonstrate the victimization of prairie natives; *Une Corde sur l'abîme* (A Rope over the Abyss, 1933), in which Monge briefly reappears, the melodramatic tale of a Frenchman who sacrifices his life while helping the Indians; and *Un Sourire dans la tempête* (A Smile in the Storm, 1934) and *Telle qu'elle était en son vivant* (As She Was in Her Lifetime, 1936), both of which explore the love of three men (including a Mountie) for a single woman in the snowy solitudes of the Canadian Northwest, and which, like *Un Homme se penche sur son passé*, were made into successful films.

After the war Constantin-Weyer was closely questioned by officials of the justice department in Paris for allegedly sympathizing with the Nazis during the occupation of France; to these charges Constantin-Weyer responded by citing his work with the Resistance movement. In April 1946 he was accepted into the Société de Gens de Lettres de France, and in the following years he traveled to Algeria and Italy. He continued to write until 1960, though his postwar books did not use Canada for their subjects and setting. Following his wife's death in May 1961, Constantin-Weyer wrote two unpublished autobiographical works—"Journal" and "Propos d'un octogénaire"—while living alternately in Vichy and with his daughter Françoise in Luxembourg. After a long and prolific career, Constantin-Weyer died in 1964 at the age of eighty-three in Vichy and is buried in the nearby cemetery of Creuzier-le-Vieux.

In summary it might be argued that this man was indeed drawn to adventure and romance because, as he said, he believed that they alone produced masterpieces that would remain intelligible to posterity. However, the modern reader does not see just intelligibility, but rather originality and insight, as major critical concerns in evaluating his work. Although the novels are often superficial examinations of character and circumstance, the irony of his ultimate success cannot have escaped him, as it did not Donatien Frémont in 1932: "L'auteur de *l'Epopée canadienne* . . . doit se demander parfois s'il est bien l'ancien colon du Manitoba, maudissant le sort qui l'avait fait échouer dans ce pays où il avait connu la misère noire. Sans doute, quand il se penche sur ce rude passé, admire-t-il qu'il ait pu si aisément le métamorphoser, au point de s'en faire un piédestal" (The author of the *Epopée*

The Constantin-Weyers in 1961 (photograph courtesy of Françoise Constantin-Weyer)

canadienne . . . must sometimes ask himself if he is the former Manitoba settler, cursing the fate that made him fail in that country where he had known utter misery. No doubt, when he scans this rough past, he is pleased that he was able to transform it so easily, to the point of putting himself on a pedestal). Still, Frémont's early attack on Constantin-Weyer is modified in the more balanced critical assessment he offered at the end of the novelist's career. In 1959 Frémont's *Les Français dans l'ouest canadien* offers this overview of Constantin-Weyer's achievement: "Quand il aborde l'histoire du pays, il la romance au point de la défigurer totalement; mais comme peintre de la nature et de la vie de l'Ouest, on peut l'admirer sans réserve. . . . La faune et la flore de l'Ouest n'ont pas de secret pour lui. Il nous associe à la vie de la forêt, de la prairie, du lac peuplés de bêtes et de cris. Il est inimitable dans la notation réaliste des minces événements journaliers du monde des Métis et des colons" (When he tackles the country's history, he fictionalizes it to the point of distorting it totally; but as a painter of the nature and of the life of the West, one can admire him without reserva-

tion. . . . The fauna and flora of the West have no secrets for him. He makes us a party to the life of the forest, of the prairie, of the lake inhabited by animals and cries. He is without equal in the realistic depiction of small daily events in the world of the Métis and the settlers).

Constantin-Weyer thus remains of interest to the modern reader of Canadian fiction for both biographical and literary reasons. His career presents the intriguing case of a man who invented his own past along with that of an entire region, then was lionized abroad for his courage and vision. While Frémont's later assessment now seems too generous, it nevertheless reminds us that, for other reasons besides the 1928 Prix Goncourt, Maurice Constantin-Weyer merits attention in any contemporary investigation of western Canadian literature.

References:

Marguerite Constantin-Fortin, *Une Femme se penche sur son passé* (Paris: Les Livres Nouveaux, 1940);

Donatien Frémont, *Les Français dans l'ouest canadien* (Winnipeg: Editions de la Liberté, 1959);

Frémont, *Sur le ranch de Constantin-Weyer* (Winnipeg: Editions de la Liberté, 1932);

Edward B. Ham, Introduction to Constantin-Weyer's *Un Homme se penche sur son passé*, edited by Ham and Eliot G. Fay (New York: Holt, 1933), pp. v-xxxi;

Roger Motut, *Maurice Constantin-Weyer: Ecrivain*

de *l'Ouest et du Grand Nord* (Sainte-Boniface, Man.: Editions des Plaines, 1982);

Valery Larbaud et ses contemporains bourbonnais: Charles-Louis Philippe, Emile Guillaumin, Maurice Constantin-Weyer 31 mai-21 juin 1981 (Vichy: Bibliothèque municipale/Centre Culturel Valery Larbaud, 1981).

Isabella Valancy Crawford

(25 December 1850-12 February 1887)

Carole Gerson
Simon Fraser University

BOOKS: *Old Spookses' Pass, Malcolm's Katie, and Other Poems* (Toronto: Bain, 1884);

The Collected Poems, edited by John W. Garvin (Toronto: Briggs, 1905);

Selected Stories, edited by Penny Petrone (Ottawa: University of Ottawa Press, 1975);

Fairy Tales, edited by Petrone (Ottawa: Borealis, 1977);

Hugh and Ion, edited by Glenn Clever (Ottawa: Borealis, 1977);

The Halton Boys, edited by Frank M. Tierney (Ottawa: Borealis, 1979).

Isabella Valancy Crawford, gifted with an extraordinary mythopoeic imagination, is today regarded as one of the major poets of late-nineteenth-century Canada. Although most of her fiction and her shorter poems were written to suit the conventions of the periodicals from which she tried to earn a living, her narrative poems (the best known of which is "Malcolm's Katie") and some of her lyrics are gripping expressions of a unified cosmological vision in which the interdependent opposites of light and darkness, good and evil, and life and death are eventually reconciled through the power of human love. She animated the Canadian landscape and the cycles of nature with vivid Indian and animal imagery, expressing the meeting of European civilization and New World wilderness in language and symbols very different from those of her leading Canadian contemporaries, Charles G. D. Roberts and Archibald Lampman.

During her brief lifetime, however, Crawford received meager recognition, and so little is known of her personal affairs that even the details of her birth are uncertain. While the records are scarce and unreliable, the place is presumed to have been Dublin and the date 25 December 1850. The number and fates of the other children born to her parents, Dr. Stephen Dennis Crawford and Sydney Scott Crawford, are also a mystery. Isabella stated that she was the sixth in a family that is believed to have numbered twelve, but by the end of their residence in Paisley, Ontario, their first home in Canada, the children numbered only three: Isabella and two younger siblings, Emma Naomi and Stephen Walter. Dr. Crawford's Dublin background and Anglo-Irish connections have been traced, yet neither the date of his family's departure from Ireland nor their itinerary has been discovered. Emma Naomi's death certificate states that she was born in Wisconsin in 1854. Her father may have gone to Australia in 1855 or 1856, but by 1857 the family had settled in the new village of Paisley in Bruce County, where, despite dubious credentials, Dr. Crawford was licensed to practice medicine and his wife purchased some land.

The Crawfords lived in this pioneer setting until 1861. Isabella spent her girlhood in close contact with nature and the Indians, whose camps she visited with her father. At the same time, she and her sisters were educated at home in English, Latin, and French (in which Isabella conversed fluently with her mother); Isabella's reading extended to Horace and Dante. She also became an accomplished musician, and both girls were adept at fine needlework. A frontier community where farm produce was often taken in payment for medical services, Paisley was less bountiful to the father than to his poetic daughter. The alcoholic physician did not acquire a reputation for medical competence and was unable to support his family comfortably. In 1862, apparently while on their way back to Ireland, the Crawfords were discovered in a hotel north of Kingston by two sons of Samuel Strickland (brother of Susanna Moodie and Catharine Parr Traill), who persuaded them to go instead to North Douro (later known as Lakefield), where a resident physician was needed. Here Isabella became acquainted with the Traills and with the family of Rev. Vincent Clementi, whose musical talents helped develop her interest in music. Undoubtedly the future poet reveled in the beauty of the nearby Kawartha Lakes, where she may

have camped and canoed, but here, too, her father failed to prosper. Six years later the family moved once again, this time to the larger town of Peterborough, where the death of Dr. Crawford in July 1875 was followed by that of Emma Naomi six months later.

According to Katharine Hale misfortune seemed to stalk the Crawfords:

> The delicate Emma Naomi . . . was always busy with beautiful and intricate designs in embroidery. On one piece she had worked for a year, and sent it, in hopes of a sale or a prize, to the Centennial Exhibition in Philadelphia. It was lost in the mails. At the same time it was announced that Isabella had won a six-hundred dollar prize in a short story competition. This meant financial salvation. But on the heels of the first cheque for a hundred dollars came the news that the prize-giving corporation had failed and nothing more was to be expected from them.

Of Crawford's earliest writing nothing remains, but during her years in Peterborough her first known published works appeared: half-a-dozen stories in the *Favourite* in 1872 and 1873, and eleven poems in the *Toronto Mail* between 24 December 1873 and 3 May 1875. However, among the Crawford papers housed at Queen's University (Kingston) are seven fairy tales, one signed "I.V.C. N. Douro." The handwriting and condition of the manuscripts suggest that they all date from her teenage years, but there is no evidence that they appeared in print before their recent publication in one volume in 1977. These visionary stories venture into the realm of fays and enchantment and contain many seeds of Crawford's later work in their symbolic use of flowers, water, gold, and magic, their balance and eventual union of polar opposites, their detailed descriptions of nature, and their happy endings (some including moral statements typical of Victorian children's literature). Several can be read as allegories of artistic experience, in which fairyland represents the world of the unconscious and the imagination briefly accessible to the poet.

During her family's residence in Peterborough, Crawford turned her talents to commercial use to help ease their chronic poverty. Her poems in the *Mail*, which earned more fame than remuneration, ceased abruptly after her father's death. Her younger brother had already left home to work in the forests of Northern Ontario; while the family received some financial aid from a relative in the Royal Navy, Isabella

Cover and three other illustrations for Penny Petrone's 1977 collection of Crawford's fairy tales
(drawings copyright 1976 by Susan Ross)

was left the main supporter of her mother and her invalid sister. From mid 1875 to mid 1879 she appears to have published nothing in Canada, turning instead to the more lucrative American market and the periodicals of Frank Leslie in New York. In Paisley, the Crawfords' home had been noted for its hospitality. In Peterborough, however, the women grew reclusive. The personal pride noted by Crawford's early biographers was further increased by her poverty. In Lakefield she often held herself apart from other young people, but when she did join their merrymakings, Hale notes that a contemporary remembered, "she became the life of the party, electrifying us with her flashes of fun and repartee." In later years her withdrawal increased; Mrs. S. Frances Harrison, literary editor of the *Week*, remembered her as "A tall, dark young woman, whom most people would feel was difficult, almost repellant in manner."

However, surprisingly little disaffection appears in her poetry. The poems written in Peterborough between 1873 and 1875 anticipate the optimism of her later verse. Poems about nightfall celebrate the beauty of the evening star, a love wish made on a falling star, or the triumph of the moon (representing the forces of light) over the hellish darkness. A poem about winter dwells on the certainty of spring, and "The Wooing of Gheezis" recounts an Indian regeneration myth of the marriage of a god to a human maiden, Segwun (Spring). Two poems, "Esther" and "Caesar's Wife," commemorate the heroism of historical women, while a patriotic piece praises Canada's growth to nationhood and kinship with England. They are all written in blank verse, the form of Crawford's best narrative poem, "Malcolm's Katie," first published in 1884 but possibly written ten years earlier. Like "Malcolm's Katie," these earlier pieces suggest that despite her family's misfortunes and her own apparent haughtiness, Crawford remained buoyant.

Although some obituaries erroneously stated that Crawford lived for a time in France, she herself wrote (as quoted by Mary F. Martin), "I was brought to Canada by my parents in my earliest childhood, and have never left the country since that period. I was educated at home, and have never left home but for a month, that amount of absence scattered over my life." Where she could not travel in person she easily ventured in her imagination. One of her hobbies, according to Hale, was "cutting out and making the most unique and beautiful little foreign fig-ures, tiny dolls, always of oriental types, made out of vivid coloured silks or satins; Rajahs and Mandarin and Hindoo priests in their robes and turbans, with their attendants perfectly costumed." One of these fabric sculptures, which Crawford made in 1880 to amuse a sick child, still survives, now housed in the Peterborough Centennial Museum. She had sufficient acquaintance with Eastern literature to select the epigraphs to "Life," a poem first published in 1882, from the *Bhagavad Gîtà* and the *Rig Veda*.

More than an exotic imagination was needed for survival, however, and in 1879 began the final phase of Crawford's career. Once again her poems appeared in Canadian publications, primarily the *Toronto Globe* and the *Toronto Evening Telegram*. In the spring of 1876 she and her mother moved from Peterborough to Toronto, presumably to be closer to the publishers upon whom they depended. From 1882 to 1886 they lived in a series of boardinghouses on Adelaide Street West and were often behind in their rent. The Toronto newspapers paid from one to three dollars for each poem, and from June 1879 to mid 1886 Crawford published approximately one or two poems a month. She also published some stories and serialized novels, few of which have been found. A serial novel titled "A Little Bacchante, or Some Black Sheep" received high praise, yet only one number of the *Evening Globe*, in which it ran in 1886, is extant. Notations on her surviving prose manuscripts indicate that Crawford, like many other writers of the period, was paid by the word or the line. She also tried to sell her poems to the *Week*, the country's leading literary periodical, founded in 1883, but was regretfully informed that it "didn't pay for poetry."

In the spring of 1884 Crawford published at her own expense the only volume of her poems to appear in her lifetime, *Old Spookses' Pass, Malcolm's Katie, and Other Poems*, printed by James Bain. Despite favorable reviews at home and in England and personal congratulations from Tennyson, only fifty of the one thousand copies printed sold in Canada. Critics partially attribute the book's failure to its awkward title. Crawford eventually took back the unsold volumes and in 1886 reissued them in new covers. In 1898 the Toronto publisher William Briggs rebound and marketed some of the remaining copies; today any of these issues is a collector's item.

The poems in this book reveal both Crawford's influences and the originality of her imagination. Imbued with Tennyson and Longfellow, yet compelled to court a popular audience whose taste leaned toward dialect verse and sentimentality, she tried her hand at a variety of forms, subjects, and styles. As a result her first volume contains some poems that are eminently forgettable and some that are central to her vision.

"Old Spookses' Pass" is the lesser of the title poems. Narrated in crudely stereotyped "cowboy" lingo, it describes a western miracle one dark night in the Rockies. The unidentified speaker, watching over the herd while his companions sleep, first muses on God's generosity to poor human sinners, then personally experiences divine munificence when an unseen hand halts the steer leading a stampede of three thousand cattle toward "a yanin' gulch." The poem's most striking features are its vigor and realism and Crawford's images of the herd, first like "a great black mist," later like "a great black wheel." In this book Crawford included similar narratives in Irish, Scots, and North American dialects, replete with country humor and homespun wisdom.

Of greater literary significance are two other narratives, "The Helot," which describes the rebellion of a slave against his tyrannical Spartan master, and "Gisli the Chieftain," in which Crawford draws on Norse and Russian mythologies to express her own vision of the coexistence of good and evil, upon which depend the regenerative powers of nature and love. This volume also contains one of Crawford's finest and most frequently discussed shorter pieces, "The Canoe" (later titled "Said the Canoe"). Using the voice of a feminized canoe to describe the relatively simple scene of two hunters (presumably Indians) preparing their evening campsite, Crawford weaves a rich tapestry of energies and images, inseparably meshing man and nature, love and the hunt, and life and death.

"Malcolm's Katie," the book's second title poem, is generally acclaimed as Crawford's masterpiece despite its absurd plot. More specifically Canadian than many of her narratives, it celebrates the power of love (symbolized as a daffodil) to subdue evil, and the power of the pioneer (represented by his ax) to conquer the wilderness. Enacting some of the situations of archetypal romance, the poem's two lovers–the pure-hearted, flower-loving Katie and the "social-soul'd," ax-wielding Maxwell–encounter the dark world of materialism and deceit embodied by Katie's uncooperative father and Alfred, her villainous suitor. By the end of the poem they conquer all obstacles and return to a state of renewed innocence, dwelling in "wild woods and plains . . . fairer far/Than Eden's self." Like "Gisli the Chieftain," this poem ends with a statement that good cannot exist without evil; Max and Katie name their first child Alfred, after the man who had tried first to dispose of Max, then to drown with Katie. Man and nature are likewise interdependent: while Max heroically chops down trees, Crawford describes the forest and the cycles of the seasons in vivid anthropomorphic images.

It has been suggested that the negligent reception of her first book contributed to Crawford's early death. In her last years she published fewer poems in the Toronto newspapers and may have been preparing a second volume of poetry. Her last home was a boardinghouse owned by Mrs. Stuart, above a grocery store at 57 John Street. According to Hale, Mrs. Stuart's daughter remembered Crawford as "like a being from another planet. There was something about her that the world in general could not be expected to understand. . . . I think Miss Crawford was really gay at heart, but at times seemed sad and depressed. Her passion for music was almost as great as her love for books and poetry. . . . Miss Crawford was not exactly beautiful, but I shall never forget the wonderful animation of her face at times, and its sadness in repose."

During this period Crawford received some public recognition for her poem "The Rose of a Nation's Thanks," first published to celebrate the return of the soldiers from the battle of Batoche in 1885 and reprinted by special request in the *Telegram* on 7 February 1887. Five days later she suddenly died of a heart attack. She was buried in Peterborough with little ceremony, but one nameless admirer sent a great white rose bearing the message, "The Rose of a Nation's Thanks."

After Crawford's death her brother selected John Garvin to be her literary executor. In 1905, with the help of the poet Agnes Ethelwyn Wetherald, Garvin issued the misleadingly titled *Collected Poems*. Far from complete, this volume omits nine poems from Crawford's first book and contains only the pieces that Garvin and Wetherald judged to be her best work, with many alterations. Reissued in 1973, it remains, despite the tampering and omissions, the standard edition of her poems. Among Crawford's papers are some complete stories and many fragments of fiction and poetry, most of them undated. During the 1970s three volumes of her previously unavailable prose appeared, *Selected Stories* (1975), *Fairy Tales* (1977), and *The Halton Boys* (1979), along with one long, unfinished poem, *Hugh and Ion* (1977). The *Fairy Tales* are of interest for the insight they provide into Crawford's youthful imagination; the other two volumes of fiction indicate her skill at constructing salable magazine stories for adult and juvenile readers.

Hugh and Ion, had Crawford lived to complete it, may have proven to be her masterpiece. As reconstructed from the manuscript, its most successful elements are its overt social criticism and a dramatic dialogue between Hugh, the exponent of Hope, and Ion, afflicted with despair. As well, it provides the contextual setting for two of Crawford's most sensual nature lyrics, "The Dark Stag" and "The Lily Bed," which had previously been published as independent pieces.

The tragedy of Crawford's lack of recognition during her short, impoverished life has been somewhat mitigated by the surge of critical attention her work has recently received, particularly during the 1970s. Her distinctive style, her eclectic interest in mythology, and her remarkable imagination distinguish her as the finest Canadian poet born before 1860 and rank her with the major Canadian poets of the nineteenth century.

Biographies:
Katharine Hale, *Isabella Valancy Crawford* (Toronto: Ryerson, 1923);
Mary F. Martin, "The Short Life of Isabella Valancy Crawford," *Dalhousie Review*, 52 (Autumn 1972): 390-400;
Dorothy Farmiloe, *Isabella Valancy Crawford: The Life and The Legends* (Ottawa: Tecumseh, 1983).

References:
Frank Bessai, "The Ambivalence of Love in the Poetry of Isabella Valancy Crawford," *Queen's Quarterly*, 77 (Winter 1970): 404-418;
James Reaney, Introduction to Crawford's *Collected Poems* (Toronto: University of Toronto Press, 1973);
Catherine S. Ross, "I. V. Crawford's Prose Fiction," *Canadian Literature*, 81 (Summer 1979): 47-58;
Frank Tierney, ed., *The Crawford Symposium* (Ottawa: University of Ottawa Press, 1979).

Papers:
Crawford's surviving manuscripts are in the Lorne Pierce Collection, Queen's University Archives, Kingston, Ontario.

Louis Dantin
(Eugène Seers)
(28 November 1865-17 January 1945)

Hans R. Runte
Dalhousie University

BOOKS: *Poètes de l'Amérique française,* 2 volumes (volume 1, Montreal & New York: Carrier, 1928; volume 2, Montreal: Lévesque, 1934);

Chanson javanaise: Journal d'un Canadien errant (Sherbrooke, Que.: La Tribune, 1930);

La Vie en rêve (Montreal: Librairie d'Action Canadienne-Française, 1930);

Chanson citadine (Sherbrooke, Que.: La Tribune, 1931);

Gloses critiques: Faits—œuvres—théories, 2 volumes (Montreal: Lévesque, 1931, 1935);

Chanson intellectuelle (N.p., 1932);

Le Coffret de Crusoé (Montreal: Lévesque, 1932);

Contes de Noël (Montreal: Lévesque, 1936);

L'Invitée: Conte de Noël (Montreal: Librairie d'Action Canadienne-Française, 1936);

Les Enfances de Fanny (Montreal: Chantecler, 1951); translated by Raymond Y. Chamberlain as *Fanny* (Montreal: Harvest House, 1974);

Poèmes d'outre-tombe (Trois-Rivières, Que.: Bien Public, 1962);

Un Manuscrit retrouvé à Kor-El-Fantin: La Chanson-Nature de Saint-Linoud (Eleutheropolis: Presses Idéales [fictitious place and imprint], 1963).

OTHER: *Franges d'autel,* edited by Dantin as Serge Usène (Montreal, 1900);

Emile Nelligan et son œuvre, edited, with a preface, by Dantin (Montreal: Beauchemin, 1903).

A poet and a novelist, Louis Dantin is, however, remembered mainly as a critic and a keen observer of the Quebec literary scene during the first half of the twentieth century. The son of Henriette-Eloise Perrin and Louis-Alexandre-Napoléon Seers, a lawyer, Dantin was born Ferdinand-Joseph-Eugène Seers on 28 November 1865 in Beauharnois, Quebec, and was educated in Montreal at the Collège de Montréal and the Séminaire de Philosophie (1874-1882).

On his passage to France, where he was to complete his education at the Seminary of Issy-les-Moulineaux, Dantin decided to enter religious orders and in July 1883 began his novitiate with the Pères du Très-Saint-Sacrement in Brussels, taking his vows on 29 September 1884. In October 1884 he was sent to the Gregorian University in Rome, where in 1887 he earned his doctorate in philosophy. In December 1887 he became secretary to the Superior of his order in Paris and was ordained on 22 December 1888 at Saint-Sulpice, Paris. He held administrative positions within the order in Brussels and Paris from 1889 until 1894, when, upon repeated requests by his parents, he returned to his order's Montreal location.

During the following seven years Dantin was unable to resolve the religious crisis he had experienced ever since his studies in Rome. His intellectual gifts and literary interests had increasingly come to dominate his spiritual vocation, limiting his role in the order to that of editor of the *Petit Messager du Saint-Sacrement* (1894-1900) and leading him into the world of poetic creation, literary criticism, and publishing.

On 25 February 1903 Dantin left his order and settled with his companion, Fanny, in Cambridge, Massachusetts, where he worked until 1938 as a typesetter for Caustic and Claffin and the Harvard University Press. In 1904 his son, Joseph-Déodat, was born. Tragically Dantin—renounced by his father, who had remarried, by his stepmother, and by his two sisters, abandoned by Fanny in 1909 and by his son in 1924—ended up living in self-imposed, lonely exile until his death in the Roxbury neighborhood of Boston on 17 January 1945.

Dantin signed his first story, "Le Froment de Bethléem," with his real name and published it in Paris in *Le Très-Saint-Sacrement* (1889), which he edited from 1888 to 1893; he reprinted it unsigned in the *Petit Messager* also in 1889. In 1900 he edited *Franges d'autel* (Altar Fringes), a collection of twenty-six poems by eight authors, under an anagram of Eugène Seers, "Serge Usène," also signing ten of the poems that way; one poem is signed "Louis Dantin." The latter name appeared the same year in the journal *Les Débats* and was eventually to eclipse his other pseudonyms: Eugène Voyant, Lucius, Lucien Danet, Louis Danet, Marjiotta, and Saint-Linoud (an anagram of Louis Dantin). His attempts to become a new man in the guise of Louis Dantin are described in poetic form in *Chanson intellectuelle* (1932). Dantin's name first came to prominence because of his serialized study of Emile Nelligan published in 1902 in *Les Débats* and in 1903 as a preface to the poet's collected works edited by Dantin, who had met Nelligan in 1896 and through him had become associated with the Ecole Littéraire de Montréal.

Dantin's voluminous literary criticism and the social criticism of his later years, as well as many of his creative writings, appeared from 1900 to 1942 in the magazines and newspapers of his time, such as *Les Débats, La Revue Moderne, Le Jour, Le Soleil,* and *La Tribune.* Dantin collected many of his critical pieces in *Poètes de l'Amérique française* (1928, 1934) and *Gloses critiques: Faits–œuvres–théories* (1931, 1935), and many of his stories and poems were reprinted in *La Vie en rêve* (The Dreamt Life, 1930), *Le Coffret de Crusoé* (Crusoe's Casket, 1932), and *Poèmes d'outre-tombe* (Poems from Beyond the Grave, 1962).

According to Dantin literature must not serve causes but must be judged on the appropriateness, authenticity, and sincerity of the writer's art alone. The critic's role, he claimed, is to be understanding and receptive and to measure a literary work against what its author set out to achieve in writing it: "L'art reste distinct, indépendant, soumis à ses lois intimes et doit être jaugé à sa mesure propre" (Art remains distinct, independent [of dominant ideologies], subject to its own laws, and must be gauged by its own measure). In judging literature Dantin studied first the writer's dominant characteristics, then defined the work's central idea and its thematic contents, and finally analyzed its formal components: choice of words, images, prosody, and poetic meter. In *Gloses critiques* (Critical Glosses), in which Dantin dealt with prose works, he did not hesitate to take iconoclastic positions regarding the literary and social issues of the day: literary regionalism, the relationship between art and ethics, and notions of literary nationalism and of

Cover for Dantin's first collection of stories and novellas, most of which had appeared from 1900 to 1930 in periodicals such as La Revue Moderne *and* Le Jour

the indigenous literary idiom that he called a "French-Canadian jargon which mankind would bury under its contempt."

Dantin's poetry (*Le Coffret de Crusoé,* the *Chansons, Poèmes d'outre-tombe,* and other works) reflects the fundamental inner division of a man torn between spiritual purity and the temptations of the flesh, a division most often represented by women (frequently of another race, like Fanny) as both "inviteuse . . . du démon" and consoling friend. Painfully Dantin's faith failed him in this lifelong crisis, leaving him to search for resolution in the realms of exoticism, art, and beauty.

Dantin's only novel, his moderately autobiographical *Les Enfances de Fanny* (1951), describes the fate of a young black woman from Virginia who at fifteen marries Lewis, the village schoolteacher twice her age, gives him four sons, but eventually leaves him to move to Boston, where she dies accidentally as a result of a feud between her lover, Donat Sylvain, and his rival, Charlie Ross. Disappointing in the characterization of the protagonists, who appear lifeless and without psychological depth, the novel nevertheless succeeds in evoking the social, cultural, and religious reality of Boston's black ghetto at the turn of the century. It also denounced, albeit plaintively rather than militantly, Anglo-Saxon America's "un crime ancien contre la dignité humaine" (age-old crime against human dignity), the crime of making Fanny and her people feel deeply inferior.

In the practice of literary creation and even more in theorizing about such practice, Dantin, who had the advantage of being able to observe Quebec from an objectivizing distance, was an ardent proponent of what was then called French-Canadian literature, of rigorous yet sympathetic literary criticism and historiography, and of the superiority of literary over popular French. Most of his contemporaries considered him the highest literary authority, whose judgments would not be called into question until the next generation.

Letters:

Les Sentiments d'un père affectueux: Lettres de Louis Dantin à son fils (Trois-Rivières, Que.: Bien Public, 1963).

Bibliography:

Marcel Mercier, *Bio-bibliographie de Louis Dantin* (Montreal: Ecole des Bibliothécaires, 1939).

Biographies:

Gabriel Nadeau, *Louis Dantin, sa vie et son œuvre* (Manchester, N.H.: Lafayette, 1948);

Yves Garon, "Louis Dantin, sa vie et son œuvre," Ph.D. dissertation, Université Laval, 1960.

Reference:

Placide Gaboury, *Louis Dantin et la critique d'identification* (Montreal: HMH, 1973).

Frank Parker Day
(9 May 1881-30 July 1950)

Eric Thompson
Université du Québec à Chicoutimi

BOOKS: *River of Strangers* (Garden City, N.Y.:
Doubleday, Page, 1926; London: Heine-
mann, 1926);
The Autobiography of a Fisherman (Garden City,
N.Y.: Doubleday, Page, 1927; London:
Heinemann, 1927);
Rockbound (Garden City, N.Y.: Doubleday, Doran,
1928);
John Paul's Rock (New York: Minton, Balch,
1932);
A Good Citizen (Sackville, N.B.: Mount Allison,
1947).

SELECTED PERIODICAL PUBLICATION
UNCOLLECTED: "The 'Iroquois,'" *Forum*, 74
(November 1925): 752-764.

*Frank Parker Day in 1929 (photograph copyright by Bach-
rach; courtesy of Schaffer Library, Union College)*

Frank Parker Day, a minor novelist of the
1920s, had been forgotten for many years until
his 1928 novel, *Rockbound*, was republished in
1973. In retrospect this sturdy tale of the harsh
life of Nova Scotia fishermen must remain his
memorial, for none of his other publications–
including two novels, an autobiography, and a
small book of lectures–has anything like its imaginative fire and strength of execution. However, it
is not too much to say that the novel belongs
among the few pioneering works of realism that
prepared the way for the modern period of Canadian fiction.

The son of a clergyman, George Frederick
Day, and Keziah Hardwick Day, the author was
born on 9 May 1881 at Shubenacadie, Nova Scotia, and died at Yarmouth in the same province
after spending much of his career in Europe and
the United States. As a boy, he grew used to his
family's itinerant existence in mission points
around Nova Scotia and early came to realize
why his father was not a successful minister. In
The Autobiography of a Fisherman (1927), Day recalled the "terrible restrictions" that hedged in
the life of a man who would rather fish inland
streams than preach conventional pieties, who
broke the Methodist injunction against smoking,

and who even stood his ground in a fistfight. But
father and son seem to have enjoyed a close relationship, from which the future novelist absorbed
lessons about religion and the outdoors that became themes in his writing.

At seventeen Day enrolled for a year's studies at Pictou Academy. He then worked briefly as
an under-master in a boarding school, supple-
menting his meager salary there by serving as a
hand on fishing boats during his holidays. At nineteen he won a scholarship to Mount Allison Uni-

versity, from which he graduated with a B.A. in 1903. Chosen that year as New Brunswick's second Rhodes Scholar, he pursued his studies in English literature at Oxford (M.A., 1909) and the University of Berlin. Apart from his academic achievements, he became known as an outstanding oarsman and boxer. Then, returning to Canada, he taught English at the University of New Brunswick for three years before moving to the Carnegie Institute of Technology in Pittsburgh in 1912. His teaching career was interrupted by World War I, during which he served with distinction as an officer in the Canadian infantry. Resuming his career in Pittsburgh as an administrator, he later taught at Swarthmore (1926-1928) and finally served as president of Union College, Schenectady, New York, until ill health forced his retirement in 1933.

Day married Mabel Eliza Killam in 1910, and they had one son. Day was the recipient of two honorary degrees: an LL.D. from Mount Allison in 1927, and a D.Litt. from New York University in 1929. For many years Day and his family kept a summer home at Lake Annie, Nova Scotia, to which he retired after his academic career. Besides his other writings, he contributed essays and poetry to such magazines as *Harper's Forum.*

It was in the mid 1920s that Day began to write fiction seriously, but his first effort was undistinguished. *River of Strangers* (1926) is a routine potboiler set in a Hudson's Bay Company post in northern Manitoba. Its chief characters are a doctor, a naive clergyman, and the clergyman's beautiful wife. Alex MacDonald, the Cape Breton-born doctor, is the first of Day's solitary heroes, men who escape to the wilderness for "a man's life; lonely sometimes [but] remote from bores, hypocrisy, and religious humbug." Predictably he falls in love with the clergyman's wife, the "Lady of his Dreams," and after some clumsy contrivances the pitiable husband is conveniently eaten by a bear, and the lovers can declare their feelings openly.

Day's second book, *The Autobiography of a Fisherman,* is more of a set of sketches about his favorite sport, trout fishing, than his life story. Inspired by Izaak Walton's *The Compleat Angler* (1653) and reminiscent of W. H. Blake's *Brown Waters* (1915)—descriptions of fishing trips in the Charlevoix and Saguenay regions of Quebec—the volume traces the author's memories of fishing various streams and tells anecdotes about his father, friends, and events in his life. The character of the prose may be gauged from the conclud-

Dust jacket for the 1973 republication of Day's 1928 novel, the story of a young man's growth to maturity, set on an island off the coast of Nova Scotia

ing passage: "One cannot go far wrong in the world if one loves fishing, horses, and beauty, for, after all, most of the things we dub wicked are simply ugly.... That things that are beautiful can be associated with wickedness is mere nonsense, an idea that puritans have invented to plague us. Enjoy all you can the beautiful, innocent diversions of life, for the future is vague and uncertain." This is as succinct a statement of his philosophy as Day ever wrote.

Yet such soft-centered romanticism reveals nothing of the more robust vision of reality he offers in *Rockbound,* his third book. Allan Bevan, who wrote the introduction for the 1973 republication, is right when he suggests that what Day wanted was to present "an isolated, primitive world stripped of all sophistication, a world in which man was brought face to face with the timeless problems of humanity." Indeed, by setting his novel in a village on the rocky outcrop of

East Ironbound Island, off the south coast of Nova Scotia, Day had found an ideal stage for an original and realistic drama, one that was perhaps close to the dark side of his own experience. The fierce struggle between the Jungs and the Krauses, Rockbound's rival fishing gangs, dominates the first half of the novel. Certainly this mise-en-scène presents a formidable obstacle for the young hero, David Jung, to overcome; but it is his slow progress from illiteracy to civilized manhood that forms the novel's main theme. When at the end he returns with his bride to Gershom's Island–transformed by his labor from barrenness to fertility–he has conquered the dark forces in his heritage and milieu. The local-color realism of the narrative's surface sustains an ageless fable of renewal.

However, not everyone thought so at the time. Bevan describes the protest of some angry citizens of Ironbound against what they perceived as Day's slanderous depiction of their society as "ignorant, immoral and superstitious." Undoubtedly Day had touched a nerve; it was neither the first nor the last time a Canadian novelist would be attacked as scurrilous, as the experiences of Frederick Philip Grove, Hugh MacLennan, Mordecai Richler, Margaret Laurence, and Margaret Atwood attest. But he also had his defenders, scholars such as Archibald MacMechan, who recognized the importance of *Rockbound* as an honest, fictional portrait.

John Paul's Rock (1932), Day's third and last novel, seems in some respects a sequel to *Rockbound*. Once again the hero is a solitary figure, a Micmac Indian, who flees the white man's world to rediscover his own people's heritage. For him the capricious god Glooscap is more sympathetic to his earthly physical and spiritual needs than "the white man's God," Jesus. In Day's study of John Paul's quest, one senses Day's own need to work out religious doubts.

Three years before his death, the author delivered the Josiah Wood lectures for 1947 at his alma mater, Mount Allison. The lectures, "The Ideal State," "The Actual State," and "The University as a Training Ground for Guardian Citizens," are collected in *A Good Citizen* (1947). What emerges most strongly from his remarks is a belief in the Platonic conception of state leadership, a belief that illustrates Day's conservative, elitist trust in the few who are fit to govern in a democracy. But beneath this rather austere theme runs a more personal appeal, one implicit in his earlier writings: trust yourself, be self-reliant, and learn all you can–from books and from life.

References:

Allan Bevan, Introduction to *Rockbound* (Toronto: University of Toronto Press, 1973);

Bevan, "Rockbound Revisited: A Reappraisal of Frank Parker Day's Novel," *Dalhousie Review*, 38 (Autumn 1958): 336-347;

John Moss, "Frank Parker Day: Rockbound," in his *A Reader's Guide to the Canadian Novel* (Toronto: McClelland & Stewart, 1981), pp. 84-86.

Papers:

Day's collected papers are in the Archives and Special Collections at Dalhousie University, Halifax.

Guy Delahaye
(François-Guillaume Lahaise)
(18 March 1888-2 October 1969)

Alexandre L. Amprimoz
Brock University

BOOKS: *Les Phases: Tryptiques* (Montreal: Déom, 1910);

Mignonne, allons voir si la rose . . . Portrait (Montreal: Déom, 1912);

Chemin de la Croix d'un ancien retraitant: L'Unique Voie à l'unique but (Montreal: Imprimerie le Messager, 1934).

At the turn of the century Guy Delahaye could have been the Guillaume Apollinaire of Quebec. But in a country where a traditional Catholic church and a conservative state controlled all cultural activity to the point of censorship, modernism was not welcome and the avant-garde would repeatedly fail. Meanwhile, in France, Apollinaire was able to reconcile Catholicism and progress. Delahaye was also a central figure in another debate that dominated the French-Canadian literary scene at the beginning of the century, the controversy that pitted the regionalist forces against the *exotistes* (exotics), including Delahaye, who had a wider, international perspective on art and life.

François-Guillaume Lahaise (later to adopt the pen name Guy Delahaye) was born at Saint-Hilaire-sur-Richelieu on 18 March 1888 to Evangéline Cheval and Pierre-Adélard Lahaise, owners of the town's general store. After only four years at L'Ecole Modèle, the local grade school, he was sent to the Séminaire de Saint-Hyacinthe. In 1905 he enrolled in philosophy at the Collège Sainte-Marie, and the following year he switched to medicine at the Université de Montréal. In 1910 he received his B.A. and published *Les Phases: Tryptiques*. On 17 November 1912 the poet left for Paris in order to specialize as a psychiatrist, and for the next twelve years he traveled extensively, working and studying in the United States and Cuba. On 21 February 1927 he married Marie Saint-Georges, a nurse who had looked after him in 1925 following a kidney operation. Back in Montreal he practiced medicine and

psychiatry at the Hôpital Saint-Jean de Dieu until 1959. There he had as a patient an old friend, the poet Emile Nelligan.

In 1964 the distinguished poet Alain Grandbois wrote an article whose title sums up what has since been repeated by many academics: "Guy Delahaye brûla trop tôt ce qu'il avait si tôt adoré" (Guy Delahaye burned too soon what he had worshiped so early). But it is not enough to repeat that an exceptional opportunity was lost when, discouraged by the conservative attitude of his contemporaries, Delahaye turned his attention to psychiatry and religion. Delahaye has been virtually ignored in anthologies, research, and teaching. As a result of such neglect, scholars are still working with the rare original editions of *Les Phases* and *Mignonne, allons voir si la rose . . . Portrait* (Lovely One, Let's Go See If the Rose . . . Portrait, 1912).

Les Phases is tightly structured, showing Delahaye to be linguistically aware and self-revealing. He dared to be himself instead of following traditional guidelines. Led by Abbé Camille Roy, critics accused Delahaye of being a symbolist, of imitating the French decadent movement, and of being intentionally obscure. *Les Phases* is a difficult but rewarding book that embodies the conflict between permanence and sudden change. This preoccupation appears in the title and is reiterated throughout the book, which is divided into two parts.

The first part is dedicated to Albert Laberge, the Canadian imitator of Zola, and includes thirty poems, two of which are repeated in strategic spots. The poems focus on the psyche and are presented in groups of three. Furthermore, each poem contains nine lines divided into three equal stanzas that follow a ternary rhyme pattern. The second part of the book is dedicated to Ozias Leduc, the noted Quebec painter and Delahaye's childhood friend. This part is made up of fifteen sonnets in three triptychs. For

Illustration by Ozias Leduc for Delahaye's Mignonne, allons voir si la rose . . . Portrait *(1912), a book of "verbal acrobatics"*

Delahaye this fundamental organizing structure was not simply a formal game; rather it corresponded to his vision of the world. As a Catholic he conceived of unity as an implicit form of trinity: he believed in truth, beauty, and goodness; in the present, the past, and the future, and so on.

"Amour," one of the poems contained in the first part of *Les Phases,* features this ternary doctrine and adds a new triad to the list: dawn, sun, and sunset. However, the same poem tells us that eternity has only one smile, a minute can only hold a single memory, and "always" is afraid of "never," so monistic and dualistic perceptions of the world also appear. Two images anchor the poem in concreteness. The smile of eternity is compared to a mark on steel, and the memory of the minute is compared to a scratch on wax. The interest here resides precisely in the lack of clarity. Simply stated, the struggle of the poet can be understood as the tension between his desire to create an imaginary universe and his urge to wrap his work in tangible reality. The opposition between wax and steel is effective, but Delahaye breaks the first imagist rule when he mixes abstract and concrete metaphors. To go beyond reality one must first try to describe it.

Mignonne, allons voir si la rose . . . Portrait is a book of jokes and plays on words—verbal acrobatics. But we also find stout replies to the critics of *Les Phases,* and beyond the ironic tone, we can see the formulation of a theory of literature. The first part of *Mignonne* constitutes the reply to the critics. To help them discover some of the writers who might have influenced him and whom they might have missed, Delahaye provided a long bibliography that includes the French dictionary. He also pointed out spelling mistakes and noted in particular that he influenced his critics since they all misspelled "tryptique" after him. The second part of *Mignonne* includes a prologue and three scenes divided into three parts. Each part is further divided into a sketch and a commentary. A scene is made up of six poems: three parts and three commentaries. No effort is spared, not even "medical verse" or typographical bravura.

As early as 1912, with *Mignonne,* Delahaye was already deconstructing poetry. Ahead of his time in his technical experimentation and attention to psychology, Delahaye deserves a place among other premodern writers who shook literary foundations, showing their arbitrary weaknesses and basic gaps, and pointing the way toward the massive renovations to come in the 1920s. And his later silence should not surprise us: before him Arthur Rimbaud had followed a similar emotional, spiritual, and aesthetic journey.

References:

Alain Grandbois, "Guy Delahaye brûla trop tôt ce qu'il avait si tôt adoré," *Le Petit Journal,* 20 September 1964, p. A-49;

P. A. Jannini, "Una meteora d'avanguardia nel Quebec degli anni dieci: Guy Delahaye," in *Canada, Ieri e Oggi: Atti del 6° Convegno Internationale di Studi Canadesi,* 3 volumes (Rome: Schena, 1986), pp. 145-154;

Robert Lahaise, *Guy Delahaye et la modernité littéraire* (Montreal: HMH, 1987).

Merrill Denison

(23 June 1893-13 June 1975)

Chris Johnson
University of Manitoba

BOOKS: *The Unheroic North: Four Canadian Plays* (Toronto: McClelland & Stewart, 1923)–comprises *Brothers in Arms, From Their Own Place, The Weather Breeder,* and *Marsh Hay*;

Boobs in the Woods: Sixteen Sketches by One of Them (Ottawa: Graphic, 1927);

The Prizewinner (New York & London: Appleton, 1928);

Henry Hudson and Other Plays: Six Plays for the Microphone from the "Romance of Canada" Series of Radio Broadcasts (Toronto: Ryerson, 1931)–comprises *Henry Hudson, Pierre Radisson, Montcalm, Seven Oaks, Laura Secord,* and *Alexander MacKenzie*;

On Christmas Night (New York, Los Angeles & London: French, 1934);

The Educational Program (New York: Radio Institute of the Audible Arts, 1935);

Advancing America: The Drama of Transportation and Communication (New York: Dodd, Mead, 1936);

An American Father Talks to His Son (New York: Council Against Intolerance in America, 1939);

Haven of the Spirit (New York: Dramatists Play Service, 1939);

The U.S. vs. Susan B. Anthony (New York: Dramatists Play Service, 1941);

Klondike Mike: An Alaskan Odyssey (New York: Morrow, 1943; London & New York: Jarrolds, 1945);

Canada, Our Dominion Neighbor (New York: Foreign Policy Association, 1944);

C.C.M.: The Story of the First Fifty Years (Toronto: McLaren, 1946);

Harvest Triumphant: The Story of Massey-Harris, a Footnote to Canadian History (Toronto: McClelland & Stewart, 1948; New York: Dodd, Mead, 1949; London: Falcon Press, 1949);

Bristles and Brushes, a Footnote to the Story of American War Production (New York: Dodd, Mead, 1949);

The Barley and the Stream: The Molson Story, a Foot-

Merrill Denison (photograph by Karsh-Ottawa)

note to Canadian History (Toronto: McClelland & Stewart, 1955);

The Power to Go: The Story of the Automotive Industry (Garden City, N.Y.: Doubleday, 1956);

The People's Power: The History of Ontario Hydro (Toronto: McClelland & Stewart, 1960);

Canada's First Bank: A History of the Bank of Montreal, 2 volumes (Toronto: McClelland & Stewart, 1966-1967).

PLAY PRODUCTIONS: *Brothers in Arms,* Toronto, Hart House Theatre, 5 April 1921;

From Their Own Place, Toronto, Hart House Theatre, 25 April 1922;

The Weather Breeder, Montreal, Community Players, at His Majesty's Theatre, 19 January

1923; Toronto, Hart House Theatre, 21 April 1924;

Balm, Toronto, Hart House Theatre, 1 August 1923;

The Prizewinner, Toronto, Hart House Theatre, 28 February 1928;

The U.S. vs. Susan B. Anthony, Toronto, Hart House Theatre, 1929;

Contract, Toronto, Hart House Theatre, 6 March 1929;

Haven of the Spirit, Toronto, Hart House Theatre, 1939;

Marsh Hay, Toronto, Hart House Theatre, 21 March 1974.

RADIO: *Henry Hudson, Discoverer, Romance of Canada,* Canadian National Railways Trans-Continental Network, 22 January 1931;

Madame La Tour, Romance of Canada, Canadian National Railways Trans-Continental Network, 29 January 1931;

The Plague of Mice, Romance of Canada, Canadian National Railways Trans-Continental Network, 5 February 1931;

The Land of Promise, 2 parts, adapted from John Herries McCulloch, *Romance of Canada,* Canadian National Railways Trans-Continental Network, 12 and 19 February 1931;

Seven Oaks, Romance of Canada, Canadian National Railways Trans-Continental Network, 26 February 1931;

The Raid on Grand Pré, adapted from Archibald McMechan's history *Red Snow on Grand Pré, Romance of Canada,* Canadian National Railways Trans-Continental Network, 5 March 1931;

Marguerite de Roberval, adapted from Thomas Guthrie Marquis's historical romance, *Romance of Canada,* Canadian National Railways Trans-Continental Network, 12 March 1931;

The Isle of Demons, adapted from Marquis, *Romance of Canada,* Canadian National Railways Trans-Continental Network, 19 March 1931;

Laura Secord, Romance of Canada, Canadian National Railways Trans-Continental Network, 26 March 1931;

Drucour at Louisberg, Romance of Canada, Canadian National Railways Trans-Continental Network, 9 April 1931;

Pierre Radisson and the Founding of the Hudson's Bay Company, Romance of Canada, Canadian Na-

tional Railways Trans-Continental Network, 16 April 1931;

Alexander MacKenzie, Romance of Canada, Canadian National Railways Trans-Continental Network, 23 April 1931;

David Thompson, Romance of Canada, Canadian National Railways Trans-Continental Network, 30 April 1931;

Montcalm, Romance of Canada, Canadian National Railways Trans-Continental Network, 7 May 1931;

Adam Dollard, Romance of Canada, Canadian National Railway Trans-Continental Network, 14 May 1931;

Nightpiece, Romance of Canada, Canadian National Railways Trans-Continental Network, 21 May 1931;

Kingston, Romance of Canada, Canadian National Railways Trans-Continental Network, 11 February 1932;

Pierre D'Iberville, Romance of Canada, Canadian National Railways Trans-Continental Network, 18 February 1932;

The Founding of Montreal, Romance of Canada, Canadian National Railways Trans-Continental Network, 25 February 1932;

Quebec, Romance of Canada, Canadian National Railways Trans-Continental Network, 3 March 1932;

The Great Race of Jean Baptiste Lagimodière, Romance of Canada, Canadian National Railways Trans-Continental Network, 10 March 1932;

The Last Stand of Almighty Voice, Romance of Canada, Canadian National Railways Trans-Continental Railway, 17 March 1932;

Valiant Hearts, Romance of Canada, Canadian National Railways Trans-Continental Network, 24 March 1932;

The Fathers of Confederation, Romance of Canada, Canadian National Railways Trans-Continental Network, 31 March 1932;

Great Moments from History, forty half-hour programs commissioned by the J. Walter Thompson Company and broadcast by seventy U.S. radio stations, 1932-1933;

Pickwick Papers, episodic dramatization of Charles Dickens's novel, NBC, 1933-1934;

America's Hour, weekly documentary program, CBS, 1936-1937;

Democracy in Action, series, CBS, 1938-1939;

An American Father Talks to His Son, CBS, 1 July 1939;

Saint Joan, adapted from George Bernard Shaw's

play, CBC, 9 February 1941;

Somewhile Before the Dawn, series, CBC, 1943-1944;

Measure of Achievement, CBC Toronto, 17 October 1943;

The Forty-Four Months, CBC Toronto, 15 August 1945;

Brothers in Arms, adapted from Denison's play, CBC, 9 March 1955.

OTHER: *The Weather Breeder, Balm,* and *Brothers in Arms,* in *Canadian Plays from Hart House Theatre,* volume 1, edited by Vincent Massey (Toronto: Macmillan, 1926);

"The Weather Breeder," in *Canadian Short Stories,* edited by Raymond Knister (Toronto: Macmillan, 1928), pp. 15-37;

"Nationalism and Drama," in *Dramatists in Canada: Selected Essays,* edited by William H. New (Vancouver: University of British Columbia Press, 1972), pp. 65-69.

Merrill Denison is held by many to be Canada's first English-language dramatist of note. During the 1920s his short comedies were the highlights of seasons at the Hart House Theatre in Toronto, whose concentration on the production of Canadian plays marked a significant turning point in the establishment of an indigenous Canadian drama. With the *Romance of Canada* series of radio plays begun in 1931, Denison was one of the pioneers of a form long considered to be Canada's "real" national theater, and later Denison played a similar seminal role in the development of American broadcasting. In the third phase of his writing career, Denison devoted most of his energy to industrial and corporate history.

Denison was born in Detroit on 23 June 1893 to Howard Denison, a commercial traveler, and Flora MacDonald Denison, a dressmaker and prominent suffragette who for some years contributed columns on women's issues to the *Sunday World* of Toronto. While Mrs. Denison came from Loyalist stock, she was a republican by conviction, and traveled to the United States shortly before the birth of her child so that he would not be born in a monarchy. Denison lived and worked in both Canada and the United States, but he remained an American citizen all his life.

Trained as an architect at the University of Toronto, the University of Pennsylvania, and the Ecole des Beaux-Arts in Bellevue-sur-Seine,

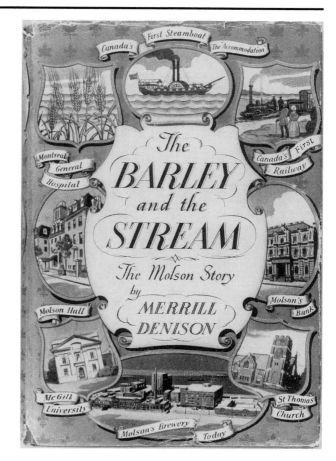

Dust jacket for Denison's 1955 book about the famous brewer

France, interrupting his studies to serve in an American ambulance unit and then in the United States Army during World War I, Denison first came to the theater as an art director. Roy Mitchell, artistic director of Hart House, urged Denison to dramatize some of the anecdotes Denison was fond of telling about his neighbors at Bon Echo, the family-owned summer resort on Lake Mazinaw in the Canadian Shield north of Kingston. The result was *Brothers in Arms,* first produced in 1921 and published in *The Unheroic North* (1923).

In this play Denison uses misunderstanding and conflict between J. Altrus Browne, a pompous businessman, and Syd White, a laconic backwoodsman, to satirize the attitudes of both, but the most telling comic effect is provided by Althea, Browne's giddy wife, whose expectations of "romance in the land of Robert Service" stand in sharp contrast to the squalor of life in the real backwoods. The play is Denison's most durable, having been revived (by the author's estimate at Hart House celebrations marking the fiftieth anniversary of the play's premiere in 1971) some fifteen hundred times since its first presentation; it is still revived from time to time by amateur companies and has doubtless contributed to Canadian drama's essentially nonromantic view of Canadian frontier life.

Realistic, antiromantic appraisal of the backwoods characterizes two other short comedies Denison wrote for Hart House, both of which are collected in *The Unheroic North*: in *From Their Own Place* (produced in 1922), the backwoodsmen who attempt to cheat the holidayers are dishonest as well as lazy and stupid, and the old farmer in *The Weather Breeder* (produced in 1923) derives masochistic pleasure from his battle with the elements. Denison examines the plight of the backwoods farmer with more sympathy in *Marsh Hay*, a serious, full-length play published with the short comedies in *The Unheroic North* but not produced until 1974. In *Marsh Hay* John Serang and his family are tied to poor and overworked land in a cycle of poverty and ignorance; the sexual escapades of daughters Tessie and Sarilin and the cyclical structure suggest that the children will repeat the mistakes of their parents. Returning to short, country comedy, Denison satirizes the attitudes of city slickers and country bumpkins toward each other in *The Prizewinner*, produced and published in 1928.

Denison's sense of social justice can be attributed to the example set by his mother. The plays he wrote for Hart House in the 1920s include several social protest plays: *Balm* (1923; published in Vincent Massey's *Canadian Plays from Hart House Theatre*, 1926) criticizes society's view of the elderly; *The U.S. vs. Susan B. Anthony* (1929; published in 1941) dramatizes the eponym's trial for the crime of voting; and in *Contract*, a full-length, unpublished comedy produced in 1929, conservationist Denison burlesques the tycoons plundering his beloved North. A later stage play, *Haven of the Spirit* (produced and published in 1939), attacks religious bigotry.

When Denison's mother died in 1921, he inherited Bon Echo and attempted to run it until 1929, assisted by his first wife, Muriel Goggin, whom he met at Hart House and married in 1926. The Bon Echo experience gave piquancy to the tone of Denison's country comedies and was recorded directly in his series of comic sketches, *Boobs in the Woods* (1927). Goggin wrote several children's novels: *Susannah, A Little Girl With the Mounties* (1936); *Susannah of the Yukon* (1937); *Susannah at Boarding School* (1938); *Su-*

sannah Rides Again (1940); and *Happy Tramp* (1942). She died in 1954 after a long illness, and Denison married Elizabeth Robert Andrews in 1957. There were no children by either marriage.

During the 1920s Denison was also engaged as a journalist, becoming a regular contributor to the *Toronto Star Weekly* in 1921 and writing articles for several other popular journals. He combined his talents for journalism and drama when, in 1930, he was asked to write the *Romance of Canada* series of radio plays dramatizing Canadian historical events from the arrival of Henry Hudson to Confederation. The twenty-five half-hour plays were produced by Tyrone Guthrie, who came to Canada to work on the project, and by Rupert Caplan, and were broadcast in 1931 and 1932 by Canadian National Railways over its chain of radio stations, forerunner of the Canadian Broadcasting Corporation. Six of the plays have been published in *Henry Hudson and Other Plays* (1931).

Broadcasting dominated Denison's career in the 1930s and early 1940s. In 1931 he began dividing his time between Bon Echo and New York and wrote *Great Moments from History*, a series similar to the *Romance of Canada* series, but dealing with American subjects. He also dramatized Charles Dickens's *Pickwick Papers* for NBC in 1933-1934, conducted the interview program *Art in America* on NBC also in 1933-1934, and in 1936 he took over as head of the writing and research team for *America's Hour*.

In 1938 and 1939 Denison wrote scripts for the CBS series *Democracy in Action*, produced in conjunction with the United States Office of Education. When war broke out in 1939, Denison became chairman of the radio committee and publicity director for the British War Relief Society. In 1943 and 1944 he wrote a series of war programs, *Somewhile Before the Dawn*, for CBC, and for BBC's *Home Hour* he provided commentaries on the American war effort. During the war Denison also wrote *Klondike Mike: An Alaskan Odyssey* (published in 1943), a fictionalized account of the exploits of Michael Ambrose Mahoney, a former sourdough who had been in the Yukon gold rushes of 1897 and 1898 and whom Denison had met at Bon Echo in 1930.

After World War II Denison wrote several corporate histories respected for an unusual objectivity and attention to detail, establishing himself as one of Canada's most significant nonacademic social historians. Considered especially important are: *Harvest Triumphant* (1948), a history of Massey-Harris, the farm-machinery manufacturers; *The Barley and the Stream* (1955), a history of Molson's breweries and the family prominent in national affairs; *The People's Power* (1960), a history of Ontario Hydro, North America's first state-owned electrical utility; and *Canada's First Bank* (1966-1967), a monumental two-volume study of the Bank of Montreal.

With the renewal of interest in Canadian drama in the 1970s, Denison finally received the recognition he deserved as a pioneer in the field. Paradoxically, he was an American citizen, a continentalist, but also a loyal regionalist who believed that Canada's contribution to North American culture had gone too long unrecognized.

Highly regarded in their day, and sometimes compared to works by Eugene O'Neill, Denison's plays have received little recent critical attention. When they are considered, they are usually placed in their historical context and put to historical ends, as in Alexander M. Leggatt's 1980 study of the change in dramatic visions of rural Ontario. However, Eugene Benson and L. W. Conolly, in *English-Canadian Theatre* (1987), single out *Marsh Hay* for their highest praise, finding it distinguished by its "uncommon honesty of vision, authenticity of speech, and a command of dramatic structure." They also cite Denison's "surprisingly mature grasp of the new medium" in their discussion of the *Romance of Canada* radio plays. While in a 1977 article Terence W. Goldie dismisses most of the one-act plays as excessively dependent on stereotypes, he declares *Marsh Hay* "the best Canadian play of the first three decades of the century."

Biography:

Dick MacDonald, *Mugwump Canadian: The Merrill Denison Story* (Montreal: Content, 1973).

References:

Howard Fink, "Beyond Naturalism: Tyrone Guthrie's Radio Theatre and the Stage Production of Shakespeare," *Theatre History in Canada/Histoire du Théâtre au Canada*, 2 (Spring 1981): 19-32;

Terence W. Goldie, "A National Drama and A National Dramatist: The First Attempt," *Canadian Drama/L'Art Dramatique Canadien*, 3 (Spring 1977): 9-19;

Tyrone Guthrie, *A Life In The Theatre* (London: Hamilton, 1961), pp. 64-68;

Alexander M. Leggatt, "Playwrights in a Landscape: The Changing Image of Rural Ontario," *Theatre History in Canada/Histoire du Théâtre au Canada*, 1 (Fall 1980): 135-148;

Anton Wagner, "The Developing Mosaic," introduction to *Canada's Lost Plays: The Developing Mosaic: English-Canadian Drama to Mid-Century*, edited by Wagner (Toronto: Canadian Theatre Review Publications, 1980), III: 4-39;

E. Austin Weir, *The Struggle for National Broadcasting in Canada* (Toronto: McClelland & Stewart, 1965), pp. 51-63.

Papers:

Denison's papers are at the Douglas Library, Queen's University, Kingston, Ontario. Some of his radio scripts are in the Broadcasting Archives at Concordia University, Montreal, and several *Romance of Canada* scripts are at the National Archives, Ottawa.

Gonzalve Desaulniers
(24 June 1863-5 April 1934)

Jean-Guy Hudon
Université du Québec à Chicoutimi

BOOKS: *L'Absolution avant la bataille: Dédié aux braves de la Butte-aux-Français* (Montreal: L'Etendard, 1886);

Pour la France: A la mémoire de nos morts (Montreal: Beauchemin, 1918);

Les Bois Qui Chantent (Montreal: Beauchemin, 1930).

OTHER: Eusèbe Senécal, ed., *Les Soirées du Château de Ramezay*, includes ten poems by Desaulniers (Montreal: Ecole Littéraire de Montréal, 1900).

The poet Gonzalve Desaulniers was born in 1863 in the village of Saint-Guillaume d'Upton, Quebec, on the same day that Quebecois celebrate their national holiday: 24 June, the feast of St. John the Baptist. The son of a medical doctor, Antoine-Lesieur Desaulniers, and of Hélène Letellier Desaulniers, he was educated first at Collège de Sorel and then at the Jesuit Collège Sainte-Marie de Montréal, from which he graduated at the age of twenty-two.

Initially Desaulniers's interests were in journalism and politics. At the age of fourteen he became one of the three editors of the *Journal d'Arthabaska,* an ephemeral Liberal daily begun with the purpose of promoting one of Wilfrid Laurier's early electoral campaigns. Later he was active as a writer for two noteworthy Montreal journals of the late nineteenth century: the *Monde Illustré* and the *Revue Canadienne.* In both of these he published poems, but his most important contribution was a column concerned with politics which he wrote for the *Revue Canadienne* from February to June 1884. Typically, in conformity with the tone of the periodical, his opinions on events–whether local, national, or international–are larded with moralism.

Desaulniers is also remembered as the editor of two Montreal newspapers, the *Etendard* (from 1883 to 1893), which espoused the ultramontane cause, and the *National* (1889-1896), which became known as a pro-Liberal publication. His name is also associated with other radical papers of the era: *Canada-Revue* and the *Avenir du Nord* which were dedicated to publicizing the liberal ideology of the Institut Canadien of Montreal. Among the periodicals to which he contributed verse in the late nineteenth century were the *Nouvelles Soirées Canadiennes,* the *Alliance Nationale,* the *Journal de Françoise,* and the *Revue Populaire.* Desaulniers also occasionally published pieces in a variety of short-lived newspapers and magazines in Montreal at the turn of the century.

In 1886 Desaulniers's first important poem, *L'Absolution avant la bataille* (Absolution Before the Battle), appeared in chapbook form; earlier in the year it had been published in the *Revue Canadienne* and in the newspaper the *Minerve.* A work of homage to the 103 officers and soldiers of a Montreal rifle battalion who fought against Cree Indians in Saskatchewan during the Rebellion of 1885, the poem has become part of the "littérature nationale" then being shaped in Quebec. In an emphatically solemn and romantic tone, and with frequent references to God and country, the poet recounts in 158 alexandrines (in rhyming couplet form) the preparations of the troops for battle after their long, difficult journey across the dry western plains.

In 1893 Desaulniers sided with Louis Fréchette during the latter's well-known quarrel with William Chapman, who had accused Fréchette of plagiarism. Desaulniers attacked Chapman in the newspaper *La Patrie,* on 27 May, in a satirical polemic entitled "Le Chêne et la Chenille" (The Oak and the Caterpillar) and dedicated to "William Chapman, premier souffleur de la troupe de M. l'abbé Baillairgé" (William Chapman, first prompter of the troupe of Father Baillairgé). A second such diatribe, "La Vipère et le socle" (The Viper and the Pedestal), appeared in the same on 8 July.

After completing studies at the University of Montreal, Desaulniers began his career in law. Admitted to the bar on 5 July 1895, he rapidly succeeded in the profession. Notably he was one of the advocates for the novelist Rodolphe Girard in 1908 during his libel proceedings against Paul Tardivel and the *Vérité* after the controversy surrounding the publication of Girard's *Marie Calumet*. Appointed K.C. in 1902, he was later elevated to the Quebec Superior Court on 15 January 1923.

The lawyer-poet was a founding member of the Ecole Littéraire de Montréal, a group of writers who turned away from the patriotic literature then in vogue in Quebec to try to improve the French-Canadian language and literature. He participated in the group's four public readings and submitted ten poems to the collection entitled *Les Soirées du Château de Ramezay* (1900). He contributed poetry to the Ecole review, the *Terroir*. In the 1920s he had a difference of opinion with Claude-Henri Grignon over the latter's article on Anatole France, published in *Les Soirées de l'Ecole littéraire de Montréal* (1925), to which Desaulniers chose not to contribute. Yet he did not completely sever his relationship with the Ecole and continued to act as host for meetings. He formed a close friendship with the poet Emile Nelligan, who had attended but withdrawn from the Ecole Littéraire. Desaulniers was instrumental in persuading the Ecole Littéraire to readmit Nelligan in 1898. Later he received Nelligan at his country house in Ahuntsic, in July 1932, during the period of Nelligan's internment at the Montreal asylum Saint-Jean-de-Dieu.

In 1909 Desaulniers was elected president of the Montreal branch of L'Alliance Française, an association founded in Paris in 1893 whose purpose was to promote French culture. The following year he became vice-president of the American federation of the Alliance. A fervent francophile, he served in these two posts until his death. In recognition of his services the French government honored him as an Officier de l'Instruction Publique and later conferred on him successively the ranks of Chevalier and Officier in the Légion d'Honneur. McGill University also recognized his services to French and Quebecois culture in granting him an honorary doctorate.

Desaulniers's second chapbook of verse, *Pour la France,* was published in 1918. Inspired by World War I, the work is in the form of a "lettre d'une petite canadienne-française à son fiancé se battant quelque part en France dans les rangs du 22e bataillon" (letter from a French-Canadian girl to her fiancé fighting somewhere in France in the ranks of the 22nd battalion). Its 180 alexandrines, again in rhyming couplets, exhort citizens

to defend their mother country, to make sacrifices, and to understand the priority of their national "duty" over their personal interests. In these words of a young girl to her lover, the message of the work is summarized lines and the religious and patriotic themes are manifest:

Réponds à cet appel de la France, mon Jean.
Laisse sans regret ta moisson sur le champ,
Et si ton pauvre coeur en la quittant se serre
Viens puiser dans le mien la force nécessaire

(Answer this call from France, my Jean.
Leave without regret your harvest in the field,
And if it wrings your poor heart to leave it
Come, draw from my heart the strength that you
    need).

Although *Pour la France* has certain technical faults, the poem is well constructed and persuasive as a call to arms.

In 1930 Desaulniers's only collection of poems, *Les Bois Qui Chantent* (The Singing Woods), appeared in a deluxe edition of 1,325 copies. This retrospective gathering includes pieces which had been published in periodicals or read aloud before such assemblies as the Ecole Littéraire, the Royal Society of Canada, and the Alliance Française. The collection is, however, not a complete record of his work. It includes, for example, with minor changes, the long poem *Pour la France*, but omits *L'Absolution avant la bataille*. The sonnet "Albani," one of ten poems published in *Les Soirées du Château de Ramezay*, is missing. Some occasional poems such as "A Antoine L***" (which appeared in the August-September 1883 issue of the *Revue Canadienne*), "Noël" and "Vive le Roi" (which appeared in the *Monde Illustré* on 27 December 1884 and 2 May 1885, respectively), and "A Benjamin Sulte" (published in the *Nouvelles Soirées canadiennes* in 1887) are also not reprinted. The long poem "La Chevrette," first published in the *Mémoires de la Société Royale du Canada* in May 1899, is included, but under the title "Le Pardon des bois," and with sixteen alexandrines omitted. With these exceptions the book covers the essential corpus of Desaulniers's poetry.

Although the poet knows classical authors, he is especially a disciple of the Romantics: "Le Vol du Silence" (The Flight of Silence) clearly illustrates this dominant tendency in his verse. More particularly, his oeuvre as a whole is reminiscent of the poetry of the French Romantic Alphonse

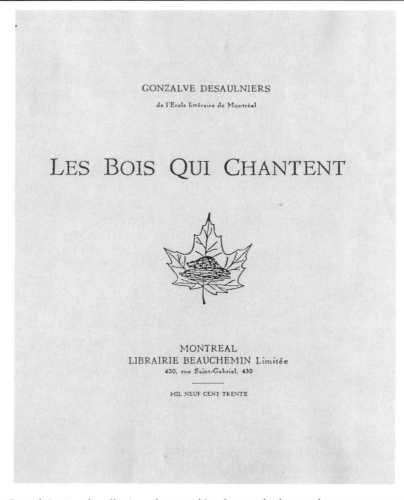

GONZALVE DESAULNIERS

de l'Ecole littéraire de Montréal

LES BOIS QUI CHANTENT

MONTREAL
LIBRAIRIE BEAUCHEMIN Limitée
430, rue Saint-Gabriel, 430

MIL NEUF CENT TRENTE

Title page for Desaulniers's only collection of poems; his other two books were long poems separately published.

de Lamartine; "Soir gaspésien" (Gaspé Evening) and "Les Voix du Golfe" (The Voices of the Gulf), especially, demonstrate Lamartine's influence. In his preface to Desaulniers's collection, the critic Louis Dantin wrote: "La plupart [des poèmes] ont jailli en face de la nature; ils en dégagent le calme, le mystère, les voix sympathiques et profondes, surtout la nostalgie pénétrante" (Most [of the poems] have sprung from facing nature; they draw from it the calmness, mystery, deep and sympathetic voices, above all, the penetrating nostalgia). Despite Desaulniers's sentimental themes, his poetry never falls into the merely affected, into religiosity or emotional narcissism. Measure and restraint, or, as Dantin notes, "enthousiasme, harmonie, justesse, éclat discret et soutenu, balance entre la pensée et l'image, correction et grâce de la strophe" (enthusiasm, harmony, precision, the discreet but sustained glitter, balance between thought and

image, propriety and grace of the strophe)—these are the qualities of the verse inspired by Desaulniers's American and European motherlands. His work has an idyllic and sylvan tone. Even in writing about war, he shows a restraint, concision, and balance that recall the objectivity of the Parnassians. And although Desaulniers often models his works on those of others, he is never a mere imitator.

Desaulniers's achievement was recognized by the Académie Française and by the Alliance Française, which awarded him its gold medal. Two years before his death, he was elected a member of the Royal Society of Canada during its annual meeting in May 1932.

Desaulniers died suddenly on the afternoon of 5 April 1934. He was survived by his wife, Elisabeth Martin Desaulniers, whom he had married on 5 July 1887, and by his son and two daughters.

References:

Germain Beaulieu, *Nos Immortels* (Montreal: Lévesque, 1931), pp. 59-69;

Gérard Bessette, *Les Images en poésie canadienne-française* (Montreal: Beauchemin, 1967), pp. 141-158;

Jean Charbonneau, *L'Ecole littéraire de Montréal. Ses Origines, ses animateurs, ses influences* (Montreal: Lévesque, 1935), pp. 161-172;

Louis Dantin, *Poètes de l'Amérique française* (Montreal: Lévesque, 1934), II: 36-46;

Paul Wyczynski, "L'Héritage poétique de l'Ecole littéraire de Montréal," in *La Poésie canadienne-française. Perspectives historiques et thématiques, profils de poètes, témoignages, bibliographie*, Archives des Lettres Canadiennes (Montreal: Fides, 1969), IV: 75-108.

Lily Dougall

(16 April 1858-9 October 1923)

Lorraine McMullen
University of Ottawa

BOOKS: *Beggars All* (London: Longmans, Green, 1892);

What Necessity Knows, 3 volumes (London: Longmans, 1893);

The Madonna of a Day (New York: Appleton, 1895; London: Bentley, 1896);

The Mermaid: A Love Tale (New York: Appleton, 1895);

A Question of Faith (London: Hutchinson/Boston: Houghton, Mifflin, 1895);

The Zeit-Geist (London: Hutchinson/New York: Appleton, 1895);

A Dozen Ways of Love (London: A. & C. Black, 1897);

The Mormon Prophet (London: A. & C. Black/New York: Appleton, 1899);

Pro Christo et Ecclesia, anonymous (London: Macmillan, 1900);

The Earthly Purgatory (London: Hutchinson, 1904); republished as *The Summit House Mystery; or, The Earthly Purgatory* (New York & London: Funk & Wagnall's, 1905);

The Spanish Dowry: A Romance (London: Hutchinson, 1906; Toronto: Copp, Clark, 1906);

Christus Futurus (London: Macmillan, 1907); also published as *The Christ That Is to Be* (New York: Macmillan, 1907);

Paths of the Righteous (London: Macmillan, 1908);

Absente Reo (London: Macmillan, 1910);

Voluntas Dei (London: Macmillan, 1912);

The Practice of Christianity (London: Macmillan, 1913);

The Christian Doctrine of Health: A Handbook on the Relation of Bodily to Spiritual and Moral Health (London: Macmillan, 1916);

Areades Ambo: Verses, by Dougall and Gilbert Sheldon (Oxford: Blackwell, 1919);

The Lord of Thought: A Study of the Problems Which Confronted Jesus Christ and the Solution He Offered, by Dougall and Cyril W. Emmet (London: Student Christian Movement, 1922);

God's Way with Man: An Exploration of the Method of the Divine Working Suggested by the Facts of History and Science (London: Student Christian Movement, 1924).

OTHER: Burnett H. Streeter, ed., *Concerning Prayer*, includes work by Dougall (London: Macmillan, 1916);

Streeter, ed., *Immortality*, includes work by Dougall (London: Macmillan, 1917);

Streeter, ed., *The Spirit: God and His Relation to Man*, includes work by Dougall (New York & London: Macmillan, 1919);

Streeter, ed., *God and the Struggle for Existence*, includes work by Dougall (New York: Association Press, 1919).

Lily Dougall was a successful writer of fiction and religious philosophical works. She was born 16 April 1858 in Montreal, the daughter of

Lily Dougall

John Dougall, a Scottish immigrant who founded a profitable religious paper, the *Montreal Witness,* and Elizabeth Redpath Dougall, the daughter of another Scottish immigrant. In 1880 Dougall moved to Edinburgh as the companion to an aunt. Here she prepared for her writing career by studying at the University of Edinburgh and the University of St. Andrews, eventually completing her degree requirements in 1887. Her first short story appeared in 1889, her first novel (*Beggars All*) in 1892. She published ten novels, one volume of short stories, and eight religious philosophical books, and contributed to several collections of essays on moral and religious topics. After 1883 Dougall lived intermittently in Great Britain and Canada, but in 1900 she decided to live permanently in England, although she continued to make extended stays in Canada. Dougall's concern with the spiritual dimension of life colors all her writings.

Beggars All, set in a small town in England, was hailed by critics and the public alike. With its unusual plot, its moral dilemmas, and its strong woman protagonist, this novel introduced features that continued to characterize Dougall's writings. The novel concerns a well-bred young woman, unequipped to make even her own living, who finds herself financially responsible for an aged mother and a crippled sister. She resolves her problem by marrying a young journalist of lesser background who has advertised in a newspaper for a wife. Their marriage, with the wife discovering that her husband is a thief, is the crux of the novel. With a suspenseful plot Dougall explores the moral problems of the protagonists and the couple's growth through experience, while challenging the moral assumptions of the day and attacking well-meaning but cold-natured philanthropists as well as the grudging charity of church representatives. Parallel to the marriage plot is one involving a friendship between the young wife and an older woman, which enriches both their lives.

Dougall's second novel, *What Necessity Knows* (1893), broader in plot, portrays the diversity of British immigrants in a small town in eastern Quebec. Five characters dominate the action: a young Anglican clergyman who had come to the town some eight years earlier and is now well established and highly respected; his younger brother, recently arrived in Canada; a well-bred young lady, whom the clergyman had loved years earlier in England, only now arrived in Canada; a young Scottish girl who has run away from an isolated farm to make a new life; and this girl's guardian, who has fallen in love with her. The interaction between these characters provides the focus for the narrative. On its deepest level, the novel concerns spiritual regeneration. Dougall's exploration of the protagonists' moral problems is philosophic and intellectual. Their response to the new land is another major concern. Dougall deals harshly with the type of British immigrant who tries to maintain a concept of superiority based on heritage without regard to intelligence, initiative, or any other personal quality, and to establish a society based on such pretensions. The key characters are the two women–of different backgrounds and ideologies–both strong, independent, and intelligent. A complex novel, *What Necessity Knows* is a study of Canadian immigrant society and its strong, independent-minded women, and an exploration of spiritual rebirth. The style is at times witty, symbolic, and lyrical–especially in the description of nature.

Dougall's next three novels are also set in Canada: *The Madonna of a Day* (1895), *The Mer-*

maid: *A Love Tale* (1895), and *The Zeit-Geist* (1895). The most overtly didactic of these is *The Zeit-Geist*. Dougall's first two novels had made it clear that she did not find the best Christians among church leaders. This fact is even more obvious in *The Zeit-Geist*, in which the wealthy and philanthropic protagonist, disapproved of by the town's clergy, belongs to no specific church. The novel, told primarily from the protagonist's viewpoint, is a retrospective account of his conversion from a dissolute life to a deeply spiritual and charitable one. He has become, finally, a freethinker, different from other religious people in viewing no one church as the only true way to God. Dougall here presents controversial ideas more openly than she did in her earlier novels. But as a novel, consisting for the most part of the protagonist's lengthy explanations of his beliefs, it is less satisfactory than her earlier novels.

Four years later Dougall published *The Mormon Prophet* (1899), a novel of the rise of Mormonism, again taking religion as a central subject. To understand the Mormon religion and its founder, Joseph Smith, Dougall spent several months visiting Mormon communities and researching in archives. By using as her protagonist an intelligent but naive young woman who gets caught up in Smith's religious movement and marries one of his supporters, Dougall could show the leader as his contemporaries perceived him. The young convert soon begins to question Smith's views but, until the death of her husband and son ten years later, feels compelled to remain among Smith's followers. Dougall captures the complexity of Smith's character and his corruption by power and success from a well-meaning Christian preacher to an increasingly self-deluded, luxury-loving demagogue.

It is not surprising that Dougall turned next to nonfiction theology. In *Pro Christo et Ecclesia* (1900) she develops the religious ideas she dramatized in her fiction, criticizing sectarianism and urging Christians to accept and adapt to new knowledge. Dougall stresses love–of God and neighbor–and voices objections to those denominations that reject art. She urges a renewal of Christianity as a religion of love and joy. Dougall published *Pro Christo et Ecclesia* anonymously. Critics were impressed by this "work of great power" (*The Church Times*, 20 July 1900) and praised the author, assumed to be an eminent clergyman.

Dougall published three more novels in the next eight years, but at the same time she continued to write religious and philosophical works. In 1911 she moved to Cumnor, near Oxford, and made her home a center for religious discussion. Four collections of essays came out of these discussions: *Concerning Prayer* (1916); *Immortality* (1917); *The Spirit: God and His Relation to Man* (1919); and *God and the Struggle for Existence* (1919), all edited by Canon Burnett H. Streeter. Contributors included specialists in history, philosophy, theology, psychology, medicine, and literature. Dougall was the leading force at these meetings and in the resulting publications. That religion was an integral part of everyday life, not a separate Sunday issue, was central to her thinking and was demonstrated by the variety of disciplines represented in the publications that came out of the Cumnor discussions. In her own works she explored such issues as the relationship between physical, mental, and spiritual health, the psychological aspects of religious experiences, the relations between science and religion and between art and religion, and the responsibilities of the churches to be concerned with justice, equality, poverty, and other social issues.

Dougall died 9 October 1923 in Cumnor, having devoted her life to expressing in fiction and nonfiction her moral and religious convictions. Dougall's best novels are her earlier ones, but all of them are characterized by unusual plots, lively dialogue, and intriguing and original characters. She admired Jane Austen and Samuel Richardson, and learned from both. Like Austen, at her best she wrote with wit and irony; like Richardson, she dealt with important moral issues. In the serious intellectual quality of her writing and in her focus on the significance of everyday actions, Dougall also resembles George Eliot. As a Canadian writer, with some of her finest fiction set in Canada, Dougall was nonetheless universal in her scope and concerns.

Reference:
Lorraine McMullen, "Lily Dougall's Vision of Canada," in *A Mazing Space*, edited by Shirley Neuman and Smaro Kambourdi (Edmonton: Longspoon/NeWest, 1986), pp. 137-147.

William Henry Drummond

(13 April 1854-6 April 1907)

Paul Matthew St. Pierre
Simon Fraser University

BOOKS: *The Habitant, and Other French-Canadian Poems* (New York & London: Putnam's, 1897);

Phil-o-rum's Canoe, and Madeleine Verchères (New York & London: Putnam's, 1898);

Johnnie Courteau, and Other Poems (New York & London: Putnam's, 1901);

The Voyageur and Other Poems (New York & London: Putnam's, 1905);

The Great Fight: Poems and Sketches, edited by May Harvey Drummond (New York & London: Putnam's, 1908);

The Poetical Works of William Henry Drummond (New York & London: Putnam's, 1912); republished as *Complete Poems* (Toronto: McClelland & Stewart, 1926); republished as *Habitant Poems* (Toronto: McClelland & Stewart, 1959).

Among minor Canadian poets who during their lifetime enjoyed unusually high reputations, William Henry Drummond is perhaps foremost. While he had a natural talent for composing French-Canadian dialect verse, he became a public and published poet more in response to the desires of his friends and (eventually) his readers than in response to any personal desire for notoriety. Yet at the turn of the century and during the years leading up to World War I he was extremely popular, not only in Canada but also in England and the United States. He made few demands on his readers, who found his poems amusing, witty, and original. If today Drummond's verse seems little more than a literary and historical curiosity, it is mainly because the community spirit that the poet and his audience shared has been diluted over the years. Arthur Phelps's 1959 remark that "Drummond today is discard material only among the undiscerning" now seems a comment more on readers' powers of discernment than on the permanent value of Drummond's verse.

Born in County Leitrim, Ireland, on 13 April 1854, Drummond spent the first ten years

William Henry Drummond

of his life in and around the villages of Mohill and Tawley, then immigrated to Canada with his parents (Elizabeth Morris Loden and George Drummond) just three years' before the country's confederation in 1867. Despite the promises of a new land, misfortune quickly struck. Within six months of their arrival Drummond's normally hardy Royal Irish Constabulary father lay dead, and his mother was faced with the prospect of bringing up Drummond and his three brothers alone, which she proceeded to do according to simple but high Christian standards. In order to help support the family Drummond withdrew from high school, training and working as a telegrapher in Bord-à-Plouffe, a Quebec lumber town where he had his first encounters with the habitants and voyageurs who were to inspire (and

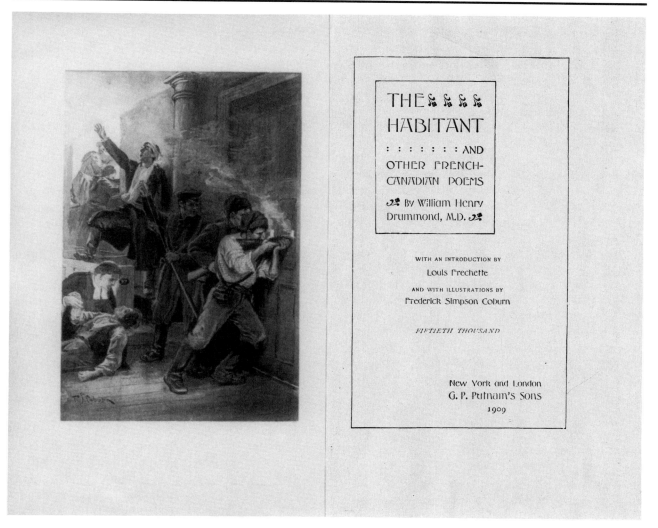

Frontispiece and title page for the 1909 edition of Drummond's popular first book. These poems in French-Canadian dialect inspired Longfellow to call Drummond the "pathfinder of a new land of song."

even to preoccupy) the poet. He would come to be known affectionately as the "Poet of the Habitant."

From one of his Bord-à-Plouffe acquaintances Drummond heard the story of "The Wreck of the 'Julie Plante,'" which was the source of the famous poem that was to appear in his first volume, *The Habitant, and Other French-Canadian Poems* (1897): "On wan dark night on Lac St. Pierre,/De win' she blow, blow, blow,/An' de crew of de wood scow 'Julie Plante'/Got scar't and run below. . . ." In the twenty years between the time he recorded the tale and the time he published the poem, Drummond pursued his education and his profession, returning to Montreal High School after several years in telegraphy,

and then advancing to McGill College in Montreal and to Bishop's Medical College in Lennoxville, from which he graduated in 1884 with an M.D. His first professional appointment was as house surgeon at Montreal's Western Hospital, a position he held briefly until establishing a practice as a private physician at Stornoway and later at Knowlton (1884-1888). Another poem from his first collection, "Ole Docteur Fiset," is very much a self-portrait: "Let her rain or snow, all he want to know/Is jus' if anywan's feelin' sick,/For Docteur Fiset's de old fashion kin'/Doin' good was de only t'ing on hees min'/So he got no use for de politique." In 1888 Drummond returned to Montreal and resumed his role as a dedicated physician and an amateur poet. His life began to change dramatically in 1892, when he met Dr. O. C. Harvey and his daughter May Isabel, who were visiting from the West Indies. In the spring of the following year Drummond traveled to Jamaica, where he and May became engaged; they were married on 18 April 1894 at Savanna le Mar, also in Jamaica.

During his stay in the Caribbean he realized the importance of the rhythms and cadences of dialect to his own self-styled French-Canadian patois, just as later, in 1902, he would become fascinated with Celtic and Anglo-Saxon speech patterns while on an otherwise unsatisfying trip to England, Scotland, and Ireland. By that time Drummond had for several years held the Chair of Medical Jurisprudence at Bishop's College, had been enrolled as a fellow of the Royal Society of Literature of England and as a fellow of the Royal Society of Canada (1899), had had an LL.D. conferred upon him by the University of Toronto (1902), and had published–largely through his wife's encouragement, since he had preferred to compose his verse for private readings–three internationally popular volumes of poetry: *The Habitant, and Other French-Canadian Poems, Phil-o-rum's Canoe, and Madeleine Verchères* (1898), and *Johnnie Courteau, and Other Poems* (1901).

The initial success of these works is attributable in part to the endorsement Drummond received from Louis Fréchette, a French-Canadian poet and politician (1839-1908), who in his introduction to *The Habitant* passed on a compliment that Henry Wadsworth Longfellow had paid to Drummond, calling him "The pathfinder of a new land of song." With Fréchette's assurances that Drummond was celebrating rather than mocking them and their language, Quebecois wholeheartedly supported his verse. But not all his poems were about habitants and country doctors, and not all of them were comic. Drummond wrote "Le Vieux Temps" (The Old Times, 1895) during his wife's convalescence following the death of their first child several hours after birth. His comforting tone as he invites her near is typical of many of his poems: "Venez ici, mon cher ami, an' sit down by me–so/An' I will tole you story of old tam long ago/W'en ev'ryt'ing is happy–w'en all de bird is sing."

At the first Christmas after another tragedy, the death of his three-year-old son, William Henry, in 1904, Drummond composed "The Last Portage," a poem about the passage from life to death, which, appropriately, appeared in his last published collection. *The Voyageur and Other Poems*

(1905) is the least original and impressive of the four volumes published during his lifetime, because Drummond tends to take the lively verse of such earlier poems as his famous "Little Bateese"– "You bad leetle boy, not moche you care/How busy you're kipin' your poor gran'-pere"–and to rework it slightly to suit new characters, as in "Dominique": "You dunno ma leetle boy Dominique?/Never see heem runnin' roun' about de place?"

Shortly after the publication of *The Voyageur* Drummond and his brothers undertook the supervision of the Drummond Mines operation at Kerr Lake in the Cobalt district of northern Ontario. However, in the spring of 1907 Drummond fell victim to fatigue while fighting an outbreak of smallpox, suffered a cerebral hemorrhage, and died on 6 April. Appearing posthumously were *The Great Fight: Poems and Sketches* (1908), consisting of previously unpublished poems and fragments, edited and with a biographical portrait by his widow, May Harvey Drummond, and *The Poetical Works of William Henry Drummond* (1912), comprising the poet's collected verse, an introduction by Fréchette, and a laudatory sketch by Drummond's friend and favorite novelist, the Scotsman Neil Munro.

William Henry Drummond is much more than a literary anachronism, though some recent criticism has seriously questioned the political presumptions that underlie such dialect verse. In any event, his sincere attempt to use language as a liaison between Canada's two founding cultures, who were separated principally by language itself, seems to have presaged everything from Hugh MacLennan's *Two Solitudes* (1945) to Canadian literatures in translation.

References:
Robert H. Craig, "Reminiscences of William Henry Drummond," *Dalhousie Review*, 5 (1925): 161-169;

May Harvey Drummond, Preface and "William Henry Drummond," in *The Great Fight: Poems and Sketches* (New York & London: Putnam's, 1908), pp. vii-xviii;

Louis Fréchette, Introduction to *The Habitant, and Other French-Canadian Poems* (New York & London: Putnam's, 1897), pp. v-x;

John Ford MacDonald, *William Henry Drummond* (Toronto: Ryerson, 1923?);

Neil Munro, "William Henry Drummond," in *The Poetical Works of William Henry Drummond*

(New York & London: Putnam's, 1912), pp.
v-xx;

Gerald Noonan, "Drummond–The Legend and
the Legacy," *Canadian Literature,* 90 (Autumn 1981): 179-187;

Arthur L. Phelps, Introduction to *Habitant Poems*
(Toronto: McClelland & Stewart, 1959), pp.
7-16;

R. E. Rashley, "W. H. Drummond and the Di-

lemma of Style," *Dalhousie Review,* 28
(1949): 387-396.

Papers:

Drummond's letter and May Harvey Drummond's unpublished biography and scrapbook
are in the Osler Library, McGill University, Montreal.

Marcel Dugas

(3 September 1883-7 January 1947)

Alexandre L. Amprimoz
Brock University

BOOKS: *Le Théâtre à Montréal: Propos d'un huron
canadien,* as Marcel Henry (Paris: Falque,
1911);

Feux de Bengale à Verlaine glorieux (Montreal: Marchand, 1915); revised as *Verlaine* (Paris: Radot, 1928);

Psyché au cinéma (Montreal: Paradis-Vincent,
1916);

*Apologies: M. Albert Lozeau, M. Paul Morin, M. Guy
Delahaye, M. Robert La Roque de Roquebrune,
M. René Chopin* (Montreal: Paradis-Vincent,
1919);

Confins, as Tristan Choiseul (Paris, 1921); enlarged as *Flacons à la mer: Proses,* as Dugas
(Paris: Gémeaux, 1923);

Littérature canadienne: Aperçus (Paris: FirminDidot, 1929);

Cordes anciennes: Prose (Paris: L'Armoire de Citronnier, 1933);

Un Romantique canadien: Louis Fréchette, 1839-1908
(Paris: Revue Mondiale, 1934);

Nocturnes, as Sixte le Débonnaire (Paris: Flory,
1936);

Notre Nouvelle Epopée (Ottawa: Service de L'Information, 1941);

Pots de fer (Quebec: Chien D'or, 1941);

Salve alma parens (Quebec: Chien D'or, 1941);

Approches (Quebec: Chien D'or, 1942);

Paroles en liberté (Montreal: L'Arbre, 1944).

Marcel Dugas (photograph from Peintres et Ecrivains
d'hier et d'aujourd'hui *by Albert Laberge, 1938)*

Marcel Dugas was born at Saint-Jacques-de-

L'Achigan, Quebec, on 3 September 1883. His mother was Rose-de-Lima Brien dit Des Roches Dugas. His father, Euclide Dugas, served as a captain in the militia and earned his living as a merchant. From 1895 to 1897 Marcel studied at the Séminaire de Joliette, then went to the Collège de l'Assomption where he received his B.A. in 1906. That same year he enrolled in law school at Laval University in Montreal. At this time he also began a literary career, often signing his articles with a nom de plume. The most important of these pseudonyms were Marcel Henry, Tristan Choiseul, and Sixte le Débonnaire. He wrote theater reviews for *Le Nationaliste, L'Action Française,* and *Le Pays* until 1910, when he received La Médaille de l'Alliance Française and left for Paris and the Sorbonne. Back in Canada in 1914, he took a position with the municipal library of Montreal and turned to journalism once again. In order to fight the abuses of nationalism he founded a literary magazine, *Le Nigog,* in 1918 with Robert de Roquebrune. From 1920 to 1940 he remained in Paris as an archivist for the Canadian government.

For his poetry and criticism he received the Prix Marcelle Guérin de l'Académie Française and the Prix David. Dugas died in Montreal on 7 January 1947. All his life he had been the enthusiastic promoter of poets such as Paul Morin, Guy Delahaye, René Chopin, Saint-Denys Garneau, and Alain Grandbois.

Dugas's first book (published in 1911) is a peculiar one. The title, *Le Théâtre à Montréal,* implies the work of a reviewer, and the subtitle, *Propos d'un huron canadien,* alludes to the tradition of the innocent yet perceptive observer that Montesquieu had established in French literature with the *Lettres persanes* (1721). The irony of the title is confirmed by the content of the book. The critic deals with works by the most popular playwrights of the time: Victorien Sardou, Alexandre Dumas, Henry Bataille, Edmond Rostand, and Maurice Leblanc, among others. However, these are French and not French-Canadian authors. In such a book, one would expect comments about staging and acting, but Marcel Dugas treated theater as textual content, sometimes showing remarkable insight. One could conclude that the absence of analysis of theater as event and the preference for theater as content was a way for Dugas to point ironically to the poor performance of French-Canadian theater. The final section of the book, "Notes et Impressions," is autobiographical and deals with the writer's romantic

discovery of Europe. Here the style is reminiscent of Chateaubriand (1768-1848).

In 1915 Dugas published the text of a public lecture he had given about Paul Verlaine: *Feux de Bengale à Verlaine glorieux.* Then he reworked the small book and republished it in Paris as *Verlaine* (1928). For today's reader, Dugas's ideas on symbolism might seem obvious and his tone too polemic. However, the beginning of the century was a culturally dark period in Quebec, where modernism was censored by the Catholic church. For this reason Dugas had to stress Verlaine's religious poetry in order to prove that his "new" ideas were not systematically diabolic.

Psyché au cinéma (1916) is another unusual book. It can best be described as a collection of eleven poetic essays. Within the framework of Quebec literature at the turn of the century this volume is distinctly modernist and resembles the works of Delahaye, Chopin, Morin, and Jean Charbonneau. While Dugas's friends produced an aggressive literature attacking the conservatism of church and state, for him reality was simply depressing and his "heart" was "in exile." His humor sometimes verged on despair, and while he had no admiration for the priests who thought France was immoral, he was not certain that political changes would suit him either. The image of the little boy "who played the violin / On a pig's tail" is typical of *Psyché au cinéma.* Thus the poet identified himself with the tradition of the sad clown, the commedia-dell'arte approach that marked the works of French symbolists and decadents.

By the time he published *Apologies* (1919), Dugas was already considered one of the most enlightened minds of his time. The very concept of *Apologies* reveals an independent thinker. Instead of writing about the noted poets of the time, like Emile Nelligan or Albert Ferland, Dugas decided to dedicate a book to five young and promising French-Canadian poets. But while showing his ability for analysis, the critic did not hesitate to exercise his judgment. For example, Dugas writes that Albert Lozeau was influenced by Georges Rodenbach (1855-1898) and spared "the worst thing": intellectual doubt. His reservations about Delahaye came from his sense that this poet was too rational and that the subtleties of his formal experiments would be missed by the average reader.

Confins (1921) was published under his pen name Tristan Choiseul; *Flacons à la mer* (1923) was published under his real name. Nonetheless the two collections constitute the same book, with the exception of a section titled "Pages oubliées" (Forgotten Pages) added to the second one. These poems seem rather romantic in form and content, reminiscent of the style of Alfred de Vigny (1797-1863). Furthermore, the basic poetic structure reminds one of *Méditations Poétiques* (1820) by Alphonse Lamartine (1790-1869). Every poem is an attempt to stretch into some type of abstract eternity a privileged moment that by its very nature is destined to death.

One must distinguish between Dugas's own poetic exploration and his theoretical position, which seems more modernist than ever in *Littérature canadienne: Aperçus* (1929). This book, published in Paris and theoretically written to introduce Frenchmen to Quebec literature, is in fact a polemic defense of Quebec's new poetry against criticism based on tradition.

In 1933, with *Cordes anciennes*, Dugas created a collection of prose poems that are at least as structured as the works of Delahaye. The content, however, reflects the same pessimistic solitude—the stance of an exiled romantic, well aware of more modern theories. By 1936, with *Nocturnes*, Dugas was able to include a new twist in his prose poems, reaching a synthesis of aesthetic and social awareness. The poetry turned to reflections on the world: "The morals of good books do not exist."

With *Un Romantique canadien: Louis Fréchette, 1839-1908* (1934), Dugas's modernist ambiguity is confirmed. Why dedicate a massive study to a pale imitator of Victor Hugo? Why analyze a "primitive poet"? This first major work on Fréchette will puzzle readers for quite a while yet with its contradictions, its vitriolic attacks, and its

reluctant confessions that recognize the "Romantique canadien" as, in some ways, an initiator. This book is fascinating, not only because in it a modernist studies a romantic but also because the critic reveals himself as much as he reveals the poet.

With *Approches* (1942) Dugas returned to the idea of writing about friends. But the circle of writers studied was a new one: Léo-Pol Morin, Alain Grandbois, François Hertel, Saint-Denys Garneau, and Simone Routier. The essay on Grandbois offers remarkable insight, perhaps because the two Canadian writers saw each other in Paris "every day, for thirteen years." In the last chapter the author states his admiration for the Canadian soldiers who defended Europe.

The final collection, *Paroles en liberté* (1944), is actually derived from his early poetry. It is composed of forty-six poems in five sections. The third section includes laudatory portraits of early modernist friends: Morin, Chopin, and Delahaye.

On one hand, Marcel Dugas remains the first promoter of modernism in Quebec. On the other, we see him as a traditional figure who had some difficulties in laying to rest the ghost of romanticism. His contributions and contradictions make him an important and fascinating figure in Canadian literary history.

References:

Etude Française, special issue, *Marcel Dugas et son temps*, 7, no. 3 (1971);

Alain Grandbois, "Marcel Dugas," *Cahiers de L'Académie Canadienne-Française*, 7 (1963): 153-165;

Albert Laberge, "Marcel Dugas," in *Peintres et Ecrivains d'hier et d'aujourd'hui* (Montreal: Privately printed, 1938), pp. 157-164.

Norman Duncan

(2 July 1871-18 October 1916)

Janet Giltrow
Simon Fraser University

BOOKS: *The Soul of the Street: Correlated Stories of the New York Syrian Quarter* (New York: McClure, Phillips, 1900);

The Way of the Sea (New York: McClure, Phillips, 1903);

Doctor Luke of the Labrador (New York: Revell, 1904);

Dr. Grenfell's Parish: The Deep Sea Fishermen (New York: Revell, 1905);

The Mother (New York: Revell, 1905);

The Adventures of Billy Topsail: A Story for Boys (New York: Revell, 1906);

The Cruise of the Shining Light (New York & London: Harper, 1907; Toronto: Frowde, 1907);

Every Man for Himself (New York & London: Harper, 1908);

Going Down from Jerusalem: The Narrative of a Sentimental Traveller (New York & London: Harper, 1909);

Higgins, a Man's Christian (New York & London: Harper, 1909);

The Suitable Child (New York: Revell, 1909);

Billy Topsail & Company: A Story for Boys (New York: Revell, 1910);

The Measure of a Man: A Tale of the Big Woods (New York: Revell, 1911);

The Best of a Bad Job: A Hearty Tale of the Sea (New York: Revell, 1912);

Finding His Soul (New York & London: Harper, 1913);

The Bird-Store Man: An Old-Fashioned Story (New York: Revell, 1914);

Australian Byways: The Narrative of a Sentimental Traveler (New York & London: Harper, 1915);

Billy Topsail, M.D.: A Tale of Adventure with Doctor Luke of the Labrador (New York: Revell, 1916);

Battles Royal Down North (New York: Revell, 1918);

Harbor Tales Down North (New York: Revell, 1918).

Norman Duncan

Best known for his descriptions of outport life in turn-of-the-century Newfoundland, Norman Duncan was a journalist, short-story writer, novelist, and travel writer. Born 2 July 1871 in Brantford, Duncan grew up in Ontario. He spent four years at the University of Toronto but left in 1895 without receiving a degree. Although he lived and worked in the United States from 1895 until his death in 1916, he remained a Canadian citizen.

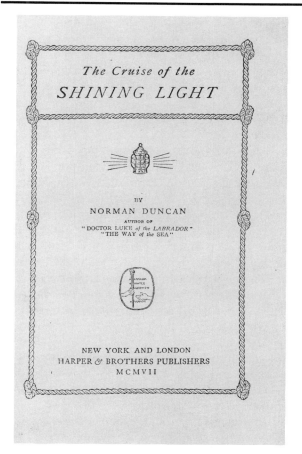

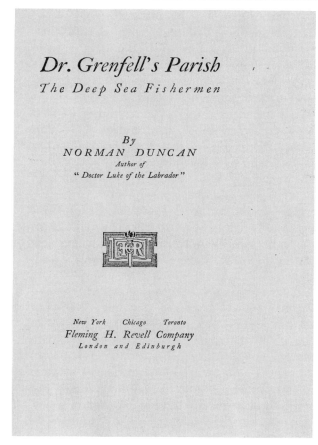

Title pages for Duncan's nonfiction book on Wilfred Grenfell's work in Labrador (1905) and his 1907 Dickensian novel narrated by an outport orphan

Duncan spent two years as a reporter on the Auburn, New York, *Bulletin* and went from there to work for four years on the *New York Evening Post,* where editors recognized his abilities as a writer of descriptive pieces capturing the flavor of neighborhood life in the city. During this period Duncan wrote several stories about the Syrian quarter of New York City, which were published in the *Atlantic* and *McClure's* and were collected as *The Soul of the Street* (1900).

In the summer of 1900 Duncan went to Newfoundland for *McClure's,* the first of his four sojourns among the people of the Newfoundland outports and the coast of Labrador. Although his total experience of this part of the world amounted only to a few months, Duncan's impressions of Newfoundland and Labrador generated the major part of his large literary output. While he was professor of rhetoric at Washington and Jefferson College in Washington, Pennsylvania, his first three books about Newfoundland ap-

peared: *The Way of the Sea* (1903), a collection of stories; *Doctor Luke of the Labrador* (1904), a novel; and *Dr. Grenfell's Parish* (1905), a description of the people of the outports and Wilfred Grenfell's work among them. All three of these books speak for Duncan's fascination with life as it was lived at the "frontier of the habitable places of the earth." They describe a meager existence on a bare coast, an existence dependent on a violent, merciless sea, which rears a hardy race of people. Awed by the "grace of heavy courage" these people exhibited, and warmed by their innocence and simplicity, Duncan wrote repeatedly of their stoical view of hunger, death, and disaster not as miseries to be lamented but as facts to be expected and accepted. In a later novel, *The Best of a Bad Job* (1912), this stoicism is the main theme.

Even Duncan's fictional accounts of outport life show his careful habits of observation. He creates a consistent picture of the economic relation between the character of these communities and their environment, and he allows his Newfoundlanders to speak with their own voice, reproducing regional phonological and grammatical structures in dialogue. But the most striking characteristic of Duncan's Newfoundlanders is their attitude of natural faith in the midst of their suffering: knowing of no other, easier life, they explain their scant surroundings in often quaint systems of belief. Duncan integrates their indigenous metaphysics into a larger pattern of Christian morality, describing a society where salvation and damnation are plausible consequences of behavior. His admiration for Grenfell's work reflects Duncan's own philanthropic Christianity, and his stories express his generous estimate of man's capacity for natural virtue under primitive conditions.

Although Duncan never married, he had strong feelings about family life, especially about relationships between parents and children. In his moves to Auburn, to New York City, and to Pennsylvania he followed his mother and brothers, and *The Mother* (1905), an urban novella about a young boy and his mother, shows just how intensely Duncan could portray family ties. In other narratives, also, death—of parent or child—heightens family sentiment. And in some of his Newfoundland and American stories adoption is a prominent theme: their hearts quickened by parental feeling, adults embrace and cherish needy children.

Duncan's most well-known novel, *Doctor Luke of the Labrador*, tells about an outport trader's children who suffer first the death of their beloved mother and then the loss of their heartbroken father. The orphans welcome into their home a young English doctor who, fleeing an immoral past, grows into robust manliness and humanitarian purpose after a few months of outport life. Sentimental as this story is, its wit and local detail save it from melodrama. Equally interesting is Duncan's *The Cruise of the Shining Light*, a novel published in 1907. Orphaned as an infant, the narrator of this story is the adopted son of Uncle Nicholas Top, a rough, rum-drinking, eccentric old fisherman whose encounters with the sea have left him grotesquely disfigured. Following the directions of Lord Chesterfield and London fashion magazines, Uncle Nicholas rears this outport orphan to be a gentleman, pampered and proud. The text has a distinctive Dickensian flavor.

After leaving his professorship at Washington and Jefferson College, Duncan was sent by *Harper's* to the Middle East in 1907. In 1909 he published *Going Down from Jerusalem: The Narrative of a Sentimental Traveller*, an account of his caravan journey from Jerusalem into Egypt. The painter Lawren Harris accompanied him on this expedition and provided the book's illustrations. In 1912 and 1913 Duncan visited Southeast Asia and Australia for *Harper's*, and in 1915 he published *Australian Byways*. He died in Fredonia, New York, 18 October 1916, having suffered heart disease.

Although he continued to write about Newfoundland and Labrador until the end of his life, Duncan's most vigorous and substantial works are those written before 1908. The two collections of Newfoundland short stories, *Battles Royal Down North* and *Harbor Tales Down North*, published posthumously in 1918, lack the intense vision of faith and endurance of the earlier works and are little more than action yarns colored with local dialect. Nevertheless, Duncan will be remembered as a talented and committed writer who could capture in lucid prose the color and emotion of real life.

References:
Fred Cogswell, "*The Way of the Sea*: A Symbolic Epic," *Dalhousie Review*, 35 (Winter 1956): 374-381;

E. J. Hathaway, "Who's Who in Canadian Literature: Norman Duncan," *Canadian Bookman*, 8 (June 1926): 171-174;

Patrick O'Flaherty, *The Rock Observed: Studies in the Literature of Newfoundland* (Toronto: University of Toronto Press, 1979), pp. 95-102.

Sara Jeannette Duncan

(22 December 1861-22 July 1922)

Thomas E. Tausky
University of Western Ontario

BOOKS: *A Social Departure: How Orthodocia and I Went Round the World by Ourselves* (New York: Appleton, 1890; London: Chatto & Windus, 1890);

An American Girl in London (New York: Appleton, 1891; London: Chatto & Windus, 1891);

Two Girls on a Barge, as V. Cecil Cotes (New York: Appleton, 1891);

The Simple Adventures of a Memsahib (New York: Appleton, 1893; London: Chatto & Windus, 1893);

A Daughter of Today (New York: Appleton, 1894; London: Chatto & Windus, 1894);

The Story of Sonny Sahib (London: Macmillan, 1894; New York: Appleton, 1895);

Vernon's Aunt: Being the Oriental Experiences of Miss Lavinia Moffat (London: Chatto & Windus, 1894; New York: Appleton, 1895);

His Honour, and a Lady (New York: Appleton, 1896; London: Macmillan, 1896);

Hilda: A Story of Calcutta (New York: Stokes, 1898); republished as *The Path of a Star* (London: Methuen, 1899);

A Voyage of Consolation (Being in the Nature of a Sequel to the Experiences of "An American Girl in London") (New York: Appleton, 1898; London: Methuen, 1898);

The Crow's Nest (New York: Dodd, Mead, 1901); published in England as *On the Other Side of the Latch* (London: Methuen, 1901);

Those Delightful Americans (New York: Appleton, 1902; London: Methuen, 1902);

The Pool in the Desert (New York: Appleton, 1903; London: Methuen, 1903);

The Imperialist (New York: Appleton, 1904; London: Constable, 1904);

Set in Authority (New York: Doubleday, Page, 1906; London: Constable, 1906);

Cousin Cinderella (New York: Macmillan, 1908; London: Methuen, 1908); also published as *A Canadian Girl in London* (New York: Macmillan, 1908);

Two in a Flat, as Jane Wintergreen (London: Hodder & Stoughton, 1908);

The Burnt Offering (London: Methuen, 1909; New York: Lane, 1910);

The Consort (London: Paul, 1912);

His Royal Highness (New York: Appleton, 1914);

Title Clear (London: Hutchinson, 1922);

The Gold Cure (London: Hutchinson, 1924);

Selected Journalism, edited by Thomas E. Tausky (Ottawa: Tecumseh, 1978).

A pioneering woman journalist and a sophisticated novelist, Sara Jeannette Duncan was one of the most important literary witnesses to the post-Confederation, pre-World War I era. Her intrepid spirit took her to all parts of the English-speaking world, and her close observation of those societies resulted in novels that show an understanding of fictional techniques possessed by few of her contemporaries.

Duncan was born on 22 December 1861 in Brantford, Ontario, to Charles and Jane Bell Duncan. Her father, who had immigrated to Canada from Scotland in 1852, was a successful merchant, and the family home, still standing, testifies to prosperity. After attending school in Brantford, Duncan went on to the Toronto Normal School. Apparently, though trained to do so, she never taught for a sustained period of time.

Her semi-autobiographical article, "How an American Girl Became a Journalist" (collected in *Selected Journalism,* 1978), tells about Duncan's early years and her start in her chosen career. Duncan's "Secret Purpose" as a child was "to distinguish herself in literature." After serving a brief apprenticeship on her hometown newspaper, "Margery Blunt" (the name Duncan gives to the protagonist of her article) gets the idea of going to the New Orleans Cotton Centennial of 1884 as a free-lance correspondent: "In the end Margery went southward, with a pleasant party, fifty dollars in her purse, and three or four engagements, all conditioned, to write about the great exhibition." Duncan's articles about the Centennial appeared principally in the *London* (Ontario) *Advertiser,* the *Toronto Globe,* and the *Memphis Appeal.*

The author, circa 1891, after her marriage to Everard Cotes

After leaving New Orleans in May 1885, she worked for the next three years as a book reviewer, editorial writer, and columnist. Some occasional writing for the *Globe* in 1885 was followed by full-time work on the *Washington Post* from October 1885 until the spring of 1886. By the summer of 1886 she had established herself at the *Globe* with a lively daily column entitled "Woman's World." In the fall of 1887 she moved to the *Montreal Star* and a similar but somewhat more general column entitled "Bric-a-Brac." In March 1888 she achieved a long-held ambition when the *Star* made her a parliamentary correspondent in Ottawa. From 1885 onward she also contributed frequently to the *Week,* the leading literary and political journal of the period, often writing two columns (one under the pseudonym "Garth Grafton") for the same issue.

One cannot help but be impressed by the range, originality, and vigor of Duncan's journalism, which deserves to be better known. Perhaps of most interest today are her stimulating essays on the literary culture of her time and on the aspirations of women. An article written for the *Week* of 30 September 1886 is Duncan's most penetrating analysis of "our character of colonists" that produces "our sins of omission in letters." Duncan's contention in this essay, that "a national literature cannot be looked for as an outcome of anything less than a complete national existence," indicates her willingness to look at literature in its social context, a tendency perhaps reinforced by her sojourn in the United States.

Duncan was one of the first women to be employed by Canadian newspapers, and a natural pride in her own achievement underlies her analysis of the position of women. Many of her articles, especially for the *Globe,* focus upon the accomplishments of women in new fields. Although Duncan clearly saw the hope of new career opportunities for women as an exhilarating prospect, she did not scorn marriage as an alternative, and she satirizes both what she perceives as overly strident feminism and what she scorns as excessive timidity.

Many of the qualities of Duncan's journalism anticipate the best aspects of her fiction. As early as in her New Orleans articles, she had the ability to turn a shrewd piece of observation into a telling and often sardonic commentary on an entire social system. She was soon able to dramatize social tendencies by inventing caricatured narrators and satirical scenes involving representative types.

Her first book, *A Social Departure* (1890), is a natural extension of these sketches. With her customary adventurousness Duncan set off in the fall of 1888 on a round-the-world trip that took her to the Canadian West, Japan, India, the Middle East, and England; in chronicling her experiences she transformed her Canadian journalist companion, Lily Lewis, into a bashful, innocent English character named Orthodocia Love. The book had its origins as a series of travel letters for the *Montreal Star;* though Orthodocia (who does not appear in the *Star* articles) serves to unify the volume, it still remains something of a patchwork. The section on India seems superficial by the standards of Duncan's later observations of that society, and the chapters on Egypt add little to the overall impact of the book. The section on the Canadian West is interesting for its glimpses of major centers like Winnipeg and Vancouver in their infancy, but the real heart of the book is the account of Japan, a country that evidently captivated Duncan: "To live a week in Tokio [*sic*] is to forget entirely how one got there, and to write about it is to disbelieve that one has ever come away." In Japan, Duncan and Lewis immersed themselves in the national culture, whereas in India and elsewhere they were kept at a safe distance from the natives by their British hosts.

The most important consequence of the trip was the fact that, while in India, Duncan met Everard Cotes, then a Calcutta museum official and subsequently a newspaper editor and Reuters correspondent. Duncan spent some months in England before returning to India to marry Cotes on 6 December 1890. Her next two works, *An American Girl in London* and *Two Girls on a Barge*, both published in 1891, have England as their setting. The latter novel, published under the pseudonym V. Cecil Cotes, is overly facetious, but *An American Girl in London* is genuinely witty and consistently entertaining.

The American girl, Mamie Wick, seems closely related to Henry James's Daisy Miller by virtue of her wealth, American character, and charming naïveté. Mamie is exposed to a series of representative British institutions: she visits Westminster Abbey, Ascot, Aldershot, and Oxford and ultimately is presented at court. With her shrewd impressions of British life, Mamie redeems the novel from being merely a travelogue. She is not the fool many Britons take her to be: she respects dignity and meaningful tradition where she finds it, but she also sees through stuffiness and snobbery.

A Social Departure and *An American Girl in London* were probably Duncan's most popular books. A 1903 advertisement indicates that they had sold sixteen thousand and eight thousand copies respectively in their American editions alone.

The first result of Duncan's two productive decades of residence in India was *The Simple Adventures of a Memsahib* (1893). Apparently some of the details are based on Duncan's own experience—she told an interviewer for the British magazine the *Idler:* "It was certainly our own house . . . and the garden was like ours as nearly as I could describe it." As in *An American Girl in London*, an innocent stands at the center of the novel: a young girl named Helen Browne who at the beginning is engaged to marry in Wiltshire and becomes an Anglo-Indian "memsahib, graduated, qualified, sophisticated" by the end. The story is told, not by the very commonplace Mrs. Browne, but by a veteran memsahib, Mrs. Perth Macintyre, who observes her with both sympathy and pity. Unlike her protégée, Mrs. Macintyre is both reflective and wise; she is also on her way to retirement in England—and oblivion—the Brownes' "first chapter has been our last." Mrs. Macintyre's delicate and subtle narration makes the story not just an account of typical Anglo-Indian life but also, especially in the novel's final pages, an account of the tragic inevitability, in the Indian physical and social climate, of English stultification and ultimate decline.

There is humor as well as melancholy in *The Simple Adventures of a Memsahib,* but the same cannot be said of the ambitious but flawed novel, *A Daughter of Today* (1894). This novel opens in Sparta, Illinois, and ends in London, by way of Paris, with the suicide of the central character, Elfrida Bell. Though Elfrida's character is revealed too melodramatically, *A Daughter of Today* fuses in its central figure two types that were to return frequently in Duncan's later work: the artist and the misguided feminist. Elfrida, in rebellion against America ("the life over there is—infernal"), first flees to Paris, in an unsuccessful

Frontispiece and title page for Duncan's first novel

attempt to be a painter, and then experiments with journalism in England. Throughout much of the novel she is contrasted with Janet Cardiff, a more cautious and conservative English girl who is at once a novelist, a friend of Elfrida's, and also her rival in the battle to win the affections of John Kendall, an English painter. Along with a few bohemian friends, Elfrida is in revolt, in true 1890s fashion, "against the dull, conventional British public." When Elfrida argues that "art has no ideal but truth, and to conventionalize truth is to damn it," Janet replies that "we're a conventional people . . . the material here is conventional." Differing conceptions of art and morality as well as their common interest in Kendall cause Elfrida and Janet to quarrel; meanwhile, Kendall has unmasked Elfrida's egotism in a portrait that she feels compelled to destroy. These unhappy events, and a conviction that her journalistic career is at a standstill, cause Elfrida to take

her own life. Kendall and Janet marry, and Kendall's English character asserts itself when he chooses to become a country squire; however, Kendall is described on the final page of the novel as "thinking of an art that has slipped away from him." *A Daughter of Today* is therefore a novel in which neither the bohemian artist nor the bourgeois artist really wins in the end. Though Duncan's portrait of Elfrida is as unflattering as Kendall's, it is possible that Duncan is dramatizing character traits in Elfrida that she was suspicious of within herself. The result is a work that is powerful in feeling, but also overly moralistic and schematic.

Duncan wrote five more works of fiction before 1900, all but one of which have India as their setting. A light comedy entitled *Vernon's Aunt: Being the Oriental Experiences of Miss Lavinia Moffat* and a children's book called *The Story of Sonny Sahib*—both published in 1894—cannot have cost Duncan much effort. *His Honour, and a Lady* (1896) is a much more substantial work, and a continuation of the exploration of Anglo-Indian society begun in *The Simple Adventures of a Memsahib*. Throughout most of her writing career Duncan alternated between a base in India and lengthy stays in England: a letter dated 19 October 1894 accepting Macmillan's offer for *His Honour, and a Lady* is written from Kensington (the setting for the novel's final scene), but the book also reveals an intimate knowledge of the ways of Anglo-Indian government.

The novel's title refers to a clever but unscrupulous lieutenant governor (conventionally referred to as "His Honour") of Bengal. Lewis Ancram destroys his personal honor by betraying his predecessor (at that time his superior), John Church, in two respects: he secretly undercuts his educational policy, and he seeks to win the love of his wife, Judith. In the course of the latter, nearly successful attempt, Ancram ungallantly breaks off an engagement with a young girl, Rhoda Daye, who subsequently marries Ancram's friend Philip Doyle. When Ancram's act of political betrayal comes to light after Church's death, he is spurned by Judith.

His Honour, and a Lady is the first of three novels—*Set in Authority* (1906) and *The Burnt Offering* (1909) are the others—in which Duncan is centrally concerned with political decisions that illuminate English attitudes toward Indians. Although the problem discussed in this work—whether Indians should be given liberal or technical education—may seem of limited interest today, the novel skillfully uses this issue as a means of exploring a more fundamental question: whether principle (represented by Church) or "exalted expediency" (represented by Ancram and his friend Doyle) is the best method of dealing with the native population. On the level of social issues this novel is the first of several that deal, rather hesitantly, with the temptations of adultery. Here, as elsewhere, the matter is seen largely from the woman's point of view, and the woman ultimately says "No," although she would like to say "Yes." Judith Church's dilemma gives her a more intriguing role than the straightforward part assigned to Rhoda Daye, but it is Rhoda, one of the best of Duncan's witty, sardonic alter egos, who has the more interesting personality.

Duncan returned to a European setting with *A Voyage of Consolation* (1898), an inferior sequel to *An American Girl in London*. *Hilda: A Story of Calcutta* (1898; published in England as *The Path of a Star*, 1899) is in some ways an Anglo-Indian version of *A Daughter of Today*: in both cases, a deliberately bohemian artist feels alienated from the main current of society and yet is attracted to more conventional people. *Hilda* also shares with *A Daughter of Today* the ambitiousness of purpose and uneven success in execution. *Hilda* touches upon the bureaucratic world of *His Honour, and a Lady*, but it also explores the artistic, religious, and commercial communities of Calcutta. The novel clearly draws upon Duncan's experiences as a staff member of the *Indian Daily News*, a Calcutta newspaper for which both she and her husband worked. An Anglo-Indian newspaper is unflatteringly described in the course of the novel; also, the religious communities in the novel were subjects for articles Duncan wrote for the newspaper.

Hilda Howe is a stage actress who is more talented and less egotistical than Elfrida Bell. Hilda's forbidden love is for Stephen Arnold, an Anglican priest whose order imposes celibacy. Hilda's friend Duff Lindsay, a stockbroker, becomes increasingly attracted to a Salvation Army missionary, but she eventually rejects him. Hilda also has a society friend, Alicia Livingstone, whose calm elegance contrasts with Hilda's impetuosity in a way that recalls the relationship of Janet Cardiff to Elfrida Bell. By the end of the novel Alicia has captured Lindsay, and Hilda, who had temporarily become a nursing sister to be near Arnold, has gone on to success on the London stage after Arnold is fatally knifed in a bazaar. The word in the novel frequently associated with Hilda is "primitive." She describes her "kind of life" as "one pure impulse." This reliance upon instinct is explicitly contrasted with Alicia's more refined but less warm-blooded "taste" and Arnold's even more spiritless spirituality. Hilda's vigorous personality and the sharply observed details of contrasting social worlds are sources of strength in the novel, but a turgid narration and some melodramatic twists of the plot undercut the book's appeal.

Before the turn of the century Duncan apparently moved from Calcutta to Simla, the small Himalayan town that each year became the headquarters of British administration in India during the hot season. Shortly afterward she had to fight off an attack of tuberculosis. *The Crow's Nest* (1901; published in England as *On the Other Side of the Latch*) describes Duncan's feelings when, in accordance with a fashionable medical treatment of the period, she had to spend months at a time in her Simla garden, exiled from the house. Duncan seems inclined, for the most part, to cope with her disease by appearing stoical and even cheerful, and by giving close attention to her narrowed environment. Her illness does, however, prompt some melancholy reflections upon death, and the far-off Canada of Duncan's childhood is occasionally evoked in nostalgic memory. Another interesting feature of the book is Duncan's skeptical account of the artificial and self-conscious Simla community, which she characteristically reveals through profiles of representative residents. As Duncan tells one visitor, conformity in such a world is inevitable: "We are round pebbles on this coral strand, worn smooth by rubbing against nothing but each other."

The same view of Simla emerges in "An Impossible Ideal," the best story in an uneven collection of Duncan's short fiction, *The Pool in the Desert* (1903). The Philistine character of the town (it is described at one point as a "remote fastness thrice barred against the arts") is galling to Ingersoll Armour, a young painter who is at first totally isolated but gradually becomes accepted by Simla society through the efforts of his fiancée, Dora Harris. Dora, the daughter of a senior official, believes that "a human being isn't an orchid, he must draw something from the soil he grows in," but the fallacy of that theory soon becomes apparent as Armour conventionalizes his art to win acceptance. The idea that the artist is inherently uneasy with society had already been developed in *A Daughter of Today* and *Hilda,* but in this novella the theme is given a carefully controlled, psychologically subtle treatment that is superior to the other versions.

Duncan returned to settings in the western world for two successful novels of this period, *Those Delightful Americans* (1902) and *The Imperialist* (1904). The former work is charmingly narrated by a young English matron who crosses the Atlantic and is therefore given an opportunity to study American girls in love. As the title implies, the narrator is much impressed by American openheartedness, which appears to great advantage in contrast with English reserve.

The Imperialist is the most well known of Duncan's novels today, and deservedly so because of its literary merit as well as its Canadian setting. Duncan evidently worked hard on the novel, seeking documents on imperialism while in India and working industriously on the proofs while on an extended visit to Brantford. She wrote a Canadian acquaintance that "I am rather anxious that none of you shall be ashamed of it. . . . I am trying very hard to make it my best book." *The Imperialist* is Duncan's most personal book, in that the town of Elgin and its central characters are clearly based on Brantford and the people most central to Duncan's youth there. The elder Murchisons in the novel are modeled on Duncan's own parents, and Advena Murchison, in her independence of mind and intellectual inclinations, has much in common with Duncan herself; Dr. Drummond, another important figure, is based on Duncan's own childhood minister, Dr. Cochrane.

The imperialist of the title, Lorne Murchison, is a bright young lawyer whose dedication to closer economic, political, and military ties with the mother country eventually proves unpalatable to his fellow citizens. Lorne fights to win Elgin for the Liberal party, and to win Dora Milburn, the daughter of one of his political opponents, for himself, but by the end of the novel he has been dumped by his party and by his fiancée and suffers a mild nervous breakdown before being rescued by his political patron, who offers him a partnership in his law firm. Meanwhile, Lorne's sister Advena has been having troubles of her own: her promising love affair with a shy but worthy minister, Hugh Finlay, has been threatened by external obstacles, but is finally resolved happily through the intervention of Dr. Drummond. The political and romantic strands of the plot are unified by the fact that each involves an encounter between idealism and pragmatism: Lorne and Advena are motivated by concern for others, whereas Octavius Milburn and his daughter think only of their own self-interest. The rejection of Lorne's idealistic vision of Canada's imperial future must be regarded as evidence of Elgin's collective narrow-mindedness, but Lorne and Advena, with all their virtues, are nevertheless presented as products of the Elgin environment. Especially in the novel's opening chapters Duncan makes it clear that her story is not just of an individual, a family, or a specific small community, but of Canadian small-town life in general. Lengthy explicit commentary by the third-person narrator analyzes the character of Elgin society, and several characters who come to Elgin from England and Scotland (a variant of the international theme) serve to underline by contrast the New World's strengths and limitations.

The Imperialist ranks with Stephen Leacock's *Sunshine Sketches of a Little Town* (1912) as an outstanding portrayal of Canadian society before the modern period. It is disconcerting to find, therefore, that *The Imperialist* was harshly attacked by English critics (because "a remote Canadian townlet" was a boring setting, and ladies should not trouble themselves about politics) and greeted with indifference by Canadian reviewers. Only the *New York Times* praised "perhaps the most worthwhile [story] which has come out here in some time."

Duncan's next novel, *Set in Authority*, was much more favorably received by the reviewers, perhaps because it was thought, in England at least, that a little town in India was intrinsically more interesting than a little town in Canada. Politics is at the center of this novel as well—the issue here is the question of whether justice or expediency prompted by fears of a backlash should prevail when an Englishman is tried for the murder of a native. The ethical dilemma is well presented, and Duncan's powers of analyzing a small, and small-minded, community are at their height, but the English scenes (leading up to a girl's implausible discovery that her fiancé has condemned her brother to death) are a weakness in the book.

Duncan had apparently planned to give "the critical colonial view of London society" as soon as she finished with *The Imperialist*, but the project, *Cousin Cinderella*, was not published until 1908. In the meantime Lorne Murchison was replaced as a Canadian abroad by Graham and Mary Trent. Though *Cousin Cinderella* is set in England, it is in its own way as much a study of the emerging Canadian character as *The Imperialist*. The Trents are the children of an English-born Canadian lumber baron who wishes to impress English society with the national virtues of his offspring. Unfortunately, English society is not disposed to be impressed by any Canadian, no matter how presentable, and Mary's initial awe upon arrival in London turns to resentment when she realizes that an American friend of theirs has been taken up more enthusiastically, and that her brother's identity is being threatened by his own excessive, self-abasing Anglophilia. A friend helps them achieve some social recognition, and the rest of the novel deals with the Trents' gallant efforts to prop up the enfeebled English aristocracy with cash and marriage alliances. Graham ends up unattached, but Mary becomes engaged to Lord Doleford, an idealistic but dim-witted young man she imagines to be like a "Crusader."

The Trents' efforts to revitalize the English aristocracy are an allegory of Canada's role within the empire as Duncan conceived of it. Yet their mixed success and concurrent disillusionment testify to the emotional difficulties faced by the sensitive youth of a country that no longer wishes to be a colony and yet is still not a nation. Under the influence of the English atmosphere the Trents are not nearly as self-confident as Lorne and Advena Murchison; the tension between cultural humility and a need for self-assertion is revealed with particular poignancy in the character of Mary Trent, the narrator of the novel.

Imperial troubles of another sort are examined in Duncan's final Indian novel, *The Burnt Offering*. At this time the internal peace that prevailed in India for half a century after the Mutiny was being seriously challenged for the first time by acts of terrorism; Duncan's novel is simultaneously a condemnation of violence and the most sympathetic image of the Indian character to be found in her fiction. The result is an uneven work, nonetheless fascinating for its revelation of the extent to which Duncan had come to realize that Indians could be complex individuals rather than merely colorful underlings, but it is also filled with melodrama and strident defenses of the principle of British rule.

Duncan lived for thirteen years after the publication of *The Burnt Offering* and wrote four more novels, as well as several commercially unsuccessful plays, but none of this work is very significant. Nearly all of it is in a light comic manner, with some of the themes and characterization, but without the cleverness, that marked Duncan's earlier ventures in this style.

Most of Duncan's novels were reasonably popular in her own time and were highly regarded by contemporary critics. Since the early 1960s her work has been studied by critics with increasing frequency and respect. Taken as a whole, Duncan's fictional output is both ambitious in scope and varied in subject. After her initial success with works of a frankly entertaining character, she began to undertake more serious themes with *The Simple Adventures of a Memsahib* and *A Daughter of Today*. Her subsequent novels deal with such important questions as the psychology of politics and race relations, the role of the artist (and more generally, the person of imagination) in an unreceptive society, and the difficulties faced by women at a time of changing morality. Her Indian novels collectively create an authentic image of that society and an intriguing picture, by implication, of her own adjustment to it; *The Simple Adventures of a Memsahib* and *His Honour, and a Lady* are the most consistently successful products of her years in India. Her two Canadian novels, *The Imperialist* and *Cousin Cinderella*, represent her greatest achievements; they are among the enduring classics of Canadian fiction.

Biography:

Marian Fowler, *Redney: A Life of Sara Jeannette Duncan* (Toronto: Anansi, 1983).

References:

Peter Allen, "Narrative Uncertainty in Duncan's *The Imperialist*," *Studies in Canadian Literature*, 9 (Winter 1984): 41-60;

Alfred G. Bailey, "The Historical Setting of Sara Duncan's *The Imperialist*," *Journal of Canadian Fiction*, 2, no. 3 (1973): 205-210;

Claude Bissell, Introduction to *The Imperialist* (Toronto: McClelland & Stewart, 1961);

G. B. Burgin, "A Chat with Sara Jeannette Duncan," *Idler*, 8 (August 1895): 113-118;

Florence Donaldson, "Mrs. Everard Cotes," *Bookman*, 14 (June 1898): 65-67;

Carole Gerson, "Duncan's Web," *Canadian Literature*, 63 (Winter 1975): 73-80;

Carrie MacMillan, "The Figure of the Artist in Late Nineteenth-Century Canadian Fiction," *Studies in Canadian Literature*, 5 (Spring 1980): 63-82;

Marjory MacMurchy, "The Bookman Gallery: Mrs. Everard Cotes," *Bookman*, 48 (May 1915): 39-40;

"M.E.R." (Mrs. Sanford Ross), "Sara Jeannette Duncan: Personal Glimpses," *Canadian Literature*, 27 (Winter 1966): 15-19;

John Moss, *Patterns of Isolation* (Toronto: McClelland & Stewart, 1974), pp. 53-79;

Michael Peterman, "Humour and Balance in *The Imperialist:* Sara Jeannette Duncan's 'Instinct of Presentation,'" *Journal of Canadian Studies*, 11 (May 1976): 56-64;

Catherine Sheldrick Ross, "Calling Back the Ghost of the Old-Time Heroine: Duncan, Montgomery, Atwood, Laurence and Munro," *Studies in Canadian Literature*, 4 (Winter 1979): 43-58;

Thomas E. Tausky, Introduction to *The Imperialist* (Ottawa: Tecumseh, 1988);

Tausky, *Sara Jeannette Duncan* (Toronto: ECW, 1989);

Tausky, *Sara Jeannette Duncan: Novelist of Empire* (Port Credit, Ont.: Meany, 1980);

Clara Thomas, "Canadian Social Mythologies in Sara Jeannette Duncan's *The Imperialist*," *Journal of Canadian Studies*, 12 (Spring 1977): 38-49;

Thomas, "*Cousin Cinderella* and the Empire Game," *Studies in Canadian Literature*, 1 (Summer 1976): 183-193;

George Woodcock, "The Changing Masks of Empire: Notes on Some Novels by Sara Jeannette Duncan," *Yearbook of English Studies*, 13 (1983): 210-227;

J. M. Zezulka, "Passionate Provincials: Imperialism, Regionalism, and Point of View," *Journal of Canadian Fiction*, 22 (1978): 80-92;

Francis Zichy, "A Portrait of the Idealist as Politician: The Individual and Society in *The Imperialist*," *English Studies in Canada*, 10 (September 1984): 330-342.

Wilfrid Eggleston

(25 March 1901-15 June 1986)

David Ingham
University of Saskatchewan

BOOKS: *Prairie Moonlight and Other Lyrics* (Toronto: Published privately, 1927);
The High Plains (Toronto: Macmillan, 1938);
Dominion-Provincial Subsidies and Grants, by Eggleston and C. T. Kraft (Ottawa: Royal Commission on Dominion-Provincial Relations, 1939); also published as *Subventions et allocations du dominion aux provinces* (Ottawa: Royal Commission, 1939);
The Road to Nationhood: A Chronicle of Dominion-Provincial Relations (Toronto: Oxford University Press, 1946);
Scientists at War (Toronto & New York: Oxford University Press, 1950);
Canada at Work (Montreal: Provincial, 1953);
The Frontier & Canadian Letters (Toronto: Ryerson, 1957);
The Queen's Choice: A Story of Canada's Capital (Ottawa: Queen's Printer, 1961); also published as *Choix de la Reine: Etude sur la Capitale du Canada* (Ottawa: Queen's Printer, 1961);
Canada's Nuclear Story (Toronto: Clarke, Irwin, 1965);
While I Still Remember: A Personal Record (Toronto: Ryerson, 1968);
Newfoundland: The Road to Confederation (Ottawa: Information Canada, 1974);
National Research in Canada: The NRC, 1916-1966 (Toronto: Clarke, Irwin, 1978);
Prairie Symphony (Ottawa: Borealis, 1978);
Literary Friends (Ottawa: Borealis, 1980);
Homestead on the Range (Ottawa: Borealis, 1982).

OTHER: Malvina Bolus, *Image of Canada,* introduction by Eggleston (Toronto: Ryerson, 1953);
"Frederick Philip Grove," in *Our Living Tradition: Seven Canadians,* edited by Claude T. Bissell (Toronto: University of Toronto Press, 1957), pp. 105-127;
The Green Gables Letters, from L. M. Montgomery to Ephraim Weber, 1905-1909, edited by Eggleston (Toronto: Ryerson, 1960).

Wilfrid Eggleston (photograph courtesy of Mrs. Wilfrid Eggleston)

SELECTED PERIODICAL PUBLICATIONS UNCOLLECTED: "Press Censorship," *Canadian Journal of Economics and Political Science,* 7 (August 1941): 313-323;
"Canadians and Canadian Books," *Queen's Quarterly,* 52 (Summer 1945): 208-213;
"Prairie Irrigation Plan Will Save Millions," *Saturday Night,* 23 August 1947, p. 7;
"Amending the Canadian Constitution," *Queen's Quarterly,* 56 (Winter 1949-1950): 576-585;
"Short Grass Prairies of Western Canada," *Canadian Geographical Journal,* 50 (April 1955): 134-145;
"Leaves from a Pressman's Log: Parliament and

the Press Gallery," *Queen's Quarterly*, 63 (Winter 1956-1957): 548-564;

"L'adaptation, par les Canadiens anglais, de leur heritage culturel," *Revue de l'Université Laval*, 16 (September 1961): 22-30.

"Once when I was a small boy," wrote Wilfrid Eggleston in his memoirs, *While I Still Remember* (1968), "I had a vivid dream in which I saw a row of books on a shelf and knew that they were mine, that I had written every one of them." When this dream finally came true, though, few were the pure literature he had hoped to write. But if his name is not widely known in literary circles, still he made a significant impact in the arena of journalism. Counting only his commissioned books, articles, and newsletters, his "bread and butter" writing, as he called it, would fill several shelves. For all his journalistic exploits, however, the fact remains that Eggleston would rather have been a poet. And the fountainhead for all his creative yearnings was his boyhood on the Alberta prairie.

Born 25 March 1901 in Lincoln, England, to Samuel and Ellen Cowham Eggleston, he moved with his family to a Canadian prairie homestead in what is now known as Palliser's Triangle. For all the grief this drought-ridden area gave his family, the virgin prairie also served to inspire poetic stirrings in the boy and a strong, lingering attachment in the man. The poems of *Prairie Moonlight and Other Lyrics* (1927), for example, celebrate love somewhat hesitantly (a fault of the novels as well, though Eggleston's marriage—to Magdalena Raskevich—proved lifelong and happy), praise and plead for the "divine gift" of poetry, and (with more success) evoke the landscapes of the prairie. But where Bliss Carman, his literary hero, sought to "paint the vision, not the view," Eggleston depicts only the view, though his reporter's instincts allowed him to depict it vividly and surely.

His career in journalism effectively began in 1926 when he was hired as a reporter by the *Toronto Star*, for which he later became the Ottawa correspondent before launching a career as a freelancer. In 1939 he accepted (with some misgivings) a post with the censorship bureau, ultimately rising to the directorship. After World War II he returned to the press gallery and also broadcast for the CBC; in 1947 he became the founding director of the School of Journalism at Carleton University, whose success owes much to his efforts and energy.

Cover for Eggleston's 1980 collection of reminiscences about his friendships with other Canadian writers

A charming, gregarious man, his openness and sincere interest in others quickly won him the trust and confidence of those with whom he came in contact; among his friends he counted prime ministers, Supreme Court jurists, and many of the leading literary figures of his day. These qualities complemented his diligence, responsibility, and talent for cutting directly to what was most essential in all he dealt with.

Eggleston's service with the Rowell-Sirois Royal Commission led to the publication in 1946 of *The Road to Nationhood: A Chronicle of Dominion-Provincial Relations*, which led to other commissioned work: *Scientists at War* (1950), *Canada at Work* (1953), *The Queen's Choice: A Story of Canada's Capital* (1961), *Canada's Nuclear Story* (1965), and *National Research in Canada: The NRC, 1916-1966* (1978). In the process he became one of Canada's leading journalistic popularizers of science and technology, with a gift for organizing complex information clearly, and for explanations that were precise without being overly technical. Most of his shorter works, though—articles and essays—dealt with politics and economics. As with much ephemeral journalism, interest in his reflections on the politics of the day has faded with interest in those politics; however, much of his output remains strikingly relevant, if largely unread, today.

Eggleston's literary output was small but noteworthy, especially so far as it reveals the man within the outward persona. His first novel, *The High Plains* (1938), is a fictionalized account of his childhood in Alberta; interwoven into the sensitively rendered story of his family and the land is a rather melodramatic subplot of murder and a woman scorned. Eggleston's surrogate in *The High Plains* wants to become an engineer, but his alter ego in *Prairie Symphony* (written a decade later but not published until 1978) burns with ambition to be a poet. Like Eggleston, he pays to have a book of his lyrics published before deciding he has more ambition, sentiment, and inspiration than he has talent, and while still a young man, he discovers that his abilities—if not his heart—

lie in journalism. As a novelist Eggleston remains a minor prairie realist, ranking well below Frederick Philip Grove and Sinclair Ross.

Of all his work, though, his literary criticism and editing will likely last the longest. In *The Green Gables Letters* (1960) Eggleston edited the letters of Lucy Maud Montgomery to his friend Ephraim Weber; *Literary Friends* (1980) recounts his experiences with Carman, Grove, Duncan Campbell Scott, Charles G. D. Roberts, and others. His most important contribution, however, is *The Frontier & Canadian Letters* (1957). A cohesive study in the tradition of Archibald MacMechan's *Headwaters of Canadian Literature* (1924), the book is a "reconnaissance," not an "assault." Its structural metaphor is botanical, and the inquiry devoutly follows the logic of science: what conditions, it asks, produce the "flower" of belles lettres? In 1982 the Alberta Writers' Guild established the Wilfrid Eggleston Award for nonfiction; nevertheless, whatever his contributions, whatever his talents, his heart clearly lay (to quote a youthful lyric) in "The hills, still golden in the sun/Where romance lurks, and poetry/Will rise when day's dull prose is done."

Hubert Evans
(9 May 1892-17 June 1986)

Catherine McLay
University of Calgary

BOOKS: *Forest Friends: Stories of Animals, Fish, and Birds West of the Rockies* (Philadelphia: Judson, 1926);

The New Front Line (Toronto: Macmillan, 1927);

Derry, Airedale of the Frontier (New York: Dodd, Mead, 1928);

Derry's Partner (New York: Dodd, Mead, 1929);

The Silent Call (New York: Dodd, Mead, 1930);

Derry of Totem Creek (New York: Dodd, Mead, 1930);

North to the Unknown: The Achievements and Adventures of David Thompson (New York: Dodd, Mead, 1949; Toronto: McClelland & Stewart, 1949);

Mist on the River (Toronto: Copp, Clark, 1954);

Mountain Dog (Philadelphia: Westminster, 1956); republished as *Son of the Salmon People* (Madeira Park, B.C.: Harbour, 1981);

Whittlings (Madeira Park, B.C.: Harbour, 1976);

Endings (Madeira Park, B.C.: Harbour, 1978);

O Time in Your Flight! (Madeira Park, B.C.: Harbour, 1979);

Mostly Coast People (Madeira Park, B.C.: Harbour, 1982).

RADIO: "A Miracle at Christmas," CBC, 26 December 1940;

"None So Blind," *Half-Hour with Mr. Jones*, CBC, 22 January 1942;

"The Way to a Man's Heart," *Vancouver Theatre*, CBC, 28 January 1955;

"A Gift at Parting," *Vancouver Theatre*, CBC, 4 February 1955;

"Men with Vision," *Vancouver Theatre*, CBC, 13 May 1955;

"Like Father, Like Son," *Vancouver Theatre*, CBC, 20 January 1956;

"Local and Personal," *Vancouver Theatre*, CBC, 27 April 1956;

"Ebb Tide," *Summer Fallow*, CBC, 18 June 1956;

"Grapevine," *Point Counterpoint*, CBC, 20 July 1956;

"They Never Yield," *Summer Fallow*, CBC, 20 August 1956;

Hubert Evans (photograph by Myrtle Hardy)

"Home for Christmas," *Vancouver Theatre*, CBC, 21 December 1956;

"Mist on the River," *Summer Stage*, CBC, 1960;

"Rory Changes Masters," *Magic Hinges*, CBC, 1960;

"O Time in Your Flight," *Book Time*, CBC, 1985.

Hubert Evans was a writer for most of his ninety-four years. He described himself as "a man who chose a varied life mostly outdoors, loved it and wanted to write about it." His classic novel *Mist on the River* (1954) William H. New has called "an historic document as much as a work of art." And for his last novel, *O Time in*

108

Your Flight! (1979), Margaret Laurence lovingly titled him "the elder of our tribe."

Evans was born in 1892 in Vankleek Hill, Ontario, and grew up in Galt near the Mohawk Reserve. He left school early to work on the *Galt Reporter* and in 1910 moved to Toronto as a reporter, first with the *Mail and Empire* and then with *Toronto World*. He enlisted in the Canadian army in 1915 and served overseas for two and a half years. After demobilization he returned to the *World* for a brief time, then for a year earned a living trapping in northern British Columbia. There he also began writing. After his marriage in 1920 to Anna Winter, a teacher he knew in Galt, he settled in British Columbia.

For the next several years Evans was employed by the Provincial Hatcheries, first in the northern Skeena area and later near Vancouver. In 1927 he built a home in Roberts Creek, and from then on he worked primarily as a writer. His first book, *Forest Friends* (1926), is a collection of sketches of animals and birds written for a newspaper column. In the tradition of Charles G. D. Roberts, Ernest Thompson Seton, and Jack London, he makes heroes of his subjects but describes them in their own habitat and with their own manners. His first adult novel, *The New Front Line* (1927), is largely autobiographical and recounts the process followed by one ex-soldier in choosing a career and a wife on the frontier of northern British Columbia. In the next three years Evans wrote three juvenile books: *Derry, Airedale of the Frontier* (1928), *Derry's Partner* (1929), and *Derry of Totem Creek* (1930). Set again in the North, they are episodic but fast-paced adventures loosely connected by the hero Ed Sibley and his dog, dramatizing their conflicts with the wilderness, wild animals, and assorted characters good and evil.

In the 1920s and 1930s Evans published two hundred stories in American and Canadian magazines, including *Saturday Night, Maclean's,* and the *Canadian Magazine;* he also wrote sixty serials and several plays for CBC radio. *The Silent Call* (1930), published the same year as *Derry of Totem Creek,* brings together fifteen stories of animals, fish, birds, and also human characters, both white and Indian. During the Depression Evans worked in commercial fishing, log-scaling, and beachcombing, although he said writing was his "cash crop." In 1945 the Evanses moved north, again to the Skeena country, where Anna Evans taught in one-room Indian schools. Here Evans wrote *North to the Unknown* (1949), a fictionalized

biography of the explorer David Thompson (1770-1857). Intended for boys, it is an account of Thompson's early career drawn from a contemporary study and from Thompson's diaries. Although it is exciting and vivid in its description and characterization, the book has been criticized for historical inaccuracy.

In the Skeena country Evans also wrote *Mist on the River*, a novel of the Gitkshan Indians whom Evans knew personally. Cy Pitt, the protagonist, is caught between the attractions of the white world as represented by Prince Rupert and Vancouver and the tribal traditions of the Indians' inland village. His sister June chooses the white world, and her future seems more optimistic than that of their cousin Dot, who survives by prostitution. But while Cy envies June her freedom, his marriage to Miriam, daughter of the old chief, Paul, binds him to the past and the local. The conflict is dramatized in the fate of Dot's boy, Steve, who dies because his grandfather will not allow him to be treated with the medicine of the white man. The death of Paul suggests that Cy, as the new chief, may be able to preserve the best of the old and reconcile it with the best of the new. While it simplifies the issues and stereotypes some of the secondary characters, the novel successfully dramatizes the conflict of cultures and creates central characters whose tensions, disappointments, and victories are memorable. *Mist on the River* has been commended by the anthropologist Harry Hawthorne for its accuracy in depicting native characters and customs, and a reviewer for the Vancouver newspaper *Indian Voice* remarked that the author "fully grasps the tragic problems of the fight of the Native Canadians. . . . Only great love could have made this possible." For many years the novel was out of print. Its republication by McClelland and Stewart in 1973 marks a renewed interest in Evans's themes and in his attempt to write from a native viewpoint.

In his next juvenile novel, *Mountain Dog* (1956), Evans returns to the setting he used in *Mist on the River* and to a similar theme. Hal Harrigan, like Cy an Indian, is more successful than Cy. Educated in Vancouver and planning to study wildlife management, he defeats the plans of an exploiter, a sawmill owner who attempts to destroy the community, and ensures the safety of both the salmon run and his people. Like the other juvenile novels, the book is melodramatic and separates heroes (and their dogs) from villains. But interest in the theme Evans treats has

Dust jacket for Evans's 1954 novel, a dramatization of the conflict between white and Indian cultures

grown in recent years, and the 1981 republication of the novel as *Son of the Salmon People* may signal a new popularity for Evans.

After Anna Evans died in 1960, Evans did not write for many years. In the 1970s and early 1980s he published three collections of poetry, *Whittlings* (1976), *Endings* (1978), and *Mostly Coast People* (1982), and an adult novel, *O Time in Your Flight!* (1979). In the introduction to *Whittlings* Evans describes his poems as "winnowings of a long life," and Earle Birney called them "outstanding for a man of any age." The novel is basically autobiographical, describing southwestern Ontario in 1899 as seen through the eyes of the boy Gilbert Egan. It recounts such historic events as the celebrations of the ending of the Boer War and of New Year's Eve at the turn of the century, side by side with vivid details of everyday living in that time and, recalling the works of W. O.

Mitchell, the universal joys, sorrows, dreams, and humiliations of the child's world. As George Woodcock has said, the novel traces the childhood not only of a boy but of Canada as well. At the time of his death Evans was working on a companion novel, set in British Columbia from 1900 to 1930.

In the later years of his writing career Hubert Evans received critical attention for his poetry and his last novel. He was awarded an honorary doctorate by Simon Fraser University in 1984 in a special ceremony at his home in Roberts Creek. His most significant work remains *Mist on the River*, which Silver Donald Cameron has called "a good man's passionate account of another's pain." Evans wrote, he once remarked, "to please myself and no one else." Yet his works seem remarkably contemporary, for he touches on some central concerns of the 1970s and 1980s: the need for preservation of wildlife and the environment and an understanding of the culture of the Indian people. For this artistic and emotional emphasis he will be remembered.

Interview:

Alan Twigg, "Why to Write," in his *For Openers: Conversations with 24 Canadian Writers* (Madeira Park, B.C.: Harbour, 1981), pp. 253-259.

Biography:

Alan Twigg, *Hubert Evans: The First Ninety-Three Years* (Madeira Park, B.C.: Harbour, 1985).

References:

Silver Donald Cameron, "After Seventy Years in

the Writing Game," *Saturday Night*, 94 (November 1979): 46-47;

Audrey Grescoe, "A Partnership with Time," *Maclean's*, 92 (3 December 1979): 6-8;

Edith Iglauer, "The Unsinkable Hubert Evans," *Today* (20 December 1980): 16-18;

William H. New, Introduction to Evans's *Mist on the River* (Toronto: McClelland & Stewart, 1973).

Papers:

Evans's papers are at the University of British Columbia Library.

Albert Ferland
(23 August 1872-9 November 1943)

Maurice Lebel
Laval University

BOOKS: *Mélodies poétiques* (Montreal: Bédard, 1893);

La Consolatrice, as B. de Flandre (Montreal: Poirier, Bessette, 1898);

Femmes rêvées: Pour lire à la femme aimée (Montreal: Privately printed, 1899); republished, with preface by Louis Fréchette (Montreal: Privately printed, 1904);

Le Canada chanté, 5 volumes: I, *Les Horizons* (Montreal: Déom, 1908); II, *Le Terroir* (Montreal: Déom, 1909); III, *L'Ame des bois* (Montreal: Granger, 1909); IV, *La Fête du Christ à Ville-Marie* (Montreal: Granger, 1910); V, *Montréal, Ma Ville natale* (Montreal: Jules Ferland, 1946).

Albert Ferland, son of Alfred and Joséphine Hogue Ferland, was born on 23 August 1872 in the oldest district of Montreal, the area that would one day be called simply "The Parish," rich in history, its buildings dating from the ancien régime. Born into the midst of these surroundings, he had the past in his blood, so to speak. He spent his childhood in Montreal, close to Mount Royal—which he saw as *his* mountain—and from there he looked off toward his first hori-

zons: the hills of Beloeil, Rougemont, and Saint-Bruno. For five years, from 1879 to 1884, he lived in the nearby Lac Simon (Labelle) area, in the heart of the Laurentian Hills; his father, a modestly successful industrialist, had decided to install his large family there in the open country on the edge of an Indian reserve. At the age of twelve Ferland returned with his family to Montreal, and he lived there for the rest of his life. But this born-again city-dweller was marked forever by his stay at Lac Simon. It was there that he became familiar with the wilderness, the forest, the Laurentians, and the Indians—"les Sauvages." The poetry he later wrote is filled with references to the world he first encountered as a youth: the world of nature, flowers, wooded hills, and the native peoples. In the city he always considered himself a country person in exile, an émigré from the heartland.

Once returned to Montreal, Ferland continued to attend the parish school. But he learned especially from his parents. His father wished at all costs to inculcate in him a strong business sense—though even the words *business* and *commerce* irritated the adolescent Ferland—and to encourage in him a taste for independent work. From his

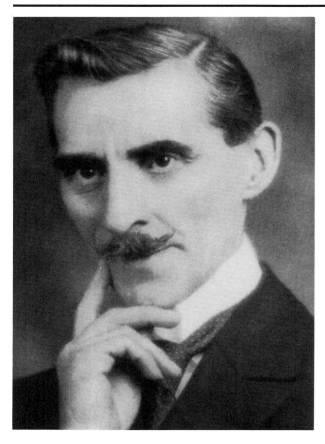

Albert Ferland

mother he inherited his subtlety, his quick spirit, his love of silence, solitude, and the interior life, and his modesty and shyness.

Because he and his father were so opposite, he had to hide himself away in order to write his poems. Self-taught in poetry, as he would be in drawing, he was a dreamer, a poet of the soul, a discriminating observer, yet he also quickly became a great help to his parents. Over the course of time he also worked successively in a grocery store, in a lawyer's office, and at Beauchemin printers before becoming an art teacher, first offering evening courses and then opening his own studio–all in the old quarter of Montreal. Today on the front of that studio building, at the corner of Rue Notre-Dame and Rue Saint-Gabriel, there is a plaque that reads "Albert Ferland, Poète et Artiste."

At the age of sixteen Ferland published his first poems in *Le Samedi* and *Le Monde Illustré*. When he was twenty his first book of verse, *Mélodies poétiques* (1893), appeared; and at twenty-two he married Eugénie Chapleau and set up his own home. He and his wife had eight children.

In 1895, at twenty-three, he participated in the setting up of the Ecole Littéraire de Montréal, in which he served for some time as secretary and president, and he published the single issue of the *Revue de l'Art* (now untraceable). A fourteen-page poem called *La Consolatrice* (The Comforter) appeared in 1898; attributed to Ferland because the pseudonym (B. de Flandre) is an anagram of his name, it is dedicated to the journalist Françoise and is a love poem cast as a dialogue between the poet and his muse. In 1899, at twenty-seven, he published his second collection of poems, *Femmes rêvées: Pour lire à la femme aimée* (Imagined Women: To Read to One's Lover). The fourth volume of *Le Canada chanté* (Canada in Song), his major work, was completed in 1910. The same year, while working in his studio as a printer, bookbinder, draftsman, and picture-framer, he was offered a job as a designer for the General Post Office in Montreal. He worked at this position until his death on 9 November 1943. His last work, *Montréal, Ma Ville natale* (Montreal, My Native City), volume 5 of *Le Canada chanté*, appeared three years later.

Mélodies poétiques, with its romantic title, comprises the works the young poet composed between the ages of fifteen and twenty, when Ferland was being most influenced by the French poets of the nineteenth century. To read several of the poems–for example, "L'automne," "Vers l'Idéal," "Voix intérieures," "Mélancolies," and "Fibres du coeur" (Autumn, Toward the Ideal, Interior Voices, Melancholy, and Heartstrings)–is to find that their gallantries, their religious sensibility, their morose thoughts, and their fantasy are sometimes awkwardly contrived.

"Alternative érotique" (Erotic Option) and "Amour divinisé" (Love Made Divine) begin the second collection, *Femmes rêvées*. This work was reissued in 1904, prepared and introduced by Louis Fréchette and illustrated by Ferland and Georges Delfosse. As the extended title, *Pour lire à la femme aimée*, suggests, this book is the work of a decadent poet amusing himself by writing a pleasant pastiche of the masters of the École Littéraire de Montréal; nevertheless, it reveals at the same time the poet's artistic temperament, torn as it was between the ideal and the real. Such poems as "Adoration," "Chants d'amour," "Exaltation," "Litanies à la femme," and "Préceptes d'amour" (Adoration, Songs of Love, Exaltation, Litanies to One's Woman, and Precepts of Love) are among the better works in the collection. But it is because the whole volume is a

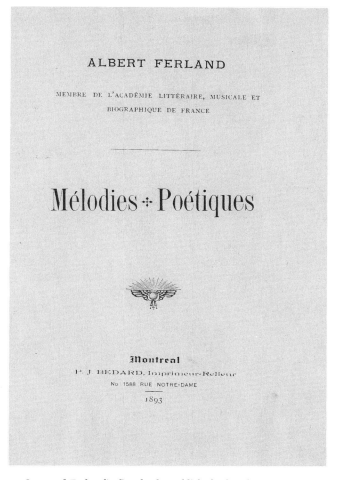

ALBERT FERLAND

MEMBRE DE L'ACADÉMIE LITTÉRAIRE, MUSICALE ET
BIOGRAPHIQUE DE FRANCE

Mélodies ⁘ Poétiques

Montreal
P. J. BEDARD, Imprimeur-Relieur
No 1588 RUE NOTRE-DAME
1893

Cover of Ferland's first book, published when he was twenty

work of *art* that its publication marks an important date in the history of Canadian poetry.

Le Canada chanté, however, is literarily superior to both the preceding collections. Its first four volumes appeared between 1908 and 1910 in the form of separate pamphlets, of which the first three were illustrated by the author. Ferland shows himself here to be a watercolorist and a naturalist of substantial quality. The poems, like the pictures, evoke Lac Simon and the rugged, picturesque mountains of northern Quebec. Finding the city to be noisy and inhumane, he set himself the task of reconstructing the Lac Simon world in these words at the start of volume 1: "Va, Barde primitif des vierges Laurentides" (Go, primitive Bard of the virgin Laurentians). Nonetheless he rises above mere nostalgia by describing the wilderness, the trees, and the flowers very precisely. Volume 3, *L'Ame des bois* (The Spirit of the

Woods), for example, abounds with excellent poems, and Ferland recognizes here only three masters: God, Nature, and Truth. A fervent believer, he shows himself to be profoundly religious in volume 4, *La Fête du Christ à Ville-Marie* (Christ's Birthday in Ville-Marie), and his approach to his subject recalls the work of Francis Jammes or Charles Peguy.

From 1910 until 1943 he published no more volumes; however, he was writing the poems that would appear in volume 5, *Montréal, Ma Ville natale*, which was published posthumously in 1946 thanks to the filial devotion of Ferland's son Jules. A few poems were also scattered among newspapers and journals such as *Le Canada Français* and the *Mémoires* of the Royal Society of Canada. *Montréal, Ma Ville natale* includes fifty-three poems, of which about forty are devoted to describing a Montreal that has today disappeared; Mount Royal, with its maple trees, its

113

birches, its apple trees, and its aspens, occupies pride of place.

A member of the École Littéraire de Montréal, the Montreal Historical Society, the Society of Quebec Poets, and the Royal Society of Canada, Albert Ferland left behind a relatively small body of poetry, but it is of high quality. Committed, sincere, serious, precise, extremely conscientious (some would say meticulous), obsessed by his devotion to formal perfection (and committed just as rigorously to his fidelity to himself), Ferland had a horror of dilettantism. He eschewed easy poetry, long discussions, and wordiness. During the thirty years from 1910 to 1940 he read and absorbed the classics, devouring the books in the Montreal Public Library and little by little assembling his own library. And yet, as well as being occupied at the same time by the raising of his eight children as best he could, and by bringing fame and prosperity to his studio, he suc-ceeded in composing numerous poems, the best of his career, during these later years. By then he had become the master of his art and attained his full maturity as a writer. True to himself, he can be compared readily with no other poet. But scholars have yet to assemble his uncollected works—which would fill two substantial volumes—and to prepare, in conjunction with the poems that have already appeared in book form, a solid critical edition of all his writings. It is a task that needs to be done. For it would be in this form only that one could finally treat Ferland with justice—he is altogether too little known—and to grant him his true place in the history of Quebec poetry.

Reference:
Soeur Jeanne Leber (Irène Branchaud), "Albert Ferland: l'homme et l'oeuvre," D. ès L. dissertation, University of Ottawa, 1965.

Françoise
(Robertine Barry)

(26 February 1863-7 January 1910)

Mary Jean Green
Dartmouth College

BOOKS: *Fleurs champêtres* (Montreal: Desaulniers, 1895);
Chroniques du lundi (Montreal, 1900);
Fleurs champêtres et Méprise, edited by Gilles Lamontagne (Montreal: Fides, 1984).

PLAY PRODUCTION: *Méprise,* Montreal, 7 November 1905.

OTHER: "Les Femmes canadiennes dans la littérature," in *Les Femmes du Canada: Leur vie et leurs œuvres* (Montreal: Conseil National des Femmes du Canada, 1900).

Robertine Barry, known to her public under the pseudonym Françoise, was Quebec's first woman journalist. The author of her own weekly column, she was also responsible for the first women's page in a Quebec newspaper. Barry was one of only a handful of Quebec women writers at the end of the nineteenth century, although her literary works are limited to a collection of sketches on rural life and customs, *Fleurs champêtres* (Rustic Flowers, 1895), and a short play, *Méprise* (Misunderstanding, produced in 1905). Her influence on Quebec literature, however, extended beyond her own literary production because of her support of women's education and literary culture in her columns and later in her own bimonthly paper, *Le Journal de Françoise,* a forerunner of the modern women's magazine.

Robertine Barry was born in L'Isle-Verte on 26 February 1863 to John Edmund Barry, who had emigrated from Ireland in 1854, and Aglaé Rouleau Barry. She received her education in a convent at Trois-Pistoles and later at the Ursuline convent in Quebec City. In 1891 Barry began contributing her own weekly column to the Montreal paper *La Patrie.* Her "Chronique du lundi" (Monday Chronicle) was the first regularly appearing column written by a woman in Quebec newspa-

Françoise (Robertine Barry)

per history. A collection of columns from the years 1891 to 1895 was published in book form in 1900. In 1897 Barry inaugurated the women's page, "Le Coin de Fanchette" (Fanchette's Corner), in *La Patrie.*

The collection of short fictional pieces *Fleurs champêtres* appeared in 1895. These sketches are remarkable for their detailed and sometimes brutally honest portrayal of rural life and language, as well as for the literary and ideological controversy they provoked. Some of the stories are little more than descriptions of village customs; others are governed by a narrative line, which often concerns love and marriage. They are unified by their focus on the lives of women, and in some cases the author does not attempt to mask harsh realities of abuse and exploitation, despite the potential conflict with the idealized vision of country life promoted at the time by Quebec's clerical elite.

Whether because of this too-realistic vision or Barry's association with the liberal views of *La Patrie*, *Fleurs champêtres* became the focus of an attack by the conservative critic Jules-Paul Tardivel, editor of *La Vérité*. In the 14 June 1895 issue he accused the book of giving "une fausse idée de notre classe agricole" (a false idea of our agricultural class), particularly by having "mis à peu près entièrement de côté la note religieuse" (almost entirely put aside the religious aspect). He said that Barry had "Rousseauistic" attitudes, a charge that became a major issue in the ensuing debate. Barry replied in her "Chronique du lundi" (*La Patrie*, 17 June 1895) that she had never read Rousseau; Joséphine Marchand-Dandurand proclaimed the high moral aims of *Fleurs champêtres* in her own magazine, *Le Coin du feu;* and Louis Fréchette delivered a stinging attack on Tardivel and a lengthy analysis of Rousseau in *La Patrie* (29 June 1895).

In 1900 Barry contributed to a document on Canadian women prepared for distribution at the Paris Exposition by the National Council of Women of Canada. She attended the exposition as an official Canadian representative and participated in the International Congress of Women held at the same time. While in Paris, she was named a member of the Lyceum, a club for women writers, and made many contacts in the French literary world. Notable among them was the feminist Juliette Adam, founder of *La Nouvelle Revue*.

When Barry founded *Le Journal de Françoise* in 1902, she was able to cite Adam as a supporter and contributor, along with the queen of Romania, who wrote under the name Carmen Sylva. Although Barry's paper included many of the features of a modern women's magazine, the primary aim of the periodical was to improve the cultural level of Quebec women by bringing them into contact with contemporary French and Canadian writers, especially women.

Although Barry never married, she inspired the love of the poet Emile Nelligan, sixteen years her junior and the son of one of her friends. His poem "Rêve d'artiste" (The Artist's Dream) is dedicated to her and reflects his feelings, as much as the sonnet "A une femme détestée" (To a Detested Woman) seems to be a response to her rejection of him. Barry is also credited with having inspired Nelligan's poems "Beauté cruelle" (Cruel Beauty), "Le Vent, le triste vent de l'automne" (The Wind, the Sad Autumn Wind), and "La Vierge noire" (The Black Virgin).

Always active in charitable and patriotic enterprises, Barry in 1895 organized a public campaign to preserve the bell from the old French fort of Louisbourg. Although she stopped short of advocating women's suffrage, she defended women's right to work outside the home and gain access to the professions.

Ceasing publication of *Le Journal de Françoise* in 1909, Barry worked as an inspector of women workers in industry. She died in Montreal the following year, on 7 January 1910.

References:

Georges Bellerive, *Brèves Apologies de nos auteurs féminins* (Quebec: Garneau, 1920), pp. 30-35;

Aurélien Boivin and Kenneth Landry, "Françoise et Madeleine, pionnières du journalisme féminin au Québec," *Voix et Images*, 4 (December 1978): 233-243;

Gilles Lamontagne, Introduction to Françoise's *Fleurs champêtres et Méprise* (Montreal: Fides, 1984), pp. 13-24;

Louise Turgeon (pseudonym: Renée des Ormes), *Robertine Barry. En littérature: Françoise. Pionnière du journalisme féminin au Canada. 1863-1910* (Quebec: Action Sociale, 1949).

John Murray Gibbon

(12 April 1875-2 July 1952)

Terrence Craig
Mount Allison University

BOOKS: *Ballads of B.C.* (Toronto: Thompson, n.d.);

Scots in Canada: A History of the Settlement of the Dominion from the Earliest Days to the Present (Toronto: Musson, 1911; London: Paul, Trench, Trübner, 1911);

Hearts and Faces (Toronto: Gundy/London & New York: Lane, 1916);

Drums Afar: An International Romance (Toronto: Gundy/London & New York: Lane, 1918);

A Canadian Calendar (Ste. Anne de Bellevue, Que.: Canadian Bookman, 1919);

The Conquering Hero (London & New York: Lane, 1920);

Pagan Love (Toronto: McClelland & Stewart, 1922; New York: Doran, 1922);

Eyes of a Gypsy (Toronto: Macmillan, 1926; London: Methuen, 1926);

The Order of Good Cheer: From the French Version of Louvigny de Montigny; Canadian Historical Ballad Opera of the First Settlers in Canada (Toronto: Dent, 1929);

Prince Charlie and Flora: A Ballad Opera (Toronto: Dent, 1929);

Melody and the Lyric from Chaucer to the Cavaliers (London & Toronto: Dent/New York: Dutton, 1930);

Magic of Melody (London & Toronto: Dent, 1933; New York: Stokes, 1933);

Steel of Empire: The Romantic History of the Canadian Pacific, The Northwest Passage of Today (Toronto: McClelland & Stewart, 1935; Indianapolis & New York: Bobbs-Merrill, 1935; London: Rich & Cowan, 1935); republished as *The Romantic History of the Canadian Pacific, The Northwest Passage of Today* (Toronto: McClelland & Stewart, 1935; New York: Tudor, 1937);

The Coureur de Bois and His Birthright (Ottawa: Royal Society of Canada, 1936);

Northland Songs, No. 1 (Toronto: Thompson, 1936); revised as *Northland Songs, Group "A"-"D"* (Toronto: Thompson/New York: Fischer, 1938);

John Murray Gibbon

The Man Comes Down from the Moon: Musical Playlet Based on "Northland Songs" (Toronto: Thompson, 1937);

Canadian Mosaic: The Making of a Northern Nation (Toronto: McClelland & Stewart, 1938; New York: Dodd, 1938);

New World Ballads (Toronto: Ryerson, 1939);

Canada in Song (Toronto: Thompson, 1941);

The New Canadian Loyalists (Toronto: Macmillan, 1941);

Pioneer Songs of Canada (Toronto: Thompson, 1941);

Brahms and Schubert Songs Transplanted (Toronto: Thompson, 1944);

Our Old Montreal (Toronto: McClelland & Stewart, 1947);

Three Centuries of Canadian Nursing, by Gibbon and Mary S. Mathewson (Toronto: Macmillan, 1947);

The Victorian Order of Nurses for Canada: 50th Anniversary, 1897-1947 (Montreal: Southam, 1947);

Canadian Cadences (Toronto: Ryerson, 1949);

New Colour for the Canadian Mosaic: The Displaced Persons (Toronto: McClelland & Stewart, 1951);

The Romance of the Canadian Canoe (Toronto: Ryerson, 1951);

Time and Tide in the Atlantic Provinces, by Gibbon and Leo Cox (Sackville, N.B.: Enamel and Heating Products, 1952).

OTHER: *Old King Cole (True Annals of Fairyland),* edited by Gibbon (London: Dent, 1901); republished as *The True Annals of Fairyland in the Reign of King Cole* (London: Dent/New York: Dutton, 1909);

Canadian Folk Songs (Old and New), edited and translated by Gibbon (London & Toronto: Dent, 1927; revised and enlarged, 1949);

French Canadian Folk Songs; French and English Texts, translated by Gibbon (Boston: Boston Music, 1928);

Adam de la Halle, *The Play of Robin and Marian (Le Jeu de Robin et Marian),* translated by Gibbon (Boston: Birchard, 1928);

Ernest MacMillan, ed., *Vingt-et-une Chansons Canadiennes,* translated, with an introduction, by Gibbon (Oakville, Ont.: Harris, 1928);

Songs of the Commonwealth: Songs of the British Empire Specially Selected for Use in Schools, edited by Gibbon and G. Roy Fenwick (Toronto: Thompson, 1945).

SELECTED PERIODICAL PUBLICATIONS
UNCOLLECTED: "The Foreign Born," *Queen's Quarterly,* 27, no. 4 (1920): 331-351;

"Radio as a Fine Art," *Canadian Forum,* 11 (March 1931): 212-214;

"Hail and Farewell," *Canadian Poetry Magazine,* 5 (September 1940): 23;

"Secular Bible for a New Canada," *Proceedings and Transactions of the Royal Society of Canada,* third series, 36, no. 2 (1942): 93-100;

"Canada's Million and More Needlecraft Workers," *Canadian Geographical Journal,* 26 (March 1943): 144-155;

"Canadian Handicrafts Old and New," *Canadian Geographical Journal,* 26 (March 1943): 130-143;

"Handicraft Among the Anglo-Canadians," *Culture,* 4 (March 1943): 44-47;

"Women as Folk-song Authors," *Proceedings and Transactions of the Royal Society of Canada,* third series, 41, no 2 (1947): 47-51;

"Folk-song and Feudalism," *Proceedings and Transactions of the Royal Society of Canada,* third series, 42, no. 2 (1948): 73-84;

"Contributions of Austro-German Music to Canadian Culture," *Proceedings and Transactions of the Royal Society of Canada,* third series, 43, no. 2 (1949): 57-71;

"Orkneymen in Canada," *Proceedings and Transactions of the Royal Society of Canada,* third series, 44, no. 2 (1950): 47-59.

John Murray Gibbon described himself as a publicist, and although the term falls short of encompassing all his published work, it does fit much of it. Between 1907 and 1945 he worked as a publicity agent for the Canadian Pacific Railway, eventually writing the history of the company, *Steel of Empire* (1935). Yet he also published verse, children's stories, romantic novels, and semi-sociological surveys of new immigrants to Canada. His writing career was long, eclectic, and prolific and saw him elected the founding president of the Canadian Authors' Association in 1921 and a fellow of the Royal Society of Canada in 1922. Despite these achievements, as well as an honorary LL.D. from the University of Montreal, a Lorne Pierce Gold Medal from the Royal Society, a Prix David from the province of Quebec, and a Governor General's Award for nonfiction, Gibbon has remained a minor figure in Canadian literature.

Gibbon was born 12 April 1875 at Udeweller, Ceylon, the son of William Duff and Katherine Murray Gibbon. His father, a wealthy tea planter, had been knighted for his contribution to the administration of the island. The young John Murray was sent to his father's birthplace, Aberdeen, Scotland, for his schooling, attending Gordon's College and King's College there before going on to Christ Church College, Oxford, where he distinguished himself, graduating with first-class honors. Apparently contemplating an academic career, he went on for further

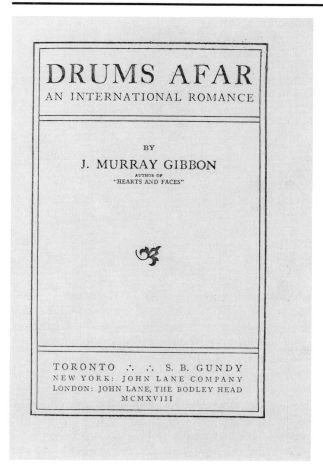

DRUMS AFAR

AN INTERNATIONAL ROMANCE

BY

J. MURRAY GIBBON

AUTHOR OF
"HEARTS AND FACES"

TORONTO ∴ ∴ S. B. GUNDY
NEW YORK: JOHN LANE COMPANY
LONDON: JOHN LANE, THE BODLEY HEAD
MCMXVIII

Title page for the Canadian edition of Gibbon's second novel, a semiautobiographical work about a young man who studies at Oxford, travels in Germany, and works as a journalist in London and Chicago during the years preceding World War I

studies at the University of Göttingen in Germany. However, his interest in journalism, stirred by undergraduate contributions at Oxford, displaced his academic ambitions, and–although he spent some time studying art in London and Paris after his marriage to Anne Fox in 1900–he turned to London's magazines to begin his professional writing career. Gibbon had worked his way up to the position of editor-in-chief of *Black and White* by 1907, when his literary style and his fluency in German earned him the position of the European publicity agent for the Canadian Pacific Railway. Spreading propaganda about the Canadian West, Gibbon traveled widely in eastern and northern Europe to recruit suitable immigrants for the colonization scheme of the C.P.R. He was so successful at this job that he was brought to Montreal in 1913 as the general publicity agent for the company, a position he retained until he retired in 1945.

Aware of Marius Barbeau's work in collecting folk material across Canada, Gibbon represented the C.P.R. in organizing fourteen folk festivals at company hotels across Canada, beginning in 1927 and ending in the Depression in 1930. Three of these were staged at the Chateau Frontenac in Quebec City, with the organizational help of Barbeau, and concentrated on showcasing French-Canadian culture. They included original compositions by prominent musicians such as Healey Willan and Alfred LaLiberté. Three Highland gatherings of Scottish Canadians were staged at Banff, Alberta, while festivals for European immigrants were held elsewhere in the prairie provinces. With his experiences of living and traveling in Europe and his knowledge of immigration both personally and professionally, Gibbon seemed to be in a uniquely qualified position to speak on the controversial issues of immigration, assimilation, and nationalism, and he wrote increasingly in the 1930s about the need for ethnic groups to respect each other's contributions to Canada, opposing any melting-pot future for the nation. Just before and during World War II he produced two books affirming the loyalty of New Canadians for Canada and reaffirming his support for what would later be called multiculturalism (*Canadian Mosaic: The Making of a Northern Nation*, 1938, and *The New Canadian Loyalists*, 1941).

Gibbon's nonfiction, while at times flagrantly ebullient in the style of a well-educated public-relations writer, is superior to his fiction, which can be unoriginal and mediocre. His five novels are embarrassingly romantic; he was unable to match the appeal of his contemporary, Ralph Connor, because he presented no clear value system in place of Connor's "red-blooded Christianity." Instead he provided his fiction with surprisingly racist characters, often under the guise of eugenics. His sense of a declining Great Britain seems to have attracted him to a rising Canada as well as giving him a sense of racial bitterness that appears disagreeably in his fiction, most blatantly in *The Conquering Hero* (1920) but also in the semiautobiographical novel, *Drums Afar: An International Romance* (1918).

Gibbon died 2 July 1952 and was buried in Banff, where a memorial to him was unveiled at the Banff School of Fine Arts in August 1955. In attendance were Stoney Indians, who had honored him by installing him as a tribal member under the name of "Chief Man-of-Many-Sides," a sobriquet that well summarizes his life and work.

References:

Watson Kirkconnell, "John Murray Gibbon," *Proceedings and Transactions of the Royal Society of Canada,* third series, 47 (1953): 79-83;

Janet McNaughton, "John Murray Gibbon and the Inter-War Folk Festivals," *Canadian Folklore Canadien,* 3, no. 1 (1981): 67-73.

Rodolphe Girard

(24 April 1879-29 March 1956)

Valerie Raoul
University of British Columbia

BOOKS: *Florence: Légende historique, patriotique et nationale* (Montreal, 1900);

Mosaïque (Montreal: Déom, 1902);

Marie Calumet (Montreal, 1904); translated by Irène Currie (Montreal: Harvest House, 1976);

Rédemption (Montreal: Guertin, 1906);

L'Algonquine: Roman des jours héroïques du Canada sous la domination française (Montreal: La Patrie, 1910);

Contes de chez nous (Montreal, 1912);

Les Ailes cassées (Ottawa: Le Courrier Fédéral, 1921).

PLAY PRODUCTIONS: *Fleur de Lys,* Montreal, Théatre National, 1 December 1902;

Le Conscrit impérial, Montreal, Théatre National, 9 March 1903;

Le Doigt de la femme, Ottawa, French-Canadian Institute, 24 April 1907.

RADIO: *Les Ailes cassées,* Radio Canada, 1953.

Rodolphe Girard is important as the author of the first satirical novel in Quebec literature, *Marie Calumet* (1904), which aroused considerable controversy at the time of its appearance and is now considered one of the best works of fiction produced in Quebec in the first quarter of the twentieth century. Girard was born in Trois-Rivières on 24 April 1879, the son of Louis Girard, a grocer and customs officer, and Marie Trottier Girard. He completed his elementary education in Trois-Rivières with the Christian Brothers before moving in 1892 to Montreal, where he studied at the Académie Commerciale et Catholique and the Collège de Montréal. In 1899 he began work as a journalist for *La Patrie,* and the following year he was employed by *La Presse.*

His first published literary work was *Florence* (1900), which was serialized in *Le Monde illustré* (3 February-28 April 1900), bearing the subtitle *Légende historique du Canada* and illustrated by Georges Delfosse. The same year an extract appeared in *La Presse* (on 22 September), and the novel was subsequently published in an edition financed by borrowed money. This work, inspired by the rebellion of 1837, is now forgotten, as is *Mosaïque*–a collection of short stories and two plays (*Le Conscrit impérial* and *A la Conquête d'un baiser*)–which followed in 1902, the year after Girard's marriage to Régine Lefaivre. In 1902 another play by Girard was produced, *Fleur de Lys,* based on the story of Madeleine de Verchères, and *Le Conscrit impérial* was performed in 1903.

The first reference to *Marie Calumet* is found in *La Presse,* where it was announced on 30 May 1903 that "un de nos hommes de lettres" (one of our men of letters) was engaged in research on Marie Calumet, the heroine of a popular song, "dont l'histoire n'a jamais été écrite" (whose story has never been written down). According to the ribald song, Marie Calumet was a fat girl who married a village priest's hired man and ate so much at the wedding that she suffered a violent attack of diarrhea. The words of one version of this song are included in Irène Currie's 1976 translation of Girard's novel. *Marie Calumet,* for which the author became notorious, was published with illustrations by various artists and preceded by an ironic letter from Jean Richepin, explaining why he refused to write a preface to

Rodolphe Girard (drawing by Napolèon Savard)

housekeeper to the village priest, the curé Flavel. The depiction of Flavel and his less-than-exemplary friend, the curé Lefranc, represents a departure from the usual solemn respect in Quebec for religious institutions and figures. Marie and Suzon, Flavel's niece, provide a disturbing female presence at the presbytery. The amorous adventures of Narcisse (the curé's hired man) in pursuit of Marie, and the vengeful tactics of his rival, the verger Zéphirin, produce scenes of Rabelaisian hilarity. Even a ceremonial visit by the bishop culminates in Narcisse receiving on his head a chamber pot containing "la sainte pisse à Monseigneur," which Marie is considering bottling as holy water. Marie herself is a snuff-sniffing, larger-than-life character, dignified yet comical, capable of solving any problem, but also of forgetting to wear underwear the day she falls over in her new, fashionable crinoline. The story unfolds in a series of twenty tableaux, all but two of which occur in the village. Marie goes to Montreal to be photographed, a memorable outing which provides a point of reference to people outside the village community. The curé Flavel visits a friend in Lachine, incidentally shooting the rapids and there saving a man from drowning. The chapter describing this incident is much longer than the others and the style is sober, in contrast with the irreverent verve of the narration, the earthiness and humor of situation and dialogue throughout the rest of the novel. The modest heroism ascribed to the curé was not enough, however, to protect Girard from attack by the defenders of the Church.

On its publication *Marie Calumet* was roundly condemned by a reviewer for *La Croix* (14 February 1904): "Pour tout dire, à lire ce livre, il y aurait danger de perversion morale, esthétique et littéraire" (In short, reading this book is an exposure to the danger of moral, aesthetic and literary perversion). The commentator for *La Semaine religieuse* (8 February 1904) pronounced it impious and immoral and expressed horror that the author had dedicated this blasphemous work to his son. The archbishop of Montreal concurred with this negative judgment in a circular to the clergy, but clerical opposition did not prevent the novel from being an enormous success with the public (one thousand copies sold at once). Girard was nevertheless forced to leave *La Presse* and to move to Ottawa, where he became editor of *Le Temps* and accepted a position in 1905 as a translator for the secretary of state at the House of Commons, a position he held

such a controversial story, in spite of his admiration for its "langue grasse, savoureuse, fleurant le terroir" (rich, full-flavored language that smells of the soil).

Marie Calumet belongs to the subgenre *roman de terroir* (novel of the land), insofar as it deals with a peasant milieu and is set in the past, in a Quebec village of the 1860s. Yet Girard's portrayal of the inhabitants of the imaginary parish of Saint-Ildefonse (which he situates near Nicolet) also represents a distinct break with the traditional idealization of rustic life. Marie is

Drawing of Marie Calumet by Edmond-J. Massicotte for Girard's 1904 novel, and the cover for the first edition in English (1976; illustration by Moe Reinblatt; design by Yair Anavi)

until his retirement. His play *Le Doigt de la femme* (The Woman's Finger) was performed in Ottawa in 1907.

Girard published two more novels, *Rédemption* in 1906 and *L'Algonquine* in 1910. In the first, about Paspébiac fishermen in the early 1890s, Girard returns to the kind of sentimental melodrama represented by *Florence*. *L'Algonquine*, a love story set in seventeenth-century New France, appeared in *La Patrie* (30 April-3 June 1910) before being published in book form with the subtitle *Roman des jours héroïques du Canada sous la domination française* (A Novel of the Heroic Days of Canada under French Rule). It was also serialized in *Le Temps* (6 October-11 November 1910) and later in *Le Courrier fédéral* (9 November-8 February 1924) and *Le Droit* (18 July-27 August 1931). This popular expression of patriotic

fervor did not suffice to rehabilitate the author in the eyes of the Church. In 1908 he had sued the Catholic journal *La Vérité* for libel. Girard had founded in Ottawa a branch of the Alliance Française, an organization associated by some Church dignitaries with freemasonry; he was accused of supporting the latter, and therefore of being a heretic. He won his case in 1911, the year in which his wife died, leaving him with three young children. The following year he married Cécile Archambault and produced his final work of fiction, a collection of stories previously published in journals, entitled *Contes de chez nous* (Stories from Around Here). Girard wrote a total of 335 short stories throughout his life, as well as a series of autobiographical articles entitled "Souvenirs," which were also published in various reviews.

During World War I Girard distinguished himself in the Canadian army, attaining the rank of lieutenant-colonel, winning the Croix de Guerre, and becoming a chevalier in the Légion d'Honneur. After the war he wrote another play, *Les Ailes cassées* (The Broken Wings), which was to be performed at the Théatre Canadien in Montreal in 1921 but was apparently canceled at the last minute. His last play, *Le Sacrifice,* was published in *La Canadienne* in May 1923.

In 1941 Girard retired and moved back to Quebec, to live in Richelieu. Five years later Serge Brousseau published a new edition of *Marie Calumet,* with a preface by Girard's friend, Albert Laberge, the author of *La Scouine* (Bitter Bread). He proclaimed the originality of Girard's novel and praised its character portrayal, realism, and vivacity of style. It was, in his opinion, the best novel ever published in Canada. Laberge lamented the fact that histories of the French-Canadian novel failed to mention *Marie Calumet,* or dismissed it with brief comments. Several even refer to it as "mediocre" or "badly written": such was the influence of the Church's condemnation.

The novel received a flurry of critical attention when a new edition appeared in 1973 with a preface by Luc Lacoursière (included in Irène Currie's translation). The aspects which have been treated are primarily the language, the role of women, the attitude to the clergy, and the de-idealization of rural life. The 1979 paperback edition, part of the Fides "Bibliothèque Québécoise," includes a dossier on the background to the novel and critical reactions to it. In 1986 Madeleine Charlebois-Dirschauer published the first study of Girard's life and works, providing extensive documentation on his numerous journal articles as well as his work for the theater and the controversy surrounding *Marie Calumet.* The fact that the latter is one of the few early-twentieth-century Quebec novels that still arouses strong reactions in readers is a tribute to Girard's lasting impact.

References:

Gérard Bachert, "Le sentiment religieux dans le roman canadien-français," *Revue de l'Université Laval,* 9 (June 1955): 868-886, and 10 (Sept. 1955): 876-877;

Jean Blouin, "Notre premier roman humoristique ne fit pas rire du tout," *Perspectives,* 12 (28 March 1970): 20-24;

Madeleine Charlebois-Dirschauer, *Rodolphe Girard (1879-1956), sa vie, son oeuvre* (Montreal: Fides, 1986);

Madeleine Ducrocq-Poirier, *Le Roman canadien de langue française de 1860 à 1958* (Paris: Nizet, 1978), pp. 192-195, 759-762;

Jean-Pierre Duquette, "*Marie Calumet,*" in *Livres et Auteurs québécois* (1973), pp. 79-80;

Jacques Ferron, "*Marie Calumet,*" *Le Petit Journal,* 45 (22 March 1970): 75;

Romain Légaré, "Le Prêtre dans le roman canadien-français," *Culture,* March 1963, pp. 3-12;

Bernard Muddiman, "The Soirées of the Château de Ramezay," *Queen's Quarterly,* 20 (July-September 1912): 73-91;

Ben-Zion Shek, *Social Realism in the French-Canadian Novel* (Montreal: Harvest House, 1977), pp. 50-52;

Paul Wyczynski, *Le Roman canadien français* (Montreal: Fides, 1964), pp. 16-17.

Papers:

One unpublished manuscript, "Le Chien d'or," is at the Bibliothèque Nationale, Ministère des Affaires Culturelles, Quebec. A handwritten manuscript of *Marie Calumet* is in the public archives, Ottawa; a typed and corrected version and the manuscript of *Rédemption* are at the Centre for French-Canadian Civilisation, University of Ottawa.

Martin Allerdale Grainger

(17 November 1874-15 October 1941)

Carole Gerson
Simon Fraser University

BOOK: *Woodsmen of the West* (London: Arnold, 1908).

Through his various careers as Cambridge mathematics scholar, international adventurer, miner, logger, civil servant, and private businessman, Martin Allerdale Grainger was known as a brilliant, gregarious, and occasionally eccentric individual. His work of greatest historical significance is his contribution to the report of the Royal Commission of Enquiry on Timber and Forestry (1909-1910), which led to the passing of the Forestry Act of 1912 and the creation of the British Columbia Forest Service. His only substantial literary work is *Woodsmen of the West* (1908), a loosely structured, realistic narrative in which his own logging experiences are given the cast of fiction.

Grainger was born in London, England, on 17 November 1874. His mother, Isobel King Grainger, took him at the age of two to Australia to join his father, Henry Allerdale Grainger, who was serving as the agent general for South Australia. From St. Peter's school in Adelaide he obtained a scholarship to Blundell's School in Tiverton, England (the hometown of his mother), and then won an Exhibition in Mathematics to King's College, Cambridge, where he distinguished himself as twenty-first Wrangler in 1896, the year he received his B.A. (Characteristically, he did not get around to acquiring his M.A. until 1926.) Several years after his death, King's College created a Studentship in his honor.

Restless upon graduation, Grainger shipped out for the Klondike, where his originality and energy were responsible for new anecdotes in the store of personal legends that had already begun to accumulate at Cambridge. In 1899 he determined to serve in the Boer War despite initial rejection by recruiters and his own lack of funds. Grainger spent all his cash on a train ticket to New York and meager supplies for the trip to Africa, only to find himself courting starvation when his food ran out because his train was de-

Caricature of Martin Allerdale Grainger (British Columbia Forest Service)

layed by a wreck. He eventually reached his destination, enlisted in the Lord Roberts' Horse division, and won the South African medal and six bars in active service. From the front he wrote letters to England, published in the *London Daily News*, detailing the miseries endured by the British troops because of mismanagement by their superiors.

After the war Grainger oscillated between the Canadian Northwest and England. He spent a year or more placer mining near British Columbia's Dease Lake and later turned to logging; in London he tutored students cramming for military exams and attempted to run a ju-

Grainger waiting for a train at Belfort Station, near Princeton, British Columbia, in 1928 following one of his camping trips
(B.C. Provincial Archives)

jitsu school. Legends about Grainger from this period include the story of his twenty-four-hour hike during which he walked seventy-five miles across two mountain ranges–in the rain; accounts of injuries to both his person and his purse resulting from his jujitsu misadventures; and the report of the month in 1907 when he was reduced to surviving on clams on an ocean beach, waiting for rescue after the Panic of 1907 had decimated western lumber markets.

On a visit to South Pender Island (between Vancouver Island and the British Columbia mainland) Grainger became interested in Mabel Higgs, the sister of his friend Leonard Higgs. Hearing later that Mabel had gone to England, Grainger sent her a telegram proposing marriage, then followed her after she accepted. To support himself in London and raise funds for wedded life, he wrote *Woodsmen of the West* in two weeks, based on his earlier letters to Mabel and dedicated: "To My Creditors, Affectionately." Only a thousand copies were printed, but the three hundred dollars they earned (because an old friend from Cambridge purchased the copyright) enabled the author to return to British Columbia on the same ship as his future wife: she

in first class, he in steerage.

In London *Woodsmen of the West* was favorably reviewed in the *Spectator,* the *Graphic,* and the *Westminster Gazette,* but in Canada (east of the Rockies) it was virtually ignored until Professor Rupert Schieder at the University of Toronto arranged to have it published as part of McClelland and Stewart's New Canadian Library in 1964. The book is now viewed as an important contribution to British Columbia literature and a classic example of the kind of narrative favored by pioneer writers who employed some of the conventions of fiction to shape their accounts of their own experiences. In the original edition the documentary quality of Grainger's detailed descriptions of the business machinations, social behavior, and physical labor of British Columbia handloggers is enhanced by a dozen photographs, some bearing captions that include the names of characters from the text. The narrator, an Englishman sometimes identified as Mart and once as Mr. Grainger, encounters characters who have been created to embody Grainger's analysis of the compelling, contradictory nature of the west-coast woodsman: independent, practical, and fearless; yet naive, foolhardy, and undisciplined. Mart signs on with Carter, one of the most ruthless bosses in the business, and spends a miserable winter working Carter's stake at Coola (that is, Knight) Inlet. Yet he foregoes an opportunity to leave, so fascinated is he with Carter's Ahab-like determination to conquer both the wilderness and the big-business interests that control the logging industry. The book ends somewhat abruptly when Mart decides to save his sanity by returning to civilization, leaving his conflict with Carter unresolved.

After their marriage the Graingers lived in Esquimalt, on Vancouver Island, where Grainger taught mathematics at a local school until he was named secretary to British Columbia's 1909 Royal Commission on Forestry. With his literary skills and firsthand knowledge of the corruption possible under the existing system of timber leases, he became the major author of the commission's report, a document that reflects Grainger's zeal to take the administration of the logging industry out of the hands of local politicians. Grainger was appointed chief of records and rose through the ranks of the B. C. Forest Service to become chief forester in 1917, a position he held until he resigned to go into the private lumber business in 1920. He remained active in lumbering associations, and as director of the Timber Industries Council of British Columbia he worked to secure international markets for Canadian lumber.

An avid outdoorsman all his life, Grainger frequently escaped the stress of business to go riding and camping in the mountainous ranching country near Princeton, close to the U.S. border. The Grainger papers (in the Provincial Archives of British Columbia) include lively sketches of these excursions dated from 1928 to 1932; if they were intended for publication, they appear not to have excited sufficient editorial interest. In 1914, during his tenure with the Forest Service, Grainger sustained the injury to his feet that resulted in his well-known habit of wearing moccasins, even in the presence of King George V at the British Empire Forestry Conference of 1920. His strenuous work habits may have contributed to his death at the age of sixty-six in 1941. Although he had been feeling unwell, he was too busy to make a medical appointment; when he finally visited his doctor, he collapsed and died of a heart attack in the physician's office.

References:

Rupert Schieder, Introduction to Grainger's *Woodsmen of the West* (Toronto: McClelland & Stewart, 1964);

Schieder, "Martin Allerdale Grainger," *Forest History*, 11 (October 1967): 6-13.

Papers:

The Provincial Archives of British Columbia, Victoria, has correspondence, manuscripts, and clippings relating to Grainger. The C. D. Orchard Papers at the University of British Columbia Library, Vancouver, include notes and correspondence on Grainger.

Alain Grandbois
(25 May 1900-18 March 1975)

David F. Rogers
University of British Columbia

BOOKS: *Né à Québec: Louis Jolliet* (Paris: Messein, 1933; Montreal: Fides, 1948); translated by Evelyn M. Brown as *Born in Quebec: A Tale of Louis Jolliet* (Montreal: Palm, 1964);

Les Voyages de Marco Polo (Montreal: Valiquette, 1941);

Les Iles de la nuit (Montreal: Parizeau, 1944; critical edition, Montreal: Fides, 1972);

Avant le chaos (Montreal: Editions Moderne, 1945); translated by Larry Shouldice as *Champagne and Opium* (Dunvegan, Ont.: Quadrant, 1984);

Rivages de l'homme (Quebec: [Charrier], 1948);

L'Etoile pourpre (Montreal: Hexagone, 1957);

Alain Grandbois: Textes choisis et présentés par Jacques Brault (Montreal & Paris: Fides, 1958; revised and enlarged edition, Paris: Seghers, 1968);

Poèmes: Les Iles de la nuit, Rivages de l'homme, L'Etoile pourpre (Montreal: Hexagone, 1963; revised and enlarged, 1979);

Selected Poems, translated by Peter Miller (Toronto: Contact, 1964);

Visages du monde: Images et souvenirs de l'entre-deux-guerres (Montreal: HMH, 1971);

Délivrance du jour et autres inédits (Montreal: Sentier, 1980);

Dossier de presse 1944-1980 (Sherbrooke, Que.: Séminaire de Sherbrooke, 1981);

Poèmes inédits, edited by Ghislaine Legendre, Marielle Saint-Amour, and Jo-Ann Stanton (Montreal: Presses de l'Université de Montreal, 1985);

Lettres à Lucienne et deux poèmes inédits (Montreal: Hexagone, 1987).

Alain Grandbois, a Quebec poet, was born to Henri Grandbois, a physician, and Bernadette Rousseau Grandbois, at Saint-Casimir de Portneuf on 25 May 1900. He was from an old family of explorers, the Guilbeaults, who came to New France around 1635. One family member was known as Guilbeault de Grandbois, and the nickname came to designate the family branch to

Alain Grandbois (photograph by André Larose)

which Grandbois belonged. Grandbois studied first at the convent of the Sisters of Providence, then at the college of the Christian Brothers; he was not a particularly assiduous pupil. In 1911 he entered the Collège de Montréal, only to leave shortly after in order to make a trip across Canada. Upon his return he studied briefly at the Séminaire de Québec and at St. Dunstan's University, Prince Edward Island. He received his B.A., enrolled in the Faculty of Law at the Université Laval, and was called to the bar in 1925. However, Grandbois had little inclination for law; he yearned to travel and "prendre l'air du siècle" (experience the spirit of the age), to use Marcel Dugas's expression. In 1925, at the zenith of the "années folles" (roaring twenties), Grandbois settled in Paris, where, around 1920, he had lived with his parents. He returned several times to Paris over the next fifteen years and once remarked that he knew Paris better than Quebec. It was in Paris that Grandbois met the poet Blaise Cendrars and his cousin Jules Supervielle; he also made the acquaintance of Alfred Pellan, who later illustrated Grandbois's *Les Iles de la nuit* (The Islands of the Night, 1944), André Malraux, and Ernest Hemingway. In Paris, too, he undertook a doctoral thesis on Rivarol, but he failed the oral exam and left for the Riviera. In France he was an assiduous theatergoer, learned boxing, and participated in swimming competitions and automobile races.

On one of the islands of the Riviera, Ile de Port-Gros, also known as Ile d'Or, he wrote part of *Né à Québec: Louis Jolliet*, which was published in Paris in 1933 (translated as *Born in Quebec: A Tale of Louis Jolliet*, 1964). Contrary to what has been said about this work, it is not historical but rather fictional, although it is clear that Grandbois drew heavily on historical documents. *Né à Québec* consists of three parts. In the introduction of the first part, Adrien d'Abancourt, maternal grandfather of the explorer Louis Jolliet, is portrayed by Grandbois as a young Frenchman who is persuaded by his readings to immigrate to New France. An account of the difficult beginnings of the colony and the struggles with the Iroquois follows. A narrative of Jolliet's voyage and discoveries constitutes the second part. Accompanied by Father Jacques Marquette, Jolliet pushed on to the heart of the North American continent, hoping to discover a new route to the Orient. After several days of navigation on the Mississippi and having realized that it flowed south, they turned back in disappointment. The third part of the work recounts the principal events that took place during the interval between Jolliet's trip down the Mississippi and his disappearance on the St. Lawrence. In Grandbois's hands Jolliet becomes a legendary hero, while French explorer Robert Cavelier de La Salle, portrayed as the antagonist, assumes a demonic character. Comparing *Né à Québec* to Chateaubriand's *Natchez*, Victor Barbeau wrote in *Liaison* (April 1949): "Les deux sont une transposition nostalgique d'un moi insatisfait et tourmenté, d'un refus d'obéissance aux servitudes du présent, une fuite ailée dans le temps et l'espace" (Both are nostalgic transpositions of an unsatisfied and tormented *I*, of a refusal to obey servi-

tudes of the present, a winged flight in time and space). *Né à Québec* is an important work for understanding the whole of Grandbois's literary production. In general, the work was well received by the critics.

Shortly before the publication of *Né à Québec*, Grandbois had set off on an extraordinary peregrination, from London to Marrakech, from Moscow to Madrid, from Cannes to Constantinople, to China, Indochina, and Japan. Grandbois was not a dilettante in his travels; like Malraux, he carried out in this way his quest to understand the human condition. On his way to Tibet, in 1934, he published his booklet *Poèmes d'Hankéou* (Hankow Poems), a collection of seven poems that a certain Vernot, a retired French colonel and the representative of an import-export firm in Bombay, had printed on tissue paper. All seven of the poems reappeared, with revisions, in *Les Iles de la nuit;* the later versions are generally less anguished in tone than the originals.

Grandbois spent some time at the island of Port-Cros before returning to Canada in 1939. The world situation in the years leading up to World War II disturbed Grandbois greatly and made his travels impossible for some time. In Deschambault, Quebec, Grandbois wrote *Les Voyages de Marco Polo*, which won him the Prix David for 1941. Certain traits of *Né à Québec* reappear in *Les Voyages de Marco Polo:* a kind of fusion of the author-hero and a fascination with time, time that would assure his hero the security of the eternal. Another dimension, that of the marvelous, also appears. The primary interest of the work is that of allowing the reader to get a glimpse of the motivations behind Grandbois the traveler; the book is a witness to the strength of Grandbois's imagination, to the real world attaining the dimension of a dream.

By the time of the publication of *Les Voyages de Marco Polo*, Grandbois had made himself known; he gave talks on the radio, lectured, contributed to several journals, worked as bibliographer at the Bibliothèque Saint-Sulpice, and in 1944 cofounded with Barbeau L'Académie Canadienne-Française. In 1945 he produced *Avant le chaos* (translated as *Champagne and Opium*, 1984), a collection of four short stories and perhaps the work in which Grandbois expresses himself most openly. In the preface of the first edition he indicates: "j'ai écrit ces nouvelles pour retrouver ces parcelles du temps perdu, pour ressuciter certains visages évanouis, pour repêcher mes propres jours" (I wrote these

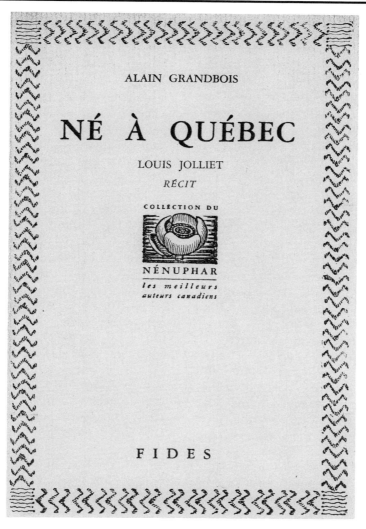

ALAIN GRANDBOIS

NÉ À QUÉBEC

LOUIS JOLLIET

RÉCIT

COLLECTION DU

NÉNUPHAR

*les meilleurs
auteurs canadiens*

F I D E S

Cover for the first Canadian edition of Grandbois's first novel (translated in 1964 as Born in Quebec:
A Tale of Louis Jolliet)

stories to rediscover these parcels of lost time, to bring back certain faded faces, to rescue my own days). *Avant le chaos* is a disconcerting work, fragmentary, with minimal plots, incorporating letters, telegrams, poems, songs, and stories within the stories. The characters are people without roots, exiled from the Paris of the interwar period. Critics described the work as "très peu québécoise" (very un-Quebecois). The principal theme of *Avant le chaos* is love, lived as an absolute, a way of transcending time. Death and fate are two other important themes of the collection.

Beginning in the early 1940s it became increasingly clear that Grandbois's real voice was that of a poet. The publication of *Les Iles de la nuit* caused Egmont (whose real name is still un-

known) to write in the *Revue populaire* in August 1944: "Nous ne croyons pas qu'un événement plus important se soit produit dans nos lettres que la publication de cet ouvrage" (We do not think there has ever been in our literature a more important event than the publication of this work). From the outset, in "O tourments," the reader is confronted with poetry that vehemently questions human and spiritual values:

Pourquoi le mur de pierre dites-moi
Pourquoi ce bloc scellé d'amitié
Pourquoi ce baiser de levres rouges
Pourquoi ce fiel et ce poison

(Why the stone wall tell me
Why this block with the seal of friendship

Why this kiss from red lips
Why this bitterness and poison).

The first poem contains the message of the whole collection, a message of anxiety and of latent revolt. What strikes the reader is the so-called modernity of the collection. Grandbois's style is disconcerting. The lack of punctuation annoyed some critics, and others called the verse anarchical and complained of its hermetism. René Chopin, in his review in *Le Devoir* (2 September 1944), regretted that certain verses "paraissent abstrus plus qu'abstraits" (seem abstruse more than abstract). It is quite true that Grandbois's poetry, compact and ambiguous, is hard to reduce to one meaning; it depends primarily for its effects on the poet's mastery of sonority and his use of repetition. The reader is spellbound by Grandbois's poetry, which often reproduces the incantatory rhythm of a litany. Critics of the period were concerned by the complexity and the bleakness of Grandbois's universe.

Les Iles de la nuit is organized around the theme of time, which in this work is the unifying element, tying together the themes of love, the search for an absolute, adventure, and fraternity. According to René Garneau, the theme of time gives the work its coherence (*Le Canada*, 22 October 1945). *Perdu* (lost) is a key word accompanying the notion of time. There has been a kind of cleavage, a breaking. But thanks to poetry, memory takes revenge on forgetting, as seen in "C'est à vous tous":

O vous tous sur ce chemin de mon passé
Je fais appel à vous de toutes mes blessures
    ouvertes
Et même si vous ne répondiez pas
Tout votre silence se dresserait soudain comme
    un grand cri emplissant ma nuit

(O all of you on this lost road of my past
I appeal to you with all of my open wounds
And even if you didn't answer
All of your silence would suddenly rise up like
    a great cry filling up my night).

Grandbois turns toward the departed and appeals for their solidarity as a means of vanquishing time. *Les Iles de la nuit* possesses a mythical dimension. Emile Bégin (*Revue de l'enseignement secondaire au Canada*, November 1944) associated this collection with the legendary couple Orpheus and Eurydice. The poem "Fermons l'armoire" (Let's Close the Cupboard), for example, brings together woman, death, and the world.

In 1948 Grandbois published *Rivages de l'homme* (Shores of Man). This work has been neglected by the critics in comparison to his other collections of poetry. *Rivages de l'homme*, like *Les Iles de la Nuit*, is a protestation against the passage of time. But in these poems the poet understands that the mystical and mythical frenzy leads nowhere. He rejects any aspiration to the beyond in favor of an orientation toward human domain; he declares the defeat of the "fantômes de la nuit" (ghosts of the night). *Rivages de l'homme* is a work of transition. The stanzas Grandbois uses are short, the poems brief; it seems to address life on a more human scale, with very pleasant rhythms. More so than in his other collections, Grandbois uses simple words. In spite of the presence of death, a constant in Grandbois's poems, *Rivages de l'homme* is written under the sign of life. The poet reaches here a new order where truth, fraternity, action, and the present reign.

A nine-year interval separates the publication of *Rivages de l'homme* and Grandbois's next verse collection, *L'Etoile pourpre* (The Purple Star, 1957). During this period Grandbois neglected poetry and devoted time to contributing to several journals and periodicals (*La Nouvelle Revue Canadienne, Les Carnets Viatoriens, Liberté, Liaison, Amérique française, Poésie 46*, and *Le Mercure de France*) and giving radio talks mainly about his travels and his literary work. He returned to France for a year, from 1955 to 1956. With *L'Etoile pourpre* the poet is again a man grappling with conflicting forces, those of life and death. This time, however, Grandbois's message is clear: the triumph of life is only possible thanks to the mediation of love. The critics were hesitant in their reception of *L'Etoile pourpre*. They denounced what they felt to be a work of odds and ends, disparate pieces put together like a jigsaw puzzle. Still others felt that the collection was too romantic. The magic of Grandbois's previous collections, in their opinion, had been lost. Some, however, had words of praise. Andrée Maillet (*Le Petit Journal*, 12 January 1958) perceived the collection as "un poem d'amour en plusieurs chants, poème d'amour bien incarné, bien charnel, bien subjectif, avoué, savouré, un poème dense si l'on veut mais assurément point obscur" (a love poem in several cantos, a poem of love incarnate, carnal, subjective, declared, savored, a dense poem, if you will, but certainly in no way obscure).

The vocabulary of this collection of poems reveals the importance of life for Grandbois. One will also notice the insistent use of the pronoun *nous* (we, us). The world of *L'Etoile pourpre* is more colorful than that of *Les Iles de la nuit*, and there are more terms evocative of pleasure and hope. Conflict is ever present; however, a kind of mutation has taken place. Ever present, too, are the sacrificial rites of which the pyres constantly remind us, but woman has become a daily companion. Grandbois seems to have discovered the object of his quest, which corresponds perhaps to that "Beau désir égaré" (Beautiful Strayed Desire):

> Je cherche les portes du ciel
> Le navire et le port
> L'autre côté du soleil
> Le silence incessant bruissant
> Ce secret d'une tremblante aurore
> Tremblante encore
> De l'odeur des lilas

> (I seek the gates of heaven
> The ship and the port
> The other side of the sun
> The incessant, rumbling silence
> This secret of a trembling dawn
> Still trembling
> With the fragrance of lilacs).

Grandbois's work did not end with *L'Etoile pourpre*. From 1957 until his death in Quebec City in 1975, he went on contributing to journals and periodicals, writing prefaces and introductions, and giving lectures and radio talks. In 1960 and 1961 he traveled again to France and Italy on a Canada Council fellowship and then set-tled in Quebec City, where he worked as a civil servant in the Musée de la Province de Québec. In July 1963 the whole of his poetry was published by the Editions de l'Hexagone, a particularly important moment in Quebec literature. In 1967 he received an honorary doctorate from the Université Laval and the following year an award from the Académie Française for his literary work; in 1970 he received, for the second time, the Prix David from the Quebec government. During this period he published various works: portraits of writers he had known, such as Dugas and Barbeau, and a series of studies on some forty-five French-Canadian poets and prose writers. Grandbois also continued composing poetry, which reflects the constants of his creation: the search for truth and for a fullness of life in this world.

References:

Jacques Blais, *Présence d'Alain Grandbois* (Quebec: Presses de l'Université Laval, 1974);

Jacques Brault, *Alain Grandbois* (Montreal: Hexagone/Paris: Seghers, 1968);

Pierre de Grandpré, "*L'Etoile pourpre*," in his *Dix ans de vie littéraire au Canada français* (Montreal: Beauchemin, 1966), pp. 32-38;

Madeleine Greffard, *Alain Grandbois* (Montreal: Fides, 1975);

Liberté 60, special double issue on Grandbois, 9-10 (May-August 1960): 145-228;

Gaston Miron and Jean-Guy Pilon, "Alain Grandbois et les jeunes poètes," *Amérique française*, 12 (December 1954): 473-476;

Lucien Parizeau, *Périples autour d'un langage: L'oeuvre poétique d'Alain Grandbois* (Montreal: Hexagone, 1988).

Wilfred Thomason Grenfell

(28 February 1865-9 October 1940)

Neil K. Besner
University of Winnipeg

BOOKS: *Vikings of Today; or, Life and Medical Work Among the Fishermen of Labrador* (London: Marshall, 1895; New York: Revell, 1896);

The Harvest of the Sea: A Tale of Both Sides of the Atlantic (New York & Chicago: Revell, 1905);

Off the Rocks: Stories of the Deep-Sea Fisherfolk of Labrador (Toronto: Briggs, 1906; Philadelphia: Sunday School Times, 1906; London: Marshall, 1907);

A Man's Faith (Boston & New York: Pilgrim, 1908; London: Marshall, 1909);

Labrador: The Country and the People, by Grenfell and others (New York: Macmillan, 1909; enlarged, 1913; enlarged again, 1922);

Adrift on an Ice-Pan (Boston & New York: Houghton Mifflin, 1909; London: Constable, 1910);

Down to the Sea: Yarns from the Labrador (New York & Chicago: Revell, 1910; London: Melrose, 1910);

A Man's Helpers (Boston & New York: Pilgrim, 1910);

What Life Means to Me (Boston & New York: Pilgrim, 1910; London: Nisbet, 1913);

What Will You Do With Jesus Christ (Boston & New York: Pilgrim, 1910);

What the Church Means to Me: A Frank Confession and a Friendly Estimate by an Insider (Boston & New York: Pilgrim, 1911);

Down North on the Labrador (New York & Chicago: Revell, 1911; London: Nisbet, 1912);

On Immortality (Boston & New York: Pilgrim, 1912; London: Nisbet, 1913);

The Adventure of Life (Boston & New York: Houghton Mifflin, 1912; London: Nisbet, 1912);

The Attractive Way (Boston & New York: Pilgrim, 1913);

The Prize of Life (Boston & New York: Pilgrim, 1914);

Tales of the Labrador (Boston & New York: Houghton Mifflin, 1916; London: Nisbet, 1916);

Labrador Days: Tales of the Sea Toilers (Boston & New York: Houghton Mifflin, 1919; London: Hodder & Stoughton, 1921);

A Labrador Doctor: The Autobiography of Wilfred Thomason Grenfell (Boston & New York: Houghton Mifflin, 1919; London: Hodder & Stoughton, 1920; enlarged edition, London: Hodder & Stoughton, 1948);

Northern Neighbours: Stories of the Labrador People (Boston & New York: Houghton Mifflin,

1923; London: Hodder & Stoughton, 1923);

That Christmas in Peace Haven and Three Eyes (Boston & New York: Houghton Mifflin, 1923);

Yourself and Your Body (New York: Scribners, 1924; London: Hodder & Stoughton, 1924);

Religion in Everyday Life (Chicago: American Library, 1926);

What Christ Means to Me (London: Hodder & Stoughton, 1926; Boston & New York: Houghton Mifflin, 1927);

Labrador Looks at the Orient: Notes of Travel in the Near and the Far East (Boston & New York: Houghton Mifflin, 1928; London: Jarrolds, 1928);

Labrador's Fight for Economic Freedom (London: Benn, 1929);

The Fishermen's Saint (New York: Scribners, 1930; London: Hodder & Stoughton, 1930);

Forty Years for Labrador (Boston & New York: Houghton Mifflin, 1932; London: Hodder & Stoughton, 1932);

Deed of Daring (London: Hodder & Stoughton, 1934);

The Romance of Labrador (New York: Macmillan/ London: Hodder & Stoughton, 1934);

A Labrador Logbook (Boston: Little, Brown, 1938; London: Hodder & Stoughton, 1939).

Grenfell with an Eskimo child (photograph by Fred C. Sears of Amherst, Massachusetts)

Wilfred Grenfell's history is that of a writer famed more for his life than for his books. He was the subject of numerous biographies, only one of which was written after his death; it is the best of them, taking the least-romanticized view of the man–J. Lennox Kerr's *Wilfred Grenfell: His Life and Work* (1959). Typically, though, it makes relatively little mention of Grenfell's writing, which includes some thirty books and hundreds of articles. At the height of his fame he was an internationally recognized figure, a compelling orator who was known to the rich and powerful and the nobility on both sides of the Atlantic. In 1958 the power of his presence for the contemporary imagination was most memorably evoked through the hero worship lavished on him by the bumbling protagonist of Saul Bellow's prize-winning novel *Henderson, the Rain King*–Eugene Henderson, would-be philanthropist, philosopher, and quintessential American idealist.

Grenfell captured the imagination of his age because he lived a life of service driven by tremendous energy and by a strong Christian faith expressed beyond the walls of any church. The remote Labrador coast became the starkly beautiful setting for his lifelong passion to minister to body and soul. In his stories and sketches he portrays the people he doctored and preached to there–the "liveyeres," the Newfoundland fishermen, the Eskimos in the North–as people who exemplified the hard-won virtue of endurance in the face of appalling poverty, isolation, and a notoriously bleak and inhospitable coastline.

Wilfred Thomason Grenfell was born on 28 February 1865 in Parkgate, England, near Chester, on the Cheshire shore of the river Dee. His father, Algernon Sydney Grenfell, was the owner and headmaster of Mostyn School House, a man who was brilliant but somewhat distant and reclusive. It was his mother, Jane Hutchinson Grenfell, who was the strongest influence on her son, instilling in him and sustaining his lifelong commitment to faith and service. All the accounts of Grenfell's childhood stress his adventurousness, his passion for the outdoors, and his love of athletics–qualities that would become legendary on the Labrador coast. He swam in the cold tidal waters of the Dee, hunted birds on its flats, and became a favorite of the local fishermen and their families, developing early a passion for boats and for the sea; many of the Grenfell stories of later years recount his impulsive daring as a navigator. From early adolescence onward Grenfell needed to challenge himself, whether this meant a dawn swim in icy seas or sailing a frail or ill-equipped boat into uncharted or unnavigable water, often in dangerous weather. He excelled at sports (boxing and rugby being his favorites) and loved physical exertion of any kind, the more strenuous the better.

His idyllic childhood and adolescence began to end when he was sent to Marlborough College in Wiltshire at fourteen, where he spent a generally undistinguished two years, interrupted by a happy interlude of a few months in the south of France, where he was sent to recover from a persistent cough. In November 1882 a more momentous change marked Grenfell's adolescence: his father, for reasons never fully explained, decided to move to the East End of London to become chaplain of a large hospital there. Pushed to decide on his future, Wilfred discarded his first idea of becoming a big-game hunter; then decided against the Church; and finally, after a visit to a family friend, the local doctor, decided on medicine. Grenfell describes the experience in his autobiography (*A Labrador Doctor*, 1919): "The only remaining memory of that visit was that the old doctor brought down from one of his shelves a large jar, out of which he produced a pickled human brain. I was thrilled with entirely new emotions. I had never thought of a man's body as a machine. That this weird, white, puckered-up mass could be the producer or transmitter of all that made man, that it controlled our physical strength and growth, and our responses to life, that it made one into 'Mad G.' and another into me—why, it was absolutely marvellous. It attracted me as did the gramophone, the camera, the automobile." According to Kerr, "This is a nice little story, with just that touch of drama Wilfred Grenfell could never resist using when he recounted an experience.... But it is likely that the boy made his decision because of his liking for his adviser and because riding along country lanes on mercy bent seemed a most attractive way to live."

Grenfell was an indifferent medical student in London but passed his examinations and was licensed to practice. The crucial event of this period was his wandering into the tent of the famous American evangelist D. L. Moody, who inspired

Grenfell, he recalls, "to make religion a real effort to do as I thought Christ would do in my place as a doctor, or frankly abandon it." Attendance at a second meeting soon after convinced Grenfell that he had "crossed the Rubicon, and must do something to prove it."

In January 1888 Grenfell embarked as a doctor on the *Thomas Grey*, a ship commissioned by the National Mission to Deep-Sea Fishermen to minister to the many fishermen in the North Sea. Grenfell's youth, his energy, and his obvious comfort with the fishermen quickly earned him admiration and respect. Kerr records an excerpt from one of Grenfell's letters to his mother about this first voyage: "He knew from the beginning that he had found the work he wanted to do and the men he wanted to serve. 'They are splendid,' he wrote to his mother, 'free and frank. I shall love them too well to be anxious to leave them.'"

In 1892 the Mission sent Grenfell, now its superintendent, on an exploratory voyage to Newfoundland aboard the *Albert;* Grenfell arrived in St. John's in late July to find the town devastated by a fire. But what most deeply impressed him was the natural setting, which he was to adopt as his chosen home for the rest of his working life, and which he describes in *A Labrador Doctor* in a passage typifying the strengths and the weaknesses of Grenfell's prose style:

> For the first time I saw the faces of its ruddy cliffs, their ledges picked out with the homes of myriad birds. Its feet were bathed in the dark, rich green of the Atlantic water, edged by the line of pure white breakers, where the gigantic swell lazily hurled immeasurable mountains of water against its titanic bastions, evoking peals of sound like thunder from its cavernous recesses—a very riot of magnificence. The great schools of whales, noisily slapping the calm surface of the sea with their huge tails as in an *abandon* of joy, dived and rose, and at times threw the whole of their mighty carcasses right out of the water for a bath in the glorious morning sunshine. The shoals of fish everywhere breaching the water, and the silver streaks which flashed beneath our bows as we lazed along, suggested that the whole vast ocean was too small to hold its riches.

Over the next forty years (Grenfell made his last summer voyage up the Labrador coast in 1932) he made a great and lasting contribution to the welfare of the fishermen and their families in Newfoundland and Labrador. He established hospitals, institutes, schools, and orphanages; he founded, and raised the funds for, numerous ven-

Grenfell Strait, Labrador, in a photograph from Labrador: The Country and the People *(1909)*

Grenfell dressed for winter hunting and with Commander Robert Peary (left) on the Roosevelt, *after Peary's trip to the North Pole*

tures, including cooperatives, designed to better the lot of the small fishing communities that lived all along the coast, in isolation from each other and from the outside world; he personally saw many thousands of patients, becoming a loved and trusted figure, revered up and down the coast. On countless voyages he helped to chart many largely unknown parts of the coastline with its innumerable inlets, reefs, and rocks; he inspired hundreds of young people from across North America to come to Newfoundland and Labrador for the summers to work without pay on his various projects. Many doctors and nurses followed Grenfell's leadership and established their careers in the same area, some of them to marry and spend their lives there. Grenfell's courage, energy, and endurance became widely celebrated: he was never known to refuse a request for help from a patient, no matter how remote the place or how threatening the conditions. His numerous scrapes with death at sea or on the ice became legendary. Perhaps the most famous of these incidents, recalled in his autobiography and in his book *Adrift on an Ice-Pan* (1909), saw Grenfell, driving himself, his dogs, and his komatik (a kind of sled) through a spring blizzard to reach an isolated patient, becoming trapped on treacherous ice in a bay he was trying to cross and being blown out to sea. Miraculously he survived, although he had to kill several of his dogs and wrap himself in their skins so that he did not freeze to death, and he erected a makeshift distress flag from the dogs' bones.

Grenfell's powerful drive and insatiable energy did not go unopposed. Local merchants who saw Grenfell's projects as a threat to their profits spoke against him, as did some of the Roman Catholic clergy, offended by his nondenominational ministry; and the Newfoundland government and press were not always wholly supportive of his efforts. Impulsive and somewhat autocratic, impatient with the slow grind of bureaucratic procedures, Grenfell also ran afoul of the Mission in England, which frequently tried to curb what it saw as his alarming excesses and expenditures. But Grenfell compensated for these shortcomings by becoming a prodigious fundraiser; although his speeches were often choppy and disjointed, they were so compelling that he regularly packed halls with crowds that he stirred to deep sympathy for his cause. Eventually the tensions between Grenfell, increasingly caught up in his Labrador projects, and the Mission in England became so pronounced that the parent

body let Grenfell have his way and establish an autonomous body, the International Grenfell Association, or I.G.A., to oversee his work. The many awards Grenfell received included an honorary M.D. from Oxford in 1907, and he was knighted in 1927; he was also honored by other universities, including Harvard, McGill, the University of Toronto, and Princeton.

Patrick O'Flaherty classifies Grenfell's books into three main groups, the first being "factual, scientific, and promotional accounts of Labrador," such as his first book, *Vikings of Today; or, Life and Medical Work Among the Fishermen of Labrador* (1895); the "Labrador storybook," such as *Tales of the Labrador* (1916); and Grenfell's religious and autobiographical works, documenting what O'Flaherty characterizes as an "unshakeable and simple faith." In this last group are works such as *What Christ Means to Me* (1926). Perhaps the most vivid and readable of Grenfell's works are the stories and sketches of Labrador life; many of these retain a sharp immediacy and vigor, and despite their fairly predictable plot lines, they present memorable portraits of a gallery of local characters.

In 1909 Grenfell married Anne Elizabeth Caldwell MacLanahan, a Chicago heiress who devoted herself to his career until her death in 1938; they had three children, two sons (Wilfred Thomason, Jr., in 1910 and Kinloch Pascoe in 1912) and a daughter (Rosamond Loveday in 1917). After a lifetime of virtually ceaseless activity, Grenfell found his health beginning to fail in his early sixties; in 1926 he suffered a heart attack while climbing a hill in Labrador and then a worse one in 1929. At the age of sixty-nine, Kerr notes, Grenfell "was forced to withdraw from active work," and he spent much of his last twelve years living in Vermont near Lake Champlain in the house his wife had had built for them. But although his health began to fail him, he was active until very near the end, writing letters and articles and raising funds for his many beloved projects.

Grenfell died on 9 October 1940. The shape of his life's work captured the imagination of much of the English-speaking world just after the turn of the century; more importantly, over the course of forty years he brought immeasurable and lasting improvements, tangible and spiritual, to the condition of a people little known in literature or in history. For his tireless efforts he became well-known in both.

Biography:
J. Lennox Kerr, *Wilfred Grenfell: His Life and Work* (London: Harrap, 1959).

Reference:
Patrick O'Flaherty, "Wilfred Thomason Grenfell," in *The Oxford Companion to Canadian Literature*, edited by William Toye (Toronto, Oxford & New York: Oxford University Press, 1983), pp. 319-320.

Papers:
Some of Grenfell's personal papers are deposited in the Yale Medical History Library.

Grey Owl
(Archibald Stansfeld Belaney)
(18 September 1888-13 April 1938)

Stanley E. McMullin
University of Waterloo

BOOKS: *The Men of the Last Frontier* (London: Country Life, 1931; Toronto: Macmillan, 1932; New York: Scribners, 1932);

Pilgrims of the Wild (London: Dickson, 1934; Toronto: Macmillan, 1934; New York: Scribners, 1935);

The Adventures of Sajo and Her Beaver People (London: Dickson, 1935; Toronto: Macmillan, 1935); republished as *Sajo and the Beaver People* (New York & London: Scribners, 1936);

Tales of an Empty Cabin (London: Dickson, 1936; Toronto: Macmillan, 1936; New York: Dodd, Mead, 1936).

From 1930, the year after his first article appeared in print, until his death in April of 1938, Archibald Stansfeld Belaney was known to the world as Grey Owl, a Canadian half-breed dedicated to the conservation of wildlife. His acute observations about the impact of man on nature were presented to an international public through books, articles, films, and public lectures. His contribution to the tradition of nature writing was so inextricably bound to his identity as Grey Owl that the literary work was largely eclipsed when that identity was exposed as a creation of Belaney's imagination. He was no half-breed: he was Archie Belaney, born and raised in Hastings, England.

In *Footsteps on Old Floors* (1968) Thomas Raddall succinctly sums up the character and appearance of one of Canada's most successful literary poseurs: "In figure he was tall and lean, with a jutting nose and a grey-blue gaze that could be bold and challenging, or shifty and furtive, or again as innocent as a child's. He was an obsessive liar, even in small matters where a lie had no purpose or advantage. He had a gift for his native English language, written or spoken, and with it he bamboozled hundreds of thousands of people, ranging from Canadian Army doctors to the King and Queen of England. And he got away with it to the very moment of his death."

Belaney's books were based upon his experiences in the wilderness of Canada. The descriptions of flora and fauna are among the most accurate recorded, but the autobiographical material is untrustworthy. While researchers have sorted out the basic details of Belaney's life, gaps remain.

Archibald Stansfeld Belaney was born in Hastings on 18 September 1888, the son of George and Katherine Cox Belaney. Four years later his parents separated. Katherine Belaney, thirteen years old at the time of Archie's birth, unable to support her two children, sent Archie to live with his grandmother Belaney and two maiden aunts who lived in Hastings. Aunt Ada was a particularly strong influence on his life; his mother, who

Grey Owl, circa 1935

later remarried, becoming Mrs. Scott-Brown, would eventually occupy another role in his life.

A solitary child attracted to nature study, Belaney decided early in life to immigrate to Canada. At the age of sixteen, he took an office job to raise passage money. He hated the job and put an end to his own employment by dropping gunpowder down the office chimney.

In the spring of 1906 Belaney sailed for Canada, arriving on 7 April. Although his ticket was for Toronto, it seems likely that he spent some time in Nova Scotia after leaving ship in Halifax. Raddall believes that Belaney lived with the Micmac Indians during this period. Lovat Dickson, in *Wilderness Man* (1973), supports Raddall but feels that the stay with the Micmacs was probably limited to about four months, after which time Belaney moved to Toronto where he found work as a clerk in a department store. After a brief stay in Toronto he traveled to Temiskaming on the Ottawa River in Ontario and took a job as a canoeman. During the winter he ran mail by dog team between Temiskaming and Temagami, and in summer he guided sportsmen on hunting and fishing trips.

While at Temiskaming he made his first contact with the Ojibwa Indians. It was during this time that he was adopted into the tribe and given the name Grey Owl, although he continued to use the name Belaney in his contacts with whites until 1930. He married Angele Eguana, a native woman, in 1910. Two years later he abandoned his wife and daughter, Agnes (born in April 1912). His next stop was Biscotasing, northwest of North Bay, Ontario, where he continued his life as a trapper and guide. One of his clients remembered that "as a guide and cook he was just a good canoeman."

Throughout his adult life, Belaney demonstrated a strong liking for both women and drink. In 1914 one or both got him into trouble. He had another child, a son, by a native woman named Marie Girard, and he departed Biscotasing for his old haunts in Nova Scotia. In

Turn-of-the-century portrait of Archibald Belaney with his dog

May of 1915 he joined the 40th Canadian Infantry Battalion for overseas duty in World War I. He sustained two injuries while in Europe. Raddall is of the opinion that the second, a wound in the foot, was self-inflicted. This wound led to his release from the army. He married (probably bigamously) an Englishwoman, Constance Holmes, an actress to whom his Aunt Ada had introduced him in 1905, but abandoned her as he had his first wife and returned to his old trapping grounds in Biscotasing. He also returned, briefly, to Angele, who bore him a second son, Robert Bernard ("Benny"), on 11 July 1918.

In 1925 Belaney met Gertrude Bernard, a full-blooded Iroquois Indian from Mattawa, Ontario. Two years later Gertrude, or Anahareo, as she became known, traveled to Doucet, in northern Quebec, to stay with Belaney. They remained together off and on for the next ten years or so.

It was in Doucet that Belaney made his first tentative move toward a writing career. He had al-

ways been an avid reader. Authors attracting his attention included Walt Whitman, James Fenimore Cooper, Sir Walter Scott, and Robert Service. He was also familiar with Shakespeare and Dickens. His reading of Longfellow's *Hiawatha* may have contributed to his choice of an Indian persona. Writing to his publishers in 1935, he suggested that "the truest definition of my status . . . is that of a modern Hiawatha."

His first article, "The Falls of Silence," was published in England by *Country Life* magazine on 2 March 1929 and earned him $150. Belaney had first sent the article to his mother, who acted as his agent. When it appeared, the author was identified as H. Scott-Brown. Katherine Scott-Brown at once wrote to the editor to say that the author was her son, A. S. Belaney. Belaney, meanwhile, in a series of letters to the editor, began to construct an image of himself as a Métis in order to establish himself as a wilderness authority among English readers. By 19 March 1930 he was claiming that Mrs. Scott-Brown was his step-mother and that his real mother was an Indian. Further articles appeared in *Country Life*, and the myth of Grey Owl was born.

While at Doucet he also decided to forgo his life as a trapper of beaver. The events leading to this decision became part of his second book, *Pilgrims of the Wild* (1934). He recounts taking a beaver from his traps and discovering two young ones orphaned by his actions. Belaney and Anahareo adopted the young beavers, taking them when they moved to Cabano, Quebec, where they established a sanctuary and a colony for the preservation of the animal.

While Belaney and Anahareo were living at Cabano, the two orphaned beaver, now named McGinnis and McGinty, mysteriously disappeared and were replaced by a successor named Jelly Roll. There is no doubt that Belaney was strongly attached to the animal; it is also true that the beaver, together with Belaney's Indian identity, quickly produced a much higher income. His next venture was lecturing. He gave his first public talk at the beach at Metis-Sur-Mer on the St. Lawrence estuary. He and Anahareo, dressed in buckskin, placed Jelly Roll on display and gave a series of public talks. Belaney was fond of saying that his first time on stage made him feel "like a snake that has swallowed an icicle, chilled from one end to another." He may have been nervous, but he had a natural bent for entertaining an audience, and the series netted him seven hundred dollars.

Anahareo also appears to have been a free spirit. Shortly after their lecture series she took off with a prospector friend to search for gold in northern Ontario, leaving Belaney on his own for eighteen months. It was during this period at Cabano that he wrote "The Vanishing Life of the Wild," his first article for a Canadian magazine, *Canadian Forest and Outdoors*. His work appeared in this magazine for the next three years. *Country Life* continued to accept material and in 1931 published his first book, *The Men of the Last Frontier*, a collection of essays on the changing frontier of Canada. The essays chronicle the hardships of the trapper, woodsman, and Indian striving to eke out a living in a wilderness already marked by the encroachment of materialism. They are laced with anecdotes and personal observations from Belaney's days before the war in the Biscotasing region of Ontario. Well received in England, the book was published in Canada by Macmillan and in the United States by Scribners. A

second British edition appeared shortly after the first. Critics praised the power of the author to conjure up "the reality and excitement of life in the woods."

Belaney acquired another beaver which he called Rawhide. His articles in the periodicals were often illustrated with his own photographs of the beaver and other wildlife. An article in *Canadian Forest and Outdoors* caught the attention of J. C. Campbell of the National Parks Service in Ottawa. Campbell visited Belaney at Cabano and saw the lean "Indian" and his beavers as ideal promoters for conservation of the wilderness. A film, *The Beaver People*, was commissioned by the Parks Service and was seen all over the world with Grey Owl, Jelly Roll, and Rawhide as central figures.

Campbell also offered Belaney the opportunity to work for the Parks Service as a supervisor for a project to introduce beaver into Riding Mountain Park in Manitoba. Belaney assumed his responsibilities in the spring of 1931. His stay in the park was brief since the setting proved to be unsuitable for beaver. His next stop was Prince Albert National Park in northern Saskatchewan, where he was provided with two cabins, one for himself and Anahareo and a second for his beavers. A daughter, Shirley Dawn, was born there in 1932.

Belaney had been working on a second book, eventually published as *Tales of an Empty Cabin* (1936), but at Prince Albert he set this manuscript aside and wrote *Pilgrims of the Wild*. He had not been pleased with editorial changes made in his first book by *Country Life*. Hugh Eayrs, who managed Macmillan of Canada, put Belaney in touch with Lovat Dickson, a Canadian who had gone to London to establish his own publishing house. Dickson became central to Belaney's success: in 1934 he published *Pilgrims of the Wild*, and it became an overnight best-seller. Seven printings appeared in the first year, and the book was eventually translated into eight languages.

Pilgrims of the Wild is generally considered to be Belaney's best book. It comes as close to an autobiography as anything he wrote, tracing his conversion to a conservationist of beaver. Anahareo, the beavers McGinnis, McGinty, Rawhide, and Jelly Roll, and Grey Owl are the central characters in this narrative that reveals Belaney's gift for detailed observation of his natural environment and his natural bent as a storyteller.

Grey Owl and Anahareo's cabin in Prince Albert National Park, where he wrote Pilgrims of the Wild
(photograph courtesy of the Canadian Parks Service)

His next book, a volume for children entitled *The Adventures of Sajo and Her Beaver People*, was published in 1935. Dedicated "to children everywhere and to all those who love the silent places," the book, illustrated with Belaney's own sketches, narrates the adventures of two Indian children, Sajo and Chapian, who befriend two young beavers, Chilawee and Shikanee. Belaney states in his preface that the events of the book grew out of personal experiences. *The Adventures of Sajo and Her Beaver People* proved to be his most popular book, with twenty-one English editions and translations in twelve languages.

Tales of an Empty Cabin returns to the essay format. The book is in many ways a mirror image of *The Men of the Last Frontier*, with the subject matter being Belaney's experiences after the war as a riverman and forest ranger. Once again, the essays reflect a dedicated naturalist exercising a fine eye for detail and a storyteller with a fondness for anecdote.

In 1935 Dickson invited Belaney to come to England to attend the annual exhibition of British books. He offered him travel expenses plus half of any profit from a lecture tour. Belaney accepted the invitation. While initial lectures were sparsely attended, it was not long before Grey Owl became a celebrity. The three-month tour

through England and Scotland saw Belaney feted by the rich and powerful. His portrait was painted by Sir John Lavery. After expenses, Belaney and Dickson split a profit from the tour of four thousands pounds and realized additional profits through increased book sales.

Returning to Prince Albert, Belaney became the subject of additional films about beavers and conservation. His habits, however, remained those of earlier days. He often disappeared on binges, with the Parks Service covering for his absences. In 1936 Anahareo finally left him. She was soon replaced by a young Métis woman, Yvonne Perrier, whom Belaney named Silver Moon.

The Parks Service was not pleased with Belaney's unpredictable life-style; however, for a time, they balanced their own inconvenience with the value he contributed as a propagandist for conservation. Their patience ran out in September of 1937, and he was "considered as separated from the Department." That year Dickson arranged a second English tour that was, he stated, "an even greater success than the first." The final triumph of the tour, which included 138 public lectures, was an invitation for Belaney to come to Buckingham Palace to give his talk for the king, queen, and two princesses. Dickson describes

*Grey Owl with Lovat Dickson, his London publisher, on a 1935 lecture tour of England and Scotland
(photograph courtesy of the Archives of Ontario)*

Grey Owl's taking leave of the royal audience: "The King held out his hand to say goodbye. Grey Owl took it. Moved by what I thought at the time was native simplicity but which I now see was a daring improvisation, he clapped the King on the shoulder and said, 'Goodbye, brother, I'll be seeing you.' "

Having triumphed in England, Belaney returned to North America and toured the United States and Canada. He was now fifty years old, and the strain of touring took its toll. His first deserted wife, Angele Eguana, had come to Prince Albert after recognizing her husband in one of his press photographs. Her case was being handled by John G. Diefenbaker, a future prime minister of Canada. Belaney returned to his cabin in Prince Albert, where he died of pneumonia on 13 April 1938. Diefenbaker eventually established that Eguana had in fact been Belaney's legal wife, and she received the widow's share of his estate.

The revelation that Grey Owl was not an Indian but an Englishman who had abandoned wives and children came with the publicity attending Eguana's claim. On the day of Belaney's death, a well-known Canadian journalist, Gregory Clark, revealed Grey Owl's true identity in the *Toronto Star*. A shocked world reacted to the news with anger and moral indignation, but Belaney's books continued to sell, even though Belaney's reputation as a "serious" writer died with his persona. One must, however, question how serious that reputation ever was. The scandal of the time suggests that the public valued Grey Owl only with some condescension in the first place–valued him *because* they thought him an Indian–and that the subsequent reaction was as strong as it was because readers were angry at themselves for having been duped.

R. E. Rashley, one of the few critics to have judged Belaney's work, has isolated its merits in a 1971 article for the *English Quarterly:* "The personal qualities which seem to emerge from the writing are intensity, conviction, earnestness, sensitivity, humour, something approaching eloquence in a cause, sadness at the approaching disappearance of a way of life, enjoyment of the goodness of comradeship at a bare human level, and elation in identity with nature." Archie Belaney knew his northern wilderness. His books documented the vanishing frontier of Canada and will continue to hold a place in the literary and social history of the country.

References:
Anahareo, *Devil in Deerskins* (Toronto: New Press, 1972);

Kenneth Brower, "Grey Owl," *Atlantic Monthly*, 265 (January 1990): 74-84;

Lovat Dickson, *Half-Breed: The Story of Grey Owl* (London: Davies, 1939);

Dickson, *Wilderness Man* (Toronto: Macmillan, 1973);

Dickson, ed., *The Green Leaf* (London: Dickson, 1938);

Thomas Raddall, *Footsteps on Old Floors* (Toronto: Doubleday, 1968);

R. E. Rashley, "Grey Owl and the Authentic Frontier," *English Quarterly*, 4 (Fall 1971): 58-64;

Donald B. Smith, "Grey Owl," *Ontario History*, 63 (September 1971): 160-176.

Frederick Philip Grove
(Felix Paul Greve)
(14 February 1879-19 August 1948)

Walter Pache
University of Augsburg

BOOKS: *Wanderungen* (Munich: Littauer, 1902);

Helena und Damon: Ein Spiel in Versen (Munich: Littauer, 1902);

Oskar Wilde (Berlin: Gose & Tetzlaff, 1903); translated by Barry Asker (Vancouver: Hoffer, 1984);

Randarabesken zu Oskar Wilde (Minden: Bruns, 1903);

Fanny Eßler (Stuttgart: Juncker, 1905); translated by Christine Helmers, A. W. Riley, and D. O. Spettigue, edited by Riley and Spettigue, 2 volumes (Ottawa: Oberon, 1984);

Maurermeister Ihles Haus (Berlin: Schnabel, 1906); translated by Paul P. Gubbins as *The Master Mason's House*, edited by Riley and Spettigue (Ottawa: Oberon, 1976);

Over Prairie Trails (Toronto: McClelland & Stewart, 1922);

The Turn of the Year (Toronto: McClelland & Stewart, 1923);

Settlers of the Marsh (Toronto: Ryerson, 1925; New York: Doran, 1925);

A Search for America (Ottawa: Graphic, 1927); republished as *A Search for America: The Odyssey of an Immigrant* (New York, London & Montreal: Carrier, 1928);

Our Daily Bread (Toronto: Macmillan, 1928; New York: Macmillan, 1928; London: Cape, 1928);

It Needs to be Said (Toronto: Macmillan, 1929);

Frederick Philip Grove (photograph courtesy of his son, Leonard Grove)

The Yoke of Life (Toronto: Macmillan, 1930; New York: Smith, 1930);

Fruits of the Earth (Toronto & Vancouver: Dent, 1933; London: Dent, 1933);

Two Generations: A Story of Present-Day Ontario (Toronto: Ryerson, 1939);

The Master of the Mill (Toronto: Macmillan, 1944);

In Search of Myself (Toronto: Macmillan, 1946);

Consider Her Ways (Toronto: Macmillan, 1947);

Tales from the Margin: The Selected Short Stories of Frederick Philip Grove, edited, with an introduction, by Desmond Pacey (Toronto & New York: Ryerson/McGraw-Hill, 1971).

TRANSLATIONS: Oscar Wilde, *Das Bildnis Dorian Grays* (Minden: Bruns, 1902);

Ernest Dowson, *Dilemmas* (Leipzig: Insel, 1903);

Wilde, *Fingerzeige* (Minden: Bruns, 1903);

H. G. Wells, *Die Riesen kommen!* (Minden: Bruns, 1904);

Wells, *Die Zeitmaschine* (Minden: Bruns, 1904);

Wilde, *Die Sphinx* (Minden: Bruns, 1904);

Wilde, *Das Granatapfelhaus* (Leipzig: Insel, 1904);

Robert Browning, *Paracelsus: Dramatische Dichtung* (Leipzig: Insel, 1904);

Browning, *Briefe von Robert Browning und Elizabeth Barrett-Browning* (Berlin: Fischer, 1905);

André Gide, *Der Immoralist* (Minden: Bruns, 1905);

Gide, *Paludes (Die Sümpfe)* (Minden: Bruns, 1905);

George Meredith, *Richard Feverels Prüfung* (Minden: Bruns, 1905);

Wilde, *Eine Frau ohne Bedeutung* (Leipzig & Wien: Wiener, 1906);

Henri Murger, *Die Bohème: Szenen aus dem Pariser Künstlerleben* (Leipzig: Insel, 1906);

Erzählungen aus den Tausendundein Nächten, 12 volumes (Leipzig: Insel, 1906-1908);

Gustave Flaubert, *Die Versuchung des heiligen Antonius,* volume 4; *Briefe über meine Werke,* volume 7; *Reiseblätter,* volume 8; and *Briefe an Zeit- und Zunftgenossen,* volume 9 of *Gesammelte Werke,* edited by E. W. Fischer (Minden: Bruns, 1907-1908);

Walter Pater, *Marius der Epikureer,* 2 volumes (Leipzig: Insel, 1908);

Honoré de Balzac, *Ein Junggesellenheim,* volume 1; *Erzählungen aus der napoleonischen Sphäre,* volume 2; *Glanz und Elend der Kurtisanen,* volumes 6 and 7; and *Das Meisterwerk,* volume 11 of *Menschliche Komödie,* 16 volumes (Leipzig: Insel, 1908-1911);

Alexandre Dumas, *Der Graf von Monte Cristo* (Berlin: Reiss, 1909);

Gide, *Die enge Pforte* (Berlin: Reiss, 1909);

Wilde, *Bunbury* [*The Importance of Being Earnest*], volume 10 of *Werke,* 12 volumes (Berlin: Globus, 1918);

Gustav Amann, *The Legacy of Sun Yatsen: A History of the Chinese Revolution* (New York & Montreal: Carrier, 1929).

OTHER: "Oskar Wilde," in *Porträts,* edited by Adalbert Luntowski (Berlin: Neues Leben, n.d.), pp. 12-51;

"Oskar Wilde und das Drama," in volume 7 of *Oskar Wildes sämtliche Werke in deutscher Sprache,* 10 volumes (Vienna & Leipzig: Wiener, 1908), pp. 7-102;

"Thoughts and Reflections: An 'Intermittent Diary,' 1933-1940," in *A Stranger to My Time,* edited by Paul Hjartarson (Edmonton: NeWest, 1986), pp. 301-342.

SELECTED PERIODICAL PUBLICATIONS
UNCOLLECTED: "Gustave Flauberts Theorien über das Künstlertum," *Rheinisch-Westfälische Zeitung* (Essen), 1065 (1904);

"Reise in Schweden," *Neue Revue,* 3 (1909): 760-766;

"Apologia pro Vita et Opere Suo," *Canadian Forum,* 11 (August 1931): 420-422;

"A Writer's Classification of Writers and Their Work," *University of Toronto Quarterly,* 1 (January 1932): 236-253;

"Thomas Hardy: a Critical Examination of a Typical Novel and his Shorter Poems," *University of Toronto Quarterly,* 1 (July 1932): 490-507;

"The Plight of Canadian Fiction? A Reply," *University of Toronto Quarterly,* 7 (July 1938): 451-467;

The Adventures of Leonard Broadus, Canadian Boy, 40 (7 April 1940-23 June 1940); republished, *Canadian Children's Literature,* 27/28 (1982): 5-126;

"Postscript to *A Search for America,*" *Queen's Quarterly,* 49 (Autumn 1942): 197-213;

"Democracy and Education," *University of Toronto Quarterly,* 12 (July 1943): 389-402;

"Morality in the Forsyte Saga," *University of Toronto Quarterly,* 15 (October 1945): 54-64.

Both as a writer and a critic Frederick Philip Grove stands at the beginning of modern literature in Canada. In his comprehensive body of work–novels, autobiographical writings, short stories, and letters and essays on literature, culture, and society–Grove breaks away from the literary conventions governing Canada's colonial century. With his emphasis on pioneer characters and prairie settings Grove writes within the tradition of realism, but his psychological and social observations are placed in a framework of ideas that is strongly influenced by the aesthetic and philosophical movements of fin-de-siècle Europe. Grove's uncompromising seriousness about the moral function of literature is remarkable.

For a long time Grove's early life was shrouded in mystery. Since the publication, in 1973, of Douglas O. Spettigue's *FPG: The European Years* there is little doubt that "Frederick Philip Grove" is the Canadian pseudonym of the German writer Felix Paul Berthold Friedrich Greve, although many biographical details still remain uncertain. Grove was born on 14 February 1879 at Radomno, Prussia, a village near the Russian border where his father, Karl Eduard Greve, worked as manager of an estate. In 1881 the family moved to Hamburg. After his parents' divorce (around 1892), Grove stayed with his mother, Bertha Reichentrog Greve, until enrolling at the University of Bonn as a student of philosophy in 1898.

Two years later Grove decided to leave Bonn to establish himself as a writer and translator of English and French literature. Probably in the summer of 1904 he married his first wife, Else Hildegard Ploetz, the former wife of the architect August Endell. Despite his prodigious energy and various contacts with influential editors and publishers such as Otto Julius Bierbaum, editor of *Die Insel,* one of Germany's leading avantgarde literary magazines at the turn of the century, Grove's success was limited. In his "Conversation avec un Allemand" (in *Œuvres Complètes,* 1932-1939), André Gide, whom Grove met in Paris in 1904, gives a vivid portrait of the young Grove as an aspiring writer proudly confessing to his "extraordinaire faculté de mentir" (outstanding ability for telling lies). Grove traveled extensively during those years. After taking up residence in Munich (1901-1902) and spending one year in prison because of an unpaid debt (1903-1904), he eventually moved to Berlin in 1906.

Grove's early literary efforts (as Greve) clearly show the influence of contemporary European movements such as aestheticism and impressionism. In 1902 he published a volume of poems (*Wanderungen*) and a lyrical verse drama (*Helena und Damon*). More significant for his later career are his two novels: *Fanny Eßler* (1905; trans-

lated, 1984) and *Maurermeister Ihles Haus* (1906; translated as *The Master Mason's House,* 1976). Drawing upon his boyhood experiences, Grove here follows in the footsteps of naturalism. Like Thomas Mann whose *Buddenbrooks* had appeared in 1901, Grove is interested in the decay of families. Both novels are, to quote Anthony W. Riley (in "The German Novels of Frederick Philip Grove," 1974), "a psychological study of the development of two German women from adolescence to maturity from a very definite social class [petit bourgeois], from a particular part of Germany (small towns in the Pomeranian lowlands near the Baltic coast), and at a specific period in German history (c. 1888 to 1903)."

The daughters' attempts to struggle free from an oppressive provincial milieu and from paternal authority, to secure financial independence as well as sexual liberation, are told through a wealth of descriptive detail and atmospheric dialogue; the plots are loosely structured. *Fanny Eßler,* a novel of over five hundred pages, reflects Grove's links with the literary *bohème* in Munich and elsewhere. Modeled on the *Künstlerroman,* it describes the progress of a young girl from the provinces through various strata of society—a search for emancipation that eventually fails. Fanny's career as an actress and her success in literary circles is accompanied by a succession of love affairs. In paralleling artistic refinement and the loss of moral respectability in a bourgeois sense, Grove uses a familiar pattern of contemporary fiction. *Maurermeister Ihles Haus,* a rambling and perhaps unfinished novel in three parts, deals with the breakup of mason Richard Ihle's marriage and the unstable relationship with his two daughters. One of them, Suse, is an interesting and psychologically convincing character who serves as a central consciousness.

Like his poetic and dramatic work, the novels did not attract the attention Grove must have hoped for. Although documentary evidence is scarce, it seems likely that their failure contributed to Grove's decision to withdraw from the European scene both in a physical and a spiritual sense. Thus in September 1909 he took the unusual step of faking a suicide. He disappeared, leaving behind him his old identity, shattered illusions, and his wife to discuss his unpaid bills with an angry and suspicious publisher. According to recently discovered sources, Else (who later married Baron Leopold von Freytag-Loringhoven) connived in Grove's "suicide" and followed her

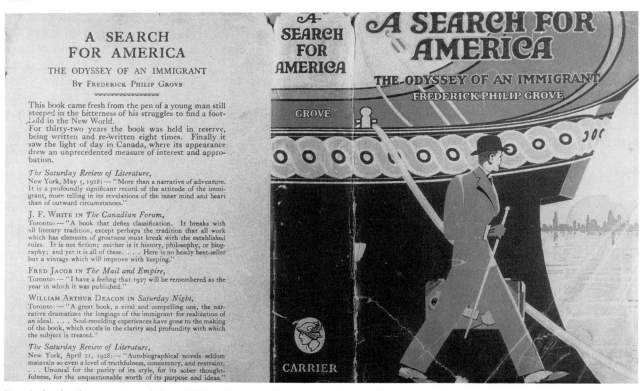

Dust jacket for the American edition (1928) of Grove's 1927 semi-autobiographical novel, which added strength to Grove's own care-fully doctored history of his early manhood

husband to North America, where they separated some time before 1912.

Grove never concealed his European background, but he was always vague about dates and details. His fictitious early life, distilled from his autobiographical writings and from other statements, deviates from the facts at significant points: Grove created as his doppelgänger the persona of an upper-middle-class gentleman, born in 1871 in Moscow, he claimed, as a son of well-to-do parents of Swedish-Russian stock, raised by his mother at a stately home in southern Sweden. Supposedly educated at the universities of Paris, Rome, and Munich, he took time off to tour Europe, Asia, and Australia. Apart from studying medicine, archaeology, and languages, he was on excellent terms with some of Europe's leading writers. When, traveling in North America in 1892, he received word that his father had gone bankrupt, he turned from dandy to self-made man. His twenty years of literary apprenticeship in Europe were followed by another twenty years devoted to gaining practical experience: washing dishes, selling encyclopedias, and working as a farmhand. In 1912 he was ready to let others

share his wisdom: he started a career as a teacher and writer in Manitoba.

The differences between the real and fictional biographies may not at first glance appear to be very striking. Grove did not completely invent a new past but gave it additional weight by a subtle shift of nuances: his parents' farming background is replaced by that of the landed gentry; the restless travels through Germany and the Continent are magnified into grand tours; and various fleeting encounters with literary celebrities are upgraded to formative relationships. By relocating his experiences between 1892 and 1912 in North America, Grove not only established a symbolic balance but responded to the anti-German mood in the years during and after World War I.

Grove first formulated this archetypal myth about the union of the Old and the New World in the novel *A Search for America* (1927; written around 1920). Phil Branden, the narrator-hero, is Grove's alter ego, who experiences the various stages from immigration to settling down, from town to country, from mass civilization to rural simplicity, as the stages of an educational process. In his "Author's Note" to the fourth edition

(1939) Grove made it clear that Branden's adventures constitute a fictional rather than an authentic autobiography: "Imaginative literature is not primarily concerned with facts; it is concerned with truth." As a story of self-discovery *A Search for America* belongs to the quest tradition, its paradigmatic mode indicated by the titles of the four parts: "The Descent," "The Relapse," "The Depths," and "The Level."

Until recently the reliability of Grove's fictional accounts of his past was never seriously questioned. While this oversight may have something to do with the state of literature and literary studies in Canada during the 1940s and 1950s, Grove's gamble ultimately worked because it provided exactly the kind of elaborate myth that appealed to the Canadian imagination. Uniting in one person the adventurous pioneer and the distinguished intellectual, Grove seemed to provide a literary tradition, a specifically Canadian synthesis of the cosmopolitan and the regional, of European culture and the wilderness of the North.

From December 1912 when Grove, at the age of thirty-three, emerged in Winnipeg, his biography ceases to be a matter of speculation. For the following twelve years, "Fred Grove" was employed as a teacher at various primary schools in Manitoba, partly in German-speaking Mennonite communities, becoming principal of the Winkler Intermediate School in September 1913. On 2 August 1914 he married Catherine ("Tena") Wiens (1892-1972), a fellow teacher. By then, as his marriage certificate shows, his new (fictitious) identity was firmly established:

The groom: Frederick Philip Grove . . .
Birthplace: Moscow
Marital Status: Widower
Parents: Charles Edward Grove and Bertha Ruth
    erford Grove
Occupation: Professor of Science (Scholastic)
Religious denomination: Lutheran.

Over Prairie Trails, published in 1922 as Grove's first Canadian work, differs from *A Search for America* in that it is an openly autobiographical sketch of his early years in rural Manitoba. Grove describes seven of the numerous trips across the prairie by horse-drawn buggy or sleigh during the autumn and winter of 1917-1918 when he and his wife were teaching at different schools. The narrative, oddly blending adventure story and essayistic reflection, was cited by Malcolm Ross (in his introduction to the

1957 edition) as evidence of Grove's "almost incredible love for the harsh, punishing, desolate Manitoba land." Grove indeed provides a vivid account of the changing landscape, of the weather conditions, and of his own physical hardships and mental frustrations, but the dominant theme is man's struggle against nature, more specifically the struggle between the planning intellect and the brutal force of the circumstances determining man's fate.

In *Over Prairie Trails*, for the first time, the traits of Grove's archetypal hero emerge. He is an outsider pitting himself with dogged determination against nature and society alike: "As soon as the storm had set in, I had instinctively started to work in order to frustrate its designs," he says at one point—not really because he expects to win the battle but because he sees it as a "supreme test" of his own personality. This challenge is taken up against all odds, and its failure is anticipated: "I had challenged a force in nature," Grove sums up, "which might defy all tireless effort and the most fearless heart." The arrogant denial of human limitations cannot be entirely explained in terms of the philosophy of naturalism because, perversely, it emerges as a kind of positive aesthetic experience: the refusal to surrender to physical danger results in artistic freedom. It is through the act of writing that man demonstrates his superiority over the inarticulate primitive elements.

With some justification *Over Prairie Trails* has been called Grove's least-flawed book. Unencumbered by involved plots, contrived characters, and twisted metaphors, and close to factual reality, it not only states the theme of most of Grove's later work with great precision but also serves as a reliable guide to his complex personality.

Grove's career during the 1920s and 1930s is symptomatic of the situation of literature in Canada. *Over Prairie Trails*, probably written in 1919, was accepted by McClelland and Stewart in the following year. After the first edition in 1922, two more editions appeared after comparatively short intervals (in 1923 and 1929). After the difficult first years Grove (who had become a naturalized Canadian citizen in December 1921) saw himself on the threshold of the success he had been denied in Germany. Encouraged by the warm reception of *Over Prairie Trails* and of the subsequent volume of essays, *The Turn of the Year*, in 1923, Grove gave up teaching in the summer of 1924 to devote himself solely to writing—a decision entirely in character with Grove's highly developed self-assurance but also testifying to his refusal to accept his real, tenuous situation.

Settlers of the Marsh, Grove's first Canadian novel, appeared in 1925. Originally planned as the first part of a trilogy, the chronicle spans eighteen years in the life of Niels Lindstedt, a Swedish immigrant and settler, who has occasionally been interpreted as a modern saint figure. Lindstedt has to find his way between innocence (represented by Ellen Amundsen) and sin (symbolized by Clara Vogel). Having been trapped in an unhappy marriage with Clara for several years, Lindstedt eventually shoots her when he becomes aware of her morally dubious life. He is imprisoned, but the end of the novel suggests that after his release a new beginning with Ellen might be possible. *Settlers of the Marsh* is the first example of what might be called Grove's symbolic realism, an attempt to adapt the naturalistic pattern of his German novels by focusing on the central conflict between the individual and circumstance, and transferring it to a prairie setting where such elementary clashes seemed more credible than elsewhere.

Settlers of the Marsh did not sell well, partly because its overtly sexual implications offended the prevailing Puritan mood and were considered scandalously immoral. But the publication of *A Search for America* in October 1927 marked the beginning of Grove's most successful period. Especially during the three lecture tours that took him across Canada in 1928 and 1929, Grove came as close as he ever did in his lifetime to widespread popularity. It was the time when, together with economic prosperity, a new wave of literary nationalism swept the country. *Canadian Forum,* established in 1920, and *Canadian Bookman* (1919-1939), the organ of the Canadian Authors' Association, served as spokesmen for the movement and tried to encourage Canadian publishers. Canada, in Douglas Bush's phrase, seemed about to take "its permanent seat in the literary league of nations" (*Canadian Forum,* December 1926).

Grove, the European and new Canadian, the prairie writer and intellectual, the man who had publicly opted for Canada over the United States, seemed to be the ideal symbolic figurehead of the new movement. All went well at first. Grove, invited by the local "Canadian Clubs" to lecture in all major cities, suddenly saw himself lionized as the undisputed teacher of the nation. In his speeches he praised the Canadian mosaic and

the ideal of individual self-determination, and he thundered against American mediocrity. *It Needs to be Said* (1929), a collection of papers and addresses delivered in these years, reflects his magisterial mood in its title. Although Grove tended to look down on the naive enthusiasm of his admirers and their lack of taste and literary refinement, he reveled in his newly acquired glory (and in the luxury of his hotel rooms). Regarding his reception in Kitchener, Ontario, for instance, he wrote to his wife on 27 March 1928, in a strange mixture of ill-concealed pride and self-irony: "Well, my deah! Drat it all! I can't sleep when I have these ovations. Had 2 in succession last night. Spoke at 4:15 till 5:30. Banquet at 6:30. Just had time to change; and that was all. Then spoke again at 7:15 till 8:30. 'The Greatest Canadian' I was called. Plup, plup! But they all know that the rest of Canadian writers are pygmies by my side; and they say so."

However, Grove was deceiving himself when he assumed that he could create a tradition of Canadian literature single-handedly from a virtual vacuum. His exuberant mood faded when the economic and cultural crisis of the 1930s crushed his—and the country's—optimistic expectations. The struggle for recognition as a leading writer proved as arduous in Canada as it had been in Germany, if for different reasons. Anticipating a much more prominent role in public life, Grove had moved from his western home in 1929. His Ottawa job as associate editor of *The Canadian Nation,* a magazine of the Canadian Clubs, ended when it ceased publication in June 1929. Again, as manager of Graphic Press in Ottawa (December 1929 to October 1931), Grove had ambitious plans, but he was unable to prevent the firm's collapse. Grove's new manuscripts were only reluctantly accepted, although publishers such as Hugh S. Eayrs (Macmillan's of Canada) and Lorne Pierce (Ryerson Press), as well as influential critics, including Arthur Leonard Phelps and Watson Kirkconnell, strongly supported him.

The Yoke of Life, a counterpart to *Settlers of the Marsh,* was published in 1930. In his following novel *Fruits of the Earth* (1933) Grove again returned to the themes of his earlier works, but with wider implications. The farmer Abe Spalding, the protagonist of this "Chronicle of Spalding District" (an earlier title), is a more mature and more powerful figure than Niels Lindstedt. A modern Prometheus—who brings light to his district by providing electricity—Spalding devotes his almost superhuman energy

The Groves, circa 1940 (photograph courtesy of Leonard Grove)

to his own ambitions, like acquiring more and more land and becoming the leading figure in the district, but also to the welfare of the community. However, the familiar pattern still holds: at the climax catastrophe strikes because (on a realistic level) his overbearing and rigid personality is unable to adapt to a changing environment, but at the same time because (according to Grove's philosophy) the strong individual is doomed by the forces of destiny. Striking a precarious balance between realistic narrative and moral fable, Spalding's rise and ultimate failure epitomize Grove's central concern: through his very efforts, man is enslaved to the powers he sets out to dominate. The question whether the blame lies with the individual or with destiny remains unanswered: Abe Spalding eventually learns to accept his limitations.

The Groves (a son, Arthur Leonard, was born in 1930; a daughter, Phyllis May, had died

in 1927 at the age of eleven) left Ottawa in October 1931 for rural Ontario, where Grove had bought a farm near Simcoe. Here Grove spent his remaining years, beset by financial worries, troubled by illness, but above all in growing bitterness and self-imposed isolation, which he saw as exemplary. "But one day," he wrote Lorne Pierce on 15 June 1936, "I wish to write the tragedy of a Canadian writer; the tragedy of the man who has something to say and tries to say it but cannot do so for sheer poverty. My personal tragedy has been that I have, throughout the forty-four years of my life in Canada, lived in exile from the realm of literature." Grove, who had proudly disclaimed all ties with contemporary Canadian literature, complained to Pierce (on 1 April 1940) that other writers did not rally around him: "I have helped many; nobody has ever helped me." Grove's letters provide fascinating evidence of his lifelong preoccupation with turning his life into fiction.

Grove's creative impulse remained unbroken, although one of his novels from the Simcoe years, *Two Generations: A Story of Present-Day Ontario* (1939), is generally regarded as among his weakest works and is the only one in which Grove tried his hand at a happy ending. His last novel, *The Master of the Mill* (1944), on the other hand, is Grove's most complex version of his favorite form, the family chronicle. Sam Clark, Ontario capitalist and mill owner, looks back on his own life and that of three generations of the prominent Clark family. A theme Grove had treated many years before in *Our Daily Bread* (1928) is taken up again on a much larger scale. In tracing the fortunes of an influential dynasty of businessmen from the pioneer days to the age of industrial civilization, Grove not only returned to his central theme of the power of technology and man's struggle to impose his will on it, but tried to come to terms with the reality of contemporary Canada, particularly its geographical variety and its social problems. Predictably this final effort to describe and interpret reality ends on a gloomy note. Shortly before he dies, old Sam has a last look at the mill, which appears as a symbol of man's ambiguous position in the universe: "When man went to rest, with the fall of darkness, [the mill] went on, with never-wearied muscles of steel, producing his food for the morrow. Man was born, suffered, and died; but the mill watched over him: this mill and others. The mill was a god to him, all-good, all-provident, all-powerful." Thus, the ultimate tragedy of human activism derives not only from man's fatal inability to control the forces he has called into being but also from the realization that man, whatever he might achieve, is unimportant, even superfluous within the universal context of cosmic evolution.

Despite Grove's innovative flashback technique and his complex vision, *The Master of the Mill* is unsatisfactory as a novel; it suffers from obtrusive symbolism and didactic explicitness, clumsy dialogue, flat characterization, and deficiencies of plot and motivation. Once more a wide gap opens between Grove's qualities as critic and thinker, and his abilities as a fiction writer whose development apparently stagnated after he left the German literary scene shortly before the onset of literary modernism and its new narrative techniques. However, Grove found another, possibly more promising way to express his views on man and his world, as is evident in *Consider Her Ways* (1947), his last published book.

With *Consider Her Ways*, the last of his narratives of travel, Grove returns to satire and allegory as vehicles for his criticism of life. The "editor" who signs himself "F. P. G." claims to have, in some trancelike state, communicated with one Wawa-quee, an ant of noble birth and leader of an expedition from the Orinoco valley in Venezuela to New York City, sent out to catalog and classify "all forms of life to be found on the continent." Here again we find Grove's hero—a female protagonist this time—tackling destiny against all odds, threatened by physical dangers, by treachery (like Faust, Wawa-quee is accompanied by a Mephistophelian rival), and above all by the lurking suspicion that all effort is ultimately futile. Gradually the well-organized expedition turns into a desperate struggle for survival. When Wawa-quee finally returns as the sole survivor, her skeptical views on man's achievements are fully justified. From the ant's point of view, man is "at present a degenerate type" who "even in a happier past . . . has never attained a level of civilization which could in any way be called comparable to our own." But the satirical invective is a double-edged sword: ironically, "antkind" itself, supposedly vastly superior to the human race, is subject to the same shortcomings and delusions about its status that it criticizes.

Whether the pessimism that overshadowed Grove's last years was entirely justified is difficult to assess. Grove's own comments are notoriously unreliable. It is true that material success forever eluded him and that his health was failing. But at the same time there is evidence that in the 1940s he was beginning to be recognized as one of Canada's leading writers. In April 1941 he was elected a fellow of the Royal Society of Canada. Oscar Pelham Edgar, professor of English at the University of Toronto, arranged for a monthly allowance to be paid by the Canadian Writer's Fund. In 1945 Desmond Pacey published his study *Frederick Philip Grove* in the Canadian Men of Letters series. Grove received an honorary doctorate from the University of Manitoba in 1946, and a year later the Governor General's Award (nonfiction) for *In Search of Myself* (1946).

In Search of Myself is the second version of Grove's fictional autobiography. Two of its four parts deal with his European period. It may seem strange today that these sections could have been read and interpreted as factual, because it is obvious that, as in *A Search for America*, Grove transposes details from his own life into a paradigmatic context. While real events and real chro-

IN SEARCH OF MYSELF

The Autobiography of

FREDERICK PHILIP GROVE

"All men of whatever quality they be, who have done anything of excellence, or which may properly resemble excellence, ought, if they are persons of truth and honesty, to describe their lives, with their own hands." Thus begins in 1559 the autobiography of Benvenuto Cellini. Whether this statement is valid or not, it remains true, very curiously, that Cellini's book, along with Pepys' *Diary* and Rousseau's *Confessions*, after centuries of crystallizing criticism, is generally regarded as one of the small number of masterpieces in that kind. However these things may be, supreme excellence in autobiography is a rare thing. Let no one attempt or expect, then, at this time, an ultimate pronouncement on this autobiography by Frederick Philip Grove.

But there can be nothing rash in pointing out, here and now, that Mr. Grove is performing what Cellini's pages set forth as a duty to humanity, and in conformity with Cellini's conditions. It would be understatement indeed to say that the work Grove has already done "properly resembles excellence". And "truth and honesty" appear on every page of this new book, written in the first person, about himself. His honesty is as transparent as sunshine. Nor can there be anything rash in the statement that the period of his life, 1872 to the present, is no less interesting or important than any period ever covered by autobiographer or historian. And we may well doubt whether many mortals have had an experience to match Grove's, remembering at once its range and variety, depth and intensity, adventures beyond any fiction.

One encounters nowadays in many places an immense desire to get down, as it were, to the skeleton form of humanity in this modern age. Here it lies, stripped and bare! As against this others wish to escape life as they have witnessed it. These readers are ever in quest of a breathlessly exciting tale. Well, here is a book that cuts straight across regular needs and slumbers, that absorbs a reader to the depths of his soul. He is lost at once in the adventures, in high life and low; he is fascinated for a while by the struggle for daily survival. Gradually, too, the reader is aware of another struggle, beyond all other strivings and questings, an endeavour pure and selfless, remarkable in its tenacity — to say something of Immortal Man to Immortal Man, in other words, to express the artist's own soul.

Only occasionally, after all, are words or pages put together in such a way as to carry us straight to a mountain of Enchantment. Mr. Grove brings to the reader an exaltation of spirit which no other autobiographer brings. For the subject of this book is the Spirit of Man, stripped of all trappings and inessentials, racial or temporal; the Spirit of Man triumphant above all human antheaps, above all human conventions and creeds.

THE MACMILLAN COMPANY OF CANADA LIMITED

St. Martin's House, Toronto 2, Canada

Dust jacket for Grove's autobiography (1946), which turned out to be nearly as fictional as his novel A Search for America *in that both recount events from a personal past Grove had partially invented*

nology are loosely preserved, it is on the narrator's education as a cosmopolitan figure that the emphasis is placed. Raised by a mother who symbolizes the decadent culture of fin-de-siècle Europe but separated from his father (symbol of bourgeois solidity and conventional morality), "Frederick Philip Grove" becomes the quintessential artist but at the same time loses his foothold in the practical world. As an exile from Europe he is ideally suited to communicate his experience to the New World. He thus takes on social responsibility but remains isolated himself. The second half of the book, which recounts Grove's life in Canada from 1912 onward, is, of course, much closer to authentic truth but firmly rests on the exile thesis put forward in the first part.

In April 1944, a few months before the publication of *The Master of the Mill*, Grove suffered a stroke; another seizure, in May 1948, paralyzed him. Grove died at his home in Simcoe on 19 August 1948. He was sixty-nine years old.

Four decades after Grove's death his elusive personality and his complex work were more than ever at the center of critical discussion. As a man Grove appears to have had many faces: arrogantly self-centered and overbearing but at times congenial and entertaining; moody and bitter but for brief periods sparkling with enthusiasm. As Wilfrid Eggleston recalls, Grove had "some wit but not much humour" ("F. P. G.: The Ottawa Interlude," 1974). As a writer Grove has been steadily gaining in popular and critical esteem during recent years, especially since most of his major works in English were reissued in the New Canadian Library series (which opened with *Over Prairie Trails* in 1957).

In a way every generation seems to create a new Grove to fit its requirements. In the 1950s critics and readers mainly saw him as a master of prairie literature, chronicling the hardships of homesteading and introducing the Canadian West into fiction. More recently the emphasis shifted to Grove's use of the prairies "as a state of mind"–to quote Henry Kreisel's famous phrase (in "The Prairie: A State of Mind," 1971)–and as a symbolic setting for a philosophical enquiry into man's position. In the 1980s Grove's considerable influence on novelists such as Robert Kroetsch and Ruby Wiebe seems to have rested on their fascination with the re-creation of reality as a fictional construct.

Many questions, however, remain unanswered. What continuity, if any, exists between Felix Paul Greve and Frederick Philip Grove? Is his work an integral part of the mainstream of English-Canadian literature, or does it stand apart as an erratic exception? Recent comparative studies have shown that the international context of Grove's oeuvre is more varied than had originally been assumed. Few critics would dispute that glib labels like "the Canadian Hardy" or "the Canadian Dreiser" are inadequate because they are gross oversimplifications that ignore Grove's heritage. "Grove arrived," as George Woodcock wrote, "bearing with him, as part of his carefully concealed mental baggage, the heritages of the two significant European movements of his time—naturalism and symbolism" ("Possessing the Land: Notes on Canadian Fiction," 1977).

Grove's "mental baggage" is of European rather than specifically German origin. Among the authors he translated as Greve, the names of Robert Browning and Gustave Flaubert, André Gide and George Meredith, Walter Pater and Arthur Symons, Oscar Wilde and H. G. Wells stand out. In Grove's essays and letters Gide and Wells, along with Matthew Arnold, Thomas Hardy, and Emile Zola, play a more prominent part than German classical authors such as Theodor Fontane and Wilhelm Raabe, or even Friedrich Nietzsche and Richard Wagner, as cultural heroes of fin-de-siècle times. (Goethe, Homer, and Shakespeare command Grove's highest respect.)

Both the number and diversity of Grove's early idols are significant because such a mind-set reveals something about his sometimes disoriented search for universal concepts: Hardy's pessimism, Zola's naturalism, and Wells's utopian belief in the perfectibility of mankind all seemed to be as attractive to Grove's eclectic mind as Pater's aestheticism and Wilde's philosophy of decadence.

While the range of Grove's European heritage by now seems clear (although many details await further investigation), comparatively little is known about exactly how it influenced his Canadian works, and, more specifically, how it blended with the influence of the American tradition Grove absorbed after his arrival in North America. The problems of chronology that arise here are particularly thorny because in Grove's case publication dates give a distorted impression. Published texts frequently represent just the final version of numerous drafts stretching over decades.

By antedating his work Grove sometimes tends to construct for it a fictitious literary context. For example, Grove claimed that *A Search for America,* though published in 1927, was in fact written around the year 1894. Spettigue, on the other hand, basing his calculation on internal evidence and on the Greve/Grove link, thinks that 1920 is a more likely date. If we accept Grove's own chronology, Phil Branden's narrative departs from the naturalistic conventions of the late nineteenth century to innovative modes of autobiographical narrative. According to Spettigue *A Search for America* follows in the wake of American realism, the classical texts of which—like Dreiser's *Sister Carrie* (1900), Frank Norris's *The Octopus* (1901), or Upton Sinclair's *The Jungle* (1906)—precede Grove's work by more than a decade. Spettigue also points out that stories of "My first reaction to America" began to come into fashion in Canada during the 1920s—Laura Goodman Salverson's *The Viking Heart* (1923) or Martha Ostenso's *Wild Geese* (1925) being typical examples.

There is another chronological coincidence that sheds some light on Grove's isolated position. If Spettigue is right, *A Search for America* is a fictional account of Grove's early American years around 1913, the year when Franz Kafka wrote *Amerika* (also called *Der Verschollene*), which his literary executor Max Brod published in 1927 as a fragment. Though there is no evidence of any direct links between Grove and Kafka, certain similarities are striking. Like Grove's Branden, Kafka's Karl Rossmann (having seduced a servant girl) finds himself in America "on probation." Both grapple with opposite aspects of the New World, which is experienced as a utopia and country of refuge, but also as a place of exile. Both texts are imaginative re-creations of reality but cast in different narrative molds. Grove's version never exceeds the limits of fictional autobiography; Kafka uses innovative quasi-objective techniques to explore a subconscious world.

It is important to view Grove in perspective because he himself went out of his way to obliterate the traces of his literary ancestry in an effort to present himself as a singular phenomenon beyond any historical context. However, Grove's

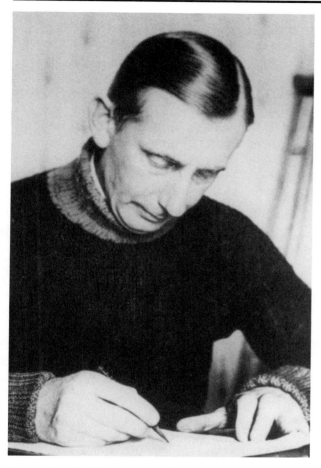

Frontispiece for The Letters of Frederick Philip Grove, *1976 (courtesy of Leonard Grove)*

dogmatic perfectionism and his effort to be recognized as a sage and a man of letters constitute just one side of his protean identity. His self-criticism, at times, could be as excessive as his conceit. "I am just a dilettante–in this as in other things," he wrote in a 1927 letter to Watson Kirkconnell in which he outlined his philosophical beliefs.

Given Grove's background, the term "dilettante," rather than simply indicating an admission of his failure to grasp abstract intellectual concepts, seems to be used here in a more specific sense. Grove introduces it after discussing (in the same letter) the thoughts of Plato and Henri Bergson. Any system of ideas, he argues, displays an aesthetic charm, irrespective of its inherent truth–a concept quite common among the writers of the decadent movement who defined the artist as a dilettante, as someone who continually masks his true identity and tries on various philosophies without fully subscribing to any. The supreme achievement of the dilettante is a playful change of identities.

Here we meet an element in Grove's mind and art that takes us back to his European years. Grove admired Oscar Wilde and in 1903 published a translation of Wilde's *Intentions* (*Fingerzeige*). In one of the essays in this collection ("The Decay of Lying") Wilde had attacked realist and naturalist tendencies in contemporary literature as perversions of the fundamental principle that life follows art. The reality of art, he claimed, is the only true reality–artificial, invented, and ahistorical: "The only real people are the people who never existed; and if a novelist is base enough to go to life for his personage, he should at least pretend that they are creations, and not boast of them as copies." Grove never forgot the lesson of the master that the young Greve had learned. Wilde regarded art as reality, but he also regarded life as an aesthetic experience. Greve, it might be argued, created "Frederick Philip Grove" in order to carry out an even more radical experiment with reality. Grove's ambitious struggle to become the "greatest Canadian author" can perhaps be interpreted as an attempt to subordinate the real world to his own artistic concept.

Seen from this point of view, there is no contradiction between Grove's highly developed self-esteem and his lifelong obsession with camouflaging his true identity. On the contrary: by inventing a new self, Grove turned his life into art, casting off all restrictions that his own past, the historical background, and contemporary literature might have placed on his existence. This approach also accounts for Grove's fascination with comprehensive systems of ideas and universal designs–like Charles Darwin's theory of evolution or Oswald Spengler's *Decline of the West* (1918-1922)–which he tried out on the real world with a vigorously experimental spirit.

"I wanted the simpler, the more elemental things, things cosmic in their associations, nearer to the beginning or end of creation," Grove had stated in *Over Prairie Trails*. Neither biographically nor artistically did his experiment turn out the way he had anticipated. Reality in the end proved stronger. Grove's role-playing led to an alternative identity that he was unable to escape, and Canada was no longer the literary desert waiting to be turned into the Garden of Eden by the wave of Grove's magic wand. Seen against the background of Canadian literature in the 1920s and 1930s, Grove's case assumes both comic and tragic dimensions: comic because Grove refused to abandon his *Lebenslüge* (life-lie) even when he had become a public figure in his own right; tragic because his ambitions made his work anachronistic. It came too late since the classic examples of realism in North America preceded *Settlers of the Marsh;* it came too early because the Canadian public was neither prepared to appreciate the extraordinary literary and intellectual challenge Grove represented, nor to offer the discriminating critical response Grove needed.

Grove's achievement remains in spite of, and in some sense because of, this ambiguity. Felix Paul Greve, hovering between naturalism and decadence, is little more than a semi-anonymous figure of literary history; Frederick Philip Grove continues to be one of the most stimulating and provocative modern authors. While the critical question of whether Grove is primarily a regionalist or a universalist has not yet been definitively answered, contemporary writers such as Robert Kroetsch have recently discovered Grove as a pioneer in a new sense. Through his stubborn refusal to accept the doctrines of realism and through his deliberate confusion of fact and fiction, Grove seems to anticipate postmodern modes of writing. Maybe his verdict on Wilde, written in 1903 (in *Oskar Wilde*), is after all a fair judgment on Grove himself: "Wilde's productions . . . were hardly ever excellent. Only few of them will stand up to serious criticism as pure works of art. What is important is Wilde's work as a whole. . . . In a hieroglyphic code, it reflects the tragic essence of a modern man's life, of a man who wanted, and did not want, to be an artist, who wanted to live and couldn't because he confused living and dreaming."

Letters:

The Letters of Frederick Philip Grove, edited, with an introduction and notes, by Desmond Pacey (Toronto & Buffalo: University of Toronto Press, 1976).

Biography:

Douglas O. Spettigue, *FPG: The European Years* (Ottawa: Oberon, 1973).

References:

Rudolf Bader, "Frederick Philip Grove and Naturalism Reconsidered," in *Gaining Ground: European Critics on Canadian Literature*, edited by R. Kroetsch and R. M. Nischik (Edmonton: NeWest, 1985), pp. 222-233;

Otto Julius Bierbaum, "*Wanderungen*, von Felix Paul Greve," *Die Insel*, 3 (1901-1902): 195-196;

E. D. Blodgett, "*Alias* Grove: Variations in Disguise," in his *Configuration: Essays on the Canadian Literatures* (Downsview: ECW, 1982), pp. 112-153;

Helmut Bonheim, "F. P. Grove's 'Snow' and Sinclair Ross' 'The Painted Door'—The Rhetoric of the Prairie," in *Encounters and Explorations: Canadian Writers and European Critics*, edited by F. K. Stanzel and W. Zacharasiewicz (Würzburg: Königshausen, 1986), pp. 58-72;

W. E. Collin, "La Tragique Ironie de Frederick Philip Grove," *Gants du Ciel*, 4 (Winter 1946): 15-40;

Lynn DeVore, "The Backgrounds of *Nightwood*: Robin, Felix, and Nora," *Journal of Modern Literature*, 10 (March 1983): 71-90;

D. J. Dooley, "Puzzled by Immensities: Grove's Double Vision in *Fruits of the Earth*," in his *Moral Vision in the Canadian Novel* (Toronto & Vancouver: Clarke, Irwin, 1979), pp. 13-23;

Louis Dudek, "The Literary Significance of Grove's *Search*," in *Reappraisals: Canadian Writers. The Grove Symposium*, edited by John Nause (Ottawa: Ottawa University Press, 1974), pp. 89-99;

Wilfrid Eggleston, "F. P. G.: The Ottawa Interlude," in *Reappraisals: Canadian Writers. The Grove Symposium*, pp. 101-110;

Eggleston, "Frederick Philip Grove," in *Our Living Tradition*, edited by Claude T. Bissell (Toronto: University of Toronto Press, 1957), pp. 105-127;

André Gide, "Conversation avec un Allemand," in *Œuvres Complètes d'André Gide*, 15 volumes edited by Louis Martin-Chauffier (Paris: NRF, 1932-1939), IX: 133-143;

Rosmarin Heidenreich, "The Search for FPG," *Canadian Literature*, 80 (Spring 1979): 63-70;

Paul Hjartarson, "Design and Truth in Grove's *In Search of Myself*," *Canadian Literature*, 90 (Autumn 1981): 73-90;

Hjartarson, ed., *A Stranger To My Time: Essays by and about Frederick Philip Grove* (Edmonton: NeWest, 1986);

W. J. Keith, "Frederick Philip Grove's 'Difficult' Novel: *The Master of the Mill*," *ARIEL*, 4 (April 1973): 34-48;

Raymond Knister, "Frederick Philip Grove," *Ontario Library Review*, 13, no. 3 (1928): 60-62;

Henry Kreisel, "The Prairie: A State of Mind," in *Contexts of Canadian Criticism,* edited by Eli Mandel (Chicago: University of Chicago Press, 1971), pp. 254-266;

Henry Makow, "Grove's Treatment of Sex: Platonic Love in *The Yoke of Life," Dalhousie Review,* 58 (Autumn 1978): 528-540;

Robin Mathews, "F. P. Grove: An Important Version of *The Master of the Mill* Discovered," *Studies in Canadian Literature,* 7, no. 2 (1982): 241-257;

Lorraine McMullen, "Women in Grove's Novels," in *Reappraisals: Canadian Writers. The Grove Symposium,* pp. 67-76;

Patricia Morley, "*Over Prairie Trails:* 'a poem woven of impressions,' " *Humanities Association Review,* 25 (Summer 1974): 225-231;

Desmond Pacey, *Frederick Philip Grove* (Toronto: Ryerson, 1945);

Pacey, ed., *Frederick Philip Grove* (Toronto: Ryerson, 1970);

Pacey, ed., Introduction to *Tales from the Margin: The Selected Short Stories of Frederick Philip Grove* (Toronto & New York: Ryerson/McGraw-Hill, 1971), pp. 1-19;

Walter Pache, "Der Fall Grove–Vorbeben und Nachleben des Schriftstellers Frederick Philip Grove," in *Deutsch Canadisches Jahrbud,* volume 5, edited by Hartmut Froeschle (Toronto: Historical Society of Mecklenburg, Upper Canada, 1979), pp. 121-136;

Pache, "Frederick Philip Grove's Loneliness: Comparative Perspectives," *World Literature Written in English,* 25 (Spring 1985): 104-111;

Arthur L. Phelps, "Frederick Philip Grove," in his *Canadian Writers* (Toronto: McClelland & Stewart, 1951), pp. 36-42;

Laurence Ricou, "The Implacable Prairie: The Fiction of Frederick Philip Grove," in his *Vertical Man/Horizontal World: Man and Landscape in Canadian Prairie Fiction* (Vancouver: University of British Columbia Press, 1973), pp. 38-64;

Anthony W. Riley, "The Case of Greve/Grove: The European Roots of a Canadian Writer," in *The Old World and the New: Literary Perspectives of German-speaking Canadians,* edited by Walter E. Riedel (Toronto: University of Toronto Press, 1984), pp. 37-58;

Riley, "The German Novels of Frederick Philip Grove," in *Reappraisals: Canadian Writers. The Grove Symposium,* pp. 55-66;

Malcolm Ross, Introduction to *Over Prairie Trails* (Toronto: McClelland & Stewart, 1957), pp. v-x;

Antoine Sirois, "Grove et Ringuet: Témoins d'une époque," *Canadian Literature,* 49 (Summer 1971): 20-27;

Isobel Skelton, "Frederick Philip Grove," *Dalhousie Review,* 19 (1939): 147-163;

Douglas O. Spettigue, *Frederick Philip Grove* (Toronto: Copp Clark, 1969);

Spettigue, "Frederick Philip Grove in Manitoba," *Mosaic,* 3 (April 1970): 19-33;

Spettigue, "The Grove Enigma Resolved," *Queen's Quarterly,* 79 (Spring 1972): 1-2;

Spettigue and Riley, "Felix Paul Greve *redivivus:* zum früheren Leben des kanadischen Schriftstellers Frederick Philip Grove," *Seminar,* 9 (June 1973): 148-155;

K. P. Stich, "Frederick Philip Grove's Language of Choice," *Journal of Commonwealth Literature,* 14 (August 1979): 9-17;

Stich, "Grove's New World Bluff," *Canadian Literature,* 90 (Autumn 1981): 111-123;

Margaret R. Stobie, *Frederick Philip Grove* (New York: Twayne, 1973);

Stobie, "Grove and the Ants," *Dalhousie Review,* 58 (Autumn 1978): 418-433;

Ronald Sutherland, *Frederick Philip Grove* (Toronto: McClelland & Stewart, 1969);

Sutherland, "What was Frederick Philip Grove?," *The New Hero: Essays in Comparative Quebec /Canadian Literature* (Toronto: Macmillan, 1977), pp. 39-50;

Rudy Wiebe, "A Novelist's Personal Notes on Frederick Philip Grove," *University of Toronto Quarterly,* 47 (Spring 1978): 189-199;

David Williams, "Oscar Wilde and a Swede from Nebraska: Masks of Autobiography in *Settlers of the Marsh* and *In Search of Myself,*" in *Canada and the Nordic Countries,* edited by Jorn Carlsen and Berge Strëyffert (Lund, Sweden: Lund University Press, 1988), pp. 365-375;

George Woodcock, "Possessing the Land: Notes on Canadian Fiction," in *The Canadian Imagination: Dimensions of a Literary Culture,* edited by David Staines (Cambridge, Mass. & London: Harvard University Press, 1977).

Papers:

Most of Grove's papers, including several unpublished manuscripts; a diary entitled "Thoughts and Reflections," covering the period from 14 March 1933 to 3 June 1940; and typescripts of the majority of stories in *Tales from the Margin* are in the Grove Collection, Elizabeth Dafoe Library, University of Manitoba.

Louis Hémon
(12 October 1880-8 July 1913)

Larry Shouldice
University of Sherbrooke

BOOKS: *Maria Chapdelaine: Récit du Canada français* (Montreal: Le Febvre, 1916; Paris: Grasset, 1921; New York: Macmillan, 1921); translated by W. H. Blake as *Maria Chapdelaine: A Tale of the Lake St. John Country* (Toronto: Macmillan, 1921; New York: Macmillan, 1921); translated by Andrew Macphail as *Maria Chapdelaine: A Romance of French Canada* (Montreal: Chapman/London: Lane, 1921);

La Belle que voilà (Paris: Grasset, 1923; Paris & New York: Nelson, 1925); translated by William Aspenwall Bradley as *My Fair Lady* (New York: Macmillan, 1923);

Colin-Maillard (Paris: Grasset, 1924); translated by Arthur Richmond as *Blind Man's Buff* (London: Macmillan, 1924; New York: Macmillan, 1925);

The Journal of Louis Hémon, translated by Bradley (New York: Macmillan, 1924);

Battling Malone, pugiliste (Paris: Grasset, 1925); translated by Bradley as *Battling Malone and Other Stories* (London: Butterworth, 1925);

Monsieur Ripois and Nemesis, translated by Bradley (New York: Macmillan, 1925); published in the original French as *Monsieur Ripois et la Némésis* (Paris: Grasset, 1950);

Récits sportifs, edited by Aurélien Boivin and Jean-Marc Bourgeois (Alma, Que.: Royaume, 1982);

Itinéraire de Liverpool à Québec (Quimper, France: Calligrammes, 1985).

Louis Hémon, author of the best-known book about French Canada, was in fact a French-man who never lived to see his masterpiece in print. *Maria Chapdelaine: Récit du Canada français*, however, has lived on to become one of the major publishing successes of the century, widely read in a variety of languages throughout the world and still a focus of controversy. Hémon's reputation rests entirely on this one book, his other writings being considered relatively minor.

Hémon was born on 12 October 1880 in Brest, France, to Louise LeBreton and Félix Hémon, an inspector-general of public education. After completing his studies in law and Asian languages at the Sorbonne, Louis then spent a year at Chartres in military service (1901-1902). Still without a profession, in 1903 he settled in London, where he worked as a free-lance journalist and sportswriter. He also completed four novels that remained unpublished until after his death. Father of a young daughter with his wife, the former Lydia O'Kelley, he abandoned both mother and child in 1911 to immigrate to Canada.

Hémon found little to interest him in either Montreal or Quebec City and soon headed to the pioneer settlements on the northern frontier. His work as a hired hand and surveyor in several farming communities around Lac Saint-Jean was interrupted only by two brief visits to Montreal, the latter in the spring of 1913 when he typed and sent off the manuscript of *Maria Chapdelaine* to his publisher in Paris.

In the summer of 1913 Hémon left Quebec en route to the western prairies. He had reached the town of Chapleau in northern Ontario when, hiking along the railway track with his packsack

LOUIS HÉMON

MARIA CHAPDELAINE

RÉCIT DU CANADA FRANÇAIS

29 BOIS ORIGINAUX DE JEAN LÉBÉDEFF

LE LIVRE DE DEMAIN
ARTHÈME FAYARD & CIE, ÉDITEURS — PARIS
18-20, rue du Saint-Gothard, 18-20

Frontispiece and title page for a 1930 edition of Hémon's first and best-known novel, which is still being read and discussed by students and critics

on his back, he was somehow struck and killed by a locomotive.

His famous novel *Maria Chapdelaine* tells the story of its heroine, a simple and sincere young woman who is close to nature, to her family, and to the traditional life of the French-Canadian habitant farmer at the turn of the century. The plot revolves around Maria's three suitors: François Paradis, a handsome young coureur de bois; Lorenzo Surprenant, a wealthy émigré to the United States; and Eutrope Gagnon, a settler, friend, and neighbor of the family. Maria is in love with François and agrees to await his return from the lumber camps; one Christmas, however, François perishes while trying to snowshoe back to visit her. Maria is too overcome with grief to be able to choose between the temptations of a magnificent life in the big city, offered by Lorenzo, and the simpler promise of a good farm and possible prosperity with Eutrope.

When her mother falls ill and dies, Maria is forced to come to a decision. While standing vigil over her mother's body, she hears three voices: the miraculous sounds of the land in springtime; the call of French civilization; and finally the voice of "the land of Quebec." Following in her mother's footsteps and heroic ideals, Maria decides to marry Eutrope the next spring.

Quite apart from its commercial success, *Maria Chapdelaine* is a remarkable novel in a variety of respects. The story is at once simple and moving, structured on the rhythm of the seasons and providing an accurate description of life and work on the farm and its northern surroundings. Hémon's somewhat naturalistic vision marks a shift away from the excessively romanticized "terroir" (land) novels, and is thus an important precursor of the later growth of realism in Canadian writing. The traditional values of Quebec—fidelity to the land, family, church, and French heritage—are presented in the light of a collective movement, heavily backed by the clergy, to transform the northern forest into agricultural land and thus assure the survival of a French-

Canadian civilization already threatened by the forces of urbanization. In this way Hémon gave sympathetic expression to many of the central themes and concerns of Quebec culture at a time when the French-speaking people of Canada, lost in the backwaters of history, were virtually unknown to the rest of the world.

Originally appearing as a popular serial in the Paris newspaper *Le Temps* (January-February 1914), *Maria Chapdelaine* was first published in Montreal after sustained efforts by Louvigny de Montigny and others, including the Quebec government, which agreed to buy two hundred copies. Initial reaction to the book was highly favorable in both Europe and Canada, although various Quebec nationalist groups were indignant at the archaic quality of the dialogue and incensed that a Frenchman had dared present French Canadians as uneducated farmers. After Bernard Grasset obtained European publishing rights in 1921, an intense marketing offensive led to prodigious sales, including more than 1.5 million copies in French alone. With translation into some twenty languages, countless republications, various radio and stage adaptations, at least two films, comic strips, illustrated and deluxe versions, and even a popular song based on it, *Maria Chapdelaine* came to be a worldwide success.

It has also been the source of lawsuits, intrigues, manipulations, misunderstandings, and endless polemical debates. Hundreds of articles have been written on it (152 in the Montreal daily *Le Devoir* alone, between 1916 and 1970), and the book has been given all manner of interpretations. Particularly popular with right-wing ideologues, for whom Maria represents the conservative values of family, fatherland, and religion, the heroine has also appealed to leftist critics who see her as a figure of alienation, colonization, and submission. It is ironic that Hémon, whose work stands apart from the French-Canadian literature of the time in virtually every respect, should nevertheless have created in his heroine an enduring symbol of traditional Quebec.

Recent critical commentary, including careful textual analyses of the various editions, has charted the many sociopolitical uses to which the book has been put. Despite continuing controversies, however, and regardless of the fact that the world portrayed by Louis Hémon is now no more than a memory from Quebec's increasingly distant past, *Maria Chapdelaine* remains the best-known work in French-Canadian literature—and perhaps also the best loved.

Letters:
Louis Hémon: Lettres à sa famille, edited by Nicole Deschamps (Montreal: Presses de l'Université de Montréal, 1968).

References:
Alfred Ayotte and Victor Tremblay, *L'aventure Louis Hémon* (Montreal: Fides, 1974);
Nicole Deschamps, Raymonde Héroux, and Normand Villeneuve, *Le Mythe de Maria Chapdelaine* (Montreal: Presses de l'Université de Montréal, 1980);
Jacques Ferron, Preface to *Colin-Maillard* (Montreal: Editions du Jour, 1972).

William Albert Hickman
(22 December 1877-10 September 1957)

Paul Matthew St. Pierre
Simon Fraser University

BOOKS: *Handbook of New Brunswick* (Fredericton: Crown Land Department, 1900);

The Canadian West and Northwest (London: Royal Colonial Institute, 1903);

The Sacrifice of the Shannon (Toronto: Briggs, 1903; New York: Stokes, 1903);

An Unofficial Love-Story (New York: Century, 1909; Toronto: Musson, 1910);

Canadian Nights (New York: Century, 1914; Toronto: McClelland, Goodchild & Stewart, 1914).

Underrated because of the brevity of his career and the paucity of his output, Albert Hickman nevertheless deserves a more important place in Canadian letters. His contributions to the adventure narrative, the romantic genre, the ironic mode, and the novella form distinguish him as a fairly innovative writer intent on ushering in a new century with fiction whose explicit self-consciousness distinguishes it refreshingly from earlier works containing implicit Victorian self-interest. Unfortunately, all his novels and stories are in first editions and out of print, but several of them are worthy of reprinting in scholarly editions because of their enduring contemporaneity. *Canadian Nights* (1914), a collection of loosely interrelated stories and short novels with vivid Maritime settings, articulate characters, and convincing narrators, is of particular interest in this respect, possibly reading even better today than when the tales first appeared in *The Century: The American Magazine* during the first decade of the century. (Ironically, it was this kind of American contact that was to draw Hickman to New England after World War I, where his vocation of marine engineering virtually overtook his avocation of story telling.) Of more exclusively historical interest are Hickman's early nonfiction publications, *Handbook of New Brunswick* (1900) and *The Canadian West and Northwest* (1903), offering insights into, respectively, one of the garrisons of confederation and the vast Canadian frontier. This early concern with history and geography

seems to have made possible Hickman's later understanding of character and situation, of persons in place, which characterizes and strengthens his literary accomplishment.

Born in 1877 in Dorchester, New Brunswick, and educated in Pictou, Nova Scotia, the area with which he is usually associated, William Albert Hickman extended his family's tradition of shipbuilding by studying marine engineering at Harvard. After graduating with a B.S. in 1899, he acted as a temporary commissioner for the New Brunswick government, producing his *Handbook of New Brunswick*. Subsequently, after returning to Pictou, he conducted extensive research into the people and landscapes of western Canada, presenting his findings on 13 January 1903 in the form of a paper to the Royal Colonial Institute, which published *The Canadian West and Northwest* in its *Proceedings*, 34. In both these works Hickman distinguishes himself from nonliterary civil servants and shows himself to be a precursor of the modern nationalist movement.

During the early 1900s Hickman simultaneously pursued his profession as an engineer and used his talent as a novelist, writing part of his first novel, *The Sacrifice of the Shannon* (1903), in February 1902 while aboard the Canadian government icebreaker *Minto* in the Strait of Northumberland off the coast of Pictou. This romantic sea adventure is successful mainly at the narrative level, Hickman having managed to transfer his own immediacy of perception and expression to his engaging narrator, Frederic Ashburn, the captain of the *Shannon* and witness to the ship's anthropomorphic "sacrifice" in its final effort to clear a channel for other ships: "The ice creaked and groaned for a moment, and the masts leaned back as the stern sank, sank while the great curved bow rose slowly high in the air, as though preparing for one last crushing blow at its lifelong enemy, the ice." In Hickman's allegorical emphases, as well as in his symbolic treatment of the setting, the novel approaches the story-telling traditions of Herman Melville and Joseph Conrad.

"Gentlemen. . . . This concert is about to begin. What the
program is to be I can tell you least of all"

CANADIAN NIGHTS

BY
ALBERT HICKMAN

Illustrated

TORONTO
McCLELLAND, GOODCHILD & STEWART, Limited
1914

*Frontispiece and title page for the Canadian edition of Hickman's last book, a collection of interrelated stories and novellas
set in the Maritimes*

Hickman's aim, however, seems to have been to produce lighthearted entertainment more than to create literature. Although in his subsequent work Hickman moved away from romance and adventure toward the common ground of humor, irony, and satire, he maintained the direct narrative stance and the nautically austere mode of address of his earliest fiction, putting it to the aesthetically higher purposes of speculating on human nature and exploring peculiarities of character.

Much more logically and thematically adventurous than *The Sacrifice of the Shannon*, the novella *An Unofficial Love-Story* (1909) and the stories collected in *Canadian Nights*—"Overproof," "The Man with the Horse's Neck," "The A-Flat Major Polonaise," "Compensated," "The New Power," and "Oriented"—in a critical sense mark

both the beginning and the end of Hickman's literary career. Through writing these works he realized his plateau of stylistic refinement and then turned to more exclusively professional, engineering concerns. Standing out in the story collection are "The A-Flat Major Polonaise" and "Compensated," which both feature inspired descriptions of executant musicianship and spare illustrations of "the law of compensation," as in the case of Mr. Spiers, in "Compensated," whose pale rendition of a Chopin ballade is eclipsed by another man's masterful playing of a Beethoven sonata yet impresses Miss Sneed enough that she goes so far as to accept his proposal of marriage. Also worthy of note are the short stories "The Man with the Horse's Neck," about a Hudson's Bay Company official, a teetotaler, who manages to drink every one of his detractors under the table, and "Oriented," about the budding romance of George Porteous Vaughan and Helen McNab: he takes her on a maniacal dash in his open Brunel automobile through the luscious mire of Montreal's Vaudreuil-Como road in the midst of the April thaw. In his last works of fiction Hickman demonstrates his narrative mastery of both the ruggedness of the New World and the refinement of the Old, and he reveals an aesthetic blending of tonal versatility and of characters in motion.

His full contribution to Canadian literature, however, remains to be seen: his fiction invites and merits closer examination. In the very phraseology of "Oriented," for example, one can recognize the ideology of realism: the incident involving the speeding car is "an artistic performance" in which a man and a woman break through the conventions of courtship; the heroine "was pretty; but if you stripped her of the aura that surrounds every pretty girl, she was not attractive"; Mr. Glover and Miss Dacoste, an ostentatiously conventional couple accompanying Mr. Vaughan and Miss McNab on their promenade on wheels, recline in the tonneau "on luxurious cushions spattered with half-dry mud"; and Mr. Vaughan, after all—the narrator concludes—"simply took the lady for a ride in a motor-car," even though, later that evening, he walks toward her home in an anticipatory mood. Such naughtily urbane writing may seem to the modern eye to belong merely in a period piece, yet it unassumingly foreshadows the intermittent rise of realism in Cana-

dian literature. Despite his subtle literary accomplishments, Hickman has received slight critical attention at best and only the obligatory interest of librarians and collectors.

In his 1924 study *Headwaters of Canadian Literature* Archibald MacMechan discusses the flourishing of popular literature during the period from the end of the nineteenth century to the beginning of World War I, the period during which Hickman wrote, yet dismisses him as merely one of a group of writers whose Canadian claim is doubtful because of their American affiliations. The *Literary History of Canada* (1965) merely places Hickman in an enumeration of Maritime writers and, like some other studies, cites *The Sacrifice of the Shannon* as the sole example of his fiction, thus overlooking his best and most characteristic writing. However, W. H. New's *Dreams of Speech and Violence* (1987) refers to his stories at slightly greater length. Like the story-telling narrator of *An Unofficial Love-Story*, who admits at the beginning of his fiction, "I was but an onlooker on the far outside," Albert Hickman became a kind of literary bystander, observing literature from a distance and Canadian literature, in particular, from an American vantage point. But his fiction continues to stand, albeit in a small corner in need of more light.

Papers:
Some of Hickman's papers, mostly concerning his engineering career, are at St. Mary's University Library, Halifax, Nova Scotia.

Pauline Johnson

(10 March 1861-7 March 1913)

Donald A. Precosky
College of New Caledonia

BOOKS: *The White Wampum* (London: Lane/ Boston: Lamson, Wolffe, 1895);
Canadian Born (Toronto: Morang, 1903);
Legends of Vancouver (Vancouver: Saturday Sunset, 1911; Toronto: McClelland, Goodchild & Stewart, 1911);
Flint and Feather (Toronto: Musson, 1912; revised and enlarged, 1913; London: Hodder & Stoughton, 1913); revised and enlarged again as *Flint and Feather: The Complete Poems of E. Pauline Johnson* (Toronto: Hodder & Stoughton, 1917);
The Shagganappi (Toronto: Briggs, 1913);
The Moccasin Maker (Toronto: Briggs, 1913).

OTHER: William D. Lighthall, ed., *Songs of the Great Dominion*, includes poems by Johnson (London: Scott, 1889).

Pauline Johnson is a symbol of the sharp division between the so-called serious and popular literary cultures in Canada. Although she has been almost entirely ignored in scholarship and academic anthologies, she is one of the few Canadian poets–Robert Service being another–whose names are familiar to the general public.

Emily Pauline Johnson was born 10 March 1861 on the Six Nations Reserve near Brantford, Ontario, the youngest of the four children of G. H. Johnson, head chief of the Six Nations, and his English wife Emily (née Howells). Despite her mixed heritage, Johnson always regarded herself as an Indian. Her Mohawk name was Tekahionwake.

Although two of her poems were included in the important anthology *Songs of the Great Dominion* (1889), Johnson's career began in earnest in June 1892 when she was included in a group of poets who read before the Young Liberal Club of Toronto. The enthusiastic reception given her led to an exclusive solo reading of her poems two weeks later. Soon she was launched on a hectic reading career that lasted almost two decades.

Pauline Johnson

The turn of the century was the golden age of traveling performers and reciters in Canada. With no television, radio, or cinema, most small communities turned to these touring entertainers for theatrical diversion. Johnson was primarily a performer, combining a large dose of theatricality with her poetry and appearing on stage in an Indian costume complete with fringed buckskins, headdress, and beaded moccasins.

In 1894 Johnson went to London to recite and arrange for the publication of her first book, *The White Wampum*, which was brought out the following year by the Bodley Head (Lane). The book is a collection of short lyrics and narratives, most with Indian subjects. In her depiction of the Indian, Johnson emphasizes his strength of character, particularly his loyalty and his refusal to deny his beliefs under even the most trying circumstances. Many of the poems may strike the modern reader as rhetorically inflated and strident; exclamation marks are rampant. There are two reasons for this failing. One is that she was writing of an injustice she felt vehemently and was consequently prone to overstate. Johnson also undoubtedly wrote with the stage in mind: a consideration that caused her to make her poems excessively theatrical. At times, however, Johnson moves beyond shrillness and poetic diction to an impassioned yet dignified statement of the Indians' rightful anger, as in "The Cattle Thief," or to a clear and gentle lyricism, as in "The Camper" and "Rainfall."

In 1903, after eight more years of almost steady touring, Johnson published her second book, *Canadian Born*. The Indian theme is far less prevalent here, replaced by the dual strains of Canadian nationalism and loyalism. The title poem, in which she claims that "we the men of Canada, can face the world and brag/That we were born in Canada beneath the British flag," is typical of the way in which she combines these two loyalties. Her many trips across the country resulted in poems that describe virtually every province then in the Dominion. Although Indian subjects play a smaller role, they do form the theme of what are possibly her two finest poems: "The Corn Husker" and "Silhouette." Both are taut, near-imagist expressions of the loss the Indian has suffered. Their muted, austere tone (derived from Charles G. D. Roberts, who was a major influence on this book) is much more effective than the shouting voice of *The White Wampum*.

Illness forced Johnson to retire to Vancouver in 1909, but though she was in steadily declining health, Johnson was not idle. In 1911 she wrote for the *Daily Province* a series of stories based on West Coast Indian legends as told by Chief Joseph Capilano. These proved so popular that in the same year they were collected into a book, *Legends of Vancouver*. This volume is possibly Johnson's finest. In it she stresses the same values of heroism and loyalty as she does in her early poems, but the stories are told in a more natural voice. Johnson provided Vancouver with a rich mythology while at the same time pointing out the sad truth that Indian ways were dying as Vancouver was growing into a major city.

Flint and Feather, Johnson's most famous book, appeared in 1912 and was an instant success. The book is made up of all the poems in her first two collections together with a selection of previously unpublished verse. The new poems

Johnson in full regalia as a Mohawk princess, as she dressed for her performances (courtesy of the Provincial Archives of British Columbia, Victoria)

share the main traits of her early works. One significant feature of the 1912 poems is that she chose to write about western Canada at a time when most poetry in the Dominion focused upon Ontario and the Maritimes.

A second volume of prose, *The Shagganappi*, was also published in 1912 (with 1913 on its title page). It consists of twenty-two romantic adventure stories, most of which are set in the West. The title is the Cree word for the buckskin pony that is common on the western plains. The collection was provided with an introduction by Ernest Thompson Seton.

Johnson died in Vancouver on 7 March 1913. After a large public procession her ashes were buried in Stanley Park. Shortly after her death Johnson's last collection of stories, *The Moccasin Maker*, was published. Although most of the pieces are excessively melodramatic, two deserve special mention. "My Mother" is not a story at all but a biography of her English mother and a portrait of her parents' marriage. It deals honestly with the touchy subjects of racial bigotry and interracial marriage. Along with "A Pagan in St. Paul's Cathedral," another personal reminiscence, "My Mother" is essential reading for anyone interested in Johnson's life.

Johnson belongs to a popular tradition that is now almost dead. In her active public career thousands of people from coast to coast turned out to hear her recite. Though she is discounted by the academic community, the fact that her collected poems are still in print as of this writing attests to Johnson's basic appeal. The appearance of a suite of poems in 1989, *Pale as Real Ladies: Poems for Pauline Johnson*, by the native writer Joan Crate, suggests also that Johnson may have special appeal to a new generation of writers and readers. As her biographer, Betty Keller, demonstrated in 1981, Pauline Johnson made theatrical use of her Mohawk heritage; she designed her writings and her performances to appeal to her audience's expectations of Indians. As Crate observes, she did so in order to allow a native voice to be heard at all. To young native writers, therefore, Johnson's career offers a challenge, for it represents both a life to be respected and a model to be overcome.

Biography:

Betty Keller, *Pauline: A Biography of Pauline Johnson* (Vancouver: Dougals & McIntyre, 1981).

References:

Walter McRaye, *Pauline Johnson and Her Friends* (Toronto: Ryerson, 1947);

Marcus Van Steen, *Pauline Johnson: Her Life and Work* (Toronto: Hodder & Stoughton, 1965).

Alice C. Jones

(26 August 1853-27 February 1933)

Gwendolyn Davies
Acadia University

BOOKS: *The Night Hawk: A Romance of the '60s,* as
   Alix John (New York: Stokes, 1901; Lon-
   don: Heinemann, 1901);
Bubbles We Buy (Boston: Turner, 1903; London:
   Richards, 1903); republished as *Isabel Brod-
   erick: Bubbles We Buy* (London & New York:
   Lane, 1904);
Gabriel Praed's Castle (Boston: Turner, 1904; Lon-
   don: Richards, 1904);
Marcus Holbeach's Daughter (New York & London:
   Appleton, 1912);
Flame of Frost (New York & London: Appleton,
   1914).

SELECTED PERIODICAL PUBLICATIONS
UNCOLLECTED:
FICTION
"A Lost Cause," *Critic,* "Jubilee Number" (1889):
   15-20;
"Hidden Treasure," *Week,* 2 January 1891, 74-76;
"The Blue Cloak," *Canadian Magazine,* 22 (March
   1904): 418-426; 23 (April 1904): 538-544;
"At the Harbour's Mouth," *Canadian Magazine,*
   26 (November 1905): 59-65; 27 (December
   1905): 162-168.
NONFICTION
"A Day In Winchester," *Week,* 27 September
   1888, 702-703;
"Treasure Hunting," *Week,* 3 October 1890, 695;
"Hidden Treasure," *Week,* 2 January 1891, 74-76;
"Christmas In Rome," *Week,* 23 January 1891,
   126;
"Stray Thoughts In Venice," *Week,* 29 May 1891,
   413-414;
"Up The River," *Week,* 11 September 1891, 655;
"All Saints' Day," *Week,* 30 October 1891, 768;
"The Misericordia in Florence," *Dominion Illus-
   trated Monthly,* 1 (January 1893): 744-747;
"The Italian Royal Family," *Week,* 27 January
   1893, 199-202;
"Nile Vignettes: Sakkarah," *Week,* 19 July 1895,
   801-802;
"Nile Vignettes: From Cairo to Luxor," *Week,* 26
   July 1895, 826-827;

Alice Jones

"Nile Vignettes: Rameses," *Week,* 2 August 1895,
   851-852;
"Nile Vignettes: Luxor to Aswan," *Week,* 9 August 1895, 872-874;
"Nile Vignettes: Luxor," *Week,* 16 August 1895,
   898-899.

During her lifetime Alice Jones enjoyed a
reputation among her contemporaries as one of
the leading female novelists in Canada. With her
international themes, independent women charac-

ters, and insistence on Canadian content, Jones managed to win a popular readership both at home and abroad. Never as socially conscious or as ironic as her contemporary Sara Jeannette Duncan, she was nonetheless consistent in counterpointing the vigor of wilderness landscapes and natural people against the decadence and hypocrisy of sophisticated urban civilization. A recurring interest in art and architecture also informed her novels, although it found more detailed expression in her travel sketches published in the *Dominion Illustrated Monthly* and the *Week* in the 1880s and 1890s. Jones's contributions to the *Week* have been described by Eva-Marie Kroller in *Canadian Travellers in Europe, 1850-1900* (1987) as ranking "among the finest in Canadian travel-writing."

The daughter of Margaret Wiseman Stairs and Alfred Gilpin Jones, a future lieutenant governor of Nova Scotia, Alice Jones was born in 1853 in Halifax into a distinguished family of Loyalist descent. Her interest in Nova Scotian history found early expression in narratives such as "A Lost Cause," *The Night Hawk* (1901), and *Bubbles We Buy* (1903), in which she integrated oral tradition and provincial settings into period contexts. Although little is known of her formal education, she pursued her study of languages in tours of Europe and North Africa in the 1880s and 1890s. The impressions and experiences she gained in these travels informed the series of descriptive sketches submitted to the *Dominion Illustrated Monthly* and the *Week* throughout that period. Describing Jones as "well-read in the works of John Ruskin and Walter Pater," Kroller argues that Jones brought an "impressionist scrutiny and aesthetic evaluation" to her descriptions of Europe's art and architecture that provided "an important antidote to the utilitarian or perfunctory approach to art among many of her fellow travellers." Sketches on Rome, Florence, Venice, and Cairo are typical in revealing Jones's wide range of reading (Washington Irving, Robert Browning, William Shakespeare, George Eliot, Henry James, and William Dean Howells) and her perception of art as an educational force. Just as Ruskin made the travel motif central, notes Kroller, so did Jones. "Her wanderings" through a city such as Florence, Kroller adds, "imply a journey through history toward aesthetic and moral revelation."

The pattern of Jones's life throughout the 1880s and 1890s seems to have been one of leisurely travel, family visitations, and the writing of short stories and journalistic sketches. Her journal for 1894 shows her in Egypt in January, in Rome in April, in Paris in May, in England in May and June, and home in Canada in July. It is punctuated with descriptions of the paintings that she sees in Paris and London; a lecture that she hears at University College, London; an archaelogical work at Thoptus; her views of several London plays; and the round of teas, croquet parties, and visitations that she attends once back in Halifax. By December her journal records that she has departed for Jamaica, the scene of an unpublished novel of that name written sometime after 1894. All of this was to change dramatically in 1900 when Jones's father was made lieutenant governor of Nova Scotia. Her journals from 1900 to 1904 record a whirl of public engagements and official entertainments as she moved into Government House with her family to become the unofficial chatelaine of the office. Halifax's significance as a major Atlantic port made it a central point for in-coming visitors, such as the writer Louis Fréchette and British officials, and outgoing Boer War military nurses and troops. Jones describes all of this in her journal in a sprightly and sometimes ironic fashion while at the same time marking the passing of a generation and an old way of life in Nova Scotia.

Jones's interest in Nova Scotian history found its most visible manifestation in this period in the publication of her first novel, *The Night Hawk*, written under the pseudonym "Alix John." Set in Paris, the American South, and Halifax during the American Civil War, the climax of the novel is based on a famous incident in local history when Confederate Captain John Taylor Wood ran the gunship *Tallahassee* through a Union blockade at the mouth of Halifax harbor. Jones introduces a charming Southern belle-cum-spy (Antoinette LeMoine) for romantic diversion, a revengeful Union agent for dramatic tension, and a noble British officer for moral victory. She took genuine pride in having copied Captain Wood's drawing of the *Tallahassee* for the cover but, according to her journal, worried when she talked to him in his exile in Halifax in August 1901 that "he will see many weak points in [the novel's] facts." Nonetheless, much of the Halifax background of the book rings true, particularly the setting in a large house on the Northwest Arm based on Jones's own girlhood home, "Bloomingdale."

The Night Hawk was the first of Jones's novels to integrate a strong, independent female character into a readable romance of intrigue or adventure. The story was heavily dependent on coincidence and was attacked by newspapers such as the *Philadelphia Times* and the *Brooklyn Times* for being untrue to history and for being melodramatic. On the whole, however, Jones's book was favorably reviewed in newspapers and magazines across the United States and Canada. She monitored responses in 1901 and 1902 through her Boston clipping service, and although she fretted in her journal at one stage over "how it is selling in New York," she was deeply gratified to find that in Halifax the book and its author seemed "to be quite a local success."

Jones's second novel, *Bubbles We Buy,* was originally entitled "Gold, the Old Man's Sword." Based on the actual tale of a Nova Scotian privateer who had become the richest man in the province through his spoils, the novel also adapted a Breton legend, a Royal Academy painting, and Guy de Maupassant's use of madness to its Boston, Nova Scotian, London, and European settings. There are psychological overtones in her description of the veiled figure painted by the increasingly mad Broderick, and a legacy of violence and tyranny from the province's past brings an almost Gothic overtone to the romance not found in Jones's other fiction.

Bubbles We Buy exposed the destructiveness of greed and money-getting, a theme that Jones was to develop further in *Gabriel Praed's Castle* (1904). However, in reviewing *Bubbles We Buy,* critics tended to focus favorably on the strong plot line and unfavorably on the nationalist issue. The *Winnipeg Telegram* was particularly vociferous in accusing Jones of downgrading her Canadian characters and content: "what appears evident is that Miss Jones seems to have imbibed the spirit of sordidness rampant among the contributors to cheap New York magazines. The book is written for United States readers" (undated clipping). Stung to the quick by this assault, Jones addressed her dilemma in letters written to Canadian newspapers and to the *Academy* periodical in London. "I am a Canadian," she stated. "But as we Canadians who attempt novel writing must necessarily try to suit the American market, either the hero or heroine must be of that nationality—better if both are. While the Americans are willing to read of Canada as a wilderness inhabited by Indians and French peasants, they do not care to hear of its civilization or progress. These," she

concluded, "are some of the difficulties of suiting one's writing to a foreign market" (*Academy,* 16 July 1904). More than one Canadian paper applauded Jones's confrontation of the issue, noting that "Miss Alice Jones has spoken out in meeting and hoisted her Canadian colours; it remains to be seen whether by doing so she has to any extent spoiled her market for the future." Possibly, "the Canadian public may have a certain share of blame in the matter. Have they not been a little slow of heart to believe in the talent of their writers?" (*Halifax Morning Chronicle,* 13 August 1904).

Gabriel Praed's Castle, Jones's next novel, represents her most polished treatment of two recurring themes: the struggle of independent women to assert themselves in a masculine world and the confrontation between North American vitality and European decadence. In Sylvia Dorr, Jones creates an artist determined to preserve the integrity of her creative ambitions, and in Julia Praed she paints an image of Canadian vigor breathing fresh life into the jadedness of Paris. The portrait of the well-intentioned but unpolished Mr. Praed verges on caricature, but Jones is skilled in depicting the incestuous, competitive world of Paris entrepreneurs and artists. Widely reviewed in the United States and Canada, *Gabriel Praed's Castle* prompted L. E. Horning of Victoria University to proclaim in *Acta Victoriana* (Toronto) that "She [Jones] now takes a front rank in the rapidly increasing list of talented Canadian authors. . . . She is one of our best" (December 1904).

In 1906 Jones's father died while in office, and she moved out of Government House to live for a brief period with her brother in Bedford, a suburb of Halifax. No lover of Canadian winters, as her journals well indicate, Jones made the decision in 1907 to move permanently to Menton in the south of France. Here she was not far away from her artist-sister, Frances Jones Bannerman, who had settled at Alassio on the French-Italian border. In the remaining twenty-six years of her life, Jones was to publish two more novels, *Marcus Holbeach's Daughter* (1912) and *Flame of Frost* (1914). Both works are set in rugged terrain in Canada and show the beneficial influence of the natural landscape in awakening the best in individuals. Marcus Holbeach is a playboy living idly on the Riviera and in London. The only decent things in his life are his daughter and the estate that he has in the Gaspé area of Quebec, and here he occasionally repairs to renew himself through salmon fishing and rural living. The clash between his lifestyles reaches a climax when his friend Lady Warrenden arrives in the Gaspé to force Holbeach to choose between his worlds. Subthemes in the novel include the investment of the Jersey fishery in Canada, a historical thread drawn from Jones's own family involvement in the east-coast fishery.

Flame of Frost once again develops the theme of cultural confrontation by interweaving native peoples, exiled French nobility, and a Canadian entrepreneur into a story of diamond mining in the northern wilderness of Ontario. This novel is very much an adventure story and lacks some of the cultural and historic touches that made Jones's earlier fiction interesting.

With an inexpensive price of $1.50, an occasional handsome illustration, and well-paced plots, Alice Jones's novels attracted a wide readership and were always published in both English and American editions. She added a popular dimension to the international themes explored by Howells and James and brought to them her own understanding of the art world, Nova Scotian history, and human folly. At the time of her death in Menton on 27 February 1933, she had not published for some time, although undated manuscript novels entitled "Jamaica," "A Well Dressed Woman," and "From The North West" in the Public Archives of Nova Scotia suggest that her body of work exceeded the five novels and the periodical publications that early in the century made her one of the most promising women writers in Canada.

Reference:

Eva-Marie Kroller, *Canadian Travellers in Europe, 1850-1900* (Vancouver: University of British Columbia Press, 1987), pp. 3, 55, 58, 82-88, 141-142.

Papers:

The Public Archives of Nova Scotia in Halifax has three manuscript novels by Jones and also possesses her journal from 1902 to 1904.

Marian Keith
(Mary Esther MacGregor)

(27 August 1874?-10 February 1961)

Misao Dean
University of Victoria

BOOKS: *Duncan Polite, the Watchman of Glenoro* (Toronto: Westminster, 1905; New York & Chicago: Revell, 1905; London: Hodder & Stoughton, 1905);

The Silver Maple (Toronto: Westminster, 1906; New York & Chicago: Revell, 1906; London: Hodder & Stoughton, 1906);

Treasure Valley (Toronto: Westminster, 1908; London: Hodder & Stoughton/New York: Doran, 1908);

'Lizbeth of the Dale (Toronto: Westminster, 1910; New York & London: Hodder & Stoughton, 1910);

The Black Bearded Barbarian: The Life of George Leslie Mackay of Formosa (Toronto: Foreign Missions Committee, Presbyterian Church of Canada, 1912; New York: Missionary Education Movement, 1912);

The End of the Rainbow (Toronto: Westminster, 1913; New York: Hodder & Stoughton/ Doran, 1913); republished as *The Pot o' Gold: At the End of the Rainbow* (London: Hodder & Stoughton, 1914);

In Orchard Glen (Toronto: McClelland, Goodchild & Stewart, 1918; New York: Doran, 1918);

Little Miss Melody (Toronto: McClelland & Stewart, 1921; New York: Doran, 1921);

The Bells of St. Stephen's (Toronto: McClelland & Stewart, 1922; New York: Doran, 1922; London: Hodder & Stoughton, 1923);

A Gentleman Adventurer: A Story of the Hudson's Bay Company (Toronto: McClelland & Stewart, 1924; New York: Doran, 1924; London: Hodder & Stoughton, 1925);

Under the Grey Olives (Toronto: McClelland & Stewart, 1927; New York: Doran, 1927);

The Forest Barrier (Toronto: McClelland & Stewart, 1930);

Courageous Women, by Keith, L. M. Montgomery, and Mabel Burns McKinley (Toronto: McClelland & Stewart, 1934);

Glad Days in Galilee; A Story of the Boyhood of Jesus (Toronto: McClelland & Stewart, 1935; New York & Cincinnati: Abingdon, 1935); revised as *Boy of Nazareth* (New York: Abingdon-Cokesbury, 1950);

As a Watered Garden (Toronto: McClelland & Stewart, 1947);

Yonder Shining Light (Toronto: McClelland & Stewart, 1948);

Lilacs in the Dooryard (Toronto: McClelland & Stewart, 1952);

The Grand Lady (Toronto: McClelland & Stewart, 1960).

Mary Esther Miller MacGregor, who wrote all her fiction under the pseudonym Marian Keith, was born (probably) on 27 August 1874 in the small town of Rugby in the Ontario township of Oro, which would become the setting for many of her early novels. Her father was John Miller, an Ontario-born schoolteacher of Scots ancestry, and her mother was Mary McIan Miller, born in Islay, Scotland. The youngest of five children, Esther (as she was known) was educated at the Collegiate Institute in Orillia and then followed her father into the profession of teaching, graduating from the Toronto Normal School in 1896.

While a teacher at the Central Public School in Orillia from 1899 to 1906, she published *Duncan Polite, the Watchman of Glenoro*, which appeared serially in the *Westminster* magazine from April 1904 to January 1905 before coming out as a book later in 1905. With the subsequent serial publication of *The Silver Maple* (1906) and *Treasure Valley* (1908), she joined Rev. Charles Gordon (Ralph Connor) as a regular contributor of serials to the *Westminster* and became one of the leading writers on the Westminster Publishing Company's fiction list.

In July 1909 Esther Miller married Donald Campbell MacGregor, the young assistant to the

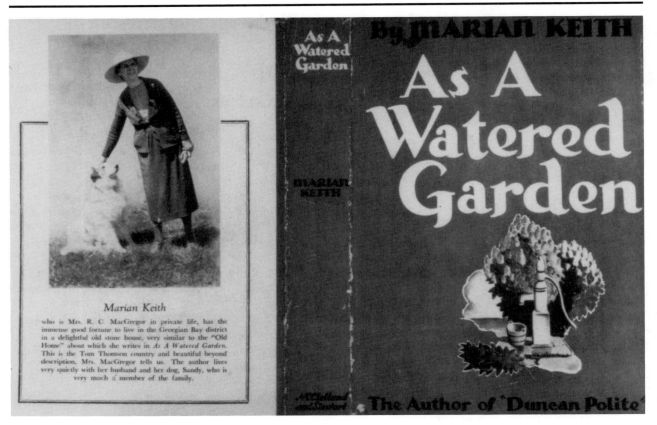

Dust jacket for Keith's 1947 novel, which became the first book of a trilogy set in the Georgian Bay area

Presbyterian minister in Orillia. MacGregor, a graduate in philosophy from the University of Toronto with a D.D. from Toronto's Knox College, had recently returned from postgraduate work in Glasgow to be ordained in Barrie, Ontario, in 1908. The couple honeymooned in the "home mission fields" of Alberta, inaugurating a lifelong interest in evangelism and missionary work. In 1910 they moved from Orillia to Toronto, where Donald MacGregor was assistant secretary to the Presbyterian church committee on social work and evangelism until 1914. His calling then took them to London (Ontario) and Brantford before they retired to his family home on the "Bay Shore Road" at Annan, near Owen Sound, the setting for *As a Watered Garden* (1947) and its sequels. After her husband's death on 11 October 1946, MacGregor moved to Owen Sound and later to Toronto, where she died on 10 February 1961.

Although MacGregor used the pseudonym Marian Keith from the beginning of her career, there seems to have been no mystery about her identity. Around the time of her move to To-

ronto she became personally known in literary circles; a profile in *Saturday Night* (22 July 1910) confidently referred to her as the author of Keith's books and grouped her with Nellie McClung and L. M. Montgomery as contributors to a revival of writing by women. When the Toronto Women's Press Club held a reception for women authors in December 1911, "Mrs. Donald MacGregor" was feted along with Montgomery, who found her "a bright little soul, full of fun and humour" (*Selected Journals of L. M. Montgomery*, 1985). MacGregor later collaborated with Montgomery (and Mabel Burns McKinley) on a volume of biographies of Canadian women (*Courageous Women*, 1934), and the two remained close friends until Montgomery's death.

MacGregor's fiction is characterized by her love of the quirky, gossipy rural Ontario community of her childhood. Her books are rich in humorous character portraits, authentic bits of Scots-Canadian dialect, information about the history of the Scots community in Canada, and the homely details of life on the farm. In MacGregor's novels the relations between the Scots,

Irish, and English, Methodists and Presbyterians, and old and young are the stuff of drama, always rendered with an eye to the comic possibilities. In one memorable incident of *In Orchard Glen* (1918), a Highland piper mistakes his audience and grandly interrupts a Methodist revival meeting with "Lochaber No More." In *The Silver Maple*, whose hero joins the 1885 expedition of Canadian lumbermen up the Nile to rescue Gen. Charles Gordon at Khartoum; *A Gentleman Adventurer: A Story of the Hudson's Bay Company* (1924), based on the Riel Rebellion; and *The Forest Barrier* (1930), set in Ontario in 1837, MacGregor joined her intimate knowledge of the rural Scots community of her parents' generation with detailed research to reveal the mythic Scots roots of British-Canadian history.

The second major impulse in MacGregor's work, her religious faith, is especially evident in *Glad Days in Galilee* (1935), a fictionalized version of the boyhood of Jesus, written for Sunday school classes. In her version Jesus learns that his mission on earth is to help the poor and destitute by giving them food and clothing and to show mercy to sinners. Similarly, in *Little Miss Melody* (1921), a kindly young pastor teaches a lonely child how good works can bring happiness; the child says his "idea of being a Christian seemed just everybody having a good time; or, rather, it was seeing that everybody else had a good time; and then you were sure to have a wonderful time yourself." In *Duncan Polite, The End of the Rainbow* (1913), and other books, the kindly church of Jesus succeeds the stern Presbyterianism of an earlier generation, and material and spiritual relief of the destitute becomes its main task. More palatable to an adult reader is *Under the Grey Olives* (1927), a fictionalized account of a trip to the Holy Land that recalls Sara Jeannette Duncan's travel books in its lively characterization of a group of all-too-human pilgrims.

MacGregor's late trilogy set near Georgian Bay—*As a Watered Garden, Yonder Shining Light* (1948), and *Lilacs in the Dooryard* (1952)—reiterates the importance of community ties, as a lonely generation of city dwellers returns to the rural home of their grandparents. The novels especially chronicle the lives of farm women, their daily tasks of cooking, gardening, preserving, and chasing chickens and children, and their underground network of supportive gossip. Contemporary reviewers sometimes complained that the novels seemed to meander; in fact, they are structured like rural women's lives: detailed, constantly interrupted, and full of dialogue. Women as caring mothers and in their traditional role as virtuous examples of self-sacrifice are essential parts of the Christian community the novels present. The central character of *As a Watered Garden*, Islay Cameron, is gradually drawn into the web of social and material relations along the "Bay Shore Road," despite her city dweller's distaste for gossip and interference; her emotional and spiritual reawakening is symbolized by the inexhaustible well at the Old Home. Nostalgia for a vanished rural home is also evident in the portrait of the generous and strong-willed Great-Aunt Flora, the "grand lady" of MacGregor's final novel (1960), whose life is recalled by the narrator for her family.

The majority of MacGregor's early books were favorably reviewed in British and American publications; with Connor and McClung she catered to a considerable audience in the early twentieth century. By the end of her life, her works, like those of her friend Montgomery, were considered suitable for juvenile readers only.

Archibald Lampman
(17 November 1861-10 February 1899)

Bruce Nesbitt

BOOKS: *Among the Millet, and Other Poems* (Ottawa: Durie, 1888);
Lyrics of Earth (Boston: Copeland & Day, 1895);
Alcyone (Ottawa: Ogilvy, 1899);
The Poems of Archibald Lampman, edited by Duncan Campbell Scott (Toronto: Morang, 1900);
Lyrics of Earth: Sonnets and Ballads, edited by Scott (Toronto: Musson, 1925);
At the Long Sault and Other New Poems, edited by Scott and E. K. Brown (Toronto: Ryerson, 1943);
Selected Poems of Archibald Lampman, edited by Scott (Toronto: Ryerson, 1947);
Lampman's Kate: Late Love Poems of Archibald Lampman, edited by Margaret Coulby Whitridge (Ottawa: Borealis, 1975);
Selected Prose of Archibald Lampman, edited by Barrie Davies (Ottawa: Tecumseh, 1975);
Lampman's Sonnets: The Complete Sonnets of Archibald Lampman, edited by Whitridge (Ottawa: Borealis, 1976).

Widely regarded by literary historians as the finest nineteenth-century poet writing in English Canada, Archibald Lampman himself recognized that he was "a minor poet of a superior order." His continuing popular reputation rests on his precise and accurate descriptions of the extremes of the Canadian environment, particularly through his sonnets. More recently he has come to be re-evaluated for his abilities in expressing the relationships between those natural extremes and human moral dilemmas, and for his few stylistic experiments that mark him as the first significant Canadian poet in English with a twentieth-century sensibility. Through both his successes and failures his work embodies the distinction between colonial romanticism and a variety of closely focused poetic imagism that articulated the essence of Canadian poetry for at least a generation. His concern with linking language and environment remains as important for Canadian poetry as Ezra Pound's dicta are for the history of poetry in English.

Archibald Lampman (reproduction made with permission from an original held in the Special Collection, Simon Fraser University, Burnaby, British Columbia)

Although Charles G. D. Roberts once suggested that Lampman was, with him, a "Canadian Republican," the core of Lampman's upbringing was counterrevolutionary. His ancestors had fought with the Loyalist forces during the American Revolution, and the American-born great-grandfathers of both his father, Archibald, and mother, Susannah, had immigrated to Canada as United Empire Loyalists. Born in Morpeth in southern Ontario on 17 November 1861, Lampman obtained his early schooling in various places depending on the appointments of his father, an Anglican priest: in Perrytown, Gore's Landing, and Cobourg, near Port Hope. With the exception of one year at the secular Cobourg

Collegiate Institute, his education was rigorously British and thoroughly Anglican. A student good in classics but not brilliant overall, he completed his secondary schooling at Trinity College School, Port Hope, as preparation for entry in fall 1879 to Trinity College, Toronto.

During his three years at Trinity College, where he took a second in classics, Lampman was drawn to a circle of acquaintances associated with the college's Literary Institute, its secret literary society Episkopon, and its student journal *Rouge et Noir*. In the unpublished records of Episkopon are to be found some of his earliest extant juvenilia: anonymous and satiric verses and sketches. To *Rouge et Noir* he contributed his first published prose and poetry: essays on Shelley's "Revolt of Islam" (1880), friendship (1881), and German patriotic poetry (1882), and a single poem in 1882. His literary ambitions had grown early and rapidly; by July 1882 he had unsuccessfully submitted two of his poems to *Harper's* and *Our Continent;* the following month *Forest and Stream* published his article on fishing.

Teaching appeared to be his inevitable career (his father and mother had started a small school at Cobourg, and his three younger sisters, Sarah Isabelle, Annie Margaret, and Caroline Stewart, were all educated at home). But after less than a month teaching classics, English, German, and history at a school in Orangeville, Ontario, he was talking of leaving for British Columbia. Through the intervention of a college friend, Archibald Campbell, whose father was minister of justice and three times previously postmaster general in John A. Macdonald's cabinets, Lampman was offered a sinecure in the Post Office Department in Ottawa. He resigned his uncongenial teaching post to become a temporary clerk at a starting salary of $450 annually, beginning in January 1883. He would remain a junior civil servant in Ottawa until his premature death on 10 February 1899, when he was thirty-seven.

Far from being inhibited by living in Ottawa, Lampman at first thrived on it. At the time a small city of fewer than twenty-eight thousand, this unlikely national capital was beginning to attract a tiny group of intellectuals. His friendship with his earliest "literary father," J. E. Collins, had already been formed while he was at Trinity; a successful Toronto journalist, amateur historian, and undistinguished novelist, Collins dedicated one of his potboilers, *Annette, the Métis Spy*, to Lampman in 1886 when the poet was only twenty-five. Lampman continued an active per-

sonal and literary correspondence until at least 1884 with his college friend John A. Ritchie (letters that unfortunately disappeared some time after 1929). His office chief was William Dawson LeSueur, one of Canada's earliest intellectual radicals and the author of two polemical pamphlets published in 1884 on evolution and agnosticism. He soon formed a close friendship with his near-contemporary Duncan Campbell Scott, then a clerk in the Department of Indian Affairs and later a poet; by the summer of 1885 they had arranged the first of several canoeing expeditions in the barely settled wilderness north of Ottawa. And by 1885 he had established his deepest personal friendship with Maud Playter, a relationship that would result both in their marriage and in profound personal anxieties later reflected in his poetry.

Maud Playter was probably sixteen when they first met; she was one of two daughters of Edward Playter, a physician and editor of the *Dominion Sanitary Journal*, later *Man*, and now *Canada Health Journal*. The couple's private letters—most of Lampman's and fragments of Maud's, recently discovered—imply that she was an affectionate, optimistic young woman, not widely read nor traveled but surrounded by supportive relatives. After an extended courtship they were married on 3 September 1887 and settled into the first of a series of small rented houses, occasionally shared with Lampman's family, notably his father, who died in 1897 at the age of seventy-five. They had three children: Natalie, on 11 January 1892; Arnold Gesner, on 12 May 1894, who died as a baby on 4 August 1894; and Archibald Otto, on 21 June 1898. Maud survived her husband until 22 November 1910. Thirty years later, however, D. C. Scott revealed that he had understood Maud to have been unsympathetic to poetry, however much she was devoted to Lampman's "study and practise of it"; more significantly, Scott believed that Lampman was looking for "spiritual affinities. . . . His wife was not such an affinity." Yet it was likely Maud's money that allowed Lampman to arrange the publication of his first volume of poetry, *Among the Millet, and Other Poems* (1888), which he dedicated to her.

During the five years before this publication Lampman confirmed to himself his own ambitions to become a poet and was ambitious to be published. His main outlet in Canada was to be the *Week*, founded by Goldwin Smith in 1883, which that year included a poem of his in its December issue, the same year in which he sold a poem to the *Canadian Illustrated News*. He was only slightly more successful in American journals, selling a handful to the *Century, Current,* and *Scribner's*. After this somewhat discouraging record Lampman was shrewd enough to send out freshly published copies of *Among the Millet* to major periodicals in Canada, the United States, and England. The resulting reviews yielded sufficient attention to confirm his reputation for a decade. In Canada two notices in the *Week* were somewhat nervous about his "true" descriptions and absence of moral significance, while praising the purity of his soul: ritual responses characteristic of contemporary literary taste in Canada. Favorable reviews in the *Statesman* and the *Academy* were (for Canadians) more important because of their appearing in English papers than for their content. At another level W. D. Howells's notice in *Harper's* served him extraordinarily well, for it helped to introduce him to several magazines and an editor who would affect his future poetry, as well as to consolidate his reputation among Canadian readers.

All the Canadian authors who would later be called the "Confederation" poets—William Wilfred Campbell, Bliss Carman, Scott, Roberts, and Lampman, all born between 1858 and 1862—had been represented in W. D. Lighthall's anthology *Songs of the Great Dominion* (1889). By then Roberts, Campbell, and Lampman had each published at least one separate collection. Within four years all of them had published books, and yet as early as 1894 the young poet and future novelist Arthur Stringer referred to Lampman among them as "the most thoroughly Canadian and in Canada the most popular . . . the strongest and broadest poet of the group." Equally interesting, on the evidence of *Among the Millet*, Stringer cited not only his technical excellence but also the fact that he had already "done his best work."

Lampman's concept of the poetic process is central to an understanding of his accomplishment in the forty-seven poems of *Among the Millet*. His technique is clearly dualistic, constantly postulating opposites, but his central attitude is inclusive: the poet is invariably between opposites in the natural world, seeing them simultaneously, watching their implied or actual conflicts. His much-misinterpreted metaphoric escape from the city into the countryside is also inclusively dualistic: both the city and the land around it are walled, and man must break through both. Although he used his particular notion of dream-

ing as a banal contrast to reality, in the sense of daydreaming, more usually Lampman was concerned with the dream as the process by which poetic and therefore human knowledge is realized. The dream approaches man's first condition of being, while the poet is the only dreamer in "this sleepless world." Although we cannot re-create the Adamic world, we may have visions of it that both allow and cause the struggle toward self-knowledge, guided by the poet living "at the uttermost tension of life." The key to the process is awareness, including an awareness that nature did not fall with man.

It is essential for man to commune with the land, then, since it provides a constant, in Lampman's view, both a symbol of man's lost state and a condition in which he can strive to regain his identity and purpose of existence. The land is "innocent"; its extremes force man to make his moral choices. It does not provide an escape from responsibility: it is morally neutral and necessary; man's inner strength will determine whether he will succeed in his struggle. The poet's superior ability to recognize that nature can afford both a model and the arena for man's moral struggles is thus a first step to man's integration with himself and a regenerated society. Hence Lampman literalizes the myth of the loss of identity, the expulsion from Eden, for a nation unwilling or unable to accept its metaphorical basis. It is characteristic of his attitude that Lampman recollects in tranquillity not the joys of summer but the hues of winter, that archetypal Canadian season, because the value of winter's extremes lies in man being made aware of his own will, which enables him to withstand his challenges. The next stage to self-knowledge is centered in the dream, at that point of balance where all forces are comprehended, together with an awareness of the struggle to come. The note of anticipation Lampman frequently associates with fall (rather than spring) implies that winter is the significant season; fall, and occasionally spring, are the times of stocktaking, of recognizing what issues confront man before the actual struggle begins.

The dream is not the ideal condition of man but the process by which that condition may be reached. Finally must come the direct confrontation with the issues challenging him. Struggle becomes not a futile encounter with fate, in which man is preordained to failure, but a positive moral action, perhaps the closest he can come to divinity. But struggle is only meaningless protest

The Archibald Lampman postage stamp

unless it is itself a condition of life; persistence is essential. Acquiescence means instant annihilation; moral stature and meaning are to be garnered by conflict with a nature indifferent to man's activities. Endurance becomes the condition of the soul's struggle, and man's apprehension of the perseverance of nature is thus a movement toward innocence, which for Lampman was a permanent state of beauty. Occasionally he described man's model of endurance as Christ, but for Lampman the corrupted church on earth can only supply a ritual reenactment of Christ's encompassing love; the precondition of that love is perseverance in the quest for self-knowledge and eventually innocence, most dramatically put in his otherwise puzzling "The King's Sabbath." There, to a priest's petulant reminder that it is Sunday, the king responds by holding a burning bush in his bare hands.

It is unlikely that the underlying intellectual complexity of the lyrics, dramatic monologues, and sonnets in Lampman's first volume had as much influence on his Canadian readers as his technical versatility and gift for sharp observation of the immediate environment. Nevertheless the exposure the book provided in the United States ensured the receptivity of *Scribner's* to his po-

etry during the next four years, and introduced it to readers of the *Atlantic, Cosmopolitan, Harper's,* the *Youth's Companion,* and the *Independent;* by the time of his death he had published approximately 150 poems in periodicals.

Late in 1891 Lampman turned to public journalism by proposing with his friend Scott that they and their new acquaintance W. W. Campbell should write for the *Toronto Globe* a weekly column of literary and social commentary. Having resigned a curacy to enter the civil service, Campbell had moved to Ottawa in the summer of 1891 to lodgings close to Lampman; Campbell's low starting salary, Lampman said, prompted their proposal, which was accepted by the *Globe* as a column that was to appear weekly for nearly a year and a half, from 6 February 1892 to 1 July 1893, collectively written. "At the Mermaid Inn," as it was called, was no influential shaper of literary taste such as the "Red Page" of the *Bulletin* in Sydney, Australia, at the same time, but it was nonetheless an unusual cultural enterprise for a Canadian daily newspaper. Lampman's eighty-seven contributions ranged from a paragraph or short review to a brief essay and included some original poetry. For the most part, however, his work consisted of literary gossip culled from other journals, unremarkable comments on the social issues of the day, and impressionistic essays. While the range of his reading eye appears wide–from New Zealand politics to the poems of Maurice Maeterlinck (1862-1949)–the substance of his observations, invariably written in a mild tone, reveal less a quiet iconoclasm than an educated literary taste. Despite this experience with popular journalism, Lampman does not appear to have been tempted by the preference of editors to pay more for prose than for poetry. After his first essays in the early 1880s, and a fairy tale published by his future father-in-law, the only other prose to appear outside the column during his lifetime was an essay on "Happiness" in *Harper's*. He had written another fairy tale before 1884 and a brief note on socialism in the mid 1880s; drafts of several other later prose works (undoubtedly lectures) survive, including "Poetic Interpretation"; "The Modern School of Poetry in England"; "Two Canadian Poets," on Roberts and G. F. Cameron, given in 1891; and "The Character and Poetry of Keats."

It was during this period of the early 1890s that Lampman's small circle of literary and social acquaintances began to broaden, and for the first time in his life he started to travel outside Canada. The most fascinating, obscure, and influential person among Lampman's new friends was a woman who possibly became a paramour, Katherine Thompson Waddell. She was twenty-one, four years younger than Lampman, when she joined his office in the Post Office Department on 18 January 1887. According to Scott, whose memories were recorded by the Canadian critic E. K. Brown in a private memorandum in August 1942, their "love began in the early nineties and was still a powerful thing at the end of Lampman's life." His sole confidant during these stormy years was Edward Thomson in Boston (who was having an affair at the same time); Scott must have been less close to Lampman than he thought, for he only learned what had happened from LeSueur after Lampman's death. Lampman's belief that he had found a "spiritual mate" more sympathetic than his wife can be inferred from his correspondence and the poems he left unpublished in his notebooks (probably written in 1892 or 1893 and afterward), which also suggest that their friendship remained "spiritual." Nevertheless what he termed his "spiritual revolution" appears to have affected him strongly. Ever since a near-fatal attack of rheumatic fever when he was seven, Lampman gave

the impression of being strongly inclined to introspection and self-doubt. By the time he was twenty-one his moodiness approached clearly defined periods of extreme depression, alternating with periods of creative volcanism; he knew, he said, that he was "constitutionally sensitive to a morbid degree." He was also an obvious hypochondriac, which he recognized. Undoubtedly his inability to resolve his personal conflicts, particularly his love for Katherine, heightened his instability to the point of creative breakdown. It is also clear that at this time his vaguely humanistic sentiments were being sharply focused into poems of social protest. His letters reveal a man disappointed in love, and in February 1896 he finally confided that, as a result, "I abuse the constitution of things," a tendency he increasingly exhibited after his eventual rejection by Katherine. Most of his poetry of social protest was written during and after his crisis with her. At the same time it is important to note that Lampman's (pale) socialism centers on the reformation of man, not of institutions.

Lampman's friendship with the Boston writer Thomson had begun in 1890, when Thomson published an article in the *Toronto Globe* urging federal sinecures for Canadian poets, Lampman in particular. The extensive literary correspondence that resulted is a major source for an understanding of Lampman's thought. Twelve years older than Lampman, Thomson was a Canadian who had seen active service in the American Civil War as a teenager, worked in western Canada as a surveyor, and become a journalist with the *Globe* (1878-1891) before joining the *Youth's Companion* as an editor in Boston, where he also wrote five volumes of fiction, mainly short stories. Thanks to Thomson, Lampman was to publish twenty-six poems in the *Youth's Companion* during their eight-year association, and it was Thomson who was instrumental in arranging the publication of Lampman's second volume of poetry, *Lyrics of Earth* (1895). Thomson was also Lampman's host on his three brief trips outside Canada, all to the Boston area: for three weeks in late summer 1891, and ten days each in spring 1893 and fall 1898. (Except for his canoeing holidays, Lampman's only other extended travel out of Ontario or farther than Montreal was to Halifax in June 1897 with the Royal Society–of which he had been made a member in 1895–and again to Nova Scotia for three weeks in September 1898.) Thomson was most encouraging about Lampman's preparation of what by 1894 would be three volumes of poetry: a version of "Lyrics of Earth" (finished in October 1892), "Alcyone," and "A Century of Sonnets." All were rejected by the American publishers to whom they were initially submitted. By 1895 Thomson came to Lampman's aid in securing the acceptance of *Lyrics of Earth* with Copeland and Day in Boston, and he undertook to edit the manuscript heavily; the final version included only twenty-nine poems. Eventually 550 copies were printed in March 1896, although the edition was dated 1895. To Lampman's disappointment (he received seventy-five cents a copy in royalties) it did not sell well, and unlike *Among the Millet*, despite his efforts at promotion, the book received little notice among reviewers. After this experience he chose once more (as he had done with his first book) to pay for the publication of his third volume, *Alcyone*, to be handsomely printed by Constable in Edinburgh. He corrected the proofs in late 1898, but died before the thirty-nine poems in *Alcyone* could be published in 1899. Scott canceled publication of the collection but had Constable pull a dozen copies from the standing type. Later Scott had the sheets bound up by James Hope (at Ogilvy) in Ottawa, who inadvertently misspelled the poet's name on the spine. It is now one of the great rarities of Canadian bibliophily.

Immediately following Lampman's death (on 10 February 1899) Scott began to prepare a large collected memorial edition, the proceeds of which were to benefit the Lampman family. With the assistance of Lampman's numerous acquaintances in Canada and the United States, the project was successful, bringing enough to allow Maud to buy a modest house in Ottawa. As Lampman's trusted friend and literary executor Scott had access to most of his papers, and he included in the memorial edition not only the contents of the three books Lampman had seen at least to the proof stage but also substantial material previously unpublished or uncollected from periodicals. *The Poems of Archibald Lampman* appeared in 1900, was republished in two volumes in 1901, and appeared in two further editions in 1905 and 1915 (Scott revised his 1900 "Memoir" in the third edition, which was reprinted in the fourth). Scott also edited a selection of work published in 1925 under the title *Lyrics of Earth: Sonnets and Ballads;* collaborated with E. K. Brown on *At the Long Sault and Other New Poems* (1943), a small collection mainly of previously unpublished

poetry from Lampman's notebooks; and edited the *Selected Poems of Archibald Lampman* (1947), drawn from the 1900 and 1943 volumes.

Lampman is said to have prompted and encouraged Scott toward a literary career that would last more than half a century; in return Scott's devotion to his friend's reputation is unequaled in Canadian literary history. Nonetheless the texts of nearly all Lampman's collected poetry are corrupt, due in part to Scott's radical editing. Lampman's normal practice when composing was to scribble ideas, lines, stanzas, and whole drafts into his notebooks, twenty-two of which survive. He then copied them into large, bound manuscript books of which seven are known to exist (one was rediscovered as recently as 1971). The *Poems* of 1900 appears to have been based on the fair-copy books, while *At the Long Sault* was taken from the rough notebooks. Yet even now, while 12,500 lines of his poetry have been published, some 6,000 remain unpublished in his manuscripts and provide substantial insights into his poetics. Most significant is the division between his "nature work" (his derogatory term for poems widely praised in his lifetime) and his "tales in verse," long narratives almost always set outside Canada, usually in the far past. Curiously, in each of these lengthy romantic creations, which represent nearly one-half his total poetic writing, Lampman consciously heightens his poetic diction with archaisms and elaborate personifications. Simultaneously he was writing poetry that exhibits few or none of these characteristics. When Lampman attempted his narratives of noble dreams, he felt obliged to imitate an already hackneyed tradition, both in what to see and how to feel. When he turned to the country around him, he dropped most of his assumed poetic baggage. He may not have abandoned all his Keatsian diction, but with that diction he expressed attitudes neither colonial nor romantic. Although he realized that he was writing derivative poetry, he continued to produce his narratives because he believed that his critical audience, sensitive to the dictates of moral earnestness, would accept them. Yet in his most significant work he instinctively realized that he had to absorb his immediate surroundings if he were to assist in what he called the "moral awakening" of Canada. No amount of revision could alter the dual sensibilities of Lampman. For Canadians he had defined the break with colonial romanticism.

Some Letters of Duncan Campbell Scott, Archibald Lampman, and Others, edited by Arthur S. Bourinot (Ottawa: Bourinot, 1959).

Bibliography:

George Wicken, "Archibald Lampman: An Annotated Bibliography," in *The Annotated Bibliography of Canada's Major Authors,* volume 2, edited by Robert Lecker and Jack David (Toronto: ECW, 1980), pp. 97-146.

Biography:

Carl Y. Connor, *Archibald Lampman, Canadian Poet of Nature,* second edition (Ottawa: Borealis, 1977).

References:

Richard Arnold, " 'The Clearer Self ': Lampman's Transcendental-Visonary Development," *Canadian Poetry,* 8 (Spring-Summer 1981): 33-35;

Munro Beattie, "Archibald Lampman," in *Our Living Tradition,* edited by Claude T. Bissell (Toronto: University of Toronto Press, 1957), pp. 63-88;

D. M. R. Bentley, "The Same Unnamed Delight: Lampman's Essay on *Happiness* and *Lyrics of Earth,*" *Essays on Canadian Writing,* 5 (Fall 1976): 25-35;

Bentley, "Watchful Dreams and Sweet Unrest: An Essay on the Vision of Archibald Lampman," *Studies in Canadian Literature,* 6 (1981): 188-210; 7 (1982): 5-26;

Barrie Davies, "Lampman and Religion," *Canadian Literature,* 56 (Spring 1973): 40-60;

Davies, "Lampman: Radical Poet of Nature," *English Quarterly,* 4 (Spring 1971): 33-43;

Sandra Djwa, "Lampman's Fleeting Vision," *Canadian Literature,* 56 (Spring 1973): 22-39;

L. R. Early, *Archibald Lampman* (Boston: Twayne, 1986);

Michael Gnarowski, ed., *Archibald Lampman* (Toronto: Ryerson, 1970);

Ralph Gustafson, "Among the Millet," *Northern Review,* 1 (February-March 1947): 26-34;

William D. Howells, "Editor's Study," *Harper's,* 78 (April 1889): 821-823;

Margaret Kennedy, "Lampman and the Canadian Thermopylae: 'At the Long Sault: May, 1660,' " *Canadian Poetry,* 1 (Fall-Winter 1977): 54-59;

Raymond Knister, "The Poetry of Archibald Lampman," *Dalhousie Review,* 7 (October 1927): 348-361;

Eli Mandel, "The City in Canadian Poetry," in his *Another Time,* (Erin, Ont.: Porcépic, 1977), pp. 114-123;

Lorraine McMullen, ed., *The Lampman Symposium* (Ottawa: University of Ottawa Press, 1976);

Kathy Mezei, "Lampman Among the Timothy," *Canadian Poetry,* 5 (Fall-Winter 1979): 57-72;

John Ower, "Portraits of the Landscape as Poet: Canadian Nature as Aesthetic Symbol in Three Confederation Writers," *Journal of Canadian Studies,* 6 (February 1971): 27-32;

Desmond Pacey, "A Reading of Lampman's 'Heat,' " *Culture,* 14 (September 1953): 292-297;

Charles R. Steele, "The Isolate 'I' (Eye): Lampman's Persona," *Essays on Canadian Writing,* 16 (Fall-Winter 1979-1980): 62-69;

George Wicken, "Prelude to Poetry: Lampman and the *Rouge et Noir,*" *Canadian Poetry,* 6 (Spring-Summer 1980): 50-60.

Papers:

Some of Lampman's juvenilia is in the papers of the Episkopon Society, Trinity College, Toronto, but unavailable to the public. Other papers are at the National Archives, Ottawa, Simon Fraser University's Special Collection, and the Douglas Library, Queen's University, Kingston, Ontario.

Napoléon-P. Landry

(30 December 1884-28 September 1956)

Hans R. Runte
Dalhousie University

BOOKS: *Poèmes de mon pays* (Montreal: Ecole Industrielle des Sourds-Muets, 1949);
Poèmes acadiens (Montreal: Fides, 1955).

Chroniclers of Acadian letters mention Father Napoléon-P. Landry's poetic attempts for the completeness of the historical record and for the particular documentary value of his two volumes (preparation of a third was interrupted by his death). Together with the long-since-forgotten creative endeavors of many others, Landry's books mark one of the points on which an Acadian literary tradition has rather tenuously been made to rest. His life roughly spanned the First Acadian Renaissance, an era of national awakening ushered in at the first Acadian Convention (Memramcook, New Brunswick, 1881) and characterized by countless initiatives aimed at affirming at last, one hundred years after the return from exile, the people's collective identity.

Landry's primary role in this era of national self-definition was that of a spiritual leader. For forty years he served his fellow Acadians in that capacity, and he was affectionately known among them as Le Père Nap'. He was born on 30 December 1884 in Memramcook, son of Mr. and Mrs. Philippe Landry; he had one brother and two sisters. After attending Notre-Dame du Sacré-Coeur convent school and the Université Saint-Joseph in Memramcook, he transferred to the Eudist Fathers' Collège Sainte-Anne in Church Point, Nova Scotia, where he received his B.A. in 1909. From 1909 to 1914 he studied for the priesthood at the Convent of the Sacred Heart in Halifax and was ordained on 29 June 1914. After a brief posting to Memramcook, he was vicar in Bouctouche, New Brunswick, from 1914 to 1917 and village priest in Sackville, New Brunswick, from 1917 to 1925. He spent the rest of his career, until his retirement in 1954, in Sainte-Marie parish, Kent County. On 27 September 1956 he was struck by a train at a level crossing in the center of Moncton and died the following day.

Napoléon-P. Landry (Centre d'Etudes Acadiennes, University of Moncton)

Landry's interest in local history led him to do research on the towns of Chipoudie, Beauséjour, and Louisbourg, and to write on historical and other matters in the newspapers and magazines of the day; he was a frequent contributor to *L'Evangéline*, the Acadian paper, from 1914 to 1927 and from 1937 to 1953. This desire to rediscover his people's past, combined with his spiritual vocation, determined the themes and purpose of his two books. Both volumes are fervent evocations of Acadia's allegedly glorious past, of her people's much-tried faithfulness to Pope and country, and of the just rewards God has reserved for his chosen flock. For instance in "A notre Acadie" (To Our Acadia), from *Poèmes de mon pays* (Poems of My Country, 1949), he writes: "Amour mystérieux/Du pays des aïeux,/De ta divine flamme,/Forge et trempe notre âme!" (Mysterious love/Of our forebears' land,/In your divine flame,/Forge and steel our soul!). Similarly, in "Marche patriotique" (*Poèmes acadiens*, 1955) these lines appear: "Debout Jeunesse! En avant! Dieu t'appelle!/Dans ton refrain le plus fier, le plus beau,/Chante au soleil la mémoire immortelle/De tes aïeux tombés sous le drapeau . . . " (Rise up, you young! Forward! God is calling you!/In your proudest, your most beautiful refrain,/Sing to the sun of the immortal remembrance/Of your forebears who fell under the flag . . .).

In his review of Landry's first book, *Poèmes de mon pays*, Lionel Groulx, in *Revue d'Histoire de l'Amérique Française* (September 1949), applauded the historical basis on which the collection is founded but avoided committing himself on the subject of Landry's poetic skills. Louis Morin, in *Lectures* (January 1953), did not demonstrate that delicacy, comparing Landry's muse to "une maraîchère travestie en marquise d'opérette" (a vegetable gardener in the costume of an operatic marquise). Such unkindness notwithstanding, Landry received an honorary diploma from the Société des Poètes Canadiens-Français in 1953 and a French-language prize from the Académie Française in 1955; on 20 May 1951 his poem "Votre

Assomption" had won him fourth prize and a laureate's diploma in an international poetry competition held by the Puy Florimontain de Lyon of the Académie des Jeux Florimontains de Lyon-Savoye-Provence.

Poèmes de mon pays and *Poèmes acadiens*, ignored by reviewers, document that period of the history of Acadia when the Church still had influence over official culture, and when the main task in the business of nation-building was still seen as a proud coming to terms with an unduly repressed collective past. As beneficiary of this completed task, the literary establishment of the Second Renaissance (since 1969), in which intellectuals and professionals have replaced priests and local politicians, has been able to turn its attention to Acadia's contradictory present and its uncertain future.

References:

Yves Bolduc, "Acadian Poetry," translated by E. Jones, in *A Literary and Linguistic History of New Brunswick*, edited by Reavley Gair and others (Fredericton: Fiddlehead & Goose Lane, 1985), pp. 83-84;

Marguerite Maillet, *Histoire de la littérature acadienne: De rêve en rêve* (Moncton: Editions d'Acadie, 1983), pp. 173-176, and passim.

Papers:

Landry's papers are at the Centre d'Etudes Acadiennes, University of Moncton.

Agnes Christina Laut

(11 February 1871-15 November 1936)

Carole Gerson
Simon Fraser University

BOOKS: *Lords of the North: A Romance of the North-west* (Toronto: Briggs, 1900; New York: Taylor, 1900);

Heralds of Empire: Being the Story of One Ramsay Stanhope, Lieutenant to Pierre Radisson in the Northern Fur Trade (Toronto: Briggs, 1902; New York: Appleton, 1902);

The Story of the Trapper (Toronto: Briggs, 1902; New York: Appleton, 1902);

Pathfinders of the West: Being the Thrilling Story of the Adventures of the Men Who Discovered the Great Northwest (Toronto: Briggs, 1904; New York & London: Macmillan, 1904);

Vikings of the Pacific: The Adventures of the Explorers Who Came from the West, Eastward (New York & London: Macmillan, 1905);

The Conquest of the Great Northwest: Being the Story of the Adventurers of England Known as the Hudson's Bay Company (New York: Outing, 1908; London: Hodder & Stoughton, 1908);

Canada, the Empire of the North: Being the Romantic Story of the New Dominion's Growth from Colony to Kingdom (Boston & London: Ginn, 1909);

The Freebooters of the Wilderness (Toronto: Musson, 1910; New York: Moffat, Yard, 1910);

The New Dawn (New York: Moffat, Yard, 1913);

Through Our Unknown Southwest, the Wonderland of the United States—Little Known and Unappreciated—The Home of the Cliff Dweller and the Hopi, the Forest Ranger and the Navajo—The Lure of the Painted Desert (New York: McBride, Nast, 1913);

The "Adventurers of England" on Hudson Bay: A Chronicle of the Fur Trade in the North (Toronto: Glasgow Brook, 1914);

Pioneers of the Pacific Coast: A Chronicle of Sea Rovers and Fur Hunters (Toronto: Glasgow Brook, 1915);

The Canadian Commonwealth (Toronto: McLeod & Allen, 1915; Indianapolis: Bobbs-Merrill, 1915);

Agnes Christina Laut

The Cariboo Trail: A Chronicle of the Gold-fields of British Columbia (Toronto: Glasgow Brook, 1916);

The Fur Trade of America (New York: Macmillan, 1921);

Canada at the Cross Roads (Toronto: Macmillan, 1921);

The Quenchless Light (New York: Appleton, 1924);

The Blazed Trail of the Old Frontier: Being the Log of the Upper Missouri Historical Expedition Under the Auspices of the Governors and Historical Associations of Minnesota, North and South Dakota and Montana for 1925 (New York: McBride, 1926);

Enchanted Trails of Glacier Park (New York: Mc-
　　Bride, 1926);

The Conquest of Our Western Empire (New York:
　　McBride, 1927);

The Romance of the Rails, 2 volumes (New York:
　　McBride, 1929);

*The Overland Trail: The Epic Path of the Pioneers to
　　Oregon* (New York: Stokes, 1929);

Antoine de la Mothe Cadillac (Toronto: Ryerson,
　　1930);

John Tanner, Captive Boy Wanderer of the Borderlands
　　(Toronto: Ryerson, 1930);

Marquette (Toronto: Ryerson, 1930);

*Cadillac, Knight Errant of the Wilderness, Founder of
　　Detroit, Governor of Louisiana from the Great
　　Lakes to the Gulf* (Indianapolis: Bobbs-
　　Merrill, 1931);

Pilgrims of the Santa Fe (New York: Stokes, 1931).

Agnes Christina Laut was a prolific author
of fiction and popular history in the first decades
of the twentieth century. Her success can be
gauged by the extensive republication of her
books during her lifetime and their current avail-
ability in most libraries today. She was born in
Stanley township, Huron County, Ontario, on 11
February 1871 to John Laut, a merchant from
Glasgow, and Eliza George Laut, a daughter of
Rev. James George, D.D., vice-principal of
Queen's University from 1853 to 1857. When
Laut was two years old her family moved to Winnipeg, where the future author became well acquainted with western frontier life. At the age of
fifteen she completed normal school, and although she was too young to receive a teaching certificate, she acted as a substitute in a prairie
school. Several years of teaching in Winnipeg preceded her enrollment at the University of Manitoba. Because of ill health Laut withdrew after
her second year and turned to writing, sending
her first articles to the *New York Evening Post* and
the *Manitoba Free Press*. From 1895 to 1897 the latter employed her as an editorial writer, after
which she enjoyed two years of "tramp life," crossing the continent to Newfoundland and contributing articles to American, English, and Canadian
periodicals.

Laut's first novel, *Lords of the North* (1900),
was an instant success, readily meeting English
Canada's desire for a national literature drawing
on the country's colorful history and modeled on
the fiction of Sir Walter Scott. It dramatizes the
struggle between the Hudson's Bay Company
and the Northwest Company for control of the

northwest fur trade as a contest between two feu-
dal robber barons. The noble characters share a
code of chivalry, refusing to yield to "the witching fascinations of a wild life in a wild, free, tame-
less land"; the Indians represent the threat of
raw wilderness to the veneer of civilization. Like
its successor, *Heralds of Empire* (1902), this romantic novel bears evidence of its author's careful research and her desire to enliven Canadian history. The two books share problems of characterization and plot, as well as clumsy archaic diction. Laut's fascination with the past was to find
better expression in her many subsequent works
of nonfiction.

In 1901 Laut moved to Wassaic, in Upstate
New York, for her health and to be nearer her
publishers. This was to be her home for the rest
of her life, although she continued to spend her
summers in the Canadian Rockies and Selkirk
Mountains and to write extensively about Canada. Some indication of her financial success can
be inferred from her 1902 contract with her Canadian publisher, William Briggs, from whom she
could command the high royalty rate of twenty
percent for *The Story of the Trapper* (1902), and
from her purchase of Wildwood, her country estate.

Laut's best and best-selling books were (in
her own words) intended "To re-create the shadowy figures of the heroic past, to clothe the dead
once more in flesh and blood, to set the puppets
of the play in life's great dramas again upon the
stage of action." Drawing upon her extensive research into published and manuscript sources, including the private records of the Hudson's Bay
Company, she reworked the same stories of early
North American explorers and fur traders
(Radisson and des Groseilliers, La Vérendrye,
Hudson, Hearne, Lewis and Clark, Vancouver)
into scores of magazine articles which formed the
basis of more than a dozen books. Those intended for younger readers include three short
books in George M. Wrong and H. H. Langton's
Chronicles of Canada series (*The "Adventurers of
England" on Hudson Bay* [1914], *Pioneers of the Pacific Coast* [1915], *The Cariboo Trail* [1916]) and a
1930 series of three school history texts for the
Ryerson Press. Her major works of history for
adults include *The Story of the Trapper*, part of
which was later incorporated into *The Fur Trade
of America* (1921), *Pathfinders of the West* (1904), *Vikings of the Pacific* (1905), *The Conquest of the Great
Northwest* (1908), and *Cadillac, Knight Errant of the
Wilderness* (1931). *The Conquest of the Great North-*

west was financially "her most satisfactory book," she claimed in 1912.

As a journalist, Laut traveled extensively through the Canadian West and American Southwest, writing about her travels in articles and books which plead the cause of wilderness conservation. A personal, anecdotal style characterizes *Through Our Unknown Southwest* (1913) and *Enchanted Trails of Glacier Park* (1926), as well as *The Romance of the Rails* (1929). An outspoken Canadian nationalist, she wrote *Canada, the Empire of the North* (1909) to support the popular notion that the twentieth century belonged to Canada. In 1912 her reputation as a national spokesperson led to an assignment from the Toronto-based magazine *Saturday Night* to investigate labor and racial issues in British Columbia. Her analysis, republished as a pamphlet, *Am I my Brother's Keeper* (1913), and later included in *The Canadian Commonwealth* (1915), summarizes some of the prevailing tensions of her era. Social issues continued to concern her, and in 1919 Laut traveled to Mexico as secretary to the Childhood Conservation League. She reported her findings to a Senate subcommittee in Washington.

From a literary point of view, her weakest works are her last three volumes of fiction. *The Freebooters of the Wilderness* (1910) and *The New Dawn* (1913), both set in the United States of her own day, are contrived thesis novels. The first supports the efforts of the United States Forest Service to conserve the wilderness against rampant exploitation, while the second denounces the self-interest and underhandedness of both big business and the international labor movement. *The Quenchless Light* (1924) marks Laut's return to historical fiction, in this case to the time of the early Christian apostles.

Laut's record of publishing success and social action represents the fields of activity that opened to North American women for her generation. Following her death (on 15 November 1936), the *American Historical Review* (January 1937) opined that her historical writing in particular had "substantial merit."

References:

Harriette Cuttino Buchanan, "Agnes Christina Laut," in *American Women Writers,* edited by Lina Mainiero (New York: Ungar, 1980), pp. 522-524;

O. J. Stevinson, *From Fort Garry, West, A People's Best* (Toronto: Musson, 1927), pp. 63-69.

Papers:

The Lorne Pierce Collection, Queen's University Archives, includes correspondence by Laut from the years 1924 to 1931, and letters by her from 1902 to 1914 are in the archives of the Century Publishing Company in the New York Public Library.

Stephen Leacock

(30 December 1869-28 March 1944)

Louis K. MacKendrick
University of Windsor

BOOKS: *Elements of Political Science* (Boston & New York: Houghton, Mifflin, 1906);

Baldwin, Lafontaine, Hincks: Responsible Government (Toronto: Morang, 1907); enlarged as *Mackenzie, Baldwin, La Fontaine, Hincks* (London & Toronto: Oxford University Press, 1926);

Literary Lapses: A Book of Sketches (Montreal: Gazette, 1910; London & New York: Lane, 1910);

Nonsense Novels (Montreal: Publishers' Press, 1911; London & New York: Lane, 1911);

Sunshine Sketches of a Little Town (Toronto: Bell & Cockburn, 1912; London & New York: Lane, 1912);

Behind the Beyond, and Other Contributions to Human Knowledge (Toronto: Bell & Cockburn, 1913; New York & London: Lane, 1913);

Adventures of the Far North: A Chronicle of the Frozen Seas (Toronto & Glasgow: Brook, 1914);

Arcadian Adventures with the Idle Rich (Toronto: Gundy, 1914; New York & London: Lane, 1914);

The Dawn of Canadian History (Toronto & Glasgow: Brook, 1914);

The Mariner of St. Malo: A Chronicle of the Voyages of Jacques Cartier (Toronto & Glasgow: Brook, 1914);

Moonbeams from the Larger Lunacy (Toronto: Gundy, 1915; New York: Lane, 1915; London: Lane, 1916);

Further Foolishness: Sketches and Satires on the Follies of the Day (Toronto: Gundy, 1916; London & New York: Lane, 1916);

Essays and Literary Studies (Toronto: Gundy, 1916; New York & London: Lane, 1916);

Frenzied Fiction (Toronto: Gundy, 1918; London & New York: Lane, 1918);

The Hohenzollerns in America; with the Bolsheviks in Berlin and Other Impossibilities (Toronto: Gundy, 1919; London & New York: Lane, 1919);

The Unsolved Riddle of Social Justice (Toronto: Gundy, 1920; London & New York: Lane, 1920);

Stephen Leacock, circa 1930

Winsome Winnie, and Other New Nonsense Novels (London & New York: Lane, 1920; Toronto: Gundy, 1922);

My Discovery of England (Toronto: Gundy, 1922; London: Lane, 1922; New York: Dodd, Mead, 1922);

College Days (Toronto: Gundy, 1923; London: Lane, 1923; New York: Dodd, Mead, 1923);

Over the Footlights (Toronto: Gundy, 1923; New York: Dodd, Mead, 1923; London: Lane, 1923);

The Garden of Folly (Toronto: Gundy, 1924; New York: Dodd, Mead, 1924; London: Lane, 1924);

Winnowed Wisdom: A New Book of Humour (Toronto: Macmillan, 1926; London: Lane, 1926; New York: Dodd, Mead, 1926);

Short Circuits (Toronto: Macmillan, 1928; New York: Dodd, Mead, 1928; London: Lane, 1928);

The Iron Man & the Tin Woman: With Other Such Futurities: A Book of Little Sketches of To-day and To-morrow (Toronto: Macmillan, 1929; New York: Dodd, Mead, 1929; London: Lane, 1929);

Economic Prosperity in the British Empire (Toronto: Macmillan, 1930; London: Constable, 1930; Boston & New York: Houghton Mifflin, 1930);

Back to Prosperity (Toronto: Macmillan, 1932; New York: Macmillan, 1932; London: Constable, 1932);

Afternoons in Utopia: Tales of the New Time (Toronto: Macmillan, 1932; New York: Dodd, Mead, 1932; London: Lane, 1932);

The Dry Pickwick and Other Incongruities (London: Lane, 1932);

Mark Twain (London: Davies, 1932; Toronto: Ryerson, 1933; New York: Appleton, 1933);

Charles Dickens: His Life and Work (London: Davies, 1933; Garden City, N.Y.: Doubleday, Doran, 1934);

Lincoln Frees the Slaves (New York: Putnam's, 1934);

The Perfect Salesman, edited by E. V. Knox (New York: McBride, 1934);

Humour: Its Theory and Technique, with Examples and Samples, a Book of Discovery (Toronto: Dodd, Mead, 1935; New York: Dodd, Mead, 1935; London: Lane, 1935);

Funny Pieces: A Book of Random Sketches (Toronto: McClelland & Stewart, 1936; New York: Dodd, Mead, 1936; London: Lane, 1937);

Hellements of Hickonomics, in Hiccoughs of Verse Done in Our Social Planning Mill (Toronto: McClelland & Stewart, 1936; New York: Dodd, Mead, 1936);

Here Are My Lectures and Stories (Toronto: McClelland & Stewart, 1937; New York: Dodd, Mead, 1937; London: Lane, 1938);

My Discovery of the West: A Discussion of East and West in Canada (Toronto: Allen, 1937; London: Lane, 1937; Boston & New York: Hale, Cushman & Flint, 1937);

LITERARY LAPSES

A Book of Sketches

BY

STEPHEN LEACOCK

MONTREAL:
GAZETTE PRINTING COMPANY, LIMITED.
1910.

Price 35 Cents.

Title page for Leacock's first collection of humorous tales, which was subsequently published in London and New York, marking the beginning of his career as a humorist

Humour and Humanity: An Introduction to the Study of Humour (London: Butterworth, 1937; New York: Holt, 1938);

Model Memoirs and Other Sketches from Simple to Serious (New York: Dodd, Mead, 1938; London: Lane, 1939);

Too Much College; or, Education Eating Up Life, with Kindred Essays in Education and Humour (New York: Dodd, Mead, 1939; London: Lane, 1940);

The British Empire: Its Structure, Its Unity, Its Strength (New York: Dodd, Mead, 1940; London: Lane, 1940);

Canada: The Foundations of Its Future (Montreal: Gazette, 1941);

Montreal: Seaport and City (Garden City, N.Y.: Doubleday, Doran, 1942; Toronto: McClelland & Stewart, 1948);

My Remarkable Uncle, and Other Sketches (New York: Dodd, Mead, 1942; London: Lane, 1942);

How to Write (New York: Dodd, Mead, 1943; London: Lane, 1944);

Happy Stories, Just to Laugh at (New York: Dodd, Mead, 1943; London: Lane, 1945);

Last Leaves (Toronto: McClelland & Stewart, 1945; New York: Dodd, Mead, 1945);

While There Is Time: The Case Against Social Catastrophe (Toronto: McClelland & Stewart, 1945);

The Boy I Left Behind Me (Garden City, N.Y.: Doubleday, 1946; London: Bodley Head, 1947).

Collections: *The Leacock Roundabout: A Treasury of the Best Works of Stephen Leacock* (New York: Dodd, Mead, 1946);

The Bodley Head Leacock, edited by J. B. Priestley (London: Bodley Head, 1957); republished as *The Best of Leacock* (Toronto: McClelland & Stewart, 1958);

The Unicorn Leacock, edited by James Reeves (London & New York: Hutchinson, 1960);

Feast of Stephen: An Anthology of Some of the Less Familiar Writings of Stephen Leacock, edited by Robertson Davies (Toronto: McClelland & Stewart, 1970);

The Social Criticism, edited by Alan Bowker (Toronto & Buffalo: University of Toronto Press, 1973).

OTHER: *The Greatest Pages of Charles Dickens,* edited, with commentary, by Leacock (Garden City, N.Y.: Doubleday, Doran, 1934);

The Greatest Pages of American Humor, edited, with commentary, by Leacock (Garden City, N.Y.: Doubleday, Doran, 1936).

Stephen Leacock is the first immortal in the ranks of Canadian humorists, and even in his lifetime his popularity and reputation were international. His work has become a touchstone for some types of comic writing, even though modern readers and critics are largely unfamiliar with the sheer extent of his publications. Some of his best work is still in print in McClelland and Stewart's New Canadian Library series. His principal form was the sketch, the joke given its own metaphorical extension, in which he could exercise his talents for incongruity, irony, and wordplay. He was also gifted in his ability to parody popular conventions in literature, entertainment, and behavior. He was an accomplished storyteller, and his work often sounds as good as it looks. Still, no analysis of his humor has denied its most fundamental and generous effect: the ability to create laughter.

Stephen Butler Leacock was born 30 December 1869 in Swanmore, Hampshire, England, but his family moved to a farm near Sutton, Ontario, when he was six. From 1882 to 1887 he attended Upper Canada College; after training at the Strathroy Collegiate Institute and teaching briefly at Uxbridge, he became a master in modern languages at Upper Canada from 1889 to 1899. He had received a B.A. from the University of Toronto in 1891 and was awarded his Ph.D. by the University of Chicago in 1903 (where he studied with Thorstein Veblen) for a thesis on the doctrine of laissez-faire. Meanwhile he had married Beatrix Hamilton in 1900. After receiving his doctorate he joined McGill University's new Department of Economics and Political Science, remaining until his mandatory retirement in 1936. He produced an internationally respected textbook, *Elements of Political Science,* in 1906 and in 1908 was appointed chairman of his department.

In 1910 a privately published collection of his early magazine pieces, *Literary Lapses: A Book of Sketches,* appeared; it was noticed and subsequently published in London by John Lane, who simultaneously brought it out in New York, and Leacock's career as a humorist began to be established. His reputation was secured with *Nonsense Novels* (1911), which had been contracted as a series by *Saturday Night,* and with *Sunshine Sketches of a Little Town* (1912), commissioned by the *Montreal Star.* He was ultimately in great demand as a speaker and made several successful circuits of lectures: an international tour for the Rhodes Trust on behalf of the imperial cause from 1907 to 1908, another in North America for the Belgian Relief Fund in 1915, addresses in Great Britain in 1921, and, late in 1936, a western Canadian tour to urge national unity. His later awards included the Mark Twain Medal, the Lorne Pierce Medal from the Royal Society of Canada, the Governor General's Award, and honorary degrees from Queen's, Dartmouth, Brown, Bishop's, and McGill universities. At his death from cancer of the throat on 28 March 1944, he left unfinished the autobiographical book *The Boy I Left Behind Me,* which was published in 1946. His manuscripts went to McGill, and later his beloved house at Old Brewery Bay on Lake Couchiching became the Stephen Leacock Memorial Home. The Leacock Medal for Humour was first struck in 1947 and is awarded annually.

A selective survey of Leacock's humorous writing and some of his other literary work reveals some persistent topics and techniques. *Liter-*

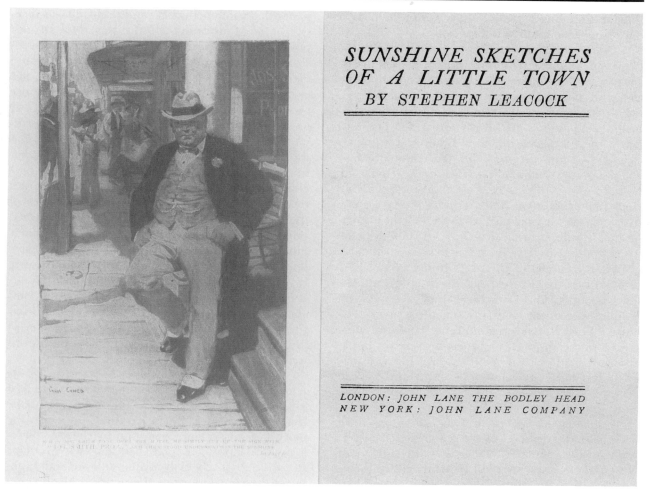

Frontispiece and title page for Leacock's most critically acclaimed book (1912). Set in the mythical small town Mariposa, the stories—such as "The Hostelry of Mr. Smith"—satirize the self-importance of various residents but also show nostalgia for simpler times.

ary Lapses, for example, his collection of miscellaneous sketches, effectively established the model against which most of his subsequent assemblages could be judged. "My Financial Career" shows a little man confronted by a forbidding institution; "The Conjurer's Revenge" realistically depicts vengeance on a spoilsport; and "Hoodoo McFiggin's Christmas" memorably combines pathos with implicit parental meanness. "A Lesson in Fiction" lampoons and explodes, in a question-and-answer format, the clichés of romantic adventure, and in "The New Food" a baby literally explodes from the effects of dehydrated food. "Saloonio: A Study in Shakespearean Criticism" features the obdurate and dramatically persistent Col. Hogshead, and "The Awful Fate of Melpomenus Jones" involves a guest's fatal inability to take his leave. There are several "how to" and

"how to be" items, a parody of the society page, and the sad comedy of the celebrated "A, B, and C: The Human Element in Mathematics." "A New Pathology," manic and brilliant, speaks of men's clothing in medical and surgical terms, as in the specific cases of "Contractio Pantalunae, or Shortening of the Legs of the Trousers" and "Mortificatio Tilis, or Greenness of the Hat." "Boarding-House Geometry" includes the same inspired invention; among its "Postulates and Propositions" is this one: "The clothes of a boarding-house bed, though produced ever so far both ways, will not meet." In *Literary Lapses* Leacock shows his command of careful malapropism and the resolutely literal reading of metaphor or cliché, which were to become favorite devices. The collection is buoyant and vivacious, rife with imaginative merriment, and its human constants remain unfailingly fresh. Many of these pieces have been frequently anthologized.

Nonsense Novels comprises hilarious burlesques of popular fiction in which Leacock twists stereotypical formulae, in effect foregrounding excesses of language, incident, and character. All the sensationalism, hyperbole, and banalities of his possible models are vividly apparent. There is a sea story, a tale of highland feud, and a homestead melodrama (in which the "Good Book" is Euclid's *Elements*); characters include a "hero in homespun," a Horatio Alger prototype, who finds that crime pays, and an obtuse Great Detective. One of the "novels" is "Q. A Psychic Pstory of the Psupernatural," which portrays the hoax of an "inter-astral psycho-monetary experiment." "Guido the Gimlet of Ghent: A Romance of Chivalry" is energized by medieval derring-do and mistaken identity, and "Gertrude the Governess: or Simple Seventeen" contains the often-cited sentence, "Lord Ronald said nothing; he flung himself from the room, flung himself upon his horse and rode madly off in all directions." Leacock manipulates metaphors and types with enthusiastic assurance throughout; his travesties are consistently treasures of verbal acrobatics.

Sunshine Sketches of a Little Town has long been acknowledged as Leacock's creative masterpiece and is deservedly his most critically celebrated book. It is a series of interrelated short stories, whereas his later collections are composed of miscellaneous sketches. A joking autobiographical preface sets the tone of genial deprecation that is the book's principal narrative device: its narrator, in familiar address to the reader, is both one of and above his townspeople. He is breezy and colloquial and attempts to play the naif with ill-concealed glee and only a token straight face.

In "The Hostelry of Mr. Smith" Leacock's prime rhetorical strategy is hyperbole, to underscore the self-importance and insular grandiosity of some of Mariposa's residents. The opportunistic hotelier, Josh Smith, is seen as heroic to the provincials, while "The Speculations of Jefferson Thorpe" is a mock-heroic burlesque of high finance concerning the overreaching personality of the town's barber. "The Marine Excursion of the Knights of Pythias," which tells of the sinking of the *Mariposa Belle*, is also subject to rhetorical inflation and builds to an effective anticlimax. The book is rampant with touches such as this description of the undertaker: "he was there in a neat suit of black, not, of course, his heavier or professional suit, but a soft clinging effect as of burnt

paper that combined gaiety and decorum to a nicety." "The Ministrations of the Rev. Mr. Drone" pokes gentler, sentimental fun at a simple, well-meaning, and unpretentious Church of England divine. Drone and Mr. Pupkin, a bank clerk, are each the subject of a trio of related stories: those on Drone carry some well-measured sympathetic touches and pathos, while Pupkin's "Extraordinary Entanglement" with Zena Pepperleigh has the whimsically innocent tone of Booth Tarkington. "The Great Election in Missinaba County" and "The Candidacy of Mr. Smith" feature "not the miserable, crooked, money-ridden politics of the cities, but the straight, real old-fashioned thing that is an honour to the country-side." Finally, "L'Envoi: The Train to Mariposa" presents evocative nostalgia for the sunshine town, from the perspective of former residents, now urbanized. The story epitomizes Leacock's deft changes of key throughout the book and confirms his implicit regret for the exaggeration of life's ordinary values, something all his humorous writing never entirely ignores.

Behind the Beyond, and Other Contributions to Human Knowledge (1913) is a miscellany typical of many to follow. The collection is substantially characterized by "Parisian Pastimes," in which the naive persona is employed, and by the title piece, a modern "problem play" written as a dramatic story. Leacock cheekily comments on and highlights the conventions of the genre ("All through a problem play it is understood that any of the characters may ring for tea and get it. Tea in a problem play is the same as whiskey in a melodrama"). Again he accents the inanities in popular culture with what proves to be relatively uniform success.

Arcadian Adventures with the Idle Rich (1914), Leacock's other major critical success, is effectively a metropolitan companion piece to *Sunshine Sketches of a Little Town*. There are clear, perhaps intentional parallels between the two books' attention to love, the church, and politics, and several characters are nearly identical in kind and degree. However, here Leacock is altogether darker, and considerably sharper with his somewhat corrupted principals, the majority of whom are comically distorted by a capitalist milieu. Sophisticated hypocrisy, voracity, and self-deception reign in the world that radiates from the Mausoleum Club on Plutoria Avenue, and those most severely caricatured are, at heart, merely fiscal hustlers. "A Little Dinner with Mr. Lucullus Fyshe," for example, is woven through with metaphors

Frontispieces for Behind the Beyond, and Other Contributions to Human Knowledge *(left, 1913) and* Further
Foolishness: Sketches and Satires on the Follies of the Day *(right, 1916)–drawings by A. H. Fish*

of wealth mixed into an Arcadian pastoral environment, as Fyshe and the impecunious Duke of Dulham are bent on getting each other's imagined reserves. The city's gilt-edged Clean Government Association turns virtually fascist to ensure its nominal goal, while the moneyed Newberrys faddishly "rough it" at their simple summer castle. "The Rival Churches of St. Asaph and St. Osoph" (in the story of the same name) are caught up in the cash flow; even at Mr. Peter Spillikins's nuptials, "The face of the young rector, Mr. Fareforth Furlong, wore the added saintliness that springs from a five-hundred dollar fee." The ultimate merger of the two institutions is financial–United Churches Limited–with doctrinal matters left to the purview of the shareholders.

In this corrupt society the innocent are victims. Tomlinson, the so-called wizard of finance who is a simple, troubled soul, is preyed upon by

Dr. Boomer, the profit-oriented president of Plutoria University. The culturally pretentious Mrs. Rasselyer-Brown and her Yahi-Bahi Oriental Society are nearly fleeced by the emissaries of Boohooism. The literally short-sighted and helpless Spillikins is captured in marriage by the worldly Mrs. Everleigh; Dr. McTeague, whose pastoral concerns are properly spiritual and fundamental, not monetary, is swept away. Though the innocents receive some sympathetic and even sentimental touches, they fall before the urban dedication to a cash nexus. The narrator uses fiscal metaphors, allegorical names, and irreverent similes with satiric frequency, and eviscerates those who strike self-righteous poses, often flatly stating the reality that underscores the ritual pretenses of the acquisitive society. In *Arcadian Adventures with the Idle Rich* may be heard Leacock's lament for the dearth of simplicity–along with a controlled irony directed at all forms of ego inflation. The book's final appalling image finds dawn "dimming with its cheap prosaic glare that shaded beauty of the artificial light," the hard unnatural sheen that Leacock despairs of and despises. Yet in his disillusionment he creates not only delightful mockeries but also some of his most effective individual narratives.

In *Moonbeams from the Larger Lunacy* (1915) Leacock continues to illustrate his variety of whimsy at the relative outset of his popular writing career, in such pieces as "Ram Spudd: The New-World Singer," "The First Newspaper: A Sort of Allegory" (about a paper that prefers the newsworthy to the factual), and the sarcastic "Passionate Paragraphs," with fictitious extracts from a crassly stylish "recent novel." Leacock's mock preface to "Spoof: A Thousand-Guinea Novel" sets out his satiric opinion of popular fiction: "The childish attempt to *interest* the reader has long since been abandoned by all the best writers. They refuse to do it. The modern novel must convey a message, or else it must paint a picture, or remove a veil, or open a new chapter in human psychology. Otherwise it is no good. SPOOF does all of these things. The reader rises from its perusal perplexed, troubled, and yet so filled with information that rising itself is a difficulty." The emphasis of the collection is primarily literary, and it is a success.

Further Foolishness: Sketches and Satires on the Follies of the Day (1916) has many individual pleasures. "The Snoopopaths, or, Fifty Stories in One" exposes false sensationalism in fiction, as other pieces present the clichés of sentimental and melodramatic culture. "Are the Rich Happy?" is a fine exercise in incongruous perspective, and popular stereotypes, ideas, and personalities are constantly undermined. The most significant argument, under the rubric "Timid Thoughts on Timely Topics," is "Humour as I See It." From a comic deflation of an English reviewer's scholarly exactitude about his work, Leacock moves from a discussion of good humor ("without harm and without malice") to great humor, that which is mixed with pathos and celebrates "the strange incongruity between our aspiration and our achievement. . . ." Leacock's perspective, which endures through much of his later criticism, is fundamentally eupeptic; though he acknowledges that there are forms of humor he is unable to appreciate, his attitude avoids extremes.

Essays and Literary Studies (1916), however, does show some vigorous and unevasive positions on the humanities. Leacock creates an amusing argument for Dickens's characters to deny that they are caricatures, and essays are offered on O. Henry (William Sydney Porter), Charles II, modern morality, women's dependence, and schoolmastering. In "The Apology of a Professor: An Essay on Modern Learning" he castigates academic specialization and the mechanistic accumulation of fact with no "wide and humane culture of the intellect"; in "Literature and Education in America" he recounts the surrender of literature to a charmless and businesslike drudgery. "American Humour," a fine serious argument, is important for its later development in *Humour and Humanity: An Introduction to the Study of Humour* (1937). Leacock approaches the "evolution of amusement" in America from the low form of discomfiture or destruction through wit and incongruity to the highest form, life's incongruities themselves. He identifies American humor by its affectation of simplicity, exaggeration (including the "Unrestrained Simile"), and, in its prime form, the freedom from convention–qualities that apply directly to his own work. In "The Lot of the Schoolmaster" he writes, "the half-truth is to me a kind of mellow moonlight in which I love to dwell. One sees better in it," and to a degree this ambiguity characterizes all his criticism, even as he writes, as here, forcefully and with a vivid use of metaphor and illustration.

Frenzied Fiction (1918) gives reasonably sustained attention to social foibles, fads, and pretensions; the collection is mostly first-person and miscellaneous; and few pieces are far removed from actuality. However, "My Revelations as a Spy" is the volume's gem, making much pleasant foolery with "the astounding ramifications and the ubiquity of the international spy system." Leacock's next (virtually annual) collection, *The Hohenzollerns in America; with the Bolsheviks in Berlin and Other Impossibilities* (1919), reflects his concession to a war mentality, and it is never completely divorced from that reality despite the puckishness of "Echoes of the War." Here former German princelings are now immigrants, and their lives are rounded with meanness, fakery, chicanery, and pathos. "The Lost Illusions of Mr. Sims" is about the remembered splendors of college days. In "Heroes and Heroines," a parody of "Ned" in children's literature and of stock figures in adult fiction, and in "The Discovery of America," a silent film described according to its staginess, Leacock mocks the artifices of public entertainments. With *Winsome Winnie, and Other New Nonsense Nov-*

els (1920) Leacock tried to capitalize on the success of *Nonsense Novels*, but the same energy of invention is not present. The new parodies include "Winsome Winnie: or, Trial and Temptation" and "Broken Barriers: or, Red Love on a Blue Island"; by far the best is "Buggam Grange: A Good Old Ghost Story." Leacock is perhaps more faithful here to the language and plots of his models, and consequently his imagination seems constrained.

This was not the case with *My Discovery of England* (1922), a uniformly accomplished book with an evenness and geniality of tone that nevertheless accommodates some spirited irreverence. Leacock considers transatlantic impression-writers, his press interviews (which "entirely failed to elicit the large fund of information which I acquired"), reflections on London as well as British government and business, the prospects of prohibition, and various introductions of himself as speaker ("We Have With Us Tonight"). In "Have the English Any Sense of Humour?" he addresses the differences between British and American comedy: the American predilection to slang, the supposed humor of bad spelling, and stories with a point, as distinct from the British dedication to puns and pedantry, literal anecdotes, and narration. "Oxford as I See It" is the book's heart, an alleged "searching scrutiny" that cleverly defines the university's virtues by their seeming opposites and invidious instances, such as that of the smoking tutor: "Men who have been systematically smoked at for four years turn into ripe scholars." Leacock's discovery of England through incongruity is vivacious and stays consistently fresh in its amiable colonial cheekiness.

College Days (1923) displays the haze and hyperbole of memory as well as the ironic and bittersweet comic deflation of romantic retrospect. However, what stands out are the satiric verses, accomplished rhymes good-naturedly directed at specific academics at the University of Toronto. *Over the Footlights* (1923) begins, like many Leacockian miscellanies, focused on a theme or form before it becomes more truly varied. Included are dramatic travesties of the seacoast melodrama, Ibsen ("done out of the original Norwegian with an axe"), a Greek tragedy, Russian and historical episodes, and a Nevada film. Despite the facetiousness, beneath it lurks a nostalgia for such predictable scenes, and some of Leacock's recreations survive the satiric thrust to stand as effective dramaturgy. (Several Leacock stories and nonsense novels actually became repertory plays

adapted by V. C. Clinton-Baddeley.) The section "Other Fancies" includes a favorite target, "Nature Men," in the pseudoserious "Personal Experiments with the Black Bass," and Leacock's not unfamiliar chauvinism in "Abolishing the Heroine," a notion for adding "sprightliness" to fictions that otherwise "start in excitement and end in slush."

The Garden of Folly (1924) prefatorily advocates humor as "essentially a comforter, reconciling us to things as they are in contrast to things as they might be" ("Concerning Humour and Humourists"). The volume contains some exquisite parodies of self-help manuals, guides, and laymen's introductions to successes. "The Human Mind Up To Date" and "The Human Body: Its Care and Prevention" are burlesque anatomies with nonchalant foolery; in them Leacock reaches a masterly comedy, as, for instance, when the prudent man watches his insides: "Are his ducts functioning? How is his great colon? And the shorter, or semi-colon, what about that? Is there an easy flow of nitric acid from the oesophagus to the proscenium? If not, what is stopping it: has perhaps a lot of sand or mud made its way into the auditorium?" Leacock's admitted subject, "the follies of the mind and body, of failure and success," cannot be taken with the hard satiric bite that he ostensibly wishes: the pleasure is too insistent.

Winnowed Wisdom: A New Book of Humour (1926) is bland in comparison to earlier collections; its sketches are loosely grouped under rubrics such as "The Outlines of Everything," "Studies in the Newer Culture" (including "Attaboy" language), "Travel and Movement," and "In the Good Old Summer Time." In *Short Circuits* (1928) there are suggestions of impatience with the disruptions Leacock finds in man's dealings with nature, society, education, the media, and literature. He points up ludicrousness and failures in his compact sketches, seeing a world riddled with manias and excesses, and with little allowance for the ordinary man. The literature section assembles some splendid creations, such as up-to-date poems ("The Cash and Carry of the Light Brigade") and "The Old Men's Page," with its former scouts: "After lunch, each scout will place his rug and cushion under a suitable tree and smoke a cigar while listening in silence for any especial calls and wood notes of birds, bees, and insects, such as the cicada, the rickshaw, the ginricki, and others that he has learned to know." Leacock also reveals the denizens of the under-

Leacock, circa 1941, at his home in Orillia, Ontario (photograph by Karsh-Ottawa)

world as exaggerated in fiction and the experts by reputation only; he savages the romantic concept of the heroine with his character Margaret Overproof, all things to all fictions ("Her graceful neck sloped away in all directions till it reached her bust, which stopped it"). The longest sketch, and an unalloyed delight, is "The Great Detective": the conventions and techniques of the genre are explained, re-created, and simultaneously parodied.

The Iron Man & the Tin Woman: With Other Such Futurities: A Book of Little Sketches of To-day and To-morrow (1929) is a racy and slick volume. In "Pictures of the Bright Time to Come" Leacock indulges his fondness for futuristic silliness, and in "Great Lives in Our Midst" he characteristically inflates the insignificant. "The Intimate Disclosures of a Wronged Woman" satirizes the public greed for confessions and memoirs–"the writer lays her soul bare and jumps on it"–and "Conversations I Can Do Without" shows the less

subtle, broader, and harder tone the book often reveals. In *Afternoons in Utopia: Tales of the New Time* (1932) Leacock looks variously at war, medicine, and college in past, present, and future. There is little real merriment to redeem a generally flat and weak collection, which depends on a mechanical formula of arrangement; the book reveals the writer's nostalgia for a simpler world and a distrust of both an increase in technology and political socialization. However, *The Dry Pickwick and Other Incongruities* (1932) succeeds with many amusing items: a medieval hole-in-one, a mock tourist guide to the stimulating refreshments of Quebec, the fervid confessions of a soda fiend, and the title story, a bad dream in which Dickens's Pickwickians, subject to the U.S. Eighteenth Amendment (prohibition), become surly as they are forced into a surreptitious pursuit of questionable beverages.

Humour: Its Theory and Technique, with Examples and Samples, a Book of Discovery (1935) does not completely represent the critical formulation Leacock had begun in earlier essays. It illustrates his major themes, in chapters on fun with words–parody, burlesque, and mistranslation–techniques of the greater humorists, national characteristics, and humor through the ages. The volume is a sampler, with commentary, a form Leacock had followed in *The Greatest Pages of Charles Dickens* (1934). Later (in 1937) he presented a more thorough and personal articulation of his position in *Humour and Humanity*. Before that, however, *Funny Pieces: A Book of Random Sketches* (1936) had again shown his theories at work, in treatments focusing on bygone schoolbooks, the invasion of human thought by mathematical symbols, papers of the Ignoramus Club, and particularly Red Riding-Hood up-to-date. *Here Are My Lectures and Stories* (1937) characteristically reuses proven material. These include his accomplished platform performances on substantially serious topics ("How Soon Can We Start the Next War?"), his burlesques ("What I Don't Know About Drama"), a trio on "Frenzied Fiction," and the personable "My Fishing Pond," with pastoral pleasantries.

Humour and Humanity is often written with what in *My Discovery of the West* (1937) he calls "the warm diction of rhetoric." For Leacock "Humour may be defined as the kindly contemplation of the incongruities of life, and the artistic expression thereof." He traces a development from exultation based on injury or destruction through incongruity to that greatest humor, which is "born, as it were, in perplexity, in contemplation of the insoluble riddle of existence." There are successive chapters on words, ideas, the humor of situation and of character, comic verse, humorous poetry, craftsmanship, and sublimity. Leacock's emphasis is always on kindliness and incongruity; he delivers his generalities with apt illustrations and humane grace, and both his conviction and the broad categories he suggests are his virtues here. *Humour and Humanity* bears with great particularity on his own comic work, and its geniality and sympathy had characterized his biographies of Mark Twain (1932) and Charles Dickens (1933). His range in *Humour and Humanity* is uncomplicated, but as aesthetic criticism the book's one failure is its sentimentality.

The autobiographical pieces and monologues of *Model Memoirs and Other Sketches from Simple to Serious* (1938) show Leacock's keen eye for incongruity, his ability to place contemporary language in humorously inappropriate mouths, and

Leacock in the early 1940s (photograph by Karsh-Ottawa)

also his skill in adapting a formula somewhat mechanically. A strong impression is left by "The Anatomy of Gloom," which sees "a gathering pall of over-seriousness pervading all our civilization, of over-apprehension, over-anxiety," and, in a related vein, a later lament for the passing of the once unshrunken imaginative world and a plea for the old fictional favorites, "real people to whom your heart responds and who mean more to you than the people of your everyday life." The collection is divided between the comic and the plaintive; as Leacock admitted, "I am aware that parts of this volume may be found offensively serious and can only plead the influence of advancing years." Similarly, *My Remarkable Uncle, and Other Sketches* (1942) does not maintain the tone of Leacock's deft, engaging portrait of the scapegrace E. P. Leacock and his "indomitable self-belief," which precedes other reminiscences that do not entirely avoid the sentimental. The volume is an unemphatic miscellany with a personal emphasis and an underlying autumnal mood. Several "Studies in Humour" do little more than *Humour and Humanity*, emphasizing the consolatory and democratic nature of humor and jokes as a reflection of sociological history.

How to Write (1943) recalls the preface to *Sunshine Sketches of a Little Town*, which presented writing as "an arduous contrivance only to be achieved in fortunate moments." Leacock looks at the desire to write, laws of grammar, sentences, narration, language, and how to or how not to write history, the historical novel, poetry, and humor. He notes the complexities of ordinary language and the "perplexing" nature of prose, distinguishes between realism and romance in narrative, remarks on garrulity, and generally frowns on sentimentality, tediousness, and affectation. The book is a series of compact simplified thoughts, ironically coming from a writer adept at burlesquing the "how-to" so wittily. Leacock's material is engaging and varied, and his essentially entertaining nature often wins over the nominal objectivity of his presentation.

Happy Stories, Just to Laugh at (1943) is characteristically Leacockian in that a first-person narrator is in contact with the foibles, eccentricities, and facades of others. His tone is bemused and is best seen in "Boom Times": actual incidents from the life of Leacock's remarkable uncle are removed "from the cramped environment of truth to the larger atmosphere of fiction," though the fictionalizing is minimal. "Mariposa Moves On" also depends on nostalgia: written in connection with the Victory Loan of 1943, these sketches, mostly focused on Jeff Thorpe's barbershop, are easy, familiar, and light, pervaded by a goodwill that does not caricature any of the "fellers."

Finally, *Last Leaves* (1945) is a posthumous collection assembled, with a prefatory reminiscence, by Leacock's niece, Barbara Nimmo. Its pieces are mature and relaxed, with no striving for rhetorical animation. The volume has a mixture of modes: quasi-literary studies, essays on the gold standard and the postwar world, "ponderous" subjects treated lightly, and comic items such as "Living With Murder," wherein the reader of detective fiction himself always has an alibi.

The bulk and reputation of Leacock's humorous writings tend to obscure his other publications, which represent a considerable range of work in political science, economics, biography, sociology, and history, and which were interspersed with his more familiar productions. For example, Leacock's clever *Hellements of Hickonomics, in Hiccoughs of Verse Done in Our Social Planning Mill* (1936) suggests the overlap of his careers as professional humorist and as political economist. As a teacher, Leacock resisted heartless practical curricula and the disciplinary method of education. This volume of lively, debunking, and demystifying verses is based on his notion that "it might be of great service if economic problems could be discussed in the form of the literature of the imagination," which gives rise to such clear and vivid rhymes as "Oh! Mr. Malthus!" In his less literary career Leacock was a persistent imperialist, patriot, conservative, and humanitarian. As well as his books in more academic fields, he published addresses, pamphlets, and articles on such subjects as responsible government in the British colonial system, Canada and the Monroe Doctrine, fiscal policy, the Canadian balance of trade, freedom and compulsion in education, democracy and social progress, the proper limitations of state interference, and the economic analysis of industrial depression.

This other writing is informative without being didactic; even with circumstantially appropriate proselytizing or special pleading it is often illuminated, like his literary criticism, by illustrative instances and a scorn for jargon. His interest was practical, not theoretical, and in his wider social and academic concerns are found conviction, sincerity, and knowledge. He tried repeatedly to remove the complexities and accommodate his readers.

Leacock's literary work over his long career was not of uniform excellence; many of his earliest books, which have attracted the greatest critical attention, were his best. Yet his writing was never totally negligible, even given his habits of repetition and dependence on formulaic devices. Even in his least distinguished collections there are uniquely comic pieces. If his popularity made his writing sometimes mechanical, his substantial corpus of humor is still seen to possess a verve and comic imagination that are remarkable, and whose subjects appeal across international boundaries. There are rich tracts of Leacock's comedy that continue to be overlooked. His robustness, wit, and good cheer were those of a good-natured man who was an ironist and sometimes a satirist but who could not be moved to a vexing indignation. Leacock's work has never lost its essentially humane appeal, and his eye on harmless follies remains invitingly genial.

Bibliography:
Gerhard R. Lomer, *Stephen Leacock: A Check-List and Index of His Writings* (Ottawa: National Library, 1954).

Biographies:

Peter McArthur, *Stephen Leacock* (Toronto: Ryerson, 1923);

Ralph L. Curry, *Stephen Leacock: Humorist and Humanist* (New York: Doubleday, 1959);

Elizabeth Kimball, *The Man in the Panama Hat* (Toronto: McClelland & Stewart, 1970);

David M. Legate, *Stephen Leacock: A Biography* (Toronto & Garden City, N.Y.: Doubleday, 1970);

Albert and Theresa Moritz, *Leacock: A Biography* (Toronto: Stoddart, 1985).

References:

Carl Berger, "The Other Mr. Leacock," *Canadian Literature*, 5 (Winter 1973): 23-40;

Claude T. Bissell, "Haliburton, Leacock and the American Humorous Tradition," *Canadian Literature*, 39 (Winter 1969): 5-19;

Douglas Bush, "Stephen Leacock," in *The Canadian Imagination: Dimensions of a Literary Culture*, edited by David Staines (Cambridge, Mass. & London: Harvard University Press, 1977);

Donald Cameron, *Faces of Leacock: An Appreciation* (Toronto: Ryerson, 1967);

Ralph L. Curry, *Stephen Leacock and His Works* (Downsview, Ont.: ECW, 1988);

Robertson Davies, *Stephen Leacock* (Toronto: McClelland & Stewart, 1970);

J. Kushner and R. D. MacDonald, "Leacock: Economist / Satirist in *Arcadian Adventures* and *Sunshine Sketches*," *Dalhousie Review*, 56 (Autumn 1976): 493-509;

Gerald Lynch, *Stephen Leacock: Humour and Humanity* (Montreal: McGill-Queen's University Press, 1988);

T. D. MacLulich, "Mariposa Revisited," *Studies in Canadian Literature*, 4 (Winter 1979): 167-176;

W. H. Magee, "Genial Humour in Stephen Leacock," *Dalhousie Review*, 56 (Summer 1976): 268-282;

Magee, "Leacock, Local Colourist," *Canadian Literature*, 39 (Winter 1969): 34-42;

Douglas Mantz, "Preposterous and Profound: A New Look at the Envoi of *Sunshine Sketches*," *Journal of Canadian Fiction*, 19 (1977): 95-105;

D. A. Norris, "Preserving Main Street: Some Lessons of Leacock's Mariposa," *Journal of Canadian Studies*, 17 (Summer 1982): 128-136;

Desmond Pacey, "Leacock as a Satirist," *Queen's Quarterly*, 58 (Summer 1951): 208-219;

B. J. Rasporich, "The Leacock Persona and the Canadian Character," *Mosaic*, 14 (Spring 1981): 76-92;

Rasporich, "New Eden Dream: The Source of Canadian Humour: McCulloch, Maliburton, and Leacock," *Studies in Canadian Literature*, 7, no. 2 (1982): 227-240;

David Staines, ed., *Leacock: A Reappraisal* (Ottawa: University of Ottawa Press, 1986);

Frank W. Watt, "Critic or Entertainer? Leacock and the Growth of Materialism," *Canadian Literature*, 5 (Summer 1960): 33-42;

R. E. Watters, "A Special Tang: Stephen Leacock's Canadian Humour," *Canadian Literature*, 5 (Summer 1960): 21-32.

Papers:

Stephen Leacock's manuscripts and papers are in the MacLennan Library, McGill University, and in the Leacock Memorial Home, Orillia, Ontario.

James Le Rossignol

(24 October 1866-4 December 1969)

John Stockdale
Laval University

BOOKS: *The Ethical Philosophy of Samuel Clarke* (Leipzig, 1892);

Monopolies Past and Present (New York: Crowell, 1901);

Taxation in Colorado (Denver: Bishop, 1902);

History of Higher Education in Colorado (Washington, D.C.: Government Printing Office, 1903);

Orthodox Socialism: A Criticism (New York: Crowell, 1907);

Little Stories of Old Quebec (New York: Eaton & Mains, 1908);

State Socialism in New Zealand, by Le Rossignol and William Downie Stewart (New York: Crowell, 1910; London: Harrap, 1911);

Jean Baptiste: A Story of French Canada (Toronto: Dent/New York: Dutton, 1915);

What is Socialism?: An Explanation and Criticism of the Doctrines and Proposals of "Scientific Socialism" (New York: Crowell, 1921);

Economics for Everyman: An Introduction to Social Economics (New York: Holt, 1923; London: Pitman, 1924);

First Economics (Chicago & New York: Shaw, 1926);

The Beauport Road (Tales of Old Quebec) (Toronto: McClelland & Stewart, 1928);

The Flying Canoe (La Chasse-galerie) (Toronto: McClelland & Stewart, 1929);

The Habitant-Merchant (Toronto: Macmillan, 1939);

From Marx to Stalin: A Critique of Communism (New York: Crowell, 1940).

James Le Rossignol was a Quebec writer and teacher whose concerns were broadly based. Publishing books on philosophy, economics, and political science, he was also well versed in psychology and literature. His detailed grasp of all these fields informs his primarily rural fiction, making for a stimulating blend of simple settings and complex issues.

Le Rossignol's father, Peter, was a native of the Isle of Jersey, and his mother, Mary Gillespi

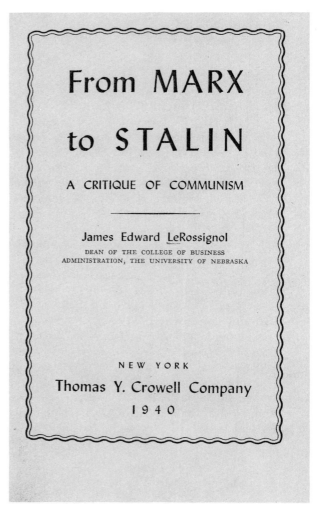

Title page for Le Rossignol's last book. His interests covered a broad range of social, economic, and psychological issues, and were reflected in both his fiction and nonfiction publications.

Le Rossignol, a native of Quebec. Le Rossignol was educated at Huntington Academy, Montreal High School, McGill University (B.A., 1888), and at Leipzig (M.A. and Ph.D., 1892). He married Jessie Catherine Ross of Montreal in 1898, and they had four children. Le Rossignol began teaching high school in Montreal and soon moved to the

United States, where he taught psychology at Clark (1892) and Ohio University (1892-1894), and then went to the University of Denver to teach economics and political science. He arrived finally at the University of Nebraska in 1908, where he remained until retirement in 1941. He first directed the School of Commerce and, in 1919, was instrumental in founding the College of Business Administration, which he headed with great distinction.

Le Rossignol was a model father, a gregarious, fun-loving man, and an ardent trout and salmon fisherman, though even on summer holidays he reserved every morning for his writing. His other activities included bridge, chess, college football, and reading. His regular diet of reading included scientific journals in English, German, and French, with the occasional foray into Western stories and detective fiction.

Le Rossignol was throughout his academic career, besides a teacher and an administrator, a writer on economics particularly. He published six volumes on this subject and a flood of newspaper and magazine articles. During the period between 1908 and 1939, he also published five books of fiction. *Little Stories of Old Quebec* (1908) is a collection of short, moralizing tales set in the countryside near Quebec City on the north bank of the Saint Lawrence and in the mountains that border the river. His second book of fiction, *Jean Baptiste: A Story of French Canada* (1915), is a rudimentary novel about a clever, ambitious young man who attempts to rise in prestige and find peace of mind by modernizing his thinking but runs into opposition from his priest and his fellow citizens. A third book, a collection of nine tales, *The Beauport Road (Tales of Old Quebec)*, published in 1928, is set in the countryside along the road that leads east from Quebec City. It was followed by *The Flying Canoe (La Chasse-galerie)* in 1929, which, in its title story, retells the old French-Canadian folktale of a compact with the devil and a cold, wild ride in a flying canoe on New Year's Eve. *The Habitant-Merchant* appeared in 1939. This is a good-humored collection of tales about a sharp, sophisticated commercial traveler in the dry-goods line and a wily shopkeeper in Quebec's Lower Town.

All the stories contained in these volumes are written in a style that recalls the poetry of William Henry Drummond. By modern literary standards they are simple and folklike, making use of stock figures and gothic elements such as witches and spells. Only one of his books approaches the novel in form, and that is *Jean Baptiste: A Story of French Canada*, which, while dealing with young Baptiste's ambitions, touches on themes common to French-Canadian novels of the early twentieth century, particularly the idea that the heart of the nation rests in the people, in the old habits of the farm communities, and in their sturdy support of the Roman Catholic religion. Unfortunately the early promise in the first chapters of this work is allowed to slide away into Le Rossignol's overuse of the supernatural rather than the natural to solve his plot problems. He clearly sets up an antagonism between Baptiste and the priest and his flock but does not exploit the situation and allows the "modern" young man to be easily defeated. Like all his other stories, this one looks back toward the past and describes a way of life, a rural idyll, then long dead, killed by the urbanization and industrialization brought about by world commerce and progress.

The best-sustained of the stories are contained in *The Habitant-Merchant;* they are the best organized and plotted stories and depend for their appeal on a juxtaposition of the commercial traveler from the big city and the rustic local merchant, who tries to get the better of his visitor by taking advantage of the salesman's lack of understanding of human nature. Today many of Le Rossignol's tales may seem to come out of a land that never existed, or existed only in the imaginations of Quebec writers of the nineteenth century—a land of farmers who loathed the interloper and who felt that their very existence depended on the defense of things as they were, or as they preferred to think that they were. It would be futile to claim great literary merit for the writings of James Le Rossignol, but he has left behind for us an enjoyable, kindly intended picture of rural Quebec life from the days of his childhood, when things were slower, gentler, and perhaps happier.

William Dawson LeSueur

(19 February 1840-23 September 1917)

Clifford G. Holland
Ontario Institute for Studies in Education

BOOKS: *Count Frontenac* (Toronto: Morang, 1906; London: Jack, 1906);

A Critical Spirit: The Thought of William Dawson LeSueur, edited by A. B. McKillop (Toronto: McClelland & Stewart, 1977);

William Lyon Mackenzie: A Reinterpretation, edited by McKillop (Toronto: Macmillan, 1979).

SELECTED PERIODICAL PUBLICATIONS UNCOLLECTED: "Sainte-Beuve," *Westminster Review* (U.S. edition), 95 (April 1871): 208-227;

" 'Progress and Poverty' and the Doctrine of Evolution," *Rose-Belford's Canadian Monthly and National Review*, 6 (March 1881): 287-296;

"The True Idea of Canadian Loyalty," *Rose-Belford's Canadian Monthly and National Review*, 8 (January 1882): 1-11;

"Evolution and the Destiny of Man," *Popular Science Monthly*, 26 (February 1885): 456-468;

"Evolution Bounded by Theology," *Popular Science Monthly*, 29 (June 1886): 145-153;

"Ex-President Porter on Evolution," *Popular Science Monthly*, 29 (September 1886): 577-594;

"Science and Its Accusers," *Popular Science Monthly*, 34 (January 1889): 367-379.

As the quintessential Canadian Victorian intellectual, William Dawson LeSueur introduced the spirit of modern criticism into Canadian life, combining a long and remarkable career as a man of letters with that of an Ottawa civil servant. Lauded by Goldwin Smith in a 17 August 1885 letter to Matthew Arnold as "the best critic Canada has," he was a distinguished essayist, persuasive journalist, historian, scientific writer, classical scholar, and positivist philosopher. Devoted as he was to truth and free, responsible thought, the rigor of LeSueur's intellect matched the spirit of Arnold, Charles Augustine Sainte-Beuve, Herbert Spencer, Thomas Henry Huxley, John Stuart Mill, and Auguste Comte, representing a synthesis of thoughts and values common to Anglo-American-Canadian Victorian society.

William Dawson LeSueur

Throughout his life LeSueur sought a foundation for morality based on the intellect, feeling that a purely intellectual life was also a moral life.

Born 19 February 1840 in Quebec, he was of French and English descent and became bilingual and bicultural. His father, Peter LeSueur, had emigrated from the island of Jersey, while his mother, Barbara Dawson, hailed from Sunderland in northern England. Little is known of his childhood other than his deep attachment to his sister Annie. The LeSueur family moved from Quebec to Montreal in the early 1850s, where he was versed in Latin and Greek at Montreal High

School. Moving to Toronto, he studied law at Osgoode Hall and graduated as a silver medalist in classics from the University of Toronto in 1863. Entering lifelong public service while still a student in 1856, he was appointed secretary of the post office department in 1888 and served until his retirement in 1902. He married Ann Jane Foster of Montreal in 1867, and they eventually had a son and a daughter (Ernest Arthur and Beatrice).

He held positions in many learned societies, including his thirty-year association with the Literary and Scientific Society of Ottawa, during which he served nine times as president. Over the years he published scores of articles in British, American, and Canadian periodicals on the social and intellectual issues of the day. In 1900, in recognition of his reputation as a serious thinker and writer, he received an honorary LL.D. from Queen's University, and in 1903 he was elected a fellow of the Royal Society of Canada, holding the position of president in 1912. For over twenty years he was an editorial writer for the *Montreal Star, Montreal Gazette,* and *Ottawa Citizen,* which had the effect of further strengthening his readable and incisive style.

He first attracted international attention with an essay on the great French critic and poet Sainte-Beuve, published in 1871 in the *Westminster Review,* when LeSueur was thirty-one. Sainte-Beuve had rejected the notion of criticism being subjected to any external authority or preconceived idea; he felt it could only be sustained by systematic intellectual inquiry. LeSueur wrote that Sainte-Beuve was "less a judge than an enquirer who tells us of his discoveries, and invites us to verify them for ourselves." Sainte-Beuve was to exercise a lifelong influence upon him and set the tone of his intellectual concerns for the next forty-six years.

LeSueur made a great impact with his political articles that detailed the abuse of the party system in North America. He suggested, in "Party Politics" (collected by A. B. McKillop in *A Critical Spirit,* 1977), that "partyism" led to "a ban on the free exercise of a man's mind" and led people "to conceal or misrepresent their real opinions," for one's party *has* to be supported even if true conscience is violated. He noted how a party in power will cheerfully sacrifice the very principles that brought its triumph at the hustings rather than relinquish the privileges and emoluments of office, while "we set the State on fire with all kinds of false and factitious issues." As for Can-

ada, he rejected its dependent position with respect to the mother country but, unlike his colleague Smith, rejected even more strongly the idea of annexation by the United States. LeSueur was also a representative Canadian who sought to reconcile the English- and French-speaking people in his native land.

In the conflict between science and religion LeSueur played a crucial role with articles such as "Materialism and Positivism," "Morality and Religion," "The Scientific Spirit," and "Science and Materialism." He denied that evolutionism sought to subvert belief in God or that science was materialistic, for he felt it could exert a moral influence. The great issue, he declared in "Ex-President Porter on Evolution" (*Popular Science Monthly,* September 1886), "however some may try to disguise it, is between dogma on the one hand and the free spirit of scientific inquiry on the other." He was influenced by Spencer, who applied evolutionary ideas to social thought but, unlike others, drew no conclusions about Social Darwinism. In "Mr. Spencer and His Critics," LeSueur defended the great philosopher. In turn, Spencer introduced LeSueur to Edward Livingston Youmans of the *Popular Science Monthly* in New York, who republished his Spencer essay as "A Vindication of Scientific Ethics." He was chosen to represent Canada when Spencer was given his famous 1882 testimonial dinner at Delmonico's Restaurant in New York. LeSueur was subsequently invited to join the influential American monthly as a contributing editor and was to be associated with it for nearly twenty years, enhancing his international reputation with a host of essays on evolutionary science, positivism, religion, ethics, and politics. It is not known whether his official position as a civil servant was threatened by his insistence on free thought and free speech, but we do know he felt compelled to use pseudonyms ("A Radical" and "Loan") in some articles written before 1876.

In 1884 he got involved in public debate with the bishop of Ontario on agnosticism. While the battle raged in pulpit and press, he was a model of rectitude, inviting comparison with Huxley. He rejected any labels for those who disbelieved in revealed religion: "Let their opponents coin names if they will; they whom the truth has made free feel their creed is too wide for limitation" ("A Defence of Modern Thought," 1884). In his 1875 essay "The Intellectual Life" he had noted how vexed people became with those who sought truth, for most people set opinion above truth. "That truth *may* be on the other side they cannot help at times suspecting, but they are determined never to be brought face to face with the proof."

After writing a biography of Comte de Frontenac for the Makers of Canada series (1906), he was urged by the publisher Morang to do one on the rebel leader William Lyon Mackenzie. After extensive research LeSueur wrote the first truly critical biography in Canada. It challenged the conventional liberal view of Canadian history and exploded the sacrosanct mythology of the reform tradition. However, the famous insurgent's grandson, William Lyon Mackenzie King, was so incensed by LeSueur's objectivity that he pressured Morang to reject the book. Having made certain papers available to the author, Mackenzie's heirs had anticipated a laudatory biography without regard to the facts; but such duplicity was impossible for LeSueur, who felt the essential nature of history was investigation and critical inquiry, not merely affirmation. In LeSueur's old age, after years of litigation, an injunction was obtained that restrained him from publishing his research. It was finally published in 1979, seventy-one years after it had been written, as edited by A. B. McKillop.

Widely known upon his death in 1917, LeSueur occupied a position as a critic that can be compared to that of Northrop Frye in the mid to late twentieth century, but he was allowed to lapse into obscurity until rediscovery by a later generation. LeSueur lived through the Darwinian revolution in thought that caused the rise of empiricism, the decline of idealism, and in Canada the emergence of democracy, nationalism, industrialization, and technology. It was an age beset by doubt as the claims of religion and science were debated and the old values eroded by the idea of progress and the burgeoning new technology. It is within this context that LeSueur must

be considered, for as John Reade noted in his obituary: "He recognized at once the significance of the new science and its destined ultimate effects on religious and philosophic thought." There was an idealistic component to LeSueur's thought that reflected his belief in a cosmic moral order harmonizing both natural and spiritual laws. In one of his greatest essays, "Idealism in Life" (1878), he points out the secret contempt of the world for the idealist and artist, for the man who does not worship Mammon: "In most pursuits, money broadly speaking is the greatest criterion and measure of success." He suggests that idealism is based upon a perception of a perfect end: "Shall we idealize life, or shall we vulgarize it? . . . [I]f we choose the former we choose struggle, but the struggle will be ever upward, and our last days shall be our best."

References:

Clifford G. Holland, "The Sage of Ottawa: William Dawson LeSueur," *Canadian Literature*, 96 (Spring 1983): 167-181;

A. B. McKillop, *A Disciplined Intelligence: Critical Inquiry and Canadian Thought in the Victorian Era* (Montreal: McGill-Queen's, 1979), chapter 5;

H. J. Morgan, ed., *The Canadian Men and Women of the Time*, second edition (Toronto: Briggs, 1912), p. 654;

John Reade, "William Dawson LeSueur," *Proceedings of the Royal Society of Canada*, 12 (May 1918): iv-vi.

Papers:

Letters, documents, and two unpublished manuscripts by LeSueur–"A History of Canada to 1763" and "The Political Development of Canada"–are on deposit in the Public Archives of Canada, Ottawa.

William Douw Lighthall

(27 December 1857-3 August 1954)

Paul Matthew St. Pierre
Simon Fraser University

BOOKS: *Thoughts, Moods and Ideals: Crimes of Leisure* (Montreal: Witness, 1887);

The Young Seigneur; or, Nation-making, as Wilfrid Châteauclair (Montreal: Drysdale, 1888);

An Account of the Battle of Chateauguay: Being a Lecture Delivered at Ormstown, March 8th, 1889 (Montreal: Drysdale, 1889);

Montreal after 250 Years (Montreal: Grafton, 1892); republished as *Sights and Shrines of Montreal: A Topographical, Romantic and Historical Description of the City and Environs* (Montreal: Grafton, 1892);

The False Chevalier; or, The Lifeguard of Marie Antoinette (Montreal: Grafton, 1898; New York: Arnold, 1898);

A New Hochelagan Burying-ground Discovered at Westmount on the Western Spur of Mount Royal, Montreal, July-September 1898 (Montreal: Pelletier, 1898);

Hochelagans and Mohawks: A Link in Iroquois History (Ottawa: Hope, 1899; London: Quaritch, 1899);

Hiawatha the Great, as Châteauclair (London: Royal Society of Literature Transactions, 1901); republished under Lighthall's real name as *The Master of Life: A Romance of the Five Nations and of Prehistoric Montreal* (Toronto: Musson, 1908; Chicago: McClung, 1909);

Canada: A Modern Nation (Montreal: Witness, 1904);

Thomas Pownall: His Part in the Conquest of Canada (Ottawa: Hope, 1904);

The Land of Manitou (Montreal: Desbarats, 1916);

Old Measures: Collected Verse (Montreal: Chapman/ Toronto: Musson, 1922);

The Outer Consciousness, 8 volumes (Montreal: Privately printed, 1923-1930); revised and published in one volume (Toronto: Macmillan, 1933).

OTHER: *Songs of the Great Dominion: Voices from the Forests and Waters, the Settlements and Cities of Canada,* edited, with an introduction, by

William Douw Lighthall

Lighthall (London: Scott, 1889); abridged as *Canadian Poems and Lays: Selections of Native Verse, Reflecting the Seasons, Legends and Life of the Dominion,* edited, with an introduction, by Lighthall (Toronto: Musson, 1891; London: Scott, 1893);

Canadian Songs and Poems: Voices from the Forests and Waters, the Settlements and Cities of Canada, edited by Lighthall (Toronto: Gage/ London: Scott, 1892).

SELECTED PERIODICAL PUBLICATIONS
UNCOLLECTED: "The Conditions of a Colonial Culture," *Royal Society of Literature of the United Kingdom, London: Essays by Divers Hands, Being the Transactions,* second series, 19 (1898): 79-91;

"Hiawatha the Great," *Royal Society of Literature of the United Kingdom, London: Essays by Divers Hands, Being the Transactions*, second series, 23 (1902): 1-18;

"Westmount: A Municipal Illustration," *University of Toronto Studies*, 2, no. 1 (1902): 25-34;

"French-Canadian Literature," *Royal Society of Literature of the United Kingdom, London: Essays by Divers Hands, Being the Transactions*, second series, 26 (1905): 231-248;

"English Settlement in Quebec," *Canada and Its Provinces*, 15 (1914): 121-164;

"City Government in the Province of Quebec," *Canada and Its Provinces*, 15 (1914): 299-320;

"Elimination of Political Parties in Canadian Cities," *National Municipal Review*, 6 (March 1917): 207-209;

"War Time Experiences of Canadian Cities," *National Municipal Review*, 7 (January 1918): 19-23;

"Law of Cosmic Evolutionary Adaptation: An Interpretation of Recent Thought," *Royal Society of Canada Transactions*, third series, 34 (1940): 135-141;

"The Way It Was in 1933," *Canadian Author and Bookman*, 52 (Spring 1977): 13-14.

In a doubly centenary life–not only nudging one hundred years itself but drawing its lifeblood from the hearts of two centuries–William Douw Lighthall was an articulate witness to Canadian literature's romantic and modernist developments and an original contributor to the arcana of aboriginal history and idiosyncratic philosophy. In his professional roles as a lawyer, historian, novelist, poet, philosopher, and editor, Lighthall distinguished himself as a Canadian achiever, mastering whatever trades he undertook. That life happened to cast him some fairly superficial and tangential tasks is attributable more to his acceptance of hazard than to any lack of ambition or ability on his part. In fact, history may eventually come to acknowledge his philosophic and historical contributions not merely as peripheral accomplishments but as the periphery defining his core accomplishments as a writer, as a poet, and especially as an editor. Lighthall was very much a territorial figure, his focus on Quebec and Montreal distinguishing him even more than his associations with literary genres and intellectual disciplines. But more than anything he was a man of culture, a truly multicultural figure, as impressed with his role as the Iroquois chief Ticonderoga (1909) as with his

roles as a fellow in the Royal Society of Canada (1902) and as the president of the Canadian Authors Association (1930). His dedication to culture was, in the widest sense of the term, political, Lighthall viewing professional and recreational, academic and parochial, administrative and domestic accomplishments as equal contributions to Canadian culture. History sees Lighthall not just as a literary figure but as a whole man contributing to history directly through society. In this respect his writings accurately document his social orientation and his societal role.

Born in Hamilton, Ontario, on 27 December 1857, to Margaret and William Lighthall, he received his education in Montreal, graduating at the top of his class from Montreal High School and winning the Shakespeare Gold Medal upon graduation with a B.A. in English literature from McGill University (1879). Continuing his studies at McGill, he received a bachelor's degree in civil law (1881) and a master of arts degree (1885). Eventually McGill awarded him an honorary LL.D. In 1890 he married Cybel Wilkes, with whom he had three children. Between 1900 and 1903 he served as mayor of Westmount (the Montreal suburb where he lived at "Chateauclair"), in 1901 helping to establish the Union of Canadian Municipalities, and during the next two decades he held numerous civic appointments, in particular on historical commissions and in antiquarian societies. He also had a long-standing commitment to the military, serving with the Prince of Wales Regiment (1877-1878) and with the Victoria Rifles (1881-1883) and the Victoria Rifles reserve (1914-1917); he founded the Canadian Association of Retired Soldiers in 1915. The middle member of three generations of Montreal legal professionals, Lighthall also practiced law in Montreal for sixty-three years (1881-1944), becoming a King's Council in 1905.

Throughout his historical writings Lighthall developed an insistently Loyalist point of view and persistent hypotheses on the Canadian national character. In 1889 he presented *An Account of the Battle of Chateauguay* to the Chateauguay Literary and Historical Society of Ormstown, Quebec, on the subject of the battle of 26 October 1813, one of the principal engagements of the War of 1812, in which outnumbered French-Canadian troops thwarted an American invasion targeted on Montreal. Lighthall re-creates the battle in fastidious detail and, with the benefit of a half-century of hindsight, concludes "that we shall always be able to preserve ourselves free in our course of development towards our own idea of a nation." This patriotically nationalistic sentiment set the tone for all his nonfiction work. In *Montreal after 250 Years* (1892), for example, he reveals both his great personal sense of place and, more important, the interconnections of the particular site of Montreal with the generalities of history. In such works as *Thomas Pownall: His Part in the Conquest of Canada* (1904) and *Canada: A Modern Nation* (1904), Lighthall consolidates his ideas on historical place through an idealistic celebration of Canadian historicity. Even in his anthropological treatises, *A New Hochelagan Burying-ground Discovered at Westmount on the Western Spur of Mount Royal* (1898) and *Hochelagans and Mohawks: A Link in Iroquois History* (1899), Lighthall teeters between the scientific and the idealistic, as in his opening observation on the Iroquois, that "the exact origin and first history of the race whose energy so stunted the growth of early Canada and made the cause of France in America impossible, have long been wrapped in mystery." In all these historical pursuits Lighthall endeavored to fortify Canada's nationhood and succeeded in doing the groundwork for his historical romances and poetic anthologies.

In his first novel, *The Young Seigneur; or, Nation-making* (1888), written under the pen name Wilfrid Châteauclair, Lighthall inaugurates his recurrent fictional theme of personal power overwhelming personality within national and cultural contexts. The seigneur of the title is an idealistic Quebecois politician who, out of dedication to the faultless Canada of the immediate future, surrenders first to free choice and ultimately to random circumstance, giving in to the temptation of political opportunism, yet, through his sudden death before detection, coincidentally upholding the appearance of idealistic nationalism. Through his protagonist as nation maker Lighthall propagates his own idiosyncratic concepts of ideal nationhood realized through idealism itself, and of a nation that, once set in motion, can survive all corruption, whether expressed through state, community, or individual. To Lighthall the Loyalist option is the one which, in the interests of Canada, all Canadians have to choose.

In his second novel, *The False Chevalier; or, The Lifeguard of Marie Antoinette* (1898), Lighthall gives his romanticism a more precisely historical focus. His protagonist, a young French Canadian from a prominent mercantile family, manages to pass himself off as a nobleman in prerevolutionary France and to secure a position in the guard of Louis Seize. Circumstance eventually exposes him not as an impostor but as a true chevalier when, falling into the hands of the revolutionaries, he elects to legitimize his adopted identity by silently facing his punishment of execution rather than by ignobly pleading his Canadian identity. Here, as in *The Young Seigneur*, Lighthall endorses the reality of appearance, positing for Canada the authentic appearance of future greatness.

The Master of Life: A Romance of the Five Nations and of Prehistoric Montreal (1908) marks a slight departure in Lighthall's fiction, bearing as it does a curiously anticipatory relationship to Canadian nationalism. Written originally under the pseudonym Châteauclair as *Hiawatha the Great* (1901), the novel focuses not on the poeticized Hiawatha of Longfellow but on the legendary Hiawatha of the Iroquois confederacy. This semihistorical figure interested Lighthall precisely because he predated the European presence in Canada, thus opening up a perspective onto a kind of primordial Canada. By describing his work as "an aboriginal romance," Lighthall seems to be acknowledging the impossible challenge of reconciling native psychology and romantic representation. The novel is impressive, however, in its descriptive detail and anthropological color, and, to a degree, in its characterization, as in Lighthall's account of the inception of the Iroquois league: "Once more the young men were hard to restrain. But the mere uplifted hand of Dekanaweda allowed the tempest of their cries, and Hiawatha's answer was awaited in a half delirium of stilled excitement. The moment desired by the Prophet had come quickly, and, his soul flaming with his mission, he stood up and drew the quick bow of his oratory." The coming together of imagination and history in this way suggests to Lighthall the future gathering of the myriad peoples of Canada, and in this respect the novel assumes an authenticity distinct from its romantic stylization.

Although he published a very early volume of verse, *Thoughts, Moods and Ideals: Crimes of Leisure* (1887), Lighthall did not produce a mature book of poetry until two decades later. The brief volume *The Land of Manitou* (1916) reappeared as the "Trembling Mountain" section in the more ambitious *Old Measures: Collected Verse* (1922), a sequence of rhythmically romantic poems on patriotism, Canada, Canadians, and philosophy. Among his most enduring verse is "Deathless," with its halting rhythm:

At Passchendale I saw it
When the battlefield was fading,
And the roar of guns grew silent
When my life stream stopped its flowing,
I saw the old hard maple
And her fire of leaves embraced me
As my life fell off in glory,
In the sunset of the year.

Although Lighthall is closely associated with Confederation poetry, much of his work documents not so much Canada's coming into being in the nineteenth century as its coming of age in the twentieth. In this regard his early editorial work in the area of anthologized verse is invaluable.

His collection *Songs of the Great Dominion: Voices from the Forests and Waters, the Settlements and Cities of Canada* (1889) holds a ground-breaking spot in Canadian literary development, in particular as a successor to the literature's first poetic anthology, Edward Hartley Dewart's *Selections from Canadian Poets* (1864). Lighthall brings together an interesting community of established (and, as it turns out, some forgettable) poets to hypothesize a truly national poetry. In his introduction he proposes no less than a national poetics based on many of the values and qualities now taken for granted in Canadian verse, such as attention to expansive landscapes and to constrictive moralities. In the voices of Canadian poets, he identifies the voice of Canada itself: "The poets whose songs fill this book are voices cheerful with the consciousness of young might, public wealth, and heroism. Through them, taken all together, you may catch something of great Niagara falling, of brown rivers rushing with foam, of the crack of the rifle in the haunts of the moose and caribou, the lament of vanishing races singing their death-song as they are swept on to the cataract of oblivion. . . ." This kind of emphasis on collective contribution and corporate experience is essential in Canadian verse even to the present day and points to the perspicacity of Lighthall's own poetic voices. Due to its critical and popular success at home, the anthology soon reappeared in an abbreviated edition intended largely for British and American consumption, under the title *Canadian Poems and Lays: Selections of Native Verse, Reflecting the Seasons, Legends and Life of the Dominion* (1891).

Toward the end of his long and ambitious writing career, Lighthall extended his voice into the philosophical range, developing in the *Outer Consciousness* series (1923-1930) a set of abstractions based on a psychic absolute, or "hypersych," and its "conscious operations" on internal human consciousness and on the evolutionary world, ranging from the protoplasmic to the cosmic, from the psychological to the astronomical. By identifying the essence of consciousness as *outside* the human mind, Lighthall argues for the survival of human consciousness, even beyond the grave: "The fall of a star is . . . the same as the fall of a leaf," as he states in the 1925 installment of the series. In the light of this very personal philosophy, one can recognize a final thrust in Lighthall's argument for the perpetuation of Canada.

Throughout his writing career Lighthall continued to practice law and to involve himself in civic affairs, ensuring for his sometimes rambling literary efforts a firm foundation in the empirical world and ensuring for himself, unfortunately, the status of dilettante. Written over the course of forty years, his fiction and verse are unadventurous for all their romantic sentiment, revealing little sense of personal artistic development, although they do serve to express his nationalistic fervor with surprisingly few aesthetic and technical encumbrances. Today, however, his creative writing is acknowledged principally because of the light it casts on his verse compilations, indisputably his major contributions to Canadian literary history. But if William Douw Lighthall is remembered more for his edition of *Songs of the Great Dominion* than for his own prose and verse, he is also to be commemorated for his singular nationalistic critical voice, enunciating a distinctly Canadian literature and culture, a quietly beautiful voice that is still to be heard in his largely forgotten publications and still to be listened for in leaves falling in Montreal streets and in stars shooting across the Canadian sky.

References:

J. M. Elson, "Who's Who in Canadian Literature: William Douw Lighthall," *Canadian Bookman*, 12 (August 1930): 151-154;

E. F. Surveyer, "William D. Lighthall, 1857-1954," *Royal Society of Canada Transactions*, third series, 49 (1955): 113-115.

Florence Randal Livesay
(3 November 1874-28 July 1953)

Carole Gerson
Simon Fraser University

BOOKS: *Shepherd's Purse* (Toronto: Macmillan, 1923);
Savour of Salt (London & Toronto: Dent, 1927).

OTHER: John Frederick Bligh Livesay, *The Making of a Canadian,* edited, with an introduction, by Florence Randal Livesay (Toronto: Ryerson, 1947).

TRANSLATIONS: *Songs of Ukraina, with Ruthenian Poems* (London: Dent/New York: Dutton, 1916);
Grigori Petrovich Kvitka, *Marusia* (New York: Dutton, 1940);
Down Singing Centuries; Folk Literature of the Ukraine, edited by Dorothy Livesay and Louisa Loeb (Winnipeg: Hyperion, 1981).

SELECTED PERIODICAL PUBLICATIONS
UNCOLLECTED: "La Bonne Sainte Anne," *Massey's Magazine,* 3 (1897): 168-170;
"The Spire of St. Ignatius," *Canadian Magazine,* 13 (June 1899): 169-171;
"A Year in a Boer School," *Canadian Magazine* (March 1904): 411-417;
"The Tenant Who Rented a Heart," *Canadian Magazine,* 23 (August 1904): 364-366;
"Natalka's Matrimonial Escapes," *Outlook,* 110 (5 May 1915): 39-41;
"When Ma'am Bid Gave a Dance in the Graveyard," *Outlook,* 133 (28 February 1923): 408-409;
"Here's Mrs. Myers with the Clothes," *Canadian Forum,* 3 (June 1923): 277-278;
"Natalka in Arcady," *Canadian Magazine,* 61 (July 1923): 225-226;
"Three Old Women and a Candle," *Canadian Forum,* 4 (May 1924): 241-242.

The mother of poet Dorothy Livesay, Florence Hamilton Randal Livesay was widely known in the first half of the twentieth century as a journalist, poet, and interpreter of Ukrainian culture. Her lyrical translations of Ukrainian songs and

Florence Randal Livesay (Provincial Archives of Manitoba)

other folk literature are credited with helping English Canada to overcome its distrust of its Eastern European immigrants.

Florence Randal was born 3 November 1874 in the English-speaking town of Compton, Quebec, the second of the six children of Stephen and Mary Louisa Andrews Randal. While attending Compton Ladies' College (now King's Hall) she published her first poem, "Remorse," which, she recalled in a 1917 interview for *Canadian Magazine,* "created no end of comment amongst her schoolmates, who were not to be convinced that it did not represent a penance for some darkly secret sin." Her father, who had been a merchant and real estate agent, died in

1888, and to help support the family she taught for a year at the Sequin school in New York. Fluent in French, she soon moved to Montreal, where she taught Latin and French at Buckingham Public School. Her literary life began in earnest in the late 1890s, with stories, articles, and poems in *Massey's Magazine* and the *Canadian Magazine* and, most important, her appointment in 1897 as the first society editor of the *Ottawa Evening Journal*.

In search of greater adventure, Randal was selected as one of forty Canadian teachers sent to South Africa in 1902 to instruct Boer children whose families were being held in concentration camps. Her experiences were transmitted home in regular reports published on the third page of the *Ottawa Journal* and occasional pieces in *Saturday Night, Canadian Good Housekeeping*, and the *Toronto Globe.* Upon her return to Canada in 1903 Randal headed for Winnipeg, believing that the west offered better employment opportunities for female journalists. She worked first as private secretary to Sanford Evans, editor of the *Telegram* (for which she earned forty-three dollars a month), and assisted on the paper; on 1 January 1906 she recorded in her diary, "I am doing the Women's Page on the Telegram but getting no more salary for it." At the end of that year she transferred to the *Winnipeg Free Press,* where she conducted her own column under the pseudonym Kilmeny.

In 1906 Randal became engaged to a fellow reporter, John Frederick Bligh Livesay, whom she had known in Ottawa. After his appointment as manager of the Western Canadian Press they could afford to marry, on 3 September 1908. Florence Livesay continued her newspaper work, becoming editor for the Children's Department at the *Free Press* in 1910. At the same time, while her daughters, Dorothy (born October 1909) and Sophie (born August 1912), were small, she became entranced with the Ukrainian songs she learned from her household help and learned to read the language although not to speak it. Her free translations were published in such periodicals as the *University Magazine* and *Poetry* (Chicago) before they were collected in her first book, *Songs of Ukraina* (1916). Characterized by concrete diction and natural syntax, some of the songs are cast into balladic rhyme and meter while others are given the shape of free verse. They celebrate the beauty of the Ukraine and the richness of its culture while commemorating the oppression of its people.

An impulsive breadwinner to whom (in his wife's words) "budgeting . . . was quite unthinkable," J. F. B. Livesay brought greater economic stability to his family in 1917 when he became one of the founders of the Canadian Press. Their finances still remained somewhat unpredictable, and one year Florence Livesay sold encyclopedias to pay for a trip to Vancouver with her daughters. Her last child, Arthur Randal, born prematurely in 1918, lived only two days. In 1920, when J. F. B. Livesay was appointed general manager of the Canadian Press, the Livesays moved to Toronto. Their summer cabin at Clarkson, named Woodlot, was next door to the home of author Mazo de la Roche, who became a friend.

In 1923 Livesay gathered many of her poems from the *Canadian Forum, Contemporary Verse,* and other periodicals into her volume *Shepherd's Purse,* dedicated to the poet Duncan Campbell Scott, whom she had known since her Ottawa days. These terse modernist verses capture moments of insight about love and time, with minimal description and scant attention to nature. Her occasional choice of archaic language and frequent use of tight formal structures suggest that she shared Scott's admiration for John Donne; her notes and epigraphs comprise an eclectic body of intertextual referrents, ranging from the Bible and folk proverbs to Richard Hakluyt, Robert Browning, and Rupert Brooke.

Livesay's interest in folk culture was not limited to the Ukraine. Two of her earliest stories were set in French Canada–"La Bonne Sainte Anne" (*Massey's Magazine,* 3 [1897]) and "The Spire of St. Ignatius" (*Canadian Magazine,* 13 [1899])–and in 1920 she translated an article on French-Canadian folk song for the *Canadian Magazine.* Her 1927 book, *Savour of Salt,* recounts the folk culture of Irish-Catholic immigrants in Ontario. A sequence of twenty-two episodes narrated from the perspective of an imaginative little girl (as would be Dorothy Livesay's *A Winnipeg Childhood,* 1973), this overlooked work is an engaging example of the linked series of stories, one of the most consistently successful forms of regional fiction in Canada.

In addition to journalism, Ukrainian literature continued to interest Livesay. In 1931 she undertook a lecture tour for the I.O.D.E. (Imperial Order of Daughters of the Empire), her translations being one of her topics, and in 1940 her translation of Grigori Kvitka's early-nineteenth-century romantic folk novel *Marusia,* which she had completed in 1929, was finally published.

Livesay as a young public-school teacher (Department of Archives & Special Collections, University of Manitoba)

Much of her Ukrainian material remained in manuscript until 1981, when Louisa Loeb, with the assistance of Dorothy Livesay, compiled *Down Singing Centuries*. After the death of J. F. B. Livesay in 1944, Florence Livesay edited her husband's autobiographical notes, published in 1947 as *The Making of a Canadian*. During her last years she returned to some of her earlier manuscripts in the hope of selling them to the CBC. Lively and energetic to the last, shortly after moving to a new home in the town of Grimsby, Ontario, Florence Randal Livesay died unexpectedly at the age of seventy-eight, from injuries sustained in a bus accident.

References:

"Florence Randal Livesay, Poet and Novelist," *Ontario Library Review*, 12 (November 1927): 41-42;

Sandra Gwyn, *The Private Capital: Ambition and Love in the Age of MacDonald and Laurier* (Toronto: McClelland & Stewart, 1984), pp. 372-387;

Louisa Loeb, "Florence Randal Livesay," in *Down Singing Centuries*, pp. 171-196;

Loeb, "The Ukrainian Translations and Interest of Florence Randal Livesay," Ph.D. dissertation, Free Ukrainian University of Munich, 1976;

The Papers of Dorothy Livesay: A Research Tool, compiled by the staff of the Department of Archives and Special Collections, University of Manitoba Libraries (Winnipeg: University of Manitoba Press, 1986);

"What Are They Like?," *Canadian Magazine*, 50 (May 1917): 78-81.

Papers:
The Provincial Archives of Manitoba, in Winnipeg, has diaries, correspondence,. and manuscripts by Livesay. The Lorne Pierce Collection at the Queen's University Archives has some of her correspondence from the years 1924-1925 and 1940-1952. The Dorothy Livesay Papers at the University of Manitoba library include correspondence and other papers by Livesay. The Thomas Fisher Rare Book Library at the University of Toronto has some correspondence and the typescript of an unpublished novel by Livesay, "The Moon and the Morning Star." Her letters to Robert Weaver (1950-1952) and to Abby Lyon Sharman (1914-1918) are in the National Archives of Canada, Ottawa.

Jean-Aubert Loranger

(16 October 1896-28 October 1942)

Maurice Lebel
Laval University

BOOKS: *Les Atmosphères* (Montreal: Morissette, 1920);
Poèmes (Montreal: Morissette, 1922);
A la recherche du régionalisme: Le Village, Contes et nouvelles du Terroir (Montreal: Garand, 1925);
Les Atmosphères, suivi des Poèmes, edited by Gilles Marcotte (Montreal: HMH, 1970);
Contes, 2 volumes: I, *Du Passeur à Joë Folcu;* II, *Le Marchand du Tabac en Feuilles*, edited by Bernadette Guilmette (Montreal: Fides, 1978).

PLAY PRODUCTION: *L'Orage,* Montreal, Théâtre Parisien, 22 January 1923.

Jean-Aubert Loranger was born in Montreal, in Saint-Jean-Baptiste parish, on 16 October 1896. His father, Joseph-Thomas Loranger, a young medical student, had married Lucie Beaudry earlier that year in the same parish. Four years later, on 30 August 1900, the young doctor (professor at Bishop's University and physician associated with Notre-Dame and the Sisters of Providence Hospital) died of typhoid fever at the age of twenty-seven. (Jean-Aubert's mother lived until 15 April 1960.) The education of the now-fatherless boy was entrusted to tutors, so that he attended neither primary nor secondary school, though he did go to Mont Saint-Louis and Le Plateau for some higher education. By then, however, he was already passionately in love with art and French literature, especially the work of Marcel Proust and Jules Romains.

It was then that his cousin, the archivist and writer Robert de Roquebrune, introduced him to the architect Fernand Préfontaine and the poet-musician Léo-Pol Morin, who in 1918 were preparing, over the course of several artistic and literary discussions at the Préfontaines' Westmount home, the review called *Le Nigog* (the title refers to an Indian fishing spear). The journal lasted for thirteen issues, from March to June 1918, and published two articles by Loranger, "Le Pays laurentien" (Laurentian Countryside) and "A Saint-Sulpice; Causerie de M. Dupuy sur Verhaeren [A Chat about The Celebrated Belgian Poet]." These showed Loranger's two centers of interest: Quebec and the exotic. At this same time his personal circumstances were beginning to alter, and his literary career began to flourish. On 5 February 1920, at the age of twenty-three, he married Alice Tétreau of the parish of Saint-Viateur d'Outremont. In the years to come they had three children: Jean De Gaspé (born 1927), Lucie-Blanche (born 1930), and François-Jean-Aubert (born 1933). Also in 1920 Loranger became a member of the Ecole Littéraire de Montréal, with which he was to remain until 1925.

Jean-Aubert Loranger (photograph from Peintres et Ecrivains d'hier et d'aujourd'hui *by Albert Laberge, 1938)*

In December 1920 his first book, *Les Atmosphères,* was published. In 1921 he participated in the creation of the French-Canadian section of the Canadian Authors' Association, and then, with his wife, spent six months in Paris and Aix. In 1922 he accepted the position of liquor commissioner in Quebec, and in the same year his second book, *Poèmes,* was published. On 22 January 1923 his one-act farce about the land, *L'Orage* (The Storm), opened at the Théâtre Parisien on Stanley Street in Montreal; but this was a work he was never very proud of, for he hastened to disavow it. (Badly printed, in pamphlet form, it is no longer locatable.) In 1925 he published his third book, *A la recherche du régionalisme* (In Search of Regionalism), a collection of stories.

From 1923 to 1927 Loranger was a journalist for *La Patrie,* then from 1927 to 1930 he was associate director of the information office of *La Presse.* Over subsequent years he changed employ-

ers frequently. From 15 August 1930 to 15 February 1932 he served in Ottawa as private secretary to Alfred Duranleau, minister of the navy. From 1932 to 1934, while working in the office of the Port of Montreal, he published seven stories in Albert Pelletier's journal *Les Idées,* and he contributed regularly during the years 1938 and 1939 to Jean-Charles Harvey's newspaper *Le Jour.* Then, from 1939 until his death in 1942, while a journalist with *La Patrie,* he saw more than a hundred other stories of his appear. Scarcely had he begun to work for another paper, *Montréal-Matin,* when he was felled by a violent attack of rheumatic fever, and he died on 28 October 1942, at Saint-Luc Hospital in Montreal, shortly after having celebrated his forty-sixth birthday.

He wrote, actively, from 1920 to 1942. Outside of two collections of poetry, his work consists of more than 150 stories (both *contes* and *nouvelles*), most of which Bernadette Guilmette collected in 1978 in two volumes. These stories first appeared in *Les Atmosphères* and *A la recherche du régionalisme* and in such papers and journals as *L'Autorité, Le Jour, Les Idées, Ecrits du Canada Français,* and especially *La Patrie.* In *Les Atmosphères* the story "Le Passeur" (The Ferryman) opens the collection, and another story, "Le Vagabond" (The Tramp), closes it; these are two tiny masterpieces, and between them appear six poems, including two poems-in-prose. *A la recherche du régionalisme,* a forty-three-page pamphlet, contains eleven tales, of which the best is undoubtedly "La partie de dames" (The Women's Game). Loranger also published seven stories in *Les Idées* between 1937 and 1939; "Le Dernier des Ouellette" (The Last of the Ouellettes), "Le Garde forestier" (The Forest Warden), "Le Long Trail" (The Long Trail), "La Savane des Cormier" (The Cormiers' Savannah), and "De miraculeuses matines" (Of Miraculous Matins) stand out from the others and are much superior to the stories of *A la recherche du régionalisme.*

The author here has perfectly mastered his art; he is in full possession of his medium, writing precisely and energetically. All these stories, however, represent his first style. His second is that of the more than 140 narratives that appeared in *La Patrie.* Those in the first group are anecdotal; those in the second pay attention to social mores. Small villages and their inhabitants, water, fire, tobacco, money, liquor, women, strong men, weak men, solitude, and death are the major motifs the author develops. A good many stories are unclassifiable: biting, irrational,

Lac Edouard, Quebec, in the 1920s, the setting for some of the stories in A la recherche du régionalisme: Le Village,
Contes et nouvelles du Terroir, *Loranger's 1925 collection of rural tales (National Archives of Quebec, Montreal)*

and based on folk sayings. But altogether they reveal a whole philosophy of life, a sincere love, a penetrating observation, and a deep knowledge of the country and its people. Reading them reminds one of the profound words of Jacques Ferron: "Le pays sans nos contes retourne à la confusion" (The country without our stories returns to chaos). In other words, a country without a past no longer has life.

As for Loranger's poetry, it dates from the period 1920-1922. The six poems in *Les Atmosphères* (with its curious plural title) were not widely admired, nor did critics welcome the works that followed in *Poèmes*. It is only thanks to later critics, and to such anthologists as Jules Fournier and Olivar Asselin (*Anthologie des poètes canadiens*, 1933), Guy Sylvestre (*Anthologie de la poésie canadienne-française*, 1942), and Laurent Mailhot (*La Poésie Québécoise*, 1980) that Loranger's poems have been rescued from oblivion. A marginal poet like Marcel Dugas, Loranger wrote in free verse and experimented with brief poetic forms inspired by the Japanese haiku and tanka. Familiar with the *Anabase* (1924) of Saint-John

Perse, with Paul Eluard and Jules Romains, Loranger broke with various received traditions, broke with the alexandrine, and with the orotund patriotic verse of Octave Crémazie and Louis Fréchette. Hence he preceded and foretold the work of Alain Grandbois and Saint-Denys Garneau. Among his best poems are "Le Retour de l'enfant prodigue" (The Return of the Prodigal Child), "Je regarde dehors par la fenêtre" (I Look about Through the Window), "Avec l'hiver soudain" (With Sudden Winter), and "Des gens sur un banc attendent l'heure d'un train" (Some Men on a Bench Wait for a Train). But many readers still prefer the storyteller to the long-unknown, or long-forgotten, recently rediscovered poet. Gilles Marcotte carefully edited *Les Atmosphères, suivi des Poèmes* in 1970. But Jean-Aubert Loranger will live because of his finest tales.

Reference:

Edouard M. Corbett, "Les contes du terroir depuis 1900," Ph. D. dissertation, Laval University, 1948.

Albert Lozeau
(23 June 1878-24 March 1924)

Jacqueline Viswanathan
Simon Fraser University

BOOKS: *L'Ame solitaire* (Montreal: Beauchemin, 1907; Paris: Rudeval, 1907);
Billets du soir, 3 volumes (Montreal: Devoir, 1911, 1912, 1918);
Le Miroir des jours (Montreal: Devoir, 1912);
Jean le précurseur: Poème lyrique religieux en trois parties (Paris: Joubert, 1914);
Lauriers et Feuilles d'érable (Montreal: Devoir, 1916);
Poésies complètes, 3 volumes (Montreal: Devoir, 1925-1926).

SELECTED PERIODICAL PUBLICATIONS
UNCOLLECTED: "Emile Nelligan et l'art canadien," *Nationaliste*, 2 (13 March 1904);
"Les Inédits," *Barre du Jour*, 2 (1966): 39-50.

Albert Lozeau in 1910 (National Archives of Quebec, Montreal)

Albert Lozeau is one of a group of young poets who in the early twentieth century gave a new direction to French-Canadian poetry. With his contemporary Emile Nelligan, Lozeau is often considered one of the most gifted and successful writers associated with the Ecole Littéraire de Montréal. His "intimiste" (intimate) poems, praised for their subtle musical harmonies and formal perfection, marked a significant change from the rather pompously patriotic or religious verse of the "Soirées Canadiennes." Whereas Octave Crémazie and Louis Fréchette had been the epigones of the French romantics, Lozeau and the other poets of the Ecole Littéraire are generally associated with the symbolists and the Parnassians.

Lozeau's life was spent in the immobility and confinement forced upon him by paralysis of the legs (caused by spinal tuberculosis, or Pott's disease), which struck him at the age of thirteen. Virtually cloistered at home until his death at forty-five, unable to lead a normal life (he was never married), he devoted himself to poetry. Although he never mentioned his illness explicitly, few critics fail to construe this personal tragedy as the background of Lozeau's often melancholy poems.

Lozeau was born on 23 June 1878 into a modest Montreal family; his father, Marie-Joseph Alphonse Lozeau, was an employee at the Justice Department; his mother, Marie Louise Gauthier Lozeau, a physician's daughter. Lozeau was a student at a "cours commercial" (business school) until his illness forced him to drop out; he did not attend the traditional "collège classique," reserved for young upper-middle-class French-Canadians. As a poet he was therefore largely self-taught, reading avidly from Rutebeuf, François Villon, the Pléiade poets, the romantics, and his contemporaries, Charles Pierre Baudelaire, Charles Marie Leconte de Lisle, Théophile Gautier, and others.

By 1904 Lozeau was an accomplished poet, publishing in newspapers and magazines and becoming well known in Quebec and even France. More and more poet friends would gather in his room, which became one of the focal points of literary life in Montreal. *L'Ame solitaire* (The Solitary Soul), his first volume of poems, was published in 1907. Another volume, *Le Miroir des jours* (The Mirror of the Days), was soon to follow in 1912. Both works were well received in Canada and France. In 1911 Lozeau had been elected a member of the Royal Society of Canada; in 1912 he was decorated by the French government. These two collections of poems represent, in the opinion of most past and present critics, the best of Lozeau's work. Themes are predictably universal: love requited and unrequited, the passage of time reflected in the seasonal changes of landscape—with a predilection for autumnal melancholy—and the heavenly and unsurpassable beauty of music. The main charm of these intimate, gently lyrical pieces lies in their lack of pretension and in the deceptively simple perfection of their versification. Lozeau's preference for the sonnet is a sign of his masterful craftsmanship.

Lozeau's restraint in the expression of his personal plight is remarkable. His situation is revealed only through the running theme of Christian resignation and through the realization that the landscapes described in the poems are always out of reach, seen from the inside of an invalid's room. The only pathetic note was struck in the last poem of *Lauriers et Feuilles d'érable* (Laurels and Maple Leaves, 1916), "Epilogue": "J'ai versé tout le sang de mon coeur dans mes vers" (I have shed all the blood of my heart into my lines). It is also only in this volume that the landscape acquires some characteristically Canadian features, such as the maple bleeding in the light of the Fall sun: "Il n'est qu'une blessure où magnifiquement/ Le rayon qui pénètre allume un flamboiement" (It is but a wound where magnificently/The ray which penetrates lightens a blaze). Generally, however, *Lauriers et Feuilles d'érable*, a series of patriotic and religious pieces inspired by various heroes and events of World War I, is too naïve and pompous to be palatable for modern readers.

The three volumes of *Billets du soir* (Notes of the Evening, 1911, 1912, 1918) are collections of short chronicles published in Montreal magazines. The entries are unpretentious "pièces de circonstance," some in verse, most in prose, dealing with aspects of daily life: from the first snow to the return of the swallows to urban traffic jams.

Poésies complètes (three volumes, 1925-1926) contains all poems published previously. Although printed after Lozeau's death, the volumes were prepared under his supervision.

A comparison between Lozeau and Nelligan, though possibly unfair, is almost unavoidable. The two were contemporaries, both associated with the Ecole Littéraire de Montréal. Lozeau wrote one of the enthusiastic articles greeting the publication of Nelligan's first volume of collected works in 1904. Above all it is tempting to see a similarity in the tragic fate of the two poets. (Nelligan was confined in insane asylums from 1899 until his death in 1941.) Was illness a price both had to pay for their poetic gifts?

Although Lozeau is far from enjoying the same attention and admiration as Nelligan, his works are generally praised, and several of his poems have been included in recent standard anthologies. Contemporary Quebec critics prefer his early poems, which opened new grounds for French-Canadian poetry. Intimate feelings and simple everyday experiences have now replaced patriotism and regionalism as sources of inspiration. Lozeau himself had a very humble view of his works: "Avec mes grandes douleurs, je fais de petites chansons" (With my great pains, I make small songs). A modern evaluation would tend to agree with this statement, possibly because Christian resignation in suffering, coyness in love, and a sentimental view of nature are not in tune with modern expectations of great poetry.

References:

Charles ab der Halden, *Nouvelles Etudes de littérature canadienne-française* (Paris: Rudeval, 1907), pp. 306-362;

Yves de Margerie, *Albert Lozeau* (Montreal: Fides, 1958);

De Margerie, "Albert Lozeau et l'Ecole littéraire de Montréal," in *L'Ecole littéraire de Montréal*, Paul Wyczynski and others (Montreal: Fides, 1972), pp. 212-254.

Madge Macbeth

(6 November 1880-20 September 1965)

Carole Gerson
Simon Fraser University

BOOKS: *The Winning Game* (New York: Broadway, 1910);

Kleath (Boston: Small, Maynard, 1917; Toronto: Musson, 1917);

The Patterson Limit (London: Hodder & Stoughton, 1923);

The Land of Afternoon: A Satire, as Gilbert Knox (Ottawa: Graphic, 1924);

Glacier, British Columbia, Canadian Pacific Rockies (N.p., 1925);

Curiosity Rewarded: A Dialogue Between Gilbert Knox and the Curious Public (Ottawa: Graphic, 1926);

The Long Day: Reminiscences of the Yukon, as W. S. Dill (Ottawa: Graphic, 1926);

Shackles (Ottawa: Graphic, 1926; New York: Waterston, 1927);

The Great Fright, Onesiphore, Our Neighbour, by Macbeth and A. R. Conway (New York & Montreal: Carrier, 1929); published in England as *Beggar Your Neighbour* (London: Paul, 1929);

Over the Gangplank to Spain (Ottawa: Graphic, 1931);

The Goose's Sauce: A Comedy in One Act (Toronto & New York: French, 1935);

The Kinder Bees, as Gilbert Knox (London: Dickson & Thompson, 1935);

Wings in the West (London: Hamilton, 1937);

Three Elysian Islands: Grand Canary, Lanzarote, Fuerteventura (Las Palmas, Canary Islands: Junta Provincial del Turismo, 194-?);

Shreds of Circumstance (London: Allen, 1947);

Lost; a Cavalier (London: Allen, 1947);

Over My Shoulder (Toronto: Ryerson, 1953);

Boulevard Career (Toronto: Kingswood House, 1957);

The Lady Stanley Institute for Trained Nurses (Ottawa: Lady Stanley Alumnae Association, 1959);

Volcano: A Novel of the Ecuadorean Andes (Philadelphia: Dorrance, 1963).

Madge Macbeth

OTHER: *Inside Government House as told by H. Willis-O'Connor to Madge Macbeth* (Toronto: Ryerson, 1954).

Well known as an Ottawa literary personality and the first woman president of the Canadian Authors' Association, Madge Hamilton Lyons Macbeth was born in Philadelphia, 6 November 1880, the elder daughter of Bessie Maffit and Hymen Hart Lyons, the latter of pioneer Jewish-American descent. Because of her father's illness the family moved to Asheville, North Carolina, and after his death in 1888 they lived in various locations in Maryland. A precocious child, Macbeth attempted to revise the Bible at the age

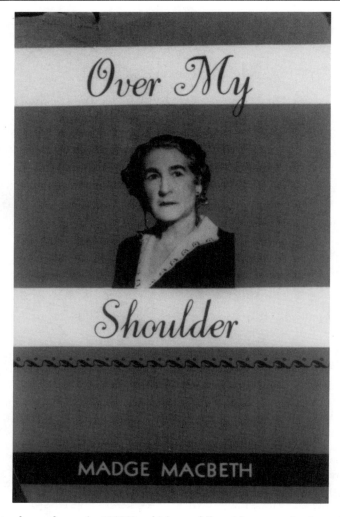

Dust jacket for Macbeth's first volume of memoirs (1953), which was followed by a second volume, Boulevard Career, *in 1957*

of three, wrote and staged neighborhood plays, and ran juvenile newspapers, including the school paper at Hellmuth College in London, Ontario, where she was sent in her early teens. This Victorian finishing school, which educated her to drink tea and mingle with the Upper-Canadian social elite, ill-prepared her for the later realities of household management and widowhood. After returning to Maryland for a brief career on the musical stage as a mandolinist from 1899 to 1901 (a phase of her life omitted from her memoirs but preserved in her scrapbooks), she married Charles William Macbeth, a Canadian civil engineer, in Baltimore on 26 October 1901. They first lived in Detroit then moved to Ottawa about 1904. Several years later Charles Macbeth died of tuberculosis, leaving his wife to support two small sons, John Douglas and Charles Lyons.

Macbeth chose writing as an occupation that would allow her to remain with her children. After a discouraging year "when stories came back like homing pigeons" (as she says in *Boulevard Career*, 1957), she established herself in fiction with the sale of two stories, "The Changeling," for sixty dollars, to *Canada West* and "Frieda's Engagement," for five dollars, to the *Canadian Magazine;* she also became known in the field of journalism for her free-lance interviews of Members of Parliament, a tactic suggested by Marjorie MacMurchy (Lady Willison), a journalist and minor author. To generate sufficient income, Macbeth said she wrote "everything but hymns" (*Ottawa Citizen*, 23 March 1964) and often submitted her work pseudonymously to avoid saturating the small Canadian magazine market.

Her first novel, *The Winning Game* (1910), is a sensational account of a woman's ruses to reform her alcoholic husband. *Kleath* (1917), set in the Yukon, promised greater financial reward when the film rights were sold, the author's share being $442. However, the resulting silent movie was given the title *The Law of the Yukon*, taken from Robert Service's famous poem, and Macbeth received no credit or royalties. Most of her later fiction, like her initial books, bears evidence of its composition for immediate sale, yet Macbeth did not hesitate to tackle pertinent political and social issues. The forest-ranger heroine of *The Patterson Limit* (1923) argues for the right of women to perform traditionally male occupations. When told that "Fire-ranging is a man's job," she retorts, "So was acting, and doctoring, and legislating, and ambulance driving, and traffic regulating, and flying ... yet women have proved their capabilities in all these spheres once they were given a chance!" *Shackles* (1926) anticipates Alice Munro's story "The Office" in its account of a woman writer's attempt to assert her independence and the validity of her work, as well as Margaret Laurence's *The Fire-Dwellers* in its depiction of women's struggles to balance inexorable family demands against personal needs.

The Land of Afternoon (1924) and *The Kinder Bees* (1935), the two satirical novels Macbeth published as Gilbert Knox, aroused considerable attention and might have elevated her reputation had she been willing to acknowledge them publicly. The first is a devastating satire of Ottawa social climbing and political intrigue, described by Arthur Stringer in a contemporary review as "a gallery of portraits etched in acid." Fresh from Pinto Plains, newly elected M.P. Raymond Dilling, the protagonist, is quickly initiated into and nearly victimized by his party's back-room power struggles, just as his wife is unwittingly drawn into parallel social schemes. While the Dillings escape with their integrity intact, Ottawa does not.

The target of *The Kinder Bees* is moral and social hypocrisy in governing circles; along with *Shackles*, Macbeth's Ottawa satires contain a degree of sexual realism rare in Canadian fiction of this era.

Macbeth's childhood interest in theater was rekindled in Ottawa. One of the founding organizers of the Ottawa Little Theatre, she continued to write, direct, and act in amateur productions throughout her life. In the 1920s she adapted her theatrical flair to put on business dramas, fashion shows, and educational dramatic classes. National and foreign travel added more grist to her mill as a free-lance journalist and lecturer. In 1923 she undertook a cross-Canada lecture tour to publicize the "bungalow camps" run by the Canadian Pacific Railroad; other travels took her to Paris and Spain, and later to South America (1936), Palestine (1938), and prewar Europe. She was also a founding member of the Canadian Authors' Association. After heading the Ottawa branch she was elected national president in 1939, 1940, and 1941, achieving a double record as the group's first woman and only three-term president. Reflections on her career and engaging personal glimpses into the past of Ottawa and the Canadian literary establishment are to be found in Macbeth's two books of memoirs, *Over My Shoulder* (1953) and *Boulevard Career.*

Reference:
Elizabeth Bailey Price, "Madge Macbeth Won Success as a Writer," *Maclean's*, 38 (1 January 1924): 50-51.

Papers:
Macbeth's papers are at the National Archives of Canada and the Ottawa City Archives.

Wilson MacDonald
(5 May 1880-8 April 1967)

Richard Duprey
Emerson College

BOOKS: *Song of the Prairie Land, and Other Poems* (Toronto: McClelland & Stewart, 1918; Buffalo: Clark, 1918);

The Miracle Songs of Jesus (Toronto: MacDonald, 1921);

Out of the Wilderness (Ottawa: Graphic, 1926; New York & London: Scribners, 1926);

An Ode on the Diamond Jubilee of Confederation (Toronto: MacDonald, 1927);

Caw-Caw Ballads (Toronto: MacDonald, 1930; Buffalo: Gay-Hagen, 1930);

A Flagon of Beauty (Toronto: Pine Tree, 1931; Buffalo: Gay-Hagen, 1932);

Paul Marchand and Other Poems (Toronto: Pine Tree, 1933); enlarged as *Quintrains of "Callender" and Other Poems* (Toronto: Saunders, 1935); republished as *Armand Dussault and Other Poems* (Buffalo: Broadway, 1948);

The Song of the Undertow, and Other Poems (Toronto: Saunders, 1935; Buffalo: Broadway, 1935);

Comber Cove (Toronto: Saunders, 1937; New York: McBride, 1939);

Greater Poems of the Bible: Metrical Versions, Biblical Forms, and Original Poems (Toronto: Macmillan, 1943; New York: Broadway, 1943);

The Lyric Year (Buffalo: Foster & Stewart, 1952);

Pigwash (Toronto: Pine Tree, 1957);

Old Samuel Cashwigger (Willowdale, Ont.: Privately printed, 1958).

OTHER: "Stigma of Colonialism," in *Open House*, edited by W. A. Deacon and Wilfred Reeves (Ottawa: Graphic, 1931).

A relatively minor poet known for being romantic, ornate, and rhetorical, Wilson Pugsley MacDonald retains a small coterie of enthusiasts even to the present. Known mainly in his own time for his considerable platform abilities in a series of public readings, he was the rarest of birds in modern society, the individual who derives his living from poetry alone.

Wilson MacDonald

Born in Cheapside, Ontario, in 1880, MacDonald attended Woodstock College and was an undergraduate at McMaster University when first published as a poet by the *Toronto Globe* in 1899. He graduated in 1902 and traveled around Britain for a period of months. Returning to Canada he worked in a bank and then later was employed by an advertising firm in the United States, where he wrote copy. In 1918, after publishing some poetry in newspapers under the name Frederick MacLean, he published his first volume of poetry under his own name, *Song of the Prairie Land, and Other Poems*.

This volume, with its strongly traditional poetry, introduces the reader to a man who loves the lakes, the rivers, and the forests of his native land, but who is less than impressed with its cities, its politics, and its despoilment by commerce.

There is a considerable degree of patriotism in this volume as there is in much of MacDonald's work, but it is clear from his tone that he loves the potential of his land without being enamored of its condition. For example, in "A Song to Canada" he writes:

My land is a woman who knows
Not the child at her breast.
All her quest has been gold.
All her joys, all her woes
With the thin yellow leaf are unrolled
And here is my grief that no longer she cares
For the tumult that crowds in a rune
When the white curving throat of a cataract bares
In a song to the high floating moon.

In 1921 the religious spirit that was as much a part of MacDonald as his patriotism was expressed in his self-published *Miracle Songs of Jesus*. Later the same year the Toronto publisher Ryerson published the work, thus spreading MacDonald's already growing reputation.

MacDonald had worked in his early years as seaman, schoolteacher, actor, newspaper reporter, advertising copywriter, bank employee, producer, composer, and bartender, and held half a dozen other jobs. Described by Albert E. S. Smythe as a "slight, lithe, graceful Italian figure, the same dark eyes and olive complexion, the same inscrutable smile of the shy but friendly soul," MacDonald was clearly a romantic with a sense of the lyrical. His work is metrical, tends to have a formal tone, and is most often rhymed, although he does demonstrate some facility for free verse. He also shows a liking for broad humor, and many of his best-known works are satiric. There is also a considerable religious flavor in much of MacDonald's work. Because after he had been published he refused to make his way in the world as anything other than a fully committed poet, MacDonald managed to supplement his income by engaging in lengthy and rather successful tours of readings and lectures. There was once a Wilson Pugsley MacDonald Poetry Society in the United States, testimony to his popularity even on that side of the border.

After *Out of the Wilderness* (1926) and *An Ode on the Diamond Jubilee of Confederation* (1927), *Caw-Caw Ballads*, self-published in Toronto in 1930, demonstrates both MacDonald's cleverness in designing the book and his interest in dialect poems that work a sometimes effective balance between pathos and humor. MacDonald's dialect poems, in which he sought to employ a narrative voice that spoke in the broken patois of a habitant attempting English, are defended by Smythe, who also points out that MacDonald should not be accused of imitating William Henry Drummond, the success of whose collection *The Habitant, and Other French-Canadian Poems* (1897) popularized that sort of dialect in poetry. *Caw-Caw Ballads* and *Paul Marchand and Other Poems* (1933) both present this facet of MacDonald's craft.

Despite publishing several other volumes in the years between 1930 and 1958, MacDonald was taken seriously by few critics. That MacDonald received little encouragement from critics in his day is not surprising in view of the fact that he came along at a watershed time when poetry was moving rapidly away from the "romantic sensibility" he adopted to a new and strikingly less sentimental realism.

Despite the evident grace of expression in the best of his works, there is something intractable and perhaps a little self-pitying about MacDonald, who clearly found it difficult, if not altogether impossible, to embrace the changing times and new movements in poetry. He remained steadfastly fixed on classical notions of beauty. In *Song of the Prairie Land* he writes: "A poet stood forlorn at break of day:/His comrades had forsaken, one by one./Yet in his ear an angel whispered: 'They/Shall cease to sup when thy feast is begun./Keep thou thine eye ahead:/They live the most who to the most are dead.'"

MacDonald also showed a censorious, critical side. In his essay "Stigma of Colonialism" (in *Open House*, 1931) he alludes to the way in which British colonialism exacerbates the literary snobbishness of Canada and makes it increasingly difficult for a worthy Canadian writing fraternity to develop. He says "definitely and without any hesitation that no country under the *aegis* of another country will ever believe in herself." He deals harshly with critics and the literary establishment as well: "Canadian literature has suffered less from foreign unfairness than from internal faultfinders who abound in Canada and whose stock-in-trade is the inferiority of colonialism." He goes on to describe specifically these individuals by saying, "These critics are for the most part university professors who know as much about the soul of Canada as a stoker at sea knows about the beauty of a storm."

MacDonald had a penchant for satire—a proclivity that seemed to intensify as it became increasingly evident that he had largely failed to carve a

MacDonald (right) with E. J. Pratt in Muskoka, Ontario, circa 1927 (photograph courtesy of Victoria University Library, Toronto)

niche for himself as a major figure in his chosen field. He rejected the perversions of contemporary life as he saw it—a kind of watering down, a betraying diminishment of the romantic spirit. Yet there was always a measure of hope in him, a reaching out to create a greater Canada, which was often to be discerned in his love for the West, the frontier. Like the railroad that tied Canada together, the railroad of which he writes in the poem "Westward," MacDonald sought to tie many of the richly disparate elements of Canadian cultural life together in his work:

> Who dropped these rails from star to sea
>   Had surely felt the cascade's thrill;
> Had known the eagle's ecstasy
>   In that long mounting of the hill.
>
> O shining rails that led me far
>   To tilt in larger lands with Fate!
> The spirit in the evening star
>   At both our comings is elate.

But in the lines to follow he expresses his discouragement with the old Canada of the East, with its swollen cities and industrial spoliation: "How sweet to race the rising sun/That flees with me the shambled East!/Better the banquet just begun/ Than debris of an ancient feast."

MacDonald was something of a Renaissance man. He was fascinated by music, a fascination that was demonstrated both in his poetry and in his personal appearances where he sang and hummed. Further, he was something of an artist, a designer. Frequently he illustrated his own poems and dabbled with illumination and typography. What MacDonald could not manage was to be taken seriously as a poet who could significantly effect a change in his beloved country. In *Comber Cove* (1937) MacDonald strongly states that the only salvation for modern man and Canada is to get back to natural things, to recapture the land with its innate harmony and beauty.

It is likely that critical hostility and indifference encouraged MacDonald to become increasingly bitter and self-pitying in his final years. And it is ironic that this poet who had little love for urbanization, who cried so loudly for a return to simple values, for a Canada more intimately linked to its natural treasures, died in the country's largest and most modern city, Toronto, in 1967.

References:

Stan Dragland, comp., *Wilson MacDonald's Western Tour, 1923-24* (Toronto: Coach House, 1975);

A. Ermantinger Fraser, "Who's Who in Canadian Literature: Wilson MacDonald," *Canadian Bookman*, 9 (January 1927): 3-6;

J. M. Hughes, "Wilson MacDonald: A Sketch of Personality," *Acta Victoriania*, 55 (February-March 1931): 9-14;

Raymond Knister, "A Poet in Arms For Poetry," *Canadian Magazine*, 19 (October 1927): 28, 38-39;

L. A. McKay, "Wilson MacDonald," *Canadian Forum*, 13 (April 1933): 262-263;

M. Joan Montgomery, "Wilson MacDonald," *Educational Record* (Quebec), 59 (January-March 1943): 35-40;

M. Orr, "Poet of Brotherhood," *Canadian Bookman*, 18 (July 1936): 10;

Desmond Pacey, "Modern Canadian Writing," in his *Creative Writing in Canada: A Short History of English-Canadian Literature*, revised edition (Toronto: Ryerson, 1961), pp. 126-128;

T. D. Rimmer, "A Canadian Genius," *Canadian Bookman*, 8 (December 1926): 365-367;

Albert E. S. Smythe, Introduction to *Song of the Prairie Land, and Other Poems* (Toronto: McClelland & Stewart, 1933).

Papers:
MacDonald's papers are in the National Archives of Canada, Ottawa.

Agnes Maule Machar

(23 January 1837-24 January 1927)

Carole Gerson
Simon Fraser University

BOOKS: *Faithful unto Death: A Memorial of John Anderson, Late Janitor of Queen's College, Kingston, C.W.* (Kingston, Ont.: Creighton, 1859);

Katie Johnstone's Cross: A Canadian Tale (Toronto: Campbell, 1870; Edinburgh: Oliphant, 1870);

Lucy Raymond; or, The Children's Watchword. By a Lady of Ontario (Toronto: Campbell, n.d.; New York: American Tract Society, 1871);

Memorials of the Life and Ministry of the Rev. John Machar, D.D., Late Minister of St. Andrew's Church, Kingston (Toronto: Campbell, 1873);

For King and Country: A Story of 1812 (Toronto: Adam, Stevenson, 1874);

Stories of New France; Being Tales of Adventure and Heroism from the Early History of Canada, first series by Machar, second series by Thomas G. Marquis (Boston: Lothrop, 1890);

Roland Graeme, Knight: A Novel of Our Time (Montreal: Drysdale, 1892; New York: Fords, Howard & Hulbert, 1892);

Marjorie's Canadian Winter; A Story of the Northern Lights (Boston: Lothrop, 1892; Toronto: Briggs, 1893);

Heroes of Canada, by Machar and Marquis (Toronto: Copp, Clark, 1893);

The Heir of Fairmount Grange (Toronto: Copp, Clark, 1895; London: Digby, Long, 190?);

Lays of the "True North" and Other Canadian Poems (Toronto: Copp, Clark, 1899; London: Stock, 1899; revised and enlarged edition, Toronto: Musson, 1902; London: Stock, 1902);

The Story of Old Kingston (Toronto: Musson, 1908);

Stories of the British Empire for Young Folks and Busy Folks (2 volumes, London: Stock, 1913; 1 volume, Toronto: Briggs, 1914);

The Thousand Islands (Toronto: Ryerson, 1935).

OTHER: *Young Soldier Hearts of France: A Wreath*

of Immortelles, edited and translated by Machar (Toronto: Musson, 1919).

SELECTED PERIODICAL PUBLICATIONS
UNCOLLECTED: "Lost and Won: A Canadian Romance," *Canadian Monthly and National Review,* 7-8 (January-December 1875);

"Parted Ways," *Week,* 19 June 1891, pp. 461-463;

"Views of Canadian Literature," *Week*, 23 March 1894, pp. 391-392.

During the second half of the nineteenth century, Agnes Maule Machar (occasionally writing as Fidelis) was an important literary and reformist figure in Victorian Canada. Described in 1892 as "our most gifted authoress," Machar wrote more than half a dozen novels, some poetry, and several volumes of history and biography. She was a leading contributor to the country's major cultural periodicals, with more than sixty-five pieces of prose and poetry published in the *Canadian Monthly* and its successor, *Rose-Belford's Canadian Monthly*, and more than one hundred items in the *Week*. She was an outstanding crusader for the causes of temperance, labor, reform, feminism, and in the defense of Christianity.

Born in Kingston, Ontario, where she remained for her entire life, she inherited her social and religious concerns from her Scottish Presbyterian parents. Her mother was Margaret Maule Machar, and her father, John Machar, was minister of the church attended by the families of John A. Macdonald and Oliver Mowat and was principal of Queen's College (later University) from 1846 to 1854. Under the later principalship of George Munro Grant, Queen's became a Canadian center of the social gospel movement which strongly influenced Agnes Machar's writings. Her earliest publications were poems and didactic religious works; her first novel, *Katie Johnstone's Cross: A Canadian Tale* (1870), won a competition sponsored by a Toronto publisher for "the book best suited to the needs of the Sunday School library." Describing the religious enlightenment of a fourteen-year-old girl, it set the pattern that was to shape most of Machar's subsequent fiction. To her message of Christian service Machar added a nationalistic dimension with *For King and Country: A Story of 1812* (1874), a historical romance which canonizes General Isaac Brock. She later expressed her patriotism in *Stories of New France* (1890), a collaboration with Thomas G. Marquis, the first of several books of historical anecdotes intended to imbue young readers with a love of country and Empire. The

1890s were the most fruitful decade for her creative writing. Published during this period was her major poetic work, *Lays of the "True North" and Other Canadian Poems* (1899), as well as four novels, including her most important, *Roland Graeme, Knight: A Novel of Our Time* (1892).

Although not set in Canada, *Roland Graeme* is one of the few pieces of nineteenth-century Canadian fiction to examine some of the social and economic problems arising from industrialization. Heroic Roland joins the Knights of Labour in an American mill town, intending "To ride abroad redressing human wrongs." Indignant about social injustice yet fearful of class warfare, Machar equally castigates greedy capitalists and sanctimonious clergymen, advocating selflessness and active Christian brotherhood as the solution to conflicts between workers and their employers. In this book, as in all her fiction, didacticism overrides artistry and romance overpowers realism.

Machar's artistic weaknesses have earned her the neglect of most modern readers and critics. Yet as a Christian, nationalist, feminist, and social reformer she was highly respected by her contemporaries, who saw reflected in her work the social conscience of Victorian Canada.

References:

Ruth Compton Brouwer, "The 'Between-Age' Christianity of Agnes Machar," *Canadian Historical Review*, 65 (September 1984): 347-370;

Ramsay Cook, *The Regenerators: Social Criticism in Late Victorian English Canada* (Toronto: University of Toronto Press, 1985), passim;

Carole Gerson, "Three Writers of Victorian Canada: Rosanna Leprohon, James De Mille, Agnes Maule Machar," in *Canadian Writers and Their Works*, Fiction Series, volume 1, edited by Robert Lecker, Jack David, and Ellen Quigley (Toronto: ECW, 1983), pp. 195-256;

Mary Vipond, "Blessed are the Peacemakers: The Labour Question in Canadian Social Gospel Fiction," *Journal of Canadian Studies*, 10 (August 1975): 32-43.

Isabel Ecclestone MacKay

(25 November 1875-15 August 1928)

Diana M. A. Relke
University of Calgary

BOOKS: *Miss Witterly's China* (Toronto: Women's Missionary Society of the Methodist Church, n.d.);

Pansies for Thoughts (Woodstock, Ont.: Woodstock Public Library, 1898);

Between the Lights (Toronto: Briggs, 1904);

The House of Windows (London & New York: Cassell, 1912);

Up the Hill and Over (Toronto: McClelland, Goodchild & Stewart, 1917; New York: Doran, 1917);

The Shining Ship and Other Verse for Children (Toronto: McClelland & Stewart, 1918; New York: Doran, 1918; revised and enlarged edition, Toronto: McClelland & Stewart, 1929);

Mist of Morning (Toronto: McClelland, 1919; New York: Doran, 1920);

The Window Gazer (Toronto: McClelland & Stewart, 1921; New York: Doran, 1921);

Fires of Driftwood (Toronto: McClelland & Stewart, 1922);

Blencarrow (Toronto: Allen, 1926; Boston & New York: Houghton, Mifflin, 1926);

The Last Cache (New York: French, 1927; London: French, 1927);

Treasure: A Play in One Act (New York & London: French, 1927);

Two Too Many: A Comedy in Three Acts (Philadelphia: Penn, 1927);

The Complete Poems (Toronto: McClelland & Stewart, 1930);

Indian Nights (Toronto: McClelland & Stewart, 1930);

Goblin Gold: A Comedy Drama in Three Acts (New York & Los Angeles: French, 1933).

OTHER: *The Second Lie: A Play in One Act*, in *Canadian Plays from Hart House Theatre*, 2 volumes, edited by Vincent Massey (Toronto: Macmillan, 1926), I: 125-151.

SELECTED PERIODICAL PUBLICATIONS
UNCOLLECTED: "The Timeless Travellers," *Canadian Magazine*, 52 (April 1919): 983-998;

"Charles Mair—Poet and Patriot," *Canadian Magazine*, 59 (June 1922): 162-165;

"Canadian Authors' Association: Annual Report of Chairman of Vancouver Branch, Isabel Ecclestone MacKay," *British Columbia Monthly*, 25 (May 1926): 7-8;

"Active Association: Vancouver Branch C.A.A.," *Canadian Bookman*, 8 (May 1926): 147-148.

Isabel Ecclestone MacKay is one of a group of Canadian literary women whose phenomenal output and active public lives are a testimony to the considerable energy that characterized the early twentieth-century female literary community. Although she was a prolific poet, novelist, playwright, and newspaperwoman, MacKay will be remembered best as a tireless champion of creative writing and journalism in Canada. She founded the British Columbia chapter of the Canadian Women's Press Club, serving as vice president in 1914 and president in 1916. She was also vice president of the Vancouver branch of the Canadian Authors' Association from 1922 to 1926. Her reports on the activities of the Vancouver C.A.A. are valuable sources of information about this important Canadian literary organization.

She was born Isabel Ecclestone Macpherson on 25 November 1875 in Woodstock, Ontario, was educated at the Woodstock Collegiate Institute, and began her literary career at the age of fifteen. From 1890 to 1900, writing under the pseudonym "Heather," she was staff contributor to the *Woodstock Daily Express* and, in 1894, began contributing poems and short stories to other Canadian newspapers as well. She married court reporter Peter John MacKay in 1895, and in 1909 the couple moved to Vancouver, where for a year she edited the social column for the *Canadian Courier*. Between 1894 and 1928 she published six novels, four collections of poems, and five plays, and contributed over three hundred poems, short stories, and sketches to the best British, American,

Isabel Ecclestone MacKay (photograph courtesy of the University of Waterloo)

and Canadian magazines, including *Harper's, Scribner's, McClure's, Youth's Companion, St. Nicholas, Ainslee's, Red Book, Life,* and others. Over fifty of her poems and stories have been reprinted in various Canadian anthologies.

MacKay's poetry and drama garnered several literary awards. Early in her career she was twice winner of the *Toronto Globe* prize for the best poem on a Canadian historical subject: her "Marguerite de Roberval" received the prize in 1907, and in 1909 the prize was awarded to her for "The Passing of Cadieux." Later her one-act play *Treasure* (1927) won the All-Canada I.O.D.E. (Imperial Order of Daughters of the Empire) award, and her three-act play *Two Too Many* (1927) received third prize in an American playwriting competition sponsored by Penn Publishing of Philadelphia. In 1929 her three-act comedy *Goblin Gold* (published in 1933) received first

prize in the drama section of the Canadian Governor-General's literary competition.

MacKay's six novels, which are sometimes melodramatic but often starkly realistic, were enthusiastically reviewed and noted for their psychological insight. For example, *The Window Gazer* (1921) was hailed as a courageous novel because of its candid treatment of the theme of sexuality. However, the favorable reception of MacKay's novels is perhaps better explained in terms of the literary nationalism that runs like a leitmotif through the book-review sections of Canadian magazines and newspapers of the period. All MacKay's novels are set in Canada, most in small-town Ontario; two of her urban novels, *Mist of Morning* (1919) and *The Window Gazer,* are set in Toronto. Unlike most Canadian novelists of the period, who uncritically celebrated rural values and condemned city life as immoral, MacKay's treatment of urban experience is considerably balanced. But what reviewers of the period rarely mention is MacKay's powerful depictions of female experience. For example, the theme of *The House of Windows* (1912) is the poverty and exploitation of working-class urban women; *Up the Hill and Over* (1917), a novel about drug addiction, features an all-female family held together by psychological tension and the meager salary of a young rural schoolteacher; and *Blencarrow* (1926), set in MacKay's hometown of Woodstock during the late nineteenth century, portrays the victimization of a woman and her daughters by an alcoholic and drug-crazed husband. Among MacKay's fiction for children, the charming *Indian Nights*, published posthumously in 1930, is a novel constructed around several west coast Indian myths. In style and content the novel demonstrates MacKay's indebtedness to Pauline Johnson's Squamish Indian tales, *Legends of Vancouver* (1911); like Johnson, MacKay accords a place of honor to the wise woman storyteller.

Like the poetry of her female contemporaries, most of MacKay's verse shows the late-Victorian romantic style and is of historical interest rather than lasting literary value. Johnson and Marjorie Pickthall, the two most widely read women poets of the day and close personal friends of MacKay, were a significant influence on her poetry. However, MacKay's verse lacks Pickthall's craftsmanship and Johnson's wide public appeal. But while MacKay's poetry for adults is dated, her children's verse still retains its charm. As cited by Myrtle Patterson in the December 1927 issue of *Canadian Bookman*, Canadian critics J. D. Logan and Donald French praised *The Shining Ship and Other Verse for Children* (1918), comparing it favorably to Robert Louis Stevenson's *A Child's Garden of Verses* (1885), and Pelham Edgar considered the book a fitting companion to Walter de la Mare's *Peacock Pie* (1913).

MacKay also made a respectable contribution to Canadian theater of the 1920s. Her one-act play *The Last Cache* was presented at Toronto's Hart House Theatre on 17 May 1927, and the following year, on 30 March, *Two Too Many* was presented by the Canadian Literature Club of Toronto at the Margaret Eaton Theatre. Both the Hart House Players and the Players' Club of the University of British Columbia mounted productions of the one-act play *The Second Lie*. And finally, two of MacKay's unpublished plays, *The Changeling* and *Matches*, were performed by the Hart House Summer School Players and the Little Theatre of Vancouver, respectively.

In the periods of time not occupied by her own writing, her activities in literary organizations, and the raising of her three daughters, MacKay found time to offer support and encouragement to other writers. For example, "bighearted Isabel MacKay," as poet and novelist Arthur Stringer called her in the 14 June 1914 issue of *Saturday Night*, nursed the ailing Pickthall through not only the writing of her last novel but also the final months of her life. As a member of the Canadian Women's Press Club, MacKay was a chief participant in a fund-raiser that helped to finance the publication of Johnson's *Legends of Vancouver*. MacKay was a generous host to many other writers, both in Vancouver and in the MacKays' summer home at Boundary Bay. She was fifty-two years old when, on 15 August 1928, she died in Vancouver of cancer. Her death was mourned and her achievements praised by many members of the Canadian literary establishment.

Bibliography:
Susan Bellingham, *Isabel Ecclestone MacKay: A Bibliography* (Waterloo, Ont.: University of Waterloo Library, 1986).

Biography:
Myrtle Patterson, "Who's Who in Canadian Literature: Isabel Ecclestone MacKay," *Canadian Bookman*, 9 (December 1927): 371-372.

Reference:
Arthur Stringer, "Wild Poets I've Known," *Saturday Night*, 14 June 1914: 41.

Andrew Macphail

(24 November 1864-23 September 1938)

Paul Matthew St. Pierre
Simon Fraser University

BOOKS: *Essays in Puritanism* (Boston & New York: Houghton, Mifflin, 1905; London: Unwin, 1905);

The Vine of Simbah: A Relation of the Puritans (New York & London: Macmillan, 1906);

Essays in Politics (London & New York: Longmans, Green, 1909);

Essays in Fallacy (London: Longmans, Green, 1910; New York: Longmans, Green, 1910);

The Land: A Play of Character in One Act with Five Scenes (Montreal: University Magazine, 1914);

Official History of the Canadian Forces in the Great War, 1914-1919: The Medical Services (Ottawa: Ministry of National Defence, 1925);

Three Persons (London: Murray, 1929; New York & Montreal: Carrier/London: Murray, 1929);

The Bible in Scotland (London: Murray, 1931);

Sir Gilbert Parker: An Appraisal (Ottawa: Royal Society of Canada, 1939);

The Master's Wife (Montreal: Macphail & Lindsay, 1939).

OTHER: *The Book of Sorrow,* edited, with poems, by Macphail (London & New York: Oxford University Press, 1916);

John McCrae, *In Flanders Fields, and Other Poems,* edited, with an introduction, by Macphail (Toronto: Briggs, 1919; London & New York: Hodder & Stoughton, 1919);

Louis Hémon, *Maria Chapdelaine,* translated by Macphail (Montreal: Chapman, 1921; Toronto: Gundy, 1921).

SELECTED PERIODICAL PUBLICATIONS

UNCOLLECTED: "British Diplomacy and Canada," *University Magazine,* 8 (April 1909): 188-214;

"The Atlantic Provinces in the Dominion," *Canada and Its Provinces,* 13 (1914): 3-12;

"John McCrae: An Essay in Character," *Canada and Its Provinces,* 13 (1914): 44-141;

"The History of Prince Edward Island," *Canada and Its Provinces,* 13 (1914): 305-375.

Andrew Macphail

Andrew Macphail was a kind of Canadian Renaissance man whose principal role as a writer was complemented by his roles as soldier and professor. Even though in his professional versatility he demonstrated the negative as well as the positive qualities of the dilettante, Macphail did seem to come as close as any Canadian to becoming at once a jack- and master-of-all-trades. An experimenter in fiction, drama, and poetry, Macphail excelled as an essayist, with profound historical, ideological, editorial, argumentative, and discursive skills. In the essay form, more than in any other literary form, he found his voice, and in the process of writing essays he discovered a voice for Canada itself during the relatively silent years preceding and following World War I. These were watershed years for Macphail personally, in that the Great War (which for a half-century thereafter assumed archetypal associations in the writings of novelists such as Robertson Davies and Timothy Findley) provided him with a world of subject matter for formal commentary and a means of concentrating the concentric medical, academic, military, and literary circles in which he moved. His receiving a knighthood during the last months of the war marked the center of his life circle.

Born 24 November 1864 in Orwell, Prince Edward Island, John Andrew Macphail attended Prince of Wales College in Charlottetown, graduating with first-class honors in 1882. After spending three years teaching in country schools, he left the island for Montreal, where, somewhat like his contemporary William Douw Lighthall (1857-1954), he began his lifelong association with McGill University, receiving his B.A. in 1888, his M.D. in 1891, and eventually his LL.D. in 1922. On 19 December 1893 he married Georgina Burland (with whom he had two children before her death in 1902). Earlier in 1893 Macphail had accepted a teaching position in the medical faculty at the University of Bishop's College in Montreal, balancing a professorship in pathology with a private medical practice until 1905. Two years later he returned to McGill as the university's first professor of the history of medicine, an appointment he held for the next three decades. This time he balanced his professorship with various literary endeavors that began with his editing the *Montreal Medical Journal* (1903-1911) and its successor, the *Canadian Medical Association Journal* (1911-1914), and ended with his veiled autobiography, *The Master's Wife*, published posthumously in 1939.

In between these contributions to medicine and memoir, Macphail established himself as a political essayist, an academic editor, and a military historian, and in each capacity as a writer with a peculiarly Canadian slant and a curiously idiosyncratic bent. The appearance of his first book coincided with the end of his tenure at Bishop's College but was inspired principally by the death of his wife. *Essays in Puritanism* (1905) not only began a brief but important series of collections of extended essays on everything from moral politics to political morality but also marked Macphail's almost exclusive commitment to the essay whose context is the academic periodical with its

chorus of voices and cacophony of ideas. If his essays on Jonathan Edwards, John Winthrop, Margaret Fuller, Walt Whitman, and John Wesley are somewhat puritanical in tone and judgment, they are also engagingly spontaneous and discursive, imaginative exercises in the free association of ideas and in a free association with the audience, although they may only go through the motions of free thinking. The pieces on Fuller and Whitman are especially perceptive, helping to identify the very shape of a century. Macphail's evaluation of Fuller is cutting: "Literary people, as a rule, are ignorant of many things, and easily swayed one way or the other by influences of slight force. It may have been that they were carried away by wonder, not that Margaret Fuller could write so well, but that this outland stranger of unprepossessing appearance and nasal voice was a woman and could write at all—like Dr. Johnson when he saw the dancing bear." Macphail is more generous in his assessment of Whitman: "His ambition was to give an expression of the Cosmos, which he understood to be the United States of America; and he spent most of his time in telling how he was going to set about it. He was to do it by a series of glittering images, and he does produce the impression which he sought upon a reader who will give himself unreservedly into his hands, a willing victim to the poet's will."

Macphail's two subsequent volumes of essays are more ambitious and of even greater historical interest. *Essays in Politics* (1909) comprises a progression of discourses on political points at issue in the still new Confederation of Canada, with particular emphasis on the value and efficacy of its diplomatic association with Britain. Although Macphail's sentiments may sound quaint to a modern ear, his treatments of such issues as protectionism, the Conservative-Liberal dichotomy, and the Canadian psyche are instructive historically and insightful when seen in their contemporary context. *Essays in Fallacy* (1910) assumes its historical importance largely because of the author's observations on the suffragist movement, pointing out some of its weaknesses of zeal and, by implication, some of the obstacles of stance and tone that women still had to overcome. By identifying the fallacious and problematical in education and theology, as well as in women on the move, however, Macphail stressed the folly of presuming any kind of absolute knowledge and thus renouncing the wisdom of critical argument, a wisdom that motivated him in his greatest project as an essayist, the editing of the *University Magazine* (in which several pieces from his three essay collections made their first appearance). Between 1907 and 1920, as head of the most influential academic quarterly of the period, Macphail found himself mediating in the history of Canadian ideas and the world at war.

Although based at McGill, the *University Magazine* also represented the University of Toronto and Dalhousie College and, with a circulation of six thousand, was highly regarded and widely read throughout anglophone eastern Canada. The journal provided Macphail and other academics, such as Stephen Leacock, with a forum for ideas, most significantly ideas outside their own professional spheres. For example, Macphail avoided medical subjects in his personal output of nearly fifty articles, focusing instead on the political topics of his published collections and later on the changing shape of Canada: the debate between imperialism and nationalism; the emergence of the economy as a determining factor in culture; the shifting relations between the provinces and the federal government; the political context of the feminist movement; and the issues leading up to and lingering after World War I. During the war years Macphail took a leave of absence from his editorial duties, serving from 1914 to 1919 with the 6th Field Ambulance Corps and reaching the rank of major. He gathered a harvest of material for future articles and for some of his most powerful prose, notably his final article for the *University Magazine* (April 1920), "The Peace and Its Consequence," in which he argues that the success of Canadian involvement in the Great War should be not a move toward national independence but a reassertion of Canada's place within the British Empire: "When the imperial thread is broken these provinces will fall into that original chaos from which they were rescued by Confederation." This statement, more than any other in his life's work, sums up Macphail's position in the political discourse he used so pointedly.

Shortly after the *University Magazine* ceased publication in 1920, Macphail published two important books on the war, both of them with eyewitness veracity. Commissioned by the historical section of the Canadian General Staff, the *Official History of the Canadian Forces in the Great War, 1914-1919: The Medical Services* (1925) is, according to his own definition of history, "something more than record and something less than praise." *Three Persons* (1929) is a more subjective work, featuring extended reviews of the memoirs of Sir Henry Wilson, Col. E. M. House, and Col. T. E. Lawrence, and profound observations on the tactics of conflict. Such remarks as "War always breaks out when it has become 'unthinkable'" and "Soldiers make war; historians make history" are pertinent not merely to World War I but also to other wars, suggesting the intense involvement that Macphail himself had in complex matters of conscience and in the crucial events of history.

The war had earlier inspired Macphail to edit a selection of poetry by his literary colleague, Great War compatriot, and fellow physician John McCrae, *In Flanders Fields, and Other Poems* (1919), to which he contributed a hundred-page biographical-critical sketch of the poet, "John McCrae: An Essay in Character," which remains a standard source of irrefutable firsthand observation. His interest in poetry was longstanding. In his protracted grief following his wife's death, he began to collect elegies and laments, eventually gathering them together in *The Book of Sorrow* (1916), which contains works by well-known poets of the time and several competent pieces by Macphail himself. His other literary ventures include a romantic novel about seventeenth-century England, New England, and New France, *The Vine of Simbah: A Relation of the Puritans* (1906); the first English translation of Louis Hémon's popular novel *Maria Chapdelaine* (1921); and his mildly fictional autobiography, *The Master's Wife*, a series of reflections on his boyhood in Orwell and on the mystique of Prince Edward Island. The book provides the most authentic commentary on Macphail's life and work, revealing through the characters of his mother and father his own dedication to cultural heritage and historical tradition, and by extension disclosing the very rationale of all his writing: the identification of sociopolitical conscience as the means of passage from an agrarian century into an industrial age, and of history-making as the means of perpetuating the values of a vanishing past.

References:

Brandon Conron, "Essays 1880-1920," in *Literary History of Canada*, second edition, 3 volumes, edited by Carl Klinck (Toronto: University of Toronto Press, 1976), I: 356-360;

O. P. Edgar, "Sir Andrew Macphail," *Queen's Quarterly*, 54 (Spring 1947): 8-22;

Stephen Leacock, "Andrew Macphail," *Queen's Quarterly*, 45 (Winter 1938): 445-452;

Ian Ross Robertson, "Sir Andrew Macphail as a Social Critic," Ph.D. dissertation, University of Toronto, 1974.

Frère Marie-Victorin
(Conrad Kirouac)
(3 April 1885-15 July 1944)

Michel Gaulin
Carleton University

BOOKS: *La Flore du Témiscouata: Mémoire sur une nouvelle exploration botanique de ce comté de la Province de Québec* (Quebec: Laflamme, 1916);

Récits laurentiens (Montreal: Frères des Ecoles Chrétiennes, 1919); translated by James Ferres as *The Chopping Bee and Other Laurentian Stories* (Toronto: Musson, 1925);

Croquis laurentiens (Montreal: Frères des Ecoles Chrétiennes, 1920);

Les Filicinées du Québec (Montreal: Populaire, 1923);

Charles Le Moyne: Drame canadien en trois actes (Montreal: Frères des Ecoles Chrétiennes, 1925);

Peuple sans histoire: Fantaisie dramatique en un acte et trois tableaux (Montreal: Frères des Ecoles Chrétiennes, 1925);

Flore laurentienne (Montreal: Imprimerie de La Salle, 1935);

Itinéraires botaniques dans l'île de Cuba, by Marie-Victorin and Frère Léon, 3 volumes (Montreal: Frères des Ecoles Chrétiennes, 1942, 1944, 1956);

Flore de l'Anticosti-Minganie, by Marie-Victorin and Frère Rolland-Germain (Montreal: Presses de l'Université de Montréal, 1969);

Pour l'amour du Québec, edited by Hermas Bastien (Sherbrooke: Editions Paulines, 1971).

Frère Marie-Victorin (Service des Archives, Université de Montréal)

Frère Marie-Victorin is one of the seminal figures who, in the 1920s and 1930s, were instrumental in bringing French Canada into the modern era. A botanist, he was one of the first French Canadians to pursue a scientific career and to achieve, in that guise, a measure of international recognition. As a scientist and educator, he tirelessly urged upon his compatriots the need to make room for science in what had, up to then, been a largely humanistic education. Marie-

Victorin, attracted from his early years to literature, was also a literary figure of some note, whose love for language informed all of his scientific writing. This was particularly true of his *Flore laurentienne* (Laurentian Flora, 1935), his most enduring work and one which strengthened the bonds French Canadians felt to the land settled by their forebears.

Marie-Victorin was born Conrad Kirouac in Kingsey Falls, Quebec, on 3 April 1885, the son of Cyrille Kirouac, a prosperous grain merchant, and Philomène Luneau Kirouac. The family having moved to Quebec City shortly after he was born, he attended the Académie de Québec, headed by the Frères des Ecoles Chrétiennes, and opted for the religious life himself, entering the novitiate in June 1901.

His early teaching career was perturbed by the chronic tuberculosis which plagued him all his life. After brief postings in Saint-Jérôme and Westmount, he was sent, in 1905, to the Collège de Longueuil, where he resided until the end of his life. There he organized a chapter of the strongly nationalistic Association Catholique de la Jeunesse Canadienne, and for this group he wrote two dramatic works, *Charles Le Moyne* and *Peuple sans histoire,* both published in 1925.

Meanwhile Marie-Victorin had found time to pursue an amateur interest in botany and to train himself in the principles of scientific methodology. He had begun publishing as a botanist in 1908, and by the time of his appointment to the Université de Montréal in 1920, he would have to his credit some forty-odd scientific papers, including a book, his first, *La Flore du Témiscouata,* published in 1916.

Those early years were also devoted to creative writing, culminating in the publication, in 1919, of *Récits laurentiens* (translated as *The Chopping Bee and Other Laurentian Stories,* 1925), to be followed, a year later, by *Croquis laurentiens* (Laurentian Sketches). The first work is a collection of short stories based on memories from childhood, while the other consists of a series of short pieces on unspoiled natural sites of the province of Quebec, places no doubt visited by the author on his botanical explorations. Both works evince a talent for the close observation and meticulous attention to detail which is the hallmark of the later *Flore laurentienne.*

It was in the 1920s and 1930s that Marie-Victorin came fully into his own as a botanist. When the Université de Montréal was constituted and a Faculty of Science, the first in French Can-

Illustration for Récits laurentiens *(1919), a collection of stories based on Marie-Victorin's childhood memories*

ada, organized, Marie-Victorin was appointed a professor of botany. Two years later, in 1922, the university awarded him one of the first two doctoral degrees in science ever conferred by a French-Canadian institution of higher learning. His thesis, *Les Filicinées du Québec,* was published in 1923 as number two of the *Contributions du Laboratoire de Botanique de l'Université de Montréal,* which he had created upon his appointment to the university.

From the start Marie-Victorin was keenly aware of the need to organize scientific activity in French Canada on a more professional basis, to transform it from a pursuit of a largely cultural nature into something worth undertaking in and of itself. Thus, he was one of the guiding spirits behind the foundation, in 1924, of both the Association Canadienne pour l'Avancement des Sciences (ACFAS) and the Société Canadienne d'Histoire Naturelle. These organizations provided meeting places where French-Canadian scientists from dif-

Title page for the 1925 translation of Récits laurentiens

ferent disciplines could exchange ideas.

The 1920s and 1930s also saw Marie-Victorin's rising reputation and influence in both Canadian and international circles. A fellow of the Royal Society of Canada from 1924, he was appointed a member of the Biological Board of Canada in 1927, was active in the British Association for the Advancement of Sciences, and served twice as Canadian representative to meetings of the Congress of the Pacific, in 1933 and 1939 respectively. He was honored by the Société Botanique de France in 1932, and the French Académie des Sciences conferred its Prix Coincy on Marie-Victorin for *Flore laurentienne.*

In the midst of such recognition, Marie-Victorin never lost his interest in youth, nor did he forget his primary role as a pedagogue. Sensitive to the drawbacks of a purely bookish knowledge, he believed that the young should, through direct contact, be awakened early to the beauty and poetry of nature. To this end he was behind the establishment of the Cercles des Jeunes Naturalistes movement in 1931, and of L'Eveil, a kind of nature kindergarten for preschoolers, in 1935. Likewise, he organized summer field-training programs for the teachers who were entrusted with the responsibility of initiating the young to the sciences.

The two driving forces of Marie-Victorin's personality, his rigorous scholarship and his abilities as a communicator, were brought powerfully to the fore in the two crowning achievements of his life and career, the Jardin Botanique de Montréal and *Flore laurentienne.* Inaugurated in 1939 and combining for the first time in French Canada public gardens with a research and teaching facility, the Jardin Botanique was yet one more way in which large segments of the population were brought into direct contact with nature and the practice of science.

In terms of intellectual achievement and emotional impact, however, *Flore laurentienne* ranks ahead of the Jardin Botanique. The volume had originated in Marie-Victorin's early dream of updating and complementing Abbé Léon Provancher's 1862 *Flore canadienne*, the only comprehensive work in the French language devoted, before his time, to the native flora of Canada.

By describing, classifying, and giving French names to some two thousand species of the flora of the St. Lawrence valley, Marie-Victorin reached well beyond his early dream and produced a work which was truly original. By naming the various species, he conferred existence upon them in the eyes of his compatriots. The work's extensive illustrations (some twenty-eight hundred in all) made it in a sense into a sumptuous "book of hours" of the native land through which French Canadians became conscious of a large part of their natural heritage that had been largely unknown and thus widely ignored.

Marie-Victorin died at the age of fifty-nine, on 15 July 1944, as the result of a car accident on the way back from a botanical exploration. He can truly be said to have been one of the founding fathers of modern intellectual enterprise in French Canada.

Letters:

Confidence et combat: Lettres, 1924-1944, edited by Gilles Beaudet (Montreal: Lidec, 1969).

Biographies:

Robert Rumilly, *Le Frère Marie-Victorin et son temps* (Montreal: Frères des Ecoles Chrétiennes, 1949);

Gilles Beaudet, *Frère Marie-Victorin* (Montreal: Lidec, 1985).

References:

Louis-Philippe Audet, *Le Frère Marie-Victorin: Ses idées pédagogiques* (Quebec: Erable, 1942);

Marcel Fournier, "Le Frère Marie-Victorin et les petites sciences," in his *L'Entrée dans la modernité: Sciences, culture et société au Québec* (Montreal: Saint-Martin, 1986), pp. 75-113.

Papers:

"Fonds de l'Institut Botanique" in the archives of the University of Montreal includes the scientific correspondence of Marie-Victorin.

Peter McArthur
(10 March 1866-28 October 1924)

John Lennox
York University

BOOKS: *To Be Taken with Salt: Being an Essay on Teaching One's Grandmother to Suck Eggs* (London: Limpus, Baker, 1903);

The Ghost and the Burglar (New York: McArthur & Ryder, 1905);

The Peacemakers (New York: McArthur & Ryder, 1905);

The Prodigal and Other Poems (New York: Kennerly, 1907);

In Pastures Green (London & Toronto: Dent, 1915);

The Red Cow and Her Friends (Toronto: Dent, 1919; New York: Lane, 1919);

Sir Wilfrid Laurier (Toronto: Dent, 1919);

The Affable Stranger (Toronto: Allen, 1920; New York: Houghton Mifflin, 1920);

The Last Law–Brotherhood (Toronto: Allen, 1921);

Stephen Leacock (Toronto: Ryerson, 1923);

Around Home (Toronto: Musson, 1925);

Familiar Fields (Toronto: Dent, 1925; London & Letchworth: Dent, 1925; New York: Dutton, 1926);

Friendly Acres (Toronto: Musson, 1927);

The Best of Peter McArthur, edited by Alec Lucas (Toronto: Clarke, Irwin, 1967).

Peter McArthur

One of the Canadian masters of the light occasional essay, Peter McArthur established his literary reputation in his rural sketches that appeared in the *Toronto Globe* between 1909 and 1924, the year of his death. These sketches were collected and published during his lifetime in *In Pastures Green* (1915) and *The Red Cow and Her Friends* (1919), and posthumously in *Around Home* (1925), *Familiar Fields* (1925), and *Friendly Acres* (1927).

Born in Ekfrid Township near Glencoe, Ontario, on 10 March 1866 of Scottish immigrant parents, Catherine McLennan and Peter McArthur, the young McArthur early became an omnivorous reader. This habit grew stronger when ill health and lack of funds interrupted his schooling between 1880 and 1885. The libraries of his family's clergyman and of the nearby Mechanics' Institute encouraged his literary curiosity and am-

bition, and he began writing articles on farm life for the *Stratford Age* while he was in high school and normal school. After obtaining his teaching certificate in December 1887, he tried being a teacher for six months and then decided to enroll in arts at the University of Toronto in the fall of 1888, where he stayed until early 1889, when debt forced him to leave. To make money he had already discovered his métier as humorist and satirist and had become a regular weekly contributor of jokes to the satirical Toronto magazine *Grip*. After leaving the university he joined the *Toronto Mail* as a reporter, continued his work for *Grip*, and began sending jokes and cartoons to New York magazines and newspapers. He moved to New York in the spring of 1890 and there joined the Canadian expatriate circle of Charles G. D. Roberts, Bliss Carman, and

McArthur in later life

C. W. Jefferys. For the next five years McArthur worked as a free-lance writer and humorist for various magazines and newspapers in the city. In 1895 he was named editor of *Truth* magazine; in this year he also married Mabel Waters of Niagara-on-the-Lake, Ontario. He left *Truth* after a disagreement in 1897, returned to free-lancing, and then, in the hope of establishing a new magazine in England, he and his family immigrated to London in 1902. The prospects for the magazine fell through, and McArthur once again resumed free-lancing, contributing several articles to *Punch*, a distinction he shared with only two other North Americans—Artemus Ward and Stephen Leacock. In England he published his first book, *To Be Taken with Salt: Being An Essay on Teaching One's Grandmother to Suck Eggs* (1903), a social satire on the Old World versus New World contrast.

Disappointed in his journalistic ambitions, McArthur returned to New York in 1904, formed a partnership in an advertising agency, and published *The Prodigal and Other Poems* (1907). Economic difficulties prompted his return to Canada in 1908; for several months he acted as public-relations man for the Liberal party and then moved permanently to the old family farm. Although he thereafter worked the land, McArthur remained a writer. In 1910 he brought out his rural magazine, *Ourselves,* to which he was practically the sole contributor and which failed in 1912 after eight issues. His articles attacking the Canadian banking system brought an invitation in 1913 to appear before the Committee on Banking and Commerce. His political and literary reputation grew. In 1919 he was asked to lead the United Farmers party—an honor he declined; in 1922 he became provisional director of the Ontario Equitable Trust Corporation; and in 1923 he organized and directed Carman's trans-Canadian poetry tour.

Primarily, however, in the years between 1908 and 1924 he contributed more than a thousand essays on rural topics to the *Globe* and some three hundred to the *Farmer's Advocate.* Of McArthur's books of this period—his anecdotal and eulogistic biography of Sir Wilfrid Laurier (1919), his nationalistic, agrarian manifesto, *The Affable Stranger* (1920), and his critical appreciation of Stephen Leacock (1923)—the last was the most perceptive and polished.

Peter McArthur had early discovered and honed his satirical talents. At the time of his death in 1924, however, his reputation rested on his command of the occasional essay form and on his sympathy for a disappearing rural Canada. William Arthur Deacon's appreciative but idiosyncratic *Peter McArthur* (1923) attempted to revise the way McArthur was popularly viewed by treating him not only as a famous rural essayist but as a poet and nationalist of admirable self-reliance. Alec Lucas's *Peter McArthur* (1975), a far more balanced and detailed assessment, confirms McArthur's forte as the essayist who remembered and celebrated the values and experiences of the Canadian countryside.

References:
Brandon Conron, "Essays (1880-1910)," in *Literary History of Canada,* 3 volumes, edited by Carl F. Klinck, second edition (Toronto: University of Toronto Press, 1976), I: 354-360;

William Arthur Deacon, *Peter McArthur* (Toronto: Ryerson, 1923);

Alec Lucas, *Peter McArthur* (Boston: Twayne, 1975);

F. W. Watt, "Peter McArthur and the Agrarian Myth," *Queen's Quarterly,* 67 (Summer 1960): 245-257.

Nellie Letitia McClung

(20 October 1873-1 September 1951)

Hilda L. Thomas
University of British Columbia

BOOKS: *Sowing Seeds in Danny* (Toronto: Briggs, 1908; New York & London: Doubleday, Page, 1908); republished as *Danny and the Pink Lady* (London: Hodder & Stoughton, 1908);

The Second Chance (Toronto: Briggs, 1910; New York: Doubleday, 1910; London: Hodder & Stoughton, 1922);

The Black Creek Stopping-House and Other Stories (Toronto: Briggs, 1912);

In Times Like These (Toronto: McLeod & Allen, 1915; New York: Appleton, 1915);

The Next of Kin: Stories of Those Who Wait and Wonder (Boston & New York: Houghton Mifflin, 1917; Toronto: Allen, 1917);

Three Times and Out: Told by Private Simmons, by McClung and Mervin C. Simmons (Toronto: Allen, 1918; New York & Boston: Houghton Mifflin, 1918);

Purple Springs (Toronto: Allen, 1921; Boston & New York: Houghton Mifflin, 1922; London: Hutchinson, 1922);

The Beauty of Martha (London: Hutchinson, 1923);

When Christmas Crossed "The Peace" (Toronto: Allen, 1923);

Painted Fires (Toronto: Allen, 1925; New York: Dodd, Mead, 1925; London: Fisher, 1926);

All We Like Sheep and Other Stories (Toronto: Allen, 1926);

Be Good to Yourself: A Book of Short Stories (Toronto: Allen, 1930);

Flowers for the Living: A Book of Short Stories (Toronto: Allen, 1931);

Clearing in the West: My Own Story, volume 1 (Toronto: Allen, 1935; New York: Revell, 1936);

Leaves from Lantern Lane (Toronto: Allen, 1936);

More Leaves from Lantern Lane (Toronto: Allen, 1937);

The Stream Runs Fast: My Own Story, volume 2 (Toronto: Allen, 1945).

Nellie Letitia McClung in 1920

Although her published work comprises sixteen volumes–including fiction, essays, and autobiography–Nellie Letitia McClung will be remembered chiefly for her contributions to the cause of feminism and women's suffrage. However, her literary efforts, too, still hold some intrinsic value, both artistically and historically.

McClung was born Nellie Letitia Mooney in Chatsworth, Ontario, on 20 October 1873 to John and Letitia McCurdy Mooney. In 1880 her family moved west to homestead land in Manitoba. Her childhood in this rural, pioneering community shaped both her imagination and her character. After graduating from normal school in

Dust jacket for McClung's last book (1945), her second volume of autobiography

1889 McClung taught in rural and semirural schools until 1896, when she married Robert Wesley McClung, a pharmacist, and settled in Manitou, Manitoba. They had five children. Here she wrote her first novel, *Sowing Seeds in Danny* (1908), which grew out of a short story composed for a magazine contest. The narrative, with its emphasis on the everyday life of a farming community, is well characterized by Desmond Pacey's term "regional idyll." As Pacey says, in this romantic version of rural life, "Trials and hardships are not completely ignored, but they are overcome or circumvented," and "Such qualities as thrift, industry, and integrity will always, in the long run, triumph." McClung's essential themes–temperance, liberal Protestantism, and feminism–are all set forth in her first novel.

In 1911, the year after the publication of *The Second Chance*, in which Pearlie Watson of *Sowing Seeds in Danny* is once again the heroine, the McClungs moved to Winnipeg. Here she helped to organize the Political Equality League and played a prominent role in the struggle for women's freedom and suffrage. In *Women's Parliament*, a burlesque of the government, which was performed at Winnipeg's Walker Theatre on 28 January 1914, McClung played the premier. In the second volume of her autobiography, *The Stream Runs Fast* (1945), she writes of this episode, "We had one desire: to make the attitude of the government ridiculous and set the whole province laughing at the old concept of chivalry, when it takes the form of hat lifting, giving up seats in street cars, opening doors and picking up handkerchiefs, pretending that this can ever be a substitute for common, old-fashioned justice!"

The struggle for the vote also provided the background for the third Pearlie Watson novel, *Purple Springs* (1921).

In 1914 the McClungs moved to Alberta, and in 1921 McClung was elected to the provincial assembly. Defeated in 1926, partly because of her uncompromising temperance views, she was active in the so-called "Persons Case," which culminated in a decision by the Privy Council in London that Canadian women were indeed "persons" under the British North America Act. This conclusion, she writes in *The Stream Runs Fast*, "came as a surprise to many women in Canada . . . who had not known that they were not persons until they heard it stated that they were."

After the publication of the first volume of her autobiography, *Clearing in the West*, in 1935 the McClungs moved to Victoria, British Columbia. In 1936 McClung was appointed the first woman member of the board of governors of the Canadian Broadcasting Corporation, and in 1938 she served as a Canadian delegate to the League of Nations. However, in 1943 illness forced her retirement from public life.

McClung's fiction is seldom more than what Northrop Frye calls "an incidental commentary on a non-literary career." Her characters are stereotypes, her work loosely structured, sentimental, and consciously designed for moral uplift. But her work remains readable for its shrewd observation of human absurdity and its detailed description of the rural countryside and people; and although she never achieves the comic inventiveness or the moral depth of the writers she most admires–George Eliot, Victor Hugo, and, especially, Charles Dickens–in her life if not in her art she was, as she claimed in *Clearing in the West*, "a voice for the voiceless . . . a defender of the weak," and there is much in the staunch feminism and hardy idealism of "Calamity Nell" that is still of value today.

Biography:

Candace Savage, *Our Nell: A Scrapbook Biography of Nellie L. McClung* (Saskatoon: Western Producer, 1979).

References:

Northrop Frye, Conclusion to *Literary History of Canada,* 3 volumes, edited by Carl F. Klinck, second edition, enlarged (Toronto: University of Toronto Press, 1976), III: 318-332;

Eleanor Harman, "Five Persons from Alberta," in *The Clear Spirit*, edited by Mary Quayle Innis (Toronto: University of Toronto Press, 1966), pp. 165-170;

Susan Jackel, "Canadian Women's Autobiography: A Problem of Criticism," in *Gynocritics* (Toronto: ECW, 1987), pp. 97-110;

Given Matheson and V. E. Lang, "Nellie McClung: 'Not a Nice Woman,' " in Matheson's *Women in the Canadian Mosaic* (Toronto: Martin, 1976), pp. 1-20;

Desmond Pacey, "Fiction 1920-1940," in *Literary History of Canada*, II: 168-204.

John McCrae

(30 November 1872-28 January 1918)

Carole Gerson
Simon Fraser University

BOOKS: *A Text-book of Pathology for Students of Medicine,* by McCrae and J. George Adami (New York: Lea & Feibenger, 1914);
In Flanders Fields, and Other Poems (Toronto: Briggs, 1919; New York: Putnam's, 1919; London: Hodder & Stoughton, 1919).

Known to his friends and colleagues as a fine physician and an outstanding soldier, John McCrae won international fame for the authorship of one poem, "In Flanders Fields," which was composed during the second battle of Ypres and published anonymously in *Punch* on 8 December 1915. It quickly became popular among the British troops and during World War I became "the poem of the army." Today, in much of the English-speaking world, the poem is memorized by schoolchildren and is an essential feature of Remembrance Day ceremonies.

John McCrae, the son of David and Janet Simpson McCrae, was born in Guelph, Ontario, where his Scots Presbyterian family had been established for several generations. He attended local schools, then won a scholarship to the University of Toronto, graduating with a degree in biology in 1894. After an unsuccessful year of teaching at the Ontario Agricultural College in Guelph, McCrae returned to the university to study medicine, graduating in 1898 with a gold medal and a scholarship in physiology and pathology. His first poems were published during these student days in the university's *Varsity*, the *Canadian Magazine*, *Massey's Magazine*, and the *Westminster*. The theme of most of them is death. In some death is described as a welcome rest after the toils of life, often in images of reaping and harvest. Others, written in a more personal manner, refer to the death of a young woman who has wronged or been wronged by her lover.

McCrae practiced at the Toronto General Hospital and the Johns Hopkins Hospital in Baltimore before receiving an appointment as a fellow in pathology at McGill University and a pathologist at the Montreal General Hospital. In 1900

John McCrae

he joined a Canadian contingent fighting with the British in the Boer War, rising to the rank of major. The military had been one of his interests since boyhood, when he had marched with the Guelph Highland Cadets and listened to his father, commander of a field battery in the Canadian militia, relate the history of the Highland regiments. McCrae's experiences in South Africa added the theme of war to his poetry. Nearly all his poems written after his return to Canada were published in McGill's *University Magazine* (edited by his friend and fellow physician Andrew Macphail), some of them anticipating the form and ideas of "In Flanders Fields." During his years in Montreal McCrae became a prominent medical figure, publishing thirty-three papers and coauthoring a textbook of pathology (1914). He was elected to the Royal College of Physicians

In Flanders Fields

—

In Flanders fields the poppies grow
Between the crosses, row on row
That mark our place : and in the sky
The larks still bravely singing, fly
Scarce heard amid the guns below.

We are the Dead. Short days ago
We lived, felt dawn, saw sunset glow,
Loved, and were loved, and now we lie
In Flanders fields.

Take up our quarrel with the foe :
To you from failing hands we throw
The Torch : be yours to hold it high !
If ye break faith with us who die
We shall not sleep, though poppies grow
In Flanders fields.

John McCrae

Autograph copy of McCrae's well-known poem, as reproduced in Putnam's first edition of In Flander Fields, and Other
Poems, *1919 (with "grow" in place of "blow" in first line)*

(London) and the Association of American Physicians.

When World War I broke out, McCrae offered his services as a medical officer. After the battle of Ypres he was appointed to the rank of lieutenant colonel and placed in charge of a military hospital in Boulogne, France, where he died of pneumonia on 28 January 1918. He left behind a total of thirty-one poems, only two of them about the Great War: "In Flanders Fields" and "The Anxious Dead."

References:
A. H. Brodie, "John McCrae—A Centenary Reassessment," *Humanities Association Bulletin,* 23 (Winter 1972): 12-22;

A. E. Byerly, *The McCraes of Guelph* (Elora, Ont.: Elora Express, 1932).

Papers:
McCrae's papers are in the National Archives of Canada, Ottawa.

Jean Newton McIlwraith
(1859-17 November 1938)

Misao Dean
University of Victoria

BOOKS: *The Making of Mary,* as Jean Forsyth (New York: Cassell, 1895; London: Unwin, 1895);

Ptarmigan, or A Canadian Carnival, by McIlwraith and J. E. P. Aldous (Hamilton: Spectator, 1895);

A Book about Shakespeare Written for Young People (London & New York: Nelson, 1898);

The Span O' Life: A Tale of Louisbourg & Quebec, by McIlwraith and William McLennan (Toronto: Copp, Clark/New York & London: Harper, 1899);

Canada (Toronto: Briggs, 1899; New York: Appleton, 1899; London: Unwin, 1899);

A Book about Longfellow (London & New York: Nelson, 1900);

The Curious Career of Roderick Campbell (Toronto: Macmillan, 1901; Boston & New York: Houghton, Mifflin, 1901; Westminster: Constable, 1901);

Sir Frederick Haldimand (Toronto: Morang, 1904; London: Jack, 1905);

A Diana of Quebec (Toronto: Bell & Cockburn, 1912; London: Smith, Elder, 1912);

The Little Admiral (London & Toronto: Hodder & Stoughton, 1924);

Kinsmen at War (Ottawa: Graphic, 1927).

SELECTED PERIODICAL PUBLICATIONS
UNCOLLECTED: "A Singing Student in Lon-

don," *Harper's,* 88 (February 1894): 385-391;

"On Georgian Bay," *Cornhill,* 3rd series, 9 (August 1900): 179-195;

"A Dialogue in Hades: Omar Khayyam and Walt Whitman," *Atlantic Monthly,* 89 (June 1902): 808-812;

"Household Budgets Abroad; Canada," *Cornhill,* 3rd series, 17 (December 1904): 806-821;

"Bracing Outings on the Great Lakes," *Country Life in America,* 8 (June 1905): 193-194;

"Winter Sports, Old and New," *Country Life in America,* 9 (December 1905): 175-180;

"Re-enacting 300 years of Quebec History," *World's Work,* 16 (June 1908): 10371-10373;

"City of Fountains," *World To-day,* 18 (February 1910): 186-196;

"On Georgian Bay," *Hampton's,* 24 (June 1910): 867-872;

"Wah-sah-yah-ben-oqua," *Cornhill,* 3rd series, 28 (June 1910): 820-831;

"The Assimilation of Christina," *Canadian Magazine,* 41 (October 1913): 607-614.

Jean Newton McIlwraith was born in 1859 in Hamilton, Canada West (now Ontario). Her father, Thomas McIlwraith, had emigrated from Ayr, Scotland, in 1853 and was a well-known merchant and a pioneer ornithologist. Her mother,

*Jean Newton McIlwraith (photograph courtesy of the
University of Guelph)*

Mary Park McIlwraith, had accompanied her husband to Canada from Ayr. One of seven children, Jean McIlwraith was educated at the Hamilton Ladies' College and by correspondence courses from Queen Margaret College, Glasgow University; she lived in Hamilton, at "Cairnbrae," her family home, until after her mother's death in 1901, writing her first novel and several works of nonfiction there. In 1902 she moved to New York, where she worked as a publisher's reader and was for some time head reader for Doubleday, Page and Company; she continued to publish articles in periodicals such as *Cornhill*, *Country Life*, *Harper's*, and *Canadian Magazine*, as well as books. She eventually retired to Burlington, Ontario, and died there on 17 November 1938.

McIlwraith's first publication was "A Singing Student in London," which appeared in *Harper's* in February 1894. The narrator, a young American girl taking lessons from a British "master," is named "Jean," suggesting an autobiographical element that is perhaps confirmed by the precise details about breath control and singing repertoire in the story. The narrator remains a rather enigmatic figure with few distinguishing characteristics besides her constant suspicion that she is being cheated by sophisticated Europeans.

She eventually cuts short her time in London, feeling uncertain about the benefits of the teaching she has received, but sure that her duty lies at home. McIlwraith's first book, *The Making of Mary* (1895), is a much more accomplished work. The first-person narrator of this short novel is a middle-aged journalist, David Gemmell, who portrays himself as the victim of his wife's eccentricities–which include theosophy, "society," good works, and Mary, an orphan girl she befriends. In a tone of ironic amusement Gemmell relates his wife's attempts to reform the intractable Mary, whose early life on the streets has made her self-centered, impertinent, and ungrateful, yet pathetically craving affection and security. Fulfilling Gemmell's prophecy, Mary fails in her chosen careers as a public speaker, cornet player, and debutante; finally showing some promise as a student nurse, Mary contracts smallpox, which, by destroying her beauty, becomes the "making of Mary," encouraging her to devote her life to serving others. The moralistic endings of both these tales, which seemed as unlikely to contemporary reviewers as they do to modern readers, nevertheless conform to the popular paradigm of "usefulness" into which much of the feminist energy of the late nineteenth century was directed.

Ptarmigan, or A Canadian Carnival (1895), another early work, is a two-act opera, a hilarious spoof on Canadian nationalism in the style of Gilbert and Sullivan, written in collaboration with J. E. P. Aldous, the proprietor of a local music academy in Hamilton. The chorus is composed of a group of young people on a winter outing who encounter and restrain a "dangerous criminal," Ptarmigan; his crime is that he applied for U.S. citizenship. After much admonition and a few songs praising winter sports, Ptarmigan is found not guilty–the judge decides that his very crime is proof of his insanity. The story concludes with a love duet between "Maple Leaf," the female lead, and her lover; the chorus declares, "while they are under British rule,/they'll never feel the cold."

Most of McIlwraith's publications in *Cornhill*, *Country Life*, and other periodicals reflect her historical interests and, in the manner of Canadians writing for foreign publication, characterize Canada as a land of lakes, ice and snow, and quaint French customs. More interesting is the short story "The Assimilation of Christina," published in October 1913 in *Canadian Magazine*, in which a newly arrived Scots maid falls in love

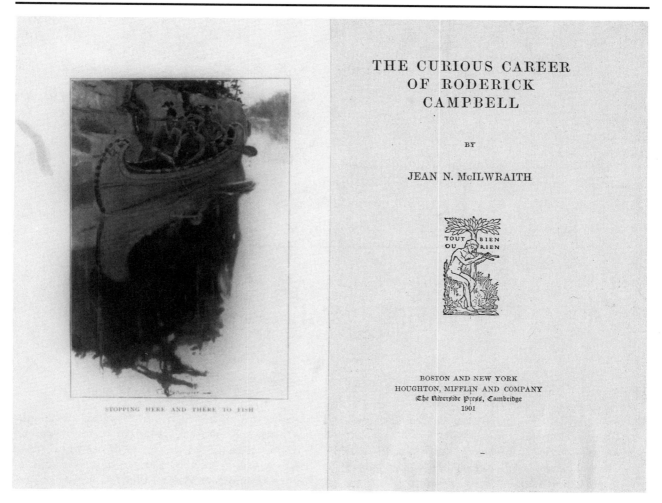

THE CURIOUS CAREER
OF RODERICK
CAMPBELL

BY

JEAN N. McILWRAITH

TOUT BIEN
OU RIEN

BOSTON AND NEW YORK
HOUGHTON, MIFFLIN AND COMPANY
The Riverside Press, Cambridge
1901

STOPPING HERE AND THERE TO FISH

*Frontispiece and title page for the American edition of McIlwraith's historical novel of 1901
concerning one of the Scottish settlers of Canada*

with the part-Indian handyman of her employer. It had also appeared in *Cornhill* (June 1910) under the title "Wah-sah-yah-ben-oqua." Another *Cornhill* story, "On Georgian Bay" (August 1900), dramatizes the reformation of a cultivated Boston gentleman with lackadaisical habits by a Canadian girl who teaches him to paddle a canoe.

With her 1899 project *The Span O' Life: A Tale of Louisbourg & Quebec*, a novel written in collaboration with Montreal folklorist and historian William McLennan, McIlwraith inaugurated a series of works that drew on her serious original research into the history of Canada. A rather stiff and slow-moving book, *The Span O' Life* follows the career of a Scots gentleman, exiled from his own country after 1745, who comes to serve in the French army; the novel is overflowing with details about the fall of Louisbourg and the siege

and defense of Quebec. *Sir Frederick Haldimand* (1904), a respected nonfiction biography of one of the first governors of Quebec for the Makers of Canada series, illustrates McIlwraith's continuing interest in the early years of British rule in Quebec. Another historical novel, *A Diana of Quebec* (1912) dramatizes Haldimand's years in Quebec, during which he settled Loyalists fleeing from persecution and fended off spies from the rebel army. The narrator is Haldimand's private secretary, and a prominent character is a youthful Horatio Nelson, who (legend has it) fell in love with a Quebec beauty during his short time in Quebec in the 1770s.

The Span O' Life and *A Diana of Quebec*, along with McIlwraith's other historical novels, *The Curious Career of Roderick Campbell* (1901), *The Little Admiral* (1924), and *Kinsmen at War* (1927), responded to the call from Goldwin Smith and other respected contemporary critics for a literature that would create a sense of unified nationhood and imaginatively lay claim to Canada and Canadian history. All are thematically concerned with showing how Scots, English, and French settlers came to found Canada. The introduction to *The Little Admiral*, a juvenile novel based on the kidnapping of the son of a British admiral by the French in 1859, refers specifically to the purpose of "instilling into young Canadians of British ex-

traction more sympathy for their fellow countrymen, the French, than is usually displayed." Some of these works, especially *The Span O' Life* and *Kinsmen at War*, seem to drown in historical detail and melodramatic coincidence, but works such as *The Curious Career of Roderick Campbell* and *A Diana of Quebec* remain interesting for their almost modern emphasis on point of view and the particularized, unified characterization of their eccentric, middle-aged narrators.

William McLennan

(8 May 1856-28 July 1904)

Neil K. Besner
University of Winnipeg

BOOKS: *As Told to His Grace, and Other Stories* (Ste. Philomène, Que., 1891);

Spanish John; Being a Memoir . . . of the Early Life and Adventures of Colonel John McDonnell, Known as "Spanish John," When a Lieutenant in the Company of St. James of the Regiment Irlandia, in the Service of the King of Spain Operating in Italy (New York & London: Harper, 1898);

In Old France and New (New York: Harper, 1899; Toronto: Copp, Clark, 1900);

The Span O' Life: A Tale of Louisbourg and Quebec, by McLennan and Jean N. McIlwraith (Toronto: Copp, Clark/New York & London: Harper, 1899);

Montreal and Some of the Makers Thereof (N.p., 1903).

OTHER: *Songs of Old Canada*, bilingual edition, with translations by McLennan (Montreal: Dawson, 1886).

Although he is largely forgotten today, William McLennan contributed significantly to two of the main currents of literary activity of his day in Canada–the rendering of French-Canadian songs and stories in English and the writing of what is loosely known as historical fiction, a form

that did not always fully suit McLennan's talents. His work with French-Canadian material was inspired by a genuine love for the history and traditions of the French in Canada; his portraits of French-Canadian life show that his strongest literary gifts lay in the domain of the short story, the humorous sketch, and the tale. As well, this work reveals McLennan's interesting ambivalence toward the origins of the French Revolution and the destruction of the monarchy. His two novels, generally less powerful and skillful than his shorter pieces, are shaped less by literary structures than by the historical and romantic forces that McLennan imagined working episodically through individual lives and by his abiding conceptions, forcefully repeated throughout both works, of what constitutes honor, integrity, and noble character.

McLennan was born in Montreal, the second son of Hugh McLennan, a grain merchant, and Isabella Stewart McLennan. His older brother, John Stewart McLennan, owned the *Sydney Post* and wrote a history, *Louisbourg from Its Foundation to Its Fall* (1918). William McLennan was raised and educated in Montreal, attending McGill University and graduating with a degree in law in 1880. He worked for twenty years as a notary public in Montreal and held many promi-

William McLennan

istocracy in the process of being swept away by the masses. Most of the stories are subtle and skillfully written, and they show that McLennan could construct fictions that at once conveyed his perspective on historical forces, rendered compelling characters, and turned on well-shaped plots for their effects. McLennan was obviously sympathetic to the French monarchy and its supporters and was appalled at the energies unleashed by the Revolution; the closing of "The Story-Tellers," a prefatory piece that introduces the three narrators of the first section, sets out the common framework and mood of the stories that follow:

> The apartment in which they sat had been that of Madame Elizabeth, the King's sister, and her dainty furniture, her prie-dieu, her paintings, her ivory and silver drawing instruments, her books, and other evidences of her devout and studious life, still lay scattered about in the track of the storm as it had rushed onward.
>
> A heavy silver candelabrum held a few lights, which flickered and flared as the fierce gusts of the December storm forced their way through the uncurtained windows to sweep through the hollow rooms, wailing over the desolation of the past and the impending horror of the future.

The second section, "Canadian Stories Old and New," is set in the New France to which McLennan was drawn so strongly. These six stories depict the social, political, and religious life of the habitants with careful attention to local detail and custom, and with a strong evocation of French-Canadian perspectives on their landscape, as well as an astute rendition of their complex relations with the English and with the Indians. McLennan's description in his preface of the origins of the last and the funniest of these stories, "The Indiscretion of Grosse Boule," shows his careful and considerable scholarship, his familiarity with the various antecedents of his stories, and his perceptions of the ways in which these tales were deeply imbued with borrowings from French tradition: "The story out of which 'The Indiscretion of Grosse Boule' has grown almost attains the dignity of a folk-tale, or at least a 'conte populaire,' with us. It was brought from France to Canada, where it is preserved with a larger proportion of Gallic salt than is necessary for its presentation in English. In France it is known as 'Le Petit Chien Bavard,' and has been told time out of mind to the delight of successive generations

nent civic posts in the city. In 1883 he married Marion Patterson of Quebec, and they had two sons and two daughters. Ill health prompted McLennan to travel to Italy in 1900, a year after he was elected a fellow of the Royal Society of Canada; he died in Vallombrosa, an Italian village resort, in 1904 and was buried in the English cemetery in Florence.

McLennan's stories of French-Canadian life first appeared in *Harper's Magazine* in 1891; *In Old France and New,* published in 1899, collects some of these. As the title suggests, the book, divided into three parts, opens with McLennan's re-creations of life in France, focusing on the upheavals during the period of the Revolution. McLennan draws on thorough historical research in all of his work; in the preface to *In Old France and New* he cites a two-volume work published in France in 1802, *Le Château des Tuileries,* as the inspiration for his stories about the Revolution. These six pieces, which constitute the section entitled "As Told to His Grace," depict from several vantage points the pathos of a noble and honorable arin slightly varying form. In 'Les Contes et Joyeux Devis' of the poet Bonaventure des Periers, who died in 1544, a foundation of the story may be found, and, I am informed, it exists as a fabliau, although not in any collection to which I have access."

The final seven pieces, all narrated in the first person by a French Canadian speaking broken English, present the experience of the French-Canadian peasant more directly. McLennan outlines the history of the habitant in the admirable ten-page concluding section of his preface, explaining his intentions in writing these last pieces. Thorough as McLennan's knowledge of French Canada may be, there is the danger, recognized by the author, that these pieces may strike the reader in some measure as quaint, patronizing, or merely grotesque renditions of English as spoken by a French Canadian. Given the current cultural climate, contemporary readers are all the more likely to react in this manner. An excerpt from "Malouin," a story of electioneering and political skulduggery among the villagers, who are either "Bleu" or "Rouge" by tradition, exemplifies the tones and textures of these pieces: "But we was pretty sick dat morning w'en we come out an' fin' de ol' Malouin 'ave bring down all dose Irish feller all de way from de Gore on de night. An' dere dey was w'ere dey 'ad no biznet for be, 'mos'a 'undre' of dem, an' every one 'ave de new h'axe-'andle on 'is 'an', an' I'll know does 'andle' come from de ol' Malouin." The inevitable problems with this kind of narration aside, *In Old France and New* remains as a whole McLennan's most substantial legacy. The portraits of French-Canadian character and custom are vibrant, and McLennan's love for his subject is more often than not complemented by his literary skills.

The other major aspect of McLennan's preservation of French-Canadian material is his translation of French songs, first published in 1885 in the *Montreal Gazette* and collected in 1886 as *Songs of Old Canada*. The original French versions of these fourteen songs are printed alongside McLennan's translations, allowing the reader to see how McLennan, as he acknowledges in his preface, had to take considerable liberties with the lyrics in order to make the English words fit the melodic lines and rhythms of the original songs. The collection is a pleasing and valuable contribution to the body of French material of the time available in English translation.

McLennan's two novels, *Spanish John* (1898) and *The Span O' Life* (1899), are generally less suc-

cessful than the works in which he draws on French-Canadian experience and traditions. *Spanish John* derives substantially from the memoirs of Capt. John McDonnell, which were originally published in 1825 in the *Canadian Magazine*. *Spanish John* recounts the experience of a loyal follower of Bonnie Prince Charlie; in fact, McLennan uses parts of the same family's history for different characters in both novels. McLennan was evidently much drawn to the history of the eighteenth-century Scottish uprising and of the men who supported King James the Pretender and Prince Charles, and both novels document and celebrate the loyalty of Bonnie Prince Charlie's followers. Both novels are narrated in the first person, and this presents readers with the first major difficulty; Spanish John (John McDonnell) is a character of unremittingly grave demeanor who holds himself in unremittingly high esteem, always on his mettle, always ready to prove his valor and honor, and although he is chastised throughout the novel for his seriousness by his companion, an Irish priest who ministers to the soldiers, there is scant evidence that Spanish John takes these jibes to heart, or that McLennan disapproves of his narrator's posturing.

But the novel does set out an interesting account of a young Scottish boy's journey from the Highlands to Rome, where he is to study for the priesthood. Shortly after he arrives in Rome, his family's soldiering heritage is aroused when he meets King James and Prince Charles, exiled in the city. The rest of the novel relates Spanish John's enlistment and rapid rise in the ranks of the rebel forces, first in the armies fighting in Italy, and then as a special envoy of Prince Charles, entrusted with money for the rebel forces in Scotland. The battle of Culloden (1746) crushes the uprising, and Spanish John plays a major role in conveying the fugitive prince aboard a ship sailing for France. The narration is basically episodic, with little evidence of fully developed relations among characters, and the novel, which closes with John's exacting revenge upon a longtime enemy by cutting off his ears, does not come to a real conclusion.

The Span O' Life: A Tale of Louisbourg and Quebec (1899), a historical romance written in collaboration with Jean N. McIlwraith, is a more ambitious and successful work that suffers from some of the same failings as *Spanish John*. Divided into three parts, it is narrated in the first person by two protagonists who are star-crossed lovers:

Hugh Maxwell, a loyal supporter of Prince Charles, and Margaret Nairn (in *Spanish John*, the sister of John McDonnell). The first part, narrated by Hugh, recounts his exile in London following the defeat at Culloden, his chance meeting with Margaret Nairn, and his flight to France. From France he journeys to Quebec in the service of the French forces, sharing in their defeat on the Plains of Abraham in 1759 but conducting himself with valor.

The second part takes up the story of Margaret, who, waited upon by a woman whom she later and fatefully discovers to have been Hugh's wife, comes to Quebec in secret pursuit of Maxwell. Captured by Indians, rescued and befriended by a French family, protected by Gen. Louis Joseph de Montcalm, Margaret makes her way to Quebec and Hugh, but the English invasion intervenes. Hugh eventually explains his ill-fated marriage to Margaret, and the lovers finally come together at novel's end as Hugh narrates the third and closing section. The story of their romance provides a background for McLennan's fictionalized history of the 1750s in Louisbourg and Quebec. As in *Spanish John*, in this novel the armies play decisive parts, and the ethos of a soldier's life is fully explored. Like Span-

ish John, Hugh Maxwell is a high-minded, noble, valorous character, ready to defend his name and principles at any moment; his love for Margaret rounds out the portrayal of his character, but he, like Margaret, is basically a stereotype and does not always succeed fully in engaging the reader's sympathies for his predicaments. Despite their failings, however, both novels, and particularly *The Span O' Life*, do succeed in dramatizing history through the resources of fiction, and provide vivid depictions of the British, the French, and the Canadians, as well as of the period McLennan looks back upon.

In Old France and New is the work of McLennan's that most deserves attention today. *Songs of Old Canada* is a valuable resource, and McLennan's two novels are serviceable and representative works of their time and form; but with *In Old France and New* McLennan succeeded not only in preserving but, more important, in rekindling the interest of successive generations of English-Canadian readers in the French-Canadian heritage that has become both inevitably distinct and inextricably a part of Canada's history and culture.

Lucy Maud Montgomery

(30 November 1874-24 April 1942)

Frances Frazer
University of Prince Edward Island

BOOKS: *Anne of Green Gables* (Boston: Page, 1908; London: Pitman, 1908);

Anne of Avonlea (Boston: Page, 1909; London: Pitman, 1909);

Kilmeny of the Orchard (Boston: Page, 1910; London: Pitman, 1910);

The Story Girl (Boston: Page, 1911; London: Pitman, 1911; Toronto: Ryerson, 1944);

Chronicles of Avonlea: In Which Anne Shirley of Green Gables and Avonlea Plays Some Part (Boston: Page, 1912; London: Low, 1912);

The Golden Road (Boston: Page, 1913; London: Cassell, 1914);

Anne of the Island (Boston: Page, 1915; London: Pitman, 1915);

The Watchman and Other Poems (Toronto: McClelland, Goodchild & Stewart, 1916; New York: Stokes, 1917; London: Constable, 1920);

Anne's House of Dreams (Toronto: McClelland, Goodchild & Stewart, 1917; New York: Stokes, 1917; London: Constable, 1917);

Rainbow Valley (Toronto: McClelland & Stewart, 1919; New York: Stokes, 1919; London: Constable, 1920);

Further Chronicles of Avonlea: Which Have to Do With Many Personalities and Events in and About Avonlea (Boston: Page, 1920);

Rilla of Ingleside (Toronto: McClelland & Stewart, 1921; New York: Stokes, 1921; London: Hodder & Stoughton, 1921);

Emily of New Moon (New York: Stokes, 1923; London: Hodder & Stoughton, 1923; Toronto: McClelland & Stewart, 1923);

Emily Climbs (Toronto: McClelland & Stewart, 1924; New York: Stokes, 1925; London: Hodder & Stoughton, 1925);

The Blue Castle (Toronto: McClelland & Stewart, 1926; New York: Stokes, 1926; London: Hodder & Stoughton, 1926);

Emily's Quest (Toronto: McClelland & Stewart, 1927; New York: Stokes, 1927; London: Hodder & Stoughton, 1927);

Lucy Maud Montgomery, age twenty-five

Magic for Marigold (Toronto: McClelland & Stewart, 1927; New York: Stokes, 1929; London: Hodder & Stoughton, 1929);

A Tangled Web (Toronto: McClelland & Stewart, 1931; New York: Stokes, 1931); republished as *Aunt Becky Began It* (London: Hodder & Stoughton, 1932);

Pat of Silver Bush (Toronto: McClelland & Stewart, 1933; New York: Stokes, 1933; London: Hodder & Stoughton, 1933);

Courageous Women, by Montgomery, Marian Keith, and Mabel Burns McKinley (Toronto: McClelland & Stewart, 1934);

Mistress Pat: A Novel of Silver Bush (Toronto: McClelland & Stewart, 1935; New York: Stokes, 1935; London: Harrap, 1935);

Anne of Windy Poplars (New York: Stokes, 1936); republished as *Anne of Windy Willows* (Toronto: McClelland & Stewart, 1936; London: Harrap, 1936);

Jane of Lantern Hill (Toronto: McClelland & Stewart, 1937; New York: Stokes, 1937; London: Harrap, 1937);

Anne of Ingleside (Toronto: McClelland & Stewart, 1939; New York: Stokes, 1939; London: Harrap, 1939);

The Alpine Path: The Story of My Career (Don Mills, Ont.: Fitzhenry & Whiteside, 1974);

The Road to Yesterday (Toronto, New York & London: McGraw-Hill Ryerson, 1974);

The Doctor's Sweetheart and Other Stories, edited, with an introduction, by Catherine McLay (Toronto, New York & London: McGraw-Hill Ryerson, 1979);

Spirit of Place: Lucy Maud Montgomery in Prince Edward Island, edited by Francis W. P. Bolger (Toronto: Oxford University Press, 1982);

The Selected Journals of L. M. Montgomery, 2 volumes, edited by Mary Rubio and Elizabeth Waterston (Toronto: Oxford University Press, 1985, 1987);

The Poetry of Lucy Maud Montgomery (Don Mills, Ont.: Fitzhenry & Whiteside, 1987);

Akin to Anne: Tales of Other Orphans, edited by Rea Wilmhurst (Toronto: McClelland, 1988);

Along the Shore: Tales by the Sea, edited by Wilmhurst (Toronto: McClelland, 1989).

If L. M. (Lucy Maud) Montgomery had never written anything else, she would still be famous and beloved the world over for *Anne of Green Gables* (1908), her first published novel. In an appreciative note to Montgomery, Mark Twain, then elderly, irascible, and no pushover for sticky sentimentality, declared Anne "the dearest and most lovable child in fiction since the immortal Alice" (*The Green Gables Letters*, 1960). The story of Montgomery's red-haired, trouble-prone orphan was first published in the United States by the Boston publisher L. C. Page, who brought out six editions in as many months. Isaac Pitman and Sons published an English edition in the same year, and the book quickly spread to other

countries. The majority of its lay readers everywhere have endorsed Twain's judgment. Established critics, however, at least until very recent times, have been less enthusiastic. At best they have dismissed Montgomery as a one-book author whose reasonably attractive first novel was followed by a series of potboilers. One or two also have favorable words for her "Emily" series (1923-1927) and *The Story Girl* (1911). But critical strictures and reservations have had little effect on the reading public. All nineteen other novels and two volumes of short stories published during her lifetime remain popular, to varying degrees. Moreover, two more collections of her short stories were published in the 1970s. *The Road to Yesterday* (1974) is an edited version of a manuscript discovered among her papers by her surviving son, Stuart Macdonald. *The Doctor's Sweetheart and Other Stories* (1979) contains fourteen tales selected by Catherine McLay out of some five hundred magazines and periodicals ranging in date from 1899 to 1935, and Rea Wilmhurst has edited two more collections of stories: *Akin to Anne* (1988) and *Along the Shore* (1989). Montgomery's international appeal, especially to young girls, whom she rightly regarded as her natural audience, has never flagged.

Maud Montgomery (she loathed "Lucy" and insisted upon "L. M." on her publications and "Maud" from her friends) was born in the village of Clifton, now New London, Prince Edward Island, on 30 November 1874 to Hugh John Montgomery, merchant, and Clara Macneill Montgomery, both descendants of Scottish immigrants to Canada and members of a large clan of interrelated families whose diverse vagaries and collective fund of familial anecdotes were to provide a wealth of material for the newborn author. The tribal stories, several of which Montgomery tells straightforwardly in her brief autobiography, *The Alpine Path: The Story of My Career* (1974), are exploited to good effect throughout her fiction.

When Montgomery was not quite two her mother died of tuberculosis, and the child was thenceforward brought up by her strict Presbyterian maternal grandparents, the Macneills, on their homestead at Cavendish, near the shore of the Gulf of St. Lawrence. In *The Alpine Path*, which originally appeared as a series in the Toronto magazine *Everywoman's World* (June-November 1917), Montgomery shows a remarkable memory for details and stresses her happier memories, shading them only slightly with the inevitable fears and pains of a sensitive youngster.

Opening page of the manuscript for Montgomery's first and most popular novel (courtesy of the Confederation Centre Art Gallery and Museum, Charlottetown, Prince Edward Island)

She celebrates the natural charms of Prince Edward Island–"the most beautiful place in America, I believe. Elsewhere are more lavish landscapes and grander scenery; but for chaste, restful loveliness it is unsurpassed." She sketches the romantic fantasies she wove around trees, flowers, kittens, brooks, and the red rocks and vast stretches of platinum-colored sand of the Cavendish shore. Although she implies some lonely times in her recollections of the shadowy friends she made out of her own reflections in a bookcase's glass doors, her obsessive affection for cats, her imposed differences in dress and routine from the other children at Cavendish School, she gives equal weight to frolics with two male cousins, who lived with the Macneills for three years, and occasional delightful visits to Park Corner, where her Montgomery grandparents and her Campbell relatives, including three female cousins, had neighboring homes.

But since her death the darker side of her childhood has gradually become perceptible in publications of her letters (1960, 1980), selections from her journals (1985, 1987), and a 1974 CBC television feature based partly upon her diaries. Though the posthumous revelations do not contradict her autobiography, they do fill in gaps and help to explain the apprehensions, anger, and rebelliousness that make her most powerful books something more than pleasantly flavored pabulum for the young.

Montgomery's childhood was crucial to the nature of her writing, for all of her successfully realized characters *are* children, in spirit if not in years. As she says in *The Alpine Path,* adults who have lost their youthful curiosity, terrible candor, and unsophisticated–even tasteless–penchants for imagining souls in flowers, ghostly "white things" in "haunted woods," princesses in birch trees, and validity in firm dates for the end of the world are not of Montgomery's "tribe of Joseph" and are depicted two-dimensionally, though the descriptive details are often picturesque, complex, and memorable. Montgomery remained a child at heart, with an exhaustive, unforgiving memory of what a thin-skinned, imaginative child can suffer and an unquenchable delight in children's pleasures.

It is now apparent that she had much to be unforgiving about: verbal assaults from her eloquent but razor-tongued Grandfather Macneill and spiritual assaults from his narrow-minded wife, who frequently reminded her that her father had abandoned her financially as well as phys-

ically (he settled permanently in Saskatchewan when Maud was seven, remarried, and proceeded to sire a new family) and compelled her to kneel and pray to God for forgiveness for childish transgressions, real or alleged, while the little girl was still aflame with rebellious anger. The enforced confessions and prayers left Montgomery with a feeling of profound humiliation and a confused sense that religion was, like sex, necessary but shameful. She learned to knuckle under and to dissemble; she even acquired her grandmother's work ethic and demonstrated it daily. But she also became an ironist. In the same letter in which she told her friend Ephraim Weber that *Anne of Green Gables* was to be published, she wrote: "I may have given up belief in foreordination and election and the Virgin Birth; *but* I have not and never shall be guilty of the heresy of asserting that it is not vital to existence that the house should be torn up once a year and scrubbed!" In fact, her saving sense of humor, which frequently acts as an antidote to overdoses of sentiment and florid imaginings in her fiction, could be cool, wry, and even mordant.

She also learned to retreat into what she called her "ideal world," and there is often a note of egotism in her references to this haven from the obtuse majority. Writing in 1905 to George Boyd MacMillan, she said: "I grew up out of that strange, dreamy childhood of mine and went into the world of reality. I met with experiences that bruised my spirit–but they never harmed my ideal world. That was always mine to retreat into at will.... I learned to hide the thoughts and dreams and fancies that had no place in the strife and clash of the market place. I found that it was useless to look for kindred souls in the multitude...."

Out of this haven came her first stories and poems. She was from girlhood "an indefatigable little scribbler," she reports in *The Alpine Path.* But her objectives were real as well as ideal. Her memoir takes its title from a platitudinous bit of magazine verse clipped and preserved by the aspiring young author as a stimulus to climb the "Alpine path, so hard, so steep" that leads to fame and the "shining scroll" whereon one may inscribe "A woman's humble name." The young Montgomery wanted approval. When her father found her blank verse "very blank," she instantly shifted to rhyme. From a precocious tendency to write lachrymose fiction she emerged to a conviction that she preferred happy endings and that the buying public probably did, too.

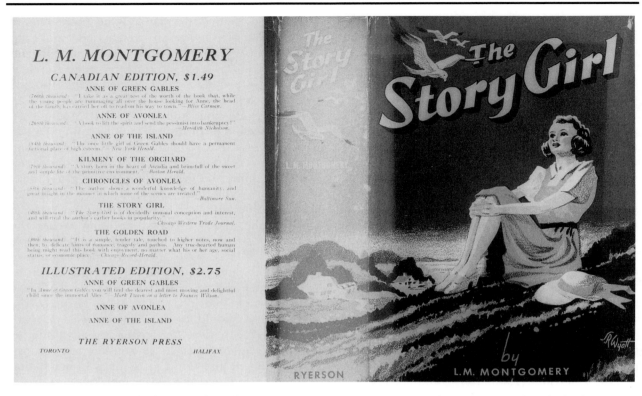

Dust jacket for the first Canadian edition (1944) of Montgomery's 1911 novel set on Prince Edward Island.
The book was one of her personal favorites.

But she served a hard apprenticeship before she reached paying markets. Her first publication, a verse rendition of a legendary murder perpetrated on the Cavendish shore, was printed in the *Charlottetown Patriot* of 26 November 1890, while its nearly sixteen-year-old author was in Prince Albert, Saskatchewan, trying to settle in with her father and his new family. The domestic experiment failed, but during that year Montgomery achieved several more small, unpaid publications and became convinced that she might be able to earn at least a part of her living with her pen. She returned to Prince Edward Island fired by this hope and thereafter wrote something virtually every day on the theory that writing must be practiced like any other skill. In the meantime she covered her bets by acquiring a teacher's license from Prince of Wales College, Charlottetown.

Her first teaching year (1894-1895), spent at rural Bideford, P.E.I., was reasonably pleasant, but she decided that as a novice writer she needed more education. She spent the following winter in Halifax, taking a special literature course at Dalhousie College (now University)

and persistently writing. In one "Big Week" she achieved three publications and a total of twenty-two dollars. But it was clear that she must still teach for an income, and she returned to P.E.I. to teach for two more years at Belmont Lot 16 and then Lower Bedeque. At the same time, she was learning to please editors, loving her work—though for a time she could do it only between six and seven in the mornings in frigid lodgings—but unreconciled to having to "drag a moral" into her stories for juveniles.

During these years of industrious writing Montgomery was also enduring romantic traumas. She became engaged to a "handsome, brilliant, cultured, successful" man (Edwin Simpson of Belmont), whom she called "B" in a letter to MacMillan, and then found that his kiss turned her "cold with horror." She fell helplessly in love with "A" (Herman Leard), who was her "inferior in every respect," and was saved from marrying him only by his premature death in 1899.

Meanwhile, her Grandfather Macneill died in 1898, and Montgomery gave up teaching to live with her grandmother. Apart from nine months (October 1901-June 1902) serving as general factotum on the *Halifax Daily Echo*, she stayed home, helping to keep house and tend her grandmother's post office, maintaining the social round required by clan and friends, and writing in every salvageable hour.

The corner in her writing career was turned, although she did not then realize it, in 1904 when she focused on an old newspaper story about an elderly couple who had applied to an orphanage for a boy and received a girl instead. The situation struck Montgomery as too good for a mere short story, and she wrote a novel about it over some sixteen months. Her fair copy, painstakingly typed on her secondhand typewriter that refused to type *w*'s, went successively to five publishers, all of whom rejected it. She put it away for two years, and then, having unearthed it one wintry day in 1907, submitted it once more. The result was L. C. Page's publication of *Anne of Green Gables* and instant fame for Montgomery.

Page immediately requested a sequel, and Montgomery obliged with *Anne of Avonlea* (1909), though her heart was not in it. The "*freshness* of the *idea* was gone," she told Weber; "I simply *built* it. Anne, grown-up, couldn't be made as quaint and unexpected as the child Anne." She was right. Anne lost her distinctive edges and, in the sequels, became a remote, beautiful heroine, almost as immobile as the graceful birch trees she loved, while her creator changed from a slight, lively, dark-haired girl into a graying, matronly looking "authoress"–although Montgomery inwardly maintained the old rebellious notions, love of drama and scandal, and hunger for experience that her young heroines always display. But she was a born storyteller, and even when forced to write about queenly Anne, whom she came to regard as "an incubus," she surrounded her with interesting subplots related in strong, often elegant prose.

By the spring of 1911, when Grandmother Macneill died, Montgomery had also published *Kilmeny of the Orchard* (1910)–a melodramatic tale of psychosomatic dumbness reworked from her old serial "Una of the Garden"–and (a personal favorite of hers) the episodic *Story Girl*, with a rainbow-voiced young protagonist whose stories, many derived from Montgomery's great-aunt Mary Lawson, punctuate the summer adventures of a group of youthful friends and cousins. On 5 July 1911 the thirty-six-year-old Montgomery married the forty-year-old Reverend Ewen Macdonald, to whom she had been engaged since 1906.

Montgomery in later life

It appears to have been an affectionate but passionless marriage. In September 1907 she had confided to MacMillan that she believed a couple could be happy together given mutual affection, shared interests, and compatibility in age and social position, "even if some of the highest upflashings of the 'flame divine' are missing." The letter continues, "If I ever marry that is the basis on which I shall found my marriage. *But*–I shall never cease to thank fate that I *knew the other kind of love too*."

After a ten-week honeymoon in Scotland and England (during which Montgomery met MacMillan in person for the first time), the Macdonalds settled into the Presbyterian manse of Leaskdale, Ontario, and the Leaskdale years (1911-1925) became her most productive ones as an author. She wrote *The Golden Road* (1913), a sequel to *The Story Girl*; *The Watchman and Other Poems* (1916), her one book of poetry (not her forte); a short-story collection, *Chronicles of Avonlea: In Which Anne Shirley of Green Gables and Avonlea Plays Some Part* (1912); four more "Anne" novels, the eponymous ones plus *Rainbow Valley* (1919) and *Rilla of Ingleside* (1921); and the first two "Emily" books (1923, 1924), about a spirited girl whose early experiences closely parallel Montgomery's.

She also became the happy mother of two

sons (Chester Cameron, born in 1912, and Ewen Stuart, born in 1915) and, in 1923, the first female Canadian fellow of England's Royal Society of Arts.

But the period was darkened by the loss of a child (Hugh Alexander, stillborn on 13 August 1914), by World War I, and by a prolonged legal battle with Page, who broke faith with her by publishing *Further Chronicles of Avonlea* (1920) from their illicit copies of old manuscripts that she had revamped or discarded. (In October 1928 Montgomery emerged from nine years of suits and countersuits exhausted but vindicated.) She was also continuously homesick for P.E.I., which she could not often visit, and worst of all, she was learning that her husband was not only prone to bodily illness but subject to increasingly severe attacks of melancholia during which he was convinced he was predestined to hell. Montgomery herself was becoming depressive and nervously inclined to believe in prophetic dreams and other psychic phenomena. Nevertheless she covered for her husband so well among parishioners and friends that only recently has something of her marital ordeal become public knowledge. Her last letter to MacMillan (23 December 1941) contains two stark sentences: "My husband's nerves are worse than mine even. I have kept the nature of his attacks from you for over 20 years but they have broken me at last."

In early 1925, however, Ewen Macdonald still felt strong enough to accept a call to Norval, Ontario, after his Leaskdale parish had split between converts to the new United Church and loyal Presbyterians. The family stayed at Norval until 1935, when a devastating breakdown forced Ewen's retirement and they moved to the handsome house Montgomery called "Journey's End" in Toronto.

In 1926 Montgomery completed her first attempt at a novel for adults, *The Blue Castle*. This ugly-duckling story of twenty-nine-year-old Valancy, who rebels from her staid life after a misdirected medical diagnosis predicts her imminent death, is full of comeuppances for horrid people and wish-fulfillments for the emotionally starved heroine. Except for some pleasingly tart dialogue, it is a sentimental romance, notable in Montgomery's canon only for its Muskoka, Ontario, setting.

During the Norval years, Montgomery also wrote *Emily's Quest* (1927), the last "Emily" novel; an entertaining novel about some "magic" for sprightly little Marigold (1927); two novels about

Pat Gardiner of "Silver Bush" (1933, 1935), whose almost pathological attachment to her P.E.I. home may reflect Montgomery's own desperate nostalgia; and *A Tangled Web* (1931), another effort at adult fiction, which turned out to be more of an overplotted, multicharactered novel for teenagers.

The move to Toronto reunited the family; her son Chester was studying law there, and Stuart medicine. June 1935 was brightened for Montgomery by her investiture as an Officer of the British Empire. But in general the tone of her letters from this point forward is melancholic. Nonetheless she managed two more commissioned "Anne" novels (1936, 1939) and, to please herself, *Jane of Lantern Hill* (1937), an upbeat story of a strong-minded little girl who defeats a steely grandmother and a silkily malevolent aunt to bring her parents back together on Montgomery's ever-beloved Prince Edward Island. There is fun as well as fighting in *Jane of Lantern Hill*, but Montgomery was sinking toward the physical and nervous collapse she suffered in 1938; she never completely recovered. On 24 April 1942, worn out in body and spirit, she died in Toronto. She was buried on 29 April in Cavendish Cemetery, P.E.I.

Anne of Green Gables remains Montgomery's greatest popular success. Performed as a play (1937), made into two filmed versions in the United States (1921, 1934), and adapted for a British television series in 1972 and two Canadian (CBC) TV films (*Anne* in 1985 and *Anne of Green Gables: The Sequel* in 1987), the story has also been enthusiastically received as a stage musical (1965), by Donald Harron and Norman Campbell, which won the London Critics' Award for 1969, was a hit at Japan's Expo in 1970 (Anne has long been a favorite with Japanese girls), and is the annual mainstay of the Charlottetown, P.E.I., Summer Festival.

But none of Montgomery's fiction is thin or dull, and she is beginning to receive some respectful attention from modern critics, as evidenced by the autumn 1975 issue of *Canadian Children's Literature* being devoted to her. Meanwhile, many teenage girls have never ceased to share her love of a good story, her preferences for "pine woods over pigsties" (as in *Emily's Quest*), and the conviction expressed by Uncle Horace of *Mistress Pat* (1935): "Real life! We get enough real life living. *I* like fairy tales."

Letters:

The Green Gables Letters from L. M. Montgomery to Ephraim Weber, 1905-1909, edited by Wilfrid Eggleston (Toronto: Ryerson, 1960);

My Dear Mr. M: Letters to G. B. MacMillan, edited by Francis W. P. Bolger and Elizabeth R. Epperly (Toronto: McGraw-Hill Ryerson, 1980).

Biographies:

Hilda M. Ridley, *The Story of L. M. Montgomery* (Toronto: McGraw-Hill Ryerson, 1956);

Francis W. P. Bolger, *The Years Before "Anne"* (Charlottetown: Prince Edward Island Heritage Foundation, 1974);

Mollie Gillen, *The Wheel of Things: A Biography of L. M. Montgomery* (Don Mills, Ont.: Fitzhenry & Whiteside, 1975).

References:

Canadian Children's Literature, special L. M. Montgomery issue, 1 (Autumn 1975);

Alice Munro, Afterword to *Emily of New Moon* (Toronto: McClelland & Stewart, 1989), pp. 357-361;

P. K. Page, Afterword to *Emily's Quest* (Toronto: McClelland & Stewart, 1989), pp. 237-242;

Thomas E. Tausky, "L. M. Montgomery and 'The Alpine Path, So Hard, So Steep,'" *Canadian Children's Literature,* 30 (1983): 5-20;

Jane Urquhart, Afterword to *Emily Climbs* (Toronto: McClelland & Stewart, 1989), pp. 330-340;

Elizabeth Waterston, "Lucy Maud Montgomery," in *The Clear Spirit: Twenty Canadian Women and Their Times,* edited by Mary Quayle Innis (Toronto: University of Toronto Press, 1966), pp. 198-220.

Louvigny de Montigny

(1 December 1876-20 May 1955)

David F. Rogers
University of British Columbia

BOOKS: *La Langue française au Canada: Son état actuel. Etude canadienne* (Ottawa: The author, 1916);
Antoine Gérin-Lajoie (Toronto: Ryerson, 1925);
Le Bouquet de Mélusine: Scènes de folklore (Montreal & New York: Carrier/Mercure, 1928);
Les Boules de neige (Montreal: Déom, 1935);
La Revanche de "Maria Chapdelaine": Essai d'initiation à un chef-d'oeuvre inspiré du pays de Québec (Montreal: Action Canadienne-Française, 1937);
Au pays de Québec: Contes et images (Montreal: Pascal, 1945);
Ecrasons le perroquet! Divertissement philologique (Montreal: Fides, 1948);
L'Epi rouge et autres scènes du pays de Québec (Montreal: Cercle du Livre de France, 1953).

PLAY PRODUCTIONS: *Je vous aime: Broderie de raison sur un thème d'amour*, Montreal, Monument National Theater, 27 April 1902;
Les Boules de neige, Montreal, Monument National Theater, 27 April 1902.

OTHER: *Etoffe du pays: Pages de Gaston de Montigny*, edited by de Montigny (Montreal: Beauchemin, 1951).

SELECTED PERIODICAL PUBLICATION
UNCOLLECTED: *Je vous aime: Broderie de raison sur un thème d'amour*, *La Revue Canadienne*, September 1903, pp. 5-21.

Louvigny de Montigny (photograph courtesy of the Collège de Sainte-Anne-de-la Pocatière)

Carolus-Glatigny-Louvigny de Montigny, the important Quebec critic, dramatist, and co-founder (with Jean Charbonneau) of the Ecole Littéraire de Montréal, was born in Saint-Jérôme on 1 December 1876. His father, Antoine Testard de Montigny, was a judge; his mother's maiden name was Marie-Louise Hétu. He studied at the Collège Sainte-Marie and then went to law school at the University of Montreal, which he soon abandoned for journalism. As early as 1894 he became a founding member of the Ecole Littéraire de Montréal, of which he was also the first secretary and archivist. In 1895 he began his literary career by publishing a few poems in the Montreal newspapers *Le Monde Illustré* and *Le Samedi*, and in 1899 he founded and began editing the newspapers *Les Débats* and *La Gazette Municipale*. In 1904 Montigny married Antoinette-Marie Helbronner. In 1910 he obtained a post as translator in the Senate of Canada, a position he kept until his death in 1955.

Montigny was named a knight (*chevalier*) of the French Légion d'Honneur in 1925, and in 1937 he received a doctoral degree from the Université de Montréal and an award from the

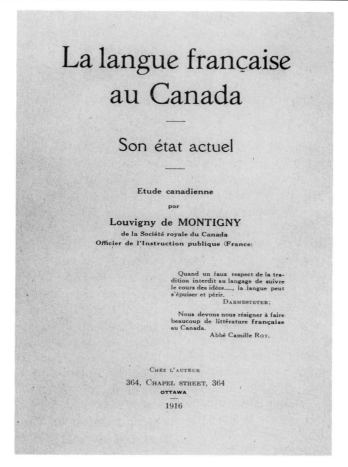

La langue française
au Canada

——

Son état actuel

——

Etude canadienne
par
Louvigny de MONTIGNY
de la Société royale du Canada
Officier de l'Instruction publique (France)

Quand un faux respect de la tradition interdit au langage de suivre
le cours des idées...., la langue peut
s'épuiser et périr.
DARMESTETER;

Nous devons nous résigner à faire
beaucoup de littérature française
au Canada.
Abbé Camille ROY.

CHEZ L'AUTEUR
364, CHAPEL STREET, 364
OTTAWA
1916

Cover for Montigny's first book, a long, controversial essay in which he discusses the origins, the forms, and the possible methods for purifying the French-Canadian language

Académie Française for his *La Revanche de "Maria Chapdelaine"* (Maria Chapdelaine's Revenge). In 1945 he received yet another award (the Prix de la Langue Française–the French language prize) from the Académie Française, as well as the Ernesta Stern Prize from the Société des Gens de Lettres de France (Society of Men of Letters of France) for his essay *Au pays de Québec: Contes et images* (In Quebec Province: Tales and Images, 1945). Montigny was a member of the Royal Society of Canada, vice president of the Société des Ecrivains Canadiens (Society of Canadian Writers), and for many years he represented French Canada in the Société des Gens de Lettres de France.

La Langue française au Canada: Son état actuel (The French Language in Canada: Its Actual State), published in 1916, is a philological essay, a study Montigny carried out "sans être équipé de tous les approvisionnements de la grammaire empirique, de la critique textuelle, de l'analogie lex-

ique, de la sémantique, de l'étymologie, de la morphologie, de la phonétique et de tout le tremblement de la psychologie du langage" (without being equipped with all the stock of empirical grammar, of textual critique, of lexical analogy, of semantics, of etymology, of morphology, of phonetics and the "whole caboodle" of the psychology of language). In twelve chapters he traces the origins of what he calls "le francocanadien primitif" (original French-Canadian); he then describes what he sees as three linguistic classes in French-Canadian society: the rural, the urban, and the educated populations. Finally, in medical terms, Montigny proposes two main remedies for purifying a language contaminated by anglicisms: the study of both English and French and a return to the sources of the French language, that is its literature, its thought. Montigny's essay met with violent criticism, mainly that of Jules Fournier, who, in two letters reproduced in his *Mon Encrier* (My Inkwell, 1922), refuted the causes for the decline of the French language in Canada put forth by Montigny. He further suggested that Montigny's remedies would be ineffective if "un sens du français . . . le génie de la langue" (a feeling for the genius of the French language) was not first restored in French Canada.

Montigny was deeply involved in the literary world of his day as attested by his membership in several literary societies and the publication of his poetry. In 1916 in Montreal, he edited Louis Hémon's *Maria Chapdelaine*, which had been published in serial form in 1914 in the Paris newspaper *Le Temps*. In 1937 he published *La Revanche de "Maria Chapdelaine": Essai d'initiation à un chef-d'oeuvre inspiré du pays de Québec* (Maria Chapdelaine's Revenge: Essay of Initiation to a Masterwork Inspired by the Province of Quebec). Montigny had found what he considered to be a "modèle de littérature canadienne" (a model of Canadian literature) in Hémon's novel, and he made a concerted effort in his study to outline the novel's sources, its literary fortunes, and the criticisms leveled against it. Despite the controversy surrounding this study–Claude-Henri Grignon and Guy Sylvestre felt vehemently that the essay was elementary and definitely did not deserve a doctorate–the Académie Française awarded Montigny both the degree and a prize for his work. Pierre Daviault was to write, in the Montreal newspaper *Le Droit* (31 March 1938), that "il vaut surtout par les renseignements précieux qu'il réunit sur la genèse et la vie du premier grand roman qu'ait inspiré notre pays" (its [the essay's] worth is above all in the precious information it brings together concerning the development and life of the first great novel our country has inspired).

Criticism, positive or negative, did not easily impress Montigny. His comedy *Les Boules de neige* (Snowballs), published in 1935, was, according to the author, "une occasion d'observer les moeurs de son temps et de son milieu" (an opportunity to observe the mores of his time and his milieu). The play denounces what its author perceives to be a "vice social" (social vice), "un travers" (a shortcoming) of the French-Canadian upper-middle class of his day, that of a tendency to gossip that "snowballs." The play remains as a witness to the French-Canadian bourgeoisie in the early 1900s, its mentality and its activities.

Louvigny de Montigny, as journalist, dramatist, literary critic, or translator, was sensitive to the problems facing the French language in Canada. On one hand he eliminated certain colloquialisms and regionalisms used by Hémon to portray the lives of the habitants (French-Canadian farmers); on the other he himself made use of the popular language in *Les Boules de neige*. His deep concern for the importance and the place of French in Canada was a constant throughout his career; his linguistic awareness was soon to be shared by many other prominent Quebec authors.

Reference:
Robert Choquette, "Louvigny de Montigny," *Cahiers de l'Académie Canadienne-Française,* 7 (1963): 139-151.

Dora Mavor Moore

(8 April 1888-15 May 1979)

Paul Leonard
Toronto Theatre Alliance

PLAY PRODUCTIONS: *Spring Thaw*, by Moore, Andrew Allen, and other members of the New Play Society, Toronto, Royal Ontario Museum, 1 April 1948 (an annual revue updated and performed through 1971);
The Way of the Spirit, Whitby, Ont., Ontario Hospital, 3 May 1956.

RADIO: *The Blue Bird*, adapted by Moore and Joan Burke from Maurice Maeterlinck's play, CBC, 3 May 1934.

When a group of theater professionals in Toronto decided in 1979 to create a series of awards to recognize the excellence of theater in Canada, it was natural that they name the new honors after Dora Mavor Moore, for she is widely considered the founder of professional theater in Canada. She has earned a place in the *Dictionary of Literary Biography* not so much by her writing as by her laying of the foundation for contemporary Canadian theater and drama through her work as an actress, a director, a teacher, and an indefatigable proponent of professionalism and dedication to the art of the theater.

Dora Mavor was born on 8 April 1888 in Glasgow, Scotland, but came to Canada with her parents, James Mavor and Christina Watt, in 1892 when she was four years old, her father having been hired as a professor of political economy at the University of Toronto. She attended the university from 1906 to 1909, and it was as a student that she gained her first experience of the theater; she appeared in a number of university productions, most notably as Rosalind in *As You Like It*. After leaving the university Dora continued to study at the Margaret Eaton School of Literature and Expression in Toronto, and the quality of her work there earned her a scholarship to the Royal Academy of Dramatic Art in London. In 1912 she became the first Canadian to graduate from that prestigious institution. From there she journeyed to New York to study acting privately with Philip Ben Greet. Besides reprising the role of Rosalind, this time on Broadway, she toured the Chautauqua Circuit with Greet's "Pastoral Players" from 1912 to 1914.

On 23 February 1916 Dora married Rev. Francis John Moore, an army padre who took his wife with him when he went to serve overseas during World War I. While in England Dora Mavor Moore played the role of Viola in *Twelfth Night* at the Old Vic Theatre in 1918; she was the first Canadian to perform in that building. After the war, the Moores returned to Toronto. While raising her three sons (Francis, Peter, and James Mavor, known as Mavor), Moore continued to act in local productions at the Royal Alexandra and Hart House theaters, and she began her career as a producer and director, working with such groups as the Margaret Eaton School, the Toronto Public Library Dramatic Club, and the University College Players. During the 1930s Moore collaborated on theater productions with Professor G. Wilson Knight, composer Healey Willan, and artist Arthur Lismer, among others.

One of the chief accomplishments of Moore's career had its genesis in the Village Players, an amateur troupe she founded in 1938. This company, which had toured productions of Shakespeare to high schools before World War II, continued to operate with meager resources until 1946. Among the projects of the Village Players were Canadian premieres of plays by Federico García Lorca and Bertolt Brecht. Once the war ended, however, Moore was determined to launch a fully professional theater company, and the Village Players gave way to the New Play Society. The first production of the N.P.S. was presented on 11 October 1946, when John Millington Synge's *Playboy of the Western World* (1907), directed by Moore, was performed at the 435-seat theater of the Royal Ontario Museum in downtown Toronto. It was followed by five other professional productions, ranging from Eugene O'Neill's *Ah, Wilderness!* (1932) to the traditional *Coventry Nativity Play* and *Wakefield Second Shepherd's Play*. This first N.P.S. project was so successful that a second series began in January 1947 and included Moore's direction of James M. Barrie's *What Every Woman Knows* (1908). These series continued until 1950, offering Torontonians the "balanced season" that would become a staple of the regional theater movement a decade later in Canada: contemporary British and American hits, classics, and original Canadian plays.

Late in the winter of 1947-1948 the New Play Society was forced to scramble for a fifth production when an anticipated adaptation of Hugh MacLennan's *Two Solitudes* (1945) was not ready. The result was *Spring Thaw*, an original satirical revue that addressed local issues and current concerns. The opening song of the show, for example, was called "We All Hate Toronto." Audiences, first in Toronto and later nationally, were hungry for the kind of lighthearted indigenous satire *Spring Thaw* provided, and the show achieved instant popularity. *Spring Thaw* became a tradition at the N.P.S., which produced a new version each year until 1971 (*Spring Thaw* was also revived for one production run during the 1979-1980 season). The New Play Society was also responsible for the premiere of John Coulter's *Riel* (1962), as well as plays by Andrew Allen, Lister Sinclair, Mavor Moore (Dora's son), and Morley Callaghan, among others.

In 1950, partly in response to increased demand for trained actors, the New Play Society created a theater school, which would demand much of Moore's attention for the next eighteen years. When the school opened Moore was the only instructor for the five students, although by the time the school closed in 1968, after several moves throughout the city of Toronto, there was a staff of nine to serve the two hundred actors in training. The New Play Society School was for much of its history Canada's major English-language drama school. Throughout her life Moore was a dedicated teacher, and many Canadian actors who began their careers in the 1950s and 1960s credit her as mentor.

Although a strong proponent of professionalism in the theater, Moore was deeply aware of the therapeutic value of drama in education and in the treatment of the mentally ill. In the early 1950s the New Play Society collaborated with the Canadian Mental Health Association to produce nine original plays dealing with a variety of problems, from disciplining children to coping with old age. These productions toured church organizations, service clubs, and other groups, and were always followed by discussions with the audience led by experts from the Mental Health Association. In the winter of 1955 and the spring of 1956 Moore directed large-scale pageants featuring patients at a provincial psychiatric hospital (the Ontario Hospital in Whitby) outside Toronto.

Until her death Moore enthusiastically followed the careers of her former students and continued to promote Canadian theater. Her contributions to Canadian culture began to be recognized formally in 1967 when the nation celebrated the hundredth anniversary of its founding; in that year Moore was awarded a Centennial Medal and was chosen by B'nai B'rith as Woman of the Year. She was awarded honorary degrees by Western College for Women, Oxford, Ohio, in 1969 and the University of Toronto in 1970; also in 1970, Moore was made an officer of the Order of Canada. In 1971, 30 November was declared Dora Mavor Moore Day by the city of Toronto. Since 1980 one of the greatest tributes to this theater pioneer is the annual presentation of the Dora Mavor Moore Awards, produced each June by the Toronto Theatre Alliance, a service organization for all the professional theater companies in the city. Moore died on 15 May 1979.

Papers:
Moore's collected papers are housed in the Thomas Fisher Library, University of Toronto; the archives of the Toronto Theatre Alliance also contain information about her career.

Paul Morin
(6 April 1889-17 July 1963)

Evelyne Voldeng
Carleton University

BOOKS: *Le Paon d'émail* (Paris: Lemerre, 1911);
Les Sources de l'œuvre de Henry Wadsworth Longfellow (Paris: Larose, 1913);
Poèmes de cendre et d'or (Montreal: Dauphin, 1922);
Textes choisis et préséntes par Jean-Paul Plante (Montreal: Fides, 1958);
Géronte et son miroir (Montreal: Cercle du Livre de France, 1960);
Oeuvres poétiques: Le Paon d'émail, Poèmes de cendre et d'or, edited by Jean-Paul Plante (Montreal: Fides, 1961).

OTHER: Louis Bertrand, *La vie privée de Louis XIV,* translated by Morin (Montreal: Carrier, 1922);
Sir Edward Beatty, *Les sources de l'activité économique,* translated by Morin (Montreal, 1922);
Henry Wadsworth Longfellow, *Evangeline,* translated by Morin (Montreal, 1924);
Pierre-Louis Morin d'Equilly, *De Paris au lac Ouinipègue en 1837,* edited by Morin, *Mémoires de la Société royale du Canada,* 21 (May 1927): 9-27.

SELECTED PERIODICAL PUBLICATIONS
UNCOLLECTED: "Prise de voile," *Journal de Françoise,* 17 (December 1903): 117;
"Le Jardin," *Le Nationaliste,* 42 (December 1907): 3;
"L'Exotisme dans la poésie contemporaine," *L'Action,* 92 (January 1913): 1-2;
"Les Sources françaises d'un poète mineur américain," *Revue Trimestrielle Canadienne,* 10 (March 1924): 1-22;
"Patriae amans," *Revue Populaire,* 20 (March 1927): 6;
"L'Exotisme en littérature: visions d'Orient et des tropiques," *La Revue Moderne,* 8 (June 1938): 7, 8, 34;
"Anniversaire," *La Patrie* (3 July 1949): 74;
"René Chopin, poète magicien," *Qui?,* 3 (March 1953): 41-46.

Paul Morin is mostly remembered as the proponent in French Canada of the Parnassian literary creed of art for art's sake and for his association with the *Nigog* (January-December 1918), an art review which, in a crusade against the regionalist writers, the "terroiristes," promulgated a new aesthetics. The main tenets were the precedence of form over content and the artist's freedom to choose his subject.

Paul Morin was born on 6 April 1889 in Montreal, the son of Henri E. Morin and Antonia Marchand Morin, the daughter of Médéric Marchand, whose wife founded a famous music school: l'Académie Marchand. Paul was educated at St. Mary's College in Montreal, the Lycée Saint-Louis de Gonzague in Paris, and the universities of Montreal and Paris. He was called to the Quebec bar in 1910 but in the fall of the same year went back to Paris to work on a doctorate in comparative literature.

In 1911 Morin, whose poems had appeared since 1903 in magazines such as *Le Journal de Françoise, Le Messager canadien du Coeur de Jésus,* and *Le Nationaliste,* published in Paris his first collection of poems, *Le Paon d'émail* (The Enamel Peacock). This book was acclaimed for the perfection of its form, although some French-Canadian critics blamed the poet for cultivating exoticism instead of writing nationalistic poetry. As the title suggests, the peacock is the symbol of enduring beauty arrested in the eternal form of art. Unlike the regionalist poets, Morin drew his inspiration from the splendor and color of the exotic lands about which he had read extensively and in which he had traveled widely. In his poems he describes, in sometimes farfetched metaphors, works of art, historical cities, landscapes, and mythological and pagan motifs, emphasizing the visual aspect of poetry. In his important poem "A Ceux de mon pays" (To My Countrymen) he explains how in a first stage he has to sing of France and its Latin heritage in order to be able in his mature years to "marier les mots canadiens aux rythmes de la France et l'érable au laurier" (join Canadian words to rhythms of France and the maple to the laurel). Although *Le Paon d'émail* shares common characteristics with Parnassian poetry, Morin in this book–which reveals his philosophical outlook on art and life–only accepts the theory of art for art's sake because of the sheer impossibility of capturing the elusive world of human emotions.

In 1913, two years after the publication of *Le Paon d'émail*, his thesis entitled "Les Sources de l'oeuvre de Henry Wadsworth Longfellow" was published in Paris. This thick volume, in which Morin discusses the sources of Longfellow's works with an emphasis on the influence of German romanticism on the American poet, enables him to clarify his antiromantic stand and his idea of the nature of a poem. The extensive research in world literature required for his doctoral work was to contribute largely to the kind of learned sophisticated poetry that was to be his trademark.

Back in North America Morin became professor of French literature first at McGill University (1914-1915), later at Smith College (Northampton, Massachusetts), and then at the University of Minnesota (1916-1917). In 1917 he married Geneviève Van Rennslaer-Bernhardt and returned to Montreal, where he worked for *Le Prix courant* and was for some time editor of another financial newspaper, *L'Information*.

In 1922 he received the Prix David for his second book of poetry, *Poèmes de cendre et d'or* (Poems of Ash and Gold), published that year in Montreal. In this volume, no longer concerned with the dialectics of regionalism and universalism, Morin chose as his main theme man torn between the ideal and the real worlds. This collection, whose title symbolizes the opposition between light and darkness, mortality and immortality, is divided into four sections entitled "Cendres," "Jades," "Soies," and "Ors" (Ashes, Jades, Silks, and Golds) and shows fewer Parnassian characteristics than *Le Paon d'émail*. The poems often reveal Morin's personal feelings as well as an ironic distanciation between the poet and the theory of *ars gratis ars*. It is through role-playing, irony, and parody that the poet expresses his difficulty at coming to terms with everyday life and drudgery. Whether the theme be love, foreign lands, or great men, the poems are all concerned with the tension between dream and reality. The same duality is expressed in poems about poetics–such as "Réveil" (Waking) and "La revanche du Paon" (The Revenge of the Peacock)–in which the art of poetry is depicted as an arduous task against which the poet at times rebels; although ultimately Morin reaffirms its worth in his "triple hommage" to his poet friends Marcel Dugas, Guy Delahaye, and René Chopin. In *Poèmes de cendre et d'or* Morin, unlike the Parnassians, expresses personal feelings and a poetic quest, but he does it through a Parnassian-like mastery of craft, shown in his use of artful and careful stanza and line patterns as well as extraordinarily rich rhymes.

In 1923 Morin became a member of the Royal Society of Canada, received the Jubilee Medal from Great Britain, and was made an "officier d'académie" by the French government. In 1924 his translation of *Evangeline* by Henry Wadsworth Longfellow was published. Morin was the editor of "La Revue Moderne" for a brief period and then acted as an interpreter for the Quebec tribunals for fifteen years. Meanwhile he was also the host of the popular Radio-Canada program "Les Fureurs d'un puriste" (The Passions of a Purist).

Two unfortunate events were to sadden the rest of his life: the death of his wife in 1952 and the burning down of the house in which he was living in Pointe aux Trembles, Quebec, on 16 April 1957. In the fire he lost valuable art objects, the manuscript of his translation of Michel de Montaigne's works into modern French, and his precious correspondence with the French writer Countess Anna de Noailles, who had facilitated his debut in Parisian literary circles.

In 1960 his last volume of poetry, *Géronte et son miroir*, was published. In this heterogeneous collection of poems (poems published in magazines, plus epigraphs and translations) the tone is set by the ironical testament-like preface. The peacock-like dandy has turned into a poor and lonely old man who through ironic distance recalls his glamorous past.

Paul Morin was at one time celebrated as French Canada's greatest poet. Now he is still remembered for his craftsmanship, for the formal beauty of his verse, and for the Parnassian aesthetics that shaped his poetry and his life.

References:

Victor Barbeau, "Paul Morin," *Cahiers de l'Académie Canadienne-Française*, 13 (1970): 45-119;

Gérard Bessette, "Les images en poésie canadienne-française," Ph.D. dissertation, Montreal University, 1950, pp. 177-190;

Léo-Paul Desrosiers, "L'Ecole du Nigog," *La Revue nationale*, 7 (July 1919): 251-257;

Henri Dombrowski, "Du Paon d'émail aux Poèmes de cendre et d'or," *L'Action Française*, 9 (January 1923): 25-32;

Marcel Dugas, "Paul Morin," in his *Apologies* (Montreal: Paradis-Vincent, 1919), pp. 39-60;

Jean-Paul Morel de la Durantaye, "Paul Morin, l'homme et l'oeuvre," Ph.D. dissertation, 3 volumes, Ottawa University, 1975;

Jean Ethier-Blais, "Un poète canadien, Paul Morin," *L'Action Universitaire*, 4 (July 1948): 303-311;

Jean-Jacques Lefebvre, "Paul Morin," *La Revue du Barreau*, 23 (November 1963): 563-568;

Bernard Muddiman, "Paul Morin," *Canadian Magazine*, 48 (November 1916): 179-184;

Jean-Paul Plante, *Paul Morin* (Montreal & Paris: Fides, 1958);

Camille Roy, "Le Paon d'émail," *Nouvelle-France*, 11 (May 1912): 204-216;

Jane Turnbull, *Essential Traits of French Canadian Poetry* (Toronto: Macmillan, 1938), pp. 184-196.

Jean Narrache
(Emile Coderre)

(10 June 1893 - 6 April 1970)

Alexandre L. Amprimoz
Brock University

BOOKS: *Les Signes sur le sable,* as Coderre (Montreal: L'auteur, 1922);

Quand j'parl' tout seul (Montreal: Lévesque, 1932);

Histoires du Canada . . . vies ramanchées (Montreal: L'Action Canadienne-Française, 1937);

J'parl' pour parler (Montreal: Valiquette, 1939);

Bonjour, les gars! Vers ramanchés et pièces nouvelles (Montreal: Pilon, 1948);

J'parle tout seul quand Jean Narrache (Montreal: L'Homme, 1961);

Jean Narrache chez le diable (Montreal: L'Homme, 1963);

Rêveries de Jean Narrache (Montreal: Pauvre Yabe, s.d.).

RECORDING: *Les Poèmes de Jean Narrache avec René Caron,* Trans-Canada TC 782.

Jean Narrache is one of the most underestimated Canadian poets and writers. His fundamental inspiration was the Depression, and he wrote about "the little guy" from the East End of Montreal. It was Narrache who introduced into French-Canadian literature the informal "habitant" language that would later develop into "joual," the slang of Montreal's working classes.

Emile Coderre, who later took the pen name of Jean Narrache, was born in Montreal on 10 June 1893 to Jeanne Marchaud and Emile Coderre, a pharmacist. He soon became an orphan and was adopted at the age of four by M.-A. Ouimet, who later sent him to be educated at the Séminaire de Nicolet. There he gave the first signs of his propensity for humor in *Le Mercredi,* a student weekly he published. When he graduated in 1912 Narrache returned to his native city where he joined the Ecole Littéraire de Montréal for a brief period (1912-1913). This was an important association of Quebec writers that stressed a romantic imagination within the framework of traditional French-Canadian life. Under their influence Narrache wrote his first poems, which he published a decade later. At the same time the young writer decided to follow in his father's footsteps and began to study pharmacy at the Université de Montréal. He obtained his B.A. in 1917 and his *licence* in 1921. That year, on 19 September, he married Marie-Rose Tassé. In 1924 he accepted a position with a paint company, Martin-Senours, as a distributor and a promoter. Besides technical publications, during the twenties and thirties Narrache contributed to such periodicals as the *Revue Moderne*

Jean Narrache (photograph by André Larose, Montreal)

and the *Grande Revue*. His poems were also regularly published by the newspaper *La Patrie du Dimanche*. In 1932 the Société des Poètes Canadiens-Français awarded him its silver medal, indicating that his peers recognized at least his originality if not his excellence. From 1943 to 1961 Narrache was secretary of the Collège des Pharmaciens de la Province du Québec. The poet died on 6 April 1970.

Narrache's first book is the only one published under his real name and appeared in the shadow of L'Ecole Littéraire de Montréal. Inspired by the mythical figure of Emile Nelligan, the movement was to dominate the literature of Quebec until 1935. As a first collection of poems, *Les Signes sur le sable* (Signs on the Sand, 1922) was published ten years too late, and a L'Ecole critic, Valdombre (Claude-Henri Grignon), dismissed it as sentimental rubbish. The poems were certainly traditional in form and content, and such contemporary reviewers as Camille Roy, Albert Pelletier, and Louis Dantin echoed, although with less virulence, the opinion of

Valdombre. The older poet Alphonse Désilets, in his introduction to *Les Signes sur le sable*, seems to have been the only one to see the altruistic themes that would later contribute to Narrache's success.

Quand j'parl' tout seul (When I Talk All Alone, 1932) proved Désilets right. The 1932 silver medal was only one sign of the increasing respect for Narrache. The pen name chosen by the poet was an indication of the roots of his new social and aesthetic vision. A pun like "Jim Nasium" or "Nick O'Teen," Jean Narrache is the homonym for the phrase "J'en arrache," which means "I'm tearing at it" or, less literally, "People give me a hard time," or "It's a tough grind." Humor and compassion for the underdog are blended in the persona of Narrache, who criticized the Quebec middle class during the Depression.

While the content and language of *Quand j'parl' tout seul* may seem radical, the poetic form remains rather conservative. All the poems in the collection are composed of quatrains of octosyllabic verse and present simple, linear narratives.

In "Les Deux Orphelines" (Two Orphan Girls), one of the best poems of *Quand j'parl' tout seul*, the reader cannot help noticing the sharp, ironic observations. It is the story of a plump, well-to-do lady who goes to see a play about two orphans. She is very moved and cannot stop sobbing until she leaves the theater and sees two real orphan girls begging. Instead of offering them something, the lady tells them to leave, accuses them of being thieves, and remarks that people should be ashamed to beg. She even threatens to call the police and have them arrested.

This populist perspective might explain why Narrache was much more popular with readers at large than with academic critics and middle-class journalists. In 1932 *Quand j'parl' tout seul* sold more than six thousand copies. Many of these poems were quickly adapted into plays by theater companies and broadcasters. The immediate impact of Narrache's second book, then, was quite considerable.

The natural strength of such a proletarian tone gave Narrache the idea to rewrite Canadian history from the point of view of the man on the street and to use this vehicle to criticize the contemporary political and economic elite. *Histoires du Canada ... vies ramanchées* (1937) depicts the adventures of men from Columbus to La Vérendrye, and yet the reader can savor the humor directed at political life in the thirties, the scandals

Dust jacket for the first book Narrache wrote under his pseudonym (1932), and an illustration by Simone Aubry for J'parl'
pour parler *(1939). These poetry collections criticize the middle class from the point of view
of a common man on the street.*

related to road construction, tax evasion, and related fraud. One of the more specific targets of Narrache is Camillien Houde (1889-1958), a colorful political figure who is presented as corrupt.

In *J'parl' pour parler* (I Speak for the Sake of Speaking, 1939) Narrache's preoccupations that surfaced in *Histoires du Canada* become more obsessive and turn into bitter attacks against the establishment. The poems themselves are not without merit and offer Narrache's vision of the role of the Christian artist. As shown in the "Jasette à saint Francois d'Assise," the poet has chosen a marginal position in order to criticize freely a society from which he does not ask anything for himself. In this collection there are some formal changes as well. Regular stanzas are abandoned for a flexible structure more able to convey the nomadic alienation of Narrache and the French-Canadian street person of the 1930s.

In *Bonjour, les gars!* (Hello, Boys! 1948) thirty-two poems are reprinted from previous collections. Only nine texts are new, but one of them, which is 206 lines long, is worth mentioning for its orthodox populism: "Méditation d'un gueux

au pied de la croix" (Meditation of a Beggar at the Foot of the Cross). The book contains an introduction by Alphonse Loiselle and a long essay entitled "Qui est Jean Narrache?" (Who Is J. N.?). It is assumed that the essay is a lecture Narrache himself prepared to state the principles of his populist poetics.

J'parle tout seul quand Jean Narrache (I Speak Alone When I Am J. N., 1961) is a collection of selected poems, fifteen of which had never been published. In an amusing introduction, Narrache examines the paradox that, in spite of apparent economic affluence, almost nothing has changed: the 1930s and 1960s are very similar.

In *Jean Narrache chez le diable* (Jean Narrache at the Devil's House, 1963), the speaker descends to the underworld and is escorted by "Contradiction"–a figure resembling the demon Asmodeus. This neglected book deserves more attention, at least for these three reasons: the text is written in standard French, a gesture of ironic surrender to the internationalist position of educator Jean-Paul Desbiens, author of *Les Insolences du frère Untel* (1960; translated as *The Impertinences of*

Brother Anonymous, 1962); the discussion of separatism might have influenced many writers, in particular Jacques Ferron, author of *La Nuit* (The Night, 1965); and the image of the limping devil links Narrache to a better-known orphan, André Langevin, author of *Poussière sur la ville* (1953; translated as *Dust Over the City*).

Although much of the particular flavor of Narrache's poetry is lost in translation, two stanzas of "Soir d'hiver dans la rue Ste-Catherine" (Winter Night on Saint Catherine Street) might give an idea of how Jean Narrache succeeded in combining art and sociopolitical commitment:

> Eh oui! la neig' blanch' en belle ouate
> Comm' nos beaux rêv's puis nos espoirs,
> Comm' c'est pas long qu'ell' r'tourn' en bouète
> Un' fois qu'elle a touché l'trottoir!

> La foule, ell', c'est comme un' marée
> Qui moutonne en se j'tant partout
> Comme un troupeau d'bêt's épeurées
> Que tout l'tapage a rendu fou.

> (Ah, yes, the snow, like cottony scud,
> White as our dreams, our hopeful talk,
> How quickly it turns into dirty mud
> As soon as it touches the sidewalk!

> The crowd itself, that's like a tide
> That whitens where it overflows,

> Becomes a herd, half-terrified
> By the noise that blares wherever it goes.)

A conservative and a populist, Narrache denounced an unjust society but found, in faith, the great consolation of the humble. Although he preached courageous acceptance, his analysis of Quebec society is similar to that of the reformists of the Quiet Revolution and even to that of the more radical separatists. But his art transcends his politics.

References:

Emile Bégin, "*Histoires du Canada*," *L'Enseignement Secondaire au Canada*, 17, no. 4 (January 1938): 314-315;

Frédéric Bronner, "Henri Grignon, Jean Narrache and the 'Chansonnier' Desrousseaux," *Culture*, 13, no. 2 (June 1952): 164-167;

Maurice Hébert, "*Quand j'parl' tout seul*," *Le Canada Français*, 20, no. 6 (February 1933): 569-573;

André Major, "Simenon et Jean Narrache," *Le Devoir*, 58, no. 90 (18 April 1967): 10;

Camille Roy, "La Poésie qui se fait," *Le Canada Français*, 9, no. 2 (October 1922): 133-143;

Rita Simard, "Bio-bibliographie d'Emile Coderre," Montreal: Ecole des Bibliothécaires de l'Université de Montréal, 1942.

Emile Nelligan

(24 December 1879-18 November 1941)

Kathy Mezei
Simon Fraser University

BOOKS: *Emile Nelligan et son oeuvre,* edited by Louis Dantin (Montreal: Beauchemin, 1904 [i.e., 1903]);

Poésies complètes: 1896-1899, edited by Luc Lacourcière (Montreal & Paris: Fides, 1952);

Selected Poems by Emile Nelligan, translated by P. F. Widdows (Toronto: Ryerson, 1960);

Poésies choisis, edited by Eloi de Grandmont (Montreal: Fides, 1966);

Poésies, edited by Gilles Corbeil (Montreal: Fides, 1967);

Poèmes chaisis, edited by Roger Chamberland (Montreal: Fides, 1980);

31 Poèmes Autographes (Trois-Rivières, Que.: Forges, 1982);

The Complete Poems of Emile Nelligan, edited and translated by Fred Cogswell (Montreal: Harvest House, 1983).

OTHER: *The Poetry of French Canada,* edited by John Glassco, includes twelve poems by Nelligan (Toronto: Oxford University Press, 1970).

The tragic and romantic Emile Nelligan is Quebec's most beloved and admired poet. One could say that the whole of the French-Canadian sensibility lives under his shadow. Called the Canadian Rimbaud because of his dramatic and short-lived literary career (he wrote his approximately 160 poems between the ages of sixteen and nineteen), Nelligan ushered the poetry of Quebec into the modern age. Attracted by the Parnassian and symbolist movements of France and Belgium, he threw off the tired old subjects of patriotism, "le terroir" (the soil), the glories of old France, and the theme of fidelity to the land, language, and religion of French Catholic Quebec to explore unusual symbols, the melodies and symbolic possibilities of language, and, most striking of all, the dark recesses of his own inner being and tormented soul. Instead of clichéd celebrations of the land and ancestors, he spun out the webs of his dreams and longings in delicate

Emile Nelligan

rhythms and moving images. In his 1907 study *Nouvelles Etudes de littérature canadienne-française,* the French critic Charles ab der Halden remarked that Nelligan was the first Quebec poet to create a poetic image.

Nelligan was born on Christmas Eve 1879 in Montreal. His parents, a microcosm of the two solitudes of Canada, had a difficult marriage. His mother, Emilie-Amanda Hudon Nelligan, who doted on her son, was a French Canadian who was musically talented, proud of her culture and heritage, and a devout Catholic, while his father, David Nelligan, a volatile Irishman who had immigrated to Canada at the age of twelve, showed little interest in speaking French. As an inspector of the postal services in the Gaspé region, he spent much time away from home. Apparently, according to Paul Wyczynski (*Emile Nelligan,* 1968), the young Nelligan once asked his mother, "Is that Irish man coming to visit us tomorrow?" In a poem dedicated to his father, "Le Voyageur," Nelligan transformed him into an absent phantom: "On ne le revoit plus dans ses plaines natales. / Fantôme, il disparut dans la nuit, emporté / Par le souffle mortel des brises hivernales" (He can be seen no more on his native sod. / He disappeared in the night, a phantom cast / On the mortal breath of a wintry blast). Evidently father and son had a stormy relationship, and later Nelligan would deny his Irish heritage, insisting that his name be pronounced in the French way, even spelling it "Nelighan."

Nelligan was, however, attached to his mother and his two younger sisters, Eva and Gertrude. The family lived in Montreal, where Nelligan attended school, and spent idyllic summers in the village of Cacouna at the Peek à Boo Villa, which may have inspired some of his more bucolic poems.

In 1896 Nelligan entered the Collège Sainte-Marie, where he proved to be a mediocre student of classics, immersing himself instead in the study and writing of poetry. During this year he also met at a bazaar his mentor and future editor, the priest Eugene Seers (later called Louis Dantin), and Joseph Melançon, who introduced Nelligan to the literary circles of Montreal. Under the pseudonym Emile Kovar he published his first poem, "Rêve fantasque" (Whimsical Dream), in *Le Samedi* (13 June 1896). Echoing Paul Verlaine's "La Nuit du Walpurgis classique," Nelligan's poem, with its plaintive violin and gloomy images of "Les bruns chêneaux altiers traçaient dans le ciel triste, . . . un bien sombre contour" (The brown proud oaks traced against the sad sky's hues, . . . dark outlines), draws the reader into what will become a familiar Nelliganian world of shadows, vague longings, and memory. By September eight other poems had also appeared in local papers and journals.

In 1897 Nelligan quit his studies in classics and on 10 February, invited by his friend Arthur de Bussières, joined the now-renowned Ecole Littéraire de Montréal, a circle of young writers and intellectuals who met weekly to discuss the arts. Begun in 1895 by students disgusted with the deteriorating state of the French language, the group soon attracted the most interesting

and dynamic writers of the day, enlivening and heightening the cultural life of the city. During several meetings the young poet read his poetry gravely and with deep feeling. His appearance matched the tone of his verse, for he was Byronically handsome, with thick, disheveled hair, dark, mournful eyes, and a distant, dreamy air. Affecting a bohemian stance, he envisioned himself as a poet in the romantic tradition. In his poem "Un poète" he presents this notion of the rebel artist: "Laissez-le vivre ainsi sans lui faire de mal! / Laissez-le s'en aller; c'est un rêveur qui passe; / C'est une âme angélique ouverte sur l'espace, / Qui porte en elle un ciel de printemps auroral" (Let him live then and harm not anything! / Let him depart, a dreamer passing by, / An angel soul, open to infinity, / Bearing his own dawn of celestial spring).

The following year his father dispatched him on a sea voyage (of which there are few details) that took the young poet to Liverpool and Belfast, and then arranged employment for him as a bookkeeper. But Nelligan had no head for figures and, much to the annoyance of his father, resolved to devote his time to poetry. Often he would escape to his friend de Bussières's attic to read and work, and he continued to publish his poems in *Le Samedi, Le Monde Illustré, La Patrie,* and other local papers.

At this time L'École Littéraire de Montréal successfully initiated a series of public readings, at the first of which Nelligan recited "Le Rêve de Watteau" (Watteau's Dream), "Le Récital des anges" (Recital of the Angels), and "L'Idiote aux cloches" (The Idiot Girl). However, at another reading, on 24 February 1899, when Nelligan read "Notre-Dame-des-Neiges" (Our Lady of the Snows), "La Négresse," and "Le Perroquet" (The Parrot), De Marchy, a minor French critic visiting Montreal, singled Nelligan out for harsh criticism. Morbidly sensitive, Nelligan was devastated by this attack and withdrew from L'Ecole Littéraire into his private world. But later, on 26 May (his last appearance at L'Ecole), Nelligan like a young god sprang up to recite with passion three poems, including "La Romance du vin" (The Song of Wine), a reply to his attacker: "C'est le règne du rire amer et de la rage / De se savoir poète et l'objet du mépris, / De se savoir un coeur et de n'être compris / Que par le clair de lune et les grands soirs d'orage!" (The bitter laugh of rage is now good form, / And I, a poet, must eat scorn for food. / I have a heart but am not understood / Except in moonlight and in great nights of storm!). The audience responded with a resounding ovation, and Nelligan was triumphantly carried home like a victor.

Then, on 9 August 1899, after a visit by his mother to de Bussières's attic, Nelligan ran to Saint-Louis Square, climbed a tree, and threatened to commit suicide. The ever-fragile thread of his sanity had snapped, as perhaps best described in his famous "Vaisseau d'or" (The Ship of Gold): "Que reste-t-il de lui dans la tempête brève? / Qu'est devenu mon coeur, navire déserté? / Hélas! Il a sombré dans l'abîme du Rêve!" (What rests at last after the hasty plunge? / What of my heart's lost fate, poor derelict? / — Foundered, alas! in the black gulf of Dream!). He was admitted to the Rétraite Saint-Benoît, where he remained for twenty-five years, after which he was transferred to the Saint-Jean-de-Dieu Hospital. Classified as a schizophrenic, he lived a passive and quiet existence until his death on 18 November 1941. Unfortunately this young "poète maudit" (damned poet), alienated from his time and place, split by his passions, his desire for liberty and the oppressive rigidity of the Catholic church, between the temptation of dreams and the encroachment of reality, could not live in late-Victorian Quebec. His schizophrenia symbolically captures the tension between the French and the English, the uneasy dual heritage of Quebec so tragically manifested in his own family.

Although he kept five notebooks in the hospital, these consist mainly of scribblings, poems in English and French by his favorite poets, and poems written earlier by himself, all jotted down from memory. His writing days were over.

Nelligan's poems were not collected and published until after his incarceration, although his manuscripts show that he had been arranging his poems into a volume. Louis Dantin, at that time still a priest, spent several years compiling a volume of Nelligan's poems. When his disapproving superiors discovered his activities, Dantin handed the manuscripts and printed papers to Nelligan's mother, who, along with Charles Gill, gave them to the publisher Beauchemin. These were then published in 1903 (with "1904" on the title page) as *Emile Nelligan et son oeuvre* with a preface by Dantin. Dantin, partly because of this incident, exiled himself to Cambridge, Massachusetts, and left the church. Then in 1952 Luc Lacourcière brought out *Poésies complètes: 1896-1899,* which contains the 107 poems gathered together by Dantin, 35 poems that had appeared in journals

from 1896 to 1939 (friends who had received poems from Nelligan published them after he was hospitalized), and 21 poems from the Nelligan-Corbeil manuscripts now at the Bibliothèque Nationale in Montreal.

Nelligan had intended to entitle his collection of poems "Motifs du récital des anges" (Motifs from the Recital of Angels) and had listed the sections as follows: "Prélude aux anges," "Clavecin céleste," "Villa d'enfance," "Petite chapelle," "Vesprées mystiques," "Mysticisme," "Choses mystiques," "Intermezzo," "Lied," and "Les Pieds sur les chenets" (Prelude to the Angels, Celestial Harpsichord, Childhood Villa, Small Chapel, Mystical Vespers, Mysticism, Mystical Matters, Intermezzo, Song, and Feet on the Fender). Dantin, apparently with recourse to a later list, entitled the sections: "L'Ame du poète," "Le Jardin de l'enfance," "Amours d'élite," "Les Pieds sur les chenets," "Virgiliennes," "Eaux-fortes funéraires," "Petite chapelle," "Pastels et Porcelaines," "Vêpres tragiques," and "Tristia" (The Poet's Soul, The Garden of Childhood, Elite Loves, Feet on the Fender, Virgilians, Funereal Etchings, Small Chapel, Pastels and Porcelains, Tragic Vespers, and Tristia), titles that reflect the thematic and formal concerns of the poet, particularly the religious motif. Lacourcière maintained Dantin's order, with the addition of "Pièces retrouvées" and "Poèmes posthumes" (Recovered Poems and Posthumous Poems), culled from manuscripts and journals.

Although Nelligan wrote persistently during his brief period of creativity and although he showed great skill in crafting his sonnets and rhymes, he was naturally influenced by the poets he read. In contrast to his tradition-bound predecessors, he turned to the symbolists, to Paul Verlaine, Charles-Pierre Baudelaire, Stéphane Mallarmé, Arthur Rimbaud, Georges Rodenbach, Maurice Rollinat, and, as he read widely in English, to Lord Byron, Sir Walter Scott, and (with great affinity) Edgar Allan Poe. His verse resounded with the decadent strains and tones of ennui common to the symbolists, yet surmounted these influences to attain the beauty and singularity upon which his fame rests.

Catholicism permeates his poems with images of chapels, priests, stained-glass windows, the release of prayer, and the specter of damnation. In "Confession nocturne" the tormented poet seeks salvation: "Prêtre, je suis hanté, c'est la nuit dans la ville, / Mon âme est le donjon des mortels péchés noirs" (Priest, I'm haunted, it's dark in the city, / A keeper of sins my soul is deadly black). Religion and the church provide a sanctuary from the terrors of the present, but frequently Nelligan's nightmare vision breaks through and the "chapelle dans le bois" (chapel in the woods), a retreat into the idyllic memories of happy childhood, is transformed into a "chapelle ruinée" (ruined chapel) or a "Chapelle de la mort" (chapel of death), shattering dreams, illusions, and visions of a peaceful haven.

Absent from Nelligan's poems are concrete references to the Canadian landscape or any local color. Only "Soir d'hiver" (Winter Evening), an eloquent expression of ennui, relies upon a central image–snow–drawn from his immediate environment:

> Ah! comme la neige a neigé!
> Ma vitre est un jardin de givre.
> Ah! comme la neige a neigé!
> Qu'est-ce que le spasme de vivre
> A la douleur que j'ai, que j'ai!
>
> (Ah! how the snow falls free!
> My pane is a frosty garden now.
> Ah! how the snow falls free!
> What is life's spasm anyhow
> To the sorrow in me, in me!).

Instead Nelligan all too often resorts to exotic or foreign images derived from literature or fantasy, as in the poems of parrots and Negresses criticized by De Marchy. Faded pillow-laces, antiques, stuffy salons, the lushness of Louisiana, a Creole fantasy, and the conventional pastorals of Silvio and Pan reflect the artificial world of ideality, a symbolic inner landscape that Nelligan sought to create.

Dominating his poems are the themes of dreaming, childhood, music, and death, all tightly entwined through recurring images. Each of these themes focuses on the poet's desire to attain an ideal, enclosed poetic universe, characterized by a nostalgic yearning for the past, by bittersweet memories, and, occasionally, by heroic acts of valor. This protean ideal world, therefore, assumes varied shapes and guises, and Nelligan's talent lay in his ability to render an abstract concept concretely. In "Clair de lune intellectuel" (The Mind's Moonlight), for example, Nelligan presents an exquisite image, "Ma pensée est couleur de lumières lointaines" (In distant lights my colored thoughts unfold); these thoughts fly from reality, from the material world, to seek an ideal realm "loin de la matière et des brutes laideurs" (far from the squalor of this material heap).

Nelligan's desire to return to the golden days of childhood is often symbolized as a sentimental garden, a "jardin d'antan" (garden of yesteryear), a "jardin d'enfance" (childhood garden). In "Rêve d'artiste" (An Artist's Dream) Nelligan illuminates the process by which he discovers his ideal world and describes how, were he to possess the elusive muse, "une soeur angélique au sourire discret" (an angel sister with a modest smile), he would fashion an equally angelic and beautiful garden:"Et pour qui je ferai si j'aborde à la gloire / Fleurir tout un jardin de lys et de soleils / Dans l'azur d'un poème offert à sa mémoire" (And for her I shall grow, if I find fame, / A whole garden of lily and sunflower bloom / In a sky-blue poem addressed to her name). "Rêve d'artiste" is an exposition of the development of the conditions of artistic creation and of his vision of an ideal poetic space. Dreaming is equated with poetic creation. Here, as in many of his poems, Nelligan embraces an innocent, platonic love, distant and ideal.

Gardens–golden, green, fragrant, and enclosed–along with musical motifs, exotic artifacts and places, and enclosed rooms laden with knickknacks are images that Nelligan favors to express his search for an ideal and private space. The journey beyond to the ideal or back down the path of childhood also circumscribes the painful dissection of the poet's soul, another enclosed and private space. In "Mon Ame" (My Soul) the poet exclaims that "Mon âme a la candeur d'une chose étoilée, / D'une neige de février" (My soul is as artless / As a flake of snow in February), and yearns to return "au seuil de l'Enfance en allée" (to childhood's threshold). His soul suffers from "le regret de vivre et l'effroi de mourir" (our living in sorrow and our dying in fear).

By plucking at the strings of remembrance (calling up in particular the image of his mother at the piano–much as D. H. Lawrence wrote of his mother in "Piano") and by its association with religious ceremony, music assumed thematic importance in Nelligan's poetry. "Clavier d'antan" (Yesterday's Keyboard) describes how, with the "Clavier vibrant de remembrance" (keyboard ringing with memories), the poet recalls "un peu des jours anciens, / Et l'Eden d'or de mon enfance" (a few days of old, / And my own childhood's Eden of gold). Other poems, "Five O'Clock," "Pour Ignace Paderewski," "Lied fantasque" (Odd Song), "Le Violin brisé" (The Shattered Violin),

Hommage à Nelligan, *a 1971 oil painting by Jean-Paul Lemieux (Collection Université de Montréal)*

"Chopin," and "Violin d'adieu," to name a few, also evoke the power of music to stir the soul.

As Nelligan's vision darkened and as he escaped more and more into dreams, his themes and images, always marked by a mournful note, grew increasingly macabre and obsessed with death. The enclosed garden, no longer a place of enchantment, was transformed into "le puits hanté," into tombs, coffins, and other dark artifacts of death. Music, no longer a delicate instrument of memory and dream, instead accompanied funerals in "Musiques funèbres" and "Marches funèbres," and the lively waltzes and mazurkas became a "Banquet macabre" where ancestors came "claquant leurs vieux os" (clacking their old bones). Enclosure was no longer creative but deadly. In a series of poems, obviously inspired by Poe's writings, "Les Chats," "Le Chat fatal," "Le Spectre," and "La Terrasse aux Spectres" (The Cats, The Deadly Cat, The Specter, and The Terrace with Its Specters), the poet creates his ultimate nightmare vision of phantoms and haunted castles.

It is the famous "Vaisseau d'or" (Ship of Gold), later set to music and sung by Quebec chansonniers, that seems to epitomize both Nelligan's tragic decline and his uncanny ability to strike the chords of emotion. The image of "un grand Vaisseau taillé dans l'or massif" (a gallant vessel wrought of gold) sailing on unknown seas with a naked Venus at the prow and carrying a treasure along with the three sailors, Hate, Disgust, and Frenzy, and finally sinking during a storm to disappear forever, effectively portrays both the sad fate of Nelligan and the perilous path of any artistic venture. In several other poems Nelligan relied upon the image of the ship to symbolize either a vehicle of escape or the poet himself. "Vaisseau d'or" is composed in sonnet form, and Nelligan, a skilled craftsman even at so young an age, wrote most of his poems in variations of the sonnet.

One indication of Nelligan's significance is the vast array of critical writings on his work; in his *Bibliographie descriptive et critique d'Emile Nelligan* (1973), Paul Wyczynski lists some six hundred texts. Each of the seven reeditions of his poems has initiated a series of memoirs and articles. Dantin's tempered and scholarly preface to *Emile Nelligan et son oeuvre* stands as one of the first and most astute commentaries on the poet's life and work. According to Dantin, Nelligan, "souvent symboliste par sa conception des entités poétiques, est presque toujours parnassien par leur expression" (often symbolist in his conception of poetic ideas, is almost always Parnassian in their expression). Gérard Bessette's studies (four published from 1946 to 1968) examine the nature of Nelligan's images and explore the reflection of his oedipal complex in his poems; while in *Emile Nelligan, sources et originalité de son oeuvre* (1960), Wyczynski exhaustively examines the influences on Nelligan's subjects, images, and forms. Wyczynski's massive *Nelligan, 1879-1941: Biographie* appeared in 1987. Nelligan continues to be analyzed, and postmodern critics are applying structuralist and semiological principles to his poems.

The spirit of Nelligan has pervaded all aspects of Quebec life; the subject of numerous colloquia, conferences, and media exposure of all types from reviews to films, Nelligan's poems have been translated into English, have been re-created in the watercolors of Louis Pelletier, and have inspired pieces by composers. Jean Drapeau's Montreal restaurant, now bankrupt, was called "Le Vaisseau d'or." "Nelligan" was also the title of a ballet choreographed by Ann Ditchburn, and an opera called "Nelligan" was scheduled to open in March 1990 in Montreal. In 1979 Le Prix Emile Nelligan, recognizing outstanding poets, was first awarded, and he has been a recurring figure and symbol in novels and the subject of many poems.

This adulation stems in part from Nelligan's eloquent and timely expression of images and themes that seem to obsess Quebec artists: entrapment, isolation, alienation, exile, and ambivalence toward one's Catholic heritage, so rich but so oppressive. He was the first Quebec poet to portray the state of his soul and to reveal the often-divided images of the self; thus he created a landscape of the soul that still reverberates in the poets of today. Although his own imagination became macabre, his expression of it proved to be a liberating force for those who followed.

Bibliography:

Paul Wyczynski, *Bibliographie descriptive et critique d'Emile Nelligan* (Ottawa: Editions de l'Université d'Ottawa, 1973).

Biography:

Paul Wyczynski, *Nelligan, 1879-1941: Biographie* (Montreal: Fides, 1987).

References:

Gérard Bessette, "Le Complexe parental chez Nelligan," in his *Une Littérature en ébullition* (Montreal: Editions du Jour, 1968);

Bessette, "Les Images chez Nelligan," *L'Action Nationale*, 28 (November 1946): 195-200;

Bessette, *Les Images en poésie canadienne-française* (Montreal: Beauchemin, 1960);

Baudouin Burger, "Nelligan, prince des poètes," *La Barre du Jour* (October-November 1968): 55-57;

Alfred Desrochers, "Nelligan a-t-il subi une influence anglaise?," *Les Carnets Viatoriens*, 16 (July 1951): 187-198;

Jean Ethier-Blais, "A l'ombre de Nelligan," in his *Signets II* (Montreal: Cercle du Livre de France, 1967);

Ethier-Blais, ed., *Nelligan: Poésie rêvée, poésie vécu* (Montreal: Cercle du Livre de France, 1969);

Thérèse Fabi, "L'Effritement de Nelligan," *L'Action nationale*, 65 (February 1976): 426-437;

Pierre de Grandpré, "Emile Nelligan," *Bulletin de la Bibliothèque Nationale du Québec*, 13 (December 1979): 2-6;

Charles ab der Halden, *Nouvelles Etudes de littérature canadienne-française* (Paris: Rudeval, 1907);

Guy Laflèche, "Sémiotique et poétique, 'Les Chats' d'Emile Nelligan," *Voix et Images*, 4 (September 1978): 50-76;

Gilles Marcotte, *Une littérature qui se fait* (Montreal: HMH, 1962), pp. 98-106;

Kathy Mezei, "Emile Nelligan, a Dreamer Passing By," *Canadian Literature*, 87 (Winter 1980): 81-99;

Jacques Michon, "La poétique d'Emile Nelligan," *Revue des sciences humaines*, 45 (January-March 1979): 25-35;

Robidoux and Paul Wyczynski, eds., *Crémazie et Nelligan* (Montreal: Fides, 1981);

R. P. Roland, M. Charland, and Jean-Noël Samson, *Emile Nelligan* (Montreal: Fides, 1968);

Emile J. Talbot, "The Poetics of Reversal: Nelligan's 'Chateaux en Espagne,'" *Quebec Studies*, 8 (Spring 1989): 58-64;

G.-André Vachon, "L'Ere du silence et l'âge de la parole," *Etudes françaises* (special issue on Nelligan), 3 (August 1967): 309-321;

Paul Wyczynski, *Emile Nelligan* (Montreal: Fides, 1968);

Wyczynski, *Emile Nelligan, sources et originalité de son oeuvre* (Ottawa: Editions de l'Université d'Ottawa, 1960);

Wyczynski, *Nelligan et la musique* (Ottawa: Editions de l'Université d'Ottawa, 1969).

Papers:
The Nelligan-Corbeil Collection, at the Bibliothèque Nationale du Québec, Montreal, consists of a scrapbook, a collection of journal articles and poems by Nelligan, and fifty-six manuscript sheets of poems.

Frederick John Niven

(31 March 1878-30 January 1944)

W. H. New
University of British Columbia

BOOKS: *The Lost Cabin Mine* (London & New York: Lane, 1908);

The Island Providence (London & New York: Lane, 1910);

A Wilderness of Monkeys (New York: Lane, 1911; London: Secker, 1911);

Dead Men's Bells: A Romance (London: Secker, 1912);

Above Your Heads (London: Secker, 1913);

Ellen Adair (London: Nash, 1913);

Hands Up! (New York: Lane, 1913; London: Secker, 1913);

The Porcelain Lady (London: Secker, 1913);

Justice of the Peace (London: Nash, 1914; New York: Boni & Liveright, 1923);

The S.S. Glory (London: Heinemann, 1915; New York: Doran, 1916);

Cinderella of Skookum Creek (London: Nash, 1916);

Two Generations (London: Nash, 1916);

Maple Leaf Songs (London: Sidgwick & Jackson, 1917);

Sage-Brush Stories (London: Nash, 1917);

Penny Scot's Treasure (London: Collins, 1918);

The Lady of the Crossing (London & New York: Hodder & Stoughton, 1919);

A Tale that Is Told (Toronto: Collins, 1920; London: Collins, 1920; New York: Doran, 1920);

Treasure Trail (New York: Dodd, Mead, 1923);

The Wolfer (New York: Dodd, Mead, 1923);

A Lover of the Land, and Other Poems (New York: Boni & Liveright, 1925);

Wild Honey (New York: Dodd, Mead, 1927); republished as *Queer Fellows* (London: Lane, 1927);

The Story of Alexander Solkirk (London: Gardner, 1929);

Canada West (London & Toronto: Dent, 1930);

The Three Marys (London: Collins, 1930);

The Paisley Shawl (New York: Dodd, Mead, 1931; London: Collins, 1931);

The Rich Wife (London: Collins, 1932);

Mrs. Barry (New York: Dutton, 1933; London: Collins, 1933);

Triumph (New York: Dutton, 1934; London: Collins, 1934);

The Flying Years (London: Collins, 1935);

Old Soldier (London: Collins, 1936);

Colour in the Canadian Rockies (Toronto: Nelson, 1937);

The Staff at Simson's (London: Collins, 1937);

Coloured Spectacles (London: Collins, 1938);

The Story of Their Days (London: Collins, 1939);

Mine Inheritance (New York: Macmillan, 1940; London: Collins, 1940); abridged and edited by E. C. Woodley (Toronto: Dent, 1945);

Brothers in Arms (London: Collins, 1942);

Under Which King (London: Collins, 1943);

The Transplanted (Toronto: Collins, 1944; London: Collins, 1944).

SELECTED PERIODICAL PUBLICATIONS
UNCOLLECTED: "A Note upon Style," *Bookman*, 51 (June 1920): 434-437;

"The Call of the West," *Canadian Magazine*, 57 (May 1921): 50-53;

Frederick John Niven (photograph courtesy of the Special Collections Division, University of British Columbia)

"The Upper Country," *World Today*, 48 (September 1926): 365-373.

One might think there are two novelists named Frederick John Niven: the Scots writer (after whom the Frederick Niven Literary Award is named) who penned a variety of historical romances and realistic, post-kailyard-school stories, and the Canadian author of westerns, reflective essays, descriptive verses, and a so-called "prairie trilogy." For Niven acquired two quite separate reputations. This was the plight of many an immigrant artist: to be rooted by tradition in one culture, by choice in another, and to be recognized in neither for the total body of work he produced. In Niven's case, nationalist critical practices in Canada and Scotland collided with his varied choice of setting and subject in his work (over thirty-seven books in all), which derived directly from his own itinerant life.

Niven was born on 31 March 1878, the youngest of three children, in Santiago, Chile, where his father was in the British consular service. His contact with South America lent a certain cachet to his life; a passion for the romantic and the New World, fed by the *Deadwood Dick* readings of his childhood, led him to reject many of the conventions of his British upbringing. A mythical Latin American country called Salvador was to become in part the setting of one of his best novels, *Triumph* (1934). But in fact he left Chile, on a clipper ship to Scotland, when he was still five years old. His schooling (at Hutcheson's Grammar School in Glasgow) was Scots; his parents were Calvinist, his mother rigorously so; and though his family, on both Niven and Barclay sides, included librarians and scholars, his father was a Glasgow muslin manufacturer and his mother was keen for him to enter theology or trade. In due course there was a break between the mother and son. He aspired to a career in art; she insisted on practicality; they compromised on a training in commercial design while he was apprenticed to the soft-goods manufacturing business. "I broke a tradition of her family," he writes in his autobiography, *Coloured Spectacles* (1938), adding, "we humoured each other. That's life." While he names his grandfather in this book (John Niven, a librarian), together with his great-grandfather (the Glasgow printer William Waterson Niven) and his maternal grandfather (George Barclay, a doctrinal essayist who was a missionary in Calcutta—where Frederick John Niven's mother was born—and then a Baptist preacher in Irvine), he never mentions his parents (John and Jane Barclay Niven) by name. Niven reconstructed them frequently, however, in the domineering parents depicted in his novels.

A certain lung weakness that required him to move to a drier climate extended the horizons of his life in unanticipated directions. Sent to live with missionary friends of his parents in the Okanagan Valley of British Columbia, Niven quickly recuperated and embarked on a series of adventures—riding the rails, digging ditches, and working in a lumber camp (experiences that are recounted in *Wild Honey*, 1927, and *The S.S. Glory*, 1915)—before he returned home. He published a few sketches of his Canadian experiences in the *Herald* (Glasgow), which led to his being discovered by Isobel Thorne, then fiction editor for Shureys' Publications in London. Three novels followed quickly: *The Lost Cabin Mine* (1908), a western adventure; *The Island Providence* (1910), a period sea story; and *A Wilderness of Monkeys* (1911), a realistic attempt to examine the nature of art, which he wrote while living in Devon. At this time he sent his manuscripts back to his editor, whose daughter, Mary Pauline Thorne-Quelch, would type them. In 1911 Niven and Mary Pauline were married. (She outlived him by twenty-four years, dying in Nelson, British Columbia, in 1968.) They had no children.

For some months during 1912 and 1913 Niven was again traveling alone in Canada, but he was in England during World War I. Rejected for active service, he served in three capacities: as assistant flood controller; in the Ministry of Food; and finally in the War Office under John Buchan, author of *The Thirty-Nine Steps* (1915), and later Lord Tweedsmuir, governor-general of Canada, as associate editor of articles for Allied and neutral powers. All this time he was writing, producing more westerns, such as *Hands Up!* (1913) and the stories in *Above Your Heads* (1913); a Jacobite romance called *Dead Men's Bells* (1912); and the realistic Scots works that were to establish his reputation: *Ellen Adair* and *The Porcelain Lady* (both 1913), *Justice of the Peace* (1914), *Two Generations* (1916), and *A Tale that Is Told* (1920). The latter three in particular brought him a measure of success; they raised issues that would mark his entire work, telling of overpowering mothers and passive fathers, of young men having to break away from their Calvinist homes, of men's bondage to insensitive women, and of the need for an artist to retire to a sanctuary where he might be "alive and free." *Dead Men's Bells* speaks of "the old necromancy in the theologians"; *Two Generations* speaks of Scotland as "that land where Calvin once gloomed"; in *Ellen Adair*, Niven writes of a family over which hangs "the curse of Calvin and a misconceived Christ"; and in *Justice of the Peace*, he distinguishes between the Christ of the New Testament and the "cruel and suburban" Christ that his main characters' relatives invent. In 1916 the critic W. L. George, casting about for Thomas Hardy's successor, listed Niven (along with several others, including James Joyce) as one of the possibilities. Rebecca West wrote in the *New Statesman* in 1920 that Niven wrote "with the rarest wisdom and technical mastery." *Justice of the Peace* was published in the United States in 1923 with laudatory introductions by Hugh Walpole and Christopher Morley. And Niven's career seemed assured. In fact he did live by his writing, but in 1920 his life

took another turn.

That year the Nivens visited Canada for the first time together. Initially he went for a three-month trip, on commission from John Murray Gibbon of the *World's Work* to gather material for more Canadian articles. But the Nivens stayed to settle at Willow Point on Kootenay Lake near Nelson, British Columbia. Literary friends pressured him to return to England, but he had come to reject London as a place of "thrice-breathed air" (*A Lover of the Land,* 1925). An article he published in the *Canadian Magazine* in 1921 spells out his fascination with the landscape: "The Alps are in a pocket of Europe, and seem almost a kind of sleeping partner of Messrs. Cook; but the Rockies run the length of the continent; and are in league with eternity. . . ." Still, the landscape reminded him of his homeland; in his autobiography he notes that "There is a season . . . when . . . Nothing is asked of imagination save to turn the odour of woodsmoke to that of peat. . . . All Scotland is mine then, from forsaken St. Kilda and the roar of the Atlantic on its cliffs to the piping of a piper, on a Saturday night, by the Broomielaw." The concluding twenty-four years of his career give ample evidence of this double loyalty. He produced works praising the freedom and beauty of the New World, not the least of which are *Colour in the Canadian Rockies* (1937; illustrated by Walter J. Phillips), and his autobiography, *Coloured Spectacles.* But Niven also continued to anatomize Scots urban life, and in novels such as *The Three Marys* (1930), *The Paisley Shawl* (1931), *The Rich Wife* (1932), *Mrs. Barry* (1933), *Triumph* (1934), *Old Soldier* (1936), and *The Staff at Simson's* (1937), he exposed the conflicting values of Calvinist mercantile culture. Increasingly he began to question the nature of the sanctuary that would aid an artist and the kind of triumph one would be morally justified to claim. Exerting triumph "over" Calvinism seemed to him a pointless tyranny; he needed to be able to claim a triumph "against" it. Hence he also calls into question his earlier belief that the author's function was not to take part in society but rather to observe it; "detachment" allows a writer, he observes in *Triumph,* to compose only fragments, never a whole work of art.

At the end of his career he was striving for unity, devoting himself to his chosen society, acquiring whatever knowledge about it he could in order adequately to live in it and to write about it. Distinguishing Canada from Scotland was not, he said, a matter of distinguishing a malign from

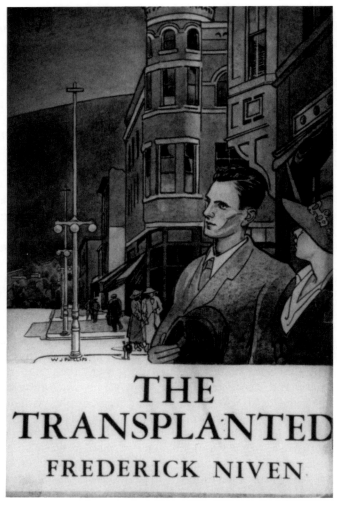

Dust jacket for Niven's last novel (1944), the third part of a trilogy set in the Canadian West

a benign wilderness. Nature was neither; it was only the knowledge that people took to it that made it appear one or the other. And civilization, moreover, was not to be simply identified with a European code of manners. So he climbed in the high country, sought out Indian communities (who knew him as "Apasto": "Talking by Signs"), read history, and wrote in due course a loose trilogy about the changing Canadian West: *The Flying Years* (1935), *Mine Inheritance* (1940), and *The Transplanted* (posthumously published in 1944). While he was revising the last novel, a series of heart attacks struck him; he was taken to a hospital in Vancouver where on 30 January 1944 he died. The connection between the Canadian novels and Niven's experience is clear; they concern the period of the "Clearances," which drew Scots emigrants to Canada, trace patterns of settle-

ment and adaptation, and follow one man's quest for his own valley in British Columbia. It was not precisely his own past, but it was a communal past to which he had access; through his writing he tried to make it available to Canadian culture at large. And in fact *Mine Inheritance* was made available to an even wider audience as a radio play adapted by Ben Lepkin (CBC, January 1959).

Niven perhaps wrote too many formulaic adventures for his reputation. Particularly in the decade following his immigration to Canada he wrote little work of any consequence and mostly wrote to survive. The fact of immigration also distanced him from London literary circles. But that he should have published so regularly during the Depression (*Mrs. Barry* and *Triumph* were both Book Society choices) itself says something about his professional skills; he was one of the most able prose writers in Canada at the time–not by any means experimental, but serious about his craft–and *The Flying Years* finally gave him the Canadian audience he desired. This book was not an isolated accomplishment; nor were the novels set in Canada divorced in theme and attitude from those set in Scotland. For Frederick John Niven, the world was various, but ultimately beautiful, and of a piece.

References:

St. John Adcock, *The Glory that Was Grub Street* (London: Low/New York: Stokes, 1928), pp. 247-257;

Jan de Bruyn, Introduction to *The Flying Years* (Toronto: McClelland & Stewart, 1974);

W. L. George, "Who Is the Man?," in his *A Novelist on Novels* (London: Collins, 1918), pp. 65-66;

Edward A. McCourt, *The Canadian West in Fiction* (Toronto: Ryerson, 1949), pp. 39-54;

Christopher Morley, Second preface to *Justice of the Peace* (New York: Boni & Liveright, 1923), pp. xiii-xviii;

W. H. New, "A Life and Four Landscapes," in his *Articulating West* (Toronto: New Press, 1972), pp. 3-19;

Alexander Reid, " 'A Scottish Chekov?,' " *Scotland's Magazine*, 58 (March 1962): 45-46;

Hugh Walpole, First preface to *Justice of the Peace* (New York: Boni & Liveright, 1923), pp. ix-xii;

Rebecca West, "Notes on Novels," *New Statesman*, 16 (9 October 1920): 22.

Papers:
Most of Niven's papers are at the University of British Columbia Library, Vancouver.

Robert Norwood
(27 March 1874-28 September 1932)

R. Alex Kizuk

University of Saskatchewan

BOOKS: *Driftwood,* by Norwood and Charles Vernon (N.p.: Privately printed, 1898);

His Lady of the Sonnets (Toronto: McClelland, Goodchild & Stewart, 1915; Boston: Sherman, French, 1915);

The Witch of Endor: A Tragedy (Toronto: McClelland, Goodchild & Stewart, 1916; New York: Doran, 1916);

The Piper and the Reed (Toronto: McClelland, Goodchild & Stewart, 1917; New York: Doran, 1917);

The Modernists (Toronto: McClelland, Goodchild & Stewart, 1918; New York: Doran, 1918);

The Man of Kerioth (New York: Doran, 1919);

Bill Boram (New York: Doran, 1921);

Mother and Son (New York: Doran, 1925);

The Heresy of Antioch: An Interpretation (Garden City, N.Y.: Doubleday, Doran, 1928);

The Steep Ascent: Noontide Meditations (New York & London: Scribners, 1928);

The Man Who Dared to Be God: A Story of Jesus (New York & London: Scribners, 1929);

His Glorious Body (New York & London: Scribners, 1930);

Issa (New York & London: Scribners, 1931);

Increasing Christhood (New York & London: Scribners, 1932);

The Hiding God: Divinity in Man (New York & London: Scribners, 1933).

OTHER: Charles Mair, *Tecumseh, a Drama, and Canadian Poems,* introduction by Norwood (Toronto: Radisson Society of Canada, 1926).

Robert Winkworth Norwood, a minister and poet, was born in New Ross, Lunenberg County, Nova Scotia, on 27 March 1874, the son of the Reverend Joseph and Edith Harding Norwood. The father, who had run away from his home in Boston at the age of eight and gone to sea, was a soldier in the American Civil War and a missionary to West Africa before he became rector of Christ Church in New Ross, then a tiny village surrounded by forest. The son inherited both his father's adventurous spirit and clerical calling. He was educated at Coaticook Academy and Bishop's College in Quebec, King's College in Nova Scotia, and Columbia University. Norwood was encouraged in poetry by his professor of English at King's, Charles G. D. Roberts, and given the freedom of Roberts's home and library. Upon graduation from King's, Norwood and his roommate, Charles Vernon, published a student chapbook of verses, *Driftwood,* in 1898 (a copy is available in the Logan Collection at Acadia University, Wolfville, Nova Scotia). He was ordained in the same year in Halifax and was highly regarded by the Cape Breton parishioners of his first charge. He married Ethel McKeen while in Cape Breton and went on to larger parishes in Quebec; London, Ontario; and, in 1917, Philadelphia, at which time he became an American citizen. From 1925 until his sudden death in 1932, Norwood enjoyed affluence and prestige as the sixth rector of New York City's St. Bartholomew's Church.

In 1915 Norwood set out to produce annual books of verse as texts for the message of his ministry. The first, *His Lady of the Sonnets* (1915), was written, along with his first verse play, *The Witch of Endor: A Tragedy* (1916), during his ministry at Cronyn Memorial Church in London, Ontario. His second religious closet drama, *The Man of Kerioth* (1919), as well as an undistinguished collection of poems, *The Piper and the Reed* (1917), and a sustained tribute to Robert Browning, *The Modernists* (1918), were all written for his growing following in Philadelphia. *Bill Boram* (1921), however, is a long, powerful narrative poem set in the Maritime villages that he knew in his youth. *Mother and Son* (1925) was inspired by the death of his only son. Aside from biographical appreciations by his friends A. D. Watson and Elsie Pomeroy, and blustery assessments in early-twentieth-century Canadian criticism, Norwood's poetry has largely been forgotten. This is regrettable, especially since *Issa* (1931),

Robert Norwood, circa 1927 (photograph by the author's nephew Robert Norwood; Public Archives of Nova Scotia)

his last poetic work, is one of the most interesting book-length poems in Canadian literature.

Norwood's poetry is not adventurous in terms of prosodic experimentation; his lyrics and blank verse are unremarkable. His experiments with the sequential long poem and narrative verse, however, shear away from the cloying conventionality of his time. In *His Lady of the Sonnets* Norwood proposes a rule of ethical conduct based on physical love. The female and male personae of the title sequence are multiple figures, reincarnated lovers evolving toward spiritual love. The sequence is unified by a kiss capable of a miracle: the transformation of void and chaos into perfection and atonement within the mystical unity of God so that "Joy and constant Certainty appear." In the sequences and dramatic monologues that follow, Norwood pursues the theme

of love between man and woman as a mutual sacrifice akin to Christ's. As a Christian verse text, the book preaches the unity of "One God,/One Law, one Hope, one Faith, and One Desire." This one desire was supposedly the vehicle of salvation for all men throughout history who have accepted love's absolute authority regarding the perfection of the human spirit. The book closes with a miscellany of songs and sonnets that reprise the themes of reincarnation and love as an expression of the divinity of the Savior.

Norwood's two verse dramas and the collection of sentimental lyrics *The Piper and the Reed* expand on the theme of love as modern man's answer to a lack of confidence in traditional methods of achieving certainty in salvation. These works also preach that one must not bind society and society's voice, poetry, to conventional rules of behavior and practice.

The nineteen personae of the dramatic monologues in *The Modernists* range from "The Cave Man" to "Darwin" and the "Voice of the Twentieth Century." The book traces the evolution of human perfection in such a way as to make sense of life as his readers knew it in 1921. In this grand design the modern common man is a king. The Second Coming will be synonymous with an age of democratic humanitarianism, once Man and the Word and Desire and the Law of God are one. The book's appeal lies in its personal, unaffected tone of voice. Like *His Lady of the Sonnets, The Modernists* attempts to bring order to a jumble of abstract and contradictory images and motifs in discursive fashion. In *Bill Boram*, however, Norwood's growing reliance on speech rhythms strikes a truly original note. This work surpasses his earlier rewritings of classical and biblical texts, producing a narrative of confidence and certainty for his parishioners. The poem presents human characters as personifications of Doubt and Certainty in a dialogue that achieves, on the one hand, a demonstration of how ordinary men and women make sense of their time and place and, on the other, a sincere and rigorously worked out treatise on the "One Desire." As a whole the poem is a composition of example and lesson, but the voice that manifests Bill Boram's blasphemy, atheism, and drunkenness neither denies nor resolves the essential incoherence of life that leads to Doubt. On the contrary, it invites the reader to respond to that ambiguity with an act of faith sustained by compassion and love.

Working toward a simpler, more colloquial poetic ministry in *Bill Boram*, Norwood questions the language of religious authority—"Them fables that made the Bible a poor book"—as well as conventional diction and prosody. The tale ends in comedy, with the community's laughter more convincing as an ending than the solemn moralizing tagged onto the close. Norwood was unable to develop this comic aspect of his writing, however. *Mother and Son* records his search for consolation following the death of his son. In two long poems, "The Mother of Cain" and "The Mother of Christ," Norwood shows that language cannot reconcile modernity and tradition, doubt and certainty, or the plain language of Cain and the stately language of the ode. Norwood strove to heal these ruptures in *Issa*, a spiritual autobiography of some eighteen hundred lines divided into seven cantos.

Issa is an unusual early-twentieth-century work, somewhat Wordsworthian as a study of local piety and the growth of a poet's mind, somewhat Poundian in its syncretism and the economy of its thematic architecture. Norwood uses his own life as an exemplum to teach the power of human love to bring order and meaning to a life such as his. The poem spins "Webbed images of life/In such a dance of words/That he who reads/May feel the flight of birds." Thousands of images of disparate things, fragments of life, faith, and homeland, well up through the poet's voice in a dialogue between himself and Issa, or Christ, the Word and the Son. Memories of localities, friends, relatives, and loved ones jostle against one another amidst everyday objects and mythological and literary allusions. "Descend, you hierarchies, be made man!" cries Issa. As in *His Lady of the Sonnets*, the beloved is a multiple figure whose fragments are rather like a mobile revolving around "one law only—love!"

Norwood's poetry, while not highly regarded today, acted as a part of Canada's literary bridge from nineteenth-century romanticism to twentieth-century modernism. He took the devout religion inherent in his own and his country's past and fused it with his particular form of the humanism of the modern age, thus creating an interesting blend of metaphysical and physical.

Biographies:
Albert Durrant Watson, *Robert Norwood* (Toronto: Ryerson, 1923);

Elsie M. Pomeroy, "Robert Norwood," in *Leading Canadian Poets*, edited by W. P. Percival (Toronto: Ryerson, 1948), pp. 158-167.

References:
R. Alex Kizuk, "Religion, Place, and Self in Early Twentieth-Century Canadian Poetry: Robert Norwood's Poetry," *Canadian Literature*, 115 (Winter 1987): 66-77;

John Daniel Logan and Donald G. French, *Highways of Canadian Literature: A Synoptic Introduction to the Literary History of Canada (English) from 1790-1924* (Toronto: McClelland & Stewart, 1924), pp. 211-212, 315-319;

Lorne Pierce, *Outline of Canadian Literature French and English* (Toronto: Ryerson, 1927), pp. 117-118;

Charles G. D. Roberts, "The Poetry of Robert Norwood," in *Issa* (New York: Scribners, 1931), pp. ix-xiv.

Martha Ostenso
(17 September 1900 - 24 November 1963)

Anthony John Harding
University of Saskatchewan

BOOKS: *A Far Land: Poems by Martha Ostenso* (New York: Seltzer, 1924);

Wild Geese (Toronto: McClelland & Stewart, 1925; New York: Dodd, Mead, 1925); republished as *The Passionate Flight* (London: Hodder & Stoughton, 1925);

The Dark Dawn (New York: Dodd, Mead, 1926; London: Hodder & Stoughton, 1927);

The Mad Carews (New York: Dodd, Mead, 1927; London: Heinemann, 1928);

The Young May Moon (New York: Dodd, Mead, 1929; London: Butterworth, 1930);

The Waters Under the Earth (New York: Dodd, Mead, 1930; London: Butterworth, 1931);

Prologue to Love (New York: Dodd, Mead, 1932);

There's Always Another Year (Toronto: McClelland & Stewart, 1933; New York: Dodd, Mead, 1933);

The White Reef (New York: Dodd, Mead, 1934; Toronto: McClelland & Stewart, 1935; London: Cassell, 1935);

The Stone Field (Toronto: McClelland & Stewart, 1937; New York: Dodd, Mead, 1937);

The Mandrake Root (New York: Dodd, Mead, 1938);

Love Passed This Way (New York: Dodd, Mead, 1942);

O River, Remember! (New York: Dodd, Mead, 1943; London: Long, 1945);

And They Shall Walk: The Life Story of Sister Elizabeth Kenny, by Ostenso and Kenny (New York: Dodd, Mead, 1943);

Milk Route (New York: Dodd, Mead, 1948);

The Sunset Tree (New York: Dodd, Mead, 1949; London: Long, 1951);

A Man Had Tall Sons (New York: Dodd, Mead, 1958).

Wild Geese (1925), Martha Ostenso's first and best novel, is an unsparing depiction of life in a farming community in northern Manitoba. With Frederick Philip Grove's *Settlers of the Marsh* (1925) and Robert J. C. Stead's *Grain* (1926), it marked an epoch in Canadian fiction, the develop-ment of a new note of realism suited to the por-trayal of the harsh climate and isolated communi-ties of western Canada in its immediate post-pioneer period. At first, however, the book was scarcely noticed in Canada, and after 1929 Ostenso lived in the United States. Even so, two of her later novels—*The Young May Moon* (1929) and *Prologue to Love* (1932)—are set in Canada and demonstrate her continued interest in Cana-dian subjects.

Ostenso was born to Sigurd Brigt and Lena Tungeland Ostenso at the home of her maternal grandparents in the mountain village of Hauke-land, Norway, on 17 September 1900. Her family immigrated to America when Martha was two years old, and she spent her childhood in various small towns in Minnesota and South Dakota. The *Minneapolis Journal* published some of her juve-nile work on its children's pages. Her father was a restless, ambitious man, and when Martha was fifteen he moved again, taking his family north to the farmlands of Manitoba. Ostenso attended high school in Brandon and entered the Univer-sity of Manitoba in 1918. There she met Douglas Leader Durkin, her close associate for the whole of her writing career. She was prevented from marrying him for many years because his first wife would not consent to a divorce, but the mar-riage eventually took place on 16 December 1944.

Ostenso came to know the remote and chal-lenging Interlake area of northern Manitoba—the setting for *Wild Geese*—by spending a year teach-ing there. She later remarked, however, that it took her grim experience of life in New York's Lower East Side in the early 1920s to make her re-alize the true value of the farm country. From 1921 to 1922 she studied the techniques of fic-tion writing at Columbia University. She was also employed by the Bureau of Charities in Brooklyn as a social worker. Valuable as these experiences may have been for her, her imagination was not deeply affected by New York: she remained all her life essentially a western writer, selecting her

Dust jacket for Ostenso's 1943 novel, a family saga spanning more than seventy years

scenes from the homesteads, settlements, and small towns of Minnesota, Manitoba, the Dakotas, and Wisconsin.

A Far Land: Poems by Martha Ostenso (1924), her only book of poetry, clearly shows her preference for rural themes. The poems have some merit but are frequently marred by sentimentality or awkwardness. "In Time of First Rain," "Before Storm," and "The Meadow" exemplify a fondness for the "touching" or "charming" in nature, which also surfaces on occasion in her prose work. More successful in their kind are the poems for children: these have a playfulness that rings truer than the vague hints at some dark knowledge in "Lexicon" and "So I Say."

With a considerable amount of technical assistance from Durkin, Ostenso completed *Wild Geese* and entered it in 1925 for a competition sponsored by the *Pictorial Review*, Dodd, Mead and Company, and Famous Players-Lasky Corporation. *Wild Geese* beat more than thirteen hundred other entries for the first prize of $13,500 and was published in October 1925.

Wild Geese tells of the battle of wills between Judith Gare, a strong and passionate young wom-

an, and her autocratic father, Caleb. Caleb grows rye and flax and raises cattle, sheep, and chickens. To save the expense of a hired man he is determined to keep Judith and his three other children on the farm to work for him. All his own energies are devoted to enlarging his property by annexing the more fertile land around the township of Oeland. He does not shrink from blackmailing and browbeating his neighbors to attain this end, which obsesses him. His wife, Amelia, is kept compliant to his wishes by his threat to disclose the fact that before she married him, she bore an illegitimate son to another man. The children have learned not to resist his commands, because they see that whenever they do stand up to him their mother is made to suffer for it; but Judith's fierce love for a neighboring widow's son, Sven Sandbo, forces her to rebel. Judith's longing for sexual and spiritual fulfillment is linked with the dominant motif of the novel, the "endless quest" of the wild geese as they fly over Oeland during each spring and fall migration.

A friend to Judith, and the focus of the narrative for much of the novel, is Lind Archer, a young schoolteacher who boards with the Gares.

She tries to draw Judith out and encourages her to wear more feminine clothes and wash with perfumed soap. Lind is attracted to Mark Jordan, an apprentice architect who is spending some time in the country for the sake of his health, but she does not know that Mark is the illegitimate son of Amelia Gare.

Historians of Canadian literature generally classify *Wild Geese* under the heading of "western realism," but one needs to define realism rather broadly in order to encompass all the techniques used in the book. Ostenso adopts a blend of realism and romance, with some touches of symbolism and even of myth and folktale. Clara Thomas has pointed out that Caleb Gare is actually "a great realization of the Grotesque" along the lines of Nathaniel Hawthorne's Roger Chillingworth in *The Scarlet Letter* (1850). Dick Harrison, in *Unnamed Country: The Struggle for a Canadian Prairie Fiction* (1977), agrees that Caleb has "the larger-than-life dimensions of a romantic villain" and suggests that his name is meant to evoke the Old Testament figure who urged Moses to seize the land of Canaan by force.

This patriarchal compulsion to possess the land and impose one's will on it is set in opposition to Judith's more instinctual, secretive, and almost religious love of the earth. Feminist critics such as Joanne Hedenstrom have rightly admired Ostenso's heroine for being so radically unlike the conventional heroines of romantic fiction, but it would be a mistake to overlook the elements of romance and myth that contribute to her character and develop Ostenso's theme. Lind Archer finds herself thinking of Judith as resembling "some fabled animal—a centauress, perhaps," and as if to reinforce this perception, while Caleb is at church one Sunday, Lind watches Judith expertly breaking a colt. Later, needing to escape from the oppressive Gare household for a time, Judith seeks out a ravine where she lies naked on the damp ground; returning to the farm, she stops to admire two young bulls prancing.

These scenes suggest that Judith possesses besides physical strength and sexuality some atavistic female understanding of the earth and its mysteries that is even more ancient than Caleb's patriarchal urge to dominate and exploit it. David Arnason has suggested that like other prairie realists Ostenso saw in the Darwinian theory of evolution a possible model for human progress. Judith's strength, in this view, links her with the future of the race, while Caleb's autocratic ha-

tred of the earth and narrow religious views indicate that he belongs to a vanishing class.

There is, however, a conflict within Judith herself, precipitated by the arrival of Lind, for Judith envies Lind's mastery of the trappings of civilized life—music, literature, and conversation (things for which Caleb has no time, of course). Though Judith admires Lind's city-bred ways, and eventually "escapes" to the city herself, it is impossible not to feel that a woman of her earthy vitality would soon wilt in an urban environment. Nevertheless, Judith Gare is a well-drawn character and is in no sense dwarfed by her father, who is himself a massive creation.

Lind's part in the novel is less convincing. At first it seems that she is to be used as observer of the main action, but she has no part in several important scenes, and her relationship with Mark is not pursued with any degree of interest. Mark himself represents intellect and culture, in opposition to the rough-hewn Caleb, but his intellect shows itself only in such pedantic pronouncements as "The austerity of nature reduces the outward expression in life. . . . We are, after all, only the mirror of our environment." Numerous lesser characters are skillfully etched in, but given nothing in particular to do.

These are not serious flaws, however, and *Wild Geese* remains a major achievement. It took two decades or more for this achievement to be recognized in Canada. In 1926, W. E. MacLellan spoke up for Ostenso in the *Dalhousie Review*, comparing her book favorably with Louis Hémon's *Maria Chapdelaine* (1916) and even invoking (rather inappropriately) Emile Zola's *La Terre* (1887). It was not until 1946, though, that *Wild Geese* was given its deserved place in the tradition of Canadian literature (by Clara Thomas in her *Canadian Novelists 1920-1945*).

The success that *Wild Geese* enjoyed in the United States launched Ostenso and Durkin on their joint career as professional writers. The novels published under Ostenso's name were almost all collaborations: Durkin would provide a plot outline based on an idea of Ostenso's, Ostenso would then write a draft of the book, and Durkin would edit it. This system produced a number of good novels, none of them (with the possible exception of *The Young May Moon*) as original as *Wild Geese*; some of them are merely respectable examples of light romantic fiction—for example, *Prologue to Love* and *The Mad Carews* (1927); but a few are deserving of more critical attention than has yet been paid to them.

The Dark Dawn (1926), like *The Mandrake Root* (1938), centers on a woman's dynastic ambitions. A strong but sexually inexperienced young man, Lucian Dorrit, is seduced by Hattie Murker, a local beauty who has inherited her dead father's ambitious nature along with his farm and neighboring quarry. To the dismay of his family, Lucian marries Hattie. He finds that the marriage also estranges him from his old friend Mons Torson, a homesteader and hunter. As Lucian works Hattie's land and starts to build the stone house she wants, he feels increasingly trapped and turns for companionship to the young, high-spirited Karen Strand; but the worst is yet to come. During a quarrel with Bert, Hattie's simpleminded younger brother, Lucian learns that Mons and Hattie were once lovers, and that Hattie married Lucian to get even with Mons, who had spurned her. Lucian tells Hattie he will no longer sleep with her; she is enraged and storms out. Later Lucian finds her lying in the quarry, badly injured. As she recuperates, Mons, still infatuated with Hattie despite his refusal to marry her, bursts in to tell her they have always loved each other. Hattie's weakened heart cannot stand this shock, and she dies in Mons's arms.

The depiction of Hattie Murker, the strong-willed, sensual woman, bears comparison with that of Judith Gare, although Hattie's energy is of a much more sinister kind. Mons and Karen are also well drawn, and Karen brings some sunlight into what might otherwise be a rather morbid tale of sexual obsession. There is a major flaw in the book, however, in that Lucian does not have enough depth to justify the amount of attention readers are forced to pay to him. His young man's idealism is crushed out of him by Hattie's forceful personality, and little remains but a sullen sense of injustice. The philosophical conversations between the town's doctor and schoolteacher, intended to provide a detached perspective on Lucian's fate, are pretentious and redundant.

Clara Thomas (in her 1973 article "Martha Ostenso's Trial of Strength") finds the *The Young May Moon*, Ostenso's fourth novel, superior to *Wild Geese* in "tightness of structure and total artistic consistency." If this is so, it is because Ostenso once more deals with the issue she knows best, a woman's struggle for independence and her need to accept her own sexuality without being dominated by it. In the novel Marcia Vorse marries Rolf Gunther and goes to live with him and

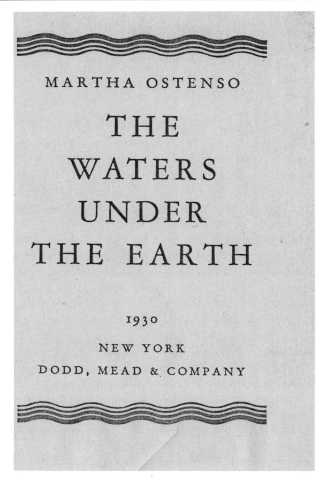

MARTHA OSTENSO

THE
WATERS
UNDER
THE EARTH

1930

NEW YORK
DODD, MEAD & COMPANY

Title page for Ostenso's 1930 novel, which like several of her other novels, features a self-righteous father

his puritanical Baptist mother, Dorcas, in the small town of Amaranth, Manitoba. Inevitably there is a clash of wills between the two women, and Rolf, forced out of the house one night, is later discovered drowned. Marcia stays on with Dorcas as a kind of penance and bears Rolf's child. She cannot withstand the oppressive, inquisitorial atmosphere of Amaranth, however, and moves out of town to an old abandoned house where she can be alone with her child. Here a bleak future stretches before her–she can see herself becoming a mad old recluse. Paul Brulé, a doctor whose wife has left him, helps Marcia to face her situation by telling her that loneliness and despair are common features of human existence. She comes to accept that the petty puritanism of Amaranth, and what she recognizes as the ever-present danger of becoming suffocated by love and concern, are conditions of existence that cannot be altered, and the book ends with her return to the town.

There is much less untidiness in the deployment of characters here than in *The Dark Dawn*. Marcia and Paul each have a depth suited to their roles in the story, and Marcia's courage throughout what Thomas calls her "trials of strength" quite outweighs the occasional overwriting in which Ostenso indulges.

The Waters Under the Earth (1930), which traces the usually unsuccessful attempts of seven young people to escape the despotism of their self-righteous father, and *O River, Remember!* (1943), an ambitious family saga spanning the period from 1870 to 1941, are not without merit. But *The Mandrake Root*, which returns to the theme of the strong-willed woman who comes close to destroying a man, has more thematic coherence. Eric Stene, the man in question, is of interest in his own right. He is one of Ostenso's more successful attempts at the intellectual male: a disillusioned university teacher who is torn between his desire to cultivate the life of the mind and his instinctual response to the sexuality of Lydie Clarence, wife of a devout, idealistic farmer, Andrew Clarence, to whom Eric rents the prairie farm he has inherited. Eric also finds himself drawn into the political conflict that besets the town, for this is the Depression, and Andrew's well-meaning efforts to relieve the poverty of the unemployed townspeople are resented and violently rejected. This promising political theme is largely undeveloped, however. Andrew, having found that Lydie is carrying Eric's child, kills himself. Lydie, now that she has the child she wanted, refuses Eric's offer of marriage, and he returns, broken, to the city. The novel recaptures some of the vitality of *Wild Geese*, and the two chief characters—Eric and Lydie—do win some measure of self-knowledge, but the dominant feeling upon finishing the book is still one of missed opportunities.

After 1929 Ostenso lived exclusively in the United States, first in New Jersey, then in St. Louis Park, a suburb of Minneapolis, and lastly in Brainerd, in the lake country of northern Minnesota. In 1943 Ostenso published a book about the experiences of Sister Elizabeth Kenny, an Australian nurse who worked with victims of polio. The book, written in collaboration with Kenny, was made into a motion picture, *The Sister Kenny Story* (1946), with Rosalind Russell playing the title role.

Ostenso and Durkin's income now enabled them to live stylishly; Ostenso's novels were translated into German, Norwegian, Polish, and other European languages; and she also acquired some fame in Scandinavia as a painter. While it would be sentimental to blame this more comfortable life for any real or supposed lack of authenticity in the later books, it remains true that the best of them still lack the power of *Wild Geese* and *The Young May Moon*. Ostenso's last book, *A Man Had Tall Sons* (1958), is another story of conflict between the members of a farming family. It starts several promising plots, but finishes only one of them.

On 22 November 1963 Ostenso arrived with her husband in Seattle, intending to visit Durkin's sons, Roy Durkin of Seattle and Stanley Durkin of Tacoma. Ostenso was taken ill and died in a local hospital two days later.

Despite the plea Thomas puts forward on behalf of *The Young May Moon*, it is likely that *Wild Geese* will remain the only novel of Martha Ostenso's to be widely known. This is regrettable because in her best work she displays a considerable understanding of the social and economic structure of small western towns, an unusual grasp of the ways in which relationships develop, and a bleak, Ibsen-like vision of human life that is tempered by a real sympathy for children and their imaginative world. In some of her more diffuse books a good novella lies buried, and her failure to see this can perhaps be attributed partly to Durkin's plot outlines and partly to the demands of her publishers and the reading public. At the very least Ostenso's strong-willed women—Judith Gare, Hattie Murker, Marcia Vorse, and Lydie Clarence, among others—deserve to be recognized as honorable precursors of the strong, questing women created by Margaret Laurence, Alice Munro, and Margaret Atwood.

References:

David Arnason, "The Development of Prairie Realism: Robert J. C. Stead, Douglas Durkin, Martha Ostenso and Frederick Philip Grove," Ph.D. dissertation, University of New Brunswick, 1980;

Arnason, Letter to author, 23 April 1981;

Nancy W. Fraser, "The Development of Realism in Canadian Literature during the 1920s," *Dalhousie Review*, 57 (Summer 1977): 287-299;

Dick Harrison, *Unnamed Country: The Struggle for a Canadian Prairie Fiction* (Edmonton: University of Alberta Press, 1977);

Joanne Hedenstrom, "Puzzled Patriarchs and Free Women: Patterns in the Canadian Novel," *Atlantis*, 4, no. 1 (1978): 2-9;

M. G. Hesse, "The Endless Quest: Dreams and Aspirations in Martha Ostenso's *Wild Geese*," *Journal of Popular Culture*, 15, no. 3 (1981): 47-52;

Susan Jackel, "The House on the Prairies," *Canadian Literature*, 42 (Autumn 1969): 46-55;

W. J. Keith, "The Death of Caleb Gare," *Studies in Canadian Literature*, 3 (Summer 1978): 274-276;

Carlyle King, Introduction to *Wild Geese* (Toronto: McClelland & Stewart, 1961), pp. v-x;

Joy Kuropatwa, Letter to author, 21 May 1981;

Robert G. Lawrence, "The Geography of Martha Ostenso's *Wild Geese*," *Journal of Canadian Fiction*, 16 (1975): 108-114;

W. E. MacLellan, "Real 'Canadian Literature,'" *Dalhousie Review*, 6 (October 1926): 18-23;

"Martha Ostenso, Novelist, Dies; Won an Award for 'Wild Geese,'" *New York Times*, 26 November 1963, p. 37;

S. G. Mullins, "Some Remarks on Theme in Martha Ostenso's *Wild Geese*," *Culture*, 23 (December 1962): 359-362;

Grant Overton, *The Women Who Make Our Novels*, revised edition (New York: Dodd, Mead, 1931), pp. 245-252;

Candace Savage, *Foremothers* (Saskatoon, Sask.: Privately printed, 1975), pp. 35-37;

Clara Thomas, *Canadian Novelists 1920-1945* (Toronto: Longmans, 1946), p. 95;

Thomas, "Martha Ostenso's Trial of Strength," in *Writers of the Prairies*, edited by Donald G. Stephens (Vancouver: University of British Columbia Press, 1973), pp. 39-50.

Marjorie Pickthall

(14 September 1883-19 April 1922)

Donald A. Precosky
College of New Caledonia

BOOKS: *Dick's Desertion: A Boy's Adventures in Canadian Forests; A Tale of the Early Settlement of Ontario* (Toronto: Musson, 1905; London: Partridge, 1905);

The Straight Road (Toronto: Musson, 1906; London: Partridge, 1909);

Billy's Hero; or, The Valley of Gold (Toronto: Musson, 1908; London: Partridge, 1908);

The Drift of Pinions (Montreal: University Magazine, 1913; London: Lane, 1913); revised and enlarged as *The Lamp of Poor Souls, and Other Poems* (London & New York: Lane, 1916; Toronto: Gundy, 1917);

Little Hearts (London: Methuen, 1915; Toronto: McClelland & Stewart, 1926);

The Bridge: A Story of the Great Lakes (London: Hodder & Stoughton, 1922; New York: Century, 1922);

The Wood Carver's Wife and Later Poems (Toronto: McClelland & Stewart, 1922);

Angels' Shoes and Other Stories (London: Hodder & Stoughton, 1923);

Little Songs: A Book of Poems (Toronto: McClelland & Stewart, 1925);

Complete Poems of Marjorie Pickthall, edited by Arthur C. Pickthall (Toronto: McClelland & Stewart, 1927);

Selected Poems, edited by Lorne Pierce (Toronto: McClelland & Stewart, 1957).

Marjorie Pickthall (Victoria University Library)

Probably no other Canadian writer has suffered such a plunge in reputation as Marjorie Pickthall. Once she was thought to be the best Canadian poet of her generation. Now her work, except for two or three anthologized pieces, goes unread. The fact is that her initial popularity was based upon extraliterary criteria. Her rejection of modernism in style and attitude made her the darling of conservative Canadian critics. She was also viewed as a genteel alternative to Robert Service and Tom MacInnes, who were widely read by the general public but abhorred by many of the literati of the day. But she has fallen victim to time. Service has retained a body of devoted readers, which Pickthall has not, and modernism has replaced nineteenth-century romantic verse.

Marjorie Lowry Christie Pickthall was born on 14 September 1883 in Gunnersby, Middlesex, England. When she was six her family moved to Toronto, where she grew up. She was a precocious child and in her teens wrote some surprisingly well-crafted stories and poems. In 1898, at the age of fifteen, Pickthall sold her first story, "Two Ears," to the *Toronto Globe*.

Pickthall's career began in earnest when she was in her early twenties. Between 1905 and 1908 she published three novels: *Dick's Desertion: A Boy's Adventures in Canadian Forests; A Tale of the Early Settlement of Ontario* (1905), *The Straight Road* (1906), and *Billy's Hero; or, The Valley of Gold* (1908). All three appeared first as magazine serials, and they were all juvenile tales of adventure in frontier areas where good, embodied in a male hero, did battle with evil and always won.

In the decade from 1913 to 1922 Pickthall produced five books: *The Drift of Pinions* (1913), her first book of verse; *Little Hearts* (1915), a historical romance set in eighteenth-century England; *The Lamp of Poor Souls, and Other Poems* (1916), a revised and enlarged version of *The Drift of Pinions*; *The Bridge: A Story of the Great Lakes* (1922), a novel; and *The Wood Carver's Wife and Later Poems* (1922). It may be that overwork contributed to her death at the age of thirty-eight on 19 April 1922 in Vancouver.

It is a sad irony that the two books that made Pickthall's reputation appeared posthumously. *Angels' Shoes and Other Stories* (1923) brings together many of her short stories. The book presents melodramatic adventures involving earthquakes, blizzards, love, mining, and outlaws in a variety of settings, including Canada, Italy, France, and Africa. The stories portray toughs or desperate men, but since Pickthall knew virtually nothing of outlaws or prospectors, her tales often lack a sense of reality.

The second famous book is her *Complete Poems* (1927). The verses are gentle, dreamy, and musical yet somehow empty. She has nothing to say but she says it harmoniously. The world of her poetry, with its ivory towers, Persian lovers, and "amber bars" of sunlight, is not drawn from life but from her reading of romantic literature.

While Marjorie Pickthall had a gentle and refined sensibility and was well skilled in traditional poetic technique, her verse now seems dated. Her narratives hold historical interest however, and recent feminist criticism has begun to examine her career in different ways. Diana M. A. Relke, for example, probes the predicament Pickthall faced as a female writer, writing against (yet being judged by) the conventional male models of romanticism. Further criticism may well follow this lead, focusing more on the late feminist observations in *The Wood Carver's Wife* than on the early lyrics of nature.

References:

Desmond Pacey, "The Poems of Marjorie Pickthall," in his *Essays in Canadian Criticism, 1938-1968* (Toronto: Ryerson, 1969);

Lorne Pierce, *Marjorie Pickthall: A Book of Remembrance* (Toronto: Ryerson, 1925);

Diana M. A. Relke, "Demeter's Daughter: Marjorie Pickthall and the Quest for Poetic Identity," *Canadian Literature*, 115 (Winter 1987): 28-43.

Papers:

The Marjorie Pickthall Collection is held at the E. J. Pratt Library, Victoria University, Toronto.

E. J. Pratt

(4 February 1882-26 April 1964)

Michael Darling
University of Western Ontario

BOOKS: *Studies in Pauline Eschatology, and Its Background* (Toronto: Briggs, 1917);

Rachel: A Sea Story of Newfoundland in Verse (New York: Privately printed, 1917);

Newfoundland Verse (Toronto: Ryerson, 1923);

The Witches' Brew (London: Selwyn & Blount, 1925; Toronto: Macmillan, 1926);

Titans (Toronto: Macmillan, 1926);

The Iron Door: An Ode (Toronto: Macmillan, 1927);

The Roosevelt and the Antinoe (New York: Macmillan, 1930);

Verses of the Sea (Toronto: Macmillan, 1930);

Many Moods (Toronto: Macmillan, 1932);

The Titanic (Toronto: Macmillan, 1935);

The Fable of the Goats and Other Poems (Toronto: Macmillan, 1937);

Brébeuf and His Brethren (Toronto: Macmillan, 1940); republished as *Brébeuf and His Brethren (the North American Martyrs)* (Detroit: Basilian, 1942);

Dunkirk (Toronto: Macmillan, 1941);

Still Life and Other Verse (Toronto: Macmillan, 1943);

Collected Poems (Toronto: Macmillan, 1944; New York: Knopf, 1945); enlarged edition, edited by Northrop Frye (Toronto: Macmillan, 1958);

They Are Returning (Toronto: Macmillan, 1945);

Behind the Log (Toronto: Macmillan, 1947);

Ten Selected Poems, with Notes (Toronto: Macmillan, 1947);

Towards the Last Spike: A Verse-Panorama of the Struggle to Build the First Transcontinental from the Time of the Proposed Terms of Union with British Columbia, 1870, to the Hammering of the Last Spike in the Eagle Pass, 1885 (Toronto: Macmillan, 1952);

Here the Tides Flow, edited by D. G. Pitt (Toronto: Macmillan, 1962);

Selected Poems of E. J. Pratt, edited by Peter Buitenhuis (Toronto: Macmillan, 1968);

E. J. Pratt (photograph courtesy of his daughter, Claire Pratt)

E. J. Pratt: On His Life and Poetry, edited by Susan Gingell (Toronto & Buffalo: University of Toronto Press, 1983);

E. J. Pratt: Complete Poems, 2 volumes, edited by Sandra Djwa and R. G. Moyles (Toronto & Buffalo: University of Toronto Press, 1989).

OTHER: Thomas Hardy, *Under the Greenwood Tree*, edited by Pratt (Toronto: Macmillan, 1937);

Heroic Tales in Verse, edited, with a preface and notes, by Pratt (Toronto: Macmillan, 1941);

Poems for Upper School, edited, with notes and questions, by Pratt (Toronto: Macmillan, 1953).

Few poets can be said to occupy a more secure position in the literary history of their countries than that held by E. J. Pratt. Often hailed in his own lifetime as Canada's unofficial poet laureate, Pratt has become, since his death in 1964, the subject of a thriving critical industry. Recent critics have stressed Pratt's significant role in the development of modernism in Canada and have taken note of the subtlety and complexity of his verse and the wide range of his learning, qualities rarely observed by his contemporaries. Though Pratt's image patterns draw heavily upon his intimate knowledge of the sea and reflect his Newfoundland heritage, his themes are not rooted in solely local concerns but reach out to embrace the struggles of men everywhere and at all times.

Edwin John ("Ned") Pratt was born on 4 February 1882 in the small fishing village of Western Bay, Newfoundland. His father, the Reverend John Pratt, was a Methodist preacher, and his mother, the former Fanny Pitts Knight, was the daughter of a sea captain. The sea deeply influenced Pratt, but it was many years before he was to give poetic expression to his formative experiences. He went to school in the outport villages ministered to by his father and then was apprenticed to a draper in St. John's from 1896 to 1898. Following attendance at St. John's Methodist College and a stint as a teacher at Moreton's Harbour, Pratt embarked on a career as itinerant preacher and probationer for the Methodist ministry in Newfoundland, but the long distances between villages and the strenuous duties of his calling adversely affected his health. To earn enough money to attend university, he concocted a medicine out of cherry bark, sarsaparilla, peppermint, and rum, which he peddled door-to-door as a cure for consumption. In September 1907 he left for Victoria College at the University of Toronto, where he was to remain for the rest of his professional life, retiring as professor emeritus of English in 1953.

Pratt received a B.A. in philosophy in 1911 and an M.A. the following year. In 1913 he earned his bachelor of divinity degree and was ordained into the Methodist ministry, which he soon abandoned to become a lecturer in psychology. He was awarded a Ph.D. in 1917, and his dissertation on Pauline eschatology was published the same year. Up to this time Pratt had published only a few poems in the college magazine *Acta Victoriana*, but in 1917 he had his first book of poetry privately printed in New York. *Rachel: A Sea Story of Newfoundland in Verse* was not highly thought of by its author and has received little attention from critics. Although Pratt's technique is immature, the subject of the poem is one that he was to return to again and again in his writing. The implacable force of the sea, source of both livelihood and death for the Newfoundlander, is depicted through the imagery of music and speech, with the description of the "grounded gutturals" of the reefs and the "lovely linguals" of the coves foreshadowing the obsession with linguistic metaphors that manifests itself in all of Pratt's great epics and in many of his shorter poems as well.

In 1918 Pratt married Viola Whitney, a gold medal graduate in English from the University of Toronto, who had at one time edited the student newspaper *Acta Victoriana*, and who became editor of the United Church young people's magazine, *World Friends*, in 1928. Their only daughter, Claire, ill during much of her childhood, later published a history of the Pratt family, *The Silent Ancestors* (1971).

The earliest work to give evidence of Pratt's technical abilities is *Newfoundland Verse* (1923), a collection of lyrics exploring different facets of the interrelationship of man and the sea. "The Shark" represents the amoral and incomprehensible power of the sea, especially with the poem's description of the carnivorous fish's mechanical shape and motion. Shipwreck and drowning are dominant motifs in the book; for example, the tragedy of sixty men who die on a seal-hunting expedition is described with ironic insight in "The Ice-Floes." In telling of "twenty thousand seals that were killed/To help to lower the price of bread," Pratt makes a bitter point about the identity of man and seal: the hunter frequently suffers the same fate as the hunted. Violent death was never far from Pratt's mind when he wrote of the sea. For all its apparent beauty, notably detailed in "Newfoundland," the sea, like the shark, is an indiscriminate and cold-blooded killer.

Though warmly praised by reviewers, the lyrical qualities of *Newfoundland Verse* gave way to fantasy and hyperbole in *The Witches' Brew* (1925),

*Pratt ready to climb Cathedral Mountain in July 1913
(Victoria University Library, Toronto)*

*Pratt with his daughter and mother in June 1925 (Victoria
University Library, Toronto)*

which recounts the efforts of three water-witches
to test the effects of alcohol on the creatures of
the sea. The powerful brew is served up with a
feast that Pratt describes in one of his characteristic mock-epic catalogues:

> Then for the more substantial fare,
> The curried quarter of a tail
> Hewn from a stranded Greenland whale,
> A liver from a Polar bear,
> A walrus heart and pancreas,
> A blind Auk from the coast of Java,
> A bull moose that had died from gas
> While eating toadstools near Ungava. . . .

To guard their potion, the witches choose the fiercest creature in the ocean–an amphibious sea-cat
named Tom. Satan shows up to observe the proceedings, accompanied by a legion of ghosts that
includes Byron, Pepys, Saint Patrick, Napoleon,
Blake, and Johnny Walker. The creature most affected by the alcohol is Tom the Cat, who goes
on a wild orgy of destruction aimed at the "trai-

tors to the sea," the whales, dolphins, seals, and
other warm-blooded creatures that have more in
common with land animals than with fish. After
the debacle Tom heads off to create havoc in the
Irish Sea, his glowing tail visible only to Satan
and the three witches.

The reviewers were quick to praise the
poem for its vitality and exuberance, noting that
nothing quite like it had ever before been written
by a Canadian, but none perceived the serious
themes that underlie it, nor the broad literary
background on which Pratt drew for his sources.
Scholars have since noted the influence of Byron
and Burns, the parallels with Milton and Goethe,
and the relationship to popular Newfoundland
ballads. In parodying St. Paul, Freud, and his
own academic study of demonology and eschatology, Pratt reveals a genuine comic voice. But
Tom the Cat's destructive impulses are not presented solely for their comic value, but equally as
a reminder of the dangers of the awakening of reason in a hitherto amoral being. Tom's racially moti-

vated killing illuminates the darker side of human nature that he represents, and the Irish Sea is not a surprising destination for a creature who has discovered how to hate.

Whereas themes of evolution and internecine warfare were hinted at in *The Witches' Brew*, they found full expression in Pratt's next volume, *Titans* (1926), consisting of two long narratives, "The Cachalot" and "The Great Feud." "The Cachalot" draws on Pratt's experiences at a Newfoundland whaling station and his reading of *Moby-Dick* to create a sympathetic portrayal of the heroic qualities of a great sperm whale. The irregularly rhymed iambic tetrameter he had experimented with in *The Witches' Brew* serves here to convey the sort of humorous exaggeration that Pratt delights in:

> . . . so large
> The lymph-flow of his active liver,
> One might believe a fair-sized barge
> Could navigate along the river;
> And the islands of his pancreas
> Were so tremendous that between 'em
> A punt would sink; while a cart might pass
> His bile-duct to the duodenum
> Without a peristaltic quiver.

The poem is divided into three sections, of which the first traces the royal line of the cachalot from the time of Leif Eriksson and Marco Polo and discusses his physical appearance and mastery of the seas, and the second deals with his titanic struggle with a kraken (a giant squid). In the final section, the whale confronts his most dangerous foe: man. Some critics have complained that the shift in focus from whale to whaler in part 3 detracts from the unity of the poem. In fact Pratt is concerned with presenting his master-whaler as a worthy opponent for the cachalot, and although Captain Taylor is no titan, and his crew is no more than "a puny batch of men," together they have as much energy and persistence as the whale, and the matchup is one that neither side can win. In his splendid concluding lines Pratt shows death as triumphant over all, while raising his cetacean protagonist to tragic proportions:

> Then, like a royal retinue,
> The slow processional of crew,
> Of inundated hull, of mast,
> Halliard and shroud and trestle-cheek,
> Of yard and topsail to the last
> Dank flutter of the ensign as a wave
> Closed in upon the skysail peak,
> Followed the Monarch to his grave.

"The Great Feud" takes place in Australasia during the Pliocene era, and concerns a fierce struggle between the creatures of the land and those of the sea. At a certain point in their evolution, the fish find too many of their kind moving onto the land, and "The fear of racial doom was thrown/Heavily upon the piscine soul." A turtle, significantly amphibious and therefore "bilingual," accidentally comes upon a mass meeting of the land creatures presided over by a female anthropoidal ape. Pratt stresses the connection between man and this tool-making, reasoning ancestor who has already fathomed "the raw/Material of the moral law" after observing the accidental death of an alligator who had eaten one of her children. The morality she has discovered is the law of an eye for an eye, and thus her reasoning powers lead to a revengeful desire for the total annihilation of all sea creatures. Recognizing the difficulty of keeping the animals united against their racial foes, the ape hopes to avert internecine strife by ordering the carnivores to refrain from eating their herbivorous brethren, knowing that this abstention will make the fiercest of her troops that much more bloodthirsty when the time comes to attack.

The battle scene is, if anything, more fantastic and grotesque than anything in *The Witches' Brew*, as Pratt's linguistic inventiveness lends a comic touch to the carnage:

> Inflammatory Bengalese,
> Starved with cherry bark and peas;
> With salicaceous jaguars,
> Leguminous leopards full of beans
> That murmured in their jugulars,—
> Swooped, with the speed of peregrines,
> Upon the red substantial meals
> Of dolphins hot and blubberous,
> And a large school of porpoises. . . .

The fight is a seesaw affair complicated by the anachronistic presence of a lone dinosaur, Tyrannosaurus Rex, an "alien Atavist" who wreaks havoc on both sides before taking a suicidal plunge into the sea. With his death the internecine warfare feared by the ape breaks out, and the poem ends with a colossal volcanic eruption. Only the anthropoidal ape escapes destruction, retreating to her lair to suckle her brood amid "moans,/And croons, and drummings of the breast."

Critics have seen the poem variously as an allegory of World War I, a stinging satire on man's pretensions to reason, or a beast fable with Chris-

Part of the first draft of "The Great Feud" (1926), corresponding to lines 23-43 and 113-128 in the finished poem (Pratt Library, Victoria University, Toronto; reproduced by permission of Claire Pratt) tian overtones. Certainly the conclusion seems pessimistic, with the burden of responsibility for the holocaust resting on the shoulders of its chief instigator, man's evolutionary ancestor. But whether viewed ultimately as comedy or tragedy, "The Great Feud" evinces Pratt's ability to treat an apocalyptic struggle in a comic tone, while mitigating the farcical element by a serious moral vision.

The Iron Door: An Ode (1927), occasioned by the death of Pratt's mother, is a quasi-mystical ode on the meaning of death and the afterlife. In a dream the poet sees a giant door bearing "the crest/Of Death upon the lintel." Before the door stands a group of people who have recently died. Among them are a ship captain who has lost three sons, a mother who stands with quiet self-assurance, and a man who has sacrificed his own life to save a drowning man, only to find that the man has subsequently died, rendering his efforts futile. Suddenly the door opens a little, and although the poet himself cannot see what lies beyond, the petitioners pass through. Then the door closes, leaving the speaker conscious only of his inability to see beyond it, but Pratt suggests the possibility of a world behind the "Theban mockery" of the iron door. The poem lacks the vigor and verbal ingenuity expected from Pratt, but it is important as a statement of his credo that life is not rendered meaningless by unexpected death.

Three years later Pratt published *The Roosevelt and the Antinoe*, the first of his narratives in pentameter, and the first to be entirely concerned with human protagonists. Pratt pursues the theme of heroism in the rescue of the crew of a sinking ship during a fierce Atlantic storm. He links man with nature to reveal that, in battling natural forces, man is actually fighting the destructive side of himself that can only be overcome by self-sacrifice. The chief antagonist in the poem can thus be seen as a universal tendency in mankind, metaphorically represented by the sea, "Contesting with its iron-alien mood,/Its pagan face, its own primordial way,/The pale heroic suasion of a rood."

Pratt's exploration of the awesome power of the sea carries over into his book *Many Moods*, published in 1932. As in *Newfoundland Verse*, the changing face of the sea is shown in all its beauty ("Sea-Gulls") and destructive potential ("The Drag-Irons" and "The Ritual"). The latter aspect is incisively presented in "Erosion": "It took the sea a thousand years . . . to trace/The granite features of this cliff,/In crag and scarp and base./It

Pratt, circa 1926 (Thomas Fisher Rare Book Library, Toronto)

took the sea an hour one night . . . to place/The sculpture of these granite seams/Upon a woman's face."

In "The Man and the Machine" Pratt expresses his fears about the effects of technology on mankind. Though some readers have seen Pratt as an apologist for technological advancement, pointing to his delight in energy and dynamism, his true reaction to mechanism, as revealed in this poem and a handful of others like it, is one of profound horror. This vision was likely prompted in part by his reaction against the mechanistic psychological theories of Wilhelm Wundt, whose work was in vogue at the time Pratt was lecturing in psychology at the University of Toronto. While the machine may appear to have the grace of a cougar, it leaves man "with slag upon his face," reducing him to subservience and impotence.

Another of Pratt's favorite themes is atavism, which he explores in one of his best-known lyrics, "From Stone to Steel." Confronting the ever-present tendency in man to revert to his basest instincts, Pratt writes: "The snarl Neanderthal is worn/Close to the smiling Aryan lips," and that contemporary reference reinforced by the juxtaposition of Java and Geneva in the first and last verses is a measure of Pratt's foresight. The onset of World War II seven years later was to prove him correct in his assertion that "Between the temple and the cave/The boundary lies tissue-thin. . . ."

In *The Titanic* (1935) Pratt treats a subject entirely congruent with his poetic genius. The sinking of the great ocean liner had been the subject of other poems, but Pratt was the first to see in the story a potential conflict of titans–the irresistible ship and the immovable iceberg–and to fully exploit the cosmic ironies of the event. The *Titanic* herself is the fullest realization of the ambitions of man to rule the seas by mechanical means; as the "Primate of the Lines," she represents the evolutionary fulfillment of her species. Pratt wastes no time in underlining the potential for ironic catastrophe that exists when "That ancient *hubris* in the dreams of men" ignores the will of fate: "No wave could sweep those upper decks–unthinkable!/No storm could hurt that hull–the papers said so./The perfect ship at last–the first unsinkable,/Proved in advance–had not the folders read so?" As the *Titanic* is launched Pratt shifts the focus to the creation of the iceberg, which, as it drifts south into the shipping lanes, gradually loses its beauty and takes on "the brute/And palaeolithic outline of a face." Alluding to the "Mechanics of its birth," Pratt hints that the best that human technology has to offer stands little chance against a hostile mechanistic nature.

Careful research gave Pratt a vast amount of data to work with in his account of the voyage. (His notes on this poem and others are collected in *E. J. Pratt: On His Life and Poetry*, edited by Susan Gingell, 1983.) He records entries in the log, the menu at dinner, and wireless messages from other ships. The central section of the poem describes a poker game that Pratt makes a metaphor for the ultimate gamble with fate the voyage of the *Titanic* represents. The game is terminated when one player calls for ice and another chances to look out the porthole just as the ship hits the iceberg. Pratt deals effectively with all aspects of the sinking of the ship–concentrating on acts both of bravery and cowardice–culminating in "Her thousand fathoms journey

to her grave," an echo of the last line of "The Cachalot," when men and monarch drown together. The iceberg remains "the master of the longitudes" but itself is doomed as long as it continues on a southward course. *The Titanic* clearly represents an advance over *The Roosevelt and the Antinoe* in its handling of source materials, which are judiciously selected to reinforce the themes of hubris and fate and the illusion of man's independence from nature. The poem is also unmistakably modern in its pervasive ironic tone.

Pratt's next narrative also features two strong protagonists, but the tone reverts to the mock-epic and no battle takes place. In fact pacifism seems to be the theme of the curious title poem in *The Fable of the Goats and Other Poems* (1937), which has not been as highly regarded as Pratt's other epics. The poem deals with a racial conflict between two bands of goats. One group, with "lyrate horns," lives on the west side of the mountain and is led by Cyrus, while the straight-horned goats to the east give their allegiance to Abimelech. Each side covets the other's territory, and mighty battles have been fought between the two groups for generations past. However, the "carrion curtain" that has closed each act in the history of this feud does not fall this final time because Cyrus, in confronting his rival, chooses to kneel rather than to lock horns. The poem concludes with a peaceful exchange of territory, a pacifist solution Pratt must have hoped would occur to the leaders of the European powers in the troubled prewar years.

The volume also features many fine shorter poems, some of which refer obliquely to the contemporary political situation, or warn explicitly of the dangers of the impending war. "The Baritone" is directed against dictatorship and Hitler in particular, while the allusion to an "Abyssinian child" in "The Prize Cat" reveals Pratt's reaction to Mussolini's brand of fascism. In the latter poem Pratt again makes the connection between man and animal, noting the cat's ability to turn from "Pure blood domestic" to predator in an instantaneous reversion to primitive savagery. "The Old Organon (1225 A.D.)" and "The New (1937 A.D.)" exhibit the poet's concern with the abuse of language, while "Silences" deals disturbingly with the consequences of a world without language: the violence under the sea is carried on without sound, "pre-reptilian" in its silent horror. Making effective use of the long line, Pratt asks that "silent hate be put away for it feeds upon the heart of the hater." Where there are words,

Dust jacket for Pratt's 1947 narrative poem, one of three celebrating the World War II heroism of the Allies

there is the possibility of communication that can lead to understanding and compassion, but without such communication, he implies, men will revert to violence like the silent killing under the sea from which they long ago emerged.

The year 1940 saw the publication of a remarkable epic on the martyrdom of the Jesuit missionaries to Huronia, *Brébeuf and His Brethren*, for which Pratt won his second Governor-General's Award. This is Pratt's longest poem, and its interpretation has been the source of some controversy, with critics maintaining that the poem proves Pratt's atheism, or his humanism, or his devout Christianity. Whatever his religious beliefs, Pratt insists here, as elsewhere, upon the importance of heroic self-sacrifice. Brébeuf himself is larger than life, a giant of a man, both in size and in his ability to withstand hardship and pain. Like the cachalot, he can trace his descent from many powerful warriors, but, as if to counterbalance his vitality, he is also imbued with a strong

sense of his own martyrdom: "*I shall be broken first before I break them.*" Significantly Pratt ascribes similar virtues to the Indians: they value endurance and impassivity, and their pride leads them to welcome death. It has been suggested that Brébeuf is equally motivated by pride, even by masochism, but Pratt clearly states that the source of his stamina lies "in the sound of invisible trumpets blowing/Around two slabs of board, right-angled, hammered/By Roman nails and hung on a Jewish hill."

Fire and water are key symbols in the development of Pratt's theme. The fire of purification that the missionaries hope to bring to the Indians is suggested in the "alphabet of flame" kindled by the "winds of God," but ironically it is fire that consumes the mission and the Jesuits themselves. Water is the means by which the French can reach the Huron nation, bringing with them the rite of baptism, but it is their own blood that flows like water as each man reenacts himself the sacrifice of Christ. Brébeuf's vision of the Cross "*huge enough to crucify us all*" foreshadows the martyrdom of the Jesuits, but also prefigures the raising of a cross three hundred years later, as Pratt suggests in an epilogue on "The Martyrs' Shrine." Despite claims to the contrary, it is difficult to believe that Pratt feels anything but admiration for the profundity of Brébeuf's faith.

The emotional heights of *Brébeuf and His Brethren* are not equaled in any of the other three narrative poems that Pratt published in the 1940s. *Dunkirk* (1941), *They Are Returning* (1945), and *Behind the Log* (1947) treat various aspects of World War II, celebrating the heroic actions of the Allied forces. *Dunkirk* specifically focuses on the English nation and its close relationship with the sea: "*The sea was their school; the storm, their friend.*" The small-craft owners and sailors, ranging from curates and valets to butchers and gardeners, are the real heroes in the evacuation of the British troops from Dunkirk.

They Are Returning expresses the debt of gratitude owed by the Canadian people to their servicemen. The musical images at the end of the poem are typical of Pratt's best work in their fusion of song and human achievement:

> And from those tonic syllables,
> Dieppe, Authie, Falaise, and Carpiquet,
> Kleve, Emmerich, Antwerp and Groningen,
> They shall learn how to wind
> Their souls into the reeds and strings
> To reach their own *Eroicas*, and find

The *Chorals, Passions, Pathétiques,*
To hymn their Iliad voyagings.

Behind the Log is the most successful of the three in its depiction of the tension and horror accompanying a North Atlantic convoy under submarine attack. Pratt's diction and tone are always sure when he is dealing with marine events, and his theme is the habitual insistence on communal action. Only by working together and subordinating the will of the individual to the needs of the group can the Allies win the war.

In the same decade appeared *Still Life and Other Verse* (1943), and most of the poems have some reference to the war. "The Submarine" recalls "The Shark" of *Newfoundland Verse;* the vessel's awesome killing power places it above all marine creatures, but as a man-made object, it remains outside the evolutionary process. Like the offspring of the tiger shark, the torpedoes of the submarine are born ready to kill. The only thing the submarine has to fear is the destroyer, "a killer whose might was as great as her own." In this poem Pratt has replaced the sperm whale and the kraken with the new titans of the sea—warships that have greater power than the natural inhabitants of the oceans, but none of the regal dignity of the cachalot.

"Come Away, Death" contrasts medieval and modern conceptions of death, concluding with a warning against the dangerous atavistic tendencies revealed whenever man makes war on his fellow men. Modern bombs presage an Armageddon that threatens to eclipse the "outmoded page of the Apocalypse." In its ironic and allusive complexity "Come Away, Death" is Pratt's finest lyric in the modernist mode.

Also published in *Still Life* is "The Truant," which Northrop Frye has called "the greatest poem in Canadian literature" (*The Bush Garden: Essays on the Canadian Imagination,* 1971). It is Pratt's most forthright assertion of man's ability to survive and triumph in a hostile, mechanistic universe. The truant, "a biped, rational, six feet high," refuses to acknowledge the superiority of the great Panjandrum, who is not God but a symbol of amoral natural power. When this "forcibly acknowledged Lord" threatens him with the pain and suffering engendered by mortality, the truant replies defiantly that it is man who by his knowledge has measured the mechanics of the universe and thus determined the limits of the Panjandrum's rule. "Composed of electronic sparks," without emotion or compassion, the Panjandrum

*Pratt, circa 1962 (*Toronto Globe and Mail*)*

will one day succumb himself to his "sergeant-major Fate." The poem ends with a strong statement of Christian faith and heroic resistance to all would-be conquerors:

We who have learned to clench
Our fists and raise our lightless sockets
To morning skies after the midnight raids,
Yet cocked our ears to bugles on the barricades,
And in cathedral rubble found a way to quench
A dying thirst within a Galilean valley–
No! by the Rood, we will not join your ballet.

Pratt's last narrative, and one of his best, appeared in 1952. *Towards the Last Spike* is the story of the building of the railroad across Canada, with themes of power and energy emerging through the vision of national unity that motivates John A. Macdonald and his supporters. In the gathering of the clans Pratt praises the qualities of the Scottish race, as he had lauded the English in *Dunkirk:* "Oatmeal was in their blood and in their names," and this traditional food of the Scots produces "fearsome racial products"–the abilities to win their goal by argument or force.

The enemies of Macdonald's project are two-fold: human opponents whose shortsighted pessimism will consign them to oblivion, and a more substantial foe in the land itself, depicted as a reptilian monster: "A hybrid that the myths might have conceived,/But not delivered, as progenitor/ Of crawling, gliding things upon the earth." That men can succeed in overcoming such odds demonstrates Pratt's optimistic view of human achievements, a balance to his darker vision of potential Armageddon in works such as "Come Away, Death" and "The Great Feud." In emphasizing the importance of collective effort and national will that make possible the building of the railroad, Pratt articulates a political vision of Canadian unity. And as Northrop Frye has remarked in his introduction to Pratt's *Collected Poems* (1958), "as long as that culture can remember its origin, there will be a central place in its memory for the poet in whom it found its tongue."

Almost simultaneously with the publication of *Towards the Last Spike* appeared John Sutherland's important reassessment of Pratt in the *Northern Review.* Though his militantly Christian interpretation of the poetry has not found many adherents, Sutherland's insistence on the complexity of Pratt's technique prompted a new interest in the formal rather than purely thematic aspects of his work. Following the lead of Sandra Djwa (whose *E. J. Pratt: The Evolutionary Vision* appeared in 1974 and who, with R. G. Moyles, is editing "The Collected Works of E. J. Pratt" in several volumes), recent critics have begun to see Pratt's poetry in its historical and cultural contexts, and to examine the literary and philosophical sources of his ideas. Further research can only enhance the reputation of a poet whose themes are universal but whose voice is unquestionably unique in Canadian literature.

Bibliographies:
Lila and Raymond Laakso, "E. J. Pratt: An Annotated Bibliography," in *The Annotated Bibliography of Canada's Major Authors,* volume 2, edited by Robert Lecker and Jack David (Downsview, Ont.: ECW Press, 1980), pp. 147-220;
Lila Laakso, "Descriptive Bibliography," in *E. J. Pratt: Complete Poems,* volume 2, edited by Sandra Djwa and R. G. Moyles (Toronto: University of Toronto Press, 1989), pp. 373-489.

Biographies:
David G. Pitt, *E. J. Pratt: The Truant Years 1882-*

1927 (Toronto: University of Toronto Press, 1984);
Pitt, *E. J. Pratt: The Master Years 1927-1964* (Toronto: University of Toronto Press, 1987).

References:
Susan Beckmann, "Java to Geneva: The Making of a Pratt Poem," *Canadian Literature,* 87 (Winter 1980): 6-23;
Earle Birney, "E. J. Pratt and His Critics," in *Our Living Tradition,* edited by Robert L. McDougall (Toronto: University of Toronto Press, 1959), pp. 123-147;
E. K. Brown, "E. J. Pratt," in his *On Canadian Poetry,* revised edition (Toronto: Ryerson, 1944), pp. 143-164;
Peter Buitenhuis, Introduction to *Selected Poems of E. J. Pratt,* edited by Buitenhuis (Toronto: Macmillan, 1968), pp. xi-xxx;
Glenn Clever, ed., *The E. J. Pratt Symposium* (Ottawa: University of Ottawa Press, 1977);
Clever, *On E. J. Pratt* (Ottawa: Borealis, 1977);
W. E. Collin, "Pleiocene Heroics," in his *The White Savannahs* (Toronto: Macmillan, 1936), pp. 119-144;
Frank Davey, "E. J. Pratt: Apostle of Corporate Man," *Canadian Literature,* 43 (Winter 1970): 54-66;
Sandra Djwa, *E. J. Pratt: The Evolutionary Vision* (Toronto: Copp Clark/Montreal: McGill-Queen's University Press, 1974);
Louis Dudek, "Poet of the Machine Age," *Tamarack Review,* 6 (Winter 1958): 74-80;
Northrop Frye, *The Bush Garden: Essays on the Canadian Imagination* (Toronto: House of Anansi, 1971);
Frye, Introduction to Pratt's *Collected Poems,* edited by Frye (Toronto: Macmillan, 1958), pp. xiii-xxviii;
Frye, *Silence in the Sea: The Pratt Lecture, 1968* (St. John's: Memorial University, 1969);
Robert Gibbs, "A Knocking in the Clay," *Canadian Literature,* 55 (Winter 1973): 50-64;
Gibbs, "Poet of Apocalypse," *Canadian Literature,* 70 (Autumn 1976): 32-41;
James F. Johnson, "*Brébeuf and His Brethren* and *Towards the Last Spike:* The Two Halves of Pratt's National Epic," *Essays on Canadian Writing,* 29 (Summer 1984): 142-151;
Dorothy Livesay, "The Polished Lens: Poetic Techniques of Pratt and Klein," *Canadian Literature,* 25 (Summer 1965): 33-42;

Jay Macpherson, *Pratt's Romantic Mythology: The Witches' Brew: The Pratt Lecture, 1972* (St. John's: Memorial University, 1972);

R. G. Moyles, "The 'Blue Pencil' Revisions of E. J. Pratt: Editorial Procedures for Modern Canadian Texts," *Essays on Canadian Writing*, 27 (Winter 1983-1984): 55-69;

W. H. New, "The Identity of Articulation: Pratt's *Towards the Last Spike*," in his *Articulating West: Essays on Purpose and Form in Modern Canadian Literature* (Toronto: New Press, 1972), pp. 32-42;

Desmond Pacey, "E. J. Pratt," in his *Ten Canadian Poets* (Toronto: Ryerson, 1958), pp. 165-193;

Catherine McKinnon Pfaff, "Pratt's Treatment of History in 'Towards the Last Spike,'" *Canadian Literature*, 97 (Summer 1983): 48-72;

David G. Pitt, ed., *E. J. Pratt* (Toronto: Ryerson, 1969);

Mildred Claire Pratt, *The Silent Ancestors: The Forebears of E. J. Pratt* (Toronto: McClelland & Stewart, 1971);

Vincent Sharman, "Illusion and an Atonement: E. J. Pratt and Christianity," *Canadian Literature*, 19 (Winter 1964): 21-32;

A. J. M. Smith, *Some Poems of E. J. Pratt: Aspects of Imagery and Theme: The Pratt Lecture, 1969* (St. John's: Memorial University, 1969);

John Sutherland, "E. J. Pratt: A Major Contemporary Poet," *Northern Review*, 5, nos. 3 and 4 (1952): 36-64;

Sutherland, *The Poetry of E. J. Pratt: A New Interpretation* (Toronto: Ryerson, 1956);

F. W. Watt, "The Gigantomachy of E. J. Pratt," *University of Toronto Quarterly*, 54 (Winter 1984-1985): 127-147;

Henry W. Wells and Carl F. Klinck, *Edwin J. Pratt: The Man and His Poetry* (Toronto: Ryerson, 1947);

Paul West, "E. J. Pratt's Four-Ton Gulliver," *Canadian Literature*, 19 (Winter 1964): 13-20;

George Whalley, "Birthright to the Sea: Some Poems of E. J. Pratt," *Queen's Quarterly*, 85 (Winter 1978-1979): 578-594;

Milton Wilson, *E. J. Pratt* (Toronto: McClelland & Stewart, 1969).

Papers:

The E. J. Pratt Library at Victoria College, University of Toronto has a large collection of Pratt's books, manuscripts, lecture notes, clippings, photographs, and other memorabilia, and an inventory of the collection is available at the library.

Adjutor Rivard
(22 January 1868-17 July 1945)

Margot Northey
University of Western Ontario

BOOKS: *Monseigneur de Laval* (Levis, Que.: Roy, 1891);

L'Art de dire: Traité de lecture et de récitation (Quebec: Chasse, 1898);

Manuel de la parole (Quebec: Garneau, 1901);

L'Origine et le parler des Canadiens français, by Rivard and S. A. Lortie (Paris: Champion, 1903);

Bibliographie du parler français au Canada, by Rivard and James Geddes (Quebec: Marcotte, 1906);

Etudes sur les parlers de France au Canada (Quebec: Garneau, 1914);

Chez nous (Quebec: L'Action Sociale Catholique, 1914); translated by W. H. Blake as *Our Old Quebec Home* (Toronto: McClelland & Stewart, 1924; New York: Doran, 1924);

Chez nos gens (Quebec: L'Action Sociale Catholique, 1918);

De la liberté de la presse (Quebec: Garneau, 1923);

Manuel de la Cour d'appel (Montreal: Editions Variétés, 1941);

Contes et Propos divers (Quebec: Garneau, 1944).

OTHER: *Glossaire du parler français au Canada,* edited, with an introduction, by Rivard and Louis-Phillipe Geoffrion (Quebec: L'Action Sociale, 1930).

SELECTED PERIODICAL PUBLICATIONS
UNCOLLECTED: "Le Parler franco-canadien," *Bulletin du Parler Français au Canada,* 2 (October 1903): 35-46; 3 (November 1903): 65-73;

"Livres et Revues (Canadiana)," *Bulletin du Parler Français au Canada,* 5 (April 1907): 301-311;

"Legendre," *Proceedings of the Royal Society of Canada,* third series, volume 3 (1909), section 1, pp. 41-44, 73-86;

"Nos adversaires," *Bulletin du Parler Français au Canada,* 7 (March 1909): 24-52;

Adjutor Rivard

"Littérature théâtrale," *Bulletin du Parler Français au Canada,* 8 (December 1909): 134.

Dust jacket for the sixth edition of Rivard's popular 1914 collection of stories about rustic life

An influential figure in Quebec society in the first half of the twentieth century, Adjutor Rivard made distinguished contributions to the fields of linguistics, literature, and law. His scientific studies of the French-Canadian language, together with his fictional evocation of traditional French-Canadian values, helped foster pride in Quebec's distinctive culture. Born on 22 January 1868 at Saint-Grégoire de Nicolet, Quebec, to Louis and Pamela Harper Rivard, he moved with his family while an infant to Quebec City, where he was educated. He eventually obtained a law degree at Laval University and was called to the bar in 1891. As a young lawyer practicing in Chicoutimi, Quebec, he began to pursue in earnest his study of language. He taught elocution at the local seminary, a course he continued in Quebec City; in 1896 he joined the faculty of arts at Laval, married a widow named Josephine Hamel, and started a family.

Developed from his teachings, *L'Art de dire: Traité de lecture et de récitation* (The Art of Speaking: A Treatise on Reading and Reciting, 1898) is a thorough and practical study of the principles of elocution. It reveals his characteristic, well-

organized approach to language, as does his next work, *Manuel de la parole* (1901), a textbook on phonetics. His main contribution as a linguist, however, was his role in founding in 1902, along with S. A. Lortie, the Société du Parler Français au Canada and the associated *Bulletin du Parler Français au Canada*. As general secretary of the society, he contributed to the journal various articles on linguistics, critical reviews of Quebec literature, and short fictional pieces of his own. Along with Louis-Phillipe Geoffrion, he later edited and provided a foreword to the society's dictionary, the *Glossaire du parler français au Canada* (1930).

In several of his writings he defended the integrity of French-Canadian language but warned against corruptive influences from within and without. On the one hand, he wanted to preserve those special characteristics of Quebec speech that were not part of classical French usage. In an important work written with Lortie, *L'Origine et le parler des Canadiens français* (1903), he showed the connection between French-Canadian speech patterns and the regional dialects of French with which the early settlers had immigrated. Fighting the widespread attitude that the Quebec dialect was an inferior form of French, he endorsed many old words and forms of expression that had disappeared in France but survived in Quebec. In this 1903 work and in *Etudes sur les parlers de France au Canada* (1914), which examined the language from various grammatical, historical, and literary perspectives, he showed that the French-Canadian language had changed, but he argued that this evolution was a sign of a vitality that assured its preservation. On the other hand, he rejected careless use of the language and the increasing number of anglicisms being adopted, especially in commercial circles. Thus he attempted a difficult juggling act, combining a progressive recognition of the evolving character of the language with a traditionalist desire to assure the survival of its essentially French character. The success he had in this regard was based on his scrupulous insistence on scientific research and his endorsement of whatever language practices produced vigor and clarity.

Rivard's linguistic views were incorporated into his fictional writing, and in turn influenced the fiction of other young Quebec writers. By the turn of the century a school of regional literature dedicated to *le terroir* (native soil) had begun to emerge. Rivard's most well-known works, *Chez nous* (1914; translated as *Our Old Quebec Home*, 1924) and *Chez nos gens* (Home of Our People,

1918), expressed and developed this regionalism. Both are collections of rustic sketches and short tales, most of which first appeared in the Société's journal; they reveal the traditional life of the habitants, for whom love of the soil and religious faith unite to produce a celebration of their community. Rivard is exacting in his use of local details, both natural and social. He describes precisely the trees and flowers of the St. Lawrence River valley, the home furnishings, and even the tools. Using his research, he recreates realistic dialect, including the old local vocabulary and way of speaking.

Yet Rivard's realism goes only so far. Along with his attachment to earlier ways of life, he tends to humanize inanimate objects in the surroundings–whether the river bordering a property or the immense stove that dominates a farmhouse. Moreover he includes none of the sordid features of rural life that are emphasized by later Quebec writers; his vision is one of beauty and serenity. Beneath the optimism, however, lies the urgent lesson of the abandoned farm, as voiced in *Chez nous*: "c'est tout le patrimoine ancestral qu'ils abandonnent, c'est la patrie qu'ils désertent" (its the entire ancestral heritage that they're giving up, it's the country that they abandon). Although by 1918 the population of Quebec was predominantly urban, the land and rural values were viewed by Rivard and other city dwellers as central to the Quebec way of life. Despite this nostalgic idealism, *Chez nous* and *Chez nos gens* are saved from excessive sentimentality by the author's sincerity and by the natural grace of the language.

While establishing a reputation in linguistics and literature Rivard was also furthering his repu-tation as a lawyer, jurist, and social critic. In 1907 he formed, with Lortie and P.-E. Roy, L'Action Sociale Catholique, a forum for discussion of social and political issues. In 1923 he wrote a legal study, *De la liberté de la presse*, and during his long tenure as a judge in the Quebec court of appeal, he produced a thorough guide to rules and procedures, *Manuel de la Cour d'appel* (1941). His last major work, *Contes et Propos divers* (Stories and Various Remarks, 1944), published a year before his death, contains sketches and reflections on a variety of topics, from history to language and religion. Although impressive in its diversity, it lacks the charm of his earlier fiction.

Rivard received many honors in his lifetime: he became a member of the Royal Society in 1908, a knight in the order of St. Gregory in 1914, and batonnier of the provincial bar in 1918. For his fiction he received the Prix Davaine of the French Academy in 1920 and the Lorne Pierce medal in 1931. Remembered now for the confidence he engendered in the culture, and especially the language, of Quebec, his best-known writings reflect his conservative conviction that the way to ensure the future of French Canada is to understand and preserve its past.

References:

Emile Chartier, "Hommage au parler des aïeux (Rivard: Etudes sur les Parlers de France au Canada, toste final)," *Enseignement Secondaire au Canada*, 6 (January 1927): 505-521;

Maurice Lebel, "Adjutor Rivard (1868-1945)," *Le Journal de L'Instruction Publique*, 3 (January 1959): 441-445;

Arthur Maheux, "Un grand Canadien: Adjutor Rivard," *Le Canada Français*, 33 (September 1945): 39-42.

Charles G. D. Roberts
(10 January 1860-26 November 1943)

Patricia Morley
Concordia University

BOOKS: *Orion, and Other Poems* (Philadelphia: Lippincott, 1880);

In Divers Tones (Montreal: Dawson, 1887; Boston: Lothrop, 1887);

The Land of Evangeline and Gateways Thither (Kentville, N.S.: Dominion Atlantic Railway, 189?);

The Canadian Guidebook (New York: Appleton, 1891);

Songs of the Common Day and Ave! An Ode for the Shelley Centenary (Toronto: Briggs, 1893; London: Longmans, 1893);

The Raid from Beauséjour and How the Carter Boys Lifted the Mortgage (New York: Hunt & Eaton, 1894);

Reube Dare's Shad Boat (New York: Hunt & Eaton, 1895);

Around the Campfire (Toronto: Musson, 1896; New York & Boston: Crowell, 1896);

The Book of the Native (Toronto: Copp, Clark, 1896; Boston & New York: Lamson, Wolffe, 1896);

The Forge in the Forest (Boston & New York: Lamson, Wolffe, 1896; Toronto: Briggs, 1897);

Earth's Enigmas (Boston: Lamson, Wolffe, 1896; enlarged edition, Boston: Page, 1903);

A History of Canada (Boston & New York: Lamson, Wolffe, 1897; Toronto: Morang, 1898);

A Sister to Evangeline (Boston & New York: Lamson, Wolffe, 1898; Toronto: Morang, 1899);

New York Nocturnes and Other Poems (Boston & New York: Lamson, Wolffe, 1898);

By the Marshes of Minas (Boston & New York: Silver, Burdett, 1900);

The Heart of the Ancient Wood (Toronto: Copp, Clark, 1900; New York: Silver, Burdett, 1900);

Poems (New York: Silver, Burdett, 1901; Toronto: Copp, 1903; enlarged edition, Toronto: Copp, Clark, 1907; Boston: Page, 1907);

Charles G. D. Roberts

Barbara Ladd (Toronto: Copp, Clark, 1902; Boston: Page, 1902);

The Kindred of the Wild (Toronto: Copp, Clark, 1902; Boston: Page, 1902);

The Book of the Rose (Toronto: Copp, Clark, 1903; Boston: Page, 1903);

Discoveries and Explorations in the Century (London & Edinburgh: Chambers/Philadelphia & Detroit: Bradley-Garretson, 1903; Toronto: Linscott, 1906);

The Watchers of the Trails (Toronto: Copp, Clark, 1904; Boston: Page, 1904; London: Duckworth, 1904);

The Prisoner of Mademoiselle (Toronto: Copp, Clark, 1904; Boston: Page, 1904);

The Return to the Trails (Boston: Page, 1905);

The Haunter of the Pine Gloom (Boston: Page, 1905);

The King of the Mamozekel (Boston: Page, 1905);

The Lord of the Air (Boston: Page, 1905);

Red Fox (Toronto: Copp, Clark, 1905; Boston: Page, 1905);

The Little People of the Sycamore (Boston: Page, 1906 [i.e., 1905]);

The Cruise of the Yacht "Dido" (Boston: Page, 1906);

The Heart That Knows (Toronto: Copp, Clark, 1906; Boston: Page, 1906);

In the Deep of the Snow (New York: Crowell, 1907);

The Haunters of the Silences (Montreal: Montreal News, 1907; Boston: Page, 1907);

The House in the Water (Boston: Page, 1908; London, Melbourne & Toronto: Ward, Lock, n.d.);

The Backwoodsmen (New York: Macmillan, 1909; London & Melbourne: Ward, Lock, 1909);

Kings in Exile (London & Melbourne: Ward, Lock, 1909; New York: Macmillan, 1910);

Neighbours Unknown (London: Ward, Lock, 1910; New York: Macmillan, 1911);

More Kindred of the Wild (London & Melbourne: Ward, Lock, 1911);

Babes of the Wild (London & New York: Cassell, 1912);

The Feet of the Furtive (London: Ward, Lock, 1912; New York: Macmillan, 1913);

A Balkan Prince (London: Everett, 1913);

Children of the Wild (New York: Macmillan, 1913);

Hoof and Claw (London: Ward, Lock, 1913; New York: Macmillan, 1914);

The Secret Trails (New York: Macmillan, 1916; London & Melbourne: Ward, Lock, 1916);

Canada in Flanders: The Story of the Canadian Expeditionary Force, volume 3 (London: Hodder & Stoughton, 1918);

The Ledge on Bald Face (London & Melbourne: Ward, Lock, 1918);

Jim: The Story of a Backwoods Police Dog (New York: Macmillan, 1919);

In the Morning of Time (New York: Stokes, 1919; London: Hutchinson, 1919; Toronto: McClelland & Stewart, 1922);

New Poems (London: Constable, 1919);

Some Animal Stories (London & Toronto: Dent, 1921);

More Animal Stories (New York: Dutton, 1922; London: Dent, 1925);

Wisdom of the Wilderness (London & Toronto: Dent, 1922; New York: Dutton, 1922);

They Who Walk in the Woods (New York: Macmillan, 1924);

Lovers in Acadie (London: Dent, 1924);

The Vagrant of Time (Toronto: Ryerson, 1927);

Eyes of the Wilderness (Toronto: Macmillan, 1933; New York: Macmillan, 1933; London: Dent, 1933);

The Iceberg and Other Poems (Toronto: Ryerson, 1934);

Selected Poems (Toronto: Ryerson, 1936); revised edition, edited by Desmond Pacey (Toronto: Ryerson, 1955);

Canada Speaks of Britain (Toronto: Ryerson, 1941);

The Last Barrier and Other Stories, edited by Alec Lucas (Toronto: McClelland & Stewart, 1958);

King of Beasts and Other Stories, edited by Joseph Gold (Toronto: Ryerson, 1967);

Selected Poetry and Critical Prose, edited by W. J. Keith (Toronto & Buffalo: University of Toronto Press, 1974);

The Collected Poems of Sir Charles G. D. Roberts, edited by Pacey and Graham Adams (Wolfville, N.S.: Wombat, 1985).

OTHER: *Poems of Wild Life*, edited by Roberts (London: Scott, 1888);

Philippe Aubert de Gaspé, *The Canadians of Old*, translated by Roberts (New York: Appleton, 1890); republished as *Cameron of Lochiel* (Boston: Page, 1905);

Northland Lyrics, edited by Roberts (Boston: Small, Maynard, 1899);

The Canadian Who's Who, edited by Roberts (Toronto: Trans-Canada, 1910);

"A Note on Modernism," in *Open House*, edited by W. A. Deacon and Wilfred Reeves (Ottawa: Graphic, 1931);

A Standard Dictionary of Canadian Biography, 2 volumes, edited by Roberts and Arthur Tunnell (Toronto: Trans-Canada, 1934, 1938);

Flying Colours: An Anthology, edited by Roberts (Toronto: Ryerson, 1942).

Charles G. D. Roberts has a secure and significant place in the literary history of Canada. His threefold importance rests on his poetry, his prose, especially his animal stories, and on the shaping influence he exerted on other Canadian writers and on the culture of the country he loved. In the last two decades of the nineteenth century Roberts was the acknowledged leader of Canada's first major group of poets, which included Bliss Carman (his cousin), Archibald

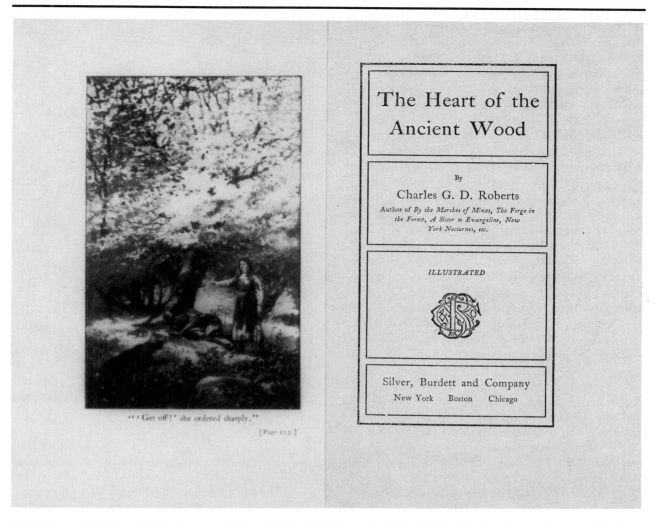

Frontispiece and title page for the American edition of Roberts's 1900 novel, which tells of a fatherless girl growing up in the Canadian wilderness with only animals for friends

Lampman, Duncan Campbell Scott, William Wilfred Campbell, and Pauline Johnson. As a creative writer and the catalyst of creativity in others, Roberts deserves the popular title he earned during his lifetime: the Father of Canadian Poetry.

Roberts was born on 10 January 1860 in the village of Douglas near Fredericton, New Brunswick, seven years before Confederation joined Canada's four existing provinces to form a nation. The first fourteen years of his life were spent at Westcock, near Sackville, in the area of the Tantramar marshes. This beautiful landscape was to dominate and inspire his work for a lifetime. In 1874 his father, the Reverend George Goodridge Roberts, was appointed rector of Fredericton. The education provided at home by his fa-

ther had been so excellent that Roberts completed Fredericton Collegiate in two years and received his B.A. from the University of New Brunswick in 1879. The primary influence on Roberts during these formative years, a time when post-Confederation national idealism was still running strong, was provided by a close-knit, conservative British society; by two classical scholars, his father and collegiate headmaster George Parkin; and by the beauty of the New Brunswick land, part pastoral, part wild. He was also proud of his maternal lineage and fond of boasting that the blood of his mother's Bliss family that had produced Ralph Waldo Emerson flowed in his veins. Roberts's *Canada Speaks of Britain* (1941) includes the autobiographical "Two Rivers," in which the poet sees his own lifelong restlessness imaged in the Tantramar's tidal flow: "In discontent content alone, / you urge and drive me, Tantramar."

Roberts's first collection, *Orion, and Other Poems* (1880), was written while he was an undergraduate and published when he was twenty. Self-conscious and imitative, the verse is strongly influenced by Alfred, Lord Tennyson, Percy Bysshe Shelley, Matthew Arnold, and John Keats. At Fredericton Collegiate the Oxford-trained Parkin had inspired his students with his own love for British poetry and its masters. Twentieth-century critics, while acknowledging the extraordinary promise represented by *Orion*, nevertheless point to the imperfect marriage of Roberts's experience with his conventional, classical subject matter. Contemporary critics in England, Canada, and the United States hailed the collection as initiating a new epoch in Canadian letters. Its effect upon Lampman is often cited. Then a student at Trinity College, Toronto, Lampman was excited to find good verse being written by a Canadian. Roberts's example inspired Lampman to begin his own career.

From 1879 to 1882 Roberts was headmaster at the grammar school in Chatham, New Brunswick. He proved a fine teacher (a Roberts family tradition) and was beloved by his pupils, some of whom were almost as old as their instructor. He married Mary Fenety in 1880 and acquired an M.A. from the University of New Brunswick in 1881. The success of *Orion* led, in 1883, to Roberts being offered the editorship of the *Week,* an important intellectual and literary magazine founded by Goldwin Smith. However, after only four months Roberts resigned from the *Week* on political principle: his views on Canadian independence collided with Smith's annexationist policies. During his short period as editor Roberts encouraged and published Canadian poets such as Carman and Lampman.

After a short free-lance period Roberts went to King's College, Nova Scotia, as professor of English. Roberts later referred to his ten years there (1885-1895) as his most fruitful period. At Kingscroft, the house provided by the college for Roberts and his family, the poet wrote his best two collections of verse, *In Divers Tones* (1887) and *Songs of the Common Day and Ave! An Ode for the Shelley Centenary* (1893), as well as the early tales of animals and of the woods that were to bring him fame and popularity. Roberts was also very much a part of college life. He organized the Arctic Club for winter sports and joined the Haliburton Club, which was devoted to fostering

Roberts, circa 1925 (Queen's University Archives)

the development of a distinctive literature in Canada.

During these years Roberts's literary reputation was established by a stream of articles, reviews, and stories in the best American and Canadian magazines. With its many literary visitors Kingscroft became for a decade a dynamic center for Canadian letters. Roberts was in demand as a public lecturer and was elected a fellow of the Royal Society of Canada in 1890. At this time Roberts was a muscular man of medium height with bespectacled, dark gray eyes that could seem both myopic and visionary. He walked like one accustomed to the woods, wore homespun or Norfolk knickers with a velvet coat, and carried a heavily knotted stick.

In Divers Tones, the first collection from this period, reflects the Westcock landscape of Roberts's youth and marks the beginning of the poet's ability to invest that area with cosmic significance. "The Tantramar Revisited," perhaps the best and best-known poem from this collection, is an elegiac treatment of chance and change, which the poet acknowledges to be at work even in the apparently changeless marshland of his youth. The long, slow-moving lines capture the spirit of place, while the detail is accurate and effective. Sonnets such as "The Sower" and "The Potato Harvest" use homely scenes to suggest subtly the eminence of a transcendent power in common things. However, some of the poems are spoiled by overt didacticism and by vague or exotic epithets.

Roberts's third volume of verse represents the peak of his poetic achievement. *Songs of the Common Day and Ave!* contains thirty-seven well-wrought sonnets on maritime life, a fine pastoral elegy for Shelley, and a miscellaneous section that is the only weak point. Sonnets such as "The Herring Weir," "The Pea-Fields," "In an Old Barn," "The Flight of the Geese," and "In the Wide Awe and Wisdom of the Night" established Roberts's reputation for a cosmic vision. Later, the religious and philosophic overtones in these sonnets came to be ignored by many critics, and Roberts and his contemporaries were charged with being mere nature poets, obsessed with the first crocus or red maple leaves.

The King's College years greatly enhanced Roberts's contemporary literary prestige. He wrote prolifically during this decade. Roberts called the nation's writers *teachers* and spoke of the heavy political responsibility they carried. His view of literature helped replace a narrow maritime provincialism with a broad nationalism.

The Canadians of Old (1890), Roberts's translation of Philippe Aubert de Gaspé's historical romance, increased his interest in Canada's French heritage, which became a lifelong concern. During his last two years at King's Roberts wrote *A History of Canada* (published in 1897) as an entry for a dominion history competition sponsored by the provincial governments. His manuscript was judged *too interesting* for a high school text—weird testimony to Victorian ideas of education. His translation, history, and numerous travel writings had been undertaken partly for money, to supplement a meager professorial salary, and had broadened Roberts's interests and increased his confidence in his ability to live by his pen. In 1895 he left King's College to embark on a free-lance career. Establishing his family in Fredericton, Roberts headed for New York, the writers' mecca, as assistant editor of the *Illustrated American*. In later years he spoke jokingly of his potboiler books, while insisting that he had never written solely for commercial purposes. Certainly, historical romances such as *The Forge in the Forest* (1896) or *Barbara Ladd* (1902), although little known today, are not merely commercial works. Roberts's de-

Roberts on Centre Island, Toronto, summer 1940 (photograph by Elsie Pomeroy)

scriptive abilities link his melodramas to his animal stories.

The break with King's College coincided with Roberts's ceasing to live with his family. The circumstances of his married life are shrouded in obscurity. Biographer Elsie M. Pomeroy passes over the break in tactful silence. Toward the end of her book, she observes that both Roberts and his wife were very young at the time of the marriage; that Mary Roberts was not an intellectual; that in the early New York years Roberts could not afford a family residence; and that after a few years he became "addicted" to living in a studio. Pomeroy credits Roberts with loyalty to his wife and with providing her financial support. As the children grew older several (especially his son Lloyd) joined Roberts from time to time in his travels.

The departure from Kingscroft also coincided with Roberts's turn to prose writing. Prose commanded a larger audience and better fees. The melancholy love lyrics of *New York Nocturnes and Other Poems* (1898) and *The Book of the Rose* (1903) do not represent Roberts's poetic genius. Some twenty-five years later a triumphant return to his homeland in a national lecture tour made Roberts aware that he was remembered and revered as a poet; several significant poetry collections followed.

In the early 1890s Roberts was experimenting with his animal stories and woodsman tales, the product of his youthful observations in the Tantramar and his many camping trips along the rivers of New Brunswick. *Earth's Enigmas* (1896) was the first of many such collections. Its first story, "Do Seek Their Meat From God," had appeared in *Harper's* (December 1892), despite the editor's misgivings. Poet Richard Hovey praised this story for representing the struggle for existence with inexorable fidelity to fact, catholic sympathy, and a sense of universality, mystery, and acceptance that achieves the effect of Greek tragedy.

Hovey's judgment could apply to many of Roberts's animal stories and to the unusual novel *The Heart of the Ancient Wood* (1900). Set in the Canadian wilderness near a human community, this extraordinary fable depicts a fatherless girl growing up with no human society save her mother and with wild animals for friends. Miranda's sensitivity toward the furry "kindred" is matched by her dangerous ignorance of human needs. The novel deals with elemental forces in humanity and nature and with mankind's relation to the environment. The same cosmic sense of a numinous presence in that environment, as in life, and of an ordered purpose in both, informs this novel and the best of the 1880-1895 sonnets.

The popular success of Ernest Thompson Seton's first collection of animal stories, *Wild Animals I Have Known* (1898), alerted Roberts to the major financial markets represented by such stories. Between 1900 and 1914 Roberts published twelve books of animal stories, many of which also appeared in magazines. He discusses the new form in prefaces to *The Kindred of the Wild* (1902), *The Watchers of the Trails* (1904), *Red Fox* (1905), and *The Haunters of the Silences* (1907). Acknowledging the hunting tale and beast fable as ancient forms, Roberts distinguishes the work of Seton and himself from the older adventurous and didactic types. In *The Kindred of the Wild* he calls the Canadian animal story "a psychological romance constructed on a foundation of natural science." He points to the exact observations that shape the Canadian tales, the attempt to understand and write from the animals' point of view, and the conviction that the furred and feathered creatures are capable of reason. Contemporary science credited them solely with instinct, with the result that Seton and Roberts were labeled shams by naturalists such as John Burroughs (*Atlantic Monthly*, March 1903). Nevertheless, Roberts's animal tales represent his finest prose writing and one of his major claims to fame.

The next quarter of a century saw Roberts traveling widely, to England, Cuba, France, Italy, Germany, Holland, and Africa. His life centered in New York until 1907, when he left for Paris. In 1912 he took up residence in London. When World War I began Roberts volunteered as a trooper in the British Legion of Frontiersmen. He later applied for a commission and was accepted, despite the fact that he was fifty-four. His excellent physique initially convinced the British army that he was younger. Roberts trained recruits, instructed officers, and eventually transferred to the Canadian Overseas Forces as a major. His wartime writings consisted of a few poems and stories and the third volume of *Canada in Flanders* (1918), the official Canadian military history of World War I.

In 1910 Roberts had been working in Germany on another unusual fiction. While living in Munich, Roberts did research for *In the Morning of Time* in the zoological gardens and museums of Hagenbeck and Hamburg. The novel, his last full-length one, appeared in 1919. It is a story of prehistoric man's evolution toward civilization, a frightening picture of primeval nature dominated by the physically fittest. Grôm, leader of The People of the Little Hills, discovers fire, the properties of cooked meat, and the making of rafts. He symbolizes the spirit of mankind, "that spirit of unquenchable expectation which has led the race of Man upwards through all obstacles—the urge to find out what lies beyond." *In the Morning of Time* draws on Roberts's skills as poet, naturalist, scholar, and romanticist and serves as a vehicle for his ideas.

The same year saw the publication of *New Poems*, his first collection in sixteen years. The optimistic mood of poems such as "The Summons" is in marked contrast to the general note of depression and futility that dominated English postwar verse. Roberts continued to live in London for several years and to write animal stories that vividly evoked the sounds and scenes of New Brunswick.

He was lured back to Canada in 1925 for the national tour that had been arranged by his son Lloyd. His arrival in Toronto's old Union Station was marked by a throng of reporters and photographers, and his first recital was to an overflow audience in a packed collegiate auditorium. A highly successful tour of western Canada taught Roberts that he was by no means forgotten in his native land and sparked his second major period of poetic productivity.

Glowing tributes to Roberts as poet and lecturer appeared in newspapers across Canada. W. A. Deacon, writing in *Saturday Night,* called him the greatest literary figure Canada had produced: "As poet, as scholar, as prose stylist, as nature student and short story writer, as novelist and historian—he is in the front rank in each capacity." Publisher and scholar Lorne Pierce noted Roberts's bardic accessories, which included a black silk ribbon on his pince-nez, a fawn vest, and festive spats. Pierce also commented that Roberts's athletic build, unpretentious dignity, and inbred gallantry contributed to his universal appeal.

Other equally successful Canadian tours followed from 1926 to 1928. In the late 1920s Roberts settled in Toronto to be near close friends such as Pierce. He resumed regular attendance at Royal Society meetings and was the first winner of the Royal Society's Gold Medal for Literature (1926), which had been established by Pierce to be awarded to a Canadian author whose entire corpus made an outstanding contribution to Canadian literature. Also in 1926 Roberts was invited to become president of the Toronto branch of the Canadian Authors' Association. The honors of his later years were capped in 1935 by a knighthood, conferred by King George V.

The Vagrant of Time (1927) marked Roberts's poetic revival after some twenty-five years devoted largely to prose. *The Iceberg and Other Poems* followed in 1934. Desmond Pacey (in *Ten Canadian Poets,* 1958) finds a development from Roberts's earlier work in the 1927 volume's new freedom of verse form, greater simplicity, and naturalness of diction. The latter collection's title poem, a long narrative in free verse about the sinking of the *Titanic,* contains fine descriptive passages and striking metaphors. In the late 1920s and early 1930s the bitter attacks mounted against the confederation group of poets were more valid in connection with their imitators and successors in the first quarter of the twentieth century than for Roberts and his early contemporaries. A. J. M. Smith, Frank Scott, and Leo Kennedy, radical young Montreal poets, had objected to what they saw as an overconcentration on nature in Canadian poetry. They called for new urban themes and for the innovative techniques introduced in Britain and the United States. Roberts's 1934 volume of verse shows him moving toward modern forms and new themes.

His last years were spent in Toronto, Canada's literary and publishing center. Older than Confederation itself, Roberts was by then as much an institution as a writer. During more than half a century Roberts had not only led Canadian literature but had impressed upon it truly national characteristics. Roberts continued to lecture, to work with literary associations, to write, and to publish until the end of his long, full life. In the mid to late 1930s, for example, he was engaged in editing *A Standard Dictionary of Canadian Biography* (1934, 1938). His last chapbook, *Canada Speaks of Britain,* was hailed as containing some of the finest war poetry that had been written in the British empire.

Tributes poured in after Roberts's death on 26 November 1943 at the age of eighty-three. Pelham Edgar called him a pivotal figure. Prophetically, Lionel Stevenson had shrewdly assessed Roberts's versatility as a quality that might act against his achieving the highest praise in any single genre but also ensured his overall literary and cultural importance: "He was not a greater poet than Carman or Duncan Campbell Scott, not a greater historical novelist than Parker, not a greater writer of animal stories than Seton, not a greater historian than Doughty or Wrong; but he rivalled these masters in their respective fields, and the aggregate achievement wins him a unique distinction." Roberts saw Canada become a nation and lived to help transform that political act of faith into a workable, vibrant reality.

Letters:

The Collected Letters of Charles G. D. Roberts, edited by Laurel Boone (Fredericton, N.B.: Goose Lane, 1989).

Biographies:

Elsie M. Pomeroy, *Sir Charles G. D. Roberts: A Biography* (Toronto: Ryerson, 1943);

J. C. Adams, *Sir Charles God-Damn: The Life of Sir Charles G. D. Roberts* (Toronto: University of Toronto Press, 1986).

References:

Anonymous, "The Animal Story," *Edinburgh Review,* 214 (July 1911): 94-118;

Diana Brydon, "Re-writing *The Tempest*," *WLWE*, 23 (Winter 1984): 75-88;

John Burroughs, "Real and Sham Natural History," *Atlantic Monthly*, 91 (March 1903): 298-309;

James Cappon, *Charles G. D. Roberts* (Toronto: Ryerson, 1925);

Cappon, *Roberts and the Influences of His Time* (Toronto: Briggs, 1905);

Edward B. Clark, "Roosevelt on the Nature Fakirs," *Everybody's Magazine*, 16 (June 1907): 770-774;

Pelham Edgar, "Sir Charles G. D. Roberts and His Times," *University of Toronto Quarterly*, 13 (October 1943); 117-126;

Joseph Gold, "The Precious Speck of Life," *Canadian Literature*, 26 (Autumn 1965): 22-32;

David Jackel, "Roberts' 'The Tantramar Revisited': Another View," *Canadian Poetry*, 5 (Fall-Winter 1979): 4-56;

W. J. Keith, *Charles G. D. Roberts* (Toronto: Copp, Clark, 1969);

R. H. MacDonald, "The Revolt Against Instinct," *Canadian Literature*, 84 (Spring 1980): 18-29;

William H. Magee, "The Animal Story: A Challenge in Technique," *Dalhousie Review*, 44 (Summer 1964): 156-164;

Robin Mathews, "Charles G. D. Roberts: Father of Canadian Poetry," in *Canadian Literature: Surrender or Revolution*, edited by Gail Dexter (Toronto: Steel Rail, 1978), pp. 45-62;

Desmond Pacey, "Sir Charles G. D. Roberts," in his *Ten Canadian Poets* (Toronto: Ryerson, 1958);

Michel Poirier, "The Animal Story in Canadian Literature," *Queen's Quarterly*, 34 (January-April 1927): 298-312, 398-419;

James Polk, "Lives of the Hunted," *Canadian Literature*, 53 (Summer 1972): 51-59;

Lloyd Roberts, *The House of Roberts* (Toronto: Ryerson, 1923);

C. Lintern Sibley, "The Voyage of the Nature Story," *Canadian Magazine*, 38 (January 1912): 287-292;

William Strong, "Charles G. D. Roberts' 'The Tantramar Revisited,'" *Canadian Poetry*, 3 (Fall-Winter 1978): 26-37;

Chantal Zabus, "A Calibanic Tempest in Anglophone and Francophone New World Writing," *Canadian Literature*, 104 (Summer 1985): 35-50.

Theodore Goodridge Roberts

(7 July 1877-24 February 1953)

Neil K. Besner
University of Winnipeg

BOOKS: *The House of Isstens* (Boston: Page, 1900);

Hemming, The Adventurer (Boston: Page, 1904);

Brothers of Peril: A Story of Old Newfoundland (Boston: Page, 1905);

The Red Feathers: A Story of Remarkable Adventures When the World Was Young (Boston: Page, 1907);

Captain Love (Boston: Page, 1908);

Flying Plover: His Stories, Told Him by Squat-by-the-fire (Boston: Page, 1909);

A Cavalier of Virginia (Boston: Page, 1910);

Comrades of the Trails (Boston: Page, 1910);

A Captain of Raleigh's (Boston: Page, 1911);

Soldier of Valley Forge, by Roberts and Robert Neilson Stephens (Boston: Page, 1911);

The Toll of the Tides (London: Laurie, 1912); republished as *The Harbor Master* (Boston: Page, 1913); republished as *Blessington's Folly* (London: Long, 1914);

Rayton: A Backwoods Mystery (Boston: Page, 1912);

Two Shall Be Born (New York: Cassell, 1913);

Love on Smoky River (London: Long, 1913);

Jess of the River (New York: Dillingham, 1914);

The Wasp (New York: Dillingham, 1914);

In the High Woods (London: Long, 1916);

Forest Fugitives (Toronto: McClelland & Stewart, 1917; London: Long, 1920);

The Islands of Adventure (London & New York: Hodder & Stoughton, 1918);

Thirty Canadian V.C.'s (London: Skeffington, 1918);

The Exiled Lover (London: Long, 1919);

The Master of the Moosehorn, and Other Backcountry Stories (London: Hodder & Stoughton, 1919);

Moonshine (London: Hodder & Stoughton, 1920);

The Lure of Piper's Glen (New York: Doubleday, 1921);

The Fighting Starkleys; or, The Test of Courage (Boston: Page, 1922);

Musket House (New York: Doubleday, 1922);

Tom Akerley: His Adventures in the Tall Timber and at Gaspard's Clearing on the Indian River (Boston: Page, 1923);

Green Timber Thoroughbreds (Garden City, N.Y.: Garden City, 1924);

The Oxbow Wizard (Garden City, N.Y.: Garden City, 1924);

The Red Pirogue: A Tale of Adventure in the Canadian Wilds (Boston: Page, 1924);

The Stranger From Up-Along (Toronto: Gundy, 1924; Garden City, N.Y.: Doubleday, Page, 1924);

Honest Fool (London: Hodder & Stoughton, 1925);

Seven Poems (Fredericton, N.B.: McMurray, 1925);

The Lost Shipmate (Toronto: Ryerson, 1926);

Prize Money (Boston: Page, 1926);

The Golden Highlander; or, The Romantic Adventures of Alastair MacIver (Boston: Page, 1929);

The Leather Bottle (Toronto: Ryerson, 1934);

Loyalists: A Compilation of Histories, Biographies, and Genealogies of United Empire Loyalists and Their Descendants (Toronto: Roberts, 1937).

OTHER: Charles G. D. Roberts, ed., *Northland Lyrics*, includes poems by T. G. Roberts (Boston: Maynard, 1899).

The life and work of George Edward Theodore Roberts—"Thede" to his friends—are striking on several counts. Driven by a peripatetic quest for adventure, Roberts's life was also strongly shaped by cycles of return to his roots in New Brunswick. His poetry and fiction, staggering in sheer quantity and variety, show at their best Roberts's most enduring gifts: in his poetry a love of nature well served by a keen eye for local color and detail, a good ear for clean, clear rhythm and rhyme, and a forceful, uncluttered narrative line; and in fiction a talent for presenting his abiding perception of universal struggles between good and evil either in mythic tales of ad-

Theodore Goodridge Roberts

venture or in regional stories animated by local settings, customs, and dialects.

Roberts was born on 7 July 1877 in the old rectory in Fredericton, the youngest child of the Reverend Goodridge Roberts, the rector of Fredericton, and Emma Wetmore Roberts. (Roberts adopted "Goodridge," the name of his paternal grandmother, in memory of a brother who died young; Goodridge is also one of the names he gave his first child, William, who became a well-known artist.) Several members and relatives of the Roberts family—most notably, Charles, Theodore's older brother by seventeen years, and Bliss Carman, the Roberts's first cousin—were already published poets when Theodore was born, and his sister Elizabeth was also writing poetry.

Roberts began writing in his school years in Fredericton, publishing his first poetry at the age of twelve in the *Independent*, a New York magazine, and in the *Dominion Illustrated*. After a brief period at the University of New Brunswick, Roberts ended his formal education, leaving Frederic-

ton for a short time for the first of several attempts at farming, this one in Stanley, New Brunswick. Later Roberts became subeditor of the *Independent* from 1897 to early 1898, and then a special correspondent reporting from Tampa and Cuba on the Spanish-American War in the spring and summer of 1898. During his time as a correspondent Roberts contracted "Cuban fever," misdiagnosed by New York doctors as consumption; in 1899 he returned to Fredericton, where he recovered but was left vulnerable to malarial attacks for the rest of his life.

After Roberts returned to Canada he edited the *Newfoundland Magazine* for two years, and in 1900 he launched his writing career in earnest with the publication of *The House of Isstens*. Around 1900 Roberts also sailed to the West Indies and South America on a full-rigged brigantine and later drew on this journey for several poems, stories, and novels set in the South seas; "Night Wind of Barbados," "Pernambuco in May," and "I Sailed a Voyage" (collected in *The Leather Bottle*, 1934), for example, are poems that vividly evoke his strong attractions to these settings.

Roberts married Frances Seymour Allan in November 1903, and the couple went to the West Indies on their honeymoon, remaining in Barbados for two years while Roberts wrote. Their first of three children, William Goodridge, was born in Barbados in 1904; shortly after, the Roberts family returned to Fredericton, confirming the shape that Desmond Pacey, in his introduction to the 1968 edition of *The Harbor Master*, sees as characteristic of Roberts's travels: "Thus the pattern of Theodore's life was established: a few months or years elsewhere–in England, France, Ottawa, or Digby [Nova Scotia]–would be followed by a return to Fredericton, which was the hub of his life's wheel."

In 1914 Roberts enlisted as an officer in the Twelfth Battalion. He established a distinguished war record, eventually serving as aide-de-camp to Gen. Sir Arthur Currie; from 1918 to 1919 Roberts was the officer in charge of Canadian Military Publications. After the war he returned to Fredericton and again embarked on his pattern of travels and brief residences elsewhere–to Ottawa, to Kingsmere, Quebec, frequently to New York, and to another farm below Fredericton; he also took one more long sea voyage, after one of his bouts with illness, around the continent via the Panama Canal to Vancouver.

Of Roberts's variegated and plenitudinous fiction, much of it based on his travels, only two books remain in print, both in McClelland and Stewart's New Canadian Library series: *The Red Feathers* (1907) and his best-known novel, *The Harbor Master* (first published in London as *The Toll of the Tides*, 1912). *The Red Feathers* has been described, with justification on both sides, as a boys' novel and as adult fare. Certainly the novel has much that would appeal to the young imagination: tales of magic and high adventure among warring Indian tribes, of good and evil magicians locked in bitter conflict, of transformations from human to animal forms, and of powers conferred upon individuals by dint of their possession of the magical "red feathers" that the good magician, Wise-as-a-she-wolf, has entrusted to the care of the good Indian chief, Run-all-day. Set in Newfoundland, the novel traces the series of struggles between Wise-as-a-she-wolf and his enemy, the evil Bright Robe, for domination over all the tribes of the region; incarnated in the development and resolution of this conflict is a more universally resonant conflict between good and evil,

and it is at this level that the novel moves beyond the domain of juvenile fiction. The tales of magic and adventure are further qualified by Roberts's psychological observations and development of character: it is clear that he admires nobility, honor, and bravery, and that he often perceives the ordinary man to be weak, gullible, and capable of being duped by powerful leaders who manipulate him for hidden ends. Greed, malice, and jealousy are shown to undermine character; courage is rewarded; and finally, the virtues of peaceful community and, above all, the promise of love are presented as the highest ideals to which people can aspire.

The Harbor Master, on the face of it a very different kind of fiction, explores some of these same concerns in another context. Set in the isolated Newfoundland village of Chance Along, the novel charts the progress of a powerful antihero, Black Dennis Nolan, in his attempts to gain control of his village; to devise strategies for making the most of the occasional shipwrecks that run onto the rocks and provide rich booty to the villagers; and finally, to win the hand of a woman from "up-along"–from anywhere beyond the immediate coast. As in *The Red Feathers,* the narrative technique–the tales of adventure, the rich Newfoundland dialect, the recurring, detailed, and compelling descriptions of landscape, of character, of skirmishes over stolen treasures, and even of hallucinatory encounters with drowned corpses aboard a wreck–might momentarily obscure the novel's important exploration of character. While Roberts obviously admires Nolan's intrepidity, he also wishes to show the process of moral education, in which Nolan is subjected to what is presented finally as the natural and powerful force of love. Because of this process, Nolan eventually surrenders his deluded desire to marry (and master) the rescued Flora Lockhart, a beautiful singer bound for New York, and then yields to the love of Mary Kavanagh, a local woman of more constant character. Again the surrounding cast is presented for the most part as easily manipulated, with some interesting exceptions, particularly Father McQueen, the visiting missionary revered above all others by Nolan. The struggles between good and evil are more complex here, and grounded more firmly in everyday life and characters, than is the case in *The Red Feathers. The Harbor Master* is further enriched by Roberts's drawing on local dialect to invigorate the dialogue, as in a representative speech of Nolan's to his men early in the novel and at the height of his powers, after subduing an incipient rebellion: "Now, men, maybe ye know who bes master of this harbor," he says. "If any one o' ye, or any four o' ye, bain't sure, say the word an' I'll pull off me coat again an' show ye. Well now, we'll git back to business."

Although in his poetry Roberts often addressed coastland subjects—as in "The Wreckers' Prayer," a plea to "Give us a wrack or two, Good Lard" (in *The Leather Bottle*)—topics that could easily have been broached by one of his fictional characters, his verse reveals more clearly than his fiction Roberts's abiding nostalgia for youth, his reverence for nature, particularly for New Brunswick rivers and woods, and the more private passions that inspired his life. *The Leather Bottle* is, at eighty-seven pages, the most substantial collection of Roberts's poetry, and the titles of its four sections identify four of the currents that run through his life and work: "Vintages of My Own Country," a selection that celebrates New Brunswick landscapes and scenes; "Stuff of Neptune's Brewing," a collection inspired by Roberts's sea voyages; "From Arcadian Vats," a group of poems that draws on mythical material to celebrate love, adventure, inspiration, and romance; and the shortest section, "Of His Majesty's Rum Jar," poems inspired by wartime experiences. The collection is prefaced by "A Note On Poetry," in which he explains his concept of the poet's art and practice: "I believe that poetry is the very essence of mankind's highest efforts to express and interpret life and our speculations concerning death, all beauty, the joyous and tragic adventures of the heart, the illuminating flashes and dark agonies of the mind, the mysteries of human behaviour and of divine acquiescence and intention, the glories of illusion and the truth of dreams."

In their evocations of New Brunswick settings the poems of the opening section sometimes recall Bliss Carman's poetic voice; nowhere is this influence clearer than in "The Desolate Cabin," which in mood, rhythm, and language seems suffused with Carman's gentle melancholy and his music: "And something stirs on the threshold/Like the ghost of a drifting leaf,/And sobs in the yellow silence/Like a lost soul of grief." Other poems from this section suggest earlier influences; "The Forsaken Canoe" indicates that he likely had read, and admired, Isabella Valancy Crawford's "Said the Canoe" (1884). Both poems imagine the canoe speaking, and in similar ways, although Roberts's poem re-creates

a more generalized past, whereas Crawford's canoe speaks of more vivid and specific settings and events. The poem in this first section that best captures Roberts's sense of the poet's calling is "Death in June," in which the third verse speaks of a poet awaking in eternity to a timeless task: "His no eternal rest! His still the quest/Of word, of phrase, to catch the spirit's gleam;/To mark the meaning of the swift stream's zest;/To fix, in ink, the radiance of a dream." Also appearing in *The Leather Bottle* is the most celebrated and most often anthologized of Roberts's poems, "The Blue Heron," justly praised for its detailed attention to the stance and stillness of the bird:

> Smoke-blue he is, and grey
> As embers of yesterday.
> Still he is, as death;
> Like stone, or shadow of stone,
> Without a pulse or breath,
> Motionless and alone,
> There in the lily stems;
> But his eyes are alive like gems.

Roberts spent his last several years in Digby, where he moved from Fredericton in the late 1940s; he had been awarded an honorary D.Litt. by the University of New Brunswick in 1930, and he became a fellow of the Royal Society of Canada in 1934. At the time of his death (24 February 1953) in Nova Scotia, he was planning what Goodridge MacDonald describes as a "New Brunswick dream epic"; one of his final poetic fragments evokes the world of myth, romance, and Arthurian legend that informs the third section of *The Leather Bottle*.

Many accounts of Roberts's life seem almost irresistibly drawn to the image of the man, as if his work were an intimate reflection of, or was intimately reflected in, his presence. Pacey's description of Roberts when he met him in Fredericton in October 1944 is representative:

He was a striking figure as he strode up and down University Avenue: he was tall, slim, and held himself erect with a bearing that suggested his military training and his strict code of honour; . . . his face was thin, the skin almost transparent and very pale yellow in hue, his hair white and fine; but in contrast with the prevailing paleness were his dark brown eyes, which shone with an eager glow. His alert eyes suggested vitality and curiosity, an appetite for experience which his dress and relaxed manner did their futile best to belie.

Pacey's description renders the lineaments of temperament and personality that lie so close to the surface of Roberts's writing: the complex weave of the ideal with the earthy, the familiar and domestic with the foreign and exotic, the local and idiomatic with the legendary and universal. All these qualities coalesce in Roberts's best work, inspired with a boyish energy and enthusiasm, tempered by a more mature, sometimes melancholy gaze toward the past. Few other Canadian writers of his time and place have received so little attention for such various accomplishments.

References:

A. G. Bailey, "T. G. Roberts," *Fiddlehead*, 18 (1953): 3;

Goodridge MacDonald, "Theodore Goodridge Roberts: Poet and Novelist," *Canadian Author and Bookman*, 21 (Spring 1953): 9-12;

Desmond Pacey, Introduction to *The Harbor Master* (Toronto: McClelland & Stewart, 1968), pp. 1-9;

Lorne Pierce, *An Outline of Canadian Literature* (Toronto: Ryerson, 1927), pp. 40-41;

Martin Ware, Introduction to *The Red Feathers* (Toronto: McClelland & Stewart, 1976), pp. i-xiv;

Ware, "Theodore Goodridge Roberts, Poet: A Neglected Voice," *Essays on Canadian Writing*, 31 (Spring 1985): 75-92.

Camille Roy

(22 October 1870-24 June 1943)

Susan Jackel
University of Alberta

BOOKS: *Chansons pour tout le monde* (Lyon, 1897);
L'Université Laval et les Fêtes du cinquantenaire (Quebec: Dussault & Proulx, 1903);
Essais sur la littérature canadienne (Quebec: Garneau, 1907);
Tableau de l'histoire de la littérature canadienne-française (Quebec: L'Action Sociale, 1907); revised and enlarged as *Manuel d'histoire de la littérature canadienne* (Quebec: L'Action Sociale, 1918);
Nos Origines littéraires (Quebec: L'Action Sociale, 1909);
Propos canadiens (Quebec: L'Action Sociale, 1912);
L'Abbé Henri-Raymond Casgrain: La Formation de son esprit, l'historien, le poète et le critique littéraire (Montreal: Beauchemin, 1913);
Propos Rustiques (Montreal: Beauchemin, 1913);
Nouveaux Essais sur la littérature canadienne (Quebec: L'Action Sociale, 1914);
La Critique littéraire au dix-neuvième siècle: De Madame de Staël à Emile Faguet. Conférences de l'Institut canadien, 1917-1918 (Quebec: L'Action Sociale, 1918);
Erables en fleurs: Pages de critique littéraire (Quebec: L'Action Sociale, 1923);
Monseigneur de Laval, 1623-1708 (Quebec: Franciscaine Missionnaire, 1923);
A l'Ombre des érables: Hommes et livres (Quebec: L'Action Sociale, 1924);
Etudes et Croquis (Montreal & New York: Carrier, 1928);
Les Leçons de notre histoire: Discours (Quebec: L'Action Sociale, 1929);
Regards sur les lettres (Quebec: L'Action Sociale, 1931);
Morceaux choisis d'auteurs canadiens (Montreal: Beauchemin, 1934);
Nos Problèmes d'enseignement (Montreal: Lévesque, 1935);
Pour Conserver notre héritage française (Montreal: Beauchemin, 1937);
Pour Former des hommes nouveaux (Montreal: Valiquette, 1941);

Camille Roy

Du Fleuve aux océans (Montreal: Beauchemin, 1943);
Semences de vie (Quebec: L'Action Catholique, 1943).

OTHER: *Les Fêtes du troisième centenaire de Québec (1608-1908)*, edited by Roy (Quebec: Laflamme & Proulx, 1911);
"French Canadian Literature," in *Canada and Its Provinces*, volume 12, edited by A. B. Doughty and Adam Shortt (Toronto: Glasgow & Brook, 1914).

As cleric, educator, and, above all, literary critic, Camille Roy championed the cause of French-Canadian *survivance* through the creation of a native literary tradition. Four times rector of Laval University, where he was professor of French literature and then of French-Canadian literature, Roy was widely recognized as *"le grand Seigneur"* of French-Canadian letters during the first half of the twentieth century.

Born on 22 October 1870 in Berthier-en-bas, Quebec, Roy was one of several children of a farming couple, Benjamin and Desanges Gosselin Roy. He was educated at the classical Seminaire de Québec and at Laval University, from which he received his doctorate in 1894. That same year he was ordained as a priest in the Roman Catholic church. (His brother Paul-Eugène also entered the priesthood, eventually becoming archbishop of Quebec.) From 1898 to 1901 Roy studied classical and contemporary literary criticism at the Institut Catholique de Paris and at the Sorbonne, being particularly influenced by the teaching and example of Vincent Brunetière.

Returning to Quebec in 1901 to take up the chair of rhetoric at the Petit Seminaire de Québec, Roy was thoroughly imbued with the power and prestige of the literary critic; at the same time, he accepted the traditional responsibility of the Quebec clergy to maintain the Catholic and rural values of his people. In terms of French-Canadian literature, however, Roy was ahead of his time: a highly trained, sensitive, and capable critic, he found little material in his native province on which to practice his talents.

With characteristic energy Roy set out to remedy this deficiency. In 1902 he founded La Société du Parler Français au Canada, and in its *Bulletin* and other journals he laid out a program for the creation of a truly national literature, one that would include the scenes, customs, values, and mentality of the French-Canadian people, in a manner distinct from that of decadent, anti-clerical France.

Roy's introduction to his *Essais sur la littérature canadienne* (1907) spelled out critical principles and methods from which he never deviated. The French-Canadian critic's four main functions, he asserted, were to judge artistic merit, assist authors to improve their work, evaluate ideas, and improve public taste. The critic should be sincere and benevolent, do everything in his power to encourage new writers, and ac-

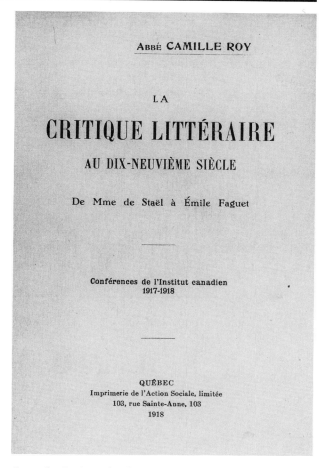

ABBÉ CAMILLE ROY

LA

CRITIQUE LITTÉRAIRE

AU DIX-NEUVIÈME SIÈCLE

De Mme de Staël à Émile Faguet

Conférences de l'Institut canadien
1917-1918

QUÉBEC
Imprimerie de l'Action Sociale, limitée
103, rue Sainte-Anne, 103
1918

Cover for Roy's study of the nineteenth-century literary critics de Staël and Faguet

cept his responsibility to act as a moral guide to writers and the reading public.

Recognizing the urgent need to raise intellectual standards among the reading public so that writers might earn respect and encouragement, Roy invested much energy in education reform. His *Tableau de l'histoire de la littérature canadienne-française* (1907), written for use in the colleges and seminaries of Quebec, was expanded and revised many times, and in the form of the *Manuel d'histoire de la littérature canadienne* played an important part in keeping before his countrymen the need to sustain and expand their literary traditions. Roy also contributed more than two hundred fifty articles and reviews to a variety of journals, three of which (*Le Bulletin du Parler Français, La Nouvelle France,* and *L'Enseignement Secondaire au Canada*) he founded and edited.

Roy was successful in encouraging a far greater volume of literary output in French Canada, and in establishing the respectability of a distinctly francophone Canadian literature. However, his commitment to the traditional pieties of his province's religious and social life led him to insist explicitly in his essay for *Canada and Its Provinces* (1914), as well as implicitly in all his early critical writing, that "French-Canadian literature . . . bears the stamp of the Christian spirit," and that its best works "breathe the perfume of the soil." Thus was nineteenth-century *terroirisme,* the reverent and nostalgic evocation of the rural Quebec scene, perpetuated into the twentieth century.

Late in his career Roy realized that his advocacy of a national (by which he meant regional) literature had unduly narrowed the scope of French-Canadian writing, exalting setting and social values at the expense of artistic merit. In *Regards*

sur les lettres (1931) and thereafter he reverted to the emphasis on universal themes that had characterized his own classical education.

References:

Frère Ludovic, *Bio-Bibliographie de Mgr. Camille Roy* (Quebec, 1941);

Clément Moisan, *L'Age de la littérature canadienne* (Montreal: HMH, 1969), pp. 85-90;

Lorne Pierce, "Monseigneur Camille Roy," *Queen's Quarterly,* 25 (Autumn 1928): 541-558;

Alan Charles Ross, "Camille Roy, Literary Critic," Ph.D. dissertation, University of Toronto, 1953.

Laura Goodman Salverson
(9 December 1890-13 July 1970)

Paul Hjartarson
University of Alberta

BOOKS: *The Viking Heart* (Toronto: McClelland & Stewart, 1923; New York: Doran, 1923);

Wayside Gleams (Toronto: McClelland & Stewart, 1925);

When Sparrows Fall (Toronto: T. Allen, 1925);

Lord of the Silver Dragon: A Romance of Lief the Lucky (Toronto: McClelland & Stewart, 1927);

The Dove (Toronto: Ryerson, 1933; London: Skeffington, 1933);

The Dark Weaver (Toronto: Ryerson, 1937; London: Low, 1937);

Black Lace (Toronto: Ryerson, 1938; London: Hutchinson, 1938);

Confessions of an Immigrant's Daughter (Toronto: Ryerson, 1939; London: Faber & Faber, 1939);

Immortal Rock: The Saga of the Kensington Stone (Toronto: Ryerson, 1954; London: Angus & Robertson, 1955).

Although Laura Goodman Salverson won a Governor General's Award (for fiction) for *The Dark Weaver* (1937), a Governor General's Award (for nonfiction) for *Confessions of an Immigrant's*

Daughter (1939), and the Ryerson Fiction Award for *Immortal Rock* (1954), she is probably best known for her first book, *The Viking Heart* (1923), which gained her recognition as one of Canada's most promising writers. She won international recognition in 1938 when the Institute of Arts and Letters in Paris awarded her its gold medal for literary merit.

Salverson was born in Winnipeg "in its plebian mudhole days," as she put it in an autobiographical sketch for the *Ontario Library Review* (1930). Her parents, Laurus and Ingiborg Gudsmundotte Goodman, were Icelandic immigrants; the family was poor and moved frequently in search of prosperity. As a child Laura Goodman lived in Manitoba, North Dakota, Minnesota, and Mississippi. She was one of many children born to the Goodmans, most of whom did not survive infancy; indeed, illness kept Laura from school until she was ten. "I had not been much of a baby," she wrote in her autobiography, *Confessions of an Immigrant's Daughter.* "I could well believe that I must have been a surprise to poor mama. Her other babies had always measured above the average in size and beauty.

Laura Goodman Salverson in 1934

Yet those sturdy little creatures had not survived. They came and departed. I was so used to it that its sole effect was a kind of fearful distaste for all babies. They were such unstable entities, predictable in nothing save the certainty of their sure departure." As a result of her childhood experiences she developed a sympathy for the poor and an awareness of the plight of women that inform her writing.

Although the family was poor, the Goodmans were intensely proud of Iceland's and of their own ancestors' literary heritage and instilled that pride and the desire to write in their daughter. She did not learn English until she entered school, but she quickly made that language her own. "Like most Icelanders," she remarked in *Confessions of an Immigrant's Daughter*, "I was a confirmed bookworm, and what is even worse, had a natural taste for stuff that either horrified or bored my friends to death." She received most of her public-school education in Duluth, Minnesota. Plans to attend normal school were sacri-

ficed to the need to make a living; however, Laura was determined to educate herself. "I have earned my living," she later declared, "in almost every way calculated by the virtuous as eminently respectable. I doubted it often and still do. But whether in office or shop, tailoring establishment or hospital (where the traditional idea of service nabbed me) my nights were spent in some dusty and highly impractical form of study."

In 1913 she married George Salverson, a Montana native of Norwegian descent, in Winnipeg. His job as a railway dispatcher involved moving frequently from one prairie town to the next, an experience for which Laura felt more than adequately prepared. "I had the advantage of being almost a tramp," she wrote of her childhood, "we jumped so much from place to place—and my married life has been cast along the same lines." In 1916 they had their only child, a son, George, who eventually adapted several of his mother's books for radio.

Although Salverson wrote prose and verse in her youth and in 1903 reportedly published her first story in a Mississippi newspaper at the age of twelve, her career was not really launched until 1922, when her short story "Hidden Fire" won a prize offered by the Women's Canadian Club of Saskatchewan and was printed in newspapers throughout western Canada. In the following years she became a regular contributor of stories, articles, and columns to numerous magazines, including the *Western Home Monthly*, the *Toronto Star Weekly*, *Maclean's*, *Chatelaine*, and others.

Encouraged by Austin Bothwell, the head of the English department at Central Collegiate Institute in Regina, to write a book about her own people, she completed *The Viking Heart* in less than a year. Originally entitled "The Price of Country," it describes the hardships suffered by the Icelanders who immigrated to Manitoba after the eruption of Mount Hecla in 1876; however, Salverson is more interested in the long-term spiritual and cultural consequences of immigration than in the immediate physical hardships the immigrants faced and so focuses not on the Icelanders who settled in the new land, represented in the book by Einar and Gudrun Halsson, but on their children's children, Borga Halsson's three offspring, Elizabeth, Ninna, and Thor. Thor's death at Passchendaele is the sacrifice that symbolically makes the Icelanders Canadians.

The Viking Heart was followed in 1925 by two books: *Wayside Gleams*, a collection of occasional verse, and *When Sparrows Fall*, a prose ro-

Salverson at eighteen (photograph courtesy of the Literary Manuscripts Collection, National Library of Canada)

mance that centers on Stephen and Vilborg Freeman's daughter, Ephemia, and traces the fortunes of a group of Norwegian and Icelandic families on the American shores of Lake Superior.

In both *The Viking Heart* and *When Sparrows Fall* Salverson writes out of her own experiences as an Icelandic immigrant's daughter. In all her remaining prose romances, except *The Dark Weaver*, she finds her inspiration in the distant past. In *Lord of the Silver Dragon* (1927) and *The Dove* (1933) she weaves a romance out of Icelandic history; in *Black Lace* (1938) she turns to seventeenth-century French history; and in *Immortal Rock* she finds her story in much-disputed evidence that

an expedition of Norsemen, commissioned by King Magnus Erikson of Norway, Sweden, and Skaane, and led by Paul Knutson, wandered the North American prairie in the fourteenth century.

In *The Dark Weaver* Salverson returns to the subject of her first book, *The Viking Heart*, but she broadens the scope considerably. Whereas in her first book she explores the fortunes of a family of Icelandic immigrants, in this one she traces the fate of several families of different national and social backgrounds. Like the earlier work, this one spans more than one generation and concludes with the immigrants' sacrifices in World War I.

In 1939 Salverson published her autobiography, *Confessions of an Immigrant's Daughter*, an account of her life up to the publication of *The Viking Heart*. Salverson was one of the pioneers of Canadian prairie fiction, perhaps Canada's first native prairie novelist. In her books she attempts to reconcile the narrative form of the Icelandic saga with that of the popular romance in order to interpret Icelandic life for English-speaking readers. Although her attempts are not entirely successful and although her style is sometimes uneven and often flowery, her tales are usually interesting and frequently compelling.

References:

Wilfrid Eggleston, *The Frontier and Canadian Letters* (Toronto: Ryerson, 1957), pp. 145, 150;

Dick Harrison, *Unnamed Country: The Struggle for a Canadian Prairie Fiction* (Edmonton: University of Alberta Press, 1977), pp. 84, 147;

Edward A. McCourt, *The Canadian West in Fiction*, revised edition (Toronto: Ryerson, 1970), pp. 75-79, 125;

Laurence Ricou, *Vertical Man/Horizontal World* (Vancouver: University of British Columbia Press, 1973), pp. 69-71, 74.

B. K. Sandwell

(6 December 1876-7 December 1954)

John Lennox
York University

BOOKS: *Westing* (Montreal: Privately printed, 1918);

The Forest Industries (Quebec: Semaine Commerciale, 1928);

The Privacity Agent and Other Modest Proposals (London & Toronto: Dent, 1928; New York: Dutton, 1928);

The Molson Family (Montreal: Privately printed, 1933);

Canada and United States Neutrality (Toronto: Oxford University Press, 1939; New York: Farrar & Rinehart, 1939);

You Take Out What You Put In (Toronto: Canadian Association for Adult Education and the Canadian Institute of International Affairs, 1940);

The Canadian Peoples (London, New York & Toronto: Oxford University Press, 1941); also published as *Canada* (London, New York & Toronto: Oxford University Press, 1941);

Post-war Finance (Ottawa: Royal Society of Canada, 1942);

The State and Human Rights (Toronto: Canadian Association for Adult Education and the Canadian Institute of International Affairs, 1947);

The Gods in Twilight (Vancouver: University of British Columbia, 1948);

Cities of Canada (Montreal: Seagram, 1953);

La Nation canadienne (Monaco: Rocher, 1954);

The Diversions of Duchesstown, and Other Essays (Toronto: Dent, 1955).

OTHER: *The Call to Arms*, edited by Sandwell (Montreal: Southam, 1914);

Poems for the Interim, edited anonymously by Sandwell (Toronto: Consolidated Press, 1946).

As editor, economist, humorist, and drama and literary critic for over half a century, B. K. Sandwell was one of Canada's outstanding public voices. Editor of the *Canadian Bookman* from 1919 to 1922, he was instrumental in founding the Canadian Authors' Association and in lobbying successfully in the early 1920s for important amendments to the proposed Canadian copyright bill. Later, under the two decades of his editorship, *Saturday Night* came to represent for its broad readership what the *Canadian Forum* was to the more restricted academic and intellectual community—an outspoken Canadian journal of in-

B. K. Sandwell (photograph by Karsh-Ottawa)

dependent opinion and an instrument of national self-definition.

Bernard Keble Sandwell was born in Ipswich, England, in 1876, the son of the Reverend George Henry Sandwell, a Congregational clergyman, and his wife, Emily Johnson Sandwell. In 1888 Sandwell's family immigrated to Canada and settled in Toronto. Here Sandwell attended Upper Canada College, where he was taught by Stephen Leacock. He went on to the University of Toronto, majored in classics, and graduated with first-class honors in 1897. Upon graduation he became a member of the editorial staff of the *Toronto News* and subsequently went to England where he also worked as a journalist. Returning to Canada in 1905, he was hired as drama editor of the *Montreal Herald*, where he remained until 1911 when he became associate editor of the *Montreal Financial Times*. Sandwell, who subsequently became editor of that journal, had married Marion Street of Albany, New York, in 1908. It was while he was with the *Times* that Sandwell directed editorial work for *The Call to Arms* (1914), a compendium of the history and of the lists of officers and men of different Montreal regiments.

In 1919, under the sponsorship of Leacock, he was appointed assistant professor of economics at McGill University, and in the same year he became editor of the *Canadian Bookman*. In 1923 his multiple talents took him away from McGill to become head of the Department of English at Queen's University, where he served as teacher and administrator until 1925 when a bitter academic dispute prompted him to resign from the university, return to Montreal, and work primarily as a free-lance writer and speaker in the lean years from 1925 to 1932. During this period he contributed to periodicals and also undertook various commissions. In 1928 he compiled for Algoma Steel a brief in support of their application for alterations and additions to the Canadian customs tariff. In the same year he prepared *The Forest Industries,* a pamphlet for public distribution, which argued for the adoption by Quebec of a complete and adequate forest policy. For these seven years Sandwell was also associated in an advisory capacity with the Alexander Hamilton Institute, a business college in New York.

His first major book was *The Privacity Agent and Other Modest Proposals* (1928). An extension of his penchant for short, humorous pieces, it is a collection that combines informal, humorous essays of whimsical or satirical charm reminiscent of the style and wit of Christopher Morley with more serious occasional pieces. They are all characterized by Sandwell's distinctive comic touch, insight, and clarity of language.

In 1932 he was appointed editor in chief of *Saturday Night,* replacing Hector Charlesworth, who had become director of the Canadian Radio Broadcasting Commission. Sandwell, fully aware of the impact of international economic and political relations on Canada in the early 1920s, sought to make *Saturday Night* even more national in its viewpoint and international in its awareness. Gradually the society columns were dropped in favor of greater emphasis on politics and the arts.

Apart from *The Molson Family* (1933), which Sandwell prepared on commission for private publication, his energies in the 1930s centered on *Saturday Night.* The threat of war prompted *Canada and United States Neutrality* (1939) for the series Oxford Pamphlets on World Affairs. His book *The Canadian Peoples* (1941), also published as *Canada,* is a well-written introduction for the general reader, addressing itself to the history and national character of Canadians and to a discussion of regionalism and continentalism. World War II in-

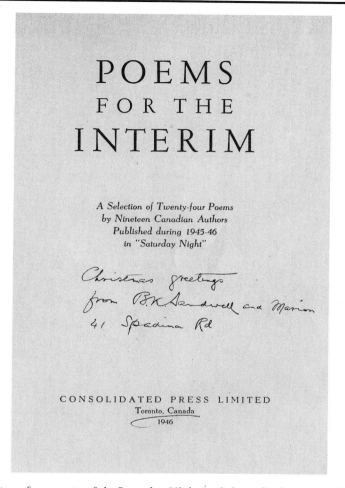

POEMS

FOR THE

INTERIM

*A Selection of Twenty-four Poems
by Nineteen Canadian Authors
Published during 1945-46
in "Saturday Night"*

*Christmas greetings
from B.K. Sandwell and Marion
41 Spadina Rd*

CONSOLIDATED PRESS LIMITED
Toronto, Canada
1946

Inscribed title page from a copy of the Saturday Night *anthology edited anonymously by Sandwell*

spired other pamphlets: *You Take Out What You Put In* (1940), on the responsibilities and privileges of the individual under democracy; and *Postwar Finance* (1942). During the war he visited Britain with a group of Canadian newspapermen and on his return wrote a series of articles in *Saturday Night* about the spirit of the British.

His publications after the war continued to reflect his wide interests. *The State and Human Rights* (1947) is a pamphlet which calls for a Canadian bill of rights. He wrote the commentary for the illustrated *Cities of Canada* published by Seagram's Distillery in 1953; the following year *La Nation canadienne* appeared in UNESCO's Profil des Nations series. Its broad emphasis on family, education, politics, economics, and religion was directed toward a general, international audience. Sandwell's final book, *The Diversions of Duchesstown, and Other Essays,* appeared posthumously in 1955, the year after Sandwell's death.

It is a collection that combines satirical sketches about a fictitious provincial Canadian small town with comic occasional essays. The book renewed the spirit and skill of his earlier drollery in *The Privacity Agent* and reconfirmed Sandwell's talent for creating the comic persona of the benign but shrewd observer.

He had been publicly honored during his career by being named to the Royal Society of Canada in 1925, by honorary degrees from Queen's University in 1942 and Bishop's University in 1943, and by his appointment as rector of Queen's from 1943 to 1947. When he retired in 1951 as editor in chief of *Saturday Night,* he was immediately designated editor emeritus and contributed a weekly column of opinion; he also wrote every week for the Toronto weekly magazine the *Financial Post.* His death in 1954 came at the end of a remarkable career. Sandwell had devoted his life to nurturing and encouraging Canada's sense of its own identity that had emerged in the aftermath of major sacrifices in World War I. In his early work for the Canadian Authors' Association, in his editorial direction of *Saturday Night*, and in his own books, pamphlets, and speeches, he sought to give Canadians a sense of themselves in a national and international context. As an accomplished humorist and satirist, he was able to balance the seriousness of his social, political, and economic themes with a delight in man's comic inconsistency.

Papers:
Sandwell's papers are at the Queen's University Archives in Kingston.

Edward Sapir
(26 January 1884-4 February 1939)

Regna Darnell
University of Alberta

BOOKS: *Takelma Texts* (Philadelphia: University Museum, 1909);

The Takelma Language of Southwestern Oregon (Washington, D.C.: Government Printing Office, 1912);

Time Perspective in Aboriginal American Culture: A Study in Method (Ottawa: Government Printing Bureau, 1916);

Dreams and Gibes (Boston: Poet Lore, 1917);

Language: An Introduction to the Study of Speech (New York: Harcourt, Brace, 1921);

The Southern Paiute Language, 3 volumes (Boston: American Academy of Arts and Sciences, 1930-1931);

International Communication: A Symposium on the Language Problem, by Sapir, Herbert N. Shenton, and Otto Jesperson (London: Paul, Trench, Trübner, 1931);

The Expression of the Ending-Point Relation in English, French, and German, by Sapir and Morris Swadesh, edited by Alice V. Morris (Baltimore: Waverly, 1932);

Selected Writings in Language, Culture and Personality, edited by David G. Mandelbaum (Berkeley & Los Angeles: University of California Press, 1949);

Yana Dictionary, by Sapir and Swadesh, edited by Mary R. Haas (Berkeley: University of California Press, 1960);

The Phonology and Morphology of the Navaho Language (Berkeley: University of California Press, 1967).

SELECTED PERIODICAL PUBLICATIONS
UNCOLLECTED: "The Musical Foundations of Verse," *Journal of English and Germanic Philology,* 20 (April 1921): 213-228;

"Culture, Genuine and Spurious," *American Journal of Sociology,* 29 (1924): 401-429.

Edward Sapir is remembered primarily as the most distinguished American-Indian linguist of his generation. Like many other social scientists of his day, however, Sapir dabbled in belles lettres and applied insights gained from aesthetic pursuits to his more conventionally academic work. He published more than two hundred poems in periodicals (approximately half of those extant in manuscript and in the possession of the Sapir family) and one volume of poetry; he wrote numerous reviews of poetry, and his interest in musical performance and composition led to several significant papers on the general nature of patterning. Sapir's poetry, however, has not been anthologized, as was that of his contemporary, friend, and fellow anthropologist Ruth Benedict (who wrote under the pseudonym of Anne Singleton). In retrospect his most significant contribution to literature may well have been his role in Ottawa social and scientific circles as a poet and supporter of the arts. Indeed, the vast majority of Sapir's aesthetic pursuits were carried out during his fifteen-year tenure as

director of the anthropological division of the Geological Survey of Canada (1910-1925).

Sapir, born in 1884 in Lauenburg, Pomerania, was the only surviving child of Eva Seagal and Jacob David Sapir, a Jewish cantor. He grew up in New York City and received his B.A., M.A., and Ph.D. from Columbia University. Initially Sapir specialized in Germanic philology and literature, also studying music; but he switched to anthropology, albeit still concentrating in linguistics, as one of the first generation of students of Franz Boas, the dominant figure of twentieth-century North American anthropology and linguistics. Sapir was fascinated by the patterned complexity of grammar, particularly in languages dramatically divergent from the Indo-European language family. Moreover, he accepted Boas's urgent mandate to record Amerindian languages before they became completely extinct, a likelihood considered inevitable in the early part of the cen-

tury. (Many of the languages Sapir studied are no longer spoken, but others have revived in their usage and symbolization of native American identity, an indirect result of the work of Sapir and his colleagues in both Canada and the United States.)

Sapir did major firsthand fieldwork on five languages before accepting his government position in 1910 (Chinook and Takelma in Oregon, Yana in California, and Ute and Southern Paiute in the Southwest). During the Ottawa years his primary fieldwork was with the Nootka of Vancouver Island. In the course of his career, Sapir worked on more than twenty different American-Indian languages. He produced exemplary descriptions of some of these, including grammar, texts, and dictionary, and wrote many comparative papers on aspects of linguistic classification and theory. As a sideline to his linguistic work Sapir collected and published ethnographic reports as well.

The tie that might have been expected between Sapir's poetry and his ethnology, however, was little exploited by him. Sapir realized that his general technique of writing poetry, as an analyst or observer, was not conducive to conveying a sense of Indian cultures. In his poetry he was more interested in his own subjective world than in anything outside his own mind. Only a handful of Sapir's poems are ethnographic; of these, the most successful is "Zuni," written for Benedict and tacitly equating her personality with the controlled, ritualistic cultural style of the Zuni.

After the initial Ottawa years Sapir became increasingly demoralized by his professional work. He sought psychic balance through poetry and music, coming to define his personal and professional identity in terms of these activities. Anyone who wrote well could write poetry–in the opinion of Sapir and many of his contemporaries. However, Sapir was disappointed with much of his poetry and blamed the failure of his work to satisfy him on an inherent conflict between the scientific spirit and the aesthetic attitude. His own temperament included both, and much of his work during the Ottawa years was devoted to an attempt at reconciling the two. By 1925 he had progressed from being a promising, perhaps even brilliant, anthropologist-linguist in the Boasian tradition to formulating a theory of culture that took account of individual variability and gave creativity a major role in cultural dynamics. Although his later work in what is now called the "culture-and-personality" field at the University

Edward and Florence Delson Sapir with their son Michael in 1913

of Chicago (1925-1931) and Yale University (1931-1939) is remembered as having emerged from interdisciplinary collaboration between psychology (particularly psychiatry), anthropology, and sociology, Sapir's position was already largely developed when he left Ottawa. Its roots, therefore, necessarily lie in his poetic explorations of the preceding decade, which were only elaborated in terms of the later work.

The date of Sapir's earliest extant poem is April 1917, appearing in his handwritten diary-notebook labeled "Subjective Notes" (in the possession of the Sapir family), which served as a record of literary ideas of various kinds: short stories, aphorisms, responses to poetry of others, and reflections on the process of writing poetry and the nature of aesthetics. Almost none of these ideas was developed further. Sapir began to write literary reviews and social commentaries in 1916 and psychoanalytic book reviews a year later, which indicate that his knowledge of this field was far from extensive and almost entirely derivative at this time. Between 1918 and 1921 more than half of his publications were literary; in 1922 literary efforts actually predominated.

After he left Ottawa in 1925, Sapir's literary activities tapered off sharply.

Sapir's only published volume of poetry, *Dreams and Gibes,* appeared in 1917, incorporating the majority of his early efforts. It was published in Boston, where Sapir had family ties; apparently he paid most of the cost himself. The book was dedicated to his wife, Florence Delson Sapir, whom he had married in 1911 and who shared his enthusiasm for poetry. In spite of his optimism, the volume received little critical attention. An anonymous reviewer in the *Dial* (23 August 1919) found it "seldom of the magic of poetry," in spite of "a free, idealistic spirit." The occasional "suggestive turn of thought" did not save the whole. Sapir must have found this ambivalent review encouraging, for he planned a second volume of his poems. He sent his efforts to various anthropological colleagues (although rarely to other poets) and accepted criticism with reasonable grace—in sharp contrast to his refusal to accept editing in his scientific works. Both he and Benedict submitted poetry manuscripts to Alfred Harcourt; both were rejected, and neither tried again.

Sapir considered himself an adequate judge of the poetry of his day, much of which he considered pretentious and second-rate. The imagist poetry of Amy Lowell and Ezra Pound seemed to Sapir inextricably linked to the currently fashionable liberal politics of John Dewey (of which Sapir also disapproved). He was also critical of poetry-journal editors, remarking in "Suggestive Notes" in January 1918 that editors were inclined to "drag the public down to their own supercilious estimate of [poetry]." Sapir corresponded extensively with Harriet Monroe, editor of *Poetry* magazine. Richard Handler (in his 1986 article for the *History of Anthropology*) reviews this correspondence in some detail, noting that Monroe attempted to avoid sentimentality and "intimate self-revelations" in favor of "hardness combined with passion and intellect." In a 1920 essay, "The Heuristic Value of Rhyme" (in *Selected Writings in Language, Culture and Personality,* 1949), Sapir uses the same images to describe his own ideals for poetry: "It is precisely the passionate temperament cutting into itself with the cold steel of the intellect" that constitutes the best of the "new poetry." However, a disagreement arose between Monroe and Sapir over what she considered his carelessness in poetic craft; at least in correspondence Sapir sometimes agreed with her assessment.

Sapir on his way to work in New Haven, 1936

Sapir described his methods of writing in his "Suggestive Notes" of 29 November 1917, musing that his thoughts seemed to dissipate between inkwell and page. Although in scientific writing he outlined his argument in advance, he suggested that the poet cease to look for a subject and build up imagery from a fragmentary, decontextualized phrase or sentence—which might not even be retained in the eventual product. The poet should deal with the underlying form of human relationships and moods. Handler (1983) argues that Sapir's poetry was fundamentally divided in its imagery between the hungry man who sought experience and the dainty man who described it in poetic terms. Sapir longed to be the former and was in practice closer to the latter, a tension reflected in many of his poems.

Sapir attempted in his notebook to develop a position on aesthetics based on his reading, and reinterpretation, of the work of Benedetto Croce. Although there is no obvious influence of Croce on his poetry, Sapir cited him in the preface to *Language: An Introduction to the Study of Speech* in 1921. Most important to Sapir was Croce's shared conviction that aesthetics was integral to both science and art. Sapir insisted, however, on the need for a cross-cultural dimension to any theory of aesthetics. The two also agreed that art was equivalent to intuition and that art included all forms of sincere self-expression.

Ottawa literary and artistic life provided Sapir with a sense of camaraderie unavailable through scientific pursuits; his professional papers, particularly in linguistics, were too technical for general interest, and their specialized audience was not in Ottawa. He was an active member of the Ottawa Arts and Letters Club, implicitly under the patronage of romantic novelist Madge Macbeth. Sapir spoke to the club on such diverse topics as an experiment in the perception of design elements, American-Indian languages, the state of contemporary poetry, and the arbitrariness of the line between prose and poetry. He also served on the executive committee and as honorary president.

Sapir's poetry served him as a catharsis during the later Ottawa years. He was profoundly depressed by the advent of World War I, partly because of the cutbacks it enforced upon his anthropological division and partly because of his basically pacifist political position. Like most intellectuals of the period, Sapir was inclined toward socialist thinking; unlike many of his contemporaries, however, he was never active in politics. The war brought considerable xenophobia in Canada, with the future of the British empire seemingly at stake. In 1919 Sapir gave an impromptu public lecture that was interpreted by the Ottawa press as critical of the Canadian political system. Since he was not a native Canadian, he was not seen as having the right to criticize his adopted country; his Jewishness was perhaps more of an issue than his birthplace. The war seemed to end the hopes of intellectuals that science and art would lead the way to a brighter future. Sapir deplored the militarism of the era, and several of the poems in *Dreams and Gibes* express his pessimism over the war. Sapir also lamented the conventionality and lack of firsthand experience in the plethora of patriotic poems then being published. However, none of these actions produced any negative public reaction.

Sapir's personal life during the late Ottawa years revolved around the physical and mental illness of his wife, Florence, beginning after the birth of her third child in 1916 and continuing intermittently until her death in 1924. He wrote some poems about death and loss of a beloved during this period; almost all of them remain unpublished, indicating that Sapir recognized their cathartic role and preferred to keep them private. His wife's illness also increased Sapir's interest in the emerging discipline of psychiatry, in spite of his failure to find an adequate diagnosis or treatment for her. Poetry, moreover, was the only form in which Sapir ever allowed himself to express the anguish of this period in his life. In later years he encouraged his students of personality and culture to undergo psychoanalysis as part of their training; but he himself refused such analysis on the grounds that he could not relive this period of his life. Such avoidance of his past may have been one of the reasons that Sapir effectively stopped writing poetry after 1925.

Sapir's explorations in the nature of creativity and the relationship of form and meaning were reflected in scientific as well as literary form. "Culture, Genuine and Spurious" (1924) argued to an audience that was as much general as sociological that modern North Americans lacked the cultural integration and, therefore, the ability to fulfill the individual, an ability taken for granted in so-called primitive societies. The genuine culture of the latter had to be achieved by modern man in a more complex society. The efforts of the "new poetry" to revitalize its own society are the clear context for this article, the first of Sapir's theoretical papers on the relationship of the individual and culture. His later development of these ideas, however, no longer attempted to speak to the popular or literary audience that was certainly part of their genesis.

Sapir's 1921 book, *Language,* also includes numerous reflections on literary endeavors, such as chapters on literature and aesthetics. But more significantly, Sapir devoted considerable attention to the nature of form in language, that is, grammar. He was later to develop his notions of linguistic patterning in relation to the effect of language on thought—a position frequently referred to as the Sapir-Whorf hypothesis (Benjamin Whorf was a student of Sapir's at Yale in the 1930s). It, too, had its genesis in Sapir's literary efforts of the period before 1925.

Sapir's concern with music cannot be fully separated from his interest in poetry and literature. He was adamant that music was part of the scope of adequate ethnography and published several papers reporting on music in American-Indian societies. His Jewish musical background and musical training at Columbia allowed more sophisticated renderings of such material than was common at the time. Many of Sapir's poems express his fascination with music and with playing the piano. His most common poetic images have to do with sound; indeed, he was one of the first to appreciate the poetry of Gerard Manley Hopkins (1844-1889). As early as 1917, in "The Music of the Spheres" (*Minaret,* June 1917), he wrote: "Oh listen to the fluting strumming singing strains, / Shot through with tinkling ringing sounds, / Upheld on booming drones." He also mused poetically on the effect that music had on his emotions and on his feelings about music education for his children.

More importantly, however, Sapir came to describe music theoretically as neither tone nor rhythm, but as a contrastive pattern of sound. He was explicitly concerned with how the creative process related to formal constraint and with the internal, structural relationship of musical and poetic units. In "The Musical Foundations of Verse" (published in 1921) Sapir uses music to counter Amy Lowell's argument regarding the atomism of free verse. Moreover, he argues that the line between poetry and prose is arbitrary and linked to the degree of "poetic receptivity of the listener." Poetry and music share the property of patterning by sound rather than primarily by idea or visual image. Music, like poetry, is an expression of the emotions.

Sapir was remembered by his professional colleagues in both anthropology and linguistics as having written poetry. Although few people have read his poems, scattered as many of them are in the small literary journals of the period or unpublished, the idea of his humanism has remained—and characterizes Sapir as a scientist, not only as a poet. For example, Sapir's former student David Mandelbaum, editor of the *Selected Writings,* wrote to Sapir's widow, Jean McClenaghan Sapir, in January 1956 (in a letter in possession of the Sapir family): "Science and art were combined in Sapir in unusual degree. He was a meticulous linguist. . . . Yet he was a humanist and artist as well. He was a poet. . . . His essays in music and literature show not only a perceptive, creative intelligence but also reveal the joy he found in those arts." And that statement may well stand as the summary of Sapir's importance as a literary figure, bridging the gap between the physical sciences, social sciences, and humanities.

Letters:

Letters from Edward Sapir to Robert H. Lowie, edited by Luella Cole Lowie (Berkeley: Published by the editor, 1965);

Edward Sapir's Correspondence, edited by Louise Dallaire (Ottawa: National Museums of Canada, 1984);

The Sapir-Kroeber Correspondence, edited by Victor Golla (Berkeley: University of California Press, 1984).

References:

Regna Darnell, *Edward Sapir: Linguist, Anthropologist, Humanist* (Berkeley & Los Angeles: University of California Press, 1990);

Darnell, "The Emergence of Edward Sapir's Ma-

ture Thought," in *New Perspectives in Language, Culture and Personality*, edited by W. Cowan, M. Foster, and K. Koerner (Amsterdam & Philadelphia: Benjamins, 1986), pp. 553-588;

Darnell, "Personality and Culture: The Fate of the Sapirian Alternative," *History of Anthropology*, 4 (1986): 156-183;

Richard Handler, "The Dainty and the Hungry Man: Literature and Anthropology in the Work of Edward Sapir," *History of Anthropology*, 1 (1983): 208-231;

Handler, "The Vigorous Male and Aspiring Female: Poetry, Personality and Culture in Edward Sapir and Ruth Benedict," *History of Anthropology*, 4 (1986): 127-155.

Margaret Marshall Saunders

(13 April 1861-15 February 1947)

Carole Gerson
Simon Fraser University

BOOKS: *My Spanish Sailor* (London: Ward & Downey, 1889); enlarged as *Her Sailor. A Love Story* (Boston: Page, 1900);

Beautiful Joe: The Autobiography of a Dog (Philadelphia: Bane, 1893); republished as *Beautiful Joe: An Autobiography* (Toronto: Baptist Book Room, 1894; Philadelphia: American Baptist Publication Society, 1894);

Charles and His Lamb (Philadelphia: Banes, 1895);

For the Other Boy's Sake, and Other Stories (Philadelphia: Banes, 1896);

The House of Armour (Philadelphia: Rowland, 1897);

The King of the Park (New York & Boston: Crowell, 1897);

Rose à Charlitte: An Acadian Romance (Boston: Page, 1898);

Deficient Saints: A Tale of Maine (Boston: Page, 1899);

For His Country and Grandmother and the Crow (Boston: Page, 1900);

'Tilda Jane: An Orphan in Search of a Home (Boston: Page, 1901);

Beautiful Joe's Paradise; or, The Island of Brotherly Love (Boston: Page, 1902);

The Story of the Graveleys (Toronto: Briggs, 1903; Boston: Page, 1904);

Nita, the Story of an Irish Setter; Containing Also Uncle Jim's Burglar and Mehitable's Chicken (Boston: Page, 1904);

Princess Sukey: The Story of a Pigeon and Her Human Friends (New York: Eaton & Mains/ Cincinnati: Jennings & Graham, 1905);

Alpatak: The Story of an Eskimo Dog (Boston: Page, 1906); republished as *The Story of an Eskimo Dog* (London: Hodder & Stoughton, 1906);

My Pets: Real Happenings in My Aviary (Philadelphia: Griffith & Rowland, 1908);

'Tilda Jane's Orphans (Boston: Page, 1909);

The Girl From Vermont: The Story of a Vacation School Teacher (Philadelphia & Boston: Griffith & Rowland, 1910);

Pussy Black-Face; or, The Story of a Kitten and Her Friends (Boston: Page, 1913);

The Wandering Dog: Adventures of a Fox Terrier (New York: Doran, 1916);

Golden Dicky: The Story of a Canary and his Friends (New York: Stokes, 1919);

Bonnie Prince Fetlar: The Story of a Pony and His Friends (New York: Doran, 1920);

Margaret Marshall Saunders with her dog

Jimmy Gold-coast; or, The Story of a Monkey and his Friends (Toronto: Hodder & Stoughton, 1923; Philadelphia: McKay, 1924);
Esther de Warren: The Story of a Mid-Victorian Maiden (New York: Doran, 1927).

At the turn of the twentieth century Margaret Marshall Saunders, author of the first Canadian novel reputed to sell over a million copies, enjoyed international renown as a vigorous campaigner for the protection of children and animals. More noteworthy for the nobility of their sentiments than the quality of their expression, most of her more than twenty books proclaim that the ills of urban, industrialized society can be cured by banning child labor, providing constructive recreation programs, and inculcating compassion by promoting kindness to animals. Her precept, as set out in a 1901 letter, was "Teach the little child his duty to the lower or-

ders, and statistics prove that he will be more mindful of his duty to the higher." Today her adult and juvenile works are out of print and virtually ignored, with the exception of *Beautiful Joe: The Autobiography of a Dog* (1893).

Saunders was born 13 April 1861 in Milton, Nova Scotia, at the home of her maternal grandparents, and spent her first six years at Berwick in the Annapolis Valley. The eldest child of Maria Freeman and Edward Manning Saunders, a popular Baptist preacher, she absorbed from her parents the religious and moral values that were to inform her writing. In 1867, when Edward Saunders accepted the position of pastor of the First Baptist Church in Halifax, the family moved from a lush rural setting to a densely populated urban environment. Saunders's initial dislike of her new home may be one source of her later tendency to depict the city less favorably than the country. Other features of her writing which may be traced to her childhood are her obsession with animals–the children were allowed numerous pets–and her preference for elaborately contrived plots, Charles Dickens and Sir Walter Scott being the only novelists deemed suitable in her Baptist household. Saunders enjoyed a happy childhood, and was so strongly attached to her parents that when she was sent abroad for two years at the age of fifteen, her stay in an Edinburgh finishing school, which was followed by a year in France, was marred by homesickness. Fifty years later she returned to this experience in *Esther de Warren: The Story of a Mid-Victorian Maiden* (1927), her last published work and her favorite book. Exhibiting a mélange of realism and romance typical of Saunders's later fiction, this novel entwines a credible depiction of a young Nova Scotian's first sea voyage and attendance at a Presbyterian boarding school with a sensational plot involving intricate family secrets, elaborate disguises, sudden wealth, the reunion of long-separated twins, and Zionism.

Upon her return from Europe, Saunders busied herself with family concerns and some teaching, eventually turning to writing almost by chance. Impressed by a letter Saunders had composed on behalf of her father, a friend suggested that she try her hand at describing "the beauty of your winter scenery, . . . the stillness of the woods, the rabbit's track in the snow." She produced instead a story about a burglar, which promptly earned her forty dollars from *Frank Leslie's Popular Monthly* (New York) and a taste for a literary career. At the age of twenty-three Saunders began to publish in popular magazines such as *Our Home* (Montreal), the *Union Signal* (Boston), the *Baptist Visitor* (Toronto), and *Godey's Lady's Book* (Philadelphia). When she turned to longer works, she retained her penchant for exciting plots. While her first book, a naively charming romance titled *My Spanish Sailor* (1889), was favorably reviewed, it was her second that established her reputation. The hero of *Beautiful Joe* was a real dog, the pet of friends in Ontario which had been mutilated by a previous owner. In her novel Saunders placed him in a family resembling her own (Miss Laura, the heroine, was based on her sister Laura, who had died at the age of seventeen) and transferred the setting to New England in order to qualify for a competition sponsored by the American Humane Educational Society. After winning a prize of two hundred dollars, Saunders eventually had the manuscript accepted for publication in Philadel-

phia. The extraordinary popularity of her homely canine hero inspired a sequel, *Beautiful Joe's Paradise; or, The Island of Brotherly Love* (1902), a whimsical account of the afterlife of deserving animals presided over by Joe himself, with his missing ears and tail restored. Narrated by a boy from San Francisco, this particular book departs from Saunders's technique of using an animal narrator, as in *Beautiful Joe* and many of her subsequent juvenile novels.

In these stories dogs, cats, birds, ponies, and monkeys are able to remember, record, and present (with the aid of a human amanuensis) complex information at the intellectual level of a nine-year-old child. Saunders's animal narrators create a distinct analogy between the subordinate position of animals in the human world and the vulnerability of children in the sphere of adult affairs. Her messages of kindness to animals and general social reform are thus communicated in the bond forged between animal narrator and juvenile reader, as well as in her repeated endorsement of Bands of Mercy, the juvenile clubs of the Society for the Prevention of Cruelty to Animals. The SPCA was one of the more than twenty reform organizations to which Saunders belonged, including the National Council of Women, the Humane Society, the Women's Christian Temperance Union, and the Playground Association of America. Saunders was also an active member of the Canadian Women's Press Club.

Although she always thought of herself as a Nova Scotian, Saunders spent much of her adult life in the United States and her last thirty-three years in Toronto. In 1895 she moved to Boston for two years, attending some university classes; in 1898 she went to California for two years; and after Rida, her only sister who married, moved to Rochester, New York, Saunders made frequent extended visits there as well. An avid traveler, she returned to Europe several times in addition to taking transcontinental North American trips. Her ostensible reason for traveling, as she put it in "The Story of My Life" (*Ontario Library Review*, 12 [1927]), was "that it was absolutely necessary that I should be on the scene where my story was laid," yet distinctive local color is not a predominant feature of much of her writing.

During the years around the turn of the century Saunders restrained her didacticism in several adult and juvenile novels which transmit their messages through the characters' experiences. In the charmingly ugly, chatterbox heroine of *'Tilda Jane: An Orphan in Search of a Home*

(1901), Saunders created a precursor of two lonely girls, Little Orphan Annie and L. M. Montgomery's Anne Shirley, whose quests for love and security have become better known. The most interesting of her adult books touch on relations between contemporary conditions and social history. *Deficient Saints* (1899), set in Maine, presents a somewhat superficial critique of New England's Puritan heritage by contrasting religiosity and religion. *Rose à Charlitte* (1898), set among contemporary Acadians living along Saint Mary's Bay in Nova Scotia, develops the popular romantic associations of the Acadian expulsion by considering the possibility of restitution, within the framework of a quaint and complex love story. Among Saunders's works, *Rose à Charlitte* stands out for its unity of plot and deftness of characterization, in contrast to her other Nova Scotian novel from this period, *The House of Armour* (1897), which has its Halifax setting as its only noteworthy feature.

It was as a writer of animal stories that Saunders was able to develop and maintain her reputation. In *My Pets: Real Happenings in My Aviary* (1908), her only work of nonfiction, she describes the elaborate accommodation made for her dozens of birds in her Halifax house, as well as the personal involvement with her pets which contributed to her public image as an eccentric. In 1911 she received an honorary M.A. from Acadia University, a rare honor for a woman at the time. In the 1920s mismanagement of her royalties and increasing difficulty in attracting publishers led her to develop popular lecture and slide presentations, "Marshall Saunders and Her Pets" and "Marshall Saunders: Her Life and Literary Adventures," with which she and her sister Grace toured the country until 1940. In 1935 she was made a Commander of the Order of the British Empire.

Saunders spent her last years in poverty and ill health and was sustained for a time by the assistance of her fellow Canadian writers through the Canadian Writers' Foundation. Upon her death, her authorship of *Beautiful Joe* and, in Dorothy Howard's words in a tribute for *Saturday Night* (1 March 1947), "her charming personality, her broad humanitarianism, and her wit and humour on the platform" earned her the accolade "Canada's Most Revered Author."

References:

Phyllis Blakely, "Margaret Marshall Saunders: The Author of *Beautiful Joe*," *Nova Scotia Historical Quarterly*, 1 (1971): 225-238;

John Elson, "Who's Who in Canadian Literature: Miss Marshall Saunders," *Canadian Bookman*, 12 (November 1930): 223-228.

Papers:

Substantial holdings of Saunders material are at the libraries of Acadia University, Wolfville, Nova Scotia; Mount Allison University, Sackville, New Brunswick; and McMaster University, Hamilton, Ontario.

Duncan Campbell Scott

(2 August 1862-19 December 1947)

Leon Slonim

BOOKS: *The Magic House, and Other Poems* (Ottawa: Durie, 1893; London: Methuen, 1893; Boston: Copeland & Day, 1895);

In the Village of Viger (Boston: Copeland & Day, 1896);

Labor and the Angel (Boston: Copeland & Day, 1898);

John Graves Simcoe (Toronto: Morang, 1905);

New World Lyrics and Ballads (Toronto: Morang, 1905);

Via Borealis (Toronto: Tyrrell, 1906);

Lundy's Lane and Other Poems (Toronto: McClelland, Goodchild & Stewart, 1916; New York: Doran, 1916);

Beauty and Life (Toronto: McClelland & Stewart, 1921);

Poetry and Progress (Ottawa: Royal Society of Canada, 1922);

The Witching of Elspie: A Book of Stories (Toronto: McClelland & Stewart, 1923; New York: Doran, 1923);

The Poems of Duncan Campbell Scott (Toronto: McClelland & Stewart, 1926; London: Dent, 1927);

The Green Cloister: Later Poems (Toronto: McClelland & Stewart, 1935);

The Circle of Affection, and Other Pieces in Prose and Verse (Toronto: McClelland & Stewart, 1947);

Selected Poems, edited by E. K. Brown (Toronto: Ryerson, 1951);

Selected Stories of Duncan Campbell Scott, edited by Glenn Clever (Ottawa: University of Ottawa Press, 1972);

At the Mermaid Inn, by Scott, William Wilfred Campbell, and others (Toronto: University of Toronto Press, 1979);

Untitled Novel, ca. 1905 (Moonbeam, Ont.: Penumbra, 1979);

Powassan's Drum: Selected Poems of Duncan Campbell Scott, edited by Raymond Souster and Douglas Lochhead (Ottawa: Tecumseh, 1985).

Duncan Campbell Scott

OTHER: *The Makers of Canada*, 22 volumes, edited by Scott, Pelham Edgar, and W. D. LeSueur (Toronto: Morang, 1903-1908, 1916); revised edition, 12 volumes, edited by W. L. Grant (London & Toronto: Oxford University Press, 1926);

Elise Aylen, *Roses of Shadow*, foreword by Scott (Toronto: Macmillan, 1930);

Archibald Lampman, *At the Long Sault and Other New Poems*, edited by Scott and E. K. Brown, with a foreword by Scott (Toronto: Ryerson, 1943);

Lampman, *Selected Poems*, edited, with a memoir, by Scott (Toronto: Ryerson, 1947).

Duncan Campbell Scott, poet and short-story writer, is one of the major Canadian literary figures of the late nineteenth and early twentieth centuries. First to make original and profound use of archetypally Canadian subjects, he is known for his harsh and, at their best, uncompromising narratives about Indians, fur traders, and other inhabitants of the Canadian North. Perhaps more than in the case of any other writer of his generation, his work forms a bridge between the romantic and the modern in Canadian literature.

Scott was born on 2 August 1862 in Ottawa, where he was to reside for his entire adult life. His father, the Reverend William Scott, was an immigrant from England; his mother, the former Janet Campbell MacCallum, was a native-born Canadian of Scottish background. Because his father was an itinerant minister of the Methodist church, Scott spent his childhood and received his formal education in several places: public school in Ottawa, high school in Smith's Falls, Ontario, and junior college in Stanstead, Quebec. More important than formal education in his creative development was Scott's early home environment: from his father, who had a large library, Scott inherited a devotion to books, and from his mother, a love of the arts, especially music.

In 1879 financial constraints forced an end to Scott's formal education, and in December of that year he entered the federal civil service as a clerk in the Department of Indian Affairs. It was to be the beginning of an illustrious career, all spent in the same branch of government. By 1893 he was chief accountant of his department, in 1909 he was appointed superintendent of Indian education, and in 1913 he was promoted to the highest nonelected position possible in his department, that of deputy superintendent general of Indian affairs, a position he held until his retirement in 1932.

In the early 1880s Scott pursued his artistic inclinations primarily through music (he was an accomplished pianist). A change in his direction occurred sometime in 1883 or 1884 when he became acquainted with Archibald Lampman, who had come to Ottawa to work with the postal service. It was a fateful meeting for, by Scott's own account, it was Lampman who provided him with the inducement to write: "It never occurred to me to write a line of prose or poetry until I was about twenty-five–and after I had met Archibald Lampman" (as quoted by E. K. Brown in his introduction to Selected Poems, 1951).

Trying his hand at both poetry and prose, Scott found himself enjoying a facility in both. As early as 1887 a story of his was accepted by Scribner's magazine, and in 1888 the second poem he

wrote appeared in the same prestigious American periodical. In the following two decades, in fact, much of Scott's output in both verse and prose–though he was not an especially prolific writer–found its way into the pages of American and Canadian magazines and newspapers. He had quickly made a name for himself, and his work was soon anthologized, appearing in W. D. Lighthall's Canadian Songs and Poems (1892) and J. E. Wetherell's Later Canadian Poems (1893). He was also one of only three Canadian writers to be discussed in William Archer's international survey Poets of the Younger Generation (1902). On the other hand, Scott did not become–indeed was never to become–a popular writer, in the sense that his peers, Charles G. D. Roberts and Bliss Carman, were popular. During the years 1892 and 1893 he collaborated with Lampman and Wilfred Campbell in writing a weekly literary column, "At the Mermaid Inn," for the Toronto Globe. But this was an act uncharacteristic of Scott, shy and reserved as he was. As the years went by he tended to take on the anonymity typical of a high-ranking civil servant, becoming less, not more, conspicuous to the public eye.

In 1893 Scott published his first book, The Magic House, and Other Poems, the only one of his books to be published in both England and the United States as well as Canada. Although the poems in The Magic House are clearly the work of an apprentice writer–the influence of such masters as John Keats, Alfred, Lord Tennyson, and Dante Gabriel Rossetti is often too apparent–they already reflect the individuality of Scott: the emphasis on the aural, rather than visual; the ubiquitous use of what was to become his trademark image–the storm; the obsession with the theme of life-in-death as opposed to death-in-life; and the fascination with the motif of drowning. And the best-known and most original poem in the volume, "At the Cedars"–a dramatic vignette about the death of a heroic French-Canadian lumberjack–anticipates Scott's later masterpieces in narrative verse. The Magic House was in general favorably received, especially in England where, according to Ezra Stafford, it "received more than usual notice" (the Week, 20 July 1894). The contemporaneous Speaker called it "one of the most remarkable books of verse of the decade."

That Scott could publish The Magic House at his own expense suggests that he had become financially more secure, as does the fact that he had bought a house on Lisgar Street in central Ottawa. In October 1894 he married Belle Warner

Botsford, an American concert violinist whom he had met when he had acted as her accompanist at a recital in Ottawa. The couple moved into the house on Lisgar Street and settled into a rather staid, cultured, and refined existence. In 1895 a daughter, Elizabeth Duncan, was born, who was to be the Scotts' only child. Her death at the age of twelve constituted the most traumatic event in their otherwise placid life.

In 1896 Scott published his first book of prose, *In the Village of Viger*, a collection of ten stories, all set in the fictional French-Canadian locale of the title. A few of the stories tend to the sentimental; others are eerie and disturbing. All are more than picturesque renditions of Quebec village life. But the book's serious treatment of such themes as materialism ("The Pedlar") and tolerance ("The Little Milliner") went largely unnoticed at the time. His second story collection, *The Witching of Elspie: A Book of Stories* (1923), tended more to employ folktale forms than to develop the social criticism inherent in the first unified collection. But by the 1920s Scott appeared to be looking to the past for security and for ideals of beauty and social coherence.

In 1898 Scott's second collection of poems, *Labor and the Angel*, was published, a book that shows an even more intense allegiance to fin-de-siècle fashions than had his first. Poems about art, dreamlike allegories, love lyrics, pastiches of Elizabethan and Romantic poets, and imitations of Scott's contemporary George Meredith dominate the volume. Among the aestheticist poems in *Labor and the Angel* undoubtedly the most successful is the ballad "The Piper of Arll." A complex, enigmatic work—perhaps Scott's only flawless major poem—"The Piper of Arll" can bear a variety of readings. One of the more persuasive ones is that of Fred Cogswell, who interprets the poem as having to do with the artist who is isolated from his fellow artists and desires communion with them. This situation is symbolized in terms of a shepherd living alone on an island and encountering a mysterious ship. The poem comes to a climax with the piper's work being absorbed, together with that of his fellow artists from afar, into the timeless realm of art, a process symbolized by the sinking of the ship:

> And down she sank till, keeled in sand,
> She rested safely, balanced true,
> With all her upward gazing band,
> The piper and the dreaming crew.
>
> And there, unmarked of any chart,

Scott at his piano. Like his mother, he never lost his love for music (photograph by Karsh-Ottawa).

> In unrecorded deeps they lie,
> Empearled within the purple heart
> Of the great sea for aye and aye.

Thus this poem may have been motivated, at least in part, by Scott's feeling of cultural isolation in Ottawa, a feeling Scott expressed more bitterly and explicitly in a letter to Pelham Edgar (4 March 1899) after his book had failed to make an impression among Canadians. "Labor & the Angel," he complained, "has hardly penetrated this wilderness."

In vain Scott tried to interest the Toronto publisher George Morang in issuing a Canadian edition of the book. Morang did, however, appoint Scott, together with Edgar and W. D. LeSueur, to edit his historical series *The Makers of Canada*. At the same time—around the turn of the century—Scott began making intensive use of Canadian material in his own writing. The titles of his next three books of verse—*New World Lyrics* and Ballads (1905), Via Borealis (1906), and Lundy's Lane and Other Poems (1916)–indicate his newfound interest. Partly this change in direction may have been a deliberate attempt to take advantage of the spirit of nationalism prevailing in Canada at the time (the same spirit that produced the turn-of-the-century "Maple Leaf" school of poetry). But there can be no doubt that it was also the result of Scott's profound and sincere response to the Canadian wilds.

In the 1890s Scott and Lampman had made canoe trips together on the lakes and rivers of northern Quebec. Lampman had died in 1899, but Scott had found himself in continued contact with the wilderness as a result of his increasing responsibilities in the civil service. The summer of 1899, for instance, was spent mostly among the Indians; in the summers of 1905 and 1906 Scott led expeditions through northern Ontario to sign treaties with native tribes, and in the summer of 1910 he toured Indian reservations in Saskatchewan and Alberta. The extent to which these four excursions were impressed upon Scott's imagination can be gauged from the fact that almost all his best-known poems were inspired by and drew upon these experiences.

At the same time, moreover, as he was making use of new material, Scott made a stylistic breakthrough, creating a kind of free verse–irregular in rhythm, plain in diction, and restrained in tone–that was eminently suited to stark narratives about Indians, trappers, and other inhabitants of the North. Scott uses this style masterfully in "The Forsaken" (in New World Lyrics and Ballads), varying the lengths of the lines to suit their meaning:

> Once in the winter
> Out on a lake
> In heart of the north-land,
> Far from the Fort
> And far from the hunters,
> A Chippewa woman
> With her sick baby,
> Crouched in the last hours
> Of a great storm.

Many years later the woman, now "old and useless," is abandoned to die:

> There one night they camped, and on the morrow
> Gathered their kettles and birch-bark
> Their rabbit-skin robes and their mink-traps,
> Launched their canoes and slunk away through
>   the islands,

> Left her alone forever. . . .

The strikingly fresh quality of New World Lyrics and Ballads did not go unnoticed by reviewers.

Via Borealis, a booklet published the next year, attracted less attention. Yet among its seven poems are two of Scott's finest: "Spring on Mattagami" and "The Half Breed Girl." The second of these is thematically central to Scott's oeuvre, as it tells of a young woman who is psychically divided between the Old World and the New (being of both Indian and Scottish blood) and who desires release from her intermediate state of neither life nor death.

Lundy's Lane and Other Poems was a much more ambitious venture than any of Scott's previous books. Issued in both Canada and the United States, it exceeded two hundred pages, carried a photographic frontispiece, and included all the poems from Via Borealis, as well as "Lines in Memory of Edmund Morris"–Scott's finest elegy–and "The Height of Land," his most philosophical Canadian wilderness poem. Unfortunately, however, Lundy's Lane also contained a mass of inferior work (such as the title poem) that detracted from the impression of the book as a whole. Thus the Toronto Mail and Empire (14 October 1916), in one of the most incisive reviews Scott was ever to receive, took the poet to task, describing him as a "distinctly Canadian" poet who is "surprisingly uneven in his work" and "not sufficiently self-critical," a writer who "at his best is found in the poems where he presents . . . scenes in the forests and in wild lands of Canada."

Lundy's Lane marks the end of what can be called Scott's "Canadian" period. His next book, Beauty and Life (1921), shows a return to the aestheticist, cosmopolitan manner he had cultivated in the 1890s. Failing at this turning point in literary history–the years during and after World War I–to make a full-fledged transition into a modern mode of writing, Scott became henceforth increasingly isolated from the forefront of literary activity, a representative of the established culture, out of touch with the new generation of Canadian writers that arose in the twenties and thirties. In his presidential address to the Royal Society of Canada in 1922 (published as Poetry and Progress and reprinted in The Circle of Affection, 1947) Scott assailed modern poetry as "wayward and discomforting, full of experiment that seems to lead nowhere." But regardless of his quarrel with current poets, the same year he was awarded an honorary doctorate by the University of Toronto, and in 1927 he received the Lorne Pierce medal in recognition of his contribution to Canadian literature.

Though Scott was to live for another two decades, *The Poems of Duncan Campbell Scott*, published in 1926, had the appearance of a book intended to bring its author's career to a distinguished close. The volume contained most of his published verse, was issued in both Canada and England, and included, in the English edition, an introduction by Poet-Laureate John Masefield. As with *Lundy's Lane*, however, the very unevenness of the book prevented its success. Thus the influential *Times Literary Supplement* (20 October 1927) praised the handful of "Canadian" poems but condemned the rest of the verse for its "tranquillizing" banal qualities. Ultimately Scott's collection made no appreciable difference to his reputation.

In 1929 Scott's wife, Belle, who had long suffered from ill health, died. Two years later Scott again married a woman who shared his interests and social rank: Elise Aylen (1904-1972) was herself a poet. She was, moreover, considerably younger than Scott, and marriage to her seemed to revitalize the sixty-nine-year-old poet. Retiring in 1932 from the civil service (after a career of fifty-three years), Scott spent much of the 1930s traveling with Elise. Europe was their principal destination, but in 1939, 1940, and 1942, with war raging there, they explored the southwestern United States and western Canada.

The Green Cloister: Later Poems (1935), Scott's last full-fledged book of verse, largely reflects these travels. But the book is really distinguished by two narratives about Indians, "A Scene at Lake Manitou" and "At Gull Lake: August, 1810," which light up brilliantly the last phase of his literary career. As one reviewer of *The Green Cloister* observed, these "graphic and interpretative studies . . . rank with his best previous work in that genre of which he is the acknowledged master" (*Mail and Empire*, 14 December 1935). Like most of Scott's books, *The Green Cloister* was not a commercial success. Ten years after its publication Scott was informed by his publisher that of 504 copies printed 281 had been sold.

After 1935 Scott wrote little, either in verse or prose. He chiefly spent the 1940s editing two selections of Lampman's poems, one of these in collaboration with E. K. Brown, who had replaced Edgar as his confidant and mentor. The last collection of Scott's writings to appear in his lifetime was published in 1947. *The Circle of Affection, and Other Pieces in Prose and Verse* (containing some of his very early and very late poetry) brought his career to an anticlimactic close. Two months after the appearance of the book, on 19 December 1947, Scott died at his Lisgar Street home in Ottawa after a short illness. (After her husband's death, Aylen left Canada to live in an ashram in India, where she published a novel called *The Night of the Lord* in 1967.)

Although Scott's work has recently received some long-overdue attention, during his lifetime his reputation had been secure but limited. If his work was never totally neglected, only a small fraction of it was appreciated. Reviewing *The Poems of Duncan Campbell Scott* in the *Canadian Bookman* in 1926, John Garvin had correctly prophesied that "Scott's fame in the future will rest more and more on his remarkable poems in 'free verse' (with or without rhyme) which have Indian and other themes of intense human interest. Who could ever tire of reading such poems as *Powassan's Drum*; *The Forsaken*; *At the Cedars*; *Night Burial in the Forest*; and *Lines in Memory of Edmund Morris?*"

For two decades after Scott's death this situation did not change: until the 1970s and 1980s his reputation continued to be based on the same small number of works (of the more than four hundred poems Scott wrote, only twelve have anything to do with Indians). However, more recently those works that originally made his reputation attracted a renewed interest. Their modern qualities became clearer (ironically so in view of Scott's overt resistance to modernism), and as a result Scott's reputation vis-à-vis his contemporaries grew stronger. Thus for Gary Geddes (in *Canadian Literature*, number 37, 1968) he is "the one breath of fresh air escaping from the mixed bag of Confederation poets." For Tom Marshall (in *Canadian Forum*, June-July 1977) Scott is "the best and most important of the Confederation poets since he goes further technically, emotionally and intellectually towards an idiom that can embody the Canadian situation." And for Glenn Clever (in *The Duncan Campbell Scott Symposium*, 1979) Scott is "a primary figure in the shift in Canadian fiction away from the tradition he inherited. . . . His fiction places him as a watershed author between the Victorian tradition and the modern. . . . Scott is an innovator."

However, Scott was a quintessentially contradictory writer. Careful and serious about the craft of poetry, he was yet prone to appalling lapses of judgment and taste. (At the end of his life he favored among his books of verse the volume of 1921, *Beauty and Life*–a volume that contains none of his finest works. Equally revealing is the fact that none of his books of verse is named after the best poem in it.) He was addicted to security and to a rooted existence, yet he also loved travel, and his greatest literary achievements came out of adventurous forays into alien territory. He disliked experimentation, yet his best work goes beyond the bounds of the conventional into what Scott himself called "the wilderness of natural accent" ("Poetry and Progress"). In daring to explore this wilderness Scott surpassed most of his contemporaries and in so doing created a unique and enduring body of work.

Letters:

Some Letters of Duncan Campbell Scott, Archibald Lampman, & Others, edited by Arthur S. Bourinot (Ottawa: Published by the editor, 1959);

More Letters of Duncan Campbell Scott, edited by Bourinot (Ottawa: The editor, 1960);

The Poet and the Critic: A Literary Correspondence Between D. C. Scott and E. K. Brown, edited by Robert L. McDougall (Ottawa: Carleton University Press, 1983).

References:

E. K. Brown, "Duncan Campbell Scott," in his *On Canadian Poetry* (Toronto: Ryerson, 1944), pp. 118-143;

Brown, Introduction to *Selected Poems of Duncan Campbell Scott*, edited by Brown (Toronto: Ryerson, 1951);

S. L. Dragland, ed., *Duncan Campbell Scott: A Book of Criticism* (Ottawa: Tecumseh, 1974);

Pelham Edgar, "Duncan Campbell Scott," *Dalhousie Review*, 7 (April 1927): 38-46;

Gary Geddes, "Piper of Many Tunes," *Canadian Literature*, 37 (Summer 1968): 15-27;

Carole Gerson, "The Piper's Forgotten Time: Notes on the Stories of D. C. Scott and a Bibliography," *Journal of Canadian Fiction*, 16 (1976): 138-143;

Keiichi Hirano, "The Aborigine in Canadian Literature," *Canadian Literature*, 14 (Autumn 1962): 43-52;

Leslie Monkman, *A Native Heritage* (Toronto: University of Toronto Press, 1981);

W. H. New, *Dreams of Speech and Violence* (Toronto: University of Toronto Press, 1987);

Leon Slonim, "D. C. Scott's 'At Gull Lake: August 1810,'" *Canadian Literature*, 81 (Summer 1979): 142-143;

A. J. M. Smith, "Duncan Campbell Scott: A Reconsideration," *Canadian Literature*, 1 (Summer 1959): 13-25;

K. P. Stich, ed., *The Duncan Campbell Scott Symposium* (Ottawa: University of Ottawa Press, 1979);

Brian Titley, *A Narrow Vision: Duncan Campbell Scott and the Administration of Indian Affairs in Canada* (Vancouver: University of British Columbia Press, 1986);

Tracy Ware, "D. C. Scott's 'The Height of Land' and the Great Romantic Lyric," *Canadian Literature*, 111 (Winter 1986): 10-25;

L. P. Weis, "D. C. Scott's View of History and the Indians," *Canadian Literature*, 111 (Winter 1986): 27-40.

Papers:

The Aylen-Scott papers at the Public Archives of Canada, Ottawa, are an important collection of manuscripts, typescripts, letters, and other miscellaneous material. The Pelham Edgar papers at the E. J. Pratt Library, University of Toronto, contain an extensive collection of Scott's correspondence and some typescripts of his poems.

Frederick George Scott

(7 April 1861-19 January 1944)

Sandra A. Djwa
Simon Fraser University

BOOKS: *Justin and Other Poems* (N.p.: Privately printed, 1885);

The Soul's Quest and Other Poems (London: Kegan Paul, Trench, 1888);

Elton Hazlewood: A Memoir by His Friend Harry Vane (New York: Whittaker, 1891; Edinburgh: Anderson & Ferrier, 1893);

My Lattice and Other Poems (Toronto: Briggs, 1894);

The Unnamed Lake and Other Poems (Toronto: Briggs, 1897);

Poems Old and New (Toronto: Briggs, 1900);

A Hymn of Empire, and Other Poems (Toronto: Briggs, 1906);

The Key of Life: A Mystery-Play (Quebec: Dussault & Proulx, 1907);

Poems (London: Constable / Toronto: Musson, 1910);

In the Battle Silences: Poems Written at the Front (Toronto: Musson / London: Constable, 1916);

The Great War as I Saw It (Toronto: Goodchild, 1922; enlarged edition, Vancouver: Clarke & Stuart, 1934);

In Sun and Shade (Quebec: Dussault & Proulx, 1926);

New Poems (Quebec: Lafrance, 1929);

Selected Poems (Quebec: Robitaille, 1933);

Collected Poems (Vancouver: Clarke & Stuart, 1934);

Poems (London: S.P.C.K., 1936);

Lift Up Your Hearts (Toronto: Ryerson, 1941).

Frederick George Scott, an Anglican priest and a lesser member of the Confederation group of poets, was celebrated by his contemporaries for his nature lyrics, his hymns of empire, and his celebration of the young Canadian soldier at the front during World War I. His regional Laurentian lyrics were important precursors of some modern Canadian poetry—especially the "Old Song" and "Laurentian Shield" of his son Francis Reginald Scott (born in 1899). The elder Scott's religious verse and fiction offer a more explicit rendering of the Victorian pessimism underlying the poetry of his more important contemporaries Charles G. D. Roberts and Archibald Lampman.

Scott was born in Montreal in April 1861. When only six he heard the bells of parliament ring out for confederation; he became a staunch Canadian, one whose poetic nationalism was rooted in the Laurentian landscape. The second strain in his poetry, the religious, also began in early childhood when he disobeyed his parents to attend a service at St. John the Evangelist Church in Montreal, where the ritual was so High Church as to be considered "Popish." But Scott (as reported by Sydenham Lindsay in 1959), "like many another small boy . . . was curious to do what was forbidden, and so he went. But when he saw surpliced choir boys preceded by a processional cross . . . he was terrified and ran out of the church." Despite his fears, or perhaps because of them, this scene was permanently imprinted upon his poetic imagination: the cross became his dominant symbol and Anglo-Catholicism his faith.

He received his early education in Montreal and in 1881 graduated with a B.A. from Bishops College, Quebec. In 1882 he studied theology at King's College, London, returning to Canada and Bishops College in September 1883, where he obtained an M.A. in 1884. His first book, a collection of verses on nature, evolution, death, and ecumenicalism, was privately printed as *Justin and Other Poems* in 1885. These early poems are informed both by personal experience and Victorian pessimism. In "A Mood," dated March 1882, he writes of his intense fear of death, speaking of a demon that had haunted him since childhood with "death and dreams of death." Like John Webster he saw the skull beneath the skin: "And, when I gaze in rapture on the face / Of whom I love, he casts a hideous light, / That lets me see, behind the sweet, warm flesh, / The lightless skull. . . ." Several of Scott's early narrative poems, including "Justin," and his novel *Elton Hazlewood: A Memoir by His Friend Harry Vane* (1891) describe the typically Victorian recogni-

337

Frederick George Scott during his service as a World War I Canadian Army chaplain

tion of "life and death as they are": Hazlewood links his own spiritual crisis with that described in John Stuart Mill's *Autobiography* (1873); and Justin asks "Why men should be, why pain and sin and death, / And where were hid the lineaments of God."

In December 1885 Scott returned to England and was ordained at Coggeshall in 1886; there he resolved his spiritual doubts. In the title poem of *The Soul's Quest and Other Poems* (1888)–the main poem being dated November 1886–the protagonist, "the old world's soul," is described as lost on life's highway where "The road is long, the hedgerows bare, / There's the chill of death in the silent air, / And a glimmer of darkness everywhere." She (the soul) finds no rest until she embraces the way of the cross and a life of active service, heartened by the solace of Anglo-Catholic ritual: "the altar lights are shining fair, / And Jesus' cross is standing there; / The darkness brightens everywhere."

This volume also includes "In Memoriam," a poem for the young Canadians killed in the North West Rebellion of 1885: "Wild the prairie grasses wave / O'er each hero's new-made grave; / . . . But the future spreads before us / Glorious in that sunset land. . . ." The last two lines were excerpted as an epigraph to W. D. Lighthall's *Songs of the Great Dominion* in 1899, the major anthology of nineteenth-century Canadian poetry. Scott had returned to Canada in February 1887 when he was appointed rector at Drummondville, Quebec, and his verse caught the epic note of heroism and the promise of Canada's future, two important strains in this post-Confederation era. On 27 April 1887 Scott married Amy Brook; they eventually had seven children.

In 1894 he published *My Lattice and Other Poems*, some of which, such as "Samson" and "Natura Victrix," are a continuation of his earlier religious didacticism; however, "My Lattice," a spontaneous description of the northern land-scape, introduces a new and fresher strain that continued in the Wordsworthian title poem of *The Unnamed Lake and Other Poems*, published in 1897. "The Unnamed Lake" depicts a Canadian wilderness where no man has been:

> Along the shore a heron flew,
>   And from a speck on high,
> That hovered in the deepening blue,
>   We heard the fish-hawk's cry.
>
> Among the cloud-capt solitudes,
>   No sound the silence broke,
> Save when, in whispers down the woods,
>   The guardian mountains spoke.

Scott's Canadianism, as was customary in this period, was closely allied with his imperialism; in 1899 he had preached to the Canadian troops leaving for the Boer War from his new parish of St. Matthews in Quebec City. In 1900 he published *Poems Old and New* and in 1906 *A Hymn of Empire, and Other Poems*, both including political poems. In 1914, two days after the declaration of the Great War, Scott volunteered for service. He was appointed chaplain in October 1914 and traveled to England. When it became apparent that he would not be dispatched to the front, he boarded a transport ship bound for France and calmly attached himself to the nearest Canadian group, the 15th Battalion of the First Division. Because of his extraordinary spirit and bravery under fire, Scott, a lieutenant colonel, returned to Canada in 1919 as a war hero decorated with the C.M.G. (Companion of St. Michael and St. George) and D.S.O. (Distinguished Service Order), the "beloved padre" who told his own story in *The Great War as I Saw It* (1922). The record of the war years is also expressed in Scott's *In the Battle Silences: Poems Written at the Front* (1916); the young soldier is seen as a Galahad in a chivalric crusade for king and country.

Scott's celebration of Canada and Canadians struck a resonant note with his contemporaries; his religious poems were appreciated, too, although as Thomas Adams noted in 1898, those "who talk of art for art's sake would perhaps decide that he is too fond of sermons in verse." In 1919 Melvin O. Hammond identified the dominant strains in Scott's poetry as a love for the Canadian northland and a pronounced imperialism. His "Hymn of Empire," Hammond shrewdly observed, was "fervent beyond the thoughts of native Britons." Scott's religious and imperialist poetry, topical in his lifetime, has seemed less relevant to later generations, and the only extended treatment of his nature poetry by a contemporary critic is Louis Dudek's analysis of the similarities between Scott's poetry and that of his son F. R. Scott.

References:

Thomas Adams, "Frederick George Scott," *Canadian Magazine* (June 1898): 160-164;

Louis Dudek, "F. R. Scott and the Modern Poets," *Northern Review*, 4 (December-January 1950-1951);

Melvin O. Hammond, "The Poet of the Laurentians," *Canadian Magazine* (March 1919);

Sydenham Lindsay, Note on Scott, *Old Boys Association of Lower Canada College News Letter*, 4 (Fall 1959): 2.

Papers:

Scott's papers are at the McCord Museum in Montreal.

Eva Senécal

(20 April 1905-   )

Mary Jean Green
Dartmouth College

BOOKS: *Un Peu d'angoisse . . . un peu de fièvre* (Montreal: La Patrie, 1927);
La Course dans l'aurore (Sherbrooke: Tribune, 1929);
Dans les ombres (Montreal: Lévesque, 1931);
Mon Jacques (Montreal: Lévesque, 1933).

Eva Senécal (née Marie-Eva) was born in La Patrie, Quebec, on 20 April 1905, to Adélard Senécal, a farmer, and Octavie Beaudry Senécal. A poet and novelist of the 1920s and 1930s, Senécal has long been classified by literary historians as part of a "feminine school" of that period, along with her contemporaries Jovette-Alice Bernier, Simone Routier, and Medjé Vézina. The works of these women share a personal lyricism and a focus on the exaltation and anguish of love, a theme that contrasts sharply with the nationalistic topics favored in Quebec at the time.

Educated at the *école normale* of Saint-Hyacinthe, Senécal was a correspondent for the *Sherbrooke Tribune* from 1920 to 1930. In 1923 she was forced to spend several months at a sanatorium on Lac-Edouard and began writing her first poems. She published her first collection of poetry, *Un Peu d'angoisse . . . un peu de fièvre* (A Little Anguish . . . A Little Fever), in 1927 and her second, *La Course dans l'aurore* (The Race into Dawn), in 1929. The second collection received favorable reviews and gained Senécal national and international recognition. One of the poems, "Vent du Nord" (North Wind), had received a prize at the Salon des Poètes de Lyon in 1928.

Senécal was also the author of two novels, *Dans les ombres* (In the Shadows, 1931), which received the Prix Lévesque, and *Mon Jacques* (1933). To date, Senécal has published nothing since her second novel. In 1936 she took a job in Ottawa, working for the minister of foreign affairs, and a few years later she became a parliamentary translator in Ottawa. In 1940 she married Clifford Cole.

Senécal's poetry shows the influence of the French Romantics, particularly Alfred de Musset and Alphonse de Lamartine, and gives much attention to the poet's relationship to the natural setting. Her short lyrics speak of the rapture of love but also of its fragility and of the inconstancy of lovers. Another recurrent theme is the appeal of dreams and visions of the ideal.

The novel *Dans les ombres* tells the story of a young woman, recently married to her childhood sweetheart, who is drawn into a relationship with an American while her husband is away working in the North. The novel traces the development of the passion as well as the heroine's attempt to resist it. In the end, after falling seriously ill, she sends her lover away and sets off for the North, vowing to become a good wife and mother. The message of the novel is ambiguous: although it ends by upholding the traditional values of fidelity and marriage, it gives a central place to a romantic passion capable of subverting them.

The emphasis on personal emotion in *Dans les ombres* was a new element in Quebec literature, and it did not pass unnoticed. Most of the early critical reception was favorable: the novel was praised for its analysis of the feminine soul and its ability to convey an impression of life and sincerity. However, Jules Larivière launched a controversy that raged for several months in the pages of *Mon Magazine* when he denounced the novel as immoral, accusing it of making a crude appeal to the physical passions unprecedented in Quebec literature (September, October, November 1931). Senécal's editor, Albert Lévesque, defended the intellectual and moral value of the novel (October 1931) and appealed to the judgment of the Dominican priest Marc-Antonin Lamarche, who supported him by finding Larivière's condemnation profoundly unjust (October 1931). This was not the last of the battles Lévesque had to sustain in defense of his series Les Romans de la Jeune Génération (Novels of the Young Generation), of which *Dans les ombres* was the first volume. Bernier's *La Chair décevante* (The Deceptive Flesh), published the same year, gave rise to even more virulent critical attacks, both for its style and its portrayal of feminine passion. It is evident that Senécal and Bernier had, each in her own way, introduced a note into Quebec fiction that clashed with the dominant ideology of their era, still concerned with rural life and the problem of cultural survival.

In her second novel, *Mon Jacques,* Senécal adopts the technique of first-person narration, which she uses effectively to explore nuances of personal emotion. This novel avoided charges of immorality, probably because its female protagonist never succumbs to illicit passion. Lina, a musician, falls in love with Jacques, a talented violinist she meets at Lake Orford, one of the many lakeside settings in Senécal's work. She is happily married to Jacques and the mother of a baby daughter when she discovers the secret of her husband's melancholy, an ill-considered youthful marriage which, for religious reasons, cannot be dissolved. Obedient to the demands of religion and morality, Lina leaves the man who can never be her husband, and the novel ends with her child's death and the suicide of Jacques.

The four volumes of Senécal's published work are dominated by the portrayal of an ephemeral and often tragic romantic passion, a theme that found few echoes in the literature of the time. She is now appreciated for her attempt, albeit short-lived, to bring about changes in the form and content of Quebec literature.

References:

Pauline Adam, "Lecture des œuvres estriennes," in *A l'ombre de DesRochers: Le Mouvement littéraire des Cantons de l'Est, 1925-1950,* edited by Joseph Bonenfant and others (Sherbrooke, Que.: Editions de l'Université de Sherbrooke, 1985), pp. 71-106;

Corine Bolla and Lucie Robert, "La Poésie féminine de 1929 à 1940," *Atlantis,* 4 (Autumn 1978): 55-62;

Janine Boynard-Frot, "L'Emergence d'une production littéraire féminine, 1925-1935," in *A l'ombre de DesRochers: Le Mouvement littéraire des Cantons de l'Est, 1925-1950* (1985), pp. 109-117.

Robert Service

(16 January 1874-11 September 1958)

Carl F. Klinck
University of Western Ontario
and
W. H. New
University of British Columbia

BOOKS: *Songs of a Sourdough* (Toronto: Briggs, 1907; London: Unwin, 1908); republished as *The Spell of the Yukon, and Other Verses* (New York: Barse & Hopkins, 1907);

Ballads of a Cheechako (Toronto: Briggs, 1909; New York: Barse & Hopkins, 1909; London: Unwin, 1910);

The Trail of '98: A Northland Romance (Toronto: Briggs, 1910; New York: Dodd, Mead, 1910; London: Stevens & Brown, 1911 [i.e., 1910]);

Rhymes of a Rolling Stone (Toronto: Briggs, 1912; New York: Dodd, Mead, 1912; London: Unwin, 1913);

The Pretender: A Story of the Latin Quarter (New York: Dodd, Mead, 1914; London: Unwin, 1915);

Rhymes of a Red Cross Man (Toronto: Briggs, 1916; New York: Barse & Hopkins, 1916; London: Unwin, 1916);

Selected Poems (London: Unwin, 1917);

Ballads of a Bohemian (Toronto & New York: Barse & Hopkins, 1921; London: Unwin, 1921);

Complete Poetical Works (New York & Newark: Barse, 1921); republished as *Collected Verse* (London: Benn, 1930) and *The Complete Poems* (New York: Dodd, Mead, 1933; enlarged, 1938; enlarged again, 1942);

The Poisoned Paradise: A Romance of Monte Carlo (New York: Dodd, Mead, 1922; London: Unwin, 1922);

The Roughneck (New York: Barse & Hopkins, 1923); republished as *The Rough-Neck: A Tale of Tahiti* (London: Unwin, 1923);

The Master of the Microbe: A Fantastic Romance (Toronto: McClelland & Stewart, 1926; New York & Newark: Barse & Hopkins, 1926; London: Unwin, 1926);

The House of Fear (New York: Dodd, Mead, 1927; London: Unwin, 1927);

Robert Service (Blower Historical Collection, Edmonton)

Why Not Grow Young? or, Living for Longevity (New York & Newark: Barse, 1928; London: Benn, 1928);

Twenty Bath-Tub Ballads (London: Francis, Day & Hunter, 1939);

Bar-Room Ballads (Toronto: Saunders, 1940; New York: Dodd, Mead, 1940; London: Benn, 1940);

Collected Poems (New York: Dodd, Mead, 1940);

Ploughman of the Moon: An Adventure into Memory (New York: Dodd, Mead, 1945; London: Benn, 1946);

Harper of Heaven (New York: Dodd, Mead, 1948; London: Benn, 1948);

Songs of a Sun-Lover (Toronto: McClelland & Stewart, 1949; New York: Dodd, Mead, 1949; London: Benn, 1949);

Rhymes of a Roughneck (New York: Dodd, Mead, 1950; London: Benn, 1950);

Lyrics of a Lowbrow (New York: Dodd, Mead, 1951; London: Benn, 1951);

Rhymes of a Rebel (New York: Dodd, Mead, 1952; London: Benn, 1952);

Songs for My Supper (New York: Dodd, Mead, 1953; London: Benn, 1953);

Carols of an Old Codger (New York: Dodd, Mead, 1954; London: Benn, 1954);

More Collected Verse (New York: Dodd, Mead, 1955; London: Benn, 1955);

Rhymes for My Rags (New York: Dodd, Mead, 1956; London: Benn, 1956);

Songs of the High North (London: Benn, 1958; Toronto: Ryerson, 1964);

Later Collected Verse (New York: Dodd, Mead, 1965).

Robert Service is known to millions of people as the poet of the Yukon Gold Rush, the author of such widely memorized parlor ballads as "The Shooting of Dan McGrew" and "The Cremation of Sam McGee." These and other verses from his first book, *Songs of a Sourdough* (1907; called *The Spell of the Yukon* in its U.S. edition), made him famous from the time of their publication until long after his death. Many readers came to believe that Service was as much of a loner and drifter as the Yukon characters he so often wrote about, but that image is far from the truth. In fact he was a bank clerk, a man who was acutely aware of the market for which he was writing (he refused the word "poetry" for his titles, insisting on calling his work "rhymes," "songs," or "ballads"), and in his final years, in the south of France, he enjoyed the pleasures that his fortune bought him.

Robert William Service was born in Preston, Lancashire, England, on 16 January 1874. His Scots father, Robert, was working in a bank there; his English mother, the former Emily Parker, was the daughter of a cotton-mill owner. When her father died and left her ten thousand pounds, the family moved to Robert Service, Sr.'s native city of Glasgow; Robert and Emily subsequently had six more sons and three daughters. When the family moved north young Robert, the eldest child, was sent to live with three maiden aunts and his paternal grandfather, who was postmaster in Kilwinning, Ayrshire. As Service recalls his youth in his 1945 autobiography, *Ploughman of the Moon*—and as he fantasizes about this time in an early novel, *The Trail of '98: A Northland Romance* (1910)—he loved freedom but was constantly thwarted by the rigors of his family's Scots Kirk affiliation. Yet his early love of humorous rhyme was encouraged—in part, his autobiography avers, because his great-grandfather had claimed to be not only Robert Burns's friend but also his second cousin. Returning to Glasgow when he was eleven, Service was enrolled in Hillhead School, a newly established private boys' school with academic and athletic ambitions. In attendance between 1885 and 1888, at which time he was expelled for defying the drillmaster, he responded warmly to such romantic poets as Alfred, Lord Tennyson, Edgar Allan Poe, and Coventry Patmore. But his family sought for him a business career, and at the age of fifteen he was apprenticed to a branch of the Commercial Bank of Scotland, with which he stayed from 1889 to 1896.

He also took to acting in amateur theatrical performances and to writing, but an attempt to study English at Glasgow University was short-lived. Achieving some local success contributing verses and serials to Glasgow newspapers (the *Herald*, *Scottish Nights*, and the *People's Friend*), he increasingly became infatuated with North America and with the idea of becoming a broncobuster and range rider. He resigned from the bank at the end of March 1896, immigrated as a steerage passenger to Montreal, took a "colonist" train to the west coast (wearing a Buffalo Bill costume), and ended up as a farm laborer near Duncan, on Vancouver Island, until in November 1897 he headed for California. Over the next few months he worked, his autobiography claims, as a tunnel builder in Oakland, a handyman in a San Diego brothel, and a guitar-playing singer in Colorado; he lived in evangelical missions and on the street and allowed his life to be governed by luck and fate. Precisely how much truth there is in these claims is difficult to verify. But from 1899 to 1903 he was again working on a Vancouver Island ranch, and on 10 October 1903 he took another bank-clerking job, this time with the Canadian Bank of Commerce in Victoria. The next year the bank transferred him to Kamloops; by November 1904 he was moved again, to Whitehorse, Yukon Territory, and at the end of the summer of 1906 he became the branch's teller. It was

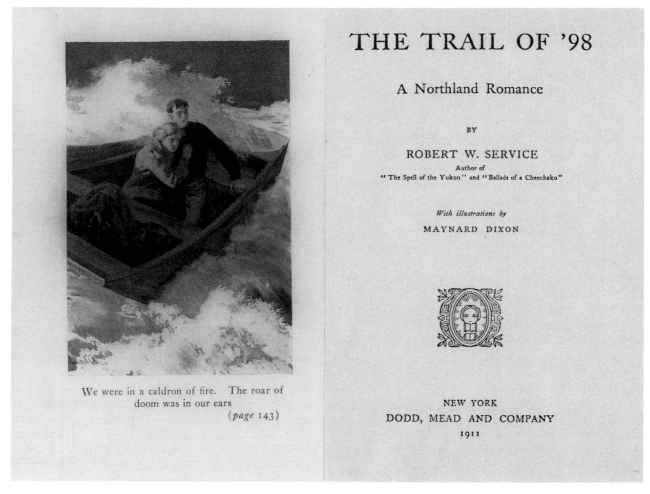

We were in a caldron of fire. The roar of
doom was in our ears
(page 143)

THE TRAIL OF '98

A Northland Romance

BY

ROBERT W. SERVICE

Author of
" The Spell of the Yukon " and " Ballads of a Cheechako "

With illustrations by
MAYNARD DIXON

NEW YORK
DODD, MEAD AND COMPANY
1911

Frontispiece and title page for the American edition of Service's first novel, a melodramatic tale of the gold rush

there that he composed "The Shooting of Dan McGrew." Its opening lines are familiar: "A bunch of the boys were whooping it up in the Malemute saloon; / The kid that handles the music-box was hitting a jag-time tune; / Back of the bar, in a solo game, sat Dangerous Dan McGrew, / And watching his luck was his light-o'-love, the lady that's known as Lou." The verse goes on to tell of the "spell" of the Yukon, the "gnawing hunger of lonely men for a home and all that it means," and the random violence that results from frustration. But, characteristically for Service, it also turns from sentimentality to ironic comedy by the end. In this case there is a shooting, then a theft of gold; Dan dies, but Lou turns out to be no lady.

Never a miner, Service learned of the Gold Rush of 1898 in conversation with old-timers, and he identified with the North, or so his poetic persona declares. In the poem "The Spell of the Yukon" the speaker tells of "a land where the mountains are nameless / And the rivers all run God knows where." In this land, although "There's gold, and it's haunting and haunting," something else brings him back: "It's the beauty that thrills me with wonder, / It's the stillness that fills me with peace." Service began to write even more verses with Yukon characters in them, and he gained a reputation doing recitations, first of Rudyard Kipling's work and "Casey at the Bat" and then with his own works. But he stuffed these ballads into a drawer, together with some more bookish lyrics, until he one day sent the collection off to his father, who (with his family) had in the meantime immigrated to Toronto. Robert Service, Sr., sent the manuscript to the Methodist publisher William Briggs in Toronto. Success was immediate and largely based on Dan

McGrew's tale and "The Cremation of Sam McGee," which opens:

> There are strange things done in the midnight sun
>   By the men who moil for gold;
> The Arctic trails have their secret tales
>   That would make your blood run cold;
> The Northern Lights have seen queer sights,
>   But the queerest they ever did see
> Was that night on the marge of Lake Lebarge
>   I cremated Sam McGee.

The rhetorical reliance on internal rhymes and stressed rhythms, the hint of sentimentality, the touch of stereotypical manliness, the ironic and slightly macabre humor, and the unconventionality of the northern references all combined to mark Service's style and reputation. Success also proved surprisingly profitable. The volume, *Songs of a Sourdough*, was in its fifteenth impression by 1907, and his royalties quickly rose to several thousand dollars a year.

After a winter holiday in Vancouver, he returned to the Yukon, where he was made the bank's teller in Dawson, even farther north. There, though the town was no longer in its Klondike heyday, he studied old records and began to draft the verses for *Ballads of a Cheechako* (1909)–"cheechako" being Yukon slang for a tenderfoot, a newcomer, as opposed to a "sourdough" or old hand. His new verses focused increasingly on vice rather than virtue because Service considered vice a more marketable subject for poetry. Monologues of individuals with checkered pasts characterize the book: "The Ballad of Pious Pete," "The Ballad of Blasphemous Bill," "The Ballad of Hard-Luck Henry," and "The Black Sheep." His novel *The Trail of '98* told the gold-rush story through another medium. He designed it to be authentic, moral, and vivid, to blend realism with romance, and to re-create vicariously the world of the gold rush. This book tells the story of a Scot named Athol Meldrum whose years wandering around North America roughly parallel Service's own; when Meldrum heads for the Klondike, however, he takes the Skagway route, and he participates melodramatically in an epic adventure with a tragic ending. The novel was transformed into a Hollywood film in 1928.

To write the novel, Service had refused promotion to the position of manager of the bank, and he left the Dawson branch in November 1909. In April 1910 he was in Toronto, delivering his manuscript personally to Briggs, and making arrangements in New York to have Dodd,

The Services in Paris, 1913 (photograph by Germaine Service)

Mead publish an American edition. After a holiday in New Orleans, Service visited his mother and family (now settled on a farm in northern Alberta) from the late fall to spring of the following year, at which time he resolved to return to Dawson–a perilous journey of over two thousand miles by wilderness waterways–mainly by canoe, alone.

His remarkable success provided material for some of the best chapters in his autobiography; and his experiences, real or imagined, inspired the Mackenzie River ballads of *Rhymes of a Rolling Stone* (1912). For example, "Barb-Wire Bill" declares: "I saw a flat and frozen shore of hideous device,/I saw a long-drawn strand of rope that vanished through the ice./And on that treeless, rockless shore I found my partner–dead." "The Song of the Camp-Fire" sounds echoes of Longfellow: "Heed me, feed me, I am hungry, I am red-tongued with desire...." "The Logger" hints of Kipling: "they'll leave me there alone, and perhaps with softened tone/Speak of me sometimes in the camp-fire's glow,/As a played-out, broken chum, who has gone to Kingdom Come,/And who went the pace in England long ago." Some poems already show signs of imitating his earlier successes, as in the opening of "Athabaska Dick": "When the boys come out from Lac Labiche in the lure of the early Spring/To take the pay of the 'Hudson's Bay'. . . ." Others continue his lyric paeans to nature, as in "The Mountain and the Lake": "I know a mountain thrilling to the stars,/Peerless and pure, and pinnacled with snow. . . ." Collectively these verses express the romantic virtues of "A Rolling Stone": "To care for the things that shall endure,/The simple, sweet and clean./To oust out envy and hate and rage,/To breathe with no alarm;/For Nature shall be my anchorage,/And none shall do me harm." Despite their sometimes explicit questioning both of God and of conventional social virtue, such verses appealed to a readership that unquestioningly accepted simple values and that would shortly take those values into World War I. But that this "simple" code condescended toward women and native peoples was something that would lead later generations of readers to question the social as well as the literary value of Service's accomplishments.

In 1912 Service planned to follow in Robert Louis Stevenson's footsteps and travel to Tahiti, but the editor of the *Toronto Star* commissioned him instead to become a foreign correspondent. He left the Yukon, never to return; by the spring of 1913 he was in Paris. He took up residence in the Latin Quarter, haunted the Dôme and the Closerie des Lilas a decade before Ernest Hemingway made them stylish, took art lessons, and embraced the bohemian life with self-styled caution. Six weekly installments describing his Paris life appeared in the *Toronto Star*, under the title "Zig-Zags of a Vagabond," between 6 December 1913 and 10 January 1914. Further accounts of this period appear in his second volume of autobiography, *Harper of Heaven* (1948), and his second novel, *The Pretender: A Story of the Latin Quarter* (1914). This anecdotal novel develops both the author's fascination with the bohemian life (both literary and sexual) and his use of irony; it tells of James Madden, who avoids marrying assorted predatory rich and loose women until he fortunately connects with Anastasia, learns to become a good husband, and undertakes to write stories in the Latin Quarter. Fundamentally the book satirizes literary snobbery and comments upon the difficulties that a successful popular writer encounters with publishers, critics, fashionable poets, and other "pretenders."

On 12 June 1913 Service married Germaine Bourgoin, the younger daughter of a distillery owner, Constant Bourgoin, of Brie-Comte-Robert; they lived first in the Latin Quarter and then at "Dream Haven," their summer home in Lancieux, Brittany. (Madden's Brittany summer home in *The Pretender* is called "Dreamhaven," but identifying the author with his character is problematic.) The Services were friends with James Bone (editor of the *Manchester Guardian*) and with John Buchan (author of *The Thirty-nine Steps;* later Lord Tweedsmuir, governor-general of Canada). And they were in Brittany when war was declared in August 1914. Refused active duty in the Seaforth Highlanders because of varicose veins, Service therefore embarked on a further career as war correspondent, sending articles to the *Toronto Star* that appeared every Saturday between 11 December 1915 and 29 January 1916 (containing material later reworked in *Harper of Heaven*). When a group of Americans organized an ambulance corps in Paris, Service joined them, and from his months as a stretcher-bearer emerged the fifty-three verses of *Rhymes of a Red Cross Man* (1916). Less jingoistic than one might anticipate from a poet still strongly influenced by Kipling, the verses here tell of lost limbs, blindness, dirt, and separation from loved ones–sometimes sentimentally, sometimes with a rough, grim humor, but always in the familiar rhymed forms that Service admired. For nine months the book headed best-seller lists in the United States.

After moving to a luxurious apartment on the Place du Panthéon (their residence from 1919 to 1929), the Services had one daughter, Iris. Service was working on the verses that appeared in *Ballads of a Bohemian* (1921) and the series of romance novels that were published over the next decade. He knew Henry Miller, James Joyce, and others who made Paris in the 1920s a literary center, but there appears little substantive connection between him and them. Increasingly Service became interested in film, and when the opportunity arose during the winter of 1920-1921, the family traveled to Los Angeles to become involved in filmmaking (and he later went alone to take his long-planned-for Tahitian trip). They returned to Paris in 1922. The film of *The Shooting of Dan McGrew*, directed by Clarence Badger, opened at the Capitol Theatre in New

York in June 1924, to dreadful reviews; *Poisoned Paradise* (a love story based on Service's 1922 novel about the roulette tables at Monte Carlo), directed by L. Gasnier and released in New York in August 1924, fared better both critically and financially.

The Roughneck (published as a novel in 1923 and released as a film in December 1924) continued his string of adventure novels. Based on notes he wrote in Tahiti, it includes details of Service's fascination with muscularity and physical fitness. This was a time when he himself was weakening. Overweight, he suffered heart trouble, then embarked on a series of spa cures at Royat, in the Auvergne region of southern France, and wrote *Why Not Grow Young? or, Living for Longevity* (1928), a handbook on exercise, diet, and male hygiene. Though he went on to write two more cinematic adventure novels, they were not filmed. *The Master of the Microbe: A Fantastic Romance* (1926) is set in the Paris slums, *The House of Fear* (1927) in Brittany. They were his last works of fiction, and the Metro-Goldwyn-Mayer film *The Trail of '98*, which premiered at the Astor Theatre in New York, 20 March 1928, was the last film to be made from his work.

The family moved from Paris in 1929, finally taking an apartment in Nice in 1931. On the Riviera they made the acquaintance of Frank Harris, Frieda Lawrence, and Emma Goldman, but again their connection with the political and literary avant-garde appears minimal. The appearance of his *Collected Verse* in England in 1930 and the American edition, *The Complete Poems*, in 1933 (replacing a less successful 1921 edition) reconfirmed his reputation, though by this time many people in North America thought he was already dead. In 1937 and 1938, however, he was visiting Russia, making notes that would appear in *Harper of Heaven*, opposing communism and what he called its doctrinaire lack of humor.

In 1940 the Services fled France, returning to Canada to a warm welcome, but moving again to Hollywood. His 1939 volume, *Twenty Bath-Tub Ballads*, had been regarded as inconsequential and was not gathered in *Collected Poems* (1940), though *Bar-Room Ballads* (1940) was. But this latter work did not significantly alter critical attitudes; it reads as an imitation of the earlier Yukon rhymes. In California Service found some work as a public lecturer, and in 1942 he had his one screen role—in the Universal film *The Spoilers*. Directed by Ray Enright, this was a Klondike adventure starring Randolph Scott, John Wayne,

and Marlene Dietrich; the director's judgment of Service's performance was, "It's lousy, but we'll let it go" (as quoted in *Harper of Heaven*). Over the next two years he was at work on *Ploughman of the Moon*. In 1946 the family returned to the Riviera and took up residence in Monte Carlo, where Service's widow, daughter (now Iris Davies), son-in-law, and two granddaughters, Anne and Armelle, continued to live after his death.

Service remained active, publishing the second volume of his autobiography in 1948 and still more volumes of verse: *Songs of a Sun-Lover* (1949), *Rhymes of a Roughneck* (1950), *Lyrics of a Lowbrow* (1951), *Rhymes of a Rebel* (1952), and *Songs for My Supper* (1953). *More Collected Verse* appeared in 1955, and the posthumous *Later Collected Verse* (1965) includes various works from the period 1954-1957, including *Carols of an Old Codger* and *Rhymes for My Rags*. Service died of a heart attack in Lancieux, 11 September 1958, and was buried in Brittany.

As with *Harper of Heaven*, subtitled in the U.S. edition *A Record of Radiant Living*, the later poems declared his commitment to compassion, humor, and the virtues of nature. Yet he is also aware of his limited critical reputation. "A Verseman's Apology" (in *Songs of a Sun-Lover*) protests:

> Alas! I am only a rhymer,
> I don't know the meaning of Art;
> But I learned in my little school primer
> To love Eugene Field and Bret Harte. . . .
> For God-sake don't call me a poet,
> For I've never been guilty of that. . . .
> And I fancy my grave-digger griping
> As he gives my last lodging a pat:
> "That guy wrote McGrew;
> 'Twas the best he would do" . . .
> So I'll go to my Maker with that.

"A Verseman's Plea," collected in *Later Collected Verse*, reflects, "If I should ever wax poetic/Please let me be apologetic;/For every verseman by mistake/A bit of poetry may make." Written late in his life, this comment nonetheless sounds like an aspiration as well as an apology.

Praised in 1921 for their spontaneity and virility, Service's rhymes have most often been lauded for their energy but criticized for their lack of "true" emotion. For many years serious criticism simply ignored Service's work, or found it of limited interest. While Arthur Phelps recoiled from the "grotesque gruesomeness" of "The Cremation of Sam McGee," he also claimed that the poem was "a folk tale of unquestioned natural vitality." Phelps further distinguished between readers with literary pretensions (who dismissed Service's pathos, sentimentality, metronomic rhythms, simplicity, and limited range) and those who used these same criteria to praise Service for being memorable, recitable, and sympathetic to ordinary people. More recently critics have attempted to isolate the folk-poetry features of his work and to analyze his structural patterns on their own terms, rather than to measure them against those of T. S. Eliot or W. H. Auden. Edward Hirsch, for example, reads the Yukon ballads as a closed structure opposing Dionysian and Apollonian elements in human behavior. Service did indeed represent tensions between nature and culture, and he recurrently claimed to espouse nature before all. The continuing appeal of the poems about Sam McGee and Dan McGrew, however—and of recent editions of these poems, with brilliant illustrations by the distinguished northern artist Ted Harrison—rests not in any intellectual paradigm they employ but in their sly humor and in the metrical regularity that initially made them so readily adaptable to parlor performance.

Biography:
Carl F. Klinck, *Robert Service: A Biography* (Toronto: McGraw-Hill Ryerson / New York: Dodd, Mead, 1976).

References:
Stanley S. Atherton, "The Klondike Muse," *Canadian Literature*, 47 (Winter 1971): 67-72;
Martin Bucco, "Folk Poetry of Robert W. Service," *Alaska Review*, 2 (Fall 1965): 16-26;
Witter Bynner, "Poetry from the Trenches," *Dial*, 61 (14 December 1916): 531-532;
Edward Hirsch, "A Structural Analysis of Robert Service's Yukon Ballads," *Southern Folklore Quarterly*, 40 (March-June 1976): 125-140;
Arthur L. Phelps, "Robert W. Service," in his *Canadian Writers* (Toronto: McClelland & Stewart, 1951), pp. 28-35;
Louis Untermeyer, "Our Living Laureates," *Bookman*, 14 (January 1922): 481-484;
W. A. Whatley, "Kipling's Influence in the Verse of Robert W. Service," *Texas Review*, 6 (July 1921): 299-308.

Ernest Thompson Seton

(14 August 1860-23 October 1946)

Patricia Morley
Concordia University

BOOKS: *Studies in the Art Anatomy of Animals* (London & New York: Macmillan, 1896);

Wild Animals I Have Known (New York: Scribners, 1898; Toronto: Morang, 1900; London: Nutt, 1902);

Lobo, Rag, and Vixen (New York: Scribners, 1899);

The Trail of the Sandhill Stag (New York: Scribners, 1899; London: Hodder & Stoughton, 1899);

The Biography of a Grizzly (New York: Century, 1900);

The Wild Animal Play for Children, with Alternate Reading for Very Young Children (Philadelphia: Curtis/New York: Doubleday, Page, 1900; Toronto: Morang, 1901);

Lives of the Hunted: A True Account of the Doings of Five Quadrupeds and Three Birds (New York: Scribners, 1901; London: Nutt, 1902);

Krag and Johnny Bear (New York: Scribners, 1902);

Two Little Savages (London & New York: Doubleday, Page, 1903);

How to Play Indian (Philadelphia: Curtis, 1903); republished as *The Red Book; or, How to Play Indian* (New York: The author, 1904);

Monarch, The Big Bear of Tallac (New York: Scribners, 1904; London: Constable, 1905);

Animal Heroes (New York: Scribners, 1905; London: Constable, 1906);

Woodmyth and Fable (Toronto: Briggs, 1905; New York: Century, 1905);

The American Bison or Buffalo (New York: Scribners, 1906);

The Natural History of the Ten Commandments (New York: Scribners, 1907); republished as *The Ten Commandments in the Animal World* (New York: Doubleday, Page, 1907);

The Birch-Bark Roll of the Outdoor Life (New York: Doubleday, Page, 1908); revised and enlarged as *The Book of Woodcraft and Indian Lore* (Garden City, N.Y.: Doubleday, Page, 1912);

Ernest Thompson Seton, circa 1900

The Biography of a Silver Fox; or, Domino Reynard of Goldur Town (New York: Century, 1909; London: Constable, 1909);

Life-Histories of Northern Animals: An Account of the Mammals of Manitoba, 2 volumes (New York: Scribners, 1909);

Boy Scouts of America: A Handbook (New York: Doubleday, Page, 1910);

Rolf in the Woods (Garden City, N.Y.: Doubleday, Page, 1911; Toronto: Briggs, 1917);

The Arctic Prairies: A Canoe Journey of 2,000 Miles in Search of The Caribou (New York: Scribners, 1911; London: Constable, 1912);

The Forester's Manual (Garden City, N.Y.: Double-
　　day, Page, 1912);

Wild Animals at Home (Toronto: Briggs, 1913; Gar-
　　den City, N.Y.: Doubleday, Page, 1913);

Wild Animal Ways (Garden City, N.Y.: Doubleday,
　　Page, 1916);

*The Preacher of Cedar Mountain: A Tale of the Open
　　Country* (Garden City, N.Y.: Doubleday,
　　Page, 1917);

Sign Talk: A Universal Signal Code (Garden City,
　　N.Y.: Doubleday, Page, 1918);

Woodland Tales (Garden City, N.Y. & Toronto: Dou-
　　bleday, Page, 1921);

Bannertail: The Story of a Gray Squirrel (New York:
　　Scribners, 1922);

Lives of Game Animals, 4 volumes (Garden City,
　　N.Y.: Doubleday, Page, 1925-1928);

Johnny Bear, Lobo, and Other Stories (New York &
　　Chicago: Scribners, 1935);

The Biography of an Arctic Fox (New York: Appleton-
　　Century, 1937);

Great Historic Animals: Mainly About Wolves (New
　　York: Scribners, 1937); republished as
　　Mainly About Wolves (London: Methuen,
　　1937);

The Buffalo Wind (Santa Fe: Seton Village Press,
　　1938);

Ernest Thompson Seton's Trail and Camp-Fire Stories,
　　edited by Julia M. Seton (New York & Lon-
　　don: Appleton-Century, 1940);

*Trail of an Artist-Naturalist: The Autobiography of
　　Ernest Thompson Seton* (New York: Scribners,
　　1940; London: Hodder & Stoughton,
　　1951);

Santana, the Hero Dog of France (Los Angeles: Phoe-
　　nix Press, 1945);

The Best of Ernest Thompson Seton, selected by W.
　　Kay Robinson (London: Hodder & Stough-
　　ton, 1949);

*Ernest Thompson Seton's America: Selections from the
　　Writings of the Artist-Naturalist*, edited by
　　Farida A. Wiley (New York: Devin-Adair,
　　1954);

The Worlds of Ernest Thompson Seton, edited by
　　John G. Samson (New York: Knopf, 1976);

Selected Stories of Ernest Thompson Seton, edited by
　　Patricia Morley (Ottawa: University of Ot-
　　tawa Press, 1977).

OTHER: *Famous Animal Stories: Myths, Fables, Fairy
　　Tales, Stories of Real Animals*, edited by Seton
　　(New York: Brentano's, 1932);

The Gospel of the Redman: An Indian Bible, com-
　　piled by Seton and Julia M. Seton (Garden
　　City, N.Y.: Doubleday, Doran, 1936).

Ernest Thompson Seton was a man of
widely diversified gifts, a writer, artist, and naturalist. He is most commonly remembered as a
writer of realistic animal stories that appeal to all
ages. He was also a painter and illustrator, an internationally famed naturalist, a conservationist,
and a youth leader who helped to found the Boy
Scout movement. It is difficult, if not impossible,
to separate these complementary talents in his
published work.

Seton was born on 14 August 1860 in South
Shields, Newcastle's seaport, on England's northeast coast. His maternal grandfather, William
Snowden, had been a prosperous shipowner and
master. His father, Joseph Thompson, had been
a wealthy partner in a shipbuilding firm. A series
of business failures drove the family to immigrate to Canada in 1866, first to a farm near Lindsay, Ontario, and four years later to Toronto. In
the 1860s and 1870s Lindsay was pioneering territory, and Toronto was a small city whose ravines
and lakeside marshes afforded Seton a rich variety of bird and animal life. Ingeniously earned
pocket money helped the young Seton to acquire
"Doctor Ross's *Birds of Canada*," an amateur work
the boy proceeded to correct and annotate.
Much later Seton connected his first serious work
as a naturalist with the inadequacies of this book.

There was initially in his publishing career
some confusion surrounding the author's name.
His father's first cousin was the grandson of
George Seton and heir to his title, earl of
Winton. The Scottish Setons had moved to South
Shields and changed their name to Thompson,
after supporting the losing side at the battle of
Culloden. The title fell to Seton's father when
the cousin died without issue. The writer assumed the name Seton legally in 1883. When his
adored mother, Alice, objected to a variety of sur-
names being used in the family, Seton adopted
Seton-Thompson as a pen name. His mother
died in 1897, and in 1902 Seton resumed using
the aristocratic name of his choice.

Seton's father was a vain, harsh, and brutal
man. He tyrannized his large family, especially
the sensitive and sickly young Seton. The artist's
temperament, fed by a reverence for his gentle,
self-sacrificing mother and a passionate hatred
for his father, was idealistic and romantic. Seton's
need to defy his father was focused, imagina-

Seton, Chief Scout, with Robert Baden-Powell, English founder of the Boy Scouts, and Daniel Carter Beard, founder of the U.S. branch, in New York, 1910 (Seton Memorial Library, Philmont Scout Ranch, Cimarron, New Mexico)

tively, in a tiny kingbird, seen first near Lindsay, routing a group of crows much larger than itself. At the age of sixteen Seton shaped the incident into a long, mawkish poem that celebrates the courage and individuality of the bird-hero. In his autobiography (1940) Seton claims that the sight of this bird was the beginning and foundation of his work as a writer of wild-animal stories.

In his early teen years illness and a doctor's prescription for rest in the country had led to a summer on the family's old farm at Lindsay, owned by the former hired man. This happy interval became the basis, years later, for *Two Little Savages* (1903), a fictionalized account of two boys living like Indians in a bark wigwam, making fire, shooting homemade bows and arrows, and interpreting animal tracks. During this summer at Lindsay, Seton resolved to be a naturalist and to win a university scholarship in zoology.

The origin and intention of *Two Little Savages* is accurately reflected in its subtitle, "A Book of American Woodcraft for Boys." Julia Moss

Seton (in *By a Thousand Fires*, 1967) tells of her husband's friendship with Rudyard Kipling, begun in 1898, and of Kipling's advice that the substance of a dictionary of woodcraft would be more readable and salable in fictional form. Kipling knew the reading public. Sales of *Two Little Savages* over the years ran to millions of copies. The book represents not only Seton's love of woodcraft, to whose "many lasting pleasures" it is dedicated, but also his deep interest in education and the training of young people. As he told Kipling, he believed that outdoor life, with woodcraft, was the proper school of manhood. The home the Setons later established in Santa Fe, New Mexico, provided facilities for a children's camp and an adult institute.

Faced with his father's objections to his becoming a naturalist, Seton enrolled in night classes at the Ontario School of Art and won a gold medal as most outstanding student. This led, in 1879, to a scholarship at the Royal Academy School of Painting and Sculpture in London, where supplementary privileges included free admission to the London zoo and (after Seton wrote to the Prince of Wales and the prime minister) a life member's ticket to the British Museum. In its natural history section he pored over books by John James Audubon, Alexander Wilson, Henry David Thoreau, John Burroughs, and other famous naturalists. Ill health, poverty, and a mysteriously prophetic "Voice" summoned him back to Canada and to his brother's homestead at Carberry, Manitoba. Later Seton called this recurring voice his "Buffalo Wind."

Manitoba in the 1880s was the scene for Seton's self-styled golden period, the best days of his life. Here began the fat notebooks crammed with sketches and measurements of birds and animals, which Seton later declared to be the first necessity for an artist-naturalist. Manitoba, together with the Lindsay and Toronto years, provided much of the material for Seton's first and most famous collection of realistic animal stories, *Wild Animals I Have Known* (1898). The subtitle declares the book to be "the Personal Histories of Lobo, Silverspot, Raggylug, Bingo, The Springfield Fox, the Pacing Mustang, Wully, and Redruff." Its preface stakes out Seton's deeply held beliefs concerning the kinship of man and beast, and mankind's moral responsibility toward the animal kingdom. Animals, Seton insists, are creatures with wants and feelings differing from our own only in degree, and hence they have *rights*. He stresses the animals' heroism and uniqueness, not-

The photograph of Seton with his wife, Julia, that appears as the frontispiece for By a Thousand Fires *(1967), her biography of Seton*

ing that his theme is "the real personality of the individual and his view of life" rather than the ways of the species. Unlike hunting stories, animal tales by Seton are written from the animals' points of view. As Seton observes, the life of a wild animal may be far more interesting and exciting than that of many human beings. His tales fascinated the public because of the perennial human interest in wild animals, and because Seton dramatized the lives of individual animals with sympathy, humor, and scientific accuracy.

Seton's attitude toward his writing and illustrating reflects a basic religious orientation. He shows the Victorian preference for truth over art; his primary intention was to write what was true, edifying, and moral. In *Wild Animals I Have Known* Seton's "Note to the Reader" begins, "These stories are true." He admits to leaving the strict line of historical truth, and to piecing together animal characters from two or more life-models. His composite method remains true to "the actual life of a veritable animal hero." Seton duly records which tales are more and less composite, preferring this technical word to any reference to imagination or art.

Seton's interest in education and social organization, which was to occupy a large portion of his later years, is evident in the story of Silverspot, leader of a band of crows observed in Toronto's Rosedale Ravine. Crow customs, called the best in the bird kingdom, are described at length. Their system is a benevolent aristocracy, or meritocracy, in which the leader and his lieutenants are the wisest and bravest of the band. As chieftain and educator Silverspot earns a eulogy with a communal slant: "His long life of usefulness to his tribe was over—slain at last by the owl that he had taught so many hundreds of young crows to beware of."

Seton was in New York frequently in the 1880s and 1890s seeking work as an illustrator and trying to find a publisher for his writings. One of his first contacts was W. Lewis Frazer of the *Century Magazine*, who gave him the job of illustrating the second edition of *The Century Dictionary*. By the late 1890s so confident was Seton of the success of his first collection of animal stories that he contracted with Scribners for no royalties on the first two thousand copies, with twenty percent on every copy thereafter. Two thousand copies sold out in three weeks, the book became an international best-seller, and Seton's days of penury were over. He received letters of congratulation from Kipling and Charles G. D. Roberts, who both acknowledged his influence on their own writing.

The Manitoba years also supplied the material for *The Trail of the Sandhill Stag* (1899), a novella published soon after Seton's first collection. The book shows again the author's reverence for nature. It describes a young man's pursuit of a noble stag in the sandhills near Carberry and the hunter's final knowledge (when the stag places his life in his hands) of his close kinship with the animal. The stag is eulogized as having precious senses that are hidden from men, while the ex-hunter claims to have found the Holy Grail in this very kinship.

Throughout his life Seton displayed a puzzling ambivalence with regard to killing animals. At times, as in *The Trail of the Sandhill Stag*, he eschews all hunting. Elsewhere he preached the legitimacy of vivisection and endorsed the right of young men to an annual hunting expedition. In his autobiography (*Trail of an Artist-Naturalist*, 1940) he speaks of killing and dissecting animals in the service of "knowledge-hunger."

In Seton's first decade of publishing his books commonly carried the following inscription: "In the Book the designs for title-page, cover, and general make-up and also the literary revision, were done by Mrs. Grace Gallatin Seton-Thompson" (or, variously, "Gallatin Thompson Seton" and "Gallatin Seton"). Grace was a wealthy American girl whom Seton met on a ship to Paris and married in 1896. They had one child, Ann, who became the writer Anya Seton. James Polk (in *Wilderness Writers*, 1972) describes Grace as a socialite and assumes that the marriage was unsatisfactory from the beginning. Grace's collaboration on Seton's publications for some fifteen years, especially the foreword to *Wild Animals at Home* (1913), discredits this assumption. In the century's second decade, however, the couple agreed to go their separate ways. Seton was not divorced until 1937, whereupon he married Julia Moss, his secretary and companion of many years.

Wild Animals I Have Known was the subject of a famous controversy in 1903. Seton was attacked, in the March issue of the *Atlantic Monthly*, as a fraud, a sham naturalist, by poet-naturalist John Burroughs. In his autobiography Seton describes Burroughs's article as bitter, unfair, and reeking with jealousy. He encountered Burroughs at a dinner party given by Andrew Carnegie for fifty New York writers, and good-naturedly kidded him about the attack. Later Seton invited the critic home to show him his library of five thousand volumes, his collection of two thousand animal photographs taken by himself, his museum with thousands of bird and mammal skins collected and skinned by himself, and his dozens of fat journals, the record of over thirty years of observation. According to Seton, the astonished and contrite Burroughs apologized and recanted in print. Seton may have exaggerated the extent of this apology, or Burroughs might have chosen to modify in print the generosity of his oral remarks. Burroughs did praise Seton as artist and raconteur but warned his readers against Seton's romantic tendencies.

Lives of the Hunted: A True Account of the Doings of Five Quadrupeds and Three Birds (1901) attempts to repeat the success of *Wild Animals I Have Known* but is, with one exception, inferior to the earlier collection. That exception is a novella, a ninety-page story of "Krag, the Kootenay Ram," a haunting tale of obsession and madness set in the Canadian Rockies. Krag's early life permits a panoramic view of the sheep's social organization.

Society and education increasingly occupied Seton in his fifties. In a Connecticut wilderness area he instructed boys in woodcraft and Indian ways and expounded on his methods and theories in a series of articles for the *Ladies' Home Journal* in 1902. In the same year Seton founded the Woodcraft League. His lectures in England in 1906 led to Gen. Robert Baden-Powell's organizing the Boy Scouts. Seton was chief scout in the United States from 1910 to 1915 and wrote the first American scout manual. His idealization of the Indian and dislike of the movement's militarism led to an open rupture with the Boy Scout board and Seton's eviction from the organization he had so largely helped to found. He continued to lead the Woodcraft League, which had over eighty thousand members by 1934.

Despite his scientific knowledge, Seton's consuming interest lay in the individual hero. It is a romantic bias as Burroughs had noted. *Animal Heroes* (1905) deals with heroic individuals with unusual gifts: in the words of the subtitle, it is "the Histories of a Cat, a Dog, a Pigeon, a Lynx, Two Wolves, and a Reindeer. . . ." Its highlights are "The Slum Cat" and "The Winnipeg Wolf." The former illustrates Seton's humor: the slum cat is shut up in an antiseptic house and garden "polluted" with roses, "without a single tenement or smokestack in sight . . . the most unlovely, unsmellable spot." "The Winnipeg Wolf," atypical in that it features human protagonists and highly melodramatic events, demonstrates Seton's narrative skill and command of mood.

By the age of forty-five Seton had achieved international fame as a writer of animal stories. For the next twenty years he was largely preoccupied with natural histories. Burroughs's attack led Theodore Roosevelt, an amateur naturalist and Seton's friend, to urge him to publish his facts. As early as 1898 Seton's daily journals numbered twenty-five volumes. The finely detailed observations were fortified with hundreds of sketches. In 1909 Seton published *Life-Histories of Northern Animals*, a set of two quarto volumes that rapidly became a definitive work on mammals. By 1919, as his notes accumulated, Seton felt these volumes should be rewritten. He worked for eight years, with Julia and several secretaries, on this monumental task. The first revised volume appeared in 1925; the second, in 1926, won (amusingly) the John Burroughs Medal; the third, in 1927, received the Daniel Giraud Elliott Medal from the National Academy of Sciences; the final volume appeared in 1928. The set contains three thousand pages, fifteen hundred ink drawings, and one hundred maps, all done by Seton. In addition he included what he called his synoptic drawings, humorous sketches that caught the essential life and character of each animal.

In 1930 Seton and Julia moved to a twenty-five-thousand-acre ranch near Santa Fe, where they established a home, library, museum, camp, and school for youth leaders. Neighbors called the main house Seton Castle, and the surrounding Seton Village became a focus for people who wished to live in harmony with nature. Seton's creative gifts continued to flower into his old age. Julia describes him as a practical architect, an excellent sculptor, a masterly portrait painter, and a distinguished graphic artist.

Seton's autobiography is a major statement but has not been reprinted and is now rare. *Trail of an Artist-Naturalist* helps to clarify the influence of Seton's parents, and the burning, mystical vision that drove Seton from the stern orthodoxy of his youth to a passionate recognition of the whole world as "the Holy Ground of the Great Spirit," a God of love and kindness. Seton's admiration for the North American Indian and his dislike of militarism are represented in the creeds and prayers used in Seton Village. He modeled his own life after Tecumseh, the Shawnee chief whom Seton saw as a physically strong, wise, and courageous leader of his people. His self-taught methods of scientific observation and his sympathetic imagination support the religious vision that underlies all his work. Seton believed that one's most important task is to know oneself and that each animal is an inexhaustible volume of information relevant to that goal. Seton's stories foster that self-knowledge with wit and artistic skill.

Seton's fictions, which some have seen as the simple case histories of a naturalist, nonetheless have beauty and strength. Most end tragically, which, as Seton observes, is realistic. The reader's interest in the fate of his animal protagonists is reinforced by a fine sense of detail, simple yet vivid and metaphoric language, and an omnipresent perception of humanity's oneness with the natural world.

Biographies:

Anonymous, *Ernest Thompson Seton: A Biographical Sketch Done by Various Hands* (New York: Doubleday, 1925);

Julia Moss Seton, *By a Thousand Fires* (Garden City, N.Y.: Doubleday, 1967);

James Polk, *Wilderness Writers* (Toronto: Clarke, Irwin, 1972);

John Henry Wadland, *Ernest Thompson Seton: Man in Nature and the Progressive Era* (New York: Arno, 1978);

Betty Keller, *Black Wolf: The Life of Ernest Thompson Seton* (Vancouver: Douglas & McIntyre, 1984).

References:

Anonymous, "The Animal Story," *Edinburgh Review*, 214 (July 1911): 94-118;

John Burroughs, "Real and Sham Natural History," *Atlantic Monthly*, 91 (March 1903): 298-309;

Edward B. Clark, "Roosevelt on the Nature Fakirs," *Everybody's Magazine*, 16 (June 1907): 770-774;

Alec Lucas, Introduction to *Wild Animals I Have Known* (Toronto: McClelland & Stewart, 1977), pp. vii-xii;

William H. Magee, "The Animal Story: A Challenge in Technique," *Dalhousie Review*, 44 (Summer 1964): 156-164;

Patricia Morley, Introduction to *Selected Stories by Ernest Thompson Seton*, edited by Morley (Ottawa: University of Ottawa Press, 1977), pp. 9-17;

Morley, "Seton's Animals," *Journal of Canadian Fiction*, special Seton issue, 2 (Summer 1973): 195-198;

Michel Poirier, "The Animal Story in Canadian Literature," *Queen's Quarterly*, 34 (January-April 1927): 298-312;

C. Lintern Sibley, "The Voyage of the Nature Story," *Canadian Magazine*, 38 (January 1912): 287-292.

Francis Sherman

(3 February 1871-15 June 1926)

Robert Gibbs
University of New Brunswick

BOOKS: *Matins* (Boston: Copeland & Day, 1896);
In Memorabilia Mortis (Cambridge, Mass.: University Press, 1896);
A Prelude (Cambridge, Mass.: Privately printed for Copeland & Day, 1897);
The Deserted City: Stray Sonnets (Cambridge, Mass.: Privately printed for Copeland & Day, 1899);
A Canadian Calendar: XII Lyrics (Havana: Privately printed, 1900);
The Complete Poems of Francis Sherman, edited by Lorne Pierce (Toronto: Ryerson, 1935).

Francis Joseph Sherman, though ten years younger than the well-known writers Charles G. D. Roberts and Bliss Carman, was closely associated with them and others of the Roberts family in the 1890s in Fredericton, New Brunswick. The work of these poets, which began appearing in the last two decades of the nineteenth century, along with that of the Ottawa poets Archibald Lampman, D. C. Scott, and Wilfred Campbell, is the first manifestation of Canada's national literary consciousness and the first flowering of romanticism in the new nation. Sherman as one of that school adapted late romantic modes to the needs of his own sensibility and created a body of consistently well-made verse.

The eldest son of Louis Walsh and Alice Maxwell Sherman, Francis Sherman was born on 3 February 1871 in Fredericton and educated at the local grammar school and high school and at the University of New Brunswick. Like Roberts and Carman he came under the influence of George R. Parkin at the high school; Parkin's twin passions were the local countryside and the English Pre-Raphaelites. Sherman also came directly under Carman's influence during the brief period when Carman taught at the school. Like the two older writers, Sherman enjoyed long hikes and canoe trips into the wilderness. Unlike them Sherman did not take a degree at the university but in 1887 took a post in Fredericton with the Merchant's Bank of Halifax. In 1897 he became the local branch manager and in 1907 assistant general manager of the parent bank, renamed in 1901 the Royal Bank of Canada.

When Roberts returned to Fredericton in 1895 he met Sherman, about whom he had heard from Carman and others. It was Roberts who encouraged Sherman to send his first poetry collection to Fred H. Day (of Copeland & Day) in Boston. *Matins*, which appeared in November 1896, consists of thirty poems in a variety of styles, from the sonnet, of which there are ten, to a ballad in thirty-four stanzas. The sonnets, though they lack the fine distinctiveness of Roberts's and Lampman's best, are no less strong in their easy control of the form. In them, as in the other poems, natural imagery is more general than local. Formal control and pleasing cadences are the chief virtues of these poems.

William Morris, whose influence can be seen in the longer poems of *Matins*, died in October 1896. Within weeks of his death Sherman wrote a sequence of six sonnets, which were printed in December of that year under the title *In Memorabilia Mortis*. These sonnets link the passing of the poet to the passing of the year. Rich sound patterns, closely controlled rhythms, along with images and allusions clearly drawn from Morris and his school, make this sequence an eloquent tribute.

In May 1899 Sherman was transferred by his bank to Havana, where in 1900 he became supervisor of the branches in Cuba. He was to remain there until 1912. After the turn of the century he wrote very little verse, but between 1897 and 1900 he published three chapbooks, the last and most interesting of which, *A Canadian Calendar: XII Lyrics*, is a seasonal cycle of poems. Lyrics and lyrical ballads, these poems are not notably different in character or quality from his earlier work.

In 1912 Sherman returned to his bank's head office in Montreal and in 1915 enlisted as a private in the army. He served in France, first in the infantry and later in the Canadian Pay Corps.

At the end of the war he was discharged with the rank of major, then resumed his position as assistant general manager of the Royal Bank, from which he retired in 1919. He then moved to Atlantic City, where he died in 1926. In 1935, his *Complete Poems*, edited, with a memoir, notes, and bibliography, by Lorne Pierce, was published. Since then Sherman's work has largely dropped from view, winning only an occasional appearance in an anthology or a footnote in an article.

Sherman's significance to Canada's literary history is not large, but he does represent well the refinement of technical skill characteristic of the poets of his generation. None of his poems has the distinctiveness of the best work of his time, but all display a quiet integrity, a genuine lyricism, and consistent formal and tonal control.

Their appeal to Sherman's contemporaries was one lodged in their music, a music modern ears are not so well attuned to. His rendering of his feelings and view of life was enhanced by the subtle control of sound and cadence.

References:

R. H. Hatheway, "Francis Sherman: Canadian Poet," *Willison's Monthly*, 2 (March 1927): 383-384;

Lorne Pierce, "Francis Sherman," in his *Three Fredericton Poets: Writers of the University of New Brunswick and the New Dominion* (Toronto: Ryerson, 1933), pp. 25-30;

Charles G. D. Roberts, "Francis Sherman," *Dalhousie Review*, 14 (January 1935): 419-427.

Jessie Georgina Sime

(12 February 1868-13 September 1958)

W. H. New
University of British Columbia

BOOKS: *The Mistress of All Work* (London: Methuen, 1916);

Canada Chaps (London: Lane/Toronto: S. B. Gundy, 1917);

Sister Woman (London: Richards, 1919);

Our Little Life: A Novel of To-day (New York: Stokes, 1921; London: Richards, 1921);

Thomas Hardy of the Wessex Novels: An Essay & Biographical Note (Montreal & New York: Carrier, 1928);

In a Canadian Shack (Toronto: Macmillan, 1937; London: Dickson, 1937);

The Land of Dreams (Toronto: Macmillan, 1940);

Orpheus in Quebec (London: Allen & Unwin, 1942);

Dreams of the World of Light (London: Privately printed, 1951);

Brave Spirits, by Sime and Frank Nicholson (London: Privately printed, 1952);

A Tale of Two Worlds, by Sime, as Georgina Sime, and Nicholson (London: Chapman & Hall, 1953);

Inez and Her Angel, by Sime and Nicholson (London: Chapman & Hall, 1954).

OTHER: "A Book About Canada," in *Golden Tales of Canada*, edited by May Lamberton Becker (New York: Dodd, Mead, 1938), pp. 116-141;

"Art," in *Canadian Short Fiction*, edited by W. H. New (Toronto: Prentice-Hall, 1986), pp. 135-139.

SELECTED PERIODICAL PUBLICATIONS
UNCOLLECTED: "The Spy," *National Review* (London), 113 (November 1939): 638-643;

"Incident in Vienna: A True Tale of a Young Refugee," *Saturday Night*, 59 (5 February 1944): 25;

"Shakespeare's Dark Lady and the Death Mask of a Lover," *Saturday Night*, 59 (3 June 1944): 29;

"Jane Welsh Carlyle as My Mother Saw Her," *Chambers's Journal*, 9th series, 8 (1954): 177-179.

Jessie Georgina Sime was born at Ivy Cottage, Hamilton, Lanark County, Scotland, on 12 February 1868, the daughter of James and Jessie Aitken Wilson Sime, who had married three years earlier at Birkenhead. She came from a literary family. Mrs. Margaret Oliphant (1828-1897), the English novelist, was her mother's second cousin, a relationship that never, apparently, bloomed into cordiality, though the connection drew technically closer when one of Mrs. Oliphant's brothers married one of Jessie Wilson Sime's sisters. Sir Daniel Wilson, for some years the influential principal of the University of Toronto, was Jessie Wilson Sime's elder brother.

Jessie Georgina Sime grew up in London. Although her birth certificate lists her father's occupation as minister, he had given up training for the ministry in 1866 and traveled to Germany to do research on Gotthold Lessing, Johann Wolfgang von Goethe, and Friedrich von Schiller in Heidelberg and Berlin, embarking on a literary career instead. The family lived in Germany when Sime was an infant, but went to London in 1869, moving again when she was about eleven to the suburb of Chiswick. Both her parents were writers, her father being the author of several biographical and historical works on Germany and also a reader for Macmillan of London. In the latter task Sime helped her father during her early maturity (he died in 1895), paying particular attention to works of fiction and travel.

Primarily educated at home, Sime briefly attended Queen's College School, London, and then the College itself for four years. She studied singing in Berlin for a year when she was seventeen, and apparently followed a career as a public singer for a short time. She also traveled to France and Italy for extended periods and briefly served as a secretary to the American philosopher William James in Edinburgh. In due course she turned again to literature, to an official position as a reader for Nelson and Company, and to a literary career of her own. Louis Carrier recorded in 1928 that during these years she published several stories, reviewed for the *Athenaeum*, briefly contributed a weekly column to the *Pall Mall Gazette* (these were among the journals to which her father was also a regular contributor), did some translating from French and German, and occasionally published under the pseudonym Jacob Salviris. (An early work entitled *Rainbow Lights,* however, cannot be traced; Duckworth publishers, to whom it is attributed, do not list it in their files.)

The best source for the biographical details of these early years remains Sime's *Brave Spirits* (1952), a collection of literary and autobiographical essays (some previously published in *Chambers's Journal* in 1949), which are full of fascinating asides. Sime acknowledges the influence of William Morris and John Galsworthy on her ideas, provides personal memoirs of George Meredith, Henry James, Oscar Wilde, George Bernard Shaw, Mrs. Oliphant, and Sarojini Naidu, and draws vignettes of people on the edges of fame: Shaw's sister Lucy, Morris's daughter May, and Rabindranath Tagore's niece Shushama. The margins fascinated her.

It does not appear that when Sime traveled to Canada in 1907 she had any immediate intention of staying, but stay she did. While she moved back to England for eye surgery in 1933, this was merely one of several trips abroad. This trip, along with her desire to place her work with the London publisher Lovat Dickson, is covered in the letters she wrote to Herman Ould, now in the Harry Ransom Humanities Research Center of the University of Texas at Austin. She may have returned to live in England after the end of World War II; there are suggestions to this effect in *A Tale of Two Worlds* (1953). But when she died at Edstone Hall, in Wootton, Warren, England (of "senile arteriosclerosis" at the age of ninety), on 13 September 1958, her death certificate listed her permanent address as the Mount Royal Hotel, Montreal. The city was her home for half her lifetime. By far the bulk of her writing was done in Canada, for Montreal and the countryside of Quebec stimulated her literarily. More fundamentally, Canada also gave her recognition and a career. She published in *Saturday Night*. She became Quebec vice president of the Canadian Women's Press Club, president of the Montreal branch of the Canadian Authors' Association, secretary of the Montreal P.E.N., and a member of other organizations. At a Vienna meeting of the P.E.N. Club, she met the American writer May Lamberton Becker, who later praised her "power to see into the sources of things." Becker excerpted "A Book About Canada" from Sime's 1921 novel *Our Little Life* for inclusion in her own 1938 anthology *Golden Tales of Canada*. The excerpt shows, in Becker's words, the author's "detached" ability to see the "rich color of Canadian life" and to dramatize it in her female characters' meditative, reflective asides on the main action.

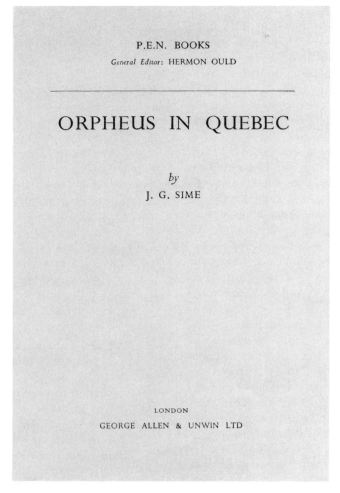

P.E.N. BOOKS
General Editor: HERMON OULD

ORPHEUS IN QUEBEC

by
J. G. SIME

LONDON
GEORGE ALLEN & UNWIN LTD

Title page for Sime's 1942 collection of anecdotal essays, one of which formed the basis for the 1953 novel A Tale of Two Worlds

This stance is recurrent in Sime's work. Repeatedly she characterizes women's perspectives by placing them alongside those of men in order to demonstrate their difference. The two views touch but are not the same. Further, although the women in her stories recognize the normative force of men's voices and roles in their society, they achieve independence from them by using rhetoric in a different way. Sime often addressed such issues directly in her work; she also broke indirectly with received standards of literary evaluation. She lectured, wrote sketches and vignettes, and sought repeatedly to portray the kind of life that was lived at tangents to the norm.

At her most direct, as in her brief general appreciation, *Thomas Hardy of the Wessex Novels* (1928)—republished from the *Westminster Review*—she praises literary men's "sympathy" for the world

but goes on to criticize their failure to connect adequately with it. Specifically the "three major" late-Victorian novelists let their intellectualism intervene between themselves and life. Hardy she praises for at least being a democrat, but Meredith is dismissed as an "aristocrat" and Rudyard Kipling as a "demagogue." Most warmly she remembers the power of personality. She met Hardy once, when she was a child, at one of Sir Alexander Macmillan's garden parties, which she attended with her father. The men talked. She observed and remembered, but she focused separately on the world, listening for the place of women.

The author of journalistic vignettes of women's lives and the roles of Canadians in the imperial war effort, she reflected, as in *Canada Chaps* (1917)—one of a propaganda series published by John Lane–the values of the time in the ways she defined patriotism and duty. In other ways she was a quiet rebel, espousing an expanded social role for women. Passive women seemed only to irritate her, and *The Mistress of All Work* (1916) is a no-nonsense pamphlet announcing how the modern woman might cope with both a career and domestic chores. At the same time, Sime recognized that self-sufficiency was not every woman's experience, and possibly her most important work, her 1919 story sequence entitled *Sister Woman*, pointedly takes an early feminist stance. Using a frame structure, the sequence begins when a man asks a woman what it is that "women really want." She answers that she can tell him only indirectly–situationally, through fiction. The stories themselves are seemingly simple sketches told with a flair for dialect speech: about the persistence of values, the effects of poverty, the offensive condescension of the "typical" English immigrant to Canada. Mostly they concern women in relation to men. The sketches portray a divorcée, a mother grief-stricken by a stillbirth, a mistress whose lover has died, a woman who becomes the victim of domestic violence, a woman who chooses single parenthood, and a woman who resists marriage because of what it did to her mother, choosing servitude instead. The sketches are an oblique education in the realities that the male norms of social order do not take into account and an implicit call for attitudinal reform. Critics, ironically, failed to understand. The first edition of Carl F. Klinck's *Literary History of Canada*, as late as 1965, acknowledged that there was some power to the stories *despite their subject*–spelling out the very kinds of preconception that Sime's interrupted narrative form was attempting to combat.

Our Little Life, too, won only modest attention when it appeared in 1921. Its portrait of urban poverty among English and Irish Catholic immigrants was ahead of its time in a decade when rural romances were still voguish forms in established Canadian literary circles. Set in the fictional Regalia in 1917 (a city whose newspaper is the *Daily Planet!*), it is loosely based on Montreal, portraying the class expectations and race biases of the Anglo-Celtic subculture of a decaying urban "apartment-house" neighborhood. Focusing on a young educated Englishman, Robert Fulton, and a forty-seven-year-old uneducated Irishwoman, Miss Katie McGee, on the surface the novel traces the growing friendship between the two. The friendship is fostered by the woman's rec-

ognition of qualities in the man that transcend speech, qualities that remain unspoken, but it is bedeviled by the man's resistant admiration of "proper" accent and grammar. Ultimately Fulton dies in the 1917 flu epidemic, while Miss McGee, having lost much with the loss of him, resolves to carry on herself, loving life and serving God.

A record of the way in which high life and low are both perceived, this narrative also carries a more reflective commentary on the effects of class, language, and money on social norms. These are related to the emerging character of Canada and to the role of the immigrant communities in it. Throughout the text, Fulton is writing a book about Canada, desperate to praise the society but recurrently at odds with it. What he reads of his manuscript to Miss McGee she only dimly understands, but by the end of the novel, the book has been completed, and it is Miss McGee who takes the manuscript a step closer to publication. He has words; she knows what needs to be done.

Fulton argues "that the nouvelle noblesse of Canada was just the manual worker enriched"–except that he is not really a manual worker, and Miss McGee is. He claims that "the workers will develop, once the restraining influences of the Old Country are withdrawn." But he remains himself restrained, always the outsider-observer. "Canada isn't a country–it's a temperament," a woman in publishing tells him, and in due course he begins to realize how much more Miss McGee's temperament accords with the country than does his own. She *is* Canada; he is not. The "romantic" side of this distinction equates with the future: the "greatness" that derives from the country's ignorance of what it lacks; that is, not knowing that it *should* value traditions, that it is free from traditional constraints, at least in theory. The more worrisome side concerns the implications of ignorance: in a middle-class milieu a reverence for aristocracy somehow gets confused with an admiration for plutocracy. In such a climate "art" is tolerated but never entirely understood. With some wit and some asperity, the novel thus probes the attitudinal borderland between manners and culture.

Sime's subsequent books all reiterate these themes. Most indirectly connected are her books on dreams. *The Land of Dreams* (1940) records (with comments) several of her own dream-memories and dream-visions from 1932 to 1939. Occasionally touching on topical symbols of wilderness and war, the book declares the author's belief in the predictive power of dreaming. The psychosexual ramifications of dream-vision also obliquely occupy the pages of *Inez and Her Angel*, a 1954 novel that asserts the metaphysical presence of an angel in Inez Sinclair's life, a presence that takes her from hate and despair to a new plane of tranquil existence.

More incidentally, *The Land of Dreams* also records various moments in Sime's own life—indicating, for example, that she was financially independent enough to successfully invest in the stock market in the 1930s. Sime also enjoyed the company of the Canadian prime minister, William Lyon Mackenzie King, though this relationship was more casual than close. A letter from King to the critic Lionel Stevenson praises Sime but misspells her name. Another letter, from King to George Doran of Doubleday, Doran in New York, dated 16 September 1929, recommends the publication of Sime's " 'Market Maxims,' a sort of wit and wisdom compilation"; King's letter was a direct response to Sime's request for one, though nothing apparently came of the proposal to publish.

In a Canadian Shack (1937)—excerpted, like *The Land of Dreams*, in Walter de la Mare's 1943 anthology *Love*—reflects autobiographically on a series of trips the author made somewhat earlier to a rural Quebec poultry farm. Every season she is drawn back (in "brazen" July, in "solidifying" autumn) to experience a life radically different from the one she knew in Europe or knew at the time of writing in urban Montreal. Why this is so she is uncertain, except that she comes to see the trips as "incursions into Canada," a way of understanding a culture still new to her. She records her observations: details of houses, families, animals, convent life, and behavior. Over time she discovers that she enjoys more intimacy with a French-Canadian neighbor, Marie Brassard, than with the Englishwoman who is her ostensible hostess. The former is at home here; the latter can be at home nowhere. Recognizing the "beauty of the unfamiliar" is one thing, she reasons; but accepting it as one's own is another. That can come about only from "long usage and slow reception." Such a change, moreover, marks the moment when an immigrant becomes rooted in a new society.

Some of Sime's essays, as in *Orpheus in Quebec* (1942), a P.E.N. book, hazard a few generalizations about the future of art in a new culture. They tend to be impressionistic. While she acknowledges the likelihood that "heterogeneity" will be a force in Canadian writing and suggests that the conventional novel will not be the appropriate form for a new literary voice, she does not examine any current writers nor pursue her idea that the roots of the new literature will have a basis in the folk culture. But her method is that of the indirect anecdote. She argues by analogy. And one of the anecdotes here, concerning a Viennese family (named Lange, becoming Long) that adapts well to Canada, becomes the basis for one of the full-scale novels she wrote late in her life in collaboration with Frank (Carr) Nicholson, *A Tale of Two Worlds* (1953).

Nicholson (1875-1962), of Keswick, was librarian of the University of Edinburgh from 1910 to 1939 and the author of a book on Old German love songs. The contribution each writer made to the later books is uncertain, though if Sime's eyesight continued to deteriorate after 1940, then Nicholson may have acted in the role of amanuensis and adviser. Certainly Sime acknowledges Nicholson's friendly collaboration in the preparation of the dream books and the essays, too, though the contents seem, from such internal evidence as biographical detail and previous history, to be hers alone.

One passage at the end of *A Tale of Two Worlds*, however, hints at some difference of judgment between them. In three sections ("The Old World," "Between Two Worlds," and "The New World"), the seven-hundred-page novel tells a three-generation saga of the Lange/Long family acculturation to Canada. The characters, largely seen from the outside, have to deal with false starts and deprivation, adapt to "turns of phrase" as much as turns of fortune. The first-person narrator (named Shoshona) who tells their tale is a writer with contacts in Vienna and Montreal who becomes a family confidante. It is a story of progress; most individuals are finally successful. At the end, however, one creative son, a musician, is killed, but in order that he acquire fame, his compositions are given over to another—who "improves" them, gives them "style," makes them "successful," finds an applauding audience for them. But according to the narrator, the "stylist" in so doing denies them the "life" they had in their less popular, original form. Convention deprives art of its reality, she declares. Such a statement might also be construed as Sime's own distinction between her early oblique, fragmentary sketches and the solid, well-tailored, but unmemorable novels of her later career.

References:

May Lamberton Becker, "Jessie Georgina Sime," in *Golden Tales of Canada,* edited by Becker (New York: Dodd, Mead, 1938), pp. 113-115;

Esther Lisabeth Bobak, "The Artist and the City," chapter five of her "Attitudes Towards the City in the Canadian Realistic Novel of the Twenties," Ph.D. dissertation, Dalhousie University, 1981, pp. 286-373;

L. C. [Louis Carrier], "Publisher's Note," appended to Sime's *Thomas Hardy of the Wessex Novels* (Montreal & New York: Carrier, 1928), pp. 55-58.

Papers:

An exchange of nineteen letters between Sime (several signed "J. Georgia Sime") and officials of the P.E.N. Club in London (primarily Herman Ould), from the period 1933-1938, is held by the Harry Ransom Humanities Research Center, University of Texas at Austin. An exchange of correspondence between Sime and the Right Honourable William Lyon Mackenzie King, 1929-1937, is held by the Public Archives of Canada. The exchange includes two letters and one telegram from King to Sime and two letters and one telegram from Sime to King. There is also one letter about Sime from King to George Doran. There are 285 documentary sheets–primarily letters exchanged by Sime with Hugh Eayrs and Ellen Elliott concerning the publication of *In a Canadian Shack* and *The Land of Dreams*–in the Macmillan Company papers, the William Ready Division of Archives and Research Collections, McMaster University Library, Hamilton, Ontario. The William Arthur Deacon Manuscript Collection, Thomas Fisher Rare Book Library, University of Toronto, has five letters by Sime and Deacon, dated 14 November 1925-14 April 1946, concerning the P.E.N. Club.

Bertrand William Sinclair

(9 January 1881-20 October 1972)

Laurie Ricou
University of British Columbia

BOOKS: *Raw Gold* (New York: Dillingham, 1908);

The Land of Frozen Suns (New York: Dillingham, 1910);

North of Fifty-Three (Toronto: Musson, 1914; Boston: Little, Brown, 1914; London: Allen, 1915);

Big Timber: A Story of the Northwest (Toronto: Copp, Clark, 1916; Boston: Little, Brown, 1916; London: Hodder & Stoughton, 1920);

Burned Bridges (Toronto: Briggs, 1919; Boston: Little, Brown, 1919; London: Hodder & Stoughton, 1920);

Poor Man's Rock (Toronto: Ryerson, 1920; Boston: Little, Brown, 1920; London: Hodder & Stoughton, 1920);

The Hidden Places (Toronto: Ryerson, 1922; Boston: Little, Brown, 1922; London: Hodder & Stoughton, 1922);

The Inverted Pyramid (Toronto: Goodchild, 1924; Boston: Little, Brown, 1924; London: Hodder & Stoughton, 1924);

Wild West (Toronto: Ryerson, 1926; Boston: Little, Brown, 1926; London: Hodder & Stoughton, 1926);

Pirates of the Plains (London: Hodder & Stoughton, 1928);

Gunpowder Lightning (Toronto: McClelland & Stewart, 1930; Boston: Little, Brown, 1930; London: Hodder & Stoughton, 1930);

Down the Dark Alley (London: Hodder & Stoughton, 1935; Boston: Little, Brown, 1936);

Both Sides of the Law (New York: Novel Selections, 1951; London: Wright & Brown, 1955);

Room for the Rolling M. (London: Wright & Brown, 1954).

MOTION PICTURE: *Shotgun Jones*, screenplay by Sinclair, Selig Polyscope, 1914.

Even at the peak of his success, when *North of Fifty-Three* (1914) was building toward sales of 340,000 copies in reprint and Little, Brown was offering a substantial contract for a novel a year, Bertrand Sinclair pined for a literary reputation. He was torn between writing for the market in order to pay his bills and writing the novel of social analysis that his intelligence and interests demanded. Ultimately an urgent need for cash won out (as it often does in his novels), and his passion for thoughtful fiction was repeatedly compromised by the market's demand for "rip-roaring adventure, the utmost conventionality in point of view [and] a liberal garnishing of sentimental slush," as he wrote to Alfred R. McIntyre on 8 February 1921. *The Oxford Companion to Canadian Literature* (1983) and *The Canadian Encyclopedia* (1988) do not mention him, nor does W. J. Keith's *Canadian Literature in English* (1985) or W. H. New's *A History of Canadian Literature* (1989).

Sinclair's own favorite (self-deprecating) term for his fiction was "yarns." A reader caught in the pell-mell opening of *North of Fifty-Three*, during which the heroine rejects an elderly suitor, splits with her fiancé, applies for a job three thousand miles away, travels from Ontario to British Columbia's Cariboo country, begins a new career as a teacher, and escapes the assault of a traveling salesman, all within sixty-five pages, will quickly recognize the aptness of the term. Adventure intertwines with more adventure in an unending spin of excitement. Speed—both in the plot and the writing—seems more important than substance, while the yarn's sly, self-conscious exaggeration touches style and character.

Much of Sinclair's life also approaches the incredible and marvelous, partly because the best sources are Sinclair's own exuberant responses to publishers. As in a yarn, he lived most of his life under a partially assumed name (taking his father's middle name, Bertrand, as part of his pen name). He was born William Brown Sinclair on 9 January 1881 in Edinburgh, Scotland, to George Bertrand and Robina Williamson Sinclair. According to an obituary in the *Vancouver Province*, William came to Canada with his mother in 1889 and settled in Regina, Saskatchewan. He ran away from home at age fourteen and became a

He felt with an odd exaltation the quick hammer of her heart against his breast. FRONTISPIECE. *See page 95.*

BURNED BRIDGES

BY

BERTRAND W. SINCLAIR

WITH FRONTISPIECE BY

RALPH P. COLEMAN

BOSTON

LITTLE, BROWN, AND COMPANY

1919

Frontispiece and title page for the American edition of Sinclair's romantic novel that is set against the background of the emergence of automobile retailing

cowboy in Montana. He was, he wrote to an admiring reader, "for seven years a range rider in Montana and the Dakotas" (to Bertha Bodger, 7 December 1924). In 1903 he quit cowpunching and wandered to Seattle, San Francisco, and back to Great Falls, Montana, where he lived for some three years. In Montana he found the subject matter and artistic friends to stimulate a writer. He began to publish magazine fiction in 1905. As he told Norrell Gregory (7 July 1937), his objective was to write a more subdued western than convention demanded: "I remember reading Owen Wister's *The Virginian* [1902] in a cowcamp . . . and wondering [why] no cowpuncher ever wrote about his own time and his own people–instead of leaving it to outsiders. . . . [W]e didn't spend all our time burning gunpowder. In Montana, when I rode there, we shipped annually over

half a million prime beef to Chicago every fall. You would never guess that from reading any western story about cowboys."

His first novels, sufficiently facile that by the 1920s he was refusing to list them among his publications, were *Raw Gold* (1908), a story featuring the adventures of Northwest Mounted Police along the Canada-U.S. boundary, and *The Land of Frozen Suns* (1910). When he returned to writing book-length accounts of range-riding toward the end of his career as a novelist, he claimed, somewhat implausibly, that *Wild West* (1926) and *Gunpowder Lightning* (1930) were "almost as much history as fiction" (to J. P. Armstrong, 24 February 1937). The *Booklist* (November 1926), drawing on a notice in the *Wisconsin Library Bulletin*, advertised the former as "a much quieter and more sanely balanced book than many another western thriller." But none of the Montana fiction offers the texture of locale or culture found in his fiction set in British Columbia.

Sinclair's love of "yarning" and his desire for a more historically accurate western were consolidated by two important relationships. In 1905 he married Bertha M. Brown, "probably the first woman, and certainly the most prolific," according to Helen Stauffer, "to write in the genre of the 'formula' Western" (*American Women Writers*, 1982). Writing under her first husband's name, as B. M. Bower, she provided Sinclair a model of rapid production and a formula (emphasizing details of ranching and keeping the violence offstage and muted). Bower published over sixty novels after her best-known *Chip of the Flying U* (first published serially in 1904). The illustrator of Bower's novel, the major western artist Charles M. Russell, was best man at the wedding. By 1905 Russell's career as an illustrator was flourishing: his passion for documenting the West in precisely observed, often whimsical sketches presumably had a considerable influence on Sinclair's own aspirations.

Sinclair and his wife spent most of the years from 1907 to 1911 in California, living in Santa Cruz, San Jose, and Jamesburg (Monterey County). Early in the marriage they had one daughter, Della Frances. In a period when he seems to have done some literary hobnobbing and sporadic studies at Stanford University, other literary influences were established, especially Jack London, with his themes of the testing of virtue in a northern wilderness, and Upton Sinclair, with his analyses of class privilege and commercial power structure. (Upton and Bertrand Sinclair were apparently cousins.) Another influence claimed, less convincingly, is O. Henry. Between 1905 and 1940 Bertrand Sinclair published at least sixty stories, as well as eleven "novelettes," mainly in pulp periodicals such as the *Popular Magazine*, *Adventure*, and *Short Stories*. Although he constantly dismissed these as potboilers, they often show a facility for presenting narration by a colloquial raconteur, telling the story from inside, a narrative stance that might have been more productively exploited in some of the often grandiloquently omniscient novels.

By 1911 Sinclair's relationship to Bertha had ended; he married Ruth, her cousin, and in March 1912 settled in Vancouver. Here he found the setting and center for his best fiction. *North of Fifty-Three* tells the predictable but improbable tale of an eastern urban sophisticate abducted by Roaring Bill Wagstaff, a personification of the rough but ultimately purifying wilderness. The novel incorporates some details of trapping, placer mining, and of the coming of the Grand Trunk Pacific railway, but it is most absorbing when Sinclair delineates the problems of corporate financing and the profiteers' unconcern for the men who are building the mine. *Big Timber: A Story of the Northwest* (1916) has a similar East-West, urban-wilderness background. Here Sinclair's strength, and now historical significance, becomes evident, as he determines to make the methods and sociology of the logging industry a more prominent part of his subject. Sinclair's racist and sexist epithets, his often telegraphed plots, and the rhetoric of affected sentimentality ("quoth," "proffered," "bespoken," "would fain have rested," etc.) are now unattractive to changed tastes, or simply distasteful. What remains of interest are his attempts to integrate fiction with precise geographical settings and the economic and cultural structures of emerging societies: the growth of automobile retailing in *Burned Bridges* (1919); the mixture of marine engineering and bootlegging in 1929 Vancouver in *Down the Dark Alley* (1935); and the economic effects of World War I on a family-controlled timber dynasty in *The Inverted Pyramid* (1924).

Sinclair and Ruth had one daughter, Cherry Whitaker, born in 1912. In 1920 they bought property at Pender Harbour, a small seaside community north of Vancouver; Sinclair spent much of his time there at the house he called "The Stopping Place," by 1922 making it their permanent residence. Life aboard the *Hoo-Hoo*, a salmon troller he bought in 1919, became an essential part of the couple's love affair with British Columbia. Consistent with the ethic of the self-educated writer—to learn by doing, not by studying—he prepared to write a novel of salmon fishing by joining the commercial fishing fleet (as he had worked for a logging crew in order to write *Big Timber*). *Poor Man's Rock* (1920) conveys an authentic firsthand experience, as it links tales of love and revenge to a study of the economics of fishing for salmon (the intricate nexus of fisherman, buyer, canner, and consumer) and to the symbolic resonances of local toponymy. *Poor Man's Rock* is the best representative of Sinclair's belief that the novel "must necessarily be an attempt to picture life, to criticise life, or to interpret life" (to Alfred McIntyre, 8 February 1921). His criticism and interpretation gain credibility from his patient detailing of the schooling habits of the salmon, the methods of gill-netters and seiners, and the scrupulous accounting of income and expenditures, profits and losses.

But even as Sinclair reflected on the positive reviews of his most engaging, socially and economically dense novel—"I am no longer in the blood and thunder business," he wrote to his agent in 1922—his market began to shrink. *Burned Bridges* had higher first-year sales than *Big Timber*, but with *Poor Man's Rock*, first-year sales began to slacken. The novel's greater attention to the intricacies of the business world may have caused the drop-off. When Sinclair tried to go too far in the direction of Upton Sinclair, the escapist-minded audience he had been attracting began to desert him. *The Hidden Places* (1922), its facially disfigured protagonist expressing Sinclair's jaundiced view of the myth of wartime heroism, accelerated the trend. By 1925 Sinclair's wife, Ruth, was hospitalized in a sanatorium in Livermore, California, suffering from a nervous breakdown. Although his later novels were aimed at reawakening the old readership and his stories continued to sell briskly, the emotional and economic blow of Ruth's illness seems to have begun a decline in the writer's commitment, which was further eroded by the drying up of his markets during the early years of the Depression.

He virtually stopped writing in the mid 1930s and fished as a licensed salmon troller from 1936 until 1966. In July 1940 he wrote poignantly to his agent, J. Chambrun, that "I would like to write one first-class novel before I die. . . ." But in 1945 his income tax return reported only $1,492 gross income from fishing and *no* interest or royalties. This account of the decline of Sinclair's writing career does not, however, suggest a decline in the man.

In many ways the life of Sinclair in the 1940s and 1950s resembles that of the hard-working adventurers portrayed in his fiction. He was living, he told his agent, "a life of useful action": "So I fish salmon and add around twenty thousand pounds of good useful food to the national effort each season." The only writing he did in this period was in the logbooks of the *Hoo-Hoo*, reporting the daily weather and catch, mapping and remapping the Gulf of Georgia, and only occasionally recording anecdotes of going to a dance or waking up halfway through the night to ride out a rollicking storm. His literary bent he saved for the people who had mattered most to him in his strongest novel, *Poor Man's Rock*, the commercial fishing community to whom he broadcast the "Sinclair Hour" on radio. When he told of his life in 1930, he once remarked, "I still get as much kick out of writing a story as any human being could," and addressing the limited audience of the "Sinclair Hour," Bertrand Sinclair, in his eighties, still got a kick out of telling a story, and the story of his life.

Reference:

Alan Twigg, *Vancouver Writers* (Madeira Park, B.C.: Harbour, 1986), pp. 137-139.

Papers:

The Bertrand W. Sinclair Papers, including typescripts, some manuscripts, correspondence, and miscellaneous items, are held in the Special Collections Division, University of British Columbia Library, Vancouver.

Constance Lindsay Skinner

(1877-March 1939)

Diana M. A. Relke
University of Calgary

BOOKS: *"Good-morning Rosamond!"* (Garden City, N.Y.: Doubleday, Page, 1917);

Pioneers of the Old Southwest: A Chronicle of the Dark and Bloody Ground (New Haven: Yale University Press/Toronto: Glasgow, Brook/London: Oxford University Press, 1920);

Adventures of Oregon: A Chronicle of the Fur Trade (New Haven: Yale University Press/Toronto: Glasgow, Brook/London: Oxford University Press, 1920);

Adventures in the Wilderness, by Skinner, Clark Wissler, and William Wood (New Haven: Yale University Press, 1925);

Silent Scot, Frontier Scout (New York: Macmillan, 1925);

The Search Relentless (London: Methuen, 1925; New York: Coward-McCann, 1928);

Becky Landers: Frontier Warrior (New York: Macmillan, 1926);

The White Leader (New York: Macmillan, 1926);

Roselle of the North (New York: Macmillan, 1927);

The Tiger Who Walks Alone (New York: Macmillan, 1927);

Andy Breaks Trail (New York: Macmillan, 1928);

The Ranch of the Golden Flowers (New York: Macmillan, 1928);

Red Willows (Toronto: McClelland & Stewart, 1929; New York: Coward-McCann, 1929);

Red Man's Luck (Toronto: McClelland & Stewart, 1930; New York: Coward-McCann, 1930);

Songs of the Coast Dwellers (New York: Coward-McCann, 1930);

Debby Barnes, Trader (New York: Macmillan, 1932);

Beaver, Kings and Cabins (New York: Macmillan, 1933; London: Dickson, 1933;

Rob Roy; The Frontier Twins (New York: Macmillan, 1934).

PLAY PRODUCTION: *David*, Carmel, Cal., Forest Theatre, July 1910.

OTHER: Epilogue to *The Path on the Rainbow*, ed-

Constance Lindsay Skinner

ited by George W. Cronyn (New York: Boni & Liveright, 1918);

The Rivers of America, six volumes, edited, with an introduction, by Skinner (New York & Toronto: Farrar & Rinehart, 1937-1939);

A. J. M. Smith, ed., *The Book of Canadian Poetry*, includes poems by Skinner (Chicago: University of Chicago Press, 1943).

SELECTED PERIODICAL PUBLICATIONS

UNCOLLECTED: "Poetry: The Swing Speech," *Poetry Review*, 5 (December 1914): 207-214;

"The Rainbow Path," *Reedy's Mirror*, 27 (13 December 1918): 666-667;

"History as Literature: And the Individual Definition," *Bookman*, 49 (August 1919): 750-754;

Title pages for Skinner's first two historical books, both published in the Chronicles of America series

"On Writing of Many Kinds," *Journal of Information for Literary Workers*, 59 (23 December 1922): 94-95;

"The Aztec Poets," *Poetry*, 26 (June 1925): 166-168;

"Cheating at Solitaire," *North American Review*, 224 (December 1927): 675-679;

"A Hudson Bay Childhood," *New York Herald Tribune Books*, 4 (26 February 1928): 8;

"What Well-Dressed Women Are Reading," *North American Review*, 227 (April 1929): 430-434;

"Feet of Clay, or Eyes of Envy?," *North American Review*, 228 (July 1929): 41-46.

Constance Lindsay Skinner is known in Canadian literary history as a minor author of the

early twentieth century who wrote adaptations of authentic West Coast Indian songs. But this reputation is misleading, for her "adaptations" are often original free-verse and imagist poems. In addition Skinner was a prolific playwright, novelist, essayist, journalist, critic, and social historian. Although she spent her adult life writing and publishing in the United States, much of her creative work is set in western Canada; it is informed by her childhood experience and her extensive knowledge of Canadian history and native Indian culture. Her work is therefore of Canadian historical interest. Skinner's poems and novels have a wider historical appeal, as well, because of their depiction of twentieth-century female experience and feminist concerns.

Skinner's interest in North American Indian culture is not surprising. She was born in 1877 to Robert and Annie Lindsay Skinner and raised in Quesnel, British Columbia, an isolated trading post where her father was a Hudson's Bay factor. She moved with her family to Vancouver when she was fourteen years old, and at sixteen she was sent to live with an aunt in California. A precocious writer, Skinner wrote her first story when she was five and her first novel when she was eleven. At fourteen she wrote the libretto and score for a three-act children's operetta, which was performed in Vancouver, circa 1891, to raise money for charity. By the age of sixteen she had published two short stories, written several musical scores, and was also writing drama and music criticism, political commentary, and fashion and social gossip for the *Los Angeles Times*, the *San Francisco Examiner*, and other newspapers.

After settling in New York in her late twenties, Skinner published fourteen novels, twenty-eight short stories, three plays, sixty poems, close to two hundred book reviews, several historical articles, and four histories of American pioneer life. One of her histories, *Adventures of Oregon: A Chronicle of the Fur Trade* (1920), was, in 1934, on the required reading list of most American high schools. The publishing house of Farrar and Rinehart commissioned her to edit and supervise a historical series on the rivers of America, a task she did not live to complete.

Toward the end of her career she wrote two articles for the *North American Review*, "Cheating at Solitaire" and "What Well-Dressed Women are Reading," which demonstrate her interest in current women's issues but betray her considerable ambivalence about the fitness of women for social equality with men. Although much of her work is devoted to enlightening her female audience, she insisted in a January 1911 interview with Vancouver's *Daily Province Magazine:* "I don't know much about Women's Movements, Suffragetteism, Women's Clubs, Councils, etc., and I am not, I think, in favor of any movement which primarily depends for its existence on sex segregation. But I recognize that at present the segregated 'Club,' the 'woman's' movement, has to exist, because men have so signally failed to keep our civic, social, and national standards high-flying in clean air. In this day of male blood-lust for money, women are leading practically all the ethical and aesthetic movements."

Among Skinner's literary forefathers were the major eighteenth- and nineteenth-century writers whose work she read as a child in her father's well-stocked library. In addition she was personally acquainted with several Indian bards of the tribes with whom her father did business. From them she learned an additional set of "literary" conventions that, combined with those she encountered in her reading of English literature, she eventually put to use in all her poetry. In 1914 the earliest of the Indian poems collected in Skinner's *Songs of the Coast Dwellers* (1930) appeared in *Poetry* (Chicago) and were singled out for an award by the magazine's editors. This positive response may explain why Skinner persisted almost exclusively in the same poetic mode for the rest of her career. Her perseverance was rewarded by two more prizes, one from the *Bookman* and the other from *Lyric West*, where many of the later Indian poems first appeared.

The poems in *Songs of the Coast Dwellers* have as their setting the Squamish Indian settlement on the north shore of Burrard Inlet in British Columbia. A series of dramatic monologues, these poems are notable for their treatment of female experience–particularly sexual experience. While ostensibly conforming in every detail to Indian poetic conventions, Skinner subverts those conventions for her own purposes; what passes for a depiction of Indian customs and traditions is below the surface an exploration of sexual politics. However, while some of the poems articulate female victimization through sexual violation, emotional brutality, and social alienation, others celebrate traditional masculinity and sanction male authority.

Skinner's novels have historical settings and reflect her interest in pioneer life, Indian culture, and the North American fur trade. Many of the juvenile novels feature female protagonists in heroic roles. *Roselle of the North* (1927), the story of a young white girl who is adopted by a tribe of Cree Indians, is one of the more interesting novels with a Canadian setting. It exhibits Skinner's ambivalence about female power. Aimed at an adolescent female audience, the moral of this novel is that immodesty in the form of heroic action is not only unfeminine but extremely dangerous and likely to be punished.

Red Willows (1929), another of Skinner's novels with a Canadian setting, is an adult adventure story set largely in British Columbia that explores the relationship between Indian and white man during the gold rush. Several critics praised the novel as a powerful sociological study, and Skinner herself felt that *Red Willows* was the best of all her books: "I put into the writing of that novel the all of all that was best in me. . . . It has been justly called a study of groups of aliens against a frontier background. If it is not a great deal more than that, then my spirit is a shallow, empty basin and my life a dreary waste." However, like most of Skinner's fiction, *Red Willows* betrays her weakness for overblown diction, which tends to deaden the book's impact.

Three of Skinner's unpublished plays were performed and received critical acclaim. *David*, a three-act drama depicting the Biblical story of the reign of King Saul, was performed in July 1910 before an audience of twelve hundred at the open-air Forest Theatre in Carmel, California. During the 1911-1912 season, *The Lady of Gray Gables*, a romantic comedy in four acts, and *Birthright*, a tragedy about a half-breed girl in a missionary household in northern British Columbia, were taken on tour across the United States and performed in Boston, Buffalo, and Chicago, as well as many smaller cities.

Although Skinner's work was not widely read in Canada during her lifetime, she was known to the female literary community through her friendship with poet and critic Florence Randall Livesay, mother of Dorothy Livesay, one of Canada's first and most important modernist poets. The young Dorothy knew Skinner personally and read her work with interest. Skinner was "repatriated" as a Canadian writer when a selection of her poems appeared in A. J. M. Smith's *Book of Canadian Poetry* (1943). She may now be viewed as a transitional figure linking the nineteenth-century poets Isabella Valancy Crawford and Pauline Johnson with contemporary poets such as Cam Hubert and Susan Musgrave, all of whom use fictions derived from North American Indian lore. Skinner died in New York City in March 1939 of complications following an attack of influenza.

Bibliography:

"Constance Lindsay Skinner," in *Literary Writings in America: A Bibliography*, 8 volumes (Millwood, N.Y.: KTO Press, 1977), VI: 9206-9217.

Biography:

Jean West Maury, "From a Fur-Trading Post to New York: Constance Lindsay Skinner's Progress from Her Earliest Days in British Columbia," *Boston Evening Transcript*, 6 May 1933, pp. 20-23.

Robert J. C. Stead

(4 September 1880-25 June 1959)

Margery Fee
Queen's University at Kingston

BOOKS: *The Empire Builders and Other Poems* (Toronto: Briggs, 1908);

Prairie Born, and Other Poems (Toronto: Briggs, 1911);

Songs of the Prairie (Toronto: Briggs, 1911; New York: Platt & Peck, 1912; London: Gay & Hancock, 1912);

The Bail Jumper (Toronto: Briggs, 1914; London: Unwin, 1914);

The Homesteaders: A Novel of the Canadian West (Toronto: Musson, 1916; London: Unwin, 1916);

Kitchener, and Other Poems (Toronto: Musson, 1917);

The Cow Puncher (Toronto: Musson, 1918; New York & London: Harper, 1918);

Why Don't They Cheer? (London: Unwin, 1918);

Dennison Grant: A Novel of Today (Toronto: Musson, 1920); revised and abridged as *Zen of the Y.D.: A Novel of the Foothills* (London: Hodder & Stoughton, 1925);

Neighbours (Toronto: Hodder & Stoughton, 1922);

The Smoking Flax (Toronto: McClelland & Stewart, 1924; New York: Doran, 1924);

Grain (Toronto: McClelland & Stewart, 1926; New York: Doran, 1926);

The Copper Disc (Garden City, N.Y.: Doubleday, Doran, 1931);

Dry Water: A Novel of Western Canada, edited by Prem Varma (Ottawa: Tecumseh, 1983).

SELECTED PERIODICAL PUBLICATIONS
UNCOLLECTED: "Literature as a National Asset," *Canadian Bookman,* 5 (December 1923): 343;

"Have We a Literature?," *Manitoba Free Press,* literary section, 4 August 1924, p. 1.

Robert J. C. Stead's novel *Grain* (1926) is considered, with Frederick Philip Grove's *Settlers of the Marsh* and Martha Ostenso's *Wild Geese,* both published in 1925, to pioneer a Canadian version of realism. During Stead's lifetime, however, *Grain* was among his least successful works. Newspaper critics dubbed him "The Canadian Laureate" for his patriotic poetry, and thousands of readers bought his more sentimental romances about prairie homesteading: *The Homesteaders* (1916) went through five printings before 1922, and *The Cow Puncher* (1918) sold seventy thousand copies. Stead's elegy "Kitchener" (1916) was published throughout the empire (eventually in book form with other poems in 1917), and this publicity ensured that his novels were read and reviewed not only in England but also in Australia, New Zealand, and even Siam, not to mention the United States.

Stead's accounts of prairie life are given authenticity by his own experience. Robert James Campbell Stead was born on 4 September 1880 in Middleville, Ontario, the sixth and youngest child of Richard Thompson Stead and May Campbell Stead. The family moved to a homestead near Cartwright, Manitoba, in 1882. Stead left the Cartwright school at fourteen; apart from some courses at the Winnipeg Business College in 1897, he had no further formal education. He was a hired man, a clerk in a general store, a grain elevator agent, and a steam engine operator before he began his early newspaper career.

Stead founded a newspaper in 1898 that was first called the *Rock Lake Review,* then the *Rock Lake Review and Cartwright Enterprise,* and in 1903 the *Southern Manitoba Review.* He sold this paper on 4 January 1910. He also published a monthly magazine, *Noble Deeds,* and edited the *Crystal City Courier* from 1908 to early 1909. When William Briggs of Toronto published Stead's first book, *The Empire Builders and Other Poems,* in 1908 Stead used his own periodicals to publicize it. During this period he owned a lumber business and a flour and feed store as well. Stead had married Nettie May Wallace on 31 December 1901, and they had three sons: Richard Lorne, Stanley Wallace, and Robert A. Stead. The family moved to High River, Alberta, in 1910, where Stead sold Buicks for two years before joining the staff of the *Calgary Herald*. While a car salesman, he had been writing for both the *High River Times* and the *Calgary Morning Albertan*.

Stead first won fame for what Laurence Ricou calls "five volumes of trivial verse." The poems, strongly influenced by Rudyard Kipling and Robert Service, deal with humorous, patriotic, and sentimental themes. His first book sold four thousand copies by 1923 because of his own skillful publicity work, and his later volumes of poetry were also popular. Despite their lack of literary merit, Stead's poems are still of interest since the attitudes and ideas they express were probably in accord with those of their typical readers: moderately educated, moderately well-to-do westerners of British background. In "The Plough" (in *Songs of the Prairie*, 1911) Stead comments that before the settlement of the West the land was "silent, useless and unused" because it had not been farmed, and concludes: "Where once the silent red-man spurned the ground, / A land of peace and plenty now is found . . . / Where loyal friends and happy homes are made, / And culture follows hard the feet of trade." Here Stead expresses the belief common in nineteenth- and early twentieth-century Canada that material progress inevitably led to a cultural flowering. In other poems the Northwest Mounted Police are eulogized, English "Remittance Men" mocked, and, in Stead's most notorious poem, "The Mixer" (in *The Empire Builders*), immigrants, however "disappointing," are welcomed as Canadians, "all but the yellow and brown." (The line was changed in the 1923 edition.) Perhaps because of his endorsement of the work ethic, Stead depicts women sympathetically. He frequently makes clear how vital the farm wife's contribution was to the farmer's success, and frequently his female characters express a wish, which is rarely granted, to be treated as equal to men.

An English review of *The Bail Jumper* (1914) (*Morning Post*, 10 July 1914) makes the best case for rereading most of Stead's novels: "As a story it leaves much to be desired, but as a series of pictures of Canadian life it has much to recommend it." When Stead's poorly realized characters and implausible and melodramatic plots begin to pall, the reader will still find the novels' detailed accounts of prairie life absorbing. His early works are a peculiar mix of popular, romantic, sentimental formula fiction and realism: his contemporar-

ies preferred the romantic side of Stead; modern readers and critics prefer the realistic side.

The Bail Jumper's hero, Raymond Burton, works, as Stead once did, in a general store, and the novel exposes many of the practices of this prairie institution. The essential plot recurs in several later novels: an uneducated young man meets an exquisite, cultivated city woman and apparently loses her. After a series of experiences that prove that the young woman's instant perception of the hero's potential quality was correct, the young man discovers (to his surprise, but not the reader's) that the young woman has waited patiently for him to reach her level of sophistication.

The Homesteaders, reprinted by the University of Toronto Press in 1973, gives a detailed description of its major characters' move to the West from Ontario. Stead shows how John Harrison, like many of Frederick Philip Grove's heroes, turns from a young idealist into a driven slave of his own materialism, a man who uses his wife and children as if they were employees.

Dave Elder of *The Cow Puncher* begins as a cowboy and ends as a real-estate speculator. Stead's interest in the boom and bust of the western land grab recurs in the peculiar theories propounded by the hero of his next novel, *Dennison Grant* (1920). (These theories were dropped in the 1925 abridgement of this novel, retitled *Zen of the Y.D.: A Novel of the Foothills*.) They are based on the idea that money should be earned by hard work rather than be gained by speculation or inheritance. All Stead's novels give a significant twist to the rags-to-riches story: the hero comes out strongly against materialism and for spiritual and cultural values.

In 1919 the Steads moved to Ottawa, where Stead became the publicity director for the Department of Immigration and Colonization. He was active in the affairs of the Canadian Authors' Association, founded in 1921, and in 1923 was its second national president, following John Murray Gibbon. In Ottawa he wrote *Neighbours* (1922), which sold over fifteen thousand copies in Canada. In this novel two young brother-and-sister couples set up adjacent homesteads. An English remittance man, mercilessly teased for his ignorance of farming, is nonetheless presented as a cultural model. The Englishman's cheerful willingness to learn from his mistakes is paralleled by the young Canadian hero's persistence in putting himself through a reading course in great literature. Willingness to learn is one of the virtues

Stead promotes most steadily; he must have possessed it himself, given his limited formal education.

The Smoking Flax (1924) is the story of Cal Beach and his nephew Reed. Cal has a degree in sociology, which allows Stead to generalize about prairie society. Reed is the illegitimate son of Cal's sister (now dead) and Jackson Stake, Jr.; the revelation of this secret after Cal becomes the hired man on the Stake farm serves to complicate the plot, not only of this novel, but also of Stead's next novel, *Grain,* in which the same characters appear.

Perhaps the simplest explanation for *Grain's* initial failure is the nature of Gander Stake, its narrator and central character. Unlike Cal, who is set up as a foil and role model for him near the end of the novel, Gander has none of the qualities considered essential for the romantic hero. He has a slouching gait, a protruding Adam's apple, and an overly high opinion of himself, based on his ability to drive a six-horse team and to run a steam thresher, regardless of his inability to distinguish between a noun and a pronoun. He has absolutely no time for the beauties of nature or poetry, refuses to go to war, and, unlike Cal, does not "get the girl" at novel's end. In *Grain* Stead has moved a long way from the reflexive patriotism and the bland heroes of his earlier works. Although one might think the young, ambitious, and literate Stead must have been completely different from the inarticulate Gander, part of this character's power may be derived from Stead's realization that he could have been trapped, as Gander nearly is, by economic necessity. Stead did, like Gander, have difficulty expressing his emotions, and fellow members of the Canadian Authors' Association dubbed him the "silent Scot." Stead obviously sympathizes with Gander's pride at being able to do "a man's work" at the age of ten, even though this pride precludes his realizing that this work robbed him of childhood, education, imagination, and the ability to cope with society or women. The novel was reprinted in 1963 as one of the first of McClelland & Stewart's New Canadian Library series.

Recent criticism has focused on how closely *Grain* fits the definition of realism. Frank Davey argues persuasively that *Grain* "is about something more elemental than the issues of historical, environmental, or biological determinism," all central to realism: "it is about man and woman. . . ." Certainly it is Gander's attraction to a woman that finally pulls him out of his rut in the country toward the possibility of education and love in the city. Yet Stead makes it clear that Gander is not alone when he abandons the farm. He is part of "the great trek from the country to the city, a trek which never could have taken place but for the application of machinery to land, so that now one farmer may raise enough wheat to feed many hundreds of city dwellers." Perhaps it is Stead's ability to show the ways in which his characters are acted upon by external forces, while at the same time making their responses to these forces seem psychologically convincing, that lifts this novel so far above the others.

Perhaps *Grain's* lack of commercial success compelled the disappointed Stead to attempt more popular work, since his last novel published in his lifetime, *The Copper Disc* (1931), is a clichéd thriller with neither literary merit nor Canadian interest. It did not do well either, however, and after its publication Stead returned to more serious work, the novel he first titled "Dry Water" and then "But Yet the Soil Remains" (finally published in 1983 as *Dry Water: A Novel of Western Canada*).

Interestingly, the Depression, central to the conclusion of the novel, had hit the book industry just when Stead was first seeking to publish it in 1936 and 1937, and despite some favorable interest from Longmans, Green and McClelland and Stewart, it did not appear. From 1936 until he retired in 1946 Stead was publicity director for the parks and resources aspects of the Department of Mines and Resources. His wife, Nettie, died in 1952, and he married Nancy Rankin in 1953. After his retirement he turned again to his manuscript, revising it and sending it to Lorne Pierce of Ryerson Press. Ryerson had just published Edward McCourt's *Music at the Close,* and Pierce felt the two novels were too similar. Prem Varma edited the version published in 1983 from the final draft.

Dry Water focuses on Donald Strand, who becomes a rich prairie farmer. The potential for misery when husband and wife or parents and children share different values is well explored, but Stead uses the stock market crash of 1929 to force a resolution of the plot. Despite its more consistent realism, or perhaps because of it, the novel is less humorous and less compelling than *Grain.* Although it might have added to Stead's reputation had he succeeded in publishing it, it would not have added much to the tradition of Canadian realism. Clearly Stead's name will figure in future discussions of Canadian realism and regionalism mainly because of *Grain*.

Bibliography:

Prem Varma, "Robert Stead: An Annotated Bibliography," *Essays on Canadian Writing*, 17 (Spring 1980): 146-204.

Biography:

Prem Varma, "The Life and Works of Robert Stead," Ph.D. dissertation, University of Ottawa, 1980.

References:

Frank Davey, "Rereading Stead's *Grain*," *Studies in Canadian Literature*, 4 (Winter 1979): 7-25;

A. T. Elder, "Western Panorama: Settings and Themes in Robert J. C. Stead," *Canadian Literature*, 17 (Summer 1963): 46-56;

Susan Wood Glicksohn, Introduction to *The Homesteaders* (Toronto: University of Toronto Press, 1973);

Dick Harrison, *Unnamed Country: The Struggle for a Canadian Prairie Fiction* (Edmonton: University of Alberta Press, 1977), pp. 89-130;

Susan Jackel, "The House on the Prairies," *Canadian Literature*, 42 (Autumn 1969): 46-55;

Edward A. McCourt, *The Canadian West in Fiction*, revised edition (Toronto: Ryerson, 1970), pp. 84-100;

Leslie Mundwiler, "Robert Stead–Home in the First Place," *Essays on Canadian Writing*, 11 (Summer 1978): 184-203;

Laurence Ricou, "The Benign Prairie: The Novels of Robert Stead," in his *Vertical Man / Horizontal World: Man and Landscape in Canadian Prairie Fiction* (Vancouver: University of British Columbia Press, 1973), pp. 20-37;

Thomas Saunders, Introduction to *Grain* (Toronto: McClelland & Stewart, 1963);

K. P. Stich, "European Immigrants in the Fiction of Robert Stead," *Studies in Canadian Literature*, 1 (Winter 1976): 76-84.

Papers:

The Public Archives of Canada, Ottawa, holds most of Stead's papers.

Arthur Stringer

(26 February 1874-13 September 1950)

Dick Harrison
University of Alberta

BOOKS: *Watchers of Twilight and Other Poems* (London, Ont.: Warren, 1894);

Pauline; and Other Poems (London, Ont.: Warren, 1895);

A Study in King Lear (N.p., 1897);

The Loom of Destiny (Boston: Small, Maynard, 1899);

Hephaestus; Persephone at Enna; and Sappho in Leucadia (Toronto: Methodist, 1903; London: Richards, 1903);

The Silver Poppy (New York: Appleton, 1903; London & New York: Methuen, 1904);

Lonely O'Malley: A Story of Boy Life (Boston & New York: Houghton, Mifflin, 1905);

The Wire Tappers (Boston: Little, Brown, 1906; London: Laurie, n.d.);

Phantom Wires (Boston: Little, Brown, 1907);

The Woman in the Rain, and Other Poems (Boston: Little, Brown, 1907);

The Under Groove (Toronto: Musson, 1908; New York: McClure, 1908);

The Gun-Runner (New York: Dodge, 1909; revised and abridged edition, Toronto: McClelland & Stewart, 1923; Indianapolis: Bobbs-Merrill, 1923);

Irish Poems (New York: Kennerley, 1911); republished as *Out of Erin (Songs in Exile)* (Indianapolis: Bobbs-Merrill, 1930);

The Shadow (Toronto: Bell & Cockburn, 1913; New York: Century, 1913); republished as *Never-Fail Blake* (New York: Burt, 1924);

Open Water (New York & London: Lane, 1914);

The Hand of Peril: A Novel of Adventure (New York: Macmillan, 1915);

The Prairie Wife (Toronto: McClelland & Stewart, 1915; Indianapolis: Bobbs-Merrill, 1915; London: Hodder & Stoughton, 1921);

The Door of Dread: A Secret Service Romance (Indianapolis: Bobbs-Merrill, 1916);

The House of Intrigue (Indianapolis: Bobbs-Merrill, 1918);

The Man Who Couldn't Sleep: Being a Relation of the Divers Strange Adventures which Befell on Wit-

Arthur Stringer

ter Kerfoot When, Sorely Troubled with Sleeplessness, He Ventured Forth along the Highways and Byways of Manhattan (Indianapolis: Bobbs-Merrill, 1919);

The Prairie Mother (Toronto: McClelland & Stewart, 1920; Indianapolis: Bobbs-Merrill, 1920; London: Hodder & Stoughton, 1920);

Twin Tales: Are All Men Alike? and The Lost Titan (Indianapolis: Bobbs-Merrill, 1921);

The Wine of Life (New York: Knopf, 1921);

The Prairie Child (Toronto: McClelland & Stewart, 1922; Indianapolis: Bobbs-Merrill, 1922; London: Hodder & Stoughton, 1923);

Prairie Stories, 3 volumes (New York: Burt, 1922?)—comprises I: *The Prairie Wife*; II: *The Prairie Mother*; and III: *The Prairie Child*;

The City of Peril (Toronto: McClelland & Stewart, 1923; New York: Knopf, 1923);

The Diamond Thieves (Indianapolis: Bobbs-Merrill, 1923);

Empty Hands (Toronto: McClelland & Stewart, 1924; Indianapolis: Bobbs-Merrill, 1924; London: Hodder & Stoughton, 1924);

Manhandled, by Stringer and Russell Holman (New York: Grosset & Dunlap, 1924; London: Hutchinson, n.d.);

The Story Without a Name, by Stringer and Holman (New York: Grosset & Dunlap, 1924);

Power (Indianapolis: Bobbs-Merrill, 1925);

In Bad With Sinbad (Indianapolis: Bobbs-Merrill, 1926);

Night Hawk (New York: Burt, 1926);

White Hands (Indianapolis: Bobbs-Merrill, 1927);

The Wolf Woman (Indianapolis: Bobbs-Merrill, 1928; London: Paul, 1929);

A Woman at Dusk, and Other Poems (Indianapolis: Bobbs-Merrill, 1928);

Cristina and I (Indianapolis: Bobbs-Merrill, 1929);

The Woman Who Couldn't Die (Indianapolis: Bobbs-Merrill, 1929);

A Lady Quite Lost (Indianapolis: Bobbs-Merrill, 1931);

The Mud Lark (Indianapolis: Bobbs-Merrill, 1932);

Dark Soil (Indianapolis: Bobbs-Merrill, 1933);

Marriage by Capture (Indianapolis: Bobbs-Merrill, 1933);

Man Lost (Indianapolis & New York: Bobbs-Merrill, 1934);

Tooloona: A Novel of the North (London: Methuen, 1936);

The Wife Traders: A Tale of the North (Toronto: McClelland & Stewart, 1936; Indianapolis & New York: Bobbs-Merrill, 1936);

Alexander Was Great: Greek Burlesque in One Act (Toronto: French, 1937);

Heather of the High Hand: A Novel of the North (Indianapolis & New York: Bobbs-Merrill, 1937);

The Lamp in the Valley: A Novel of Alaska (Indianapolis & New York: Bobbs-Merrill, 1938);

The Old Woman Remembers, and Other Irish Poems (Indianapolis & New York: Bobbs-Merrill, 1938);

The Cleverest Woman in the World and Other One-Act Plays (Indianapolis & New York: Bobbs-Merrill, 1939);

The Dark Wing (Indianapolis & New York: Bobbs-Merrill, 1939);

The Ghost Plane: A Novel of the North (Indianapolis & New York: Bobbs-Merrill, 1940);

The King Who Loved Old Clothes, and Other Irish Poems (Indianapolis & New York: Bobbs-Merrill, 1941);

Intruders in Eden (Indianapolis & New York: Bobbs-Merrill, 1942);

Shadowed Victory (Indianapolis & New York: Bobbs-Merrill, 1943; London: Hodder & Stoughton, 1944);

Star in a Mist (Indianapolis & New York: Bobbs-Merrill, 1943);

The Devastator (Toronto: McClelland & Stewart, 1944; Indianapolis & New York: Bobbs-Merrill, 1944);

New York Nocturnes (Toronto: Ryerson, 1948);

Red Wine of Youth: A Life of Rupert Brooke (Indianapolis: Bobbs-Merrill, 1948);

The Woman in the Rain, and Other Poems (Toronto: McClelland & Stewart, 1949).

Arthur Stringer will probably be remembered by Canadians for his trilogy of prairie novels (1915-1922), despite the fact that he spent his long and prolific writing career in Ontario, New York, and New Jersey. He experienced the prairies only during a brief and expensive failed attempt at grain-farming in southern Alberta just before World War I.

Arthur John Arbuthnott Stringer was born in Chatham, Ontario, on 26 February 1874, the son of Hugh Arbuthnott and Sally Delmege Stringer. His childhood in Chatham and in London, Ontario, where his family moved ten years later, provided the raw material for one of his Canadian books, *Lonely O'Malley* (1905). For all its heavily ironic tone, the novel sentimentalizes the forms of lying, cheating, and petty theft traditionally thought to distinguish a healthy boyhood.

Stringer enjoyed early recognition for his writing. While a student at the University of Toronto (from which he did not graduate) he contributed poems and prose sketches to magazines including *Toronto Saturday Night, Canadian Magazine,* and Goldwin Smith's *Week* and published his first two volumes of verse, *Watchers of Twilight and Other Poems* (1894) and *Pauline; and Other Poems* (1895). Stringer retained his early interest in poetry throughout his life, publishing fifteen volumes of generally unnoteworthy verse.

After a year spent at Oxford and elsewhere in Europe, Stringer found his first job in the car-record office of the Père Marquette Railway at Saginaw, Michigan. His continued efforts at writing and publication soon won him a reporting and editing job with the *Montreal Herald,* and by 1898

I stooped over the trap-door and lifted it up   "Get down there quick!"   Page 109   The Prairie Wife.

THE
PRAIRIE WIFE

By
ARTHUR STRINGER

INDIANAPOLIS
THE BOBBS-MERRILL COMPANY
PUBLISHERS

Frontispiece and title page for the American edition of the first novel in Stringer's prairie trilogy (1915-1922)

he was working for the American Press Association in New York and contributing to such prestigious magazines as *Harper's* and *Atlantic Monthly*. His first book of prose sketches, *The Loom of Destiny* (1899), and his first novel, *The Silver Poppy* (1903), which went through five printings, established Stringer in his career as a capable producer of light popular fiction. His New York experience, including a carefully acquired knowledge of street life and criminal activity, equipped Stringer for a popular series of crime adventure novels written chiefly for serial publication, beginning with *The Wire Tappers* (1906). Stringer later developed a series of wilderness adventure novels of the North, following from *Empty Hands* (1924). He occasionally set his plots in contexts of social or artistic life, but at their center can always be found the formulae of sentimental romance popular around the turn of the century. His biographer, Victor Lauriston, credits Stringer

with a degree of realism uncommon in his day, but the authenticity he applauds remains largely extrinsic to the plots—undigested "research" fleshing out the circumstances. Stringer's heroes still win the abject devotion of the heroines by saving them from such exigencies as drowning and by beating up bullies.

At the time of his success with *The Silver Poppy* Stringer married the actress Jobyna Howland, the original "Gibson Girl," and moved to a farm at Cedar Springs, Ontario, on the north shore of Lake Erie. This eventually unsuccessful marriage probably supplied the actress-heroine and the sober psychological depth for *The Wine of Life* (1921), which Lauriston considers Stringer's best novel. The marriage ended in divorce in 1914, about the time of Stringer's Alberta farming debacle. He subsequently married his cousin, Margaret Arbuthnott Stringer of Chatham, who bore him three sons. Stringer sold his Cedar

Springs farm in 1921, and the family moved to another farm in New Jersey, where they were to reside permanently. He became an American citizen in 1937 and was awarded an honorary D.Litt. by the University of Western Ontario in 1946.

Stringer's prairie trilogy is his most enduring work partly because there he managed with some success to resist his tendencies to use clichéd situations, melodramatic scenes, and improbable wish-fulfillment outcomes. Prairie life in 1914, of course, would not have offered a well-established set of clichés to depend upon. But the strength of the trilogy depends more particularly on Stringer's skillful creation of the first-person narrator, Chaddy McKail. Chaddy, as a New England socialite married to a dour Scots-Canadian wheat farmer, is convincing, and her personality justifies the romantic portrayal of the plains, just as the epistolary form disarms the frequently improbable dialogue. *The Prairie Wife* (1915) has the plot of a conventional romance of pioneering, in which Chaddy's doubts and fears are swept away by a bumper crop and the promise of a future in which refinement will have its place. This central theme of the fruitful marriage between eastern refinement and western vitality is further emphasized by the marriage of a splendidly physical Finnish hired girl to a frail, effete English aristocrat. In *The Prairie Mother* (1920) and *The Prairie Child* (1922) Stringer goes beyond the optimism of the first novel to explore the dangers of that combination of opposites. He follows the deterioration of the McKail marriage through financial setbacks, amatory triangles, the grind of daily farm life, and the effects of hu-

man pride and perversity to its ultimate breakup. With his trilogy Stringer unwittingly contributed to a central tradition of prairie fiction running from the nineteenth century to Sinclair Ross's *As For Me and My House* (1941) and Margaret Laurence's *The Stone Angel* (1964) and involving the confessions of a person of refined sensibility exposed to the crudity of prairie life. Stringer attempted to exploit the success of his prairie trilogy with *The Mud Lark* (1932), but the later novel loses its power through a series of melodramatic excesses.

The limited reach of Stringer's fiction should be judged in relation to his immense and varied output. In addition to his poetry and more than forty volumes of fiction, he contributed regularly to magazines and also wrote for the stage and for Hollywood, including "The Perils of Pauline." His books of nonfiction prose include *A Study in King Lear* (1897) and a biography of Rupert Brooke, *Red Wine of Youth* (1948). Through it all, he seems to have had the vigor to remain active with his family, friends, and community until his death in 1950 in Mountain Lakes, New Jersey.

Biography:

Victor Lauriston, *Arthur Stringer: Son of the North* (New York: Bobbs-Merrill, 1941).

References:

Victor Lauriston, *Postscript to a Poet* (Chatham, Ont.: The Tiny Tree Club, 1941);

McKenzie Porter, "The Purple Prose and Purple Life of Arthur Stringer," *MacLean's*, 76 (9 February 1963): 26-30.

Alan Sullivan

(29 November 1868-6 August 1947)

W. H. New

University of British Columbia

BOOKS: *The White Canoe and Other Verse* (Toronto: Bryant, 1891);

Venice and Other Verse (Toronto: Bryant, 1893);

I Believe That– (Toronto: Tyrrell, 1912);

The Passing of Oul-I-But, and Other Tales (London & Toronto: Dent/New York: Dutton, 1913);

The Power That Serves (Belleville, Ont.: Trenton Electric & Water Power, 1913);

Blantyre–Alien (London & Toronto: Dent/New York: Dutton, 1914);

The Inner Door (Toronto: Gundy, 1917; New York: Century, 1917);

The Rapids (New York & London: Appleton, 1920; Toronto: Copp Clark, 1922);

Brother Eskimo (Toronto: McClelland & Stewart, 1921; New York: Century, 1921; London: Sampson Low, 1923);

Our Silent Partner. Electricity and Its Usage in Modern Life (London: Eyre & Spottiswoode, 1923);

The Birthmark (London: Arnold, 1924);

The Jade God (Toronto: Goodchild, 1925; New York & London: Century, 1925);

The Crucible, as Sinclair Murray (London: Bles, 1925);

John Frensham, K.C., as Murray, with B. V. Shann (London: Murray, 1925); republished, as Murray alone (Toronto: Ryerson, 1925; New York: Dutton, 1928);

The Days of Their Youth (New York & London: Century, 1926);

Human Clay, as Murray, with Shann (London: Murray, 1926);

Under the Northern Lights (London & Toronto: Dent/New York: Dutton, 1926);

In the Beginning (London: Hurst & Blackett, 1926; New York: Dutton, 1927);

Brother Blackfoot (New York & London: Century, 1927);

Sands of Fortune, as Murray (London: Murray, 1927; New York: Dutton, 1928);

The Verdict of the Sea (London: Hurst & Blackett, 1927; Chicago: White House, 1927);

Alan Sullivan, 1928

Whispering Lodge, as Murray (London: Murray, 1927; Toronto: Ryerson, 1928);

The Broken Marriage, as Murray (New York: Dutton, 1929);

Double Lives, as Murray (Toronto: Macmillan, 1929; London: Murray, 1929);

A Little Way Ahead (London: Murray, 1929; Toronto: Macmillan, 1930; New York: Dutton, 1930);

The Splendid Silence (London: Murray, 1929; New York: Dutton, 1929);

The Story of One-Ear (London: Philip, 1929);

The Training of Chiliqui (London: Philip, 1929);

378

The Magic Makers (London: Murray, 1930);

Mr. Absalom (London: Murray, 1930);

Queer Partners, as Murray (Toronto: Macmillan, 1930; London: Murray, 1930);

The Golden Foundling, as Murray (Toronto: Macmillan, 1931; London: Murray, 1931);

The Ironmaster (London: Murray, 1931);

No Secrets Island (London: Murray, 1931);

Antidote, as Murray (London: Murray, 1932);

Colonel Pluckett (London & Melbourne: Ward, Lock, 1932);

Cornish Interlude, as Murray (London: Murray, 1932);

The Man at Lone Tree (London & Melbourne: Ward, Lock, 1933);

What Fools Men Are!, as Murray (London: Low, 1933);

Obstinate Virgin (London: Low, Marston, 1934);

The Great Divide: A Romance of The Canadian Pacific Railway (Toronto: Macmillan, 1935; London: Dickson & Thompson, 1935);

The Money Spinners, as Murray (London: Low, Marston, 1936);

With Love from Rachel (London: Low, 1937; Toronto: Oxford University Press, 1938);

The Cycle of the North (London: Dent, 1938);

The Fur Masters (London: Murray, 1938; New York: Coward-McCann, 1947);

Three Came to Ville Marie (Toronto: Oxford University Press, 1941; New York: Coward-McCann, 1943; London: Aldor, 1947);

"And From That Day" (Toronto: Ryerson, 1944);

Cariboo Road (Toronto & New York: Nelson, 1946).

OTHER: *Aviation in Canada: 1917-1918,* compiled by Sullivan (Toronto: Rous & Mann, 1919);

John Melly of Ethiopia, edited by Sullivan and Kathleen Nelson (London: Faber & Faber, 1937);

Félix-Antoine Savard, *Boss of the River,* translated, with an introduction, by Sullivan (Toronto: Ryerson, 1947).

SELECTED PERIODICAL PUBLICATION

UNCOLLECTED: "In the Matter of Alan Sullivan," *Ontario Library Review,* 14 (November 1929): 35-37.

Bessie Hees Sullivan on her wedding day, 12 December 1900

In the foreword to his 1947 translation of Félix-Antoine Savard's *Boss of the River (Menaud, maître-draveur,* 1937), Alan Sullivan wrote that he hoped this story would show the "wealth of cre- ative treasure" in Quebec and that it would "ad- vance the cause of Canadian unity." This Anglo- centric focus was characteristic of both the time and the man: it typifies the idea about nationhood that dominated English-Canadian culture between the wilderness stories of Charles G. D. Roberts and the railway poems of E. J. Pratt. When a bishop, in one of Sullivan's most widely read novels, *The Rapids* (1920), advises another character to read Henry Drummond and Marcus Aurelius, the point is underlined. Drummond's patois verses were long considered in English Canada to be realistic portraits of the quaintness of rural Quebec culture, a culture that was destined (it was thought) to be absorbed by English rationalism. Anglo-Protestant values also prized the male stoicism of Aurelius. All these attitudes permeated Sullivan's writings; they derived from his upbringing and from the kind of life he chose to lead.

Born in Montreal on 29 November 1868, Edward Alan Sullivan was the son of the Reverend Edward Sullivan and his second wife, Frances Mary Renaud Sullivan, the Scottish-born daughter of a Swiss businessman, whom he had married in 1866. Of Alan's four siblings, one became a poet in New York, one a Toronto journalist, one a member of a socially prominent family, and one sister died of typhoid in 1895 while nursing Alan through the disease. Irish-born (in 1832), Edward Sullivan had been ordained a Church of England priest in Montreal in 1859; his clerical advancement directly influenced Alan's life. Named rector of Trinity Church in Chicago in 1869, Edward Sullivan took his family to Illinois (journals in the family's possession record the great Chicago fire of 1872), then to Montreal when he became rector of St. George's Church in 1878, then to Sault Ste. Marie, Ontario, in 1882 when he was elected bishop of Algoma. (He held this position until his retirement in 1896, and for the last three years of his life served as dean of St. James Cathedral in Toronto.) Alan absorbed the cultures of these various locations, and he also learned to value the accoutrements of a British upper-middle-class upbringing (property, nanny, governess, and servants) and an educational system that stressed athletic achievement and the outdoors. While he particularly appreciated the wilderness life of the Algoma region, his childhood experience of it was largely confined to summertime. At the age of nine he had been sent to a private school near London, Ontario, and in the fall of 1882 he was installed in the rigorous, spartan Loretto School at Musselburgh, near Edinburgh (hinted at in *The Ironmaster*, 1931), where he spent four years. In 1887, withdrawing from the second year of his training in civil engi-

neering at the University of Toronto, he embarked on a twenty-year series of outdoor occupations that was to establish his career and his social position, and that would simultaneously shape the circumstances of his subsequent fiction.

In the years after the transcontinental Canadian Pacific Railway had been completed, Sullivan was working on C.P.R. geological survey crews, a job he continued until 1892, the year he accompanied his father on a Riviera holiday (the setting of *Colonel Pluckett*, 1932). In a mid-1930s address in England (quoted by Gordon D. McLeod in *Essentially Canadian: The Life and Fiction of Alan Sullivan 1868-1947*, 1982), he revealed the attitudes that these early years defined: "By profession I was for many years an engineer and explorer.... My life ... meant for long periods what is described as solitude so far as my own kind were concerned. My companions were mostly primitives. But ... it seems that perhaps they helped to stimulate ... the life of certain compartments of the mind.... May I suggest to you that the thinking man need never feel alone." During these formative years, too, his first literary publications appeared, the conventional poems of *The White Canoe and Other Verse* (1891) and *Venice and Other Verse* (1893).

Back in Ontario (after his vacation in France), Sullivan became involved in surveying, contracting, and timber and mineral exploration on his own. His career took another turn when the American entrepreneur Francis Clergues arrived in Sault Ste. Marie—originally as a guest in Bishop Sullivan's house. Clergues went on to found an industrial empire that (before it collapsed in 1903) included Algoma Steel, Michigan Lake Superior Power, and other corporations. All his life Alan Sullivan was fascinated by Clergues, and in his later years he was completing a biography of him (never published, but now in the possession of the Toronto historian Michael Bliss). Clergues's contemporaries, seeking metaphoric parallels, referred to him as the "Napoleon" or "Cecil Rhodes" of Canada, one of the "Captains Courageous"; Sullivan (despite Clergues's limitations) turned him into the prototype of the kind of figure he admired: the hero-prophet-dreamer whose possessive ambition drives him to act. In the last years of this age of laissez-faire capitalism in North America, the businessman was perceived as a social model.

In 1917 in *The Inner Door* Sullivan blamed absentee owners—those who were off in Europe playing at being aristocrats—for industrial unrest in

Sullivan with his son D'Arcy, 1910

Canada; his interest in the workings of labor and management, in the power of the syndicate or board of management, and in the way power makes things happen, shows up again in *The Great Divide* (1935), a narrative of the building of the C.P.R. But in *The Rapids* (published in 1920, although written immediately after *Blantyre–Alien* in 1914), Sullivan presents his clearest analysis of business practice and his clearest portrait of Clergues–in the character named Robert Fisher Clark. Set in "St. Marys" (a loosely disguised Sault Ste. Marie), this romance traces Clark's financial rise and fall. Before he arrives the town is an Arcadia (hence the novel does question whether progress is always good); St. Marys falls under Clark's "mesmeric" spell, and soon there is blasting equipment everywhere, pulp, iron ore, running water, electric lights, cigars, and fast women unsettling the order that had been in place–in large part with the active collaboration of existing social institutions. Details of the bishop's garden party read with a certain sharpness. Allu-

sions to the Japanese cook, the half-breed worker, and the spread of Clark's influence to Philadelphia are interesting for their glimpse of social history. The plot comes to a climax with a workers' riot, when there is no money for the payroll. Sullivan's sympathies are divided–between the rights of the workers and the industrialist's dream of expansion.

Always, however–as in all his novels, from *Blantyre–Alien* to *The Great Divide*–Sullivan focuses primarily on the ideal character of the individual. Bureaucracies impede dreams, his novels say. "Natural wealth" lies in the unconquerable spirit of the self. Hence enterprise, however much a struggle, is always perceived to be glorious. Success, although called by spiritual names, is always measured in financial terms and is deemed good. *The Rapids* was scripted for film in 1922 by Faith Green, directed by David Hartford, and produced by the Canadian filmmaker Ernest G. Shipman for Sault Ste. Marie Films (starring Harry Morey and Mary Astor); it was filmed on location and premiered at Sault Ste. Marie on 30 October 1922.

In the late 1890s, mingling with the social elite, Sullivan acquired gold lands in northern Ontario and negotiated arrangements with the Anglo-Canadian Gold Estates in 1899 that led to the development of the Elizabeth Mine. Until the mine closed in 1903 Sullivan's fortunes expanded rapidly; but his career then took another turn. From 1908 to 1913 he was mechanical superintendent of the Gutta Percha and Rubber Manufacturing Company in Toronto (the setting of *The Inner Door*); during this period he began to devote more time to his writing. By then, too, he was married, settled, and financially secure. On 12 December 1900 he had married New York-born Elizabeth (Bessie) Salisbury Hees (1874-1974), daughter of the well-to-do Toronto businessman George Hees. Hees had one house built for the Sullivans in Toronto in 1908; in 1913 they moved to another, which Sullivan himself designed. Though they remained on the edge of the truly powerful in Toronto society (the Eatons and the Masseys), they were clearly in the establishment. In 1917 Sullivan enlisted in the RAF, an experience that resulted in *Aviation in Canada: 1917-1918* (1919). Other pamphlets on industry and electricity followed. In 1920 George Hees died (while Sullivan was prospecting in Alaska); the inheritance allowed the Sullivans to move to England. Though Sullivan continued to spend long periods of time in Canada, the family be-

Sullivan with Will Rogers at Coronation Gulf in the Northwest Territories, July 1936

came settled abroad. Alan and Bessie had five children (who had the benefit, variously, of Fonthill/Rugby/Oxbridge educations and presentation at court): Kathleen, Lady Liddell Hart (b. 1902); D'Arcy (b. 1905); Natalie (b. 1907); Barry Seaghan (b. 1915); and Donovan Michael (b. 1916).

Sullivan's nearly four dozen books of fiction are primarily popular romances, which were regularly published in Britain, Canada, and the United States. Many of them were published under the pseudonym Sinclair Murray. The pseudonym, Sullivan observed, gave him freedom from usual forms—which meant in practice that he tried his hand at the English mystery (*The Jade God*, 1925, later dramatized by William Edward Barry), the thriller (*Whispering Lodge*, 1927; *Mr. Absalom*, 1930), science fiction (*In the Beginning*, 1926; *Human Clay*, 1926—the latter with B. V. Shann, a friend from the Savage Club, one of London's men-only writers' clubs, of which Sullivan was a member), the love story (*The Broken Marriage*, 1929; *Double Lives*, 1929), the gambling tale (*Queer Partners*, 1930), the adventure (*The Golden Foundling*, 1931; *No Secrets Island*, 1931), the story of an amoral woman (*Antidote*, 1932), the allegory about the mass psychology of war-

fare (*What Fools Men Are!*, 1933), and other romances. In *The Splendid Silence* (1929) an Englishman goes to British Columbia, is attacked by the I.W.W. (Industrial Workers of the World) in a lumber camp, survives, and ends up marrying, living half his time in England and the other half in Canada. *A Little Way Ahead* (1929), which tells of stock market failures, was published the year after some of Bessie Sullivan's fortune was lost. *Three Came to Ville Marie* (1941) won the Governor-General's Award for fiction; it, too, is in the romantic mold, reasserting conventional Anglo-Protestant beliefs about the Catholic history of New France. Set in the eighteenth century, it features Louis XIV, Frontenac, and the Indians, tells a story of a love triangle, exposes French scandals, and attacks the Jesuits.

In the early 1940s Sullivan was reestablishing himself in Canada. He and Bessie spent the war years in Toronto, and the Governor-General's Award for 1941 was one sign of his renewed visibility. Another was his radio scriptwriting: from 5 January 1942 to 26 June 1942, Sullivan's domestic serial "The Town of Newbridge" was broadcast on CBC radio every weekday evening. In 1943 Sullivan was in the Yukon, again prospecting; in 1944 his fictional account of the crucifixion, *"And From That Day,"* appeared, and at Easter time that year, the Toronto Arts & Letters Club performed his (still unpublished) religious play, "The Law and the Prophet," directed by Earl Grey. *Cariboo Road,* his last novel, appeared two years later. The Sullivans returned to England in 1945 to settle at the Liddell Hart residence of their daughter in Surrey, where Alan Sullivan died 6 August 1947.

Gordon O. McLeod (on whose research the biographical details of this article are based) emphasizes various recurrent elements in Sullivan's fiction: the character of the ideal man and woman, the struggle for survival in the natural wilderness, and the virtues of manly behavior (identified as courage, loyalty, stoicism, resilience, physical strength, and often involving what is considered visionary single-mindedness). Some of these attitudes appear in print as early as 1912, in Sullivan's book of maxims *I Believe That–* (for example: "Only an unintelligent man will say that he understands a woman"). More characteristically, they are couched in the characterization and narrative line of the many stories of Arctic wilderness and transcontinental travail. In *The Passing of Oul-I-But* (1913), for instance–a collection of sixteen stories that first appeared in *Atlantic, Harper's,* and *Scribner's* magazines, several to be reassembled in *The Cycle of the North* (1938)– appeared "The Essence of a Man," a tale of a Noble Métis, who takes a three-hundred-pound load on a toboggan, is attacked by blizzard and lynx, and after the death of his dogs, pulls the load himself, refusing all the while to eat the food that he is pulling because it belongs not to him but to the company he works for. *Brother Eskimo* (1921) also tells of the "manliness" of survival, and the eleven stories of *Under the Northern Lights* (1926), often in patois and Scots dialect, reiterate similar themes.

In *The Magic Makers* (1930), the central character uses his technical ingenuity to establish his authority in the Arctic, extending Sullivan's presumptions about the rights of "civilized man"; in *With Love from Rachel* (1937), a quarter-breed woman falls in love with an Arctic pilot, the whole story wedding prophetic dreams with "manly adventure." Two much-reprinted school readers, *The Story of One-Ear* (1929–about an Eskimo dog) and *The Training of Chiliqui* (1929–about an Indian boy), also project these attitudes. In hindsight many of Sullivan's judgments of native peoples (as in one of his unpublished

speeches quoted by McLeod: "the Indian dislikes cold, and the Eskimo heat. . . . The Indian . . . is subjective, the Eskimo objective") can at best be described as sympathetic but simplistic.

Repeatedly the wilderness is perceived in nobly alien terms–distanced from humanity and sentimentalized–as in the adjectival profusion of the opening of *The Great Divide:*

SHAPED like a gigantic "S" with shallow curves, the pass lay between a tangle of mountains on whose precipitous flanks wild goats sprang from ledge to ledge: above it towered scarred peaks, first to blush under the rising sun, last to retain the dying glory: eastward, westward, the land fell away to ravines and hanging valleys and glacier-fed lakes in whose shining surface shimmered the reflection of gaunt, inaccessible summits.

Each lake, lonely in its beauty, smiled up, bordered with stretches of dark green conical spruce of which the multitudinous spires were guarded by ten thousand feet of solid rock, and swayed by no disturbing winds. Here in a season of the year stalked the gigantic elk, deliberate and unafraid: here were meadows of a lighter green, traversed by winding streams where the beaver built his heavy-roofed home of earth and sticks, damming the vagrant creeks till only a rounded crown was unsubmerged.

Always in Sullivan's work it is the arrival of visionary individual men that humanizes the wilderness and that coincidentally testifies to what Sullivan considers real heroism. In *The Fur Masters* (1938), a historical tale of the rivalry between the Hudson's Bay Company and the Northwest Company, the honest Scots immigrants are the heroes, the men who counteract the dishonesty of previous traders, which had soured relations between Europeans and the native people. In *The Great Divide* (filmed in British Columbia in 1936 by the Gaumont-British Picture Corporation as *The Great Barrier,* a film released in Canada and the United States as *Silent Barriers*), the railway planners and engineers Sir William Van Horne and Andrew Onderdonk fulfill this heroic role. So does the prime minister, Sir John A. Macdonald, who with his "Jewish cast of face" is repeatedly likened in the novel to Benjamin Disraeli. *Cariboo Road* (1946), telling of one family's adventures as they move from San Francisco north to the gold rush and the gaming tables of the Cariboo, divides the heroic role between a fictional mother, whose devotion to family shows compassionate determination (therefore, in Sullivan's terms, "ideal" female character), and the historical figure of Matthew Baillie Begbie (known in popular history as the peremptory "Hanging Judge" but designed in this novel to be a model of ideal values for men).

In many ways more interesting than these cultural models are the many character types Sullivan required to move his historical narratives forward: figures characterized by their names— Bulldog, The Rake, and Big Mouth, for example. Through them, and through formal details of speech and setting (like the record of work songs such as "Drill, ye tarriers, drill!" in *The Great Divide*, or the particulars of railway camp life and social organization), contemporary readers may catch glimpses of the inequities of social history. Sullivan, himself, fastened more centrally on other matters: on history's romance, on Anglo-Protestant conservatism, and on the expedience and efficiency of industrial systems.

Biography:
Gordon D. McLeod, *Essentially Canadian: The Life and Fiction of Alan Sullivan 1868-1947* (Waterloo: Wilfrid Laurier University Press, 1982).

References:
Michael Bliss, Introduction to Sullivan's *The Rapids* (Toronto: University of Toronto Press, 1972), pp. vii-xx;

Peter Morris, *Embattled Shadows: A History of Canadian Cinema 1895-1939* (Montreal: McGill-Queen's University Press, 1978).

Edward William Thomson
(12 February 1849-5 March 1924)

Eric Thompson
Université du Québec à Chicoutimi

BOOKS: *Old Man Savarin, and Other Stories* (Toronto: Briggs, 1895; New York & Boston: Crowell, 1895); revised as *Old Man Savarin Stories: Tales of Canada and Canadians* (Toronto: Gundy, 1917; New York: Doran, 1917; London: Laurie, 1919);
Smoky Days (New York: Crowell, 1896);
Walter Gibbs, the Young Boss; and Other Stories: A Book for Boys (Toronto: Briggs, 1896; New York: Crowell, 1896);
Between Earth and Sky, and Other Strange Stories of Deliverance (Toronto: Briggs, 1897; Philadelphia: Rowland, 1897);
When Lincoln Died, and Other Poems (Boston & New York: Houghton Mifflin, 1909; London & Cambridge, Mass.: Constable, 1909); republished as *The Many-Mansioned House, and Other Poems* (Toronto: Briggs, 1909);
Selected Stories of E. W. Thomson, edited by Lorraine McMullen (Ottawa: University of Ottawa Press, 1973).

Edward William Thomson is usually remembered as the author of a few short stories about life in the French-Canadian, Irish, and Scottish settlements along the Ottawa River in the closing years of the nineteenth century. He was, in fact, one of the pioneers of the modern short story in Canada, and he might well have become one of the best writers of his generation had he devoted as much attention to his stories and verse as he did to his journalism.

Born on 12 February 1849 to William and Margaret Hamilton Foley Thomson, on the family farm in Peel County, Ontario, near Toronto, Thomson came from a sturdy line of Upper Canadian patriots. From an early age he wanted to emulate the soldierly exploits of his ancestors. A casual meeting with Abraham Lincoln while visiting an uncle in Philadelphia proved decisive. Even though a British subject and underage–he had just completed his schooling at Trinity College School, then at Weston, Ontario–he ran away to the United States and enlisted in the Army of the

Potomac in 1864. His service with the Union cause was cut short because of parental intervention, but in 1866 he was once more in the field as a soldier with the Queen's Own Rifles during a skirmish with Fenian raiders. After these adventures he decided to pursue studies in civil engineering. Between 1872 and 1878 he worked as a land surveyor in various lumbering and railway-building operations in eastern Ontario. In 1873 he married Adelaide St.-Denis of Pointe Fortune, Quebec, described by a contemporary (according to Linda Sheshko) as "a lady of high intellectual attainments." Their son, Bernard, graduated in law from Harvard and subsequently worked for many years on the editorial staff of the *New York Times*.

After his marriage Thomson's interests turned increasingly to politics. Accepting a position as an editorial writer with the *Toronto Globe* in 1878, he soon acquired a reputation for the soundness of his views. However, in 1891 he resigned from the paper following a disagreement with its support of the Liberal policy of "unrestricted reciprocity" in trade between Canada and the United States. He then took a job as revising editor and short-story writer with the *Youth's Companion*, a magazine for boys published in Boston.

Thomson remained with the *Youth's Companion* for the next ten years. He appears to have enjoyed the sophisticated cultural life of New England, but occasionally he yearned for his old contacts and the society of his native province. His duties with the magazine were hardly onerous and allowed him time to further his knowledge of new trends in European and American literature. He was especially interested in the realistic techniques of W. D. Howells and Henry James, and he urged his Canadian friends to read their novels. Among his correspondents was the young Ottawa poet Archibald Lampman, then suffering the neglect of an indifferent reading public. Thomson was one of the first to recognize Lampman's genius and did his utmost to promote his work. This aid was appreciated both by

Edward William Thomson (portrait from Canadian Poets, *edited by John W. Garvin, 1926)*

Lampman and by their mutual friend, Duncan Campbell Scott, who later wrote of Thomson: "He was a prince of friends whose helpfulness was inexhaustible and whose courage often understayed Lampman's ship when it was in stress of weather" (quoted by Sheshko). Moreover, through his letter writing and periodic visits to Canada, Thomson kept himself abreast of developments in the creation of a genuinely national literature and played his own part in shaping it.

In 1901 Thomson resigned his post at the *Youth's Companion,* partly because as a journalist and litterateur he felt the need to be more active in these roles in Canada. Yet he kept his ties with the United States: from 1902 until his retirement in 1923 he was the Ottawa correspondent for the *Boston Evening Transcript.* He thus came to know

the leading Canadian politicians, including Prime Minister Wilfrid Laurier and Quebec's nationalist leader, Henri Bourassa. Thomson's articles and speeches on various national and international issues were widely respected, and, in the decade prior to World War I, he enhanced his reputation as a poet. For all these activities he was made a fellow of the Royal Society of Literature in 1909 and was elected to the Royal Society of Canada the following year. Thomson's last years were marred by ill health, and he died on 5 March 1924 in Boston where he had returned to live with relatives after his retirement.

Clearly Thomson had led an active life, attaining success in several fields of professional endeavor, and he drew liberally on his experiences as a soldier, land surveyor, editor, and journalist in his creative work. It was while he was working at the *Globe* that Thomson first began to write short fiction. His tale "Petherick's Peril" won a prize for the best adventure story in a competition sponsored by the *Youth's Companion*. In form it is typical of later stories he wrote for the magazine and of juvenilia such as *Walter Gibbs, the Young Boss; and Other Stories: A Book for Boys* (1896). Far more substantial are three kinds of stories he published in *Old Man Savarin, and Other Stories* (1895) and its revised version of 1917, collections that enjoyed a good critical reception. They include stories of the Ottawa Valley, Glengarry County, and lumbering camps in the West; tales of war; and stories set in Boston. Of the first kind, "Privilege of the Limits," "Old Man Savarin," and "Little Baptiste" are good examples of Thomson's use of local-color realism to vivify village and regional attitudes, dialects, and customs. His war stories—notably "The Ride by Night" (set in the Civil War) and "The Swartz Diamond" (set in the Boer War)—are equally effective in atmosphere. And "Miss Minnely's Management" is an excellent satire of the writing trade as Thomson knew it in Boston; after reading it we can well understand Lampman's refusal to accept his friend's offer of a post at the *Youth's Companion:* "A sort of employment like that persisted in for any length of time would be ten times more deadly than anything I do now" (in Lampman's *Selected Prose,* edited by Barrie Davies, 1975).

Undoubtedly Thomson's worldliness and taste in literature enabled him to take such remarks in stride. Still, the fact remains that he accomplished less as a creative writer than might have been expected of a man of his talents. Certainly his poetry is negligible in quality, although one work, "Aspiration," was selected by Arthur Quiller-Couch for the *Oxford Book of Victorian Verse.* However, as a journalist he did have some impact on broadening Canadians' appreciation of their literary culture; and, in his "Savarin" stories at least, he made a solid contribution to it.

Letters:

Arthur Stanley Bourinot, ed., *The Letters of Edward William Thomson to Archibald Lampman (1891-1897), with Notes, a Bibliography, and Other Material on Thomson and Lampman* (Ottawa: Bourinot, 1957);

An Annotated Edition of the Correspondence Between Archibald Lampman and Edward William Thomson, 1890-1898 (Ottawa: Tecumseh, 1980).

References:

John W. Dafoe, "E. W. Thomson: Canadian Journalist and Poet," *Manitoba Free Press,* 7 April 1924;

Barrie Davies, ed., *Archibald Lampman: Selected Prose* (Ottawa: Tecumseh, 1975);

Lorraine McMullen, "E. W. Thomson and the *Youth's Companion," Canadian Children's Literature,* 13 (1979): 7-20;

McMullen, "Tales of Canada and Canadians: The Stories of Edward William Thomson," *Journal of Canadian Fiction,* 2 (Summer 1973): 191-194;

Linda Sheshko, Introduction to *Old Man Savarin Stories: Tales of Canada and Canadians,* edited by Sheshko (Toronto: University of Toronto Press, 1974).

Joanna E. Wood

(28 December 1867-1 May 1927)

Carole Gerson
Simon Fraser University

BOOKS: *The Untempered Wind* (New York: Tait, 1894);

Judith Moore; or, Fashioning a Pipe (Toronto: Ontario Publishing, 1898);

A Daughter of Witches (Toronto: Gage, 1900; London: Hurst & Blackett, 1900);

Farden Ha' (London: Hurst & Blackett, 1902).

SELECTED PERIODICAL PUBLICATIONS
UNCOLLECTED: "Unto the Third Generation," anonymous, *All the Year Round*, 67 (1890): 395-404;

"Malhalla's Revenge," *New England Magazine*, 12 (April 1895): 184-187;

"The Mother," *Canadian Magazine*, 8 (October 1896): 558-561;

"A Martyr to Love," *Tales from Town Topics*, no. 23 (1897): 7-104;

"The Mystery of the Carved Coconut," *Christmas Globe* (Toronto), 1898, pp. 9, 12, 13;

"Algernon Charles Swinburne. An Appreciation," *Canadian Magazine*, 17 (May 1901): 2-11;

"Presentation at Court," *Canadian Magazine*, 17 (October 1901): 506-510;

"The Last Cock Fight at San Mateo," *Christmas Globe* (Toronto), 1902;

"Where Waters Beckon," *Tales from Town Topics*, no. 45 (1902): 1-112.

From 1894 to 1902, when novelist Joanna Wood was being hailed as the bright new star on the Canadian literary horizon, she received considerable attention from the Canadian and American press, especially in the *Canadian Magazine*. Yet the early and later years of her life and career remain shrouded in obscurity. So little is known of her work and circumstances after 1902, when her last verified work was published, that reference books have erroneously reported the year of her death to be 1919; recently, however, a 1927 death certificate has been discovered.

Wood was born in the town of Lesmahagow in Lanarkshire, Scotland, 28 December 1867, the youngest daughter in the large family of Robert and Agnes Tod Wood. The Canadian census of 1881 recorded the Presbyterian family settled on a farm at Queenston, in the Niagara area, which was to be Joanna Wood's home until it was sold in 1906. Like most aspiring young writers of her day, she first published in popular American periodicals, reportedly under the pseudonym Jean D'Arc. Yet there survives no concrete evidence of this work to substantiate the 1901 account in the *Canadian Magazine* of her "success in New York short story competitions where she has picked up several thousands of dollars, . . . most of the stories having been sent in under pen-names. In one short story competition, so the gossips say, she captured three of the largest prizes with three stories, two being sent in to the credit of two male friends whose names she secured for the purpose–temporarily of course." Equally untraceable is the 1898 story "The Mind of a God," which, again according to the *Canadian Magazine*, had won a prize of five hundred dollars.

The topic of Wood's first novel, *The Untempered Wind* (1894), announced the seriousness of its author's ambition and her possible influence by Thomas Hardy. The people of Jamestown, a "cruel, sordid, babbling little village," harass an unwed mother with all the single-mindedness of the Puritans in Nathaniel Hawthorne's *The Scarlet Letter* (to which Wood alludes), making her promise when she finally leaves that she will inform everyone she meets that she was a mother but not a wife. Although the incisiveness of Wood's social satire is undermined by her penchant for melodrama (including a deathbed marriage), she is credited with having been one of the first Canadian authors to represent in fiction the puritan ethos of small-town life. Clues in the text suggest that Jamestown was modeled on Queenston; however, Wood's decision to blur the nationality of her setting allowed her book to be heralded by one New York reviewer as "the strongest and best American novel of the year." In Canada this

Ioanna E. Wood

work received less attention than her second novel, which made her the darling of the *Canadian Magazine*.

For *Judith Moore; or, Fashioning a Pipe* (1898) Wood selected a less controversial theme. The book is a pastoral account of love between an exhausted world-class singer seeking rest and solitude in a remote Canadian farming community, and a stalwart Canadian farmer. In the conflict between the determination of Judith's manager and the yearning of her heart, love triumphs, with Judith eventually renouncing her international career in favor of marriage and an Ontario farm. (However, Wood was enough of a feminist to include in the same book an argument in favor of paying women schoolteachers the same wages as men.) John A. Cooper, editor of the *Canadian Magazine,* was so impressed with Wood's "faultless prose" that he named her one of Canada's three leading novelists, in company with Gilbert Parker and Charles G. D. Roberts; in New York the reviewer for the *Nation* took a cooler view of

Wood's self-consciously poetical style, finding the book's greatest merits to be "brevity and cleanliness." The exaltation of romantic love is also the keynote of Wood's last known work, the lengthy story entitled "Where Waters Beckon" (published in *Tales from Town Topics* in 1902). Its ill-starred lovers enact their drama along the shores of the Niagara River and at the falls, the river's characterization as a mesmerizing presence drawing on Wood's own familiarity with the region.

In 1898 and 1899 Wood earned the distinction of being the first Canadian author to have a novel serialized in the *Canadian Magazine*. She received $12.50 for each installment, becoming the magazine's best-paid Canadian contributor for a time. Set in New England and playing upon that region's puritan heritage, *A Daughter of Witches,* published in book form in 1900, demonstrates Wood's growing adeptness with characterization and incident. The narrative follows the lives and loves of a pair of cousins: serene, innocent Mabella, whose goodness is made surprisingly credible; and passionate, malevolent Vashti, who reverts to the infamy of a diabolical ancestress when she attempts to mold her husband into an instrument of her revenge.

Wood's identified periodical publications indicate her mastery of many different forms of popular fiction. Her two stories in the Toronto *Christmas Globe* are masculine adventure stories, "The Mystery of the Carved Coconut" (1898), set in Mexico, and "The Last Cock Fight in San Mateo" (1902), narrated in the idiom of prospectors in the American Southwest. In contrast, "A Martyr to Love" (in an 1897 issue of *Tales from Town Topics*) is a rather lurid account of the career of a New York courtesan. One of the previously untraced titles listed by Henry Morgan in his *Canadian Men and Women of the Time* (1912), "Unto the Third Generation," has been located, published anonymously in *All the Year Round* in 1890; another piece listed by Morgan, "The Lynchpin Sensation," has not been discovered. Only one copy of Wood's 1902 novel, *Farden Ha'*, set in the border country of northern England, exists, in the British Library in London.

Wood is believed to have sojourned in France and to have spent some of her winters in major American cities, including New York, Boston, and Philadelphia. In 1900 she traveled to England to develop her contacts with British publishers. Two articles published in the *Canadian Magazine* in 1901 suggest that she was presented at court and made the acquaintance of Algernon Charles Swinburne. After this time she virtually disappeared and no work by her has been found published after 1902. In 1907 Wood moved with her mother to the town of Niagara-on-the-Lake, where her occasional talks on her travels and on regional history were reported in the local press. After her mother's death in 1910 she appears to have left Canada; according to one obituary, she ceased writing after a nervous breakdown. When she was not traveling, she lived alternately with her brother, William Wood, in New York, and her sister, Jessie Wood Maxwell, at whose Detroit home she died in 1927 after a lengthy illness.

References:

Barbara Godard, "A Portrait with Three Faces: The New Woman in Fiction by Canadian Women, 1880-1920," *Literary Criterion*, 19, nos. 3-4 (1984): 72-92;

Elsie M. Stevens, "She's Canada's Charlotte Brontë," *Early Canadian Life* (April 1980): B3, B15.

Papers:

A scrapbook on Joanna Wood, compiled by Elsie Stevens, is in the records of the Women's Literary Club of St. Catharines, held by the Brock University Library, St. Catherines, Ontario.

Supplementary Reading List

Atlantic Provinces Literature Colloquium. Saint John, New Brunswick: Atlantic Canada Institute, 1977.

Atwood, Margaret. *Survival: A Thematic Guide to Canadian Literature.* Toronto: Anansi, 1972.

Avis, Walter, and others. *A Concise Dictionary of Canadianisms.* Toronto: Gage, 1973.

Bailey, A. G. *Culture and Nationality: Essays.* Toronto: McClelland & Stewart, 1972.

Baillargeon, Samuel. *Littérature canadienne-française,* third edition, revised. Montreal & Paris: Fides, 1960.

Ballstadt, Carl, ed. *The Search for English-Canadian Literature.* Toronto & Buffalo: University of Toronto Press, 1975.

Bélisle, Louis-Alexandre. *Dictionnaire général de la langue française au Canada.* Quebec: Bélisle, 1957.

Bélisle. *Dictionnaire nord-américaine de la langue française.* Montreal: Beauchemin, 1979.

Beraud, Jean. *350 Ans de théâtre au Canada français.* Montreal: Cercle du Livre de France, 1958.

Berger, Carl. *The Sense of Power.* Toronto: University of Toronto Press, 1970.

Berger. *The Writing of Canadian History.* Toronto: Oxford University Press, 1976.

Bissell, C. T., and R. L. McDougall, eds. *Our Living Tradition,* 4 volumes. Toronto: University of Toronto Press, 1957-1965.

Boivin, Aurélien. *Le Conte littéraire québécois au 19e siècle: Essai de bibliographie critique et analytique.* Montreal: Fides, 1975.

Bourinot, John George. *Our Intellectual Strength and Weakness.* Montreal: F. Brown, 1893; republished, Toronto: University of Toronto Press, 1973.

Brown, E. K. *Responses and Evaluations: Essays on Canada.* Toronto: McClelland & Stewart, 1977.

Brunet, Berthelot. *Histoire de la littérature canadienne-française.* Montreal: L'Arbre, 1946.

Brym, Robert J., and Bonnie J. Fox. *From Culture to Power: The Sociology of English Canada.* Toronto: Oxford University Press, 1989.

Buitenhuis, Peter. *The Great War of Words: British, American, and Canadian Propaganda and Fiction 1914-33.* Vancouver: University of British Columbia Press, 1989.

Burnet, Jean. *"Coming Canadians": An Introduction to a History of Canada's Peoples.* Toronto: McClelland & Stewart, 1968.

The Canadian Encyclopedia, second edition, 4 volumes. Edmonton: Hurtig, 1985.

Capone, Giovanna. *Canada: il villaggio della terra.* Bologna: Pàtron Editore, 1978.

Cappon, Paul, ed., *In Our House: Social Perspectives on Canadian Literature.* Toronto: McClelland & Stewart, 1978.

Cleverdon, Catherine Lyle. *The Woman Suffrage Movement in Canada.* Toronto: University of Toronto Press, 1950.

Codignola, Luca, ed. *Canadiana.* Venice: Marsilio, 1978.

Collet, Paulette. *L'Hiver dans le roman canadien français.* Quebec: Laval, 1965.

Collin, W. E. *The White Savannahs.* 1936; republished, Toronto & Buffalo: University of Toronto Press, 1975.

Colombo, John Robert. *Colombo's Canadian Quotations.* Edmonton: Hurtig, 1974.

Colombo, comp. *Colombo's Canadian References.* Toronto, Oxford & New York: Oxford University Press, 1976.

Colombo and others, comps. *CDN SF & F: A Bibliography of Science Fiction and Fantasy.* Toronto: Hounslow, 1979.

Cook, Ramsay. *The Regenerators: Social Criticism in Late Victorian English Canada.* Toronto & Buffalo: University of Toronto Press, 1985.

Costisella, Joseph. *L'Esprit révolutionnaire dans la littérature canadienne-française de 1837 à la fin du 19e siècle.* Montreal: Beauchemin, 1968.

Daymond, Douglas. *Towards a Canadian Literature,* volume 1. Ottawa: Tecumseh, 1984.

Daymond, and Leslie Monkman, eds. *Canadian Novelists and the Novel.* Ottawa: Borealis, 1981.

Dictionary of Canadian Biography, 12 volumes, ongoing. Toronto: University of Toronto Press, 1966-   .

Dooley, D. J. *Moral Vision in the Canadian Novel.* Toronto: Clarke, Irwin, 1981.

Dostaler, Yves. *Les Infortunes du roman dans le Quebec du XIXe siècle.* Montreal: HMH, 1977.

Doyle, James. *North of America: Images of Canada in the Literature of the United States, 1775-1900.* Toronto: ECW, 1983.

Ducrocq-Poirier, Madeleine. *Le Roman canadien de langue française de 1860 à 1958.* Paris: Nizet, 1978.

Dudek, Louis and Michael Gnarowski, eds., *The Making of Modern Poetry in Canada.* Toronto: Ryerson, 1967.

Duffy, Dennis. *Gardens, Covenants, Exiles: Loyalism in the Literature of Upper Canada/Ontario.* Toronto: University of Toronto Press, 1982.

Duhamel, Roger. *Manuel de littérature canadienne-française.* Montreal: Renouveau Pédagogiques, 1967.

Egoff, Sheila. *The Republic of Childhood.* Toronto: Oxford University Press, 1967.

Fairbanks, Carol. *Prairie Women: Images in American and Canadian Fiction*. New Haven & London: Yale University Press, 1986.

Falardeau, Jean-Charles. *Imaginaire social et littérature*. Montreal: HMH, 1974.

Fowke, Edith. *Canadian Folklore*. Toronto: Oxford University Press, 1988.

Fowke, and Carole Henderson Carpenter, comps. *A Bibliography of Canadian Folklore in English*. Toronto & Buffalo: University of Toronto Press, 1981.

Fowke and Carpenter, eds. *Explorations in Canadian Folklore*. Toronto: McClelland & Stewart, 1985.

Frye, Northrop. *The Bush Garden: Essays on the Canadian Imagination*. Toronto: Anansi, 1971.

Frye. *Divisions on a Ground*. Toronto: Anansi, 1982.

Gagnon, Serge. *Quebec and Its Historians*, 2 volumes, translated by Jane Brierly. Montreal: Harvest House, 1982, 1985.

Gauvin, Lise, and Laurent Mailhot. *Guide culturel de Québec*. Montreal: Boréal Express, 1982.

Gerson, Carole. *A Purer Taste: The Writing and Reading of Fiction in English in Nineteenth-Century Canada*. Toronto, Buffalo & London: University of Toronto Press, 1989.

Gnarowski, Michael. *A Concise Bibliography of English-Candian Literature*. Toronto: McClelland & Stewart, 1973.

Godard, Barbara, ed. *Gynocritics/Gynocritiques: Feminist Approaches to Canadian and Quebec Writing*. Toronto: ECW, 1987.

Goldie, Terry. *Fear and Temptation: The Image of the Indigene in Canadian, Australian, and New Zealand Literatures*. Kingston, Ont., Montreal & London: McGill-Queen's University Press, 1989.

Gross, Konrad, and Wolfgang Kloss, eds. *English Literature of the Dominions*. Würzburg: Königshausen & Neumann, 1981.

Guillaume, Pierre, Jean-Michel Lacroix, and Pierre Spriet, eds. *Canada et canadiens*. Bordeaux: Presses Universitaires de Bordeaux, 1984.

Hall, Roger, and Gordon Dodds. *Canada: A History in Photographs*. Edmonton: Hurtig, 1981.

Halpenny, Francess G., ed. *Editing Canadian Texts*. Toronto: Hakkert, 1975.

Harper, J. Russell. *Painting in Canada: A History*. Toronto: University of Toronto Press, 1970.

Harrison, Dick. *Unnamed Country: The Struggle for a Canadian Prairie Fiction*. Edmonton: University of Alberta Press, 1977.

Harrison, ed. *Crossing Frontiers*. Edmonton: University of Alberta Press, 1979.

Hayne, David M., and Marcel Tirol. *Bibliographie critique du roman canadien-français, 1837-1900*. Toronto: University of Toronto Press, 1968.

Heath, Jeffrey M., ed. *Profiles in Canadian Literature*, volumes 1-4. Toronto & Charlottetown: Dundurn, 1980-1982.

Hébert, Chantal. *Le Burlesque au Québec*. Montreal: HMH, 1981.

Hébert, Pierre. *Le Journal intime au Québec*. Montreal: Fides, 1988.

Hinchcliffe, Peter, ed. *Family Fictions in Canadian Literature*. Waterloo, Ont.: University of Waterloo Press, 1988.

Innis, Mary Quayle, ed. *The Clear Spirit: Twenty Canadian Women and Their Times*. Toronto: University of Toronto Press, 1966.

Jones, D. G. *Butterfly on Rock*. Toronto: University of Toronto Press, 1970.

Kallmann, Helmut, and others. *The Encyclopedia of Music in Canada*. Toronto: University of Toronto Press, 1981.

Keith, W. J. *Canadian Literature in English*. London & New York: Longman, 1985.

Keitner, Wendy, ed. *"Surveying the Territory"* and *"Staking Claims,"* Canadian issues of *Literary Criterion*, 19, 3-4 (1984) and 20, 1 (1985).

King, Thomas, and others, eds. *The Native in Literature*. Toronto: ECW, 1988.

Klinck, Carl F., ed. *Literary History of Canada*, 3 volumes, second edition. Toronto: University of Toronto Press, 1976.

Kline, Marcia B. *Beyond the Land Itself: Views of Nature in Canada and the United States*. Cambridge, Mass.: Harvard University Press, 1970.

Kröller, Eva-Marie. *Canadian Travellers in Europe 1851-1900*. Vancouver: University of British Columbia Press, 1987.

Laflamme, Jean, and Rémi Tourangeau. *L'Eglise et le théâtre au Québec*. Montreal: Fides, 1979.

Lecker, Robert, and Jack David, eds. *The Annotated Bibliography of Canada's Major Authors*, 6 volumes, ongoing. Downsview, Ontario: ECW, 1979- .

Lecker and David, eds. *Canadian Writers and Their Works*, 6 volumes, ongoing. Toronto: ECW, 1983- .

Lee, Dennis. *Savage Fields: An Essay in Literature and Cosmology*. Toronto: Anansi, 1977.

Léger, Jules. *Le Canada français et son expression littéraire*. Paris: Nizet & Bastard, 1938.

Legris, Renée, and others. *Le Théâtre au Quebec 1825-1980: Repères et perspectives*. Montreal: VLB, 1988.

Lemieux, Louise. *Pleins feux sur la littérature de jeunesse au Canada français*. Montreal: Leméac, 1972.

Lemire, Maurice. *Les Grands Thèmes nationalistes du roman historique canadien-français*. Quebec: Presses de l'Université Laval, 1970.

Lemire, ed. *Dictionnaire des oeuvres littéraires du Quebec*. Montreal: Fides. Volume 1 (*Des Origines à 1900*, 1978); volume 2 (*1900 à 1939*, 1980).

Lewis, Merrill, and L. L. Lee. *The Westering Experience in American Literature*. Bellingham, Wash.: Western Washington University Press, 1977.

Lewis, Paula Gilbert, ed. *Traditionalism, Nationalism, and Feminism: Women Writers of Quebec*. Westport, Conn. & London: Greenwood Press, 1985.

Lochhead, Douglas, comp. *Bibliography of Canadian Bibliographies*, second edition, revised and enlarged. Toronto: University of Toronto Press, 1972.

MacLulich, T. D. *Between Europe and America*. Toronto: ECW, 1988.

MacMechan, Archibald. *Headwaters of Canadian Literature*. Toronto: McClelland & Stewart, 1924.

MacMurchy, Archibald. *Handbook of Canadian Literature (English)*. Toronto: Briggs, 1906.

Mailhot, Laurent. *La Littérature québécoise*. Paris: Presses Universitaires de France, 1974.

Mandel, Eli, ed. *Contexts of Canadian Criticism*. Chicago & London: University of Chicago Press, 1971.

Marshall, Tom. *Harsh and Lovely Land: Major Canadian Poets and the Making of a Canadian Tradition*. Vancouver: University of British Columbia Press, 1979.

Mathews, Robin. *Canadian Literature: Surrender or Revolution*. Toronto: Steel Rail, 1978.

Matthews, John. *Tradition in Exile*. Toronto: University of Toronto Press/Melbourne: Cheshire, 1962.

May, Cedric. *Breaking the Silence: The Literature of Quebec*. Birmingham, U.K.: University of Birmingham, 1981.

McConnell, R. E. *Our Own Voice: Canadian English and How It Is Studied*. Toronto: Gage, 1979.

McGregor, Gaile. *The Wacousta Syndrome: Explorations in the Canadian Langscape*. Toronto, Buffalo & London: University of Toronto Press, 1985.

McKillop, A. B. *Contours of Canadian Thought*. Toronto: University of Toronto Press, 1987.

McKillop. *A Disciplined Intelligence*. Montreal: McGill-Queen's University Press, 1979.

McKillop, ed. *Contexts of Canada's Past: Selected Essays of W. L. Morton*. Toronto: Macmillan, 1980.

McMullen, Lorraine, ed. *Twentieth Century Essays on Confederation Literature*. Ottawa: Tecumseh, 1977.

Moisan, Clément. *L'Age de la littérature canadienne*. Montreal: HMH, 1969.

Monkman, Leslie. *A Native Heritage: Images of the Indian in English-Canadian Literature*. Toronto: University of Toronto Press, 1981.

Moss, John. *Patterns of Isolation in English Canadian Fiction*. Toronto: McClelland & Stewart, 1974.

Moss. *A Reader's Guide to the Canadian Novel*. Toronto: McClelland & Stewart, 1981.

Moss. *Sex and Violence in the Canadian Novel.* Toronto: McClelland & Stewart, 1977.

Moyles, R. G., and Doug Owram. *Imperial Dreams and Colonial Realities: British Views of Canada 1880-1914.* Toronto, Buffalo & London: University of Toronto Press, 1988.

Narasimhaiah, C. D., ed. *Awakened Conscience.* New Delhi: Sterling, 1978.

Neuman, Shirley, and Smaro Kamboureli, eds. *A Mazing Space: Writing Canadian Women Writing.* Edmonton: Longspoon/NeWest, 1986.

New, W. H. *Among Worlds: An Introduction to Modern Commonwealth and South African Fiction.* Erin, Ont.: Porcépic, 1975.

New. *Dreams of Speech and Violence: The Art of the Short Story in Canada and New Zealand.* Toronto, Buffalo & London: University of Toronto Press, 1987.

New. *A History of Canadian Literature.* London: Macmillan, 1989.

New, comp. *Critical Writings on Commonwealth Literatures: A Selective Bibliography to 1970, With a List of Theses and Dissertations.* University Park: Pennsylvania State University Press, 1975.

New, ed. *Dramatists in Canada: Selected Essays.* Vancouver: University of British Columbia Press, 1972.

New, ed. *Literary History of Canada,* volume 4. Toronto: University of Toronto Press, 1990.

New, ed. *A Political Art.* Vancouver: University of British Columbia Press, 1978.

Northey, Margot. *The Haunted Wilderness: The Gothic and Grotesque in Canadian Fiction.* Toronto & Buffalo: University of Toronto Press, 1976.

OKanada. Ottawa: Canada Council, 1982.

O'Leary, Dostaler. *Le Roman canadien-français.* Montreal: Cercle du Livre de France, 1954.

Olinder, Britta, ed. *A Sense of Place: Essays in Post-Colonial Literatures.* Göteburg: Gothenburg University Press, 1984.

Pacey, Desmond. *Creative Writing in Canada,* second edition, revised. Toronto: Ryerson, 1961.

Pacey. *Essays in Canadian Criticism 1938-1968.* Toronto: Ryerson, 1969.

Pacey. *Ten Canadian Poets.* Toronto: Ryerson, 1958.

Pache, Walter. *Einführung in die Kanadistik.* Darmstadt: Wissenschaftliche Buchgesellschaft, 1981.

Paradis, Suzanne. *Femme fictive, femme réelle: Le Personnage féminin dans le roman féminin canadien-français, 1884-1966.* Quebec: Garneau, 1966.

Parker, George L. *The Beginnings of the Book Trade in Canada.* Toronto & Buffalo: University of Toronto Press, 1985.

Paul-Crouzet, Jeanne. *Poésie au Canada.* Paris: Didier, 1946.

Petrone, Penny. *Northern Voices: Inuit Writing in English.* Toronto, Buffalo & London: University of Toronto Press, 1988.

Petrone, ed. *First People, First Voices.* Toronto: Ryerson, 1927.

Pierce, Lorne. *An Outline of Canadian Literature.* Toronto: Ryerson, 1927.

Polk, James. *Wilderness Writers.* Toronto: Clarke, Irwin, 1972.

Rabb, J. D. *Religion and Science in Early Canada.* Toronto: Frye, 1988.

Rashley, R. E. *Poetry in Canada: The First Three Steps.* Toronto: Ryerson, 1958.

Reid, Dennis. *A Concise History of Canadian Painting.* Toronto, Oxford & New York: Oxford University Press, 1973.

Rhodenizer, V. B. *A Handbook of Canadian Literature.* Ottawa: Graphic, 1930.

Ricou, Laurence R. *Vertical Man/Horizontal World.* Vancouver: University of British Columbia Press, 1973.

Riedel, Walter E. *Das Literarische Kanadabild.* Bonn: Bouvier, 1980.

Riemenschneider, Dieter, ed. *The History and Historiography of Commonwealth Literature.* Tübingen: Gunter Narr Verlag, 1983.

Rièse, Laure. *L'Ame de la poésie canadienne-française.* Toronto: Macmillan, 1955.

Ross, Malcolm. *The Impossible Sum of Our Traditions: Reflections on Canadian Literature.* Toronto: McClelland & Stewart, 1986.

Roy, Camille. *Manuel d'histoire de la littérature canadienne de langue française.* Quebec: L'Action Sociale, 1918.

Rutherford, Paul. *A Victorian Authority: The Daily Press in Late Nineteenth-Century Canada.* Toronto & Buffalo: University of Toronto Press, 1982.

Sarkonak, Ralph, ed. "The Language of Difference: Writing in QUEBEC(ois)," special issue of *Yale French Studies,* no. 65 (1983).

Shortt, S. E. D. *The Search for an Ideal.* Toronto & Buffalo: University of Toronto Press, 1976.

Sirois, Antoine. *Montréal dans le roman canadien.* Montreal: Didier, 1970.

Smith, A. J. M. *Towards a View of Canadian Letters.* Vancouver: University of British Columbia Press, 1973.

Smith, ed. *Masks of Poetry.* Toronto: McClelland & Stewart, 1962.

Staines, David, ed. *The Canadian Imagination.* Cambridge, Mass.: Harvard University Press, 1977.

Stevenson, Lionel. *Appraisals of Canadian Literature.* Toronto: Macmillan, 1926.

Stich, K. P., ed. *Reflections: Autobiography and Canadian Literature*. Ottawa: University of Ottawa Press, 1988.

Story, G. M., and others, eds. *Dictionary of Newfoundland English*. Toronto: University of Toronto Press, 1982.

Stouck, David. *Major Canadian Authors*. Lincoln: University of Nebraska Press, 1984.

Stratford, Philip. *Bibliography of Canadian Books in Translation: French to English and English to French. Bibliographie de livres canadiens traduits de l'anglais au français et du français à l'anglais*. Ottawa: CCRH, 1977.

Stuart, E. Ross. *The History of Prairie Theatre*. Toronto: Simon & Pierre, 1984.

Sutherland, Fraser. *The Monthly Epic: A History of Canadian Magazines 1789-1989*. Toronto: Fitzhenry & Whiteside, 1989.

Taylor, Charles. *Six Journeys: A Canadian Pattern*. Toronto: Anansi, 1977.

Thomas, Clara. *Our Nature—Our Voices: A Guidebook to English-Canadian Literature*. Toronto: New Press, 1972.

Tougas, Gérard. *Histoire de la littérature canadienne-française*. Paris: Presses Universitaires de France, 1960. Translated by Alta Lind Cook as *History of French-Canadian Literature*. Toronto: Ryerson, 1966.

Toye, William, ed. *The Oxford Companion to Canadian Literature*. Toronto: Oxford University Press, 1983.

Trudel, Marcel. *L'Influence de Voltaire au Canada*, 2 volumes. Montreal: Fides, 1945.

Turnbull, Jane-M. *Essential Traits of French-Canadian Poetry*. Toronto: Macmillan, 1938.

Viatte, Auguste. *Histoire littéraire de l'Amérique française des origines à 1950*. Quebec: Presses Universitaires Laval, 1954.

Wagner, Anton, ed. *The Brock Bibliography of Published Canadian Plays in English 1766-1978*. Toronto: Playwrights, 1980.

Wardhaugh, Ronald. *Language & Nationhood: The Canadian Experience*. Vancouver: New Star, 1983.

Warwick, Jack. *The Long Journey: Literary Themes of French Canada*. Toronto: University of Toronto Press, 1968.

Waterston, Elizabeth. *Survey: A Short History of Canadian Literature*. Toronto: Methuen, 1973.

Watters, R. E. *A Check List of Canadian Literature and Background Material 1628-1950*, revised edition. Toronto: University of Toronto Press, 1972.

Winks, Robin W. *The Myth of the American Frontier*. Leicester: Leicester University Press, 1971.

Woodcock, George. *Canada and the Canadians*. Toronto: Macmillan, 1970.

Woodcock. *Odysseus Ever Returning: Essays on Canadian Writers and Writing*. Toronto: McClelland & Stewart, 1970.

Woodcock, comp. *Colony and Confederation: Early Canadian Poets and Their Background.* Vancouver: University of British Columbia Press, 1974.

Woodcock, ed. *The Canadian Novel in the Twentieth Century.* Toronto: McClelland & Stewart, 1975.

Wyzynski, Paul, and others. *Archives des lettres canadiennes.* Montreal: Fides. No. 2 (*Ecole littéraire de Montréal,* 1972); no. 3 (*Roman,* 1971); no. 4 (*Poésie,* 1969); no. 5 (*Théâtre,* 1976).

Contributors

Alexandre L. Amprimoz ....*Brock University*
Neil K. Besner ....*University of Winnipeg*
E. D. Blodgett ....*University of Alberta*
Peyton Brien ....*Toronto, Ontario*
Terrence Craig ....*Mount Allison University*
Michael Darling ....*University of Western Ontario*
Regna Darnell ....*University of Alberta*
Gwendolyn Davies ....*Acadia University*
Misao Dean ....*University of Victoria*
Sandra A. Djwa ....*Simon Fraser University*
Richard Duprey ....*Emerson College*
Margery Fee ....*Queen's University at Kingston*
Edith Fowke ....*York University*
Frances Frazer ....*University of Prince Edward Island*
Rosanna Furgiuele ....*York University*
Michel Gaulin ....*Carleton University*
Carole Gerson ....*Simon Fraser University*
Robert Gibbs ....*University of New Brunswick*
Janet Giltrow ....*Simon Fraser University*
Mary Jean Green ....*Dartmouth College*
Anthony John Harding ....*University of Saskatchewan*
Dick Harrison ....*University of Alberta*
Paul Hjartarson ....*University of Alberta*
Clifford G. Holland ....*Ontario Institute for Studies in Education*
Jean-Guy Hudon ....*Université du Québec à Chicoutimi*
Michael Hurley ....*Queen's University*
David Ingham ....*University of Saskatchewan*
Susan Jackel ....*University of Alberta*
Chris Johnson ....*University of Manitoba*
Kathleen L. Kellett ....*University of Toronto*
R. Alex Kizuk ....*University of Saskatchewan*
Carl F. Klinck ....*University of Western Ontario*
Maurice Lebel ....*Laval University*
John Lennox ....*York University*
Paul Leonard ....*Toronto Theatre Alliance*
Louis K. MacKendrick ....*University of Windsor*
Catherine McLay ....*University of Calgary*
Lorraine McMullen ....*University of Ottawa*
Stanley E. McMullin ....*University of Waterloo*
Kathy Mezei ....*Simon Fraser University*
Patricia Morley ....*Concordia University*
Bruce Nesbitt ....*Rockcliffe Park, Ontario*
W. H. New ....*University of British Columbia*
Margot Northey ....*University of Western Ontario*
John J. O'Connor ....*University of Toronto*
Walter Pache ....*University of Augsburg*
John Parr ....*Winnipeg, Manitoba*
Donald A. Precosky ....*College of New Caledonia*

Valerie Raoul...*University of British Columbia*
Diana M. A. Relke..*University of Calgary*
Laurie Ricou ....*University of British Columbia*
David F. Rogers ....*University of British Columbia*
Hans R. Runte...*Dalhousie University*
Larry Shouldice...*University of Sherbrooke*
Leon Slonim ....*Toronto, Ontario*
Donald Stephens..*University of British Columbia*
John Stockdale...*Laval University*
Paul Matthew St. Pierre..*Simon Fraser University*
Thomas E. Tausky ....*University of Western Ontario*
Hilda L. Thomas ....*University of British Columbia*
Eric Thompson..*Université du Québec à Chicoutimi*
Jacqueline Viswanathan ....*Simon Fraser University*
Evelyne Voldeng...*Carleton University*
Jack Warwick...*York University*

Cumulative Index

Dictionary of Literary Biography, Volumes 1-92
Dictionary of Literary Biography Yearbook, 1980-1988
Dictionary of Literary Biography Documentary Series, Volumes 1-7

Cumulative Index

DLB before number: *Dictionary of Literary Biography*, Volumes 1-92
Y before number: *Dictionary of Literary Biography Yearbook*, 1980-1988
DS before number: *Dictionary of Literary Biography Documentary Series*, Volumes 1-7

A

Abbey Press...DLB-49

The Abbey Theatre and Irish
  Drama, 1900-1945 ....DLB-10

Abbot, Willis J. 1863-1934 ....DLB-29

Abbott, Jacob 1803-1879 ....DLB-1

Abbott, Lyman 1835-1922 ....DLB-79

Abbott, Robert S. 1868-1940 ....DLB-29, 91

Abelard-Schuman DLB-46

Abell, Arunah S. 1806-1888 ....DLB-43

Abercrombie, Lascelles 1881-1938 ....DLB-19

Abrams, M. H. 1912- DLB-67

Abse, Dannie 1923- DLB-27

Academy Chicago Publishers DLB-46

Ace Books DLB-46

Acorn, Milton 1923-1986 ....DLB-53

Acosta, Oscar Zeta 1935?- DLB-82

Actors Theatre of Louisville DLB-7

Adair, James 1709?-1783? DLB-30

Adame, Leonard 1947- DLB-82

Adamic, Louis 1898-1951....................................DLB-9

Adams, Alice 1926- Y-86

Adams, Brooks 1848-1927 ....DLB-47

Adams, Charles Francis, Jr. 1835-1915.............DLB-47

Adams, Douglas 1952- Y-83

Adams, Franklin P. 1881-1960 ....DLB-29

Adams, Henry 1838-1918..........................DLB-12, 47

Adams, Herbert Baxter 1850-1901 ....DLB-47

Adams, J. S. and C. [publishing house].............DLB-49

Adams, James Truslow 1878-1949.....................DLB-17

Adams, John 1735-1826 ....DLB-31

Adams, John Quincy 1767-1848...........................DLB-37

Adams, Léonie 1899-1988 ....DLB-48

Adams, Samuel 1722-1803...........................DLB-31, 43

Adams, William Taylor 1822-1897 ....DLB-42

Adcock, Fleur 1934- DLB-40

Ade, George 1866-1944 ....DLB-11, 25

Adeler, Max (see Clark, Charles Heber)

Advance Publishing Company DLB-49

AE 1867-1935 ....DLB-19

Aesthetic Poetry (1873), by Walter Pater............DLB-35

Afro-American Literary Critics:
  An Introduction DLB-33

Agassiz, Jean Louis Rodolphe 1807-1873 ....DLB-1

Agee, James 1909-1955...............................DLB-2, 26

Aichinger, Ilse 1921- DLB-85

Aiken, Conrad 1889-1973.............................DLB-9, 45

Ainsworth, William Harrison 1805-1882 ....DLB-21

Aitken, Robert [publishing house].....................DLB-49

Akins, Zoë 1886-1958......................................DLB-26

Alain-Fournier 1886-1914 ....DLB-65

Alba, Nanina 1915-1968...................................DLB-41

Albee, Edward 1928- DLB-7

Alcott, Amos Bronson 1799-1888 ....DLB-1

Alcott, Louisa May 1832-1888 ....DLB-1, 42, 79

Alcott, William Andrus 1798-1859......................DLB-1

Alden, Henry Mills 1836-1919 ....DLB-79

Alden, Isabella 1841-1930.................................DLB-42

Alden, John B. [publishing house] DLB-49

Alden, Beardsley and Company DLB-49

Aldington, Richard 1892-1962 ....DLB-20, 36

Aldis, Dorothy 1896-1966 ....DLB-22

Aldiss, Brian W. 1925- DLB-14

Aldrich, Thomas Bailey 1836-1907
  ....DLB-42, 71, 74, 79

Alexander, Charles 1868-1923...........................DLB-91

Alexander, Charles Wesley
  [publishing house] DLB-49

Alexander, James 1691-1756 ....DLB-24

Alexander, Lloyd 1924- DLB-52

Alger, Horatio, Jr. 1832-1899...........................DLB-42

Algonquin Books of Chapel Hill DLB-46

Algren, Nelson 1909-1981 ....DLB-9; Y-81, 82

Allan, Andrew 1907-1974 ....DLB-88

Allan, Ted 1916- DLB-68

Allbeury, Ted 1917- DLB-87

Alldritt, Keith 1935- DLB-14

Allen, Ethan 1738-1789 ....DLB-31

Allen, George 1808-1876 ....DLB-59

Allen, Grant 1848-1899 ....DLB-70, 92

Allen, Henry W. 1912- Y-85

Allen, Hervey 1889-1949 ....DLB-9, 45

Allen, James 1739-1808....................................DLB-31

Allen, James Lane 1849-1925 ....DLB-71

Allen, Jay Presson 1922- DLB-26

Allen, John, and Company DLB-49

Allen, Samuel W. 1917- DLB-41

Allen, Woody 1935- DLB-44

Allingham, Margery 1904-1966........................DLB-77

Allingham, William 1824-1889 ....DLB-35

Allison, W. L. [publishing house] DLB-49

Allott, Kenneth 1912-1973...............................DLB-20

Allston, Washington 1779-1843 ....DLB-1

Alsop, George 1636-post 1673.........................DLB-24

Alsop, Richard 1761-1815................................DLB-37

Altemus, Henry, and Company........................DLB-49

Altenberg, Peter 1885-1919 ....DLB-81

Alurista 1947- DLB-82

Alvarez, A. 1929- DLB-14, 40

Ambler, Eric 1909- DLB-77

*America: or, a Poem on the Settlement of the
    British Colonies* (1780?), by Timothy
    Dwight..DLB-37

American Conservatory Theatre DLB-7

American Fiction and the 1930s.........................DLB-9

American Humor: A Historical Survey
    East and Northeast
    South and Southwest
    Midwest
    West..DLB-11

American News Company.................................DLB-49

The American Poets' Corner: The First
    Three Years (1983-1986)................................Y-86

American Publishing Company DLB-49

American Stationers' Company..........................DLB-49

American Sunday-School Union DLB-49

American Temperance Union............................DLB-49

American Tract Society DLB-49

The American Writers Congress
    (9-12 October 1981) Y-81

The American Writers Congress: A Report
    on Continuing Business...................................Y-81

Ames, Fisher 1758-1808...................................DLB-37

Ames, Mary Clemmer 1831-1884 ....DLB-23

Amini, Johari M. 1935- DLB-41

Amis, Kingsley 1922- DLB-15, 27

Amis, Martin 1949- DLB-14

Ammons, A. R. 1926- DLB-5

Amory, Thomas 1691?-1788............................DLB-39

Anaya, Rudolfo A. 1937- DLB-82

Andersch, Alfred 1914-1980............................DLB-69

Anderson, Margaret 1886-1973.....................DLB-4, 91

Anderson, Maxwell 1888-1959 ....DLB-7

Anderson, Patrick 1915-1979...........................DLB-68

Anderson, Paul Y. 1893-1938...........................DLB-29

Anderson, Poul 1926- DLB-8

Anderson, Robert 1917- DLB-7

Anderson, Sherwood 1876-1941......DLB-4, 9, 86; DS-1

Andreas-Salomé, Lou 1861-1937......................DLB-66

Andres, Stefan 1906-1970.................................DLB-69

Andrews, Charles M. 1863-1943.......................DLB-17

Andrews, Miles Peter ?-1814............................DLB-89

Andrieux, Louis (see Aragon, Louis)

Andrian, Leopold von 1875-1951 ....DLB-81

Andrus, Silas, and Son DLB-49

Angell, James Burrill 1829-1916 ....DLB-64

Angelou, Maya 1928- DLB-38

The "Angry Young Men".................................DLB-15

Anhalt, Edward 1914- DLB-26

Anners, Henry F. [publishing house]................DLB-49

Anthony, Piers 1934- DLB-8

Anthony Burgess's *99 Novels:* An Opinion Poll Y-84

Antin, Mary 1881-1949 ....Y-84

Antschel, Paul (see Celan, Paul)

Apodaca, Rudy S. 1939- DLB-82

Appleton, D., and Company DLB-49

Appleton-Century-Crofts DLB-46

Apple-wood Books DLB-46

Aquin, Hubert 1929-1977 ....DLB-53

Aragon, Louis 1897-1982 ....DLB-72

Arbor House Publishing Company DLB-46

Arcadia House DLB-46

Arce, Julio G. (see Ulica, Jorge)

Archer, William 1856-1924 ....DLB-10

Arden, John 1930- DLB-13

Arden of Faversham DLB-62

The Arena Publishing Company DLB-49

Arena Stage DLB-7

Arensberg, Ann 1937- Y-82

Arias, Ron 1941- DLB-82

Arland, Marcel 1899-1986 ....DLB-72

Arlen, Michael 1895-1956 ....DLB-36, 77

Armed Services Editions DLB-46

Arndt, Ernst Moritz 1769-1860 ....DLB-90

Arnim, Achim von 1781-1831 ....DLB-90

Arnim, Bettina von 1785-1859 ....DLB-90

Arno Press DLB-46

Arnold, Edwin 1832-1904 ....DLB-35

Arnold, Matthew 1822-1888 ....DLB-32, 57

Arnold, Thomas 1795-1842 ....DLB-55

Arnow, Harriette Simpson 1908-1986 ....DLB-6

Arp, Bill (see Smith, Charles Henry)

Arthur, Timothy Shay 1809-1885 ....DLB-3, 42, 79

Artmann, H. C. 1921- DLB-85

As I See It, by Carolyn Cassady DLB-16

Asch, Nathan 1902-1964 ....DLB-4, 28

Ash, John 1948- DLB-40

Ashbery, John 1927- DLB-5; Y-81

Asher, Sandy 1942- Y-83

Ashton, Winifred (see Dane, Clemence)

Asimov, Isaac 1920- DLB-8

Asselin, Olivar 1874-1937 ....DLB-92

Atheneum Publishers DLB-46

Atherton, Gertrude 1857-1948 ....DLB-9, 78

Atkins, Josiah circa 1755-1781 ....DLB-31

Atkins, Russell 1926- DLB-41

The Atlantic Monthly Press DLB-46

Attaway, William 1911-1986 ....DLB-76

Atwood, Margaret 1939- DLB-53

Aubert, Alvin 1930- DLB-41

Aubin, Penelope 1685-circa 1731 ....DLB-39

Aubrey-Fletcher, Henry Lancelot (see Wade, Henry)

Auchincloss, Louis 1917- DLB-2; Y-80

Auden, W. H. 1907-1973 ....DLB-10, 20

Audio Art in America: A Personal
    Memoir Y-85

Auernheimer, Raoul 1876-1948 ....DLB-81

Austin, Alfred 1835-1913 ....DLB-35

Austin, Mary 1868-1934 ....DLB-9, 78

Austin, William 1778-1841 ....DLB-74

The Author's Apology for His Book
    (1684), by John Bunyan DLB-39

An Author's Response, by Ronald Sukenick Y-82

Authors and Newspapers Association DLB-46

Authors' Publishing Company DLB-49

Avalon Books DLB-46

Avendaño, Fausto 1941- DLB-82

Avison, Margaret 1918- DLB-53

Avon Books DLB-46

Ayckbourn, Alan 1939- DLB-13

Aymé, Marcel 1902-1967 ....DLB-72

Aytoun, William Edmondstoune 1813-1865 ......DLB-32

B

Babbitt, Irving 1865-1933 ....DLB-63

Babbitt, Natalie 1932- DLB-52

Babcock, John [publishing house] DLB-49

Bache, Benjamin Franklin 1769-1798 ....DLB-43

Bachmann, Ingeborg 1926-1973 ....DLB-85

Bacon, Delia 1811-1859 ....DLB-1

Bacon, Thomas circa 1700-1768 ....DLB-31

Badger, Richard G., and Company DLB-49

Bage, Robert 1728-1801.....................................DLB-39

Bagehot, Walter 1826-1877.............................DLB-55

Bagley, Desmond 1923-1983.............................DLB-87

Bagnold, Enid 1889-1981 ....DLB-13

Bahr, Hermann 1863-1934.............................DLB-81

Bailey, Alfred Goldsworthy 1905- DLB-68

Bailey, Francis [publishing house] DLB-49

Bailey, H. C. 1878-1961 ....DLB-77

Bailey, Paul 1937- DLB-14

Bailey, Philip James 1816-1902.........................DLB-32

Baillargeon, Pierre 1916-1967 ....DLB-88

Baillie, Hugh 1890-1966 ....DLB-29

Bailyn, Bernard 1922- DLB-17

Bainbridge, Beryl 1933- DLB-14

Baird, Irene 1901-1981 ....DLB-68

The Baker and Taylor Company DLB-49

Baker, Houston A., Jr. 1943- DLB-67

Baker, Walter H., Company
    ("Baker's Plays").....................................DLB-49

Bald, Wambly 1902- DLB-4

Balderston, John 1889-1954 ....DLB-26

Baldwin, James 1924-1987 ....DLB-2, 7, 33; Y-87

Baldwin, Joseph Glover 1815-1864 ....DLB-3, 11

Ballantine Books...DLB-46

Ballard, J. G. 1930- DLB-14

Ballou, Maturin Murray 1820-1895.................DLB-79

Ballou, Robert O. [publishing house]................DLB-46

Bambara, Toni Cade 1939- DLB-38

Bancroft, A. L., and Company DLB-49

Bancroft, George 1800-1891 ....DLB-1, 30, 59

Bancroft, Hubert Howe 1832-1918 ....DLB-47

Bangs, John Kendrick 1862-1922.................DLB-11, 79

Banks, John circa 1653-1706 ....DLB-80

Bantam Books...DLB-46

Banville, John 1945- DLB-14

Baraka, Amiri 1934- DLB-5, 7, 16, 38

Barbeau, Marius 1883-1969.............................DLB-92

Barber, John Warner 1798-1885 ....DLB-30

Barbour, Ralph Henry 1870-1944.....................DLB-22

Barbusse, Henri 1873-1935.............................DLB-65

Barclay, E. E., and Company DLB-49

Bardeen, C. W. [publishing house]...................DLB-49

Baring, Maurice 1874-1945.............................DLB-34

Barker, A. L. 1918- DLB-14

Barker, George 1913- DLB-20

Barker, Harley Granville 1877-1946 ....DLB-10

Barker, Howard 1946- DLB-13

Barker, James Nelson 1784-1858.......................DLB-37

Barker, Jane 1652-1727?.................................DLB-39

Barks, Coleman 1937- DLB-5

Barlach, Ernst 1870-1938.................................DLB-56

Barlow, Joel 1754-1812 ....DLB-37

Barnard, John 1681-1770 ....DLB-24

Barnes, A. S., and Company............................DLB-49

Barnes, Djuna 1892-1982 ....DLB-4, 9, 45

Barnes, Margaret Ayer 1886-1967 ....DLB-9

Barnes, Peter 1931- DLB-13

Barnes, William 1801-1886..............................DLB-32

Barnes and Noble Books.................................DLB-46

Barney, Natalie 1876-1972..............................DLB-4

Baron, Richard W., Publishing Company DLB-46

Barr, Robert 1850-1912 ....DLB-70, 92

Barrax, Gerald William 1933- DLB-41

Barrie, James M. 1860-1937 ....DLB-10

Barrio, Raymond 1921- DLB-82

Barry, Philip 1896-1949.................................DLB-7

Barry, Robertine (see Françoise)

Barse and Hopkins...DLB-46

Barstow, Stan 1928- DLB-14

Barth, John 1930- DLB-2

Barthelme, Donald 1931-1989...................DLB-2; Y-80

Barthelme, Frederick 1943- Y-85

Bartlett, John 1820-1905.................................DLB-1

Bartol, Cyrus Augustus 1813-1900....................DLB-1

Bartram, John 1699-1777 ....DLB-31

Bartram, William 1739-1823.............................DLB-37

Basic Books...DLB-46

Bass, T. J. 1932- Y-81

Bassett, John Spencer 1867-1928 ....DLB-17

Bassler, Thomas Joseph (see Bass, T. J.)

Bate, Walter Jackson 1918- DLB-67

Bates, Katharine Lee 1859-1929.........................DLB-71

Baum, L. Frank 1856-1919..............................DLB-22

Baum, Vicki 1888-1960.................................DLB-85

Baumbach, Jonathan 1933- Y-80

Bawden, Nina 1925- DLB-14

Bax, Clifford 1886-1962...............................DLB-10

Bayer, Eleanor (see Perry, Eleanor)

Bayer, Konrad 1932-1964...............................DLB-85

Bazin, Hervé 1911- DLB-83

Beach, Sylvia 1887-1962...............................DLB-4

Beacon Press...DLB-49

Beadle and Adams.....................................DLB-49

Beagle, Peter S. 1939- Y-80

Beal, M. F. 1937- Y-81

Beale, Howard K. 1899-1959............................DLB-17

Beard, Charles A. 1874-1948...........................DLB-17

A Beat Chronology: The First Twenty-five
    Years, 1944-1969 ....DLB-16

Beattie, Ann 1947- Y-82

Beauchemin, Nérée 1850-1931..........................DLB-92

Beauchemin, Yves 1941- DLB-60

Beaulieu, Victor-Lévy 1945- DLB-53

Beaumont, Francis circa 1584-1616
    and Fletcher, John 1579-1625 ....DLB-58

Beauvoir, Simone de 1908-1986..............Y-86, DLB-72

Becher, Ulrich 1910- DLB-69

Becker, Carl 1873-1945................................DLB-17

Becker, Jurek 1937- DLB-75

Becker, Jürgen 1932- DLB-75

Beckett, Samuel 1906-1989.......................DLB-13, 15

Beckford, William 1760-1844...........................DLB-39

Beckham, Barry 1944- DLB-33

Beecher, Catharine Esther 1800-1878..................DLB-1

Beecher, Henry Ward 1813-1887..................DLB-3, 43

Beer, George L. 1872-1920.............................DLB-47

Beer, Patricia 1919- DLB-40

Beerbohm, Max 1872-1956...............................DLB-34

Beer-Hofmann, Richard 1866-1945.......................DLB-81

Beers, Henry A. 1847-1926 ....DLB-71

Behan, Brendan 1923-1964 ....DLB-13

Behn, Aphra 1640?-1689...........................DLB-39, 80

Behn, Harry 1898-1973 ....DLB-61

Behrman, S. N. 1893-1973 ....DLB-7, 44

Belaney, Archibald Stansfeld (see Grey Owl)

Belasco, David 1853-1931 ....DLB-7

Belford, Clarke and Company...........................DLB-49

Belitt, Ben 1911- DLB-5

Belknap, Jeremy 1744-1798.........................DLB-30, 37

Bell, James Madison 1826-1902.........................DLB-50

Bell, Marvin 1937- DLB-5

Bell, Robert [publishing house] DLB-49

Bellamy, Edward 1850-1898.............................DLB-12

Bellamy, Joseph 1719-1790.............................DLB-31

Belloc, Hilaire 1870-1953 ....DLB-19

Bellow, Saul 1915- DLB-2, 28; Y-82; DS-3

Belmont Productions..................................DLB-46

Bemelmans, Ludwig 1898-1962...........................DLB-22

Bemis, Samuel Flagg 1891-1973.........................DLB-17

Benchley, Robert 1889-1945............................DLB-11

Benedictus, David 1938- DLB-14

Benedikt, Michael 1935- DLB-5

Benét, Stephen Vincent 1898-1943.................DLB-4, 48

Benét, William Rose 1886-1950.........................DLB-45

Benford, Gregory 1941- Y-82

Benjamin, Park 1809-1864 ....DLB-3, 59, 73

Benn, Gottfried 1886-1956 ....DLB-56

Bennett, Arnold 1867-1931 ....DLB-10, 34

Bennett, Charles 1899- DLB-44

Bennett, Gwendolyn 1902- DLB-51

Bennett, Hal 1930- DLB-33

Bennett, James Gordon 1795-1872 ....DLB-43

Bennett, James Gordon, Jr. 1841-1918 ....DLB-23

Bennett, John 1865-1956 ....DLB-42

Benoit, Jacques 1941- DLB-60

Benson, Stella 1892-1933 ....DLB-36

Bentley, E. C. 1875-1956..............................DLB-70

Benton, Robert 1932- and Newman,
    David 1937- DLB-44

Benziger Brothers....................................DLB-49

Beresford, Anne 1929- DLB-40

Beresford-Howe, Constance 1922- DLB-88

Berford, R. G., Company..............................DLB-49

Berg, Stephen 1934- DLB-5

Bergengruen, Werner 1892-1964 ....DLB-56

Berger, John 1926- DLB-14

Berger, Meyer 1898-1959 ....DLB-29

Berger, Thomas 1924- DLB-2; Y-80

Berkeley, Anthony 1893-1971 ....DLB-77

Berkeley, George 1685-1753 ....DLB-31

The Berkley Publishing Corporation DLB-46

Bernal, Vicente J. 1888-1915 ....DLB-82

Bernanos, Georges 1888-1948 ....DLB-72

Bernard, Harry 1898-1979 ....DLB-92

Bernard, John 1756-1828 ....DLB-37

Bernhard, Thomas 1931-1989 ....DLB-85

Berrigan, Daniel 1921- DLB-5

Berrigan, Ted 1934-1983 ....DLB-5

Berry, Wendell 1934- DLB-5, 6

Berryman, John 1914-1972 ....DLB-48

Bersianik, Louky 1930- DLB-60

Berton, Pierre 1920- DLB-68

Bessette, Gerard 1920- DLB-53

Bessie, Alvah 1904-1985 ....DLB-26

Bester, Alfred 1913- DLB-8

The Bestseller Lists: An Assessment Y-84

Betjeman, John 1906-1984 ....DLB-20; Y-84

Betts, Doris 1932- Y-82

Beveridge, Albert J. 1862-1927 ....DLB-17

Beverley, Robert circa 1673-1722.................DLB-24, 30

Bibaud, Adèle 1854-1941..................................DLB-92

Bichsel, Peter 1935- DLB-75

Bickerstaff, Isaac John 1733-circa 1808 ....DLB-89

Biddle, Drexel [publishing house] DLB-49

Bidwell, Walter Hilliard 1798-1881 ....DLB-79

Bienek, Horst 1930- DLB-75

Bierbaum, Otto Julius 1865-1910 ....DLB-66

Bierce, Ambrose 1842-1914?......DLB-11, 12, 23, 71, 74

Bigelow, William F. 1879-1966 ....DLB-91

Biggle, Lloyd, Jr. 1923- DLB-8

Biglow, Hosea (see Lowell, James Russell)

Billings, Josh (see Shaw, Henry Wheeler)

Binding, Rudolf G. 1867-1938..........................DLB-66

Bingham, Caleb 1757-1817 ....DLB-42

Binyon, Laurence 1869-1943 ....DLB-19

Biographical Documents I...................................Y-84

Biographical Documents II Y-85

Bioren, John [publishing house]........................DLB-49

Bird, William 1888-1963 ....DLB-4

Birney, Earle 1904- DLB-88

Bishop, Elizabeth 1911-1979..............................DLB-5

Bishop, John Peale 1892-1944 ....DLB-4, 9, 45

Bissett, Bill 1939- DLB-53

Black, David (D. M.) 1941- DLB-40

Black, Walter J. [publishing house] DLB-46

Black, Winifred 1863-1936 ....DLB-25

The Black Arts Movement, by Larry Neal.........DLB-38

Black Theaters and Theater Organizations in
     America, 1961-1982: A Research List DLB-38

Black Theatre: A Forum [excerpts]....................DLB-38

Blackamore, Arthur 1679-? DLB-24, 39

Blackburn, Alexander L. 1929- Y-85

Blackburn, Paul 1926-1971 ....DLB-16; Y-81

Blackburn, Thomas 1916-1977..........................DLB-27

Blackmore, R. D. 1825-1900 ....DLB-18

Blackmur, R. P. 1904-1965 ....DLB-63

Blackwood, Caroline 1931- DLB-14

Blair, Eric Arthur (see Orwell, George)

Blair, Francis Preston 1791-1876......................DLB-43

Blair, James circa 1655-1743 ....DLB-24

Blair, John Durburrow 1759-1823 ....DLB-37

Blais, Marie-Claire 1939- DLB-53

Blaise, Clark 1940- DLB-53

Blake, Nicholas 1904-1972 ....DLB-77
     (see also Day Lewis, C.)

The Blakiston Company DLB-49

Blanchot, Maurice 1907- DLB-72

Bledsoe, Albert Taylor 1809-1877 ....DLB-3, 79

Blelock and Company DLB-49

Blish, James 1921-1975 ....DLB-8

Bliss, E., and E. White [publishing house] DLB-49

Bloch, Robert 1917- DLB-44

Block, Rudolph (see Lessing, Bruno)

Blondal, Patricia 1926-1959 ....DLB-88

Bloom, Harold 1930- DLB-67

Bloomer, Amelia 1818-1894 ....DLB-79

Blume, Judy 1938- DLB-52

Blunck, Hans Friedrich 1888-1961....................DLB-66

Blunden, Edmund 1896-1974...........................DLB-20

Blunt, Wilfrid Scawen 1840-1922......................DLB-19

Bly, Nellie (see Cochrane, Elizabeth)

Bly, Robert 1926- DLB-5

Boaden, James 1762-1839..................................DLB-89

The Bobbs-Merrill Company...........................DLB-46

Bobrowski, Johannes 1917-1965.....................DLB-75

Bodenheim, Maxwell 1892-1954 ....DLB-9, 45

Bodkin, M. McDonnell 1850-1933 ....DLB-70

Bodmershof, Imma von 1895-1982...................DLB-85

Bodsworth, Fred 1918- DLB-68

Boehm, Sydney 1908- DLB-44

Boer, Charles 1939- DLB-5

Bogan, Louise 1897-1970...................................DLB-45

Bogarde, Dirk 1921- DLB-14

Bok, Edward W. 1863-1930.............................DLB-91

Boland, Eavan 1944- DLB-40

Böll, Heinrich 1917-1985.........................Y-85, DLB-69

Bolling, Robert 1738-1775...............................DLB-31

Bolt, Carol 1941- DLB-60

Bolt, Robert 1924- DLB-13

Bolton, Herbert E. 1870-1953 ....DLB-17

Bonaventura..DLB-89

Bond, Edward 1934- DLB-13

Boni, Albert and Charles [publishing house].....DLB-46

Boni and Liveright DLB-46

Robert Bonner's Sons......................................DLB-49

Bontemps, Arna 1902-1973........................DLB-48, 51

The Book League of America DLB-46

Book Reviewing in America: I Y-87

Book Reviewing in America: II Y-88

Book Supply Company DLB-49

The Booker Prize
    Address by Anthony Thwaite, Chairman
      of the Booker Prize Judges
      Comments from Former Booker Prize
        Winners Y-86

Boorstin, Daniel J. 1914- DLB-17

Booth, Mary L. 1831-1889................................DLB-79

Booth, Philip 1925- Y-82

Booth, Wayne C. 1921- DLB-67

Borchardt, Rudolf 1877-1945...........................DLB-66

Borchert, Wolfgang 1921-1947.........................DLB-69

Borges, Jorge Luis 1899-1986..............................Y-86

Börne, Ludwig 1786-1837................................DLB-90

Borrow, George 1803-1881...........................DLB-21, 55

Bosco, Henri 1888-1976...................................DLB-72

Bosco, Monique 1927- DLB-53

Botta, Anne C. Lynch 1815-1891 ....DLB-3

Bottomley, Gordon 1874-1948...........................DLB-10

Bottoms, David 1949- Y-83

Bottrall, Ronald 1906- DLB-20

Boucher, Anthony 1911-1968............................DLB-8

Boucher, Jonathan 1738-1804 ....DLB-31

Boudreau, Daniel (see Coste, Donat)

Bourjaily, Vance Nye 1922- DLB-2

Bourne, Edward Gaylord 1860-1908.................DLB-47

Bourne, Randolph 1886-1918...........................DLB-63

Bousquet, Joë 1897-1950 ....DLB-72

Bova, Ben 1932- Y-81

Bove, Emmanuel 1898-1945 ....DLB-72

Bovard, Oliver K. 1872-1945............................DLB-25

Bowen, Elizabeth 1899-1973............................DLB-15

Bowen, Francis 1811-1890...........................DLB-1, 59

Bowen, John 1924- DLB-13

Bowen-Merrill Company...................................DLB-49

Bowering, George 1935- DLB-53

Bowers, Claude G. 1878-1958...........................DLB-17

Bowers, Edgar 1924- DLB-5

Bowles, Paul 1910- DLB-5, 6

Bowles, Samuel III 1826-1878...........................DLB-43

Bowman, Louise Morey 1882-1944 ....DLB-68

Boyd, James 1888-1944.....................................DLB-9

Boyd, John 1919- DLB-8

Boyd, Thomas 1898-1935 ....DLB-9

Boyesen, Hjalmar Hjorth 1848-1895 ....DLB-12, 71

Boyle, Kay 1902- DLB-4, 9, 48, 86

Boyle, Roger, Earl of Orrery
    1621-1679 ....DLB-80

Boyle, T. Coraghessan 1948- Y-86

Brackenbury, Alison 1953- DLB-40

Brackenridge, Hugh Henry 1748-1816........DLB-11, 37

Brackett, Charles 1892-1969 ....DLB-26

Brackett, Leigh 1915-1978 ....DLB-8, 26

Bradburn, John [publishing house] DLB-49

Bradbury, Malcolm 1932- DLB-14

Bradbury, Ray 1920- DLB-2, 8

Braddon, Mary Elizabeth 1835-1915...........DLB-18, 70

Bradford, Andrew 1686-1742......................DLB-43, 73

Bradford, Gamaliel 1863-1932.........................DLB-17

Bradford, John 1749-1830 ....DLB-43

Bradford, Roark 1896-1948 ....DLB-86

Bradford, William 1590-1657 ....DLB-24, 30

Bradford, William III 1719-1791 ....DLB-43, 73

Bradlaugh, Charles 1833-1891..........................DLB-57

Bradley, David 1950- DLB-33

Bradley, Ira, and Company...............................DLB-49

Bradley, J. W., and Company DLB-49

Bradley, Marion Zimmer 1930- DLB-8

Bradley, William Aspenwall 1878-1939...............DLB-4

Bradstreet, Anne 1612 or 1613-1672 ....DLB-24

Brady, Frederic A. [publishing house] DLB-49

Bragg, Melvyn 1939- DLB-14

Brainard, Charles H. [publishing house]...........DLB-49

Braine, John 1922-1986 ....DLB-15; Y-86

Braithwaite, William Stanley
    1878-1962 ....DLB-50, 54

Bramah, Ernest 1868-1942...............................DLB-70

Branagan, Thomas 1774-1843 ....DLB-37

Branch, William Blackwell 1927- DLB-76

Branden Press..DLB-46

Brault, Jacques 1933- DLB-53

Braun, Volker 1939- DLB-75

Brautigan, Richard 1935-1984 ....DLB-2, 5; Y-80, 84

Braxton, Joanne M. 1950- DLB-41

Bray, Thomas 1656-1730 ....DLB-24

Braziller, George [publishing house] DLB-46

The Bread Loaf Writers' Conference 1983.............Y-84

The Break-Up of the Novel (1922),
    by John Middleton Murry...........................DLB-36

Breasted, James Henry 1865-1935....................DLB-47

Brecht, Bertolt 1898-1956...................................DLB-56

Bredel, Willi 1901-1964....................................DLB-56

Bremser, Bonnie 1939- DLB-16

Bremser, Ray 1934- DLB-16

Brentano, Bernard von 1901-1964 ....DLB-56

Brentano, Clemens 1778-1842 ....DLB-90

Brentano's DLB-49

Brenton, Howard 1942- DLB-13

Breton, André 1896-1966 ....DLB-65

Brewer, Warren and Putnam...............................DLB-46

Brewster, Elizabeth 1922- DLB-60

Bridgers, Sue Ellen 1942- DLB-52

Bridges, Robert 1844-1930....................................DLB-19

Bridie, James 1888-1951....................................DLB-10

Briggs, Charles Frederick 1804-1877 ....DLB-3

Brighouse, Harold 1882-1958..........................DLB-10

Brimmer, B. J., Company DLB-46

Brinnin, John Malcolm 1916- DLB-48

Brisbane, Albert 1809-1890................................DLB-3

Brisbane, Arthur 1864-1936 ....DLB-25

Broadway Publishing Company DLB-46

Broch, Hermann 1886-1951 ....DLB-85

Brochu, André 1942- DLB-53

Brock, Edwin 1927- DLB-40

Brod, Max 1884-1968..DLB-81

Brodhead, John R. 1814-1873 ....DLB-30

Brome, Richard circa 1590-1652 ....DLB-58

Bromfield, Louis 1896-1956 ....DLB-4, 9, 86

Broner, E. M. 1930- DLB-28

Brontë, Anne 1820-1849....................................DLB-21

Brontë, Charlotte 1816-1855..............................DLB-21

Brontë, Emily 1818-1848 ....DLB-21, 32

Brooke, Frances 1724-1789................................DLB-39

Brooke, Henry 1703?-1783 ....DLB-39

Brooke, Rupert 1887-1915................................DLB-19

Brooker, Bertram 1888-1955 ....DLB-88

Brooke-Rose, Christine 1926- DLB-14

Brookner, Anita 1928- Y-87

Brooks, Charles Timothy 1813-1883....................DLB-1

Brooks, Cleanth 1906- DLB-63

Brooks, Gwendolyn 1917- DLB-5, 76

Brooks, Jeremy 1926- DLB-14

Brooks, Mel 1926- DLB-26

Brooks, Noah 1830-1903.................................DLB-42

Brooks, Richard 1912- DLB-44

Brooks, Van Wyck 1886-1963.................DLB-45, 63

Brophy, Brigid 1929- DLB-14

Brossard, Chandler 1922- DLB-16

Brossard, Nicole 1943- DLB-53

Brother Antoninus (see Everson, William)

Brougham, John 1810-1880.................................DLB-11

Broughton, James 1913- DLB-5

Broughton, Rhoda 1840-1920.................................DLB-18

Broun, Heywood 1888-1939.................................DLB-29

Brown, Alice 1856-1948 ....DLB-78

Brown, Bob 1886-1959.................................DLB-4, 45

Brown, Cecil 1943- DLB-33

Brown, Charles Brockden 1771-1810.....DLB-37, 59, 73

Brown, Christy 1932-1981.................................DLB-14

Brown, Dee 1908- Y-80

Browne, Francis Fisher 1843-1913 ....DLB-79

Brown, Frank London 1927-1962 ....DLB-76

Brown, Fredric 1906-1972 ....DLB-8

Brown, George Mackay 1921- DLB-14, 27

Brown, Harry 1917-1986 ....DLB-26

Brown, Marcia 1918- DLB-61

Brown, Margaret Wise 1910-1952 ....DLB-22

Brown, Morna Doris (see Ferrars, Elizabeth)

Brown, Oliver Madox 1855-1874.................................DLB-21

Brown, Sterling 1901-1989 ....DLB-48, 51, 63

Brown, T. E. 1830-1897.................................DLB-35

Brown, William Hill 1765-1793 ....DLB-37

Brown, William Wells 1814-1884.................DLB-3, 50

Browne, Charles Farrar 1834-1867.................................DLB-11

Browne, Michael Dennis 1940- DLB-40

Browne, Wynyard 1911-1964.................................DLB-13

Brownell, W. C. 1851-1928 ....DLB-71

Browning, Elizabeth Barrett 1806-1861 ....DLB-32

Browning, Robert 1812-1889.................................DLB-32

Brownjohn, Allan 1931- DLB-40

Brownson, Orestes Augustus
    1803-1876.................................DLB-1, 59, 73

Bruce, Charles 1906-1971 ....DLB-68

Bruce, Leo 1903-1979 ....DLB-77

Bruce, Philip Alexander 1856-1933.................................DLB-47

Bruce Humphries [publishing house] DLB-46

Bruce-Novoa, Juan 1944- DLB-82

Bruckman, Clyde 1894-1955.................................DLB-26

Brundage, John Herbert (see Herbert, John)

Bryant, William Cullen 1794-1878.................DLB-3, 43, 59

Buchan, John 1875-1940.................................DLB-34, 70

Buchanan, Robert 1841-1901 ....DLB-18, 35

Buchman, Sidney 1902-1975 ....DLB-26

Buck, Pearl S. 1892-1973 ....DLB-9

Buckingham, Joseph Tinker 1779-1861 and
    Buckingham, Edwin 1810-1833.................................DLB-73

Buckler, Ernest 1908-1984.................................DLB-68

Buckley, William F., Jr. 1925- Y-80

Buckminster, Joseph Stevens 1784-1812.................................DLB-37

Buckner, Robert 1906- DLB-26

Budd, Thomas ?-1698.................................DLB-24

Budrys, A. J. 1931- DLB-8

Buechner, Frederick 1926- Y-80

Buell, John 1927- DLB-53

Buffum, Job [publishing house].................................DLB-49

Bugnet, Georges 1879-1981.................................DLB-92

Bukowski, Charles 1920- DLB-5

Bullins, Ed 1935- DLB-7, 38

Bulwer-Lytton, Edward (also Edward Bulwer)
    1803-1873 ....DLB-21

Bumpus, Jerry 1937- Y-81

Bunce and Brother.................................DLB-49

Bunner, H. C. 1855-1896 ....DLB-78, 79

Bunting, Basil 1900-1985 ....DLB-20

Bunyan, John 1628-1688.................................DLB-39

Burch, Robert 1925- DLB-52

Burciaga, José Antonio 1940- DLB-82

Burgess, Anthony 1917- DLB-14

Burgess, Gelett 1866-1951 ....DLB-11

Burgess, John W. 1844-1931.................................DLB-47

Burgess, Thornton W. 1874-1965 ....DLB-22

Burgess, Stringer and Company.................................DLB-49

Burk, John Daly circa 1772-1808.................................DLB-37

Burke, Kenneth 1897- DLB-45, 63

Burlingame, Edward Livermore 1848-1922.......DLB-79

Burnett, Frances Hodgson 1849-1924...............DLB-42

Burnett, W. R. 1899-1982...................................DLB-9

Burney, Fanny 1752-1840...................................DLB-39

Burns, Alan 1929- DLB-14

Burns, John Horne 1916-1953..............................Y-85

Burnshaw, Stanley 1906- DLB-48

Burr, C. Chauncey 1815?-1883..........................DLB-79

Burroughs, Edgar Rice 1875-1950 ....DLB-8

Burroughs, John 1837-1921...............................DLB-64

Burroughs, Margaret T. G. 1917- DLB-41

Burroughs, William S., Jr. 1947-1981 ....DLB-16

Burroughs, William Seward 1914-
    ....DLB-2, 8, 16; Y-81

Burroway, Janet 1936- DLB-6

Burt, A. L., and Company DLB-49

Burt, Maxwell S. 1882-1954...............................DLB-86

Burton, Miles (see Rhode, John)

Burton, Richard F. 1821-1890 ....DLB-55

Burton, Virginia Lee 1909-1968........................DLB-22

Burton, William Evans 1804-1860.....................DLB-73

Busch, Frederick 1941- DLB-6

Busch, Niven 1903- DLB-44

Bussières, Arthur de 1877-1913 ....DLB-92

Butler, E. H., and Company DLB-49

Butler, Juan 1942-1981 ....DLB-53

Butler, Octavia E. 1947- DLB-33

Butler, Samuel 1835-1902........................DLB-18, 57

Butor, Michel 1926- DLB-83

Butterworth, Hezekiah 1839-1905.....................DLB-42

B. V. (see Thomson, James)

Byars, Betsy 1928- DLB-52

Byatt, A. S. 1936- DLB-14

Byles, Mather 1707-1788...................................DLB-24

Bynner, Witter 1881-1968.................................DLB-54

Byrd, William II 1674-1744 ....DLB-24

Byrne, John Keyes (see Leonard, Hugh)

C

Cabell, James Branch 1879-1958...................DLB-9, 78

Cable, George Washington 1844-1925 ....DLB-12, 74

Cahan, Abraham 1860-1951.....................DLB-9, 25, 28

Cain, George 1943- DLB-33

Caldwell, Ben 1937- DLB-38

Caldwell, Erskine 1903-1987 ....DLB-9, 86

Caldwell, H. M., Company................................DLB-49

Calhoun, John C. 1782-1850 ....DLB-3

Calisher, Hortense 1911- DLB-2

Callaghan, Morley 1903- DLB-68

Callaloo..Y-87

A Call to Letters and an Invitation
    to the Electric Chair,
    by Siegfried Mandel DLB-75

Calmer, Edgar 1907- DLB-4

Calverley, C. S. 1831-1884 ....DLB-35

Calvert, George Henry 1803-1889 ....DLB-1, 64

Cambridge Press...DLB-49

Cameron, Eleanor 1912- DLB-52

Camm, John 1718-1778 ....DLB-31

Campbell, Gabrielle Margaret Vere
    (see Shearing, Joseph)

Campbell, James Edwin 1867-1896 ....DLB-50

Campbell, John 1653-1728 ....DLB-43

Campbell, John W., Jr. 1910-1971 ....DLB-8

Campbell, Roy 1901-1957.................................DLB-20

Campbell, William Wilfred
    1858-1918 ....DLB-92

Campion, Thomas 1567-1620...........................DLB-58

Camus, Albert 1913-1960 ....DLB-72

Canby, Henry Seidel 1878-1961 ....DLB-91

Candelaria, Cordelia 1943- DLB-82

Candelaria, Nash 1928- DLB-82

Candour in English Fiction (1890),
    by Thomas Hardy DLB-18

Canetti, Elias 1905- DLB-85

Cannan, Gilbert 1884-1955...............................DLB-10

Cannell, Kathleen 1891-1974............................DLB-4

Cannell, Skipwith 1887-1957 ....DLB-45

Cantwell, Robert 1908-1978..............................DLB-9

Cape, Jonathan, and Harrison Smith
    [publishing house] DLB-46

Capen, Joseph 1658-1725 ....DLB-24

Capote, Truman 1924-1984.................DLB-2; Y-80, 84

Cardinal, Marie 1929- DLB-83

Carey, Henry circa 1687-1689-1743 ....DLB-84

Carey, M., and Company DLB-49

Carey, Mathew 1760-1839 ....DLB-37, 73

Carey and Hart...DLB-49

Carlell, Lodowick 1602-1675 ....DLB-58

Carleton, G. W. [publishing house] DLB-49

Carman, Bliss 1861-1929.....................................DLB-92

Carossa, Hans 1878-1956.....................................DLB-66

Carr, Emily 1871-1945 ....DLB-68

Carrier, Roch 1937- DLB-53

Carlyle, Jane Welsh 1801-1866 ....DLB-55

Carlyle, Thomas 1795-1881 ....DLB-55

Carpenter, Stephen Cullen ?-1820?....................DLB-73

Carroll, Gladys Hasty 1904- DLB-9

Carroll, John 1735-1815.......................................DLB-37

Carroll, Lewis 1832-1898 ....DLB-18

Carroll, Paul 1927- DLB-16

Carroll, Paul Vincent 1900-1968 ....DLB-10

Carroll and Graf Publishers DLB-46

Carruth, Hayden 1921- DLB-5

Carryl, Charles E. 1841-1920.............................DLB-42

Carswell, Catherine 1879-1946 ....DLB-36

Carter, Angela 1940- DLB-14

Carter, Henry (see Leslie, Frank)

Carter, Landon 1710-1778...................................DLB-31

Carter, Lin 1930- Y-81

Carter, Robert, and Brothers..............................DLB-49

Carter and Hendee...DLB-49

Caruthers, William Alexander 1802-1846...........DLB-3

Carver, Jonathan 1710-1780.................................DLB-31

Carver, Raymond 1938-1988 ....Y-84, 88

Cary, Joyce 1888-1957...DLB-15

Casey, Juanita 1925- DLB-14

Casey, Michael 1947- DLB-5

Cassady, Carolyn 1923- DLB-16

Cassady, Neal 1926-1968.....................................DLB-16

Cassell Publishing Company DLB-49

Cassill, R. V. 1919- DLB-6

Castlemon, Harry (see Fosdick, Charles Austin)

Caswall, Edward 1814-1878................................DLB-32

Cather, Willa 1873-1947.................DLB-9, 54, 78; DS-1

Catherwood, Mary Hartwell 1847-1902.............DLB-78

Catton, Bruce 1899-1978.....................................DLB-17

Causley, Charles 1917- DLB-27

Caute, David 1936- DLB-14

Cawein, Madison 1865-1914 ....DLB-54

The Caxton Printers, Limited...............................DLB-46

Cayrol, Jean 1911- DLB-83

Celan, Paul 1920-1970...DLB-69

Céline, Louis-Ferdinand 1894-1961....................DLB-72

Center for the Book Research Y-84

Centlivre, Susanna 1669?-1723 ....DLB-84

The Century Company DLB-49

Cervantes, Lorna Dee 1954- DLB-82

Chacón, Eusebio 1869-1948 ....DLB-82

Chacón, Felipe Maximiliano
    1873-?..DLB-82

Challans, Eileen Mary (see Renault, Mary)

Chalmers, George 1742-1825..............................DLB-30

Chamberlain, Samuel S. 1851-1916....................DLB-25

Chamberland, Paul 1939- DLB-60

Chamberlin, William Henry 1897-1969 ....DLB-29

Chambers, Charles Haddon 1860-1921 ....DLB-10

Chamisso, Albert von 1781-1838.........................DLB-90

Chandler, Harry 1864-1944.................................DLB-29

Chandler, Raymond 1888-1959 ....DS-6

Channing, Edward 1856-1931 ....DLB-17

Channing, Edward Tyrrell 1790-1856 ....DLB-1, 59

Channing, William Ellery 1780-1842 ....DLB-1, 59

Channing, William Ellery II 1817-1901 ....DLB-1

Channing, William Henry 1810-1884 ....DLB-1, 59

Chaplin, Charlie 1889-1977 ....DLB-44

Chapman, George 1559 or 1560-1634 ....DLB-62

Chappell, Fred 1936- DLB-6

Charbonneau, Jean 1875-1960 ....DLB-92

Charbonneau, Robert 1911-1967 ....DLB-68

Charles, Gerda 1914- DLB-14

Charles, William [publishing house]...................DLB-49

The Charles Wood Affair:
    A Playwright Revived Y-83

Charlotte Forten: Pages from her Diary............DLB-50

Charteris, Leslie 1907- DLB-77

Charyn, Jerome 1937- Y-83

Chase, Borden 1900-1971 ....DLB-26

Chase, Edna Woolman 1877-1957 ....DLB-91

Chase-Riboud, Barbara 1936- DLB-33

Chauncy, Charles 1705-1787 ....DLB-24

Chávez, Fray Angélico 1910- DLB-82

Chayefsky, Paddy 1923-1981................DLB-7, 44; Y-81

Cheever, Ezekiel 1615-1708................................DLB-24

Cheever, George Barrell 1807-1890..................DLB-59

Cheever, John 1912-1982 ....DLB-2; Y-80, 82

Cheever, Susan 1943- Y-82

Chelsea House DLB-46

Cheney, Ednah Dow (Littlehale) 1824-1904 ....DLB-1

Cherry, Kelly 1940 ....Y-83

Cherryh, C. J. 1942- Y-80

Chesnutt, Charles Waddell 1858-1932...DLB-12, 50, 78

Chester, George Randolph 1869-1924 ....DLB-78

Chesterton, G. K. 1874-1936............DLB-10, 19, 34, 70

Cheyney, Edward P. 1861-1947..........................DLB-47

Chicano History..DLB-82

Chicano Language..DLB-82

Child, Francis James 1825-1896 ....DLB-1, 64

Child, Lydia Maria 1802-1880........................DLB-1, 74

Child, Philip 1898-1978 ....DLB-68

Childers, Erskine 1870-1922................................DLB-70

Children's Book Awards and Prizes DLB-61

Childress, Alice 1920- DLB-7, 38

Childs, George W. 1829-1894............................DLB-23

Chilton Book Company....................................DLB-46

Chittenden, Hiram Martin 1858-1917..............DLB-47

Chivers, Thomas Holley 1809-1858 ....DLB-3

Chopin, Kate 1850-1904............................DLB-12, 78

Chopin, Rene 1885-1953....................................DLB-92

Choquette, Adrienne 1915-1973......................DLB-68

Choquette, Robert 1905- DLB-68

The Christian Publishing Company DLB-49

Christie, Agatha 1890-1976 ....DLB-13, 77

Church, Benjamin 1734-1778............................DLB-31

Church, Francis Pharcellus 1839-1906..............DLB-79

Church, William Conant 1836-1917..................DLB-79

Churchill, Caryl 1938- DLB-13

Ciardi, John 1916-1986............................DLB-5; Y-86

Cibber, Colley 1671-1757..................................DLB-84

City Lights Books DLB-46

Cixous, Hélène 1937- DLB-83

Clapper, Raymond 1892-1944 ....DLB-29

Clare, John 1793-1864 ....DLB-55

Clark, Alfred Alexander Gordon (see Hare, Cyril)

Clark, Ann Nolan 1896- DLB-52

Clark, C. M., Publishing Company....................DLB-46

Clark, Catherine Anthony 1892-1977 ....DLB-68

Clark, Charles Heber 1841-1915 ....DLB-11

Clark, Davis Wasgatt 1812-1871 ....DLB-79

Clark, Eleanor 1913- DLB-6

Clark, Lewis Gaylord 1808-1873 ....DLB-3, 64, 73

Clark, Walter Van Tilburg 1909-1971..................DLB-9

Clarke, Austin 1896-1974 ....DLB-10, 20

Clarke, Austin C. 1934- DLB-53

Clarke, Gillian 1937- DLB-40

Clarke, James Freeman 1810-1888................DLB-1, 59

Clarke, Rebecca Sophia 1833-1906..................DLB-42

Clarke, Robert, and Company DLB-49

Clausen, Andy 1943- DLB-16

Claxton, Remsen and Haffelfinger....................DLB-49

Clay, Cassius Marcellus 1810-1903 ....DLB-43

Cleary, Beverly 1916- DLB-52

Cleaver, Vera 1919-   and
    Cleaver, Bill 1920-1981..............................DLB-52

Cleland, John 1710-1789....................................DLB-39

Clemens, Samuel Langhorne
    1835-1910............................DLB-11, 12, 23, 64, 74

Clement, Hal 1922- DLB-8

Clemo, Jack 1916- DLB-27

Clifton, Lucille 1936- DLB-5, 41

Clode, Edward J. [publishing house]................DLB-46

Clough, Arthur Hugh 1819-1861......................DLB-32

Cloutier, Cécile 1930- DLB-60

Coates, Robert M. 1897-1973 ....DLB-4, 9

Coatsworth, Elizabeth 1893- DLB-22

Cobb, Jr., Charles E. 1943- DLB-41

Cobb, Frank I. 1869-1923 ....DLB-25

Cobb, Irvin S. 1876-1944........................DLB-11, 25, 86

Cobbett, William 1762-1835 ....DLB-43

Cochran, Thomas C. 1902- DLB-17

Cochrane, Elizabeth 1867-1922 ....DLB-25

Cockerill, John A. 1845-1896............................DLB-23

Cocteau, Jean 1889-1963..................................DLB-65

Coderre, Emile (see Jean Narrache)

Coffee, Lenore J. 1900?-1984 ....DLB-44

Coffin, Robert P. Tristram 1892-1955 ....DLB-45

Cogswell, Fred 1917- DLB-60

Cogswell, Mason Fitch 1761-1830 ....DLB-37

Cohen, Arthur A. 1928-1986............................DLB-28

Cohen, Leonard 1934- DLB-53

Cohen, Matt 1942- DLB-53

Colden, Cadwallader 1688-1776...................DLB-24, 30

Cole, Barry 1936- DLB-14

Colegate, Isabel 1931- DLB-14

Coleman, Emily Holmes 1899-1974 ....DLB-4

Coleridge, Mary 1861-1907...............................DLB-19

Colette 1873-1954...DLB-65

Colette, Sidonie Gabrielle (see Colette)

Collier, John 1901-1980 ....DLB-77

Collier, P. F. [publishing house] DLB-49

Collier, Robert J. 1876-1918.............................DLB-91

Collin and Small DLB-49

Collins, Isaac [publishing house] DLB-49

Collins, Mortimer 1827-1876.........................DLB-21, 35

Collins, Wilkie 1824-1889 ....DLB-18, 70

Collyer, Mary 1716?-1763? DLB-39

Colman, Benjamin 1673-1747............................DLB-24

Colman, George, the Elder
    1732-1794 ....DLB-89

Colman, George, the Younger
    1762-1836 ....DLB-89

Colman, S. [publishing house] DLB-49

Colombo, John Robert 1936- DLB-53

Colter, Cyrus 1910- DLB-33

Colum, Padraic 1881-1972 ....DLB-19

Colwin, Laurie 1944- Y-80

Comden, Betty 1919-   and Green,
    Adolph 1918- DLB-44

The Comic Tradition Continued
    [in the British Novel]..................................DLB-15

Commager, Henry Steele 1902- DLB-17

The Commercialization of the Image of
    Revolt, by Kenneth Rexroth DLB-16

Community and Commentators: Black
    Theatre and Its Critics DLB-38

Compton-Burnett, Ivy 1884?-1969 ....DLB-36

Conference on Modern Biography........................Y-85

Congreve, William 1670-1729 ....DLB-39, 84

Conkey, W. B., Company...................................DLB-49

Connell, Evan S., Jr. 1924- DLB-2; Y-81

Connelly, Marc 1890-1980........................DLB-7; Y-80

Connolly, James B. 1868-1957............................DLB-78

Connor, Ralph 1860-1937.................................DLB-92

Connor, Tony 1930- DLB-40

Conquest, Robert 1917- DLB-27

Conrad, John, and Company..............................DLB-49

Conrad, Joseph 1857-1924 ....DLB-10, 34

Conroy, Jack 1899- Y-81

Conroy, Pat 1945- DLB-6

The Consolidation of Opinion: Critical
    Responses to the Modernists DLB-36

Constantin-Weyer, Maurice
    1881-1964 ....DLB-92

Constantine, David 1944- DLB-40

Contempo Caravan: Kites in a Windstorm Y-85

A Contemporary Flourescence of Chicano
    Literature Y-84

The Continental Publishing Company DLB-49

A Conversation with Chaim Potok........................Y-84

Conversations with Publishers I: An Interview
    with Patrick O'Connor...............................Y-84

The Conversion of an Unpolitical Man,
    by W. H. Bruford DLB-66

Conway, Moncure Daniel 1832-1907...................DLB-1

Cook, David C., Publishing Company DLB-49

Cook, Ebenezer circa 1667-circa 1732................DLB-24

Cook, Michael 1933- DLB-53

Cooke, George Willis 1848-1923 ....DLB-71

Cooke, Increase, and Company DLB-49

Cooke, John Esten 1830-1886............................DLB-3

Cooke, Philip Pendleton 1816-1850 ....DLB-3, 59

Cooke, Rose Terry 1827-1892 ....DLB-12, 74

Coolbrith, Ina 1841-1928................................DLB-54

Coolidge, George [publishing house] DLB-49

Coolidge, Susan (see Woolsey, Sarah Chauncy)

Cooper, Giles 1918-1966................................DLB-13

Cooper, James Fenimore 1789-1851....................DLB-3

Cooper, Kent 1880-1965................................DLB-29

Coover, Robert 1932- DLB-2; Y-81

Copeland and Day...DLB-49

Coppel, Alfred 1921- Y-83

Coppola, Francis Ford 1939- DLB-44

Corcoran, Barbara 1911- DLB-52

Corelli, Marie 1855-1924................................DLB-34

Corle, Edwin 1906-1956.....................................Y-85

Corman, Cid 1924- DLB-5

Cormier, Robert 1925- DLB-52

Corn, Alfred 1943- Y-80

Cornish, Sam 1935- DLB-41

Cornwell, David John Moore
      (see le Carré, John)

Corpi, Lucha 1945- DLB-82

Corrington, John William 1932- DLB-6

Corrothers, James D. 1869-1917 ....DLB-50

Corso, Gregory 1930- DLB-5, 16

Cortez, Jayne 1936- DLB-41

Corvo, Baron (see Rolfe, Frederick William)

Cory, William Johnson 1823-1892....................DLB-35

Cosmopolitan Book Corporation....................DLB-46

Costain, Thomas B. 1885-1965.........................DLB-9

Coste, Donat 1912-1957.................................DLB-88

Cotter, Joseph Seamon, Sr.
      1861-1949 ....DLB-50

Cotter, Joseph Seamon, Jr.
      1895-1919 ....DLB-50

Cotton, John 1584-1652....................................DLB-24

Coulter, John 1888-1980................................DLB-68

Cournos, John 1881-1966 ....DLB-54

Coventry, Francis 1725-1754 ....DLB-39

Coverly, N. [publishing house] DLB-49

Covici-Friede...DLB-46

Coward, Noel 1899-1973 ....DLB-10

Coward, McCann and Geoghegan....................DLB-46

Cowles, Gardner 1861-1946............................DLB-29

Cowley, Hannah 1743-1809............................DLB-89

Cowley, Malcolm 1898-1989................DLB-4, 48; Y-81

Cox, A. B. (see Berkeley, Anthony)

Cox, Palmer 1840-1924 ....DLB-42

Coxe, Louis 1918- DLB-5

Coxe, Tench 1755-1824................................DLB-37

Cozzens, James Gould 1903-1978 ....DLB-9; Y-84; DS-2

Craddock, Charles Egbert (see Murfree, Mary N.)

Cradock, Thomas 1718-1770.........................DLB-31

Craig, Daniel H. 1811-1895 ....DLB-43

Craik, Dinah Maria 1826-1887 ....DLB-35

Cranch, Christopher Pearse 1813-1892.........DLB-1, 42

Crane, Hart 1899-1932....................................DLB-4, 48

Crane, R. S. 1886-1967 ....DLB-63

Crane, Stephen 1871-1900 ....DLB-12, 54, 78

Crapsey, Adelaide 1878-1914 ....DLB-54

Craven, Avery 1885-1980................................DLB-17

Crawford, Charles 1752-circa 1815 ....DLB-31

Crawford, F. Marion 1854-1909.......................DLB-71

Crawford, Isabel Valancy
      1850-1887 ....DLB-92

Crawley, Alan 1887-1975 ....DLB-68

Crayon, Geoffrey (see Irving, Washington)

Creasey, John 1908-1973 ....DLB-77

Creative Age Press...DLB-46

Creel, George 1876-1953 ....DLB-25

Creeley, Robert 1926- DLB-5, 16

Creelman, James 1859-1915 ....DLB-23

Cregan, David 1931- DLB-13

Creighton, Donald Grant 1902-1979................DLB-88

Crèvecoeur, Michel Guillaume Jean de
      1735-1813 ....DLB-37

Crews, Harry 1935- DLB-6

Crichton, Michael 1942- Y-81

A Crisis of Culture: The Changing Role
      of Religion in the New Republic DLB-37

Crispin, Edmund 1921-1978.........................DLB-87

Cristofer, Michael 1946- DLB-7

"The Critic as Artist" (1891), by Oscar Wilde....DLB-57

Criticism In Relation To Novels (1863),
     by G. H. Lewes DLB-21

Crockett, David (Davy) 1786-1836.................DLB-3, 11

Croft-Cooke, Rupert (see Bruce, Leo)

Crofts, Freeman Wills 1879-1957 ....DLB-77

Croly, Herbert 1869-1930.................................DLB-91

Croly, Jane Cunningham 1829-1901 ....DLB-23

Crosby, Caresse 1892-1970 ....DLB-48

Crosby, Caresse 1892-1970 and Crosby,
     Harry 1898-1929 ....DLB-4

Crosby, Harry 1898-1929.................................DLB-48

Crossley-Holland, Kevin 1941- DLB-40

Crothers, Rachel 1878-1958.............................DLB-7

Crowell, Thomas Y., Company.........................DLB-49

Crowley, John 1942- Y-82

Crowley, Mart 1935- DLB-7

Crown Publishers...DLB-46

Crowne, John 1641-1712 ....DLB-80

Crowninshield, Frank 1872-1947......................DLB-91

Croy, Homer 1883-1965 ....DLB-4

Crumley, James 1939- Y-84

Cruz, Victor Hernández 1949- DLB-41

Csokor, Franz Theodor 1885-1969 ....DLB-81

Cullen, Countee 1903-1946....................DLB-4, 48, 51

Culler, Jonathan D. 1944- DLB-67

The Cult of Biography
     Excerpts from the Second Folio Debate:
       "Biographies are generally a disease of
       English Literature"–Germaine Greer,
       Victoria Glendinning, Auberon Waugh,
       and Richard Holmes.....................................Y-86

Cumberland, Richard 1732-1811 ....DLB-89

Cummings, E. E. 1894-1962 ....DLB-4, 48

Cummings, Ray 1887-1957 ....DLB-8

Cummings and Hilliard DLB-49

Cummins, Maria Susanna 1827-1866 ....DLB-42

Cuney, Waring 1906-1976................................DLB-51

Cuney-Hare, Maude 1874-1936........................DLB-52

Cunningham, J. V. 1911- DLB-5

Cunningham, Peter F. [publishing house]..........DLB-49

Cuomo, George 1929- Y-80

Cupples and Leon DLB-46

Cupples, Upham and Company.........................DLB-49

Cuppy, Will 1884-1949 ....DLB-11

Currie, Mary Montgomerie Lamb Singleton,
     Lady Currie (see Fane, Violet)

Curti, Merle E. 1897- DLB-17

Curtis, Cyrus H. K. 1850-1933 ....DLB-91

Curtis, George William 1824-1892.................DLB-1, 43

D

D. M. Thomas: The Plagiarism Controversy Y-82

Dabit, Eugène 1898-1936..................................DLB-65

Daborne, Robert circa 1580-1628......................DLB-58

Daggett, Rollin M. 1831-1901...........................DLB-79

Dahlberg, Edward 1900-1977 ....DLB-48

Dale, Peter 1938- DLB-40

Dall, Caroline Wells (Healey) 1822-1912.............DLB-1

Dallas, E. S. 1828-1879.....................................DLB-55

The Dallas Theater Center DLB-7

D'Alton, Louis 1900-1951 ....DLB-10

Daly, T. A. 1871-1948......................................DLB-11

Damon, S. Foster 1893-1971 ....DLB-45

Damrell, William S. [publishing house]..............DLB-49

Dana, Charles A. 1819-1897 ....DLB-3, 23

Dana, Richard Henry, Jr. 1815-1882 ....DLB-1

Dandridge, Ray Garfield DLB-51

Dane, Clemence 1887-1965...............................DLB-10

Danforth, John 1660-1730 ....DLB-24

Danforth, Samuel I 1626-1674 ....DLB-24

Danforth, Samuel II 1666-1727........................DLB-24

Dangerous Years: London Theater,
     1939-1945 ....DLB-10

Daniel, John M. 1825-1865 ....DLB-43

Daniel, Samuel 1562 or 1563-1619....................DLB-62

Daniells, Roy 1902-1979...................................DLB-68

Daniels, Josephus 1862-1948 ....DLB-29

Danner, Margaret Esse 1915- DLB-41

Dantin, Louis 1865-1945..................................DLB-92

Darwin, Charles 1809-1882...............................DLB-57

Daryush, Elizabeth 1887-1977 ....DLB-20

Dashwood, Edmée Elizabeth Monica
de la Pasture (see Delafield, E. M.)

d'Aulaire, Edgar Parin 1898- and
d'Aulaire, Ingri 1904- DLB-22

Davenant, Sir William 1606-1668 ....DLB-58

Davenport, Robert ?-? DLB-58

Daves, Delmer 1904-1977 ....DLB-26

Davey, Frank 1940- DLB-53

Davidson, Avram 1923- DLB-8

Davidson, Donald 1893-1968 ....DLB-45

Davidson, John 1857-1909 ....DLB-19

Davidson, Lionel 1922- DLB-14

Davie, Donald 1922- DLB-27

Davies, Robertson 1913- DLB-68

Davies, Samuel 1723-1761 ....DLB-31

Davies, W. H. 1871-1940 ....DLB-19

Daviot, Gordon 1896?-1952 ....DLB-10
(see also Tey, Josephine)

Davis, Charles A. 1795-1867 ....DLB-11

Davis, Clyde Brion 1894-1962 ....DLB-9

Davis, Dick 1945- DLB-40

Davis, Frank Marshall 1905-? DLB-51

Davis, H. L. 1894-1960 ....DLB-9

Davis, John 1774-1854 ....DLB-37

Davis, Margaret Thomson 1926- DLB-14

Davis, Ossie 1917- DLB-7, 38

Davis, Rebecca Harding 1831-1910 ....DLB-74

Davis, Richard Harding 1864-1916 ....DLB-12,
23, 78, 79

Davis, Samuel Cole 1764-1809 ....DLB-37

Davison, Peter 1928- DLB-5

Davys, Mary 1674-1732 ....DLB-39

DAW Books DLB-46

Dawson, William 1704-1752 ....DLB-31

Day, Benjamin Henry 1810-1889 ....DLB-43

Day, Clarence 1874-1935 ....DLB-11

Day, Dorothy 1897-1980 ....DLB-29

Day, Frank Parker 1881-1950 ....DLB-92

Day, John circa 1574-circa 1640 ....DLB-62

Day, The John, Company DLB-46

Day Lewis, C. 1904-1972 ....DLB-15, 20
(see also Blake, Nicholas)

Day, Mahlon [publishing house] DLB-49

Day, Thomas 1748-1789 ....DLB-39

Deacon, William Arthur 1890-1977 ....DLB-68

Deal, Borden 1922-1985 ....DLB-6

de Angeli, Marguerite 1889-1987 ....DLB-22

De Bow, James Dunwoody Brownson
1820-1867 ....DLB-3, 79

de Bruyn, Günter 1926- DLB-75

de Camp, L. Sprague 1907- DLB-8

The Decay of Lying (1889),
by Oscar Wilde [excerpt] DLB-18

Dedication, *Ferdinand Count Fathom* (1753),
by Tobias Smollett DLB-39

Dedication, *Lasselia* (1723), by Eliza
Haywood [excerpt] DLB-39

Dedication, *The History of Pompey the
Little* (1751), by Francis Coventry DLB-39

Dedication, *The Wanderer* (1814),
by Fanny Burney DLB-39

Defense of *Amelia* (1752), by Henry Fielding DLB-39

Defoe, Daniel 1660-1731 ....DLB-39

de Fontaine, Felix Gregory 1834-1896 ....DLB-43

De Forest, John William 1826-1906 ....DLB-12

de Graff, Robert 1895-1981 ....Y-81

Deighton, Len 1929- DLB-87

DeJong, Meindert 1906- DLB-52

Dekker, Thomas circa 1572-1632 ....DLB-62

Delacorte, Jr., George T. 1894- DLB-91

Delafield, E. M. 1890-1943 ....DLB-34

Delahaye, Guy 1888-1969 ....DLB-92

de la Mare, Walter 1873-1956 ....DLB-19

Deland, Margaret 1857-1945 ....DLB-78

Delaney, Shelagh 1939- DLB-13

Delany, Martin Robinson 1812-1885 ....DLB-50

Delany, Samuel R. 1942- DLB-8, 33

de la Roche, Mazo 1879-1961 ....DLB-68

Delbanco, Nicholas 1942- DLB-6

De León, Nephtalí 1945- DLB-82

Delgado, Abelardo Barrientos 1931- DLB-82

DeLillo, Don 1936- DLB-6

Dell, Floyd 1887-1969 ....DLB-9

Dell Publishing Company ....DLB-46 delle Grazie, Marie Eugene 1864-1931 ....DLB-81

del Rey, Lester 1915- DLB-8

de Man, Paul 1919-1983 ....DLB-67

Demby, William 1922- DLB-33

Deming, Philander 1829-1915 ....DLB-74

Demorest, William Jennings 1822-1895 ....DLB-79

Denham, Sir John 1615-1669 ....DLB-58

Denison, Merrill 1893-1975 ....DLB-92

Denison, T. S., and Company DLB-49

Dennie, Joseph 1768-1812..............DLB-37, 43, 59, 73

Dennis, Nigel 1912-1989...................... DLB-13, 15

Dent, Tom 1932- DLB-38

Denton, Daniel circa 1626-1703........................DLB-24

DePaola, Tomie 1934- DLB-61

Derby, George Horatio 1823-1861 ....DLB-11

Derby, J. C., and Company..............................DLB-49

Derby and Miller DLB-49

Derleth, August 1909-1971 ....DLB-9

The Derrydale Press.......................................DLB-46

Desaulniers, Gonsalve 1863-1934 ....DLB-92

Desbiens, Jean-Paul 1927- DLB-53

des Forêts, Louis-René 1918- DLB-83

DesRochers, Alfred 1901-1978........................DLB-68

Desrosiers, Léo-Paul 1896-1967.......................DLB-68

Destouches, Louis-Ferdinand (see Céline,
      Louis-Ferdinand)

De Tabley, Lord 1835-1895 ....DLB-35

Deutsch, Babette 1895-1982 ....DLB-45

Deveaux, Alexis 1948- DLB-38

The Development of Lighting in the Staging
      of Drama, 1900-1945 [in Great Britain]......DLB-10

de Vere, Aubrey 1814-1902 ....DLB-35

The Devin-Adair Company..............................DLB-46

De Voto, Bernard 1897-1955 ....DLB-9

De Vries, Peter 1910- DLB-6; Y-82

Dewdney, Christopher 1951- DLB-60

Dewdney, Selwyn 1909-1979 ....DLB-68

DeWitt, Robert M., Publisher DLB-49

DeWolfe, Fiske and Company..........................DLB-49

Dexter, Colin 1930- DLB-87

de Young, M. H. 1849-1925............................DLB-25

The Dial Press...DLB-46

Diamond, I. A. L. 1920-1988 ....DLB-26

Di Cicco, Pier Giorgio 1949- DLB-60

Dick, Philip K. 1928- DLB-8

Dick and Fitzgerald DLB-49

Dickens, Charles 1812-1870....................DLB-21, 55, 70

Dickey, James 1923- DLB-5; Y-82; DS-7

Dickey, William 1928- DLB-5

Dickinson, Emily 1830-1886 ....DLB-1

Dickinson, John 1732-1808 ....DLB-31

Dickinson, Jonathan 1688-1747 ....,....................DLB-24

Dickinson, Patric 1914- DLB-27

Dickinson, Peter 1927- DLB-87

Dickson, Gordon R. 1923- DLB-8

Didion, Joan 1934- DLB-2; Y-81, 86

Di Donato, Pietro 1911- DLB-9

Dillard, Annie 1945- Y-80

Dillard, R. H. W. 1937- DLB-5

Dillingham, Charles T., Company.....................DLB-49

The G. W. Dillingham Company.......................DLB-49

Dintenfass, Mark 1941- Y-84

Diogenes, Jr. (see Brougham, John)

DiPrima, Diane 1934- DLB-5, 16

Disch, Thomas M. 1940- DLB-8

Disney, Walt 1901-1966....................................DLB-22

Disraeli, Benjamin 1804-1881.......................DLB-21, 55

Ditzen, Rudolf (see Fallada, Hans)

Dix, Dorothea Lynde 1802-1887 ....DLB-1

Dix, Dorothy (see Gilmer, Elizabeth Meriwether)

Dix, Edwards and Company DLB-49

Dixon, Paige (see Corcoran, Barbara)

Dixon, Richard Watson 1833-1900.....................DLB-19

Dobell, Sydney 1824-1874................................DLB-32

Döblin, Alfred 1878-1957 ....DLB-66

Dobson, Austin 1840-1921 ....DLB-35

Doctorow, E. L. 1931- DLB-2, 28; Y-80

Dodd, William E. 1869-1940 ....DLB-17

Dodd, Mead and Company...............................DLB-49

Doderer, Heimito von 1896-1968......................DLB-85

Dodge, B. W., and Company DLB-46

Dodge, Mary Mapes 1831?-1905 ....DLB-42, 79

Dodge Publishing Company DLB-49

Dodgson, Charles Lutwidge (see Carroll, Lewis)

Dodson, Owen 1914-1983 ....DLB-76

Doesticks, Q. K. Philander, P. B. (see Thomson, Mortimer)

Donahoe, Patrick [publishing house]..................DLB-49

Donald, David H. 1920- DLB-17

Donleavy, J. P. 1926- DLB-6

Donnadieu, Marguerite (see Duras, Marguerite)

Donnelley, R. R., and Sons Company DLB-49

Donnelly, Ignatius 1831-1901............................DLB-12

Donohue and Henneberry.................................DLB-49

Doolady, M. [publishing house]........................DLB-49

Dooley, Ebon (see Ebon)

Doolittle, Hilda 1886-1961...............................DLB-4, 45

Dor, Milo 1923- DLB-85

Doran, George H., Company............................DLB-46

Dorgelès, Roland 1886-1973 ....DLB-65

Dorn, Edward 1929- DLB-5

Dorr, Rheta Childe 1866-1948 ....DLB-25

Dorst, Tankred 1925- DLB-75

Dos Passos, John 1896-1970 ....DLB-4, 9; DS-1

Doubleday and Company...................................DLB-49

Dougall, Lily 1858-1923 ....DLB-92

Doughty, Charles M. 1843-1926....................DLB-19, 57

Douglas, Keith 1920-1944 ....DLB-27

Douglas, Norman 1868-1952 ....DLB-34

Douglass, Frederick 1817?-1895.........DLB-1, 43, 50, 79

Douglass, William circa 1691-1752.....................DLB-24

Dover Publications...DLB-46

Dowden, Edward 1843-1913..............................DLB-35

Downes, Gwladys 1915- DLB-88

Downing, J., Major (see Davis, Charles A.)

Downing, Major Jack (see Smith, Seba)

Dowson, Ernest 1867-1900................................DLB-19

Doxey, William [publishing house]....................DLB-49

Doyle, Sir Arthur Conan 1859-1930 ....DLB-18, 70

Doyle, Kirby 1932- DLB-16

Drabble, Margaret 1939- DLB-14

Drach, Albert 1902- DLB-85

The Dramatic Publishing Company DLB-49

Dramatists Play Service.....................................DLB-46

Draper, John W. 1811-1882...............................DLB-30

Draper, Lyman C. 1815-1891 ....DLB-30

Dreiser, Theodore 1871-1945 ....DLB-9, 12; DS-1

Drewitz, Ingeborg 1923-1986 ....DLB-75

Drieu La Rochelle, Pierre 1893-1945................DLB-72

Drinkwater, John 1882-1937 ....DLB-10, 19

The Drue Heinz Literature Prize
        Excerpt from "Excerpts from a Report
        of the Commission," in David
        Bosworth's *The Death of Descartes*
        An Interview with David Bosworth.................Y-82

Drummond, William Henry
        1854-1907 ....DLB-92

Dryden, John 1631-1700....................................DLB-80

Duane, William 1760-1835.................................DLB-43

Dubé, Marcel 1930- DLB-53

Dubé, Rodolphe (see Hertel, François)

Du Bois, W. E. B. 1868-1963.................DLB-47, 50, 91

Du Bois, William Pène 1916- DLB-61

Ducharme, Réjean 1941- DLB-60

Dudek, Louis 1918- DLB-88

Duell, Sloan and Pearce DLB-46

Duffield and Green DLB-46

Duffy, Maureen 1933- DLB-14

Dugan, Alan 1923- DLB-5

Dugas, Marcel 1883-1947...................................DLB-92

Duhamel, Georges 1884-1966...........................DLB-65

Dukes, Ashley 1885-1959 ....DLB-10

Dumas, Henry 1934-1968 ....DLB-41

Dunbar, Paul Laurence 1872-1906 ....DLB-50, 54, 78

Duncan, Norman 1871-1916..............................DLB-92

Duncan, Robert 1919-1988 ....DLB-5, 16

Duncan, Ronald 1914-1982................................DLB-13

Duncan, Sara Jeannette
        1861-1922 ....DLB-92

Dunigan, Edward, and Brother DLB-49

Dunlap, John 1747-1812 ....DLB-43

Dunlap, William 1766-1839....................DLB-30, 37, 59

Dunn, Douglas 1942- DLB-40

Dunne, Finley Peter 1867-1936 ....DLB-11, 23

Dunne, John Gregory 1932- Y-80

Dunne, Philip 1908- DLB-26

Dunning, Ralph Cheever 1878-1930 ....DLB-4

Dunning, William A. 1857-1922 ....DLB-17

Plunkett, Edward John Moreton Drax,
    Lord Dunsany 1878-1957 ....DLB-10, 77

Durand, Lucile (see Bersianik, Louky)

Duranty, Walter 1884-1957 ....DLB-29

Duras, Marguerite 1914- DLB-83

Durfey, Thomas 1653-1723 ....DLB-80

Durrell, Lawrence 1912- DLB-15, 27

Durrell, William [publishing house] DLB-49

Dürrenmatt, Friedrich 1921- DLB-69

Dutton, E. P., and Company DLB-49

Duvoisin, Roger 1904-1980 ....DLB-61

Duyckinck, Evert Augustus 1816-1878 ....DLB-3, 64

Duyckinck, George L. 1823-1863 ....DLB-3

Duyckinck and Company DLB-49

Dwight, John Sullivan 1813-1893 ....DLB-1

Dwight, Timothy 1752-1817 ....DLB-37

Dyer, Charles 1928- DLB-13

Dylan, Bob 1941- DLB-16

E

Eager, Edward 1911-1964 ....DLB-22

Earle, James H., and Company DLB-49

Early American Book Illustration,
    by Sinclair Hamilton DLB-49

Eastlake, William 1917- DLB-6

Eastman, Carol ?- DLB-44

Eastman, Max 1883-1969 ....DLB-91

Eberhart, Richard 1904- DLB-48

Ebner, Jeannie 1918- DLB-85

Ebner-Eschenbach, Marie von
    1830-1916 ....DLB-81

Ebon 1942- DLB-41

Ecco Press DLB-46

Edes, Benjamin 1732-1803 ....DLB-43

Edgar, David 1948- DLB-13

The Editor Publishing Company DLB-49

Edmonds, Randolph 1900- DLB-51

Edmonds, Walter D. 1903- DLB-9

Edschmid, Kasimir 1890-1966 ....DLB-56

Edwards, Jonathan 1703-1758 ....DLB-24

Edwards, Jonathan, Jr. 1745-1801 ....DLB-37

Edwards, Junius 1929- DLB-33

Edwards, Richard 1524-1566 ....DLB-62

Effinger, George Alec 1947- DLB-8

Eggleston, Edward 1837-1902 ....DLB-12

Eggleston, Wilfred 1901-1986 ....DLB-92

Ehrenstein, Albert 1886-1950 ....DLB-81

Eich, Günter 1907-1972 ....DLB-69

Eichendorff, Joseph Freiherr von
    1788-1857 ....DLB-90

1873 Publishers' Catalogues DLB-49

Eighteenth-Century Aesthetic Theories DLB-31

Eighteenth-Century Philosophical
    Background DLB-31

Eigner, Larry 1927- DLB-5

Eisenreich, Herbert 1925-1986 ....DLB-85

Eisner, Kurt 1867-1919 ....DLB-66

Eklund, Gordon 1945- Y-83

Elder, Lonne III 1931- DLB-7, 38, 44

Elder, Paul, and Company DLB-49

Elements of Rhetoric (1828; revised, 1846),
    by Richard Whately [excerpt] DLB-57

Elie, Robert 1915-1973 ....DLB-88

Eliot, George 1819-1880 ....DLB-21, 35, 55

Eliot, John 1604-1690 ....DLB-24

Eliot, T. S. 1888-1965 ....DLB-7, 10, 45, 63

Elizondo, Sergio 1930- DLB-82

Elkin, Stanley 1930- DLB-2, 28; Y-80

Elles, Dora Amy (see Wentworth, Patricia)

Ellet, Elizabeth F. 1818?-1877 ....DLB-30

Elliott, George 1923- DLB-68

Elliott, Janice 1931- DLB-14

Elliott, William 1788-1863 ....DLB-3

Elliott, Thomes and Talbot DLB-49

Ellis, Edward S. 1840-1916 ....DLB-42

The George H. Ellis Company DLB-49

Ellison, Harlan 1934- DLB-8

Ellison, Ralph 1914- DLB-2, 76

Ellmann, Richard 1918-1987 ....Y-87

The Elmer Holmes Bobst Awards
  in Arts and Letters Y-87

Emanuel, James Andrew 1921- DLB-41

Emerson, Ralph Waldo 1803-1882..........DLB-1, 59, 73

Emerson, William 1769-1811 ....DLB-37

Empson, William 1906-1984 ....DLB-20

The End of English Stage Censorship,
  1945-1968 ....DLB-13

Ende, Michael 1929- DLB-75

Engel, Marian 1933-1985 ....DLB-53

Engle, Paul 1908- DLB-48

English Composition and Rhetoric (1866),
  by Alexander Bain [excerpt].......................DLB-57

The English Renaissance of Art (1908),
  by Oscar Wilde DLB-35

Enright, D. J. 1920- DLB-27

Enright, Elizabeth 1909-1968 ....DLB-22

L'Envoi (1882), by Oscar Wilde DLB-35

Epps, Bernard 1936- DLB-53

Epstein, Julius 1909- and
  Epstein, Philip 1909-1952 ....DLB-26

Equiano, Olaudah circa 1745-1797 ....DLB-37, 50

Erichsen-Brown, Gwethalyn Graham
  (see Graham, Gwethalyn)

Ernst, Paul 1866-1933 ....DLB-66

Erskine, John 1879-1951....................................DLB-9

Ervine, St. John Greer 1883-1971 ....DLB-10

Eshleman, Clayton 1935- DLB-5

Ess Ess Publishing Company............................DLB-49

Essay on Chatterton (1842),
  by Robert Browning DLB-32

Estes, Eleanor 1906-1988 ....DLB-22

Estes and Lauriat..DLB-49

Etherege, George 1636-circa 1692.....................DLB-80

Ets, Marie Hall 1893- DLB-22

Eudora Welty: Eye of the Storyteller....................Y-87

Eugene O'Neill Memorial Theater Center...........DLB-7

Eugene O'Neill's Letters: A Review....................Y-88

Evans, Donald 1884-1921.................................DLB-54

Evans, George Henry 1805-1856.......................DLB-43

Evans, Hubert 1892-1986 ....DLB-92

Evans, M., and Company DLB-46

Evans, Mari 1923- DLB-41

Evans, Mary Ann (see Eliot, George)

Evans, Nathaniel 1742-1767..............................DLB-31

Evans, Sebastian 1830-1909 ....DLB-35

Everett, Alexander Hill 1790-1847....................DLB-59

Everett, Edward 1794-1865 ....DLB-1, 59

Everson, R. G. 1903- DLB-88

Everson, William 1912- DLB-5, 16

Every Man His Own Poet; or, The
  Inspired Singer's Recipe Book (1877),
  by W. H. Mallock DLB-35

Ewart, Gavin 1916- DLB-40

Ewing, Juliana Horatia 1841-1885....................DLB-21

Exley, Frederick 1929- Y-81

Experiment in the Novel (1929),
  by John D. Beresford DLB-36

F

"F. Scott Fitzgerald: St. Paul's Native Son
  and Distinguished American Writer":
  University of Minnesota Conference,
  29-31 October 1982..Y-82

Faber, Frederick William 1814-1863 ....DLB-32

Fair, Ronald L. 1932- DLB-33

Fairfax, Beatrice (see Manning, Marie)

Fairlie, Gerard 1899-1983 ....DLB-77

Fallada, Hans 1893-1947..................................DLB-56

Fancher, Betsy 1928- Y-83

Fane, Violet 1843-1905.....................................DLB-35

Fantasy Press Publishers DLB-46

Fante, John 1909-1983...Y-83

Farber, Norma 1909-1984.................................DLB-61

Farigoule, Louis (see Romains, Jules)

Farley, Walter 1920- DLB-22

Farmer, Philip José 1918- DLB-8

Farquhar, George circa 1677-1707 ....DLB-84

Farquharson, Martha (see Finley, Martha)

Farrar and Rinehart..DLB-46

Farrar, Straus and Giroux................................DLB-46

Farrell, James T. 1904-1979............DLB-4, 9, 86; DS-2

Farrell, J. G. 1935-1979......................................DLB-14

Fast, Howard 1914- DLB-9

Faulkner, William 1897-1962
....DLB-9, 11, 44; DS-2; Y-86

Fauset, Jessie Redmon 1882-1961......................DLB-51

Faust, Irvin 1924- DLB-2, 28; Y-80

Fawcett Books DLB-46

Fearing, Kenneth 1902-1961.............................DLB-9

Federal Writers' Project....................................DLB-46

Federman, Raymond 1928- Y-80

Feiffer, Jules 1929- DLB-7, 44

Feinberg, Charles E. 1899-1988.............................Y-88

Feinstein, Elaine 1930- DLB-14, 40

Fell, Frederick, Publishers.................................DLB-46

Fels, Ludwig 1946- DLB-75

Felton, Cornelius Conway 1807-1862 ....DLB-1

Fennario, David 1947- DLB-60

Fenno, John 1751-1798 ....DLB-43

Fenno, R. F., and Company DLB-49

Fenton, James 1949- DLB-40

Ferber, Edna 1885-1968 ....DLB-9, 28, 86

Ferdinand, Vallery III (see Salaam, Kalamu ya)

Ferguson, Sir Samuel 1810-1886 ....DLB-32

Ferguson, William Scott 1875-1954 ....DLB-47

Ferland, Albert 1872-1943 ....DLB-92

Ferlinghetti, Lawrence 1919- DLB-5, 16

Fern, Fanny (see Parton, Sara
    Payson Willis)

Ferrars, Elizabeth 1907- DLB-87

Ferret, E., and Company....................................DLB-49

Ferrini, Vincent 1913- DLB-48

Ferron, Jacques 1921-1985 ....DLB-60

Ferron, Madeleine 1922- DLB-53

Fetridge and Company..DLB-49

Feuchtwanger, Lion 1884-1958...........................DLB-66

Fichte, Johann Gottlieb 1762-1814.....................DLB-90

Ficke, Arthur Davison 1883-1945........................DLB-54

Fiction Best-Sellers, 1910-1945 ....DLB-9

Fiction into Film, 1928-1975: A List of Movies
    Based on the Works of Authors in
    British Novelists, 1930-1959 ....DLB-15

Fiedler, Leslie A. 1917- DLB-28, 67

Field, Eugene 1850-1895 ....DLB-23, 42

Field, Nathan 1587-1619 or 1620......................DLB-58

Field, Rachel 1894-1942.................................DLB-9, 22

A Field Guide to Recent Schools of
    American Poetry Y-86

Fielding, Henry 1707-1754 ....DLB-39, 84

Fielding, Sarah 1710-1768 ....DLB-39

Fields, James Thomas 1817-1881 ....DLB-1

Fields, Julia 1938- DLB-41

Fields, W. C. 1880-1946 ....DLB-44

Fields, Osgood and Company............................DLB-49

Fifty Penguin Years...Y-85

Figes, Eva 1932- DLB-14

Filson, John circa 1753-1788..............................DLB-37

Finch, Robert 1900- DLB-88

Findley, Timothy 1930- DLB-53

Finlay, Ian Hamilton 1925- DLB-40

Finley, Martha 1828-1909 ....DLB-42

Finney, Jack 1911- DLB-8

Finney, Walter Braden (see Finney, Jack)

Firbank, Ronald 1886-1926................................DLB-36

Firmin, Giles 1615-1697 ....DLB-24

First Strauss "Livings" Awarded to Cynthia
    Ozick and Raymond Carver
    An Interview with Cynthia Ozick
    An Interview with Raymond Carver Y-83

Fish, Stanley 1938- DLB-67

Fisher, Clay (see Allen, Henry W.)

Fisher, Dorothy Canfield 1879-1958 ....DLB-9

Fisher, Leonard Everett 1924- DLB-61

Fisher, Roy 1930- DLB-40

Fisher, Rudolph 1897-1934................................DLB-51

Fisher, Sydney George 1856-1927......................DLB-47

Fisher, Vardis 1895-1968.....................................DLB-9

Fiske, John 1608-1677 ....DLB-24

Fiske, John 1842-1901.....................................DLB-47, 64

Fitch, Thomas circa 1700-1774...........................DLB-31

Fitch, William Clyde 1865-1909...........................DLB-7

FitzGerald, Edward 1809-1883 ....DLB-32

Fitzgerald, F. Scott 1896-1940
....DLB-4, 9, 86; Y-81; DS-1

Fitzgerald, Penelope 1916- DLB-14

Fitzgerald, Robert 1910-1985...................................Y-80

Fitzgerald, Thomas 1819-1891 ....DLB-23

Fitzgerald, Zelda Sayre 1900-1948......................Y-84

Fitzhugh, Louise 1928-1974................................DLB-52

Fitzhugh, William circa 1651-1701.....................DLB-24

Flanagan, Thomas 1923- Y-80

Flanner, Hildegarde 1899-1987..........................DLB-48

Flanner, Janet 1892-1978...................................DLB-4

Flavin, Martin 1883-1967...................................DLB-9

Flecker, James Elroy 1884-1915 ....DLB-10, 19

Fleeson, Doris 1901-1970...................................DLB-29

Fleidser, Marieluise 1901-1974 ....DLB-56

Fleming, Ian 1908-1964 ....DLB-87

The Fleshly School of Poetry and Other
    Phenomena of the Day (1872), by Robert
    Buchanan DLB-35

The Fleshly School of Poetry: Mr. D. G.
    Rossetti (1871), by Thomas Maitland
    (Robert Buchanan) DLB-35

Fletcher, J. S. 1863-1935....................................DLB-70

Fletcher, John (see Beaumont, Francis)

Fletcher, John Gould 1886-1950 ....DLB-4, 45

Flieg, Helmut (see Heym, Stefan)

Flint, F. S. 1885-1960...DLB-19

Flint, Timothy 1780-1840 ....DLB-73

Follen, Eliza Lee (Cabot) 1787-1860....................DLB-1

Follett, Ken 1949- Y-81, DLB-87

Follett Publishing Company DLB-46

Folsom, John West [publishing house]................DLB-49

Foote, Horton 1916- DLB-26

Foote, Samuel 1721-1777 ....DLB-89

Foote, Shelby 1916- DLB-2, 17

Forbes, Calvin 1945- DLB-41

Forbes, Ester 1891-1967 ....DLB-22

Forbes and Company...DLB-49

Force, Peter 1790-1868.......................................DLB-30

Forché, Carolyn 1950-..DLB-5

Ford, Charles Henri 1913- DLB-4, 48

Ford, Corey 1902-1969..DLB-11

Ford, Ford Madox 1873-1939 ....DLB-34

Ford, J. B., and Company DLB-49

Ford, Jesse Hill 1928- DLB-6

Ford, John 1586-? DLB-58

Ford, R. A. D. 1915- DLB-88

Ford, Worthington C. 1858-1941 ....DLB-47

Fords, Howard, and Hulbert DLB-49

Foreman, Carl 1914-1984....................................DLB-26

Forester, Frank (see Herbert, Henry William)

Fornés, Maria Irene 1930- DLB-7

Forrest, Leon 1937- DLB-33

Forster, E. M. 1879-1970....................................DLB-34

Forsyth, Frederick 1938- DLB-87

Forten, Charlotte L. 1837-1914..........................DLB-50

Fortune, T. Thomas 1856-1928..........................DLB-23

Fosdick, Charles Austin 1842-1915.....................DLB-42

Foster, Genevieve 1893-1979..............................DLB-61

Foster, Hannah Webster 1758-1840....................DLB-37

Foster, John 1648-1681 ....DLB-24

Foster, Michael 1904-1956...................................DLB-9

Fouquë, Caroline de la Motte
    1774-1831 ....DLB-90

Fouqué, Friedrich de la Motte
    1777-1843 ....DLB-90

Four Essays on the Beat Generation,
    by John Clellon Holmes DLB-16

Four Seas Company...DLB-46

Four Winds Press..DLB-46

Fournier, Henri Alban (see Alain-Fournier)

Fowler and Wells Company.................................DLB-49

Fowles, John 1926- DLB-14

Fox, John, Jr. 1862 or 1863-1919 ....DLB-9

Fox, Paula 1923- DLB-52

Fox, Richard K. [publishing house] DLB-49

Fox, Richard Kyle 1846-1922..............................DLB-79

Fox, William Price 1926- DLB-2; Y-81

Fraenkel, Michael 1896-1957 ....DLB-4

France, Richard 1938- DLB-7

Francis, C. S. [publishing house] DLB-49

Francis, Convers 1795-1863..................................DLB-1

Francis, Dick 1920-...DLB-87

François 1863-1910..DLB-92

Francke, Kuno 1855-1930...................................DLB-71

Frank, Leonhard 1882-1961 ....DLB-56

Frank, Melvin (see Panama, Norman)

Frank, Waldo 1889-1967................................DLB-9, 63

Franken, Rose 1895?-1988 ....Y-84

Franklin, Benjamin 1706-1790.............DLB-24, 43, 73

Franklin, James 1697-1735 ....DLB-43

Franklin Library DLB-46

Frantz, Ralph Jules 1902-1979............................DLB-4

Fraser, G. S. 1915-1980.................................DLB-27

Frayn, Michael 1933- DLB-13, 14

Frederic, Harold 1856-1898 ....DLB-12, 23

Freeling, Nicolas 1927- DLB-87

Freeman, Douglas Southall 1886-1953...............DLB-17

Freeman, Legh Richmond 1842-1915 ....DLB-23

Freeman, Mary E. Wilkins 1852-1930.........DLB-12, 78

Freeman, R. Austin 1862-1943 ....DLB-70

French, Alice 1850-1934 ....DLB-74

French, David 1939- DLB-53

French, James [publishing house].......................DLB-49

French, Samuel [publishing house] DLB-49

Freneau, Philip 1752-1832.............................DLB-37, 43

Fried, Erich 1921-1988.................................DLB-85

Friedman, Bruce Jay 1930- DLB-2, 28

Friel, Brian 1929- DLB-13

Friend, Krebs 1895?-1967? DLB-4

Fries, Fritz Rudolf 1935- DLB-75

Fringe and Alternative Theater
    in Great Britain..DLB-13

Frisch, Max 1911- DLB-69

Frischmuth, Barbara 1941- DLB-85

Fritz, Jean 1915- DLB-52

Frost, Robert 1874-1963 ....DLB-54; DS-7

Frothingham, Octavius Brooks 1822-1895...........DLB-1

Froude, James Anthony 1818-1894.............DLB-18, 57

Fry, Christopher 1907- DLB-13

Frye, Northrop 1912- DLB-67, 68

Fuchs, Daniel 1909- DLB-9, 26, 28

The Fugitives and the Agrarians:
    The First Exhibition Y-85

Fuller, Charles H., Jr. 1939- DLB-38

Fuller, Henry Blake 1857-1929 ....DLB-12

Fuller, John 1937- DLB-40

Fuller, Roy 1912- DLB-15, 20

Fuller, Samuel 1912- DLB-26

Fuller, Sarah Margaret, Marchesa
    D'Ossoli 1810-1850 ....DLB-1, 59, 73

Fulton, Len 1934- Y-86

Fulton, Robin 1937- DLB-40

Furman, Laura 1945- Y-86

Furness, Horace Howard 1833-1912.................DLB-64

Furness, William Henry 1802-1896.....................DLB-1

Furthman, Jules 1888-1966.............................DLB-26

The Future of the Novel (1899),
    by Henry James....................................DLB-18

G

Gaddis, William 1922- DLB-2

Gág, Wanda 1893-1946.....................................DLB-22

Gagnon, Madeleine 1938- DLB-60

Gaine, Hugh 1726-1807.....................................DLB-43

Gaine, Hugh [publishing house].......................DLB-49

Gaines, Ernest J. 1933- DLB-2, 33; Y-80

Gaiser, Gerd 1908-1976 ....DLB-69

Galaxy Science Fiction Novels...........................DLB-46

Gale, Zona 1874-1938 ....DLB-9, 78

Gallagher, William Davis 1808-1894 ....DLB-73

Gallant, Mavis 1922- DLB-53

Gallico, Paul 1897-1976.....................................DLB-9

Galsworthy, John 1867-1933.....................DLB-10, 34

Galvin, Brendan 1938- DLB-5

Gambit...DLB-46

Gammer Gurton's Needle...................................DLB-62

Gannett, Frank E. 1876-1957...........................DLB-29

García, Lionel G. 1935- DLB-82

Gardam, Jane 1928- DLB-14

Garden, Alexander circa 1685-1756...................DLB-31

Gardner, John 1933-1982 ....DLB-2; Y-82

Garis, Howard R. 1873-1962 ....DLB-22

Garland, Hamlin 1860-1940.................DLB-12, 71, 78

Garneau, Hector de Saint-Denys 1912-1943......DLB-88

Garneau, Michel 1939- DLB-53

Garner, Hugh 1913-1979.................................DLB-68

Garnett, David 1892-1981 ....DLB-34

Garraty, John A. 1920- DLB-17

Garrett, George 1929- DLB-2, 5; Y-83

Garrick, David 1717-1779 ....DLB-84

Garrison, William Lloyd 1805-1879 ....DLB-1, 43

Garve, Andrew 1908- DLB-87

Gary, Romain 1914-1980 ....DLB-83

Gascoyne, David 1916- DLB-20

Gaskell, Elizabeth Cleghorn 1810-1865..............DLB-21

Gass, William Howard 1924- DLB-2

Gates, Doris 1901- DLB-22

Gates, Henry Louis, Jr. 1950- DLB-67

Gates, Lewis E. 1860-1924 ....DLB-71

Gauvreau, Claude 1925-1971.............................DLB-88

Gay, Ebenezer 1696-1787..................................DLB-24

Gay, John 1685-1732..DLB-84

The Gay Science (1866),
    by E. S. Dallas [excerpt] DLB-21

Gayarré, Charles E. A. 1805-1895 ....DLB-30

Gaylord, Charles [publishing house]..................DLB-49

Geddes, Gary 1940- DLB-60

Geddes, Virgil 1897- DLB-4

Geis, Bernard, Associates DLB-46

Geisel, Theodor Seuss 1904- DLB-61

Gelber, Jack 1932- DLB-7

Gélinas, Gratien 1909- DLB-88

Gellhorn, Martha 1908- Y-82

Gems, Pam 1925- DLB-13

A *General Idea of the College of Mirania* (1753),
    by William Smith [excerpts].........................DLB-31

Genet, Jean 1910-1986 ....Y-86, DLB-72

Genevoix, Maurice 1890-1980 ....DLB-65

Genovese, Eugene D. 1930- DLB-17

Gent, Peter 1942- Y-82

George, Henry 1839-1897...................................DLB-23

George, Jean Craighead 1919- DLB-52

Gerhardie, William 1895-1977............................DLB-36

Germanophilism, by Hans Kohn DLB-66

Gernsback, Hugo 1884-1967...............................DLB-8

Gerould, Katharine Fullerton 1879-1944...........DLB-78

Gerrish, Samuel [publishing house]...................DLB-49

Gerrold, David 1944- DLB-8

Geston, Mark S. 1946- DLB-8

Gibbon, John Murray 1875-1952.......................DLB-92

Gibbon, Lewis Grassic (see Mitchell, James Leslie)

Gibbons, Floyd 1887-1939 ....DLB-25

Gibbons, William ?-?...DLB-73

Gibson, Graeme 1934- DLB-53

Gibson, Wilfrid 1878-1962.................................DLB-19

Gibson, William 1914- DLB-7

Gide, André 1869-1951.....................................DLB-65

Giguère, Diane 1937- DLB-53

Giguère, Roland 1929- DLB-60

Gilbert, Anthony 1899-1973 ....DLB-77

Gilbert, Michael 1912- DLB-87

Gilder, Jeannette L. 1849-1916..........................DLB-79

Gilder, Richard Watson 1844-1909 ....DLB-64, 79

Gildersleeve, Basil 1831-1924 ....DLB-71

Giles, Henry 1809-1882 ....DLB-64

Gill, William F., Company DLB-49

Gillespie, A. Lincoln, Jr. 1895-1950 ....DLB-4

Gilliam, Florence ?-?...DLB-4

Gilliatt, Penelope 1932- DLB-14

Gillott, Jacky 1939-1980 ....DLB-14

Gilman, Caroline H. 1794-1888 ....DLB-3, 73

Gilman, W. and J. [publishing house]................DLB-49

Gilmer, Elizabeth Meriwether 1861-1951 ....DLB-29

Gilmer, Francis Walker 1790-1826 ....DLB-37

Gilroy, Frank D. 1925- DLB-7

Ginsberg, Allen 1926- DLB-5, 16

Ginzkey, Franz Karl 1871-1963 ....DLB-81

Giono, Jean 1895-1970......................................DLB-72

Giovanni, Nikki 1943- DLB-5, 41

Gipson, Lawrence Henry 1880-1971..................DLB-17

Girard, Rodolphe 1879-1956 ....DLB-92

Giraudoux, Jean 1882-1944 ....DLB-65

Gissing, George 1857-1903 ....DLB-18

Gladstone, William Ewart 1809-1898 ....DLB-57

Glaeser, Ernst 1902-1963 ....DLB-69

Glanville, Brian 1931- DLB-15

Glapthorne, Henry 1610-1643? DLB-58

Glasgow, Ellen 1873-1945 ....DLB-9, 12

Glaspell, Susan 1876-1948 ....DLB-7, 9, 78

Glass, Montague 1877-1934 ....DLB-11

Glassco, John 1909-1981 ....DLB-68

Glauser, Friedrich 1896-1938 ....DLB-56

F. Gleason's Publishing Hall DLB-49

Glück, Louise 1943- DLB-5

Godbout, Jacques 1933- DLB-53

Goddard, Morrill 1865-1937 ....DLB-25

Goddard, William 1740-1817 ....DLB-43

Godey, Louis A. 1804-1878 ....DLB-73

Godey and McMichael.........................DLB-49

Godfrey, Dave 1938- DLB-60

Godfrey, Thomas 1736-1763 ....DLB-31

Godine, David R., Publisher DLB-46

Godkin, E. L. 1831-1902......................DLB-79

Godwin, Gail 1937- DLB-6

Godwin, Parke 1816-1904.................DLB-3, 64

Godwin, William 1756-1836 ....DLB-39

Goes, Albrecht 1908- DLB-69

Goffe, Thomas circa 1592-1629...........DLB-58

Goffstein, M. B. 1940- DLB-61

Gogarty, Oliver St. John 1878-1957 ....DLB-15, 19

Goines, Donald 1937-1974...................DLB-33

Gold, Herbert 1924- DLB-2; Y-81

Gold, Michael 1893-1967 ....DLB-9, 28

Goldberg, Dick 1947- DLB-7

Golding, William 1911- DLB-15

Goldman, William 1931- DLB-44

Goldsmith, Oliver 1730?-1774 ....DLB-39, 89

Goldsmith Publishing Company DLB-46

Gomme, Laurence James
    [publishing house] DLB-46

González-T., César A. 1931- DLB-82

The Goodman Theatre.........................DLB-7

Goodrich, Frances 1891-1984 and
    Hackett, Albert 1900- DLB-26

Goodrich, S. G. [publishing house] DLB-49

Goodrich, Samuel Griswold 1793-1860 ...DLB-1, 42, 73

Goodspeed, C. E., and Company DLB-49

Goodwin, Stephen 1943- Y-82

Gookin, Daniel 1612-1687 ....DLB-24

Gordon, Caroline 1895-1981 ....DLB-4, 9; Y-81

Gordon, Giles 1940- DLB-14

Gordon, Mary 1949- DLB-6; Y-81

Gordone, Charles 1925- DLB-7

Gorey, Edward 1925- DLB-61

Görres, Joseph 1776-1848....................DLB-90

Gosse, Edmund 1849-1928...................DLB-57

Gotlieb, Phyllis 1926- DLB-88

Gould, Wallace 1882-1940 ....DLB-54

Goyen, William 1915-1983............DLB-2; Y-83

Gracq, Julien 1910- DLB-83

Grady, Henry W. 1850-1889................DLB-23

Graf, Oskar Maria 1894-1967..............DLB-56

Graham, George Rex 1813-1894 ....DLB-73

Graham, Gwethalyn 1913-1965 ....DLB-88

Graham, Lorenz 1902-1989 ....DLB-76

Graham, Shirley 1896-1977 ....DLB-76

Graham, W. S. 1918- DLB-20

Graham, William H. [publishing house] DLB-49

Graham, Winston 1910- DLB-77

Grahame, Kenneth 1859-1932..............DLB-34

Grainger, Martin Allerdale
    1874-1941 ....DLB-92

Gramatky, Hardie 1907-1979 ....DLB-22

Grandbois, Alain 1900-1975 ....DLB-92

Granich, Irwin (see Gold, Michael)

Grant, George 1918-1988....................DLB-88

Grant, Harry J. 1881-1963...................DLB-29

Grant, James Edward 1905-1966..........DLB-26

Grass, Günter 1927- DLB-75

Grasty, Charles H. 1863-1924..............DLB-25

Grau, Shirley Ann 1929- DLB-2

Graves, John 1920- Y-83

Graves, Richard 1715-1804..................DLB-39

Graves, Robert 1895-1985 ....DLB-20; Y-85

Gray, Asa 1810-1888 ....DLB-1

Gray, David 1838-1861.........................DLB-32

Gray, Simon 1936- DLB-13

Grayson, William J. 1788-1863.........DLB-3, 64

The Great War and the Theater, 1914-1918
    [Great Britain]..............................DLB-10

Greeley, Horace 1811-1872 ....DLB-3, 43

Green, Adolph (see Comden, Betty)

Green, Duff 1791-1875 ....DLB-43

Green, Gerald 1922- DLB-28

Green, Henry 1905-1973 ....DLB-15

Green, Jonas 1712-1767 ....DLB-31

Green, Joseph 1706-1780 ....DLB-31

Green, Julien 1900- DLB-4, 72

Green, Paul 1894-1981 ....DLB-7, 9; Y-81

Green, T. and S. [publishing house] DLB-49

Green, Timothy [publishing house] DLB-49

Greenberg: Publisher DLB-46

Green Tiger Press...........................DLB-46

Greene, Asa 1789-1838 ....DLB-11

Greene, Benjamin H. [publishing house]...........DLB-49

Greene, Graham 1904- DLB-13, 15, 77; Y-85

Greene, Robert 1558-1592 ....DLB-62

Greenhow, Robert 1800-1854 ....DLB-30

Greenough, Horatio 1805-1852 ....DLB-1

Greenwell, Dora 1821-1882 ....DLB-35

Greenwillow Books.........................DLB-46

Greenwood, Grace (see Lippincott, Sara Jane Clarke)

Greenwood, Walter 1903-1974 ....DLB-10

Greer, Ben 1948- DLB-6

Greg, W. R. 1809-1881.....................DLB-55

Gregg Press DLB-46

Persse, Isabella Augusta,
    Lady Gregory 1852-1932 ....DLB-10

Gregory, Horace 1898-1982.............DLB-48

Grenfell, Wilfred Thomason
    1865-1940 ....DLB-92

Greve, Felix Paul (see Grove, Frederick Philip)

Greville, Fulke, First Lord Brooke
    1554-1628 ....DLB-62

Grey, Zane 1872-1939.......................DLB-9

Grey Owl 1888-1938.........................DLB-92

Grier, Eldon 1917- DLB-88

Grieve, C. M. (see MacDiarmid, Hugh)

Griffith, Elizabeth 1727?-1793...........DLB-39, 89

Griffiths, Trevor 1935- DLB-13

Griggs, S. C., and Company...............DLB-49

Griggs, Sutton Elbert 1872-1930 ....DLB-50

Grignon, Claude-Henri 1894-1976.........DLB-68

Grigson, Geoffrey 1905- DLB-27

Grimké, Angelina Weld 1880-1958.........DLB-50, 54

Grimm, Hans 1875-1959.....................DLB-66

Grimm, Jacob 1785-1863 ....DLB-90

Grimm, Wilhelm 1786-1859 ....DLB-90

Griswold, Rufus Wilmot 1815-1857 ....DLB-3, 59

Gross, Milt 1895-1953......................DLB-11

Grosset and Dunlap........................DLB-49

Grossman Publishers DLB-46

Grosvenor, Gilbert H. 1875-1966.........DLB-91

Groulx, Lionel 1878-1967 ....DLB-68

Grove, Frederick Philip
    1879-1949 ....DLB-92

Grove Press DLB-46

Grubb, Davis 1919-1980....................DLB-6

Gruelle, Johnny 1880-1938................DLB-22

Guare, John 1938- DLB-7

Guest, Barbara 1920- DLB-5

Guèvremont, Germaine 1893-1968 ....DLB-68

Guilloux, Louis 1899-1980.................DLB-72

Guiney, Louise Imogen 1861-1920.........DLB-54

Guiterman, Arthur 1871-1943.............DLB-11

Günderrode, Caroline von
    1780-1806 ....DLB-90

Gunn, Bill 1934-1989.......................DLB-38

Gunn, James E. 1923- DLB-8

Gunn, Neil M. 1891-1973 ....DLB-15

Gunn, Thom 1929- DLB-27

Gunnars, Kristjana 1948- DLB-60

Gurik, Robert 1932- DLB-60

Gustafson, Ralph 1909- DLB-88

Gütersloh, Albert Paris 1887-1973 ....DLB-81

Guthrie, A. B., Jr. 1901- DLB-6

Guthrie, Ramon 1896-1973................DLB-4

The Guthrie Theater.........................DLB-7

Guy, Ray 1939- DLB-60

Guy, Rosa 1925- DLB-33

Gwynne, Erskine 1898-1948 ....DLB-4

Gysin, Brion 1916- DLB-16

H

H. D. (see Doolittle, Hilda)

Hackett, Albert (see Goodrich, Frances)

Hadden, Briton 1898-1929 ....DLB-91

Hagelstange, Rudolf 1912-1984.........................DLB-69

Haggard, H. Rider 1856-1925 ....DLB-70

Haig-Brown, Roderick 1908-1976 ....DLB-88

Hailey, Arthur 1920- DLB-88; Y-82

Haines, John 1924- DLB-5

Hake, Thomas Gordon 1809-1895 ....DLB-32

Haldeman, Joe 1943- DLB-8

Haldeman-Julius Company..............................DLB-46

Hale, E. J., and Son.....................................DLB-49

Hale, Edward Everett 1822-1909 ....DLB-1, 42, 74

Hale, Leo Thomas (see Ebon)

Hale, Lucretia Peabody 1820-1900.....................DLB-42

Hale, Nancy 1908-1988 ....DLB-86; Y-80, 88

Hale, Sarah Josepha (Buell) 1788-1879 ...DLB-1, 42, 73

Haley, Alex 1921- DLB-38

Haliburton, Thomas Chandler 1796-1865.........DLB-11

Hall, Donald 1928- DLB-5

Hall, James 1793-1868 ....DLB-73, 74

Hall, Samuel [publishing house]........................DLB-49

Hallam, Arthur Henry 1811-1833......................DLB-32

Halleck, Fitz-Greene 1790-1867 ....DLB-3

Hallmark Editions DLB-46

Halper, Albert 1904-1984 ....DLB-9

Halstead, Murat 1829-1908...............................DLB-23

Hamburger, Michael 1924- DLB-27

Hamilton, Alexander 1712-1756 ....DLB-31

Hamilton, Alexander 1755?-1804.......................DLB-37

Hamilton, Cicely 1872-1952.............................DLB-10

Hamilton, Edmond 1904-1977 ....DLB-8

Hamilton, Gail (see Corcoran, Barbara)

Hamilton, Ian 1938- DLB-40

Hamilton, Patrick 1904-1962............................DLB-10

Hamilton, Virginia 1936- DLB-33, 52

Hammett, Dashiell 1894-1961 ....DS-6

Hammon, Jupiter 1711-died between
    1790 and 1806....................................DLB-31, 50

Hammond, John ?-1663 ....DLB-24

Hamner, Earl 1923- DLB-6

Hampton, Christopher 1946- DLB-13

Handel-Mazzetti, Enrica von
    1871-1955 ....DLB-81

Handke, Peter 1942- DLB-85

Handlin, Oscar 1915- DLB-17

Hankin, St. John 1869-1909 ....DLB-10

Hanley, Clifford 1922- DLB-14

Hannah, Barry 1942- DLB-6

Hannay, James 1827-1873................................DLB-21

Hansberry, Lorraine 1930-1965 ....DLB-7, 38

Hapgood, Norman 1868-1937.........................DLB-91

Harcourt Brace Jovanovich DLB-46

Hardenberg, Friedrich von (see Novalis)

Hardwick, Elizabeth 1916- DLB-6

Hardy, Thomas 1840-1928.........................DLB-18, 19

Hare, Cyril 1900-1958....................................DLB-77

Hare, David 1947- DLB-13

Hargrove, Marion 1919- DLB-11

Harlow, Robert 1923- DLB-60

Harness, Charles L. 1915- DLB-8

Harper, Fletcher 1806-1877 ....DLB-79

Harper, Frances Ellen Watkins
    1825-1911 ....DLB-50

Harper, Michael S. 1938- DLB-41

Harper and Brothers.....................................DLB-49

Harris, Benjamin ?-circa 1720 ....DLB-42, 43

Harris, Christie 1907- DLB-88

Harris, George Washington 1814-1869..........DLB-3, 11

Harris, Joel Chandler 1848-1908................................
    DLB-11, 23, 42, 78, 91

Harris, Mark 1922- DLB-2; Y-80

Harrison, Charles Yale 1898-1954.....................DLB-68

Harrison, Frederic 1831-1923...........................DLB-57

Harrison, Harry 1925- DLB-8

Harrison, James P., Company...........................DLB-49

Harrison, Jim 1937- Y-82

Harrison, Paul Carter 1936- DLB-38

Harrison, Tony 1937- DLB-40

Harrisse, Henry 1829-1910..............................DLB-47

Harsent, David 1942- DLB-40

Hart, Albert Bushnell 1854-1943 ....DLB-17

Hart, Moss 1904-1961 ....DLB-7

Hart, Oliver 1723-1795 ....DLB-31

Harte, Bret 1836-1902 ....DLB-12, 64, 74, 79

Hartlaub, Felix 1913-1945.......................DLB-56

Hartley, L. P. 1895-1972.......................DLB-15

Hartley, Marsden 1877-1943 ....DLB-54

Härtling, Peter 1933- DLB-75

Hartman, Geoffrey H. 1929- DLB-67

Hartmann, Sadakichi 1867-1944 ....DLB-54

Harvey, Jean-Charles 1891-1967 ....DLB-88

Harwood, Lee 1939- DLB-40

Harwood, Ronald 1934- DLB-13

Haskins, Charles Homer 1870-1937.......................DLB-47

The Hatch-Billops Collection DLB-76

Hauff, Wilhelm 1802-1827 ....DLB-90

A Haughty and Proud Generation (1922),
    by Ford Madox Hueffer.......................DLB-36

Hauptmann, Carl 1858-1921 ....DLB-66

Hauptmann, Gerhart 1862-1946 ....DLB-66

Hauser, Marianne 1910- Y-83

Hawker, Robert Stephen 1803-1875 ....DLB-32

Hawkes, John 1925- DLB-2, 7; Y-80

Hawkins, Walter Everette 1883-?.......................DLB-50

Hawthorne, Nathaniel 1804-1864 ....DLB-1, 74

Hay, John 1838-1905 ....DLB-12, 47

Hayden, Robert 1913-1980.......................DLB-5, 76

Hayes, John Michael 1919- DLB-26

Hayne, Paul Hamilton 1830-1886.......................DLB-3, 64, 79

Haywood, Eliza 1693?-1756 ....DLB-39

Hazard, Willis P. [publishing house] DLB-49

Hazzard, Shirley 1931- Y-82

Headley, Joel T. 1813-1897 ....DLB-30

Heaney, Seamus 1939- DLB-40

Heard, Nathan C. 1936- DLB-33

Hearn, Lafcadio 1850-1904 ....DLB-12, 78

Hearst, William Randolph 1863-1951.......................DLB-25

Heath, Catherine 1924- DLB-14

Heath-Stubbs, John 1918- DLB-27

Hebel, Johann Peter 1760-1826.......................DLB-90

Hébert, Anne 1916- DLB-68

Hébert, Jacques 1923- DLB-53

Hecht, Anthony 1923- DLB-5

Hecht, Ben 1894-1964.......................DLB-7, 9, 25, 26, 28, 86

Hecker, Isaac Thomas 1819-1888 ....DLB-1

Hedge, Frederic Henry 1805-1890 ....DLB-1, 59

Hegel, Georg Wilhelm Friedrich
    1770-1831 ....DLB-90

Heidish, Marcy 1947- Y-82

Heine, Heinrich 1797-1856.......................DLB-90

Heinlein, Robert A. 1907- DLB-8

Heinrich, Willi 1920- DLB-75

Heidsenbüttel 1921- DLB-75

Heller, Joseph 1923- DLB-2, 28; Y-80

Hellman, Lillian 1906-1984.......................DLB-7; Y-84

Helprin, Mark 1947- Y-85

Helwig, David 1938- DLB-60

Hemingway, Ernest 1899-1961
    ....DLB-4, 9; Y-81, 87; DS-1

Hemingway: Twenty-Five Years Later Y-85

Hémon, Louis 1880-1913.......................DLB-92

Hemphill, Paul 1936- Y-87

Hénault, Gilles 1920- DLB-88

Henchman, Daniel 1689-1761 ....DLB-24

Henderson, Alice Corbin 1881-1949.......................DLB-54

Henderson, David 1942- DLB-41

Henderson, George Wylie 1904- DLB-51

Henderson, Zenna 1917- DLB-8

Henisch, Peter 1943- DLB-85

Henley, Beth 1952- Y-86

Henley, William Ernest 1849-1903.......................DLB-19

Henry, Buck 1930- DLB-26

Henry, Marguerite 1902- DLB-22

Henry, Robert Selph 1889-1970.......................DLB-17

Henry, Will (see Allen, Henry W.)

Henschke, Alfred (see Klabund)

Henty, G. A. 1832-1902 ....DLB-18

Hentz, Caroline Lee 1800-1856.......................DLB-3

Herbert, Alan Patrick 1890-1971 ....DLB-10

Herbert, Frank 1920-1986.......................DLB-8

Herbert, Henry William 1807-1858.......................DLB-3, 73

Herbert, John 1926- DLB-53

Herbst, Josephine 1892-1969 ....DLB-9

Herburger, Günter 1932- DLB-75

Hercules, Frank E. M. 1917- DLB-33

Herder, B., Book Company DLB-49

Hergesheimer, Joseph 1880-1954 ....DLB-9

Heritage Press DLB-46

Hermlin, Stephan 1915- DLB-69

Hernton, Calvin C. 1932- DLB-38

"The Hero as Man of Letters: Johnson,
    Rousseau, Burns" (1841), by Thomas
    Carlyle [excerpt] DLB-57

The Hero as Poet. Dante; Shakspeare (1841),
    by Thomas Carlyle DLB-32

Herrick, E. R., and Company DLB-49

Herrick, Robert 1868-1938 ....DLB-9, 12, 78

Herrick, William 1915- Y-83

Herrmann, John 1900-1959 ....DLB-4

Hersey, John 1914- DLB-6

Hertel, François 1905-1985 ....DLB-68

Hervé-Bazin, Jean Pierre Marie (see Bazin, Hervé)

Herzog, Emile Salomon Wilhelm (see Maurois, André)

Hesse, Hermann 1877-1962 ....DLB-66

Hewat, Alexander circa 1743-circa 1824 ....DLB-30

Hewitt, John 1907- DLB-27

Hewlett, Maurice 1861-1923 ....DLB-34

Heyen, William 1940- DLB-5

Heyer, Georgette 1902-1974 ....DLB-77

Heym, Stefan 1913- DLB-69

Heyward, Dorothy 1890-1961 and
    Heyward, DuBose 1885-1940 ....DLB-7

Heyward, DuBose 1885-1940 ....DLB-7, 9, 45

Heywood, Thomas 1573 or 1574-1641 ....DLB-62

Hickman, William Albert
    1877-1957 ....DLB-92

Hiebert, Paul 1892-1987 ....DLB-68

Higgins, Aidan 1927- DLB-14

Higgins, Colin 1941-1988 ....DLB-26

Higgins, George V. 1939- DLB-2; Y-81

Higginson, Thomas Wentworth
    1823-1911 ....DLB-1, 64

Highwater, Jamake 1942?- DLB-52; Y-85

Hildesheimer, Wolfgang 1916- DLB-69

Hildreth, Richard 1807-1865 ....DLB-1, 30, 59

Hill, Aaron 1685-1750 ....DLB-84

Hill, Geoffrey 1932- DLB-40

Hill, George M., Company DLB-49

Hill, "Sir" John 1714?-1775 ....DLB-39

Hill, Lawrence, and Company, Publishers DLB-46

Hill, Leslie 1880-1960 ....DLB-51

Hill, Susan 1942- DLB-14

Hill, Walter 1942- DLB-44

Hill and Wang DLB-46

Hilliard, Gray and Company DLB-49

Hillyer, Robert 1895-1961 ....DLB-54

Hilton, James 1900-1954 ....DLB-34, 77

Hilton and Company DLB-49

Himes, Chester 1909-1984 ....DLB-2, 76

Hine, Daryl 1936- DLB-60

Hinojosa-Smith, Rolando 1929- DLB-82

The History of the Adventures of Joseph Andrews
    (1742), by Henry Fielding [excerpt] DLB-39

Hirsch, E. D., Jr. 1928- DLB-67

Hoagland, Edward 1932- DLB-6

Hoagland, Everett H. III 1942- DLB-41

Hoban, Russell 1925- DLB-52

Hobsbaum, Philip 1932- DLB-40

Hobson, Laura Z. 1900- DLB-28

Hochman, Sandra 1936- DLB-5

Hodgins, Jack 1938- DLB-60

Hodgman, Helen 1945- DLB-14

Hodgson, Ralph 1871-1962 ....DLB-19

Hodgson, William Hope 1877-1918 ....DLB-70

Hoffenstein, Samuel 1890-1947 ....DLB-11

Hoffman, Charles Fenno 1806-1884 ....DLB-3

Hoffman, Daniel 1923- DLB-5

Hoffmann, E. T. A. 1776-1822 ....DLB-90

Hofmann, Michael 1957- DLB-40

Hofmannsthal, Hugo von 1874-1929 ....DLB-81

Hofstadter, Richard 1916-1970 ....DLB-17

Hogan, Desmond 1950- DLB-14

Hogan and Thompson DLB-49

Hohl, Ludwig 1904-1980 ....DLB-56

Holbrook, David 1923- DLB-14, 40

Holcroft, Thomas 1745-1809........................DLB-39, 89

Holden, Molly 1927-1981 ....DLB-40

Hölderlin, Friedrich 1770-1843 ....DLB-90

Holiday House DLB-46

Holland, Norman N. 1927- DLB-67

Hollander, John 1929- DLB-5

Holley, Marietta 1836-1926 ....DLB-11

Hollingsworth, Margaret 1940- DLB-60

Hollo, Anselm 1934- DLB-40

Holloway, John 1920- DLB-27

Holloway House Publishing Company DLB-46

Holme, Constance 1880-1955 ....DLB-34

Holmes, Oliver Wendell 1809-1894......................DLB-1

Holmes, John Clellon 1926-1988 ....DLB-16

Holst, Hermann E. von 1841-1904....................DLB-47

Holt, Henry, and Company DLB-49

Holt, John 1721-1784..DLB-43

Holt, Rinehart and Winston..............................DLB-46

Holthusen, Hans Egon 1913- DLB-69

Home, Henry, Lord Kames 1696-1782..............DLB-31

Home, John 1722-1808 ....DLB-84

Home Publishing Company DLB-49

Home, William Douglas 1912- DLB-13

Homes, Geoffrey (see Mainwaring, Daniel)

Honig, Edwin 1919- DLB-5

Hood, Hugh 1928- DLB-53

Hooker, Jeremy 1941- DLB-40

Hooker, Thomas 1586-1647 ....DLB-24

Hooper, Johnson Jones 1815-1862 ....DLB-3, 11

Hopkins, Gerard Manley 1844-1889............DLB-35, 57

Hopkins, John H., and Son DLB-46

Hopkins, Lemuel 1750-1801............................DLB-37

Hopkins, Pauline Elizabeth 1859-1930..............DLB-50

Hopkins, Samuel 1721-1803 ....DLB-31

Hopkinson, Francis 1737-1791 ....DLB-31

Horgan, Paul 1903- Y-85

Horizon Press..DLB-46

Horne, Frank 1899-1974....................................DLB-51

Horne, Richard Henry (Hengist) 1802
    or 1803-1884..DLB-32

Hornung, E. W. 1866-1921................................DLB-70

Horovitz, Israel 1939- DLB-7

Horton, George Moses 1797?-1883?..................DLB-50

Horváth, Ödön von 1901-1938........................DLB-85

Horwood, Harold 1923- DLB-60

Hosford, E. and E. [publishing house]..............DLB-49

Hotchkiss and Company DLB-49

Hough, Emerson 1857-1923..............................DLB-9

Houghton Mifflin Company DLB-49

Houghton, Stanley 1881-1913 ....DLB-10

Household, Geoffrey 1900-1988......................DLB-87

Housman, A. E. 1859-1936..............................DLB-19

Housman, Laurence 1865-1959......................DLB-10

Houwald, Ernst von 1778-1845 ....DLB-90

Hovey, Richard 1864-1900................................DLB-54

Howard, Maureen 1930- Y-83

Howard, Richard 1929- DLB-5

Howard, Roy W. 1883-1964..............................DLB-29

Howard, Sidney 1891-1939..........................DLB-7, 26

Howe, E. W. 1853-1937 ....DLB-12, 25

Howe, Henry 1816-1893 ....DLB-30

Howe, Irving 1920- DLB-67

Howe, Julia Ward 1819-1910............................DLB-1

Howell, Clark, Sr. 1863-1936..........................DLB-25

Howell, Evan P. 1839-1905..............................DLB-23

Howell, Soskin and Company..........................DLB-46

Howells, William Dean 1837-1920...DLB-12, 64, 74, 79

Hoyem, Andrew 1935- DLB-5

de Hoyos, Angela 1940- DLB-82

Hoyt, Henry [publishing house].......................DLB-49

Hubbard, Elbert 1856-1915 ....DLB-91

Hubbard, Kin 1868-1930 ....DLB-11

Hubbard, William circa 1621-1704....................DLB-24

Huber, Therese 1764-1829................................DLB-90

Huch, Friedrich 1873-1913..............................DLB-66

Huch, Ricarda 1864-1947 ....DLB-66

Huck at 100: How Old Is
    Huckleberry Finn?..............................Y-85

Hudson, Henry Norman 1814-1886 ....DLB-64

Hudson and Goodwin DLB-49

Huebsch, B. W. [publishing house]..................DLB-46

Hughes, David 1930- DLB-14

Hughes, John 1677-1720 ....DLB-84

Hughes, Langston 1902-1967 ....DLB-4, 7, 48, 51, 86

Hughes, Richard 1900-1976 ....DLB-15

Hughes, Ted 1930- DLB-40

Hughes, Thomas 1822-1896...............................DLB-18

Hugo, Richard 1923-1982.................................DLB-5

Hugo Awards and Nebula Awards......................DLB-8

Hull, Richard 1896-1973.................................DLB-77

Hulme, T. E. 1883-1917 ....DLB-19

Humboldt, Alexander von 1769-1859................DLB-90

Humboldt, Wilhelm von 1767-1835 ....DLB-90

Hume, Fergus 1859-1932.................................DLB-70

Humorous Book Illustration..............................DLB-11

Humphrey, William 1924- DLB-6

Humphreys, David 1752-1818...........................DLB-37

Humphreys, Emyr 1919- DLB-15

Huncke, Herbert 1915- DLB-16

Huneker, James Gibbons 1857-1921 ....DLB-71

Hunt, Irene 1907- DLB-52

Hunt, William Gibbes 1791-1833 ....DLB-73

Hunter, Evan 1926- Y-82

Hunter, Jim 1939- DLB-14

Hunter, Kristin 1931- DLB-33

Hunter, N. C. 1908-1971 ....DLB-10

Hurd and Houghton.......................................DLB-49

Hurst and Company..DLB-49

Hurst, Fannie 1889-1968.................................DLB-86

Hurston, Zora Neale 1901?-1960 ....DLB-51, 86

Huston, John 1906- DLB-26

Hutcheson, Francis 1694-1746...........................DLB-31

Hutchinson, Thomas 1711-1780 ....DLB-30, 31

Hutton, Richard Holt 1826-1897.......................DLB-57

Huxley, Aldous 1894-1963................................DLB-36

Huxley, Elspeth Josceline
    1907- DLB-77

Huxley, T. H. 1825-1895..................................DLB-57

Hyman, Trina Schart 1939- DLB-61

I

The Iconography of Science-Fiction Art..............DLB-8

Ignatow, David 1914- DLB-5

Iles, Francis (see Berkeley, Anthony)

Imbs, Bravig 1904-1946 ....DLB-4

Inchbald, Elizabeth 1753-1821 ....DLB-39, 89

Inge, William 1913-1973..................................DLB-7

Ingelow, Jean 1820-1897..................................DLB-35

The Ingersoll Prizes Y-84

Ingraham, Joseph Holt 1809-1860......................DLB-3

Inman, John 1805-1850 ....DLB-73

Innerhofer, Franz 1944- DLB-85

Innis, Harold Adams 1894-1952 ....DLB-88

Innis, Mary Quayle 1899-1972 ....DLB-88

International Publishers Company DLB-46

An Interview with Peter S. Prescott.......................Y-86

An Interview with Tom Jenks...............................Y-86

Introduction to Paul Laurence Dunbar,
    Lyrics of Lowly Life (1896),
    by William Dean Howells............................DLB-50

Introductory Essay: *Letters of Percy Bysshe
    Shelley* (1852), by Robert Browning DLB-32

Introductory Letters from the Second Edition
    of *Pamela* (1741), by Samuel Richardson.....DLB-39

Irving, John 1942- DLB-6; Y-82

Irving, Washington
    1783-1859 ....DLB-3, 11, 30, 59, 73, 74

Irwin, Grace 1907- DLB-68

Irwin, Will 1873-1948 ....DLB-25

Isherwood, Christopher 1904-1986..........DLB-15; Y-86

The Island Trees Case: A Symposium on School
        Library Censorship
    An Interview with Judith Krug
    An Interview with Phyllis Schlafly
    An Interview with Edward B. Jenkinson
    An Interview with Lamarr Mooneyham
    An Interview with Harriet Bernstein Y-82

Ivers, M. J., and Company................................DLB-49

J

Jackmon, Marvin E. (see Marvin X)

Jackson, Angela 1951- DLB-41

Jackson, Helen Hunt 1830-1885 ....DLB-42, 47

Jackson, Laura Riding 1901- DLB-48

Jackson, Shirley 1919-1965 ....DLB-6

Jacob, Piers Anthony Dillingham (see Anthony, Piers)

Jacobs, George W., and Company DLB-49

Jacobson, Dan 1929- DLB-14

Jahnn, Hans Henny 1894-1959 ....DLB-56

Jakes, John 1932- Y-83

James, Henry 1843-1916 ....DLB-12, 71, 74

James, John circa 1633-1729............................DLB-24

James Joyce Centenary: Dublin, 1982 ....Y-82

James Joyce Conference Y-85

James, P. D. 1920- DLB-87

James, U. P. [publishing house].........................DLB-49

Jameson, Fredric 1934- DLB-67

Jameson, J. Franklin 1859-1937 ....DLB-17

Jameson, Storm 1891-1986 ....DLB-36

Jarrell, Randall 1914-1965....................DLB-48, 52

Jasmin, Claude 1930- DLB-60

Jay, John 1745-1829 ....DLB-31

Jeffers, Lance 1919-1985 ....DLB-41

Jeffers, Robinson 1887-1962............................DLB-45

Jefferson, Thomas 1743-1826...........................DLB-31

Jelinek, Elfriede 1946- DLB-85

Jellicoe, Ann 1927- DLB-13

Jenkins, Robin 1912- DLB-14

Jenkins, William Fitzgerald (see Leinster, Murray)

Jennings, Elizabeth 1926- DLB-27

Jens, Walter 1923- DLB-69

Jensen, Merrill 1905-1980................................DLB-17

Jephson, Robert 1736-1803..............................DLB-89

Jerome, Jerome K. 1859-1927 ....DLB-10, 34

Jesse, F. Tennyson 1888-1958..........................DLB-77

Jewett, John P., and Company..........................DLB-49

Jewett, Sarah Orne 1849-1909.....................DLB-12, 74

The Jewish Publication Society DLB-49

Jewsbury, Geraldine 1812-1880 ....DLB-21

Joans, Ted 1928- DLB-16, 41

John Edward Bruce: Three Documents............DLB-50

John O'Hara's Pottsville Journalism.......................Y-88

John Steinbeck Research Center............................Y-85

John Webster: The Melbourne Manuscript............Y-86

Johnson, B. S. 1933-1973..............................DLB-14, 40

Johnson, Benjamin [publishing house]...............DLB-49

Johnson, Benjamin, Jacob, and
     Robert [publishing house]...........................DLB-49

Johnson, Charles 1679-1748 ....DLB-84

Johnson, Charles R. 1948- DLB-33

Johnson, Charles S. 1893-1956....................DLB-51, 91

Johnson, Diane 1934- Y-80

Johnson, Edward 1598-1672............................DLB-24

Johnson, Fenton 1888-1958 ....DLB-45, 50

Johnson, Georgia Douglas 1886-1966 ....DLB-51

Johnson, Gerald W. 1890-1980.........................DLB-29

Johnson, Helene 1907- DLB-51

Johnson, Jacob, and Company...........................DLB-49

Johnson, James Weldon 1871-1938 ....DLB-51

Johnson, Lionel 1867-1902 ....DLB-19

Johnson, Nunnally 1897-1977 ....DLB-26

Johnson, Owen 1878-1952 ....Y-87

Johnson, Pamela Hansford 1912- DLB-15

Johnson, Pauline 1861-1913 ....DLB-92

Johnson, Samuel 1696-1772.............................DLB-24

Johnson, Samuel 1709-1784.............................DLB-39

Johnson, Samuel 1822-1882.............................DLB-1

Johnson, Uwe 1934-1984 ....DLB-75

Johnston, Annie Fellows 1863-1931...................DLB-42

Johnston, Basil H. 1929- DLB-60

Johnston, Denis 1901-1984 ....DLB-10

Johnston, George 1913- DLB-88

Johnston, Jennifer 1930- DLB-14

Johnston, Mary 1870-1936...............................DLB-9

Johnston, Richard Malcolm 1822-1898 ....DLB-74

Johnstone, Charles 1719?-1800? DLB-39

Jolas, Eugene 1894-1952................................DLB-4, 45

Jones, Alice C. 1853-1933 ....DLB-92

Jones, Charles C., Jr. 1831-1893......................DLB-30

Jones, D. G. 1929- DLB-53

Jones, David 1895-1974....................................DLB-20

Jones, Ebenezer 1820-1860 ....DLB-32

Jones, Ernest 1819-1868...................................DLB-32

Jones, Gayl 1949- DLB-33

Jones, Glyn 1905- DLB-15

Jones, Gwyn 1907- DLB-15

Jones, Henry Arthur 1851-1929 ....DLB-10

Jones, Hugh circa 1692-1760 ....DLB-24

Jones, James 1921-1977.....................................DLB-2

Jones, LeRoi (see Baraka, Amiri)

Jones, Lewis 1897-1939 ....DLB-15

Jones, Major Joseph (see Thompson, William Tappan)

Jones, Preston 1936-1979...................................DLB-7

Jones, William Alfred 1817-1900 ....DLB-59

Jones's Publishing House DLB-49

Jong, Erica 1942- DLB-2, 5, 28

Jonke, Gert F. 1946- DLB-85

Jonson, Ben 1572?-1637...................................DLB-62

Jordan, June 1936- DLB-38

Joseph, Jenny 1932- DLB-40

Josephson, Matthew 1899-1978 ....DLB-4

Josiah Allen's Wife (see Holley, Marietta)

Josipovici, Gabriel 1940- DLB-14

Josselyn, John ?-1675.......................................DLB-24

Joudry, Patricia 1921- DLB-88

Joyaux, Philippe (see Sollers, Philippe)

Joyce, Adrien (see Eastman, Carol)

Joyce, James 1882-1941 ....DLB-10, 19, 36

Judd, Orange, Publishing Company..................DLB-49

Judd, Sylvester 1813-1853...................................DLB-1

June, Jennie (see Croly, Jane Cunningham)

Jünger, Ernst 1895- DLB-56

Justice, Donald 1925- Y-83

K

Kacew, Romain (see Gary, Romain)

Kafka, Franz 1883-1924 ....DLB-81

Kalechofsky, Roberta 1931- DLB-28

Kaler, James Otis 1848-1912...........................DLB-12

Kandel, Lenore 1932-.......................................DLB-16

Kanin, Garson 1912- DLB-7

Kant, Hermann 1926-.......................................DLB-75

Kantor, Mackinlay 1904-1977 ....DLB-9

Kaplan, Johanna 1942- DLB-28

Kasack, Hermann 1896-1966...........................DLB-69

Kaschnitz, Marie Luise 1901-1974.....................DLB-69

Kästner, Erich 1899-1974.................................DLB-56

Kattan, Naim 1928- DLB-53

Katz, Steve 1935- Y-83

Kauffman, Janet 1945- Y-86

Kaufman, Bob 1925- DLB-16, 41

Kaufman, George S. 1889-1961.........................DLB-7

Kavanagh, Patrick 1904-1967 ....DLB-15, 20

Kavanagh, P. J. 1931- DLB-40

Kaye-Smith, Sheila 1887-1956 ....DLB-36

Kazin, Alfred 1915- DLB-67

Keane, John B. 1928- DLB-13

Keating, H. R. F. 1926- DLB-87

Keats, Ezra Jack 1916-1983.............................DLB-61

Keble, John 1792-1866................................DLB-32, 55

Keeble, John 1944- Y-83

Keeffe, Barrie 1945- DLB-13

Keeley, James 1867-1934 ....DLB-25

W. B. Keen, Cooke and Company.....................DLB-49

Keillor, Garrison 1942- Y-87

Keith, Marian 1874?-1961................................DLB-92

Keller, Gary D. 1943- DLB-82

Kelley, Edith Summers 1884-1956 ....DLB-9

Kelley, William Melvin 1937- DLB-33

Kellogg, Ansel Nash 1832-1886........................DLB-23

Kellogg, Steven 1941- DLB-61

Kelly, George 1887-1974....................................DLB-7

Kelly, Hugh 1739-1777 ....DLB-89

Kelly, Piet and Company DLB-49

Kelly, Robert 1935- DLB-5

Kemble, Fanny 1809-1893................................DLB-32

Kemelman, Harry 1908- DLB-28

Kempowski, Walter 1929- DLB-75

Kendall, Claude [publishing company] DLB-46

Kendell, George 1809-1867 ....DLB-43

Kenedy, P. J., and Sons.....................................DLB-49

Kennedy, Adrienne 1931- DLB-38

Kennedy, John Pendleton 1795-1870...................DLB-3

Kennedy, Leo 1907- DLB-88

Kennedy, Margaret 1896-1967 ....DLB-36

Kennedy, William 1928- Y-85

Kennedy, X. J. 1929- DLB-5

Kennelly, Brendan 1936- DLB-40

Kenner, Hugh 1923- DLB-67

Kennerley, Mitchell [publishing house].............DLB-46

Kent, Frank R. 1877-1958................................DLB-29

Keppler and Schwartzmann............................DLB-49

Kerner, Justinus 1776-1862 ....DLB-90

Kerouac, Jack 1922-1969.....................DLB-2, 16; DS-3

Kerouac, Jan 1952- DLB-16

Kerr, Charles H., and Company.......................DLB-49

Kerr, Orpheus C. (see Newell, Robert Henry)

Kesey, Ken 1935- DLB-2, 16

Kessel, Joseph 1898-1979.................................DLB-72

Kessel, Martin 1901- DLB-56

Kesten, Hermann 1900- DLB-56

Keun, Irmgard 1905-1982.................................DLB-69

Key and Biddle...DLB-49

Keyserling, Eduard von 1855-1918 ....DLB-66

Kiely, Benedict 1919- DLB-15

Kiggins and Kellogg..DLB-49

Kiley, Jed 1889-1962 ....DLB-4

Killens, John Oliver 1916- DLB-33

Killigrew, Thomas 1612-1683............................DLB-58

Kilmer, Joyce 1886-1918..................................DLB-45

King, Clarence 1842-1901 ....DLB-12

King, Florence 1936 ....Y-85

King, Francis 1923- DLB-15

King, Grace 1852-1932 ....DLB-12, 78

King, Solomon [publishing house]....................DLB-49

King, Stephen 1947- Y-80

King, Woodie, Jr. 1937- DLB-38

Kinglake, Alexander William 1809-1891............DLB-55

Kingsley, Charles 1819-1875.....................DLB-21, 32

Kingsley, Henry 1830-1876..............................DLB-21

Kingsley, Sidney 1906- DLB-7

Kingston, Maxine Hong 1940- Y-80

Kinnell, Galway 1927- DLB-5; Y-87

Kinsella, Thomas 1928- DLB-27

Kipling, Rudyard 1865-1936 ....DLB-19, 34

Kirk, John Foster 1824-1904..............................DLB-79

Kirkconnell, Watson 1895-1977.........................DLB-68

Kirkland, Caroline M. 1801-1864 ....DLB-3, 73, 74

Kirkland, Joseph 1830-1893 ....DLB-12

Kirkup, James 1918- DLB-27

Kirouac, Conrad (see Marie-Victorin, Frère)

Kirsch, Sarah 1935- DLB-75

Kirst, Hans Hellmut 1914-1989.........................DLB-69

Kitchin, C. H. B. 1895-1967 ....DLB-77

Kizer, Carolyn 1925- DLB-5

Klabund 1890-1928 ....DLB-66

Klappert, Peter 1942- DLB-5

Klass, Philip (see Tenn, William)

Klein, A. M. 1909-1972....................................DLB-68

Kleist, Heinrich von 1777-1811 ....DLB-90

Kluge, Alexander 1932- DLB-75

Knapp, Joseph Palmer 1864-1951 ....DLB-91

Knapp, Samuel Lorenzo 1783-1838 ....DLB-59

Knickerbocker, Diedrich (see Irving, Washington)

Knight, Damon 1922- DLB-8

Knight, Etheridge 1931- DLB-41

Knight, John S. 1894-1981................................DLB-29

Knight, Sarah Kemble 1666-1727......................DLB-24

Knister, Raymond 1899-1932 ....DLB-68

Knoblock, Edward 1874-1945............................DLB-10

Knopf, Alfred A. 1892-1984................................Y-84

Knopf, Alfred A. [publishing house].................DLB-46

Knowles, John 1926- DLB-6

Knox, Frank 1874-1944 ....DLB-29

Knox, John Armoy 1850-1906...........................DLB-23

Knox, Ronald Arbuthnott 1888-1957................DLB-77

Kober, Arthur 1900-1975 ....DLB-11

Koch, Howard 1902- DLB-26

Koch, Kenneth 1925- DLB-5

Koenigsberg, Moses 1879-1945 ....DLB-25

Koeppen, Wolfgang 1906- DLB-69

Koestler, Arthur 1905-1983 ....Y-83

Kolb, Annette 1870-1967 ....DLB-66

Kolbenheyer, Erwin Guido 1878-1962..............DLB-66

Kolleritsch, Alfred 1931- DLB-85

Kolodny, Annette 1941- DLB-67

Komroff, Manuel 1890-1974 ....DLB-4

Konigsburg, E. L. 1930- DLB-52

Kopit, Arthur 1937- DLB-7

Kops, Bernard 1926?- DLB-13

Kornbluth, C. M. 1923-1958................................DLB-8

Körner, Theodor 1791-1813 ....DLB-90

Kosinski, Jerzy 1933- DLB-2; Y-82

Kraf, Elaine 1946- Y-81

Krasna, Norman 1909-1984.............................DLB-26

Krauss, Ruth 1911- DLB-52

Kreisel, Henry 1922- DLB-88

Kreuder, Ernst 1903-1972 ....DLB-69

Kreymborg, Alfred 1883-1966 ....DLB-4, 54

Krieger, Murray 1923- DLB-67

Krim, Seymour 1922- DLB-16

Krock, Arthur 1886-1974 ....DLB-29

Kroetsch, Robert 1927- DLB-53

Krutch, Joseph Wood 1893-1970......................DLB-63

Kubin, Alfred 1877-1959 ....DLB-81

Kubrick, Stanley 1928- DLB-26

Kumin, Maxine 1925- DLB-5

Kunnert, Günter 1929- DLB-75

Kunitz, Stanley 1905- DLB-48

Kunjufu, Johari M. (see Amini, Johari M.)

Kunze, Reiner 1933- DLB-75

Kupferberg, Tuli 1923- DLB-16

Kurz, Isolde 1853-1944.....................................DLB-66

Kusenberg, Kurt 1904-1983 ....DLB-69

Kuttner, Henry 1915-1958..................................DLB-8

Kyd, Thomas 1558-1594 ....DLB-62

Kyger, Joanne 1934- DLB-16

Kyne, Peter B. 1880-1957 ....DLB-78

L

Laberge, Albert 1871-1960 ....DLB-68

Laberge, Marie 1950- DLB-60

Lacretelle, Jacques de 1888-1985......................DLB-65

Ladd, Joseph Brown 1764-1786........................DLB-37

La Farge, Oliver 1901-1963...............................DLB-9

Lafferty, R. A. 1914- DLB-8

Lahaise, Guillaume (see Delahaye, Guy)

Laird, Carobeth 1895- Y-82

Laird and Lee...DLB-49

Lalonde, Michèle 1937- DLB-60

Lamantia, Philip 1927- DLB-16

Lambert, Betty 1933-1983 ....DLB-60

L'Amour, Louis 1908?- Y-80

Lampman, Archibald 1861-1899 ....DLB-92

Lamson, Wolffe and Company DLB-49

Lancer Books...DLB-46

Landesman, Jay 1919- and
      Landesman, Fran 1927- DLB-16

Landry, Napoléon-P. 1884-1956........................DLB-92

Lane, Charles 1800-1870...................................DLB-1

The John Lane Company DLB-49

Lane, Laurence W. 1890-1967...........................DLB-91

Lane, M. Travis 1934- DLB-60

Lane, Patrick 1939- DLB-53

Lane, Pinkie Gordon 1923- DLB-41

Laney, Al 1896- DLB-4

Langevin, André 1927- DLB-60

Langgässer, Elisabeth 1899-1950......................DLB-69

Lanham, Edwin 1904-1979 ....DLB-4

Lanier, Sidney 1842-1881 ....DLB-64

Lapointe, Gatien 1931-1983.............................DLB-88

Lapointe, Paul-Marie 1929- DLB-88

Lardner, Ring 1885-1933 ....DLB-11, 25, 86

Lardner, Ring, Jr. 1915- DLB-26

Lardner 100: Ring Lardner
      Centennial Symposium......................................Y-85

Larkin, Philip 1922-1985 ....DLB-27

La Rocque, Gilbert 1943-1984..........................DLB-60

Laroque de Roquebrune, Robert
      (see Roquebrune, Robert de)

Larrick, Nancy 1910- DLB-61

Larsen, Nella 1893-1964 ....DLB-51

Lasker-Schüler, Else 1869-1945 ....DLB-66

Lasnier, Rina 1915- DLB-88

Lathrop, Dorothy P. 1891-1980........................DLB-22

Lathrop, George Parsons 1851-1898.................DLB-71

Lathrop, John, Jr. 1772-1820 ....DLB-37

Latimore, Jewel Christine McLawler (see Amini, Johari M.)

Laughlin, James 1914- DLB-48

Laumer, Keith 1925- DLB-8

Laurence, Margaret 1926-1987...........................DLB-53

Laurents, Arthur 1918- DLB-26

Laurie, Annie (see Black, Winifred)

Laut, Agnes Christiana 1871-1936 ....DLB-92

Lavin, Mary 1912- DLB-15

Lawless, Anthony (see MacDonald, Philip)

Lawrence, David 1888-1973...............................DLB-29

Lawrence, D. H. 1885-1930...................DLB-10, 19, 36

Lawson, John ?-1711.......................................DLB-24

Lawson, Robert 1892-1957 ....DLB-22

Lawson, Victor F. 1850-1925...............................DLB-25

Layton, Irving 1912- DLB-88

Lea, Henry Charles 1825-1909............................DLB-47

Lea, Tom 1907- DLB-6

Leacock, John 1729-1802.................................DLB-31

Leacock, Stephen 1869-1944 ....DLB-92

Lear, Edward 1812-1888...................................DLB-32

Leary, Timothy 1920- DLB-16

Leary, W. A., and Company DLB-49

Léautaud, Paul 1872-1956................................DLB-65

Leavitt and Allen...DLB-49

le Carré, John 1931- DLB-87

Lécavelé, Roland (see Dorgelès, Roland)

Lechlitner, Ruth 1901- DLB-48

Leclerc, Félix 1914- DLB-60

Le Clézio, J. M. G. 1940-.................................DLB-83

Lectures on Rhetoric and Belles Lettres (1783),
    by Hugh Blair [excerpts]............................DLB-31

Leder, Rudolf (see Hermlin, Stephan)

Lederer, Charles 1910-1976...............................DLB-26

Ledwidge, Francis 1887-1917 ....DLB-20

Lee, Dennis 1939- DLB-53

Lee, Don L. (see Madhubuti, Haki R.)

Lee, George W. 1894-1976................................DLB-51

Lee, Harper 1926- DLB-6

Lee, Harriet (1757-1851) and
    Lee, Sophia (1750-1824) DLB-39

Lee, Laurie 1914- DLB-27

Lee, Nathaniel circa 1645 - 1692.......................DLB-80

Lee, Vernon 1856-1935...................................DLB-57

Lee and Shepard DLB-49

Le Fanu, Joseph Sheridan 1814-1873 ....DLB-21, 70

Leffland, Ella 1931- Y-84

le Fort, Gertrud von 1876-1971 ....DLB-66

Le Gallienne, Richard 1866-1947 ....DLB-4

Legaré, Hugh Swinton 1797-1843 ....DLB-3, 59, 73

Legaré, James M. 1823-1859.............................DLB-3

Léger, Antoine-J. 1880-1950...............................DLB-88

Le Guin, Ursula K. 1929- DLB-8, 52

Lehman, Ernest 1920- DLB-44

Lehmann, John 1907- DLB-27

Lehmann, Rosamond 1901- DLB-15

Lehmann, Wilhelm 1882-1968 ....DLB-56

Leiber, Fritz 1910- DLB-8

Leinster, Murray 1896-1975 ....DLB-8

Leitch, Maurice 1933- DLB-14

Leland, Charles G. 1824-1903 ....DLB-11

Lemelin, Roger 1919- DLB-88

Le Moyne, Jean 1913- DLB-88

L'Engle, Madeleine 1918- DLB-52

Lennart, Isobel 1915-1971 ....DLB-44

Lennox, Charlotte 1729 or 1730-1804 ....DLB-39

Lenski, Lois 1893-1974 ....DLB-22

Lenz, Hermann 1913- DLB-69

Lenz, Siegfried 1926- DLB-75

Leonard, Hugh 1926- DLB-13

Leonard, William Ellery 1876-1944 ....DLB-54

LePan, Douglas 1914- DLB-88

Le Queux, William 1864-1927...........................DLB-70

Lerner, Max 1902- DLB-29

Lernet-Holenia, Alexander 1897-1976..............DLB-85

Le Rossignol, James 1866-1969 ....DLB-92

LeSieg, Theo. (see Geisel, Theodor Seuss)

Leslie, Frank 1821-1880...............................DLB-43, 79

The Frank Leslie Publishing House DLB-49

Lessing, Bruno 1870-1940...............................DLB-28

Lessing, Doris 1919- DLB-15; Y-85

LeSueur, William Dawson 1840-1917 ....DLB-92

Lettau, Reinhard 1929- DLB-75

Letter to [Samuel] Richardson on *Clarissa*
    (1748), by Henry Fielding...........................DLB-39

Lever, Charles 1806-1872 ....DLB-21

Levertov, Denise 1923- DLB-5

Levi, Peter 1931- DLB-40

Levien, Sonya 1888-1960 ....DLB-44

Levin, Meyer 1905-1981 ....DLB-9, 28; Y-81

Levine, Norman 1923- DLB-88

Levine, Philip 1928- DLB-5

Levy, Benn Wolfe 1900-1973...................DLB-13; Y-81

Lewes, George Henry 1817-1878 ....DLB-55

Lewis, Alfred H. 1857-1914............................DLB-25

Lewis, Alun 1915-1944...................................DLB-20

Lewis, C. Day (see Day Lewis, C.)

Lewis, Charles B. 1842-1924...........................DLB-11

Lewis, C. S. 1898-1963 ....DLB-15

Lewis, Henry Clay 1825-1850 ....DLB-3

Lewis, Janet 1899- Y-87

Lewis, Matthew Gregory 1775-1818 ....DLB-39

Lewis, Richard circa 1700-1734 ....DLB-24

Lewis, Sinclair 1885-1951 ....DLB-9; DS-1

Lewis, Wyndham 1882-1957............................DLB-15

Lewisohn, Ludwig 1882-1955...................DLB-4, 9, 28

The Library of America DLB-46

The Licensing Act of 1737.................................DLB-84

Liebling, A. J. 1904-1963 ....DLB-4

Lieutenant Murray (see Ballou, Maturin Murray)

Lighthall, William Douw 1857-1954..................DLB-92

Lilar, Françoise (see Mallet-Joris, Françoise)

Lillo, George 1691-1739.....................................DLB-84

Lilly, Wait and Company DLB-49

Limited Editions Club DLB-46

Lincoln and Edmands DLB-49

Lindsay, Jack 1900- Y-84

Lindsay, Vachel 1879-1931...............................DLB-54

Linebarger, Paul Myron Anthony (see
    Smith, Cordwainer)

Link, Arthur S. 1920- DLB-17

Linn, John Blair 1777-1804 ....DLB-37

Linton, Eliza Lynn 1822-1898...........................DLB-18

Linton, William James 1812-1897 ....DLB-32

Lion Books..DLB-46

Lionni, Leo 1910- DLB-61

Lippincott, J. B., Company DLB-49

Lippincott, Sara Jane Clarke 1823-1904.............DLB-43

Lippmann, Walter 1889-1974 ....DLB-29

Lipton, Lawrence 1898-1975 ....DLB-16

Literary Documents: William Faulkner
    and the People-to-People Program Y-86

Literary Documents II: *Library Journal*–
    Statements and Questionnaires from
    First Novelists..Y-87

Literary Effects of World War II
    [British novel] DLB-15

Literary Prizes [British] DLB-15

Literary Research Archives: The Humanities
    Research Center, University of Texas..............Y-82

Literary Research Archives II: Berg
    Collection of English and American Literature
    of the New York Public Library......................Y-83

Literary Research Archives III:
    The Lilly Library Y-84

Literary Research Archives IV:
    The John Carter Brown Library......................Y-85

Literary Research Archives V:
    Kent State Special Collections........................Y-86

Literary Research Archives VI: The Modern
    Literary Manuscripts Collection in the
    Special Collections of the Washington
    University Libraries Y-87

"Literary Style" (1857), by William
    Forsyth [excerpt]...DLB-57

Literatura Chicanesca:
    The View From Without.............................DLB-82

Literature at Nurse, or Circulating Morals (1885),
    by George Moore DLB-18

Littell, Eliakim 1797-1870...............................DLB-79

Littell, Robert S. 1831-1896.............................DLB-79

Little, Brown and Company...............................DLB-49

Littlewood, Joan 1914- DLB-13

Lively, Penelope 1933- DLB-14

Livesay, Dorothy 1909- DLB-68

Livesay, Florence Randal
    1874-1953 ....DLB-92

Livings, Henry 1929- DLB-13

Livingston, Anne Howe 1763-1841 ....DLB-37

Livingston, Myra Cohn 1926- DLB-61

Livingston, William 1723-1790 ....DLB-31

Lizárraga, Sylvia S. 1925- DLB-82

Llewellyn, Richard 1906-1983 ....DLB-15

Lobel, Arnold 1933- DLB-61

Lochridge, Betsy Hopkins (see Fancher, Betsy)

Locke, David Ross 1833-1888 ....DLB-11, 23

Locke, John 1632-1704..................................DLB-31

Locke, Richard Adams 1800-1871 ....DLB-43

Locker-Lampson, Frederick 1821-1895..............DLB-35

Lockridge, Ross, Jr. 1914-1948......................Y-80

Locrine and *Selimus*....................................DLB-62

Lodge, David 1935- DLB-14

Lodge, George Cabot 1873-1909......................DLB-54

Lodge, Henry Cabot 1850-1924 ....DLB-47

Loeb, Harold 1891-1974 ....DLB-4

Logan, James 1674-1751 ....DLB-24

Logan, John 1923- DLB-5

Logue, Christopher 1926- DLB-27

London, Jack 1876-1916..........................DLB-8, 12, 78

Long, H., and Brother DLB-49

Long, Haniel 1888-1956................................DLB-45

Longfellow, Henry Wadsworth 1807-1882 ....DLB-1, 59

Longfellow, Samuel 1819-1892............................DLB-1

Longley, Michael 1939- DLB-40

Longmans, Green and Company......................DLB-49

Longstreet, Augustus Baldwin
      1790-1870.................................DLB-3, 11, 74

Longworth, D. [publishing house].....................DLB-49

Lonsdale, Frederick 1881-1954..........................DLB-10

A Look at the Contemporary Black Theatre
      Movement.....................................DLB-38

Loos, Anita 1893-1981.....................DLB-11, 26; Y-81

Lopate, Phillip 1943- Y-80

López, Diana (see Isabella, Ríos)

Loranger, Jean-Aubert
      1896-1942 ....DLB-92

The Lord Chamberlain's Office and Stage
      Censorship in England....................DLB-10

Lorde, Audre 1934- DLB-41

Lorimer, George Horace 1867-1939 ....DLB-91

Loring, A. K. [publishing house].....................DLB-49

Loring and Mussey..............................DLB-46

Lossing, Benson J. 1813-1891........................DLB-30

Lothar, Ernst 1890-1974 ....DLB-81

Lothrop, D., and Company..............................DLB-49

Lothrop, Harriet M. 1844-1924........................DLB-42

The Lounger, no. 20 (1785), by Henry
      Mackenzie DLB-39

Lounsbury, Thomas R. 1838-1915 ....DLB-71

Lovell, John W., Company................................DLB-49

Lovell, Coryell and Company DLB-49

Lovesey, Peter 1936- DLB-87

Lovingood, Sut (see Harris, George Washington)

Low, Samuel 1765-? DLB-37

Lowell, Amy 1874-1925...................................DLB-54

Lowell, James Russell 1819-1891 ....DLB-1, 11, 64, 79

Lowell, Robert 1917-1977...............................DLB-5

Lowenfels, Walter 1897-1976...............................DLB-4

Lowndes, Marie Belloc 1868-1947.....................DLB-70

Lowry, Lois 1937- DLB-52

Lowry, Malcolm 1909-1957................................DLB-15

Lowther, Pat 1935-1975 ....DLB-53

Loy, Mina 1882-1966 ....DLB-4, 54

Lozeau, Albert 1878-1924................................DLB-92

Lucas, Fielding, Jr. [publishing house]..............DLB-49

Luce, Henry R. 1898-1967................................DLB-91

Luce, John W., and Company DLB-46

Lucie-Smith, Edward 1933- DLB-40

Ludlum, Robert 1927- Y-82

Ludwig, Jack 1922- DLB-60

Luke, Peter 1919- DLB-13

The F. M. Lupton Publishing Company DLB-49

Lurie, Alison 1926- DLB-2

Lyall, Gavin 1932- DLB-87

Lyly, John circa 1554-1606 ....DLB-62

Lyon, Matthew 1749-1822................................DLB-43

Lytle, Andrew 1902- DLB-6

Lytton, Edward (see Bulwer-Lytton, Edward)

Lytton, Edward Robert Bulwer 1831-1891 ....DLB-32

M

Maass, Joachim 1901-1972 ....DLB-69

Mabie, Hamilton Wright 1845-1916.................DLB-71

Mac A'Ghobhainn, Iain (see Smith, Iain Crichton)

MacArthur, Charles 1895-1956 ....DLB-7, 25, 44

Macaulay, David 1945- DLB-61

Macaulay, Rose 1881-1958 ....DLB-36

Macaulay, Thomas Babington 1800-1859 ....DLB-32, 55

Macaulay Company DLB-46

MacBeth, George 1932- DLB-40

Macbeth, Madge 1880-1965 ....DLB-92

MacCaig, Norman 1910- DLB-27

MacDiarmid, Hugh 1892-1978 ....DLB-20

MacDonald, George 1824-1905 ....DLB-18

MacDonald, John D. 1916-1986 ....DLB-8; Y-86

MacDonald, Philip 1899?-1980 ....DLB-77

Macdonald, Ross (see Millar, Kenneth)

MacDonald, Wilson 1880-1967 ....DLB-92

MacEwen, Gwendolyn 1941- DLB-53

Macfadden, Bernarr 1868-1955 ....DLB-25, 91

MacGregor, Mary Esther (see Keith, Marian)

Machar, Agnes Maule 1837-1927 ....DLB-92

Machen, Arthur Llewelyn Jones 1863-1947.......DLB-36

MacInnes, Colin 1914-1976 ....DLB-14

MacInnes, Helen 1907-1985 ....DLB-87

MacKay, Isabel Ecclestone
        1875-1928 ....DLB-92

MacKaye, Percy 1875-1956 ....DLB-54

Macken, Walter 1915-1967................................DLB-13

Mackenzie, Compton 1883-1972........................DLB-34

Mackenzie, Henry 1745-1831 ....DLB-39

Mackey, William Wellington 1937- DLB-38

Mackintosh, Elizabeth (see Tey, Josephine)

Macklin, Charles 1699-1797...........................DLB-89

MacLean, Katherine Anne 1925- DLB-8

MacLeish, Archibald 1892-1982.......DLB-4, 7, 45; Y-82

MacLennan, Hugh 1907- DLB-68

MacLeod, Alistair 1936- DLB-60

Macleod, Norman 1906- DLB-4

The Macmillan Company....................DLB-49

MacNamara, Brinsley 1890-1963 ....DLB-10

MacNeice, Louis 1907-1963 ....DLB-10, 20

MacPhail, Andrew 1864-1938............................DLB-92

Macpherson, Jay 1931- DLB-53

Macpherson, Jeanie 1884-1946........................DLB-44

Macrae Smith Company......................DLB-46

Macy-Masius.......................................DLB-46

Madden, David 1933- DLB-6

Maddow, Ben 1909- DLB-44

Madgett, Naomi Long 1923- DLB-76

Madhubuti, Haki R. 1942- DLB-5, 41

Madison, James 1751-1836 ....DLB-37

Mahan, Alfred Thayer 1840-1914......................DLB-47

Maheux-Forcier, Louise 1929- DLB-60

Mahin, John Lee 1902-1984 ....DLB-44

Mahon, Derek 1941- DLB-40

Mailer, Norman 1923-
        ....DLB-2, 16, 28; Y-80, 83; DS-3

Maillet, Adrienne 1885-1963 ....DLB-68

Maillet, Antonine 1929- DLB-60

Main Selections of the Book-of-the-Month Club,
        1926-1945 ....DLB-9

Main Trends in Twentieth-Century
        Book Clubs DLB-46

Mainwaring, Daniel 1902-1977..........................DLB-44

Major, André 1942- DLB-60

Major, Clarence 1936- DLB-33

Major, Kevin 1949- DLB-60

Major Books....................................DLB-46

Makemie, Francis circa 1658-1708.....................DLB-24

The Making of a People,
        by J. M. Ritchie............................DLB-66

Malamud, Bernard 1914-1986 ....DLB-2, 28; Y-80, 86

Malleson, Lucy Beatrice (see Gilbert, Anthony)

Mallet-Joris, Françoise 1930- DLB-83

Mallock, W. H. 1849-1923 ....DLB-18, 57

Malone, Dumas 1892-1986.................................DLB-17

Malraux, André 1901-1976................................DLB-72

Malzberg, Barry N. 1939- DLB-8

Mamet, David 1947- DLB-7

Mandel, Eli 1922- DLB-53

Mandiargues, André Pieyre de 1909- DLB-83

Manfred, Frederick 1912- DLB-6

Mangan, Sherry 1904-1961................................DLB-4

Mankiewicz, Herman 1897-1953 ....DLB-26

Mankiewicz, Joseph L. 1909- DLB-44

Mankowitz, Wolf 1924- DLB-15

Manley, Delarivière 1672?-1724 ....DLB-39, 80

Mann, Abby 1927- DLB-44

Mann, Heinrich 1871-1950 ....DLB-66

Mann, Horace 1796-1859..................................DLB-1

Mann, Klaus 1906-1949 ....DLB-56

Mann, Thomas 1875-1955 ....DLB-66

Manning, Marie 1873?-1945 ....DLB-29

Manning and Loring DLB-49

Mano, D. Keith 1942- DLB-6

Manor Books DLB-46

March, William 1893-1954............................DLB-9, 86

Marchessault, Jovette 1938- DLB-60

Marcus, Frank 1928- DLB-13

Marek, Richard, Books....................................DLB-46

Marie-Victorin, Frère
        1885-1944 ....DLB-92

Marion, Frances 1886-1973..............................DLB-44

Marius, Richard C. 1933- Y-85

The Mark Taper Forum.....................................DLB-7

Markfield, Wallace 1926- DLB-2, 28

Markham, Edwin 1852-1940............................DLB-54

Markle, Fletcher 1921- DLB-68

Marlatt, Daphne 1942- DLB-60

Marlowe, Christopher 1564-1593 ....DLB-62

Marlyn, John 1912- DLB-88

Marmion, Shakerley 1603-1639 ....DLB-58

Marquand, John P. 1893-1960...........................DLB-9

Marquis, Don 1878-1937................................DLB-11, 25

Marriott, Anne 1913- DLB-68

Marryat, Frederick 1792-1848 ....DLB-21

Marsh, George Perkins 1801-1882 ....DLB-1, 64

Marsh, James 1794-1842................................DLB-1, 59

Marsh, Capen, Lyon and Webb DLB-49

Marsh, Ngaio 1899-1982 ....DLB-77

Marshall, Edward 1932- DLB-16

Marshall, James 1942- DLB-61

Marshall, Joyce 1913- DLB-88

Marshall, Paule 1929- DLB-33

Marshall, Tom 1938- DLB-60

Marston, John 1576-1634................................DLB-58

Marston, Philip Bourke 1850-1887....................DLB-35

Martens, Kurt 1870-1945 ....DLB-66

Martien, William S. [publishing house].............DLB-49

Martin, Abe (see Hubbard, Kin)

Martin, Claire 1914- DLB-60

Martin du Gard, Roger 1881-1958....................DLB-65

Martineau, Harriet 1802-1876.....................DLB-21, 55

Martínez, Max 1943- DLB-82

Martyn, Edward 1859-1923 ....DLB-10

Marvin X 1944- DLB-38

Marzials, Theo 1850-1920................................DLB-35

Masefield, John 1878-1967 ....DLB-10, 19

Mason, A. E. W. 1865-1948 ....DLB-70

Mason, Bobbie Ann 1940- Y-87

Mason Brothers..DLB-49

Massey, Gerald 1828-1907 ....DLB-32

Massinger, Philip 1583-1640............................DLB-58

Masters, Edgar Lee 1868-1950 ....DLB-54

Mather, Cotton 1663-1728...........................DLB-24, 30

Mather, Increase 1639-1723 ....DLB-24

Mather, Richard 1596-1669 ....DLB-24

Matheson, Richard 1926- DLB-8, 44

Matheus, John F. 1887- DLB-51

Mathews, Cornelius 1817?-1889 ....DLB-3, 64

Mathias, Roland 1915- DLB-27

Mathis, June 1892-1927 ....DLB-44

Mathis, Sharon Bell 1937- DLB-33

Matthews, Brander 1852-1929.....................DLB-71, 78

Matthews, Jack 1925- DLB-6

Matthews, William 1942- DLB-5

Matthiessen, F. O. 1902-1950 ....DLB-63

Matthiessen, Peter 1927- DLB-6

Maugham, W. Somerset 1874-1965 ....DLB-10, 36, 77

Mauriac, Claude 1914- DLB-83

Mauriac, François 1885-1970............................DLB-65

Maurice, Frederick Denison 1805-1872 ....DLB-55

Maurois, André 1885-1967 ....DLB-65

Maury, James 1718-1769......................................DLB-31

Mavor, Elizabeth 1927- DLB-14

Mavor, Osborne Henry (see Bridie, James)

Maxwell, H. [publishing house] DLB-49

Maxwell, William 1908- Y-80

May, Elaine 1932- DLB-44

May, Thomas 1595 or 1596-1650......................DLB-58

Mayer, Mercer 1943- DLB-61

Mayer, O. B. 1818-1891 ....DLB-3

Mayes, Wendell 1919- DLB-26

Mayfield, Julian 1928-1984.....................DLB-33; Y-84

Mayhew, Henry 1812-1887.........................DLB-18, 55

Mayhew, Jonathan 1720-1766...........................DLB-31

Mayne, Seymour 1944- DLB-60

Mayor, Flora Macdonald 1872-1932.................DLB-36

Mayröcker, Friederike 1924- DLB-85

Mazursky, Paul 1930- DLB-44

McAlmon, Robert 1896-1956 ....DLB-4, 45

McArthur, Peter 1866-1924 ....DLB-92

McBride, Robert M., and Company DLB-46

McCaffrey, Anne 1926- DLB-8

McCarthy, Cormac 1933- DLB-6

McCarthy, Mary 1912-1989 ....DLB-2; Y-81

McCay, Winsor 1871-1934 ....DLB-22

McClatchy, C. K. 1858-1936 ....DLB-25

McClellan, George Marion 1860-1934 ....DLB-50

McCloskey, Robert 1914- DLB-22

McClung, Nellie Letitia
    1873-1951 ....DLB-92

McClure, Joanna 1930- DLB-16

McClure, Michael 1932- DLB-16

McClure, Phillips and Company.........................DLB-46

McClure, S. S. 1857-1949...................................DLB-91

McClurg, A. C., and Company DLB-49

McCluskey, John A., Jr. 1944- DLB-33

McCollum, Michael A. 1946...............................Y-87

McConnell, William C. 1917- DLB-88

McCord, David 1897- DLB-61

McCorkle, Jill 1958- Y-87

McCorkle, Samuel Eusebius 1746-1811 ....DLB-37

McCormick, Anne O'Hare 1880-1954...............DLB-29

McCormick, Robert R. 1880-1955 ....DLB-29

McCourt, Edward 1907-1972.............................DLB-88

McCoy, Horace 1897-1955..................................DLB-9

McCrae, John 1872-1918 ....DLB-92

McCullagh, Joseph B. 1842-1896 ....DLB-23

McCullers, Carson 1917-1967..........................DLB-2, 7

McDonald, Forrest 1927- DLB-17

McDougall, Colin 1917-1984 ....DLB-68

McDowell, Obolensky DLB-46

McEwan, Ian 1948- DLB-14

McFadden, David 1940- DLB-60

McFarlane, Leslie 1902-1977.............................DLB-88

McGahern, John 1934- DLB-14

McGeehan, W. O. 1879-1933.............................DLB-25

McGill, Ralph 1898-1969 ....DLB-29

McGinley, Phyllis 1905-1978.......................DLB-11, 48

McGirt, James E. 1874-1930 ....DLB-50

McGough, Roger 1937- DLB-40

McGraw-Hill DLB-46

McGuane, Thomas 1939- DLB-2; Y-80

McGuckian, Medbh 1950- DLB-40

McGuffey, William Holmes 1800-1873 ....DLB-42

McIlvanney, William 1936- DLB-14

McIlwraith, Jean Newton
    1859-1938 ....DLB-92

McIntyre, O. O. 1884-1938................................DLB-25

McKay, Claude 1889-1948......................DLB-4, 45, 51

The David McKay Company..............................DLB-49

McKean, William V. 1820-1903........................DLB-23

McKinley, Robin 1952- DLB-52

McLaren, Floris Clark 1904-1978......................DLB-68

McLaverty, Michael 1907- DLB-15

McLean, John R. 1848-1916 ....DLB-23

McLean, William L. 1852-1931..........................DLB-25

McLennan, William 1856-1904..........................DLB-92

McLoughlin Brothers DLB-49

McLuhan, Marshall 1911-1980..........................DLB-88

McMaster, John Bach 1852-1932.......................DLB-47

McMurtry, Larry 1936- DLB-2; Y-80, 87

McNally, Terrence 1939- DLB-7

McNeil, Florence 1937- DLB-60

McNeile, Herman Cyril 1888-1937 ....DLB-77

McPherson, James Alan 1943- DLB-38

McPherson, Sandra 1943- Y-86

McWhirter, George 1939- DLB-60

Mead, Matthew 1924- DLB-40

Mead, Taylor ?- DLB-16

Medill, Joseph 1823-1899 ....DLB-43

Medoff, Mark 1940- DLB-7

Meek, Alexander Beaufort 1814-1865 ....DLB-3

Meinke, Peter 1932- DLB-5

Melançon, Robert 1947- DLB-60

Mell, Max 1882-1971.......................................DLB-81

Meltzer, David 1937- DLB-16

Meltzer, Milton 1915- DLB-61

Melville, Herman 1819-1891 ....DLB-3, 74

Memoirs of Life and Literature (1920),
    by W. H. Mallock [excerpt].........................DLB-57

Mencken, H. L. 1880-1956 ....DLB-11, 29, 63

Méndez M., Miguel 1930- DLB-82

Mercer, Cecil William (see Yates, Dornford)

Mercer, David 1928-1980.................................DLB-13

Mercer, John 1704-1768 ....DLB-31

Meredith, George 1828-1909.................DLB-18, 35, 57

Meredith, Owen (see Lytton, Edward Robert Bulwer)

Meredith, William 1919- DLB-5

Meriwether, Louise 1923- DLB-33

Merriam, Eve 1916- DLB-61

The Merriam Company DLB-49

Merrill, James 1926- DLB-5; Y-85

Merrill and Baker...DLB-49

The Mershon Company DLB-49

Merton, Thomas 1915-1968 ....DLB-48; Y-81

Merwin, W. S. 1927- DLB-5

Messner, Julian [publishing house].....................DLB-46

Metcalf, J. [publishing house] DLB-49

Metcalf, John 1938- DLB-60

The Methodist Book Concern DLB-49

Mew, Charlotte 1869-1928................................DLB-19

Mewshaw, Michael 1943- Y-80

Meyer, E. Y. 1946- DLB-75

Meyer, Eugene 1875-1959 ....DLB-29

Meynell, Alice 1847-1922...............................DLB-19

Meyrink, Gustav 1868-1932 ....DLB-81

Micheaux, Oscar 1884-1951..............................DLB-50

Micheline, Jack 1929- DLB-16

Michener, James A. 1907?- DLB-6

Micklejohn, George circa 1717-1818 ....DLB-31

Middleton, Christopher 1926- DLB-40

Middleton, Stanley 1919- DLB-14

Middleton, Thomas 1580-1627.......................DLB-58

Miegel, Agnes 1879-1964................................DLB-56

Miles, Josephine 1911-1985 ....DLB-48

Milius, John 1944- DLB-44

Mill, John Stuart 1806-1873 ....DLB-55

Millar, Kenneth 1915-1983 ....DLB-2; Y-83; DS-6

Millay, Edna St. Vincent 1892-1950 ....DLB-45

Miller, Arthur 1915- DLB-7

Miller, Caroline 1903- DLB-9

Miller, Eugene Ethelbert 1950- DLB-41

Miller, Henry 1891-1980 ....DLB-4, 9; Y-80

Miller, J. Hillis 1928- DLB-67

Miller, James [publishing house] DLB-49

Miller, Jason 1939- DLB-7

Miller, May 1899- DLB-41

Miller, Perry 1905-1963 ....DLB-17, 63

Miller, Walter M., Jr. 1923- DLB-8

Miller, Webb 1892-1940 ....DLB-29

Millhauser, Steven 1943- DLB-2

Millican, Arthenia J. Bates 1920- DLB-38

Milne, A. A. 1882-1956...........................DLB-10, 77

Milner, Ron 1938- DLB-38

Milnes, Richard Monckton (Lord Houghton)
    1809-1885 ....DLB-32

Minton, Balch and Company.............................DLB-46

Miron, Gaston 1928- DLB-60

Mitchel, Jonathan 1624-1668 ....DLB-24

Mitchell, Adrian 1932- DLB-40

Mitchell, Donald Grant 1822-1908 ....DLB-1

Mitchell, Gladys 1901-1983 ....DLB-77

Mitchell, James Leslie 1901-1935......................DLB-15

Mitchell, John (see Slater, Patrick)

Mitchell, John Ames 1845-1918.......................DLB-79

Mitchell, Julian 1935- DLB-14

Mitchell, Ken 1940- DLB-60

Mitchell, Langdon 1862-1935 ....DLB-7

Mitchell, Loften 1919- DLB-38

Mitchell, Margaret 1900-1949...........................DLB-9

Mitchell, W. O. 1914- DLB-88

Mitterer, Erika 1906- DLB-85

Modern Age Books DLB-46

"Modern English Prose" (1876),
    by George Saintsbury DLB-57

The Modern Language Association of America
    Celebrates Its Centennial Y-84

The Modern Library DLB-46

Modern Novelists–Great and Small (1855), by
    Margaret Oliphant......................................DLB-21

"Modern Style" (1857), by Cockburn
    Thomson [excerpt].....................................DLB-57

The Modernists (1932), by Joseph Warren
    Beach...DLB-36

Modiano, Patrick 1945- DLB-83

Moffat, Yard and Company DLB-46

Monkhouse, Allan 1858-1936 ....DLB-10

Monro, Harold 1879-1932 ....DLB-19

Monroe, Harriet 1860-1936.......................DLB-54, 91

Monsarrat, Nicholas 1910-1979 ....DLB-15

Montague, John 1929- DLB-40

Montgomery, John 1919- DLB-16

Montgomery, Lucy Maud 1874-1942 ....DLB-92

Montgomery, Marion 1925- DLB-6

Montgomery, Robert Bruce (see Crispin, Edmund)

Montherlant, Henry de 1896-1972....................DLB-72

Montigny, Louvigny de 1876-1955....................DLB-92

Moody, Joshua circa 1633-1697..........................DLB-24

Moody, William Vaughn 1869-1910..............DLB-7, 54

Moorcock, Michael 1939- DLB-14

Moore, Catherine L. 1911- DLB-8

Moore, Clement Clarke 1779-1863....................DLB-42

Moore, Dora Mavor 1888-1979 ....DLB-92

Moore, George 1852-1933....................DLB-10, 18, 57

Moore, Marianne 1887-1972 ....DLB-45; DS-7

Moore, Mavor 1919- DLB-88

Moore, T. Sturge 1870-1944 ....DLB-19

Moore, Ward 1903-1978 ....DLB-8

Moore, Wilstach, Keys and Company DLB-49

The Moorland-Spingarn
    Research Center DLB-76

Moraga, Cherríe 1952- DLB-82

Morales, Alejandro 1944- DLB-82

Morency, Pierre 1942- DLB-60

Morgan, Berry 1919- DLB-6

Morgan, Charles 1894-1958...............................DLB-34

Morgan, Edmund S. 1916- DLB-17

Morgan, Edwin 1920- DLB-27

Morgner, Irmtraud 1933- DLB-75

Morin, Paul 1889-1963......................................DLB-92

Morison, Samuel Eliot 1887-1976......................DLB-17

Morley, Christopher 1890-1957.........................DLB-9

Morley, John 1838-1923.....................................DLB-57

Morris, George Pope 1802-1864 ....DLB-73

Morris, Lewis 1833-1907 ....DLB-35

Morris, Richard B. 1904-1989 ....DLB-17

Morris, William 1834-1896....................DLB-18, 35, 57

Morris, Willie 1934- Y-80

Morris, Wright 1910- DLB-2; Y-81

Morrison, Arthur 1863-1945 ....DLB-70

Morrison, Charles Clayton 1874-1966................DLB-91

Morrison, Toni 1931- DLB-6, 33; Y-81

Morrow, William, and Company DLB-46

Morse, James Herbert 1841-1923.......................DLB-71

Morse, Jedidiah 1761-1826 ....DLB-37

Morse, John T., Jr. 1840-1937...........................DLB-47

Mortimer, John 1923- DLB-13

Morton, John P., and Company DLB-49

Morton, Nathaniel 1613-1685...........................DLB-24

Morton, Sarah Wentworth 1759-1846 ....DLB-37

Morton, Thomas circa 1579-circa 1647.............DLB-24

Mosley, Nicholas 1923- DLB-14

Moss, Arthur 1889-1969 ....DLB-4

Moss, Howard 1922- DLB-5

The Most Powerful Book Review in America
    [*New York Times Book Review*] Y-82

Motion, Andrew 1952- DLB-40

Motley, John Lothrop 1814-1877............DLB-1, 30, 59

Motley, Willard 1909-1965..................DLB-76

Motteux, Peter Anthony 1663-1718 ....DLB-80

Mottram, R. H. 1883-1971..................DLB-36

Mouré, Erin 1955- DLB-60

Movies from Books, 1920-1974 ....DLB-9

Mowat, Farley 1921- DLB-68

Mowrer, Edgar Ansel 1892-1977..................DLB-29

Mowrer, Paul Scott 1887-1971..................DLB-29

Mucedorus..................DLB-62

Muhajir, El (see Marvin X)

Muhajir, Nazzam Al Fitnah (see Marvin X)

Muir, Edwin 1887-1959..................DLB-20

Muir, Helen 1937- DLB-14

Mukherjee, Bharati 1940- DLB-60

Muldoon, Paul 1951- DLB-40

Müller, Wilhelm 1794-1827 ....DLB-90

Mumford, Lewis 1895- DLB-63

Munby, Arthur Joseph 1828-1910..................DLB-35

Munday, Anthony 1560-1633 ....DLB-62

Munford, Robert circa 1737-1783 ....DLB-31

Munro, Alice 1931- DLB-53

Munro, George [publishing house]..................DLB-49

Munro, H. H. 1870-1916 ....DLB-34

Munro, Norman L. [publishing house] DLB-49

Munroe, James, and Company DLB-49

Munroe, Kirk 1850-1930 ....DLB-42

Munroe and Francis DLB-49

Munsell, Joel [publishing house]..................DLB-49

Munsey, Frank A. 1854-1925 ....DLB-25, 91

Munsey, Frank A., and Company..................DLB-49

Murdoch, Iris 1919- DLB-14

Murfree, Mary N. 1850-1922 ....DLB-12, 74

Muro, Amado 1915-1971..................DLB-82

Murphy, Arthur 1727-1805 ....DLB-89

Murphy, Beatrice M. 1908- DLB-76

Murphy, John, and Company DLB-49

Murphy, Richard 1927- DLB-40

Murray, Albert L. 1916- DLB-38

Murray, Gilbert 1866-1957 ....DLB-10

Murray, Judith Sargent 1751-1820..................DLB-37

Murray, Pauli 1910-1985..................DLB-41

Muschg, Adolf 1934- DLB-75

Musil, Robert 1880-1942..................DLB-81

Mussey, Benjamin B., and Company..................DLB-49

Myers, Gustavus 1872-1942 ....DLB-47

Myers, L. H. 1881-1944 ....DLB-15

Myers, Walter Dean 1937- DLB-33

N

Nabbes, Thomas circa 1605-1641 ....DLB-58

Nabl, Franz 1883-1974..................DLB-81

Nabokov, Vladimir 1899-1977 ....DLB-2; Y-80; DS-3

Nabokov Festival at Cornell..................Y-83

Nafis and Cornish..................DLB-49

Naipaul, Shiva 1945-1985..................Y-85

Naipaul, V. S. 1932- Y-85

Nancrede, Joseph [publishing house]..................DLB-49

Narrache, Jean 1893-1970 ....DLB-92

Nasby, Petroleum Vesuvius (see Locke, David Ross)

Nash, Ogden 1902-1971..................DLB-11

Nast, Condé 1873-1942..................DLB-91

Nathan, Robert 1894-1985..................DLB-9

The National Jewish Book Awards..................Y-85

The National Theatre and the Royal Shakespeare
    Company: The National Companies..................DLB-13

Naughton, Bill 1910- DLB-13

Neagoe, Peter 1881-1960 ....DLB-4

Neal, John 1793-1876 ....DLB-1, 59

Neal, Joseph C. 1807-1847..................DLB-11

Neal, Larry 1937-1981..................DLB-38

The Neale Publishing Company DLB-49

Neely, F. Tennyson [publishing house] DLB-49

"The Negro as a Writer," by
    G. M. McClellan DLB-50

"Negro Poets and Their Poetry," by
    Wallace Thurman..................DLB-50

Neihardt, John G. 1881-1973 ....DLB-9, 54

Nelligan, Emile 1879-1941..................DLB-92

Nelson, Alice Moore Dunbar
    1875-1935 ....DLB-50

Nelson, Thomas, and Sons..................DLB-49

Nelson, William Rockhill 1841-1915 ....DLB-23

Nemerov, Howard 1920- DLB-5, 6; Y-83

Ness, Evaline 1911-1986....................................DLB-61

Neugeboren, Jay 1938- DLB-28

Neumann, Alfred 1895-1952............................DLB-56

Nevins, Allan 1890-1971 ....DLB-17

The New American Library.............................DLB-46

New Directions Publishing Corporation.............DLB-46

A New Edition of *Huck Finn* Y-85

New Forces at Work in the American Theatre:
 1915-1925 ....DLB-7

New Literary Periodicals: A Report
 for 1987..Y-87

New Literary Periodicals: A Report
 for 1988..Y-88

The New *Ulysses* Y-84

The New Variorum Shakespeare...........................Y-85

A New Voice: The Center for the Book's First
 Five Years...Y-83

The New Wave [Science Fiction] DLB-8

Newbolt, Henry 1862-1938................................DLB-19

Newbound, Bernard Slade (see Slade, Bernard)

Newby, P. H. 1918- DLB-15

Newcomb, Charles King 1820-1894 ....DLB-1

Newell, Peter 1862-1924 ....DLB-42

Newell, Robert Henry 1836-1901.......................DLB-11

Newman, David (see Benton, Robert)

Newman, Frances 1883-1928 ....Y-80

Newman, John Henry 1801-1890 ....DLB-18, 32, 55

Newman, Mark [publishing house]....................DLB-49

Newsome, Effie Lee 1885-1979 ....DLB-76

Newspaper Syndication of American Humor....DLB-11

Nichol, B. P. 1944- DLB-53

Nichols, Dudley 1895-1960 ....DLB-26

Nichols, John 1940- Y-82

Nichols, Mary Sargeant (Neal) Gove
 1810-1884 ....DLB-1

Nichols, Peter 1927- DLB-13

Nichols, Roy F. 1896-1973 ....DLB-17

Nichols, Ruth 1948- DLB-60

Nicholson, Norman 1914- DLB-27

Ní Chuilleanáin, Eiléan 1942- DLB-40

Nicol, Eric 1919- DLB-68

Nicolay, John G. 1832-1901 and
 Hay, John 1838-1905 ....DLB-47

Niebuhr, Reinhold 1892-1971 ....DLB-17

Niedecker, Lorine 1903-1970 ....DLB-48

Nieman, Lucius W. 1857-1935............................DLB-25

Niggli, Josefina 1910- Y-80

Niles, Hezekiah 1777-1839 ....DLB-43

Nims, John Frederick 1913- DLB-5

Nin, Anaïs 1903-1977......................................DLB-2, 4

1985: The Year of the Mystery:
 A Symposium..Y-85

Nissenson, Hugh 1933- DLB-28

Niven, Frederick John 1878-1944 ....DLB-92

Niven, Larry 1938- DLB-8

Nizan, Paul 1905-1940 ....DLB-72

Nobel Peace Prize
 The 1986 Nobel Peace Prize
  Nobel Lecture 1986: Hope, Despair
  and Memory
  Tributes from Abraham Bernstein,
   Norman Lamm, and John R. Silber Y-86

The Nobel Prize and Literary
 Politics..Y-88

Nobel Prize in Literature
 The 1982 Nobel Prize in Literature
  Announcement by the Swedish Academy
  of the Nobel Prize
  Nobel Lecture 1982: The Solitude of Latin
  America
  Excerpt from *One Hundred Years
  of Solitude*
  The Magical World of Macondo
  A Tribute to Gabriel García Márquez Y-82
 The 1983 Nobel Prize in Literature
  Announcement by the Swedish
  Academy
  Nobel Lecture 1983
  The Stature of William Golding................Y-83
 The 1984 Nobel Prize in Literature
  Announcement by the Swedish
  Academy
  Jaroslav Seifert Through the Eyes of the
  English-Speaking Reader
  Three Poems by Jaroslav Seifert............Y-84
 The 1985 Nobel Prize in Literature
  Announcement by the Swedish
  Academy
  Nobel Lecture 1985...................................Y-85

The 1986 Nobel Prize in Literature
Nobel Lecture 1986: This Past Must
Address Its Present.................................Y-86

The 1987 Nobel Prize in Literature
Nobel Lecture 1987.................................Y-87

The 1988 Nobel Prize in Literature
Nobel Lecture 1988.................................Y-88

Noel, Roden 1834-1894 ....DLB-35

Nolan, William F. 1928- DLB-8

Noland, C. F. M. 1810?-1858............................DLB-11

Noonday Press DLB-46

Noone, John 1936- DLB-14

Nordhoff, Charles 1887-1947...........................DLB-9

Norman, Marsha 1947- Y-84

Norris, Charles G. 1881-1945..........................DLB-9

Norris, Frank 1870-1902..................................DLB-12

Norris, Leslie 1921- DLB-27

Norse, Harold 1916- DLB-16

North Point Press...DLB-46

Norton, Alice Mary (see Norton, Andre)

Norton, Andre 1912- DLB-8, 52

Norton, Andrews 1786-1853............................DLB-1

Norton, Caroline 1808-1877 ....DLB-21

Norton, Charles Eliot 1827-1908...................DLB-1, 64

Norton, John 1606-1663 ....DLB-24

Norton, Thomas (see Sackville, Thomas)

Norton, W. W., and Company..........................DLB-46

Norwood, Robert 1874-1932 ....DLB-92

Nossack, Hans Erich 1901-1977 ....DLB-69

A Note on Technique (1926), by Elizabeth
A. Drew [excerpts]..................................DLB-36

Nourse, Alan E. 1928- DLB-8

Novalis 1772-1801 ....DLB-90

The Novel in [Robert Browning's] "The Ring
and the Book" (1912), by Henry James DLB-32

The Novel of Impressionism,
by Jethro Bithell DLB-66

Novel-Reading: *The Works of Charles Dickens,
The Works of W. Makepeace Thackeray* (1879),
by Anthony Trollope................................DLB-21

The Novels of Dorothy Richardson (1918), by
May Sinclair DLB-36

Novels with a Purpose (1864),
by Justin M'Carthy DLB-21

Nowlan, Alden 1933-1983................................DLB-53

Noyes, Alfred 1880-1958 ....DLB-20

Noyes, Crosby S. 1825-1908..............................DLB-23

Noyes, Nicholas 1647-1717 ....DLB-24

Noyes, Theodore W. 1858-1946.........................DLB-29

Nugent, Frank 1908-1965 ....DLB-44

Nye, Edgar Wilson (Bill) 1850-1896 ....DLB-11, 23

Nye, Robert 1939- DLB-14

O

Oakes, Urian circa 1631-1681 ....DLB-24

Oates, Joyce Carol 1938- DLB-2, 5; Y-81

Oberholtzer, Ellis Paxson 1868-1936 ....DLB-47

O'Brien, Edna 1932- DLB-14

O'Brien, Fitz-James 1828-1862.........................DLB-74

O'Brien, Kate 1897-1974..................................DLB-15

O'Brien, Tim 1946- Y-80

O'Casey, Sean 1880-1964.................................DLB-10

Ochs, Adolph S. 1858-1935 ....DLB-25

O'Connor, Flannery 1925-1964..................DLB-2; Y-80

O'Dell, Scott 1903- DLB-52

Odell, Jonathan 1737-1818 ....DLB-31

Odets, Clifford 1906-1963 ....DLB-7, 26

O'Donnell, Peter 1920- DLB-87

O'Faolain, Julia 1932- DLB-14

O'Faolain, Sean 1900- DLB-15

Off Broadway and Off-Off-Broadway DLB-7

Off-Loop Theatres DLB-7

Offord, Carl Ruthven 1910- DLB-76

O'Flaherty, Liam 1896-1984 ....DLB-36; Y-84

Ogilvie, J. S., and Company..............................DLB-49

O'Grady, Desmond 1935- DLB-40

O'Hagan, Howard 1902-1982 ....DLB-68

O'Hara, Frank 1926-1966..............................DLB-5, 16

O'Hara, John 1905-1970 ....DLB-9, 86; DS-2

O. Henry (see Porter, William Sydney)

O'Keeffe, John 1747-1833 ....DLB-89

Old Franklin Publishing House DLB-49

Older, Fremont 1856-1935 ....DLB-25

Oliphant, Laurence 1829?-1888.........................DLB-18

Oliphant, Margaret 1828-1897 ....DLB-18

Oliver, Chad 1928- DLB-8

Oliver, Mary 1935- DLB-5

Ollier, Claude 1922- DLB-83

Olsen, Tillie 1913?- DLB-28; Y-80

Olson, Charles 1910-1970..............................DLB-5, 16

Olson, Elder 1909- DLB-48, 63

On Art in Fiction (1838), by
  Edward Bulwer.....................................DLB-21

On Learning to Write...Y-88

On Some of the Characteristics of Modern
  Poetry and On the Lyrical Poems of Alfred
  Tennyson (1831), by Arthur Henry
  Hallam DLB-32

"On Style in English Prose" (1898), by Frederic
  Harrison..DLB-57

"On Style in Literature: Its Technical Elements"
  (1885), by Robert Louis Stevenson.............DLB-57

"On the Writing of Essays" (1862),
  by Alexander Smith...................................DLB-57

Ondaatje, Michael 1943- DLB-60

O'Neill, Eugene 1888-1953............................DLB-7

Oppen, George 1908-1984..................................DLB-5

Oppenheim, E. Phillips 1866-1946....................DLB-70

Oppenheim, James 1882-1932........................DLB-28

Oppenheimer, Joel 1930- DLB-5

Optic, Oliver (see Adams, William Taylor)

Orczy, Emma, Baroness 1865-1947 ....DLB-70

Orlovitz, Gil 1918-1973...................................DLB-2, 5

Orlovsky, Peter 1933- DLB-16

Ormond, John 1923- DLB-27

Ornitz, Samuel 1890-1957 ....DLB-28, 44

Orton, Joe 1933-1967......................................DLB-13

Orwell, George 1903-1950............................DLB-15

The Orwell Year Y-84

Osbon, B. S. 1827-1912....................................DLB-43

Osborne, John 1929- DLB-13

Osgood, Herbert L. 1855-1918........................DLB-47

Osgood, James R., and Company.....................DLB-49

O'Shaughnessy, Arthur 1844-1881....................DLB-35

O'Shea, Patrick [publishing house]....................DLB-49

Ostenso, Martha 1900-1963............................DLB-92

Oswald, Eleazer 1755-1795 ....DLB-43

Otero, Miguel Antonio 1859-1944 ....DLB-82

Otis, James (see Kaler, James Otis)

Otis, James, Jr. 1725-1783 ....DLB-31

Otis, Broaders and Company...........................DLB-49

Ottendorfer, Oswald 1826-1900 ....DLB-23

Otway, Thomas 1652-1685 ....DLB-80

Ouellette, Fernand 1930- DLB-60

Ouida 1839-1908 ....DLB-18

Outing Publishing Company............................DLB-46

Outlaw Days, by Joyce Johnson..........................DLB-16

The Overlook Press..DLB-46

Overview of U.S. Book Publishing, 1910-1945....DLB-9

Owen, Guy 1925- DLB-5

Owen, John [publishing house]..........................DLB-49

Owen, Wilfred 1893-1918................................DLB-20

Owsley, Frank L. 1890-1956 ....DLB-17

Ozick, Cynthia 1928- DLB-28; Y-82

P

Pacey, Desmond 1917-1975 ....DLB-88

Pack, Robert 1929- DLB-5

Packaging Papa: *The Garden of Eden* Y-86

Padell Publishing Company DLB-46

Padgett, Ron 1942- DLB-5

Page, L. C., and Company DLB-49

Page, P. K. 1916- DLB-68

Page, Thomas Nelson 1853-1922 ....DLB-12, 78

Page, Walter Hines 1855-1918.....................DLB-71, 91

Paget, Violet (see Lee, Vernon)

Pain, Philip ?-circa 1666.....................................DLB-24

Paine, Robert Treat, Jr. 1773-1811 ....DLB-37

Paine, Thomas 1737-1809 ....DLB-31, 43, 73

Paley, Grace 1922- DLB-28

Palfrey, John Gorham 1796-1881....................DLB-1, 30

Palgrave, Francis Turner 1824-1897 ....DLB-35

Paltock, Robert 1697-1767 ....DLB-39

Panama, Norman 1914-   and
  Frank, Melvin 1913-1988 ....DLB-26

Pangborn, Edgar 1909-1976 ....DLB-8

"Panic Among the Philistines": A Postscript,
An Interview with Bryan Griffin Y-81

Panneton, Philippe (see Ringuet)

Panshin, Alexei 1940- DLB-8

Pansy (see Alden, Isabella)

Pantheon Books DLB-46

Paperback Library DLB-46

Paperback Science Fiction DLB-8

Paquet, Alfons 1881-1944 ....DLB-66

Paradis, Suzanne 1936- DLB-53

Parents' Magazine Press DLB-46

Parisian Theater, Fall 1984: Toward
A New Baroque Y-85

Parizeau, Alice 1930- DLB-60

Parke, John 1754-1789 ....DLB-31

Parker, Dorothy 1893-1967 ....DLB-11, 45, 86

Parker, James 1714-1770 ....DLB-43

Parker, Theodore 1810-1860 ....DLB-1

Parkman, Francis, Jr. 1823-1893 ....DLB-1, 30

Parks, Gordon 1912- DLB-33

Parks, William 1698-1750 ....DLB-43

Parks, William [publishing house] DLB-49

Parley, Peter (see Goodrich, Samuel Griswold)

Parrington, Vernon L. 1871-1929 ....DLB-17, 63

Parton, James 1822-1891 ....DLB-30

Parton, Sara Payson Willis 1811-1872 ....DLB-43, 74

Pastan, Linda 1932- DLB-5

Pastorius, Francis Daniel 1651-circa 1720 ....DLB-24

Patchen, Kenneth 1911-1972 ....DLB-16, 48

Pater, Walter 1839-1894 ....DLB-57

Paterson, Katherine 1932- DLB-52

Patmore, Coventry 1823-1896 ....DLB-35

Paton, Joseph Noel 1821-1901 ....DLB-35

Patrick, John 1906- DLB-7

Pattee, Fred Lewis 1863-1950 ....DLB-71

Pattern and Paradigm: History as
Design, by Judith Ryan DLB-75

Patterson, Eleanor Medill 1881-1948 ....DLB-29

Patterson, Joseph Medill 1879-1946 ....DLB-29

Pattillo, Henry 1726-1801 ....DLB-37

Paul, Elliot 1891-1958 ....DLB-4

Paul, Peter, Book Company DLB-49

Paulding, James Kirke 1778-1860 ....DLB-3, 59, 74

Paulin, Tom 1949- DLB-40

Pauper, Peter, Press DLB-46

Paxton, John 1911-1985 ....DLB-44

Payn, James 1830-1898 ....DLB-18

Payne, John 1842-1916 ....DLB-35

Payne, John Howard 1791-1852 ....DLB-37

Payson and Clarke DLB-46

Peabody, Elizabeth Palmer 1804-1894 ....DLB-1

Peabody, Elizabeth Palmer [publishing
house] DLB-49

Peabody, Oliver William Bourn 1799-1848 ....DLB-59

Peachtree Publishers, Limited DLB-46

Pead, Deuel ?-1727 ....DLB-24

Peake, Mervyn 1911-1968 ....DLB-15

Pearson, H. B. [publishing house] DLB-49

Peck, George W. 1840-1916 ....DLB-23, 42

Peck, H. C., and Theo. Bliss [publishing
house] DLB-49

Peck, Harry Thurston 1856-1914 ....DLB-71, 91

Peele, George 1556-1596 ....DLB-62

Pellegrini and Cudahy DLB-46

Pelletier, Aimé (see Vac, Bertrand)

Pemberton, Sir Max 1863-1950 ....DLB-70

Penguin Books DLB-46

Penn Publishing Company DLB-49

Penn, William 1644-1718 ....DLB-24

Penner, Jonathan 1940- Y-83

Pennington, Lee 1939- Y-82

Percy, Walker 1916- DLB-2; Y-80

Perec, Georges 1936-1982 ....DLB-83

Perelman, S. J. 1904-1979 ....DLB-11, 44

Periodicals of the Beat Generation DLB-16

Perkins, Eugene 1932- DLB-41

Perkoff, Stuart Z. 1930-1974 ....DLB-16

Permabooks DLB-46

Perry, Bliss 1860-1954 ....DLB-71

Perry, Eleanor 1915-1981 ....DLB-44

"Personal Style" (1890), by John Addington
Symonds DLB-57

Perutz, Leo 1882-1957 ....DLB-81

Peter, Laurence J. 1919-1990.............................DLB-53

Peterkin, Julia 1880-1961.....................................DLB-9

Petersham, Maud 1889-1971 and
　　Petersham, Miska 1888-1960.......................DLB-22

Peterson, Charles Jacobs 1819-1887..................DLB-79

Peterson, Len 1917-　...DLB-88

Peterson, Louis 1922-　.....................................DLB-76

Peterson, T. B., and Brothers............................DLB-49

Petry, Ann 1908-　..DLB-76

Pharr, Robert Deane 1916-1989........................DLB-33

Phelps, Elizabeth Stuart 1844-1911...................DLB-74

Philippe, Charles-Louis 1874-1909....................DLB-65

Phillips, David Graham 1867-1911.................DLB-9, 12

Phillips, Jayne Anne 1952-　..................................Y-80

Phillips, Stephen 1864-1915...............................DLB-10

Phillips, Ulrich B. 1877-1934.............................DLB-17

Phillips, Willard 1784-1873................................DLB-59

Phillips, Sampson and Company........................DLB-49

Phillpotts, Eden 1862-1960...........................DLB-10, 70

Philosophical Library...DLB-46

"The Philosophy of Style" (1852), by
　　Herbert Spencer..DLB-57

Phinney, Elihu [publishing house]....................DLB-49

Phoenix, John (see Derby, George Horatio)

PHYLON (Fourth Quarter, 1950),
　　The Negro in Literature:
　　The Current Scene.......................................DLB-76

Pickard, Tom 1946-　...DLB-40

Pickthall, Marjorie 1883-1922............................DLB-92

Pictorial Printing Company...............................DLB-49

Pike, Albert 1809-1891.......................................DLB-74

Pilon, Jean-Guy 1930-　.....................................DLB-60

Pinckney, Josephine 1895-1957 ....DLB-6

Pinero, Arthur Wing 1855-1934........................DLB-10

Pinget, Robert 1919-　.......................................DLB-83

Pinnacle Books..DLB-46

Pinsky, Robert 1940-　..Y-82

Pinter, Harold 1930-　.......................................DLB-13

Piontek, Heinz 1925-　.......................................DLB-75

Piper, H. Beam 1904-1964 ....DLB-8

Piper, Watty..DLB-22

Pisar, Samuel 1929-　...Y-83

Pitkin, Timothy 1766-1847 ....DLB-30

The Pitt Poetry Series: Poetry
　　Publishing Today Y-85

Pitter, Ruth 1897-　..DLB-20

Pix, Mary 1666-1709 ....DLB-80

The Place of Realism in Fiction (1895), by
　　George Gissing...DLB-18

Plante, David 1940-　...Y-83

Platen, August von 1796-1835...........................DLB-90

Plath, Sylvia 1932-1963 ....DLB-5, 6

Platt and Munk Company..................................DLB-46

Playboy Press...DLB-46

Plays, Playwrights, and Playgoers......................DLB-84

Playwrights and Professors, by Tom
　　Stoppard DLB-13

Playwrights on the Theater................................DLB-80

Plenzdorf, Ulrich 1934-　..................................DLB-75

Plessen, Elizabeth 1944-　.................................DLB-75

Plievier, Theodor 1892-1955 ....DLB-69

Plomer, William 1903-1973...............................DLB-20

Plumly, Stanley 1939-　.......................................DLB-5

Plumpp, Sterling D. 1940-　..............................DLB-41

Plunkett, James 1920-　.....................................DLB-14

Plymell, Charles 1935-　....................................DLB-16

Pocket Books...DLB-46

Poe, Edgar Allan 1809-1849...............DLB-3, 59, 73, 74

Poe, James 1921-1980..DLB-44

The Poet Laureate of the United States
　　Statements from Former Consultants
　　in Poetry..Y-86

Pohl, Frederik 1919-　...DLB-8

Poirier, Louis (see Gracq, Julien)

Poliakoff, Stephen 1952-　.................................DLB-13

Polite, Carlene Hatcher 1932-　.........................DLB-33

Pollard, Edward A. 1832-1872...........................DLB-30

Pollard, Percival 1869-1911...............................DLB-71

Pollard and Moss...DLB-49

Pollock, Sharon 1936-　.....................................DLB-60

Polonsky, Abraham 1910-　...............................DLB-26

Poole, Ernest 1880-1950....................................DLB-9

Poore, Benjamin Perley 1820-1887....................DLB-23

Popular Library..DLB-46

Porlock, Martin (see MacDonald, Philip)

Porter, Eleanor H. 1868-1920...............DLB-9

Porter, Henry ?-?.................................DLB-62

Porter, Katherine Anne 1890-1980........DLB-4, 9; Y-80

Porter, Peter 1929- DLB-40

Porter, William Sydney 1862-1910.........DLB-12, 78, 79

Porter, William T. 1809-1858.........................DLB-3, 43

Porter and Coates..................................DLB-49

Portis, Charles 1933- DLB-6

Poston, Ted 1906-1974.........................DLB-51

Postscript to [the Third Edition of] *Clarissa*
    (1751), by Samuel Richardson DLB-39

Potok, Chaim 1929- DLB-28; Y-84

Potter, David M. 1910-1971 ....DLB-17

Potter, John E., and Company..............DLB-49

Pottle, Frederick A. 1897-1987 ....Y-87

Poulin, Jacques 1937- DLB-60

Pound, Ezra 1885-1972..........................DLB-4, 45, 63

Powell, Anthony 1905- DLB-15

Pownall, David 1938- DLB-14

Powys, John Cowper 1872-1963 ....DLB-15

Powys, T. F. 1875-1953 ....DLB-36

The Practice of Biography: An Interview with
    Stanley Weintraub............................Y-82

The Practice of Biography II: An Interview with
    B. L. Reid..Y-83

The Practice of Biography III: An Interview with
    Humphrey Carpenter Y-84

The Practice of Biography IV: An Interview with
    William Manchester...........................Y-85

The Practice of Biography V: An Interview with
    Justin Kaplan Y-86

The Practice of Biography VI: An Interview with
    David Herbert Donald Y-87

Praeger Publishers.................................DLB-46

Pratt, E. J. 1882-1964...........................DLB-92

Pratt, Samuel Jackson 1749-1814 ....DLB-39

Preface to *Alwyn* (1780), by Thomas
    Holcroft..DLB-39

Preface to *Colonel Jack* (1722), by Daniel
    Defoe...DLB-39

Preface to *Evelina* (1778), by Fanny Burney.......DLB-39

Preface to *Ferdinand Count Fathom* (1753), by

Tobias Smollett DLB-39

Preface to *Incognita* (1692), by William
    Congreve.......................................DLB-39

Preface to *Joseph Andrews* (1742), by
    Henry Fielding DLB-39

Preface to *Moll Flanders* (1722), by Daniel
    Defoe...DLB-39

Preface to *Poems* (1853), by Matthew
    Arnold..DLB-32

Preface to *Robinson Crusoe* (1719), by Daniel
    Defoe...DLB-39

Preface to *Roderick Random* (1748), by Tobias
    Smollett..DLB-39

Preface to *Roxana* (1724), by Daniel Defoe DLB-39

Preface to *St. Leon* (1799),
    by William Godwin...........................DLB-39

Preface to Sarah Fielding's *Familiar Letters*
    (1747), by Henry Fielding [excerpt]...........DLB-39

Preface to Sarah Fielding's *The Adventures of
    David Simple* (1744), by Henry Fielding.......DLB-39

Preface to *The Cry* (1754), by Sarah Fielding DLB-39

Preface to *The Delicate Distress* (1769), by
    Elizabeth Griffin DLB-39

Preface to *The Disguis'd Prince* (1733), by Eliza
    Haywood [excerpt] DLB-39

Preface to *The Farther Adventures of Robinson
    Crusoe* (1719), by Daniel Defoe DLB-39

Preface to the First Edition of *Pamela* (1740), by
    Samuel Richardson...........................DLB-39

Preface to the First Edition of *The Castle of
    Otranto* (1764), by Horace Walpole.............DLB-39

Preface to *The History of Romances* (1715), by
    Pierre Daniel Huet [excerpts]....................DLB-39

Preface to *The Life of Charlotta du Pont* (1723),
    by Penelope Aubin DLB-39

Preface to *The Old English Baron* (1778), by
    Clara Reeve.....................................DLB-39

Preface to the Second Edition of *The Castle of
    Otranto* (1765), by Horace Walpole.............DLB-39

Preface to *The Secret History, of Queen Zarah, and
    the Zarazians* (1705), by Delarivière
    Manley...DLB-39

Preface to the Third Edition of *Clarissa* (1751),
    by Samuel Richardson [excerpt].................DLB-39

Preface to *The Works of Mrs. Davys* (1725), by
    Mary Davys.....................................DLB-39

Preface to Volume 1 of *Clarissa* (1747), by
Samuel Richardson.........................DLB-39

Preface to Volume 3 of *Clarissa* (1748), by
Samuel Richardson.........................DLB-39

Préfontaine, Yves 1937- DLB-53

Prelutsky, Jack 1940- DLB-61

Premisses, by Michael Hamburger DLB-66

Prentice, George D. 1802-1870.........................DLB-43

Prentice-Hall DLB-46

Prescott, William Hickling 1796-1859......DLB-1, 30, 59

The Present State of the English Novel (1892),
by George Saintsbury DLB-18

Preston, Thomas 1537-1598 ....DLB-62

Price, Reynolds 1933- DLB-2

Price, Richard 1949- Y-81

Priest, Christopher 1943- DLB-14

Priestley, J. B. 1894-1984 ....DLB-10, 34, 77; Y-84

Prime, Benjamin Young 1733-1791..................DLB-31

Prince, F. T. 1912- DLB-20

Prince, Thomas 1687-1758 ....DLB-24

The Principles of Success in Literature (1865), by
George Henry Lewes [excerpt]...................DLB-57

Pritchett, V. S. 1900- DLB-15

Procter, Adelaide Anne 1825-1864 ....DLB-32

The Progress of Romance (1785), by Clara Reeve
[excerpt]...DLB-39

Prokosch, Frederic 1906-1989 ....DLB-48

The Proletarian Novel......................DLB-9

Propper, Dan 1937- DLB-16

The Prospect of Peace (1778), by Joel Barlow DLB-37

Proud, Robert 1728-1813.......................DLB-30

Proust, Marcel 1871-1922 ....DLB-65

Prynne, J. H. 1936- DLB-40

Przybyszewski, Stanislaw 1868-1927 ....DLB-66

The Public Lending Right in America
Statement by Sen. Charles McC. Mathias, Jr.
PLR and the Meaning of Literary Property
Statements on PLR by American Writers.........Y-83

The Public Lending Right in the United Kingdom
Public Lending Right: The First Year in the
United Kingdom Y-83

The Publication of English Renaissance
Plays DLB-62

Publications and Social Movements
[Transcendentalism] DLB-1

Publishers and Agents: The Columbia
Connection Y-87

Publishing Fiction at LSU Press..........................Y-87

Pugin, A. Welby 1812-1852....................DLB-55

Pulitzer, Joseph 1847-1911 ....DLB-23

Pulitzer, Joseph, Jr. 1885-1955 ....DLB-29

Pulitzer Prizes for the Novel, 1917-1945 ....DLB-9

Purdy, Al 1918- DLB-88

Purdy, James 1923- DLB-2

Pusey, Edward Bouverie 1800-1882...................DLB-55

Putnam, George Palmer 1814-1872 ....DLB-3, 79

Putnam, Samuel 1892-1950 ....DLB-4

G. P. Putnam's Sons DLB-49

Puzo, Mario 1920- DLB-6

Pyle, Ernie 1900-1945 ....DLB-29

Pyle, Howard 1853-1911 ....DLB-42

Pym, Barbara 1913-1980 ....DLB-14; Y-87

Pynchon, Thomas 1937- DLB-2

Pyramid Books...............................DLB-46

Pyrnelle, Louise-Clarke 1850-1907....................DLB-42

Q

Quad, M. (see Lewis, Charles B.)

The Queen City Publishing House.....................DLB-49

Queneau, Raymond 1903-1976 ....DLB-72

The Question of American Copyright
in the Nineteenth Century
Headnote
Preface, by George Haven Putnam
The Evolution of Copyright, by Brander
Matthews
Summary of Copyright Legislation in the
United States, by R. R. Bowker
Analysis of the Provisions of the Copyright
Law of 1891, by George Haven Putnam
The Contest for International Copyright,
by George Haven Putnam
Cheap Books and Good Books,
by Brander Matthews....................DLB-49

Quin, Ann 1936-1973.........................DLB-14

Quincy, Samuel of Georgia ?-? DLB-31

Quincy, Samuel of Massachusetts 1734-1789.....DLB-31

Quintana, Leroy V. 1944- DLB-82

Quist, Harlin, Books...DLB-46

Quoirez, Françoise (see Sagan, Françoise)

R

Rabe, David 1940- DLB-7

Radcliffe, Ann 1764-1823 ....DLB-39

Raddall, Thomas 1903- DLB-68

Radiguet, Raymond 1903-1923.......................DLB-65

Radványi, Netty Reiling (see Seghers, Anna)

Raimund, Ferdinand Jakob 1790-1836..............DLB-90

Raine, Craig 1944- DLB-40

Raine, Kathleen 1908- DLB-20

Ralph, Julian 1853-1903...................................DLB-23

Ralph Waldo Emerson in 1982 ....Y-82

Rambler, no. 4 (1750), by Samuel Johnson
    [excerpt]...DLB-39

Ramée, Marie Louise de la (see Ouida)

Ramsay, David 1749-1815 ....DLB-30

Rand, Avery and Company................................DLB-49

Rand McNally and Company.............................DLB-49

Randall, Dudley 1914- DLB-41

Randall, Henry S. 1811-1876...........................DLB-30

Randall, James G. 1881-1953...........................DLB-17

The Randall Jarrell Symposium: A Small
    Collection of Randall Jarrells
    Excerpts From Papers Delivered at
    the Randall Jarrell Symposium Y-86

Randolph, A. Philip 1889-1979 ....DLB-91

Randolph, Anson D. F. [publishing house]........DLB-49

Randolph, Thomas 1605-1635..........................DLB-58

Random House..DLB-46

Ranlet, Henry [publishing house].......................DLB-49

Ransom, John Crowe 1888-1974 ....DLB-45, 63

Raphael, Frederic 1931- DLB-14

Raphaelson, Samson 1896-1983.......................DLB-44

Raskin, Ellen 1928-1984..................................DLB-52

Rattigan, Terence 1911-1977 ....DLB-13

Rawlings, Marjorie Kinnan 1896-1953..........DLB-9, 22

Raworth, Tom 1938- DLB-40

Ray, David 1932- DLB-5

Ray, Henrietta Cordelia 1849-1916 ....DLB-50

Raymond, Henry J. 1820-1869.....................DLB-43, 79

Raymond Chandler Centenary Tributes
    from Michael Avallone, James Elroy, Joe Gores,
    and William F. Nolan Y-88

Reach, Angus 1821-1856..................................DLB-70

Read, Herbert 1893-1968 ....DLB-20

Read, Opie 1852-1939.......................................DLB-23

Read, Piers Paul 1941- DLB-14

Reade, Charles 1814-1884................................DLB-21

Reader's Digest Condensed Books DLB-46

Reading, Peter 1946- DLB-40

Reaney, James 1926- DLB-68

Rechy, John 1934- Y-82

Redding, J. Saunders 1906-1988 ....DLB-63, 76

Redfield, J. S. [publishing house] DLB-49

Redgrove, Peter 1932- DLB-40

Redmon, Anne 1943- Y-86

Redmond, Eugene B. 1937- DLB-41

Redpath, James [publishing house] DLB-49

Reed, Henry 1808-1854 ....DLB-59

Reed, Henry 1914- DLB-27

Reed, Ishmael 1938- DLB-2, 5, 33

Reed, Sampson 1800-1880 ....DLB-1

Reedy, William Marion 1862-1920....................DLB-91

Reese, Lizette Woodworth 1856-1935 ....DLB-54

Reese, Thomas 1742-1796 ....DLB-37

Reeve, Clara 1729-1807....................................DLB-39

Reeves, John 1926- DLB-88

Regnery, Henry, Company DLB-46

Reid, Alastair 1926- DLB-27

Reid, Christopher 1949- DLB-40

Reid, Helen Rogers 1882-1970..........................DLB-29

Reid, James ?-?..DLB-31

Reid, Mayne 1818-1883.....................................DLB-21

Reid, Thomas 1710-1796 ....DLB-31

Reid, Whitelaw 1837-1912 ....DLB-23

Reilly and Lee Publishing Company DLB-46

Reimann, Brigitte 1933-1973 ....DLB-75

Reisch, Walter 1903-1983.................................DLB-44

Remarque, Erich Maria 1898-1970....................DLB-56

"Re-meeting of Old Friends": The Jack Kerouac Conference..Y-82

Remington, Frederic 1861-1909 ....DLB-12

Renaud, Jacques 1943- DLB-60

Renault, Mary 1905-1983 ....Y-83

Rendell, Ruth 1930- DLB-87

Representative Men and Women: A Historical Perspective on the British Novel, 1930-1960 ....DLB-15

(Re-)Publishing Orwell Y-86

Reuter, Gabriele 1859-1941 ....DLB-66

Revell, Fleming H., Company............................DLB-49

Reventlow, Franziska Gräfin zu 1871-1918 ....DLB-66

Review of [Samuel Richardson's] *Clarissa* (1748), by Henry Fielding DLB-39

The Revolt (1937), by Mary Colum [excerpts] DLB-36

Rexroth, Kenneth 1905-1982 ....DLB-16, 48; Y-82

Rey, H. A. 1898-1977 ....DLB-22

Reynal and Hitchcock DLB-46

Reynolds, G. W. M. 1814-1879...........................DLB-21

Reynolds, Mack 1917- DLB-8

Reznikoff, Charles 1894-1976.......................DLB-28, 45

"Rhetoric" (1828; revised, 1859), by Thomas de Quincey [excerpt] DLB-57

Rhett, Robert Barnwell 1800-1876.....................DLB-43

Rhode, John 1884-1964 ....DLB-77

Rhodes, James Ford 1848-1927 ....DLB-47

Rhys, Jean 1890-1979..DLB-36

Ricardou, Jean 1932- DLB-83

Rice, Elmer 1892-1967.....................................DLB-4, 7

Rice, Grantland 1880-1954 ....DLB-29

Rich, Adrienne 1929- DLB-5, 67

Richards, David Adams 1950- DLB-53

Richards, George circa 1760-1814 ....DLB-37

Richards, I. A. 1893-1979 ....DLB-27

Richards, Laura E. 1850-1943 ....DLB-42

Richards, William Carey 1818-1892 ....DLB-73

Richardson, Charles F. 1851-1913.....................DLB-71

Richardson, Dorothy M. 1873-1957 ....DLB-36

Richardson, Jack 1935- DLB-7

Richardson, Samuel 1689-1761..........................DLB-39

Richardson, Willis 1889-1977 ....DLB-51

Richler, Mordecai 1931- DLB-53

Richter, Conrad 1890-1968................................DLB-9

Richter, Hans Werner 1908- DLB-69

Rickword, Edgell 1898-1982..............................DLB-20

Riddell, John (see Ford, Corey)

Ridge, Lola 1873-1941 ....DLB-54

Ridler, Anne 1912- DLB-27

Riffaterre, Michael 1924- DLB-67

Riis, Jacob 1849-1914 ....DLB-23

Riker, John C. [publishing house] DLB-49

Riley, John 1938-1978 ....DLB-40

Rilke, Rainer Maria 1875-1926 ....DLB-81

Rinehart and Company DLB-46

Ringuet 1895-1960 ....DLB-68

Ringwood, Gwen Pharis 1910-1984....................DLB-88

Rinser, Luise 1911- DLB-69

Ríos, Isabella 1948- DLB-82

Ripley, Arthur 1895-1961 ....DLB-44

Ripley, George 1802-1880 ....DLB-1, 64, 73

The Rising Glory of America: Three Poems DLB-37

The Rising Glory of America: Written in 1771 (1786), by Hugh Henry Brackenridge and Philip Freneau DLB-37

Riskin, Robert 1897-1955..................................DLB-26

Risse, Heinz 1898- DLB-69

Ritchie, Anna Mowatt 1819-1870 ....DLB-3

Ritchie, Anne Thackeray 1837-1919 ....DLB-18

Ritchie, Thomas 1778-1854 ....DLB-43

Rites of Passage [on William Saroyan]....................Y-83

The Ritz Paris Hemingway Award..........................Y-85

Rivard, Adjutor 1868-1945 ....DLB-92

Rivera, Tomás 1935-1984..................................DLB-82

Rivers, Conrad Kent 1933-1968 ....DLB-41

Riverside Press...DLB-49

Rivington, James circa 1724-1802......................DLB-43

Rivkin, Allen 1903- DLB-26

Robbe-Grillet, Alain 1922- DLB-83

Robbins, Tom 1936- Y-80

Roberts, Charles G. D. 1860-1943 ....DLB-92

Roberts, Dorothy 1906- DLB-88

Roberts, Elizabeth Madox 1881-1941............DLB-9, 54

Roberts, Kenneth 1885-1957 ....DLB-9

Roberts Brothers..DLB-49

Robertson, A. M., and Company.......................DLB-49

Robinson, Casey 1903-1979 ....DLB-44

Robinson, Edwin Arlington 1869-1935 ....DLB-54

Robinson, James Harvey 1863-1936..................DLB-47

Robinson, Lennox 1886-1958 ....DLB-10

Robinson, Mabel Louise 1874-1962...................DLB-22

Robinson, Therese 1797-1870 ....DLB-59

Roblès, Emmanuel 1914- DLB-83

Rodgers, Carolyn M. 1945- DLB-41

Rodgers, W. R. 1909-1969 ....DLB-20

Rodriguez, Richard 1944- DLB-82

Roethke, Theodore 1908-1963 ....DLB-5

Rogers, Will 1879-1935 ....DLB-11

Rohmer, Sax 1883-1959..DLB-70

Roiphe, Anne 1935- Y-80

Rojas, Arnold R. 1896-1988...............................DLB-82

Rolfe, Frederick William 1860-1913..................DLB-34

Rolland, Romain 1866-1944 ....DLB-65

Rolvaag, O. E. 1876-1931.......................................DLB-9

Romains, Jules 1885-1972 ....DLB-65

Roman, A., and Company......................................DLB-49

Romero, Orlando 1945- DLB-82

Roosevelt, Theodore 1858-1919.........................DLB-47

Root, Waverley 1903-1982 ....DLB-4

Roquebrune, Robert de 1889-1978 ....DLB-68

Rose, Reginald 1920- DLB-26

Rosei, Peter 1946- DLB-85

Rosen, Norma 1925- DLB-28

Rosenberg, Isaac 1890-1918 ....DLB-20

Rosenfeld, Isaac 1918-1956.................................DLB-28

Rosenthal, M. L. 1917- DLB-5

Ross, Leonard Q. (see Rosten, Leo)

Ross, Sinclair 1908- DLB-88

Ross, W. W. E. 1894-1966.....................................DLB-88

Rossen, Robert 1908-1966 ....DLB-26

Rossetti, Christina 1830-1894.............................DLB-35

Rossetti, Dante Gabriel 1828-1882.....................DLB-35

Rossner, Judith 1935- DLB-6

Rosten, Leo 1908- DLB-11

Roth, Gerhard 1942- DLB-85

Roth, Henry 1906?- DLB-28

Roth, Joseph 1894-1939 ....DLB-85

Roth, Philip 1933- DLB-2, 28; Y-82

Rothenberg, Jerome 1931- DLB-5

Routier, Simone 1901-1987..................................DLB-88

Rowe, Elizabeth 1674-1737 ....DLB-39

Rowe, Nicholas 1674-1718 ....DLB-84

Rowlandson, Mary circa 1635-circa 1678...........DLB-24

Rowley, William circa 1585-1626.........................DLB-58

Rowson, Susanna Haswell circa 1762-1824........DLB-37

Roy, Camille 1870-1943 ....DLB-92

Roy, Gabrielle 1909-1983.....................................DLB-68

Roy, Jules 1907- DLB-83

The Royal Court Theatre and the English
     Stage Company...DLB-13

The Royal Court Theatre and the New
     Drama DLB-10

The Royal Shakespeare Company
     at the Swan..Y-88

Royall, Anne 1769-1854.......................................DLB-43

The Roycroft Printing Shop DLB-49

Rubens, Bernice 1928- DLB-14

Rudd and Carleton...DLB-49

Rudkin, David 1936- DLB-13

Ruffin, Josephine St. Pierre 1842-1924.............DLB-79

Ruggles, Henry Joseph 1813-1906 ....DLB-64

Rukeyser, Muriel 1913-1980 ....DLB-48

Rule, Jane 1931- DLB-60

Rumaker, Michael 1932- DLB-16

Rumens, Carol 1944- DLB-40

Runyon, Damon 1880-1946........................DLB-11, 86

Rush, Benjamin 1746-1813 ....DLB-37

Ruskin, John 1819-1900.......................................DLB-55

Russ, Joanna 1937- DLB-8

Russell, B. B., and Company DLB-49

Russell, Benjamin 1761-1845..............................DLB-43

Russell, Charles Edward 1860-1941 ....DLB-25

Russell, George William (see AE)

Russell, R. H., and Son DLB-49

Rutherford, Mark 1831-1913.......................DLB-18

Ryan, Michael 1946- Y-82

Ryan, Oscar 1904- DLB-68

Ryga, George 1932- DLB-60

Ryskind, Morrie 1895-1985 ....DLB-26

S

The Saalfield Publishing Company DLB-46

Saberhagen, Fred 1930- DLB-8

Sackler, Howard 1929-1982.........................DLB-7

Sackville, Thomas 1536-1608
    and Norton, Thomas 1532-1584 ....DLB-62

Sackville-West, V. 1892-1962 ....DLB-34

Sadlier, D. and J., and Company......................DLB-49

Saffin, John circa 1626-1710...........................DLB-24

Sagan, Françoise 1935- DLB-83

Sage, Robert 1899-1962 ....DLB-4

Sagel, Jim 1947- DLB-82

Sahkomaapii, Piitai (see Highwater, Jamake)

Sahl, Hans 1902- DLB-69

Said, Edward W. 1935- DLB-67

Saiko, George 1892-1962 ....DLB-85

St. Johns, Adela Rogers 1894-1988 ....DLB-29

St. Martin's Press DLB-46

Saint-Exupéry, Antoine de 1900-1944 ....DLB-72

Saint Pierre, Michel de 1916-1987.....................DLB-83

Saintsbury, George 1845-1933...........................DLB-57

Saki (see Munro, H. H.)

Salaam, Kalamu ya 1947- DLB-38

Salas, Floyd 1931- DLB-82

Salemson, Harold J. 1910-1988 ....DLB-4

Salinas, Luis Omar 1937- DLB-82

Salinger, J. D. 1919- DLB-2

Salt, Waldo 1914- DLB-44

Salverson, Laura Goodman 1890-1970 ....DLB-92

Sampson, Richard Henry (see Hull, Richard)

Sanborn, Franklin Benjamin 1831-1917 ....DLB-1

Sánchez, Ricardo 1941- DLB-82

Sanchez, Sonia 1934- DLB-41

Sandburg, Carl 1878-1967 ....DLB-17, 54

Sanders, Ed 1939- DLB-16

Sandoz, Mari 1896-1966.................................DLB-9

Sandwell, B. K. 1876-1954.............................DLB-92

Sandys, George 1578-1644...............................DLB-24

Santayana, George 1863-1952 ....DLB-54, 71

Santmyer, Helen Hooven 1895-1986......................Y-84

Sapir, Edward 1884-1939.................................DLB-92

Sapper (see McNeile, Herman Cyril)

Sargent, Pamela 1948- DLB-8

Saroyan, William 1908-1981.............DLB-7, 9, 86; Y-81

Sarraute, Nathalie 1900- DLB-83

Sarrazin, Albertine 1937-1967 ....DLB-83

Sarton, May 1912- DLB-48; Y-81

Sartre, Jean-Paul 1905-1980 ....DLB-72

Sassoon, Siegfried 1886-1967 ....DLB-20

Saturday Review Press...................................DLB-46

Saunders, James 1925- DLB-13

Saunders, John Monk 1897-1940 ....DLB-26

Saunders, Margaret Marshall
    1861-1947 ....DLB-92

Savage, James 1784-1873 ....DLB-30

Savage, Marmion W. 1803?-1872 ....DLB-21

Savard, Félix-Antoine 1896-1982.......................DLB-68

Sawyer, Ruth 1880-1970 ....DLB-22

Sayers, Dorothy L. 1893-1957 ....DLB-10, 36, 77

Sayles, John Thomas 1950- DLB-44

Scannell, Vernon 1922- DLB-27

Scarry, Richard 1919- DLB-61

Schaeffer, Albrecht 1885-1950 ....DLB-66

Schaeffer, Susan Fromberg 1941- DLB-28

Schaper, Edzard 1908-1984 ....DLB-69

Scharf, J. Thomas 1843-1898 ....DLB-47

Schelling, Friedrich Wilhelm Joseph von
    1775-1854 ....DLB-90

Schickele, René 1883-1940...............................DLB-66

Schlegel, Dorothea 1763-1839 ....DLB-90

Schlegel, Friedrich 1772-1829..........................DLB-90

Schleiermacher, Friedrich 1768-1834.................DLB-90

Schlesinger, Arthur M., Jr. 1917- DLB-17

Schlumberger, Jean 1877-1968..........................DLB-65

Schmid, Eduard Hermann Wilhelm
(see Edschmid, Kasimir)

Schmidt, Arno 1914-1979 ....DLB-69

Schmidt, Michael 1947- DLB-40

Schmitz, James H. 1911- DLB-8

Schnitzler, Arthur 1862-1931 ....DLB-81

Schnurre, Wolfdietrich 1920- DLB-69

Schocken Books DLB-46

The Schomburg Center for Research
in Black Culture DLB-76

Schopenhauer, Arthur 1788-1860 ....DLB-90

Schopenhauer, Johanna 1766-1838 ....DLB-90

Schouler, James 1839-1920 ....DLB-47

Schrader, Paul 1946- DLB-44

Schreiner, Olive 1855-1920 ....DLB-18

Schroeder, Andreas 1946- DLB-53

Schubert, Gotthilf Heinrich 1780-1860 ....DLB-90

Schulberg, Budd 1914- DLB-6, 26, 28; Y-81

Schulte, F. J., and Company DLB-49

Schurz, Carl 1829-1906 ....DLB-23

Schuyler, George S. 1895-1977 ....DLB-29, 51

Schuyler, James 1923- DLB-5

Schwartz, Delmore 1913-1966 ....DLB-28, 48

Schwartz, Jonathan 1938- Y-82

Science Fantasy DLB-8

Science-Fiction Fandom and Conventions DLB-8

Science-Fiction Fanzines: The Time Binders DLB-8

Science-Fiction Films DLB-8

Science Fiction Writers of America and the
Nebula Awards DLB-8

Scott, Duncan Campbell 1862-1947 ....DLB-92

Scott, Evelyn 1893-1963 ....DLB-9, 48

Scott, F. R. 1899-1985 ....DLB-88

Scott, Frederick George
1861-1944 ....DLB-92

Scott, Harvey W. 1838-1910 ....DLB-23

Scott, Paul 1920-1978 ....DLB-14

Scott, Sarah 1723-1795 ....DLB-39

Scott, Tom 1918- DLB-27

Scott, William Bell 1811-1890 ....DLB-32

Scott, William R. [publishing house] DLB-46

Scott-Heron, Gil 1949- DLB-41

Charles Scribner's Sons DLB-49

Scripps, E. W. 1854-1926 ....DLB-25

Scudder, Horace Elisha 1838-1902 ....DLB-42, 71

Scudder, Vida Dutton 1861-1954 ....DLB-71

Scupham, Peter 1933- DLB-40

Seabrook, William 1886-1945 ....DLB-4

Seabury, Samuel 1729-1796 ....DLB-31

Sears, Edward I. 1819?-1876 ....DLB-79

Sears Publishing Company DLB-46

Seaton, George 1911-1979 ....DLB-44

Seaton, William Winston 1785-1866 ....DLB-43

Sedgwick, Arthur George 1844-1915 ....DLB-64

Sedgwick, Catharine Maria 1789-1867 ....DLB-1, 74

Sedgwick, Ellery 1872-1930 ....DLB-91

Seeger, Alan 1888-1916 ....DLB-45

Seers, Eugene (see Dantin, Louis)

Segal, Erich 1937- Y-86

Seghers, Anna 1900-1983 ....DLB-69

Seid, Ruth (see Sinclair, Jo)

Seidel, Frederick Lewis 1936- Y-84

Seidel, Ina 1885-1974 ....DLB-56

Séjour, Victor 1817-1874 ....DLB-50

Séjour Marcou et Ferrand,
Juan Victor (see Séjour, Victor)

Selby, Hubert, Jr. 1928- DLB-2

Selden, George 1929- DLB-52

Selected English-Language Little Magazines and
Newspapers [France, 1920-1939] DLB-4

Selected Humorous Magazines (1820-1950) DLB-11

Selected Science-Fiction Magazines and
Anthologies DLB-8

Seligman, Edwin R. A. 1861-1939 ....DLB-47

Seltzer, Chester E. (see Muro, Amado)

Seltzer, Thomas [publishing house] DLB-46

Sendak, Maurice 1928- DLB-61

Senécal, Eva 1905- DLB-92

Sensation Novels (1863), by H. L. Manse DLB-21

Seredy, Kate 1899-1975 ....DLB-22

Serling, Rod 1924-1975 ....DLB-26

Service, Robert 1874-1958 ....DLB-92

Seton, Ernest Thompson
1860-1942 ....DLB-92

Settle, Mary Lee 1918- DLB-6

Seuss, Dr. (see Geisel, Theodor Seuss)

Sewall, Joseph 1688-1769...................DLB-24

Sewell, Samuel 1652-1730...................DLB-24

Sex, Class, Politics, and Religion [in the British
    Novel, 1930-1959] DLB-15

Sexton, Anne 1928-1974....................DLB-5

Shaara, Michael 1929-1988 ....Y-83

Shadwell, Thomas 1641?-1692 ....DLB-80

Shaffer, Anthony 1926- DLB-13

Shaffer, Peter 1926- DLB-13

Shairp, Mordaunt 1887-1939...............DLB-10

Shakespeare, William 1564-1616.........DLB-62

Shange, Ntozake 1948- DLB-38

Shapiro, Karl 1913- DLB-48

Sharon Publications DLB-46

Sharpe, Tom 1928- DLB-14

Shaw, Albert 1857-1947 ....DLB-91

Shaw, Bernard 1856-1950...........DLB-10, 57

Shaw, Henry Wheeler 1818-1885.........DLB-11

Shaw, Irwin 1913-1984 ....DLB-6; Y-84

Shaw, Robert 1927-1978 ....DLB-13, 14

Shay, Frank [publishing house]............DLB-46

Shea, John Gilmary 1824-1892............DLB-30

Shearing, Joseph 1886-1952...............DLB-70

Shebbeare, John 1709-1788 ....DLB-39

Sheckley, Robert 1928- DLB-8

Shedd, William G. T. 1820-1894..........DLB-64

Sheed, Wilfred 1930- DLB-6

Sheed and Ward DLB-46

Sheldon, Alice B. (see Tiptree, James, Jr.)

Sheldon, Edward 1886-1946................DLB-7

Sheldon and Company.........................DLB-49

Shepard, Sam 1943- DLB-7

Shepard, Thomas I 1604 or 1605-1649 ....DLB-24

Shepard, Thomas II 1635-1677...........DLB-24

Shepard, Clark and Brown DLB-49

Sheridan, Frances 1724-1766.........DLB-39, 84

Sheridan, Richard Brinsley 1751-1816...........DLB-89

Sherman, Francis 1871-1926...............DLB-92

Sherriff, R. C. 1896-1975....................DLB-10

Sherwood, Robert 1896-1955 ....DLB-7, 26

Shiels, George 1886-1949...................DLB-10

Shillaber, B.[enjamin] P.[enhallow]
    1814-1890 ....DLB-1, 11

Shine, Ted 1931- DLB-38

Ship, Reuben 1915-1975 ....DLB-88

Shirer, William L. 1904- DLB-4

Shirley, James 1596-1666..................DLB-58

Shockley, Ann Allen 1927- DLB-33

Shorthouse, Joseph Henry 1834-1903...............DLB-18

Showalter, Elaine 1941- DLB-67

Shulevitz, Uri 1935- DLB-61

Shulman, Max 1919-1988 ....DLB-11

Shute, Henry A. 1856-1943 ....DLB-9

Shuttle, Penelope 1947- DLB-14, 40

Sidney, Margaret (see Lothrop, Harriet M.)

Sidney's Press....................................DLB-49

Siegfried Loraine Sassoon: A Centenary Essay
    Tributes from Vivien F. Clarke and
        Michael Thorpe Y-86

Sierra Club Books...............................DLB-49

Sigourney, Lydia Howard (Huntley)
    1791-1865 ....DLB-1, 42, 73

Silkin, Jon 1930- DLB-27

Silliphant, Stirling 1918- DLB-26

Sillitoe, Alan 1928- DLB-14

Silman, Roberta 1934- DLB-28

Silverberg, Robert 1935- DLB-8

Simak, Clifford D. 1904-1988 ....DLB-8

Simcox, George Augustus 1841-1905...............DLB-35

Sime, Jessie Georgina
    1868-1958 ....DLB-92

Simenon, Georges 1903-1989 ....DLB-72

Simmel, Johannes Mario 1924- DLB-69

Simmons, Herbert Alfred 1930- DLB-33

Simmons, James 1933- DLB-40

Simms, William Gilmore 1806-1870
    ....DLB-3, 30, 59, 73

Simon, Claude 1913- DLB-83

Simon, Neil 1927- DLB-7

Simon and Schuster.............................DLB-46

Simons, Katherine Drayton Mayrant 1890-1969.....Y-83

Simpson, Helen 1897-1940 ....DLB-77

Simpson, Louis 1923- DLB-5

Simpson, N. F. 1919- DLB-13

Sims, George 1923- DLB-87

Sims, George R. 1847-1922..........DLB-35, 70

Sinclair, Andrew 1935- DLB-14

Sinclair, Bertrand William
1881-1972 ....DLB-92

Sinclair, Jo 1913- DLB-28

Sinclair Lewis Centennial Conference Y-85

Sinclair, Lister 1921- DLB-88

Sinclair, May 1863-1946 ....DLB-36

Sinclair, Upton 1878-1968...............DLB-9

Sinclair, Upton [publishing house] DLB-46

Singer, Isaac Bashevis 1904- DLB-6, 28, 52

Singmaster, Elsie 1879-1958 ....DLB-9

Siodmak, Curt 1902- DLB-44

Sissman, L. E. 1928-1976 ....DLB-5

Sisson, C. H. 1914- DLB-27

Sitwell, Edith 1887-1964 ....DLB-20

Skelton, Robin 1925- DLB-27, 53

Skinner, Constance Lindsay
1877-1939 ....DLB-92

Skinner, John Stuart 1788-1851 ....DLB-73

Skipsey, Joseph 1832-1903.................DLB-35

Slade, Bernard 1930- DLB-53

Slater, Patrick 1880-1951 ....DLB-68

Slavitt, David 1935- DLB-5, 6

A Slender Thread of Hope: The Kennedy
Center Black Theatre Project DLB-38

Slick, Sam (see Haliburton, Thomas Chandler)

Sloane, William, Associates DLB-46

Small, Maynard and Company DLB-49

Small Presses in Great Britain and Ireland,
1960-1985 ....DLB-40

Small Presses I: Jargon Society Y-84

Small Presses II: The Spirit That
Moves Us Press Y-85

Small Presses III: Pushcart Press...........Y-87

Smart, Elizabeth 1913-1986 ....DLB-88

Smiles, Samuel 1812-1904..................DLB-55

Smith, A. J. M. 1902-1980 ....DLB-88

Smith, Alexander 1829-1867 ....DLB-32, 55

Smith, Betty 1896-1972 ....Y-82

Smith, Carol Sturm 1938- Y-81

Smith, Charles Henry 1826-1903 ....DLB-11

Smith, Charlotte 1749-1806 ....DLB-39

Smith, Cordwainer 1913-1966 ....DLB-8

Smith, Dave 1942- DLB-5

Smith, Dodie 1896- DLB-10

Smith, Doris Buchanan 1934- DLB-52

Smith, E. E. 1890-1965......................DLB-8

Smith, Elihu Hubbard 1771-1798.........DLB-37

Smith, Elizabeth Oakes (Prince) 1806-1893 ....DLB-1

Smith, George O. 1911-1981 ....DLB-8

Smith, H. Allen 1907-1976..............DLB-11, 29

Smith, Harrison, and Robert Haas
[publishing house] DLB-46

Smith, Iain Crichten 1928- DLB-40

Smith, J. Allen 1860-1924..................DLB-47

Smith, J. Stilman, and Company DLB-49

Smith, John 1580-1631 ....DLB-24, 30

Smith, Josiah 1704-1781....................DLB-24

Smith, Ken 1938- DLB-40

Smith, Lee 1944- Y-83

Smith, Mark 1935- Y-82

Smith, Michael 1698-circa 1771 ....DLB-31

Smith, Red 1905-1982......................DLB-29

Smith, Roswell 1829-1892 ....DLB-79

Smith, Samuel Harrison 1772-1845...................DLB-43

Smith, Samuel Stanhope 1751-1819..................DLB-37

Smith, Seba 1792-1868...................DLB-1, 11

Smith, Stevie 1902-1971 ....DLB-20

Smith, Sydney Goodsir 1915-1975 .....DLB-27

Smith, W. B., and Company DLB-49

Smith, William 1727-1803.................DLB-31

Smith, William 1728-1793.................DLB-30

Smith, William Gardner 1927-1974...................DLB-76

Smith, William Jay 1918- DLB-5

Smollett, Tobias 1721-1771................DLB-39

Snellings, Rolland (see Touré, Askia Muhammad)

Snodgrass, W. D. 1926- DLB-5

Snow, C. P. 1905-1980 ....DLB-15, 77

Snyder, Gary 1930- DLB-5, 16

Sobiloff, Hy 1912-1970 ....DLB-48

The Society for Textual Scholarship
    and *TEXT*....................................Y-87

Solano, Solita 1888-1975 ....DLB-4

Sollers, Philippe 1936- DLB-83

Solomon, Carl 1928- DLB-16

Solway, David 1941- DLB-53

Solzhenitsyn and America Y-85

Sontag, Susan 1933- DLB-2, 67

Sorrentino, Gilbert 1929- DLB-5; Y-80

Soto, Gary 1952- DLB-82

Sources for the Study of Tudor
    and Stuart Drama...........................DLB-62

Souster, Raymond 1921- DLB-88

Southerland, Ellease 1943- DLB-33

Southern, Terry 1924- DLB-2

Southern Writers Between the Wars DLB-9

Southerne, Thomas 1659-1746 ....DLB-80

Spark, Muriel 1918- DLB-15

Sparks, Jared 1789-1866 ....DLB-1, 30

Sparshott, Francis 1926- DLB-60

Späth, Gerold 1939- DLB-75

Spellman, A. B. 1935- DLB-41

Spencer, Anne 1882-1975 ....DLB-51, 54

Spencer, Elizabeth 1921- DLB-6

Spencer, Herbert 1820-1903 ....DLB-57

Spencer, Scott 1945- Y-86

Spender, Stephen 1909- DLB-20

Spicer, Jack 1925-1965 ....DLB-5, 16

Spielberg, Peter 1929- Y-81

Spier, Peter 1927- DLB-61

Spinrad, Norman 1940- DLB-8

Spofford, Harriet Prescott 1835-1921 ....DLB-74

Squibob (see Derby, George Horatio)

Stafford, Jean 1915-1979 ....DLB-2

Stafford, William 1914- DLB-5

Stage Censorship: "The Rejected Statement"
    (1911), by Bernard Shaw [excerpts] DLB-10

Stallings, Laurence 1894-1968 ....DLB-7, 44

Stallworthy, Jon 1935- DLB-40

Stampp, Kenneth M. 1912- DLB-17

Stanford, Ann 1916- DLB-5

Stanton, Elizabeth Cady 1815-1902 ....DLB-79

Stanton, Frank L. 1857-1927 ....DLB-25

Stapledon, Olaf 1886-1950....................DLB-15

Star Spangled Banner Office DLB-49

Starkweather, David 1935- DLB-7

Statements on the Art of Poetry DLB-54

Stead, Robert J. C. 1880-1959 ....DLB-92

Steadman, Mark 1930- DLB-6

The Stealthy School of Criticism (1871), by
    Dante Gabriel Rossetti...................DLB-35

Stearns, Harold E. 1891-1943................DLB-4

Stedman, Edmund Clarence 1833-1908.........DLB-64

Steele, Max 1922- Y-80

Steele, Richard 1672-1729....................DLB-84

Steele, Wilbur Daniel 1886-1970 ....DLB-86

Steere, Richard circa 1643-1721 ....DLB-24

Stegner, Wallace 1909- DLB-9

Stehr, Hermann 1864-1940 ....DLB-66

Steig, William 1907- DLB-61

Stein, Gertrude 1874-1946 ....DLB-4, 54, 86

Stein, Leo 1872-1947............................DLB-4

Stein and Day Publishers....................DLB-46

Steinbeck, John 1902-1968...............DLB-7, 9; DS-2

Steiner, George 1929- DLB-67

Stephen, Leslie 1832-1904 ....DLB-57

Stephens, Alexander H. 1812-1883...........DLB-47

Stephens, Ann 1810-1886............DLB-3, 73

Stephens, Charles Asbury 1844?-1931 ....DLB-42

Stephens, James 1882?-1950 ....DLB-19

Sterling, George 1869-1926 ....DLB-54

Sterling, James 1701-1763..................DLB-24

Stern, Richard 1928- Y-87

Stern, Stewart 1922- DLB-26

Sterne, Laurence 1713-1768 ....DLB-39

Sternheim, Carl 1878-1942 ....DLB-56

Stevens, Wallace 1879-1955 ....DLB-54

Stevenson, Anne 1933- DLB-40

Stevenson, Robert Louis 1850-1894 ....DLB-18, 57

Stewart, Donald Ogden 1894-1980 ....DLB-4, 11, 26

Stewart, Dugald 1753-1828 ....DLB-31

Stewart, George R. 1895-1980 ....DLB-8

Stewart and Kidd Company DLB-46

Stickney, Trumbull 1874-1904 ....DLB-54

Stiles, Ezra 1727-1795 ....DLB-31

Still, James 1906- DLB-9

Stith, William 1707-1755 ....DLB-31

Stockton, Frank R. 1834-1902 ....DLB-42, 74

Stoddard, Ashbel [publishing house] DLB-49

Stoddard, Richard Henry 1825-1903 ....DLB-3, 64

Stoddard, Solomon 1643-1729 ....DLB-24

Stoker, Bram 1847-1912 ....DLB-36, 70

Stokes, Frederick A., Company DLB-49

Stokes, Thomas L. 1898-1958 ....DLB-29

Stone, Herbert S., and Company DLB-49

Stone, Lucy 1818-1893 ....DLB-79

Stone, Melville 1848-1929 ....DLB-25

Stone, Samuel 1602-1663 ....DLB-24

Stone and Kimball DLB-49

Stoppard, Tom 1937- DLB-13; Y-85

Storey, Anthony 1928- DLB-14

Storey, David 1933- DLB-13, 14

Story, Thomas circa 1670-1742 ....DLB-31

Story, William Wetmore 1819-1895 ....DLB-1

Storytelling: A Contemporary Renaissance Y-84

Stoughton, William 1631-1701 ....DLB-24

Stowe, Harriet Beecher 1811-1896 ....DLB-1, 12, 42, 74

Stowe, Leland 1899- DLB-29

Strand, Mark 1934- DLB-5

Stratemeyer, Edward 1862-1930 ....DLB-42

Stratton and Barnard DLB-49

Straub, Peter 1943- Y-84

Street, Cecil John Charles (see Rhode, John)

Street and Smith DLB-49

Streeter, Edward 1891-1976 ....DLB-11

Stribling, T. S. 1881-1965 ....DLB-9

Stringer and Townsend DLB-49

Stringer, Arthur 1874-1950 ....DLB-92

Strittmatter, Erwin 1912- DLB-69

Strother, David Hunter 1816-1888 ....DLB-3

Stuart, Jesse 1906-1984 ....DLB-9, 48; Y-84

Stuart, Lyle [publishing house] DLB-46

Stubbs, Harry Clement (see Clement, Hal)

The Study of Poetry (1880), by Matthew
    Arnold DLB-35

Sturgeon, Theodore 1918-1985 ....DLB-8; Y-85

Sturges, Preston 1898-1959 ....DLB-26

"Style" (1840; revised, 1859), by Thomas
    de Quincey [excerpt] DLB-57

"Style" (1888), by Walter Pater DLB-57

Style (1897), by Walter Raleigh [excerpt] DLB-57

"Style" (1877), by T. H. Wright [excerpt] DLB-57

"Le Style c'est l'homme" (1892),
    by W. H. Mallock DLB-57

Styron, William 1925- DLB-2; Y-80

Suárez, Mario 1925- DLB-82

Such, Peter 1939- DLB-60

Suckling, Sir John 1609-1642 ....DLB-58

Suckow, Ruth 1892-1960 ....DLB-9

Suggs, Simon (see Hooper, Johnson Jones)

Sukenick, Ronald 1932- Y-81

Suknaski, Andrew 1942- DLB-53

Sullivan, Alan 1868-1947 ....DLB-92

Sullivan, C. Gardner 1886-1965 ....DLB-26

Sullivan, Frank 1892-1976 ....DLB-11

Summers, Hollis 1916- DLB-6

Sumner, Henry A. [publishing house] DLB-49

Surtees, Robert Smith 1803-1864 ....DLB-21

A Survey of Poetry
    Anthologies, 1879-1960 ....DLB-54

Surveys of the Year's Biography
    A Transit of Poets and Others: American
        Biography in 1982 ....Y-82
    The Year in Literary Biography Y-83
    The Year in Literary Biography Y-84
    The Year in Literary Biography Y-85
    The Year in Literary Biography Y-86
    The Year in Literary Biography Y-87
    The Year in Literary Biography Y-88

Surveys of the Year's Book Publishing
    The Year in Book Publishing Y-86

Surveys of the Year's Drama
    The Year in Drama Y-82
    The Year in Drama Y-83
    The Year in Drama Y-84
    The Year in Drama Y-85

The Year in Drama.......................................Y-87
The Year in Drama.......................................Y-88

Surveys of the Year's Fiction
    The Year's Work in Fiction: A Survey.............Y-82
    The Year in Fiction: A Biased View.................Y-83
    The Year in Fiction.....................................Y-84
    The Year in Fiction.....................................Y-85
    The Year in Fiction.....................................Y-86
    The Year in the Novel..................................Y-87
    The Year in Short Stories..............................Y-87
    The Year in the Novel..................................Y-88
    The Year in Short Stories..............................Y-88

Surveys of the Year's Poetry
    The Year's Work in American Poetry.............Y-82
    The Year in Poetry......................................Y-83
    The Year in Poetry......................................Y-84
    The Year in Poetry......................................Y-85
    The Year in Poetry......................................Y-86
    The Year in Poetry......................................Y-87
    The Year in Poetry......................................Y-88

Sutherland, John 1919-1956............................DLB-68

Sutro, Alfred 1863-1933.................................DLB-10

Swados, Harvey 1920-1972..............................DLB-2

Swain, Charles 1801-1874...............................DLB-32

Swallow Press...DLB-46

Swenson, May 1919-1989................................DLB-5

Swerling, Jo 1897- DLB-44

Swift, Jonathan 1667-1745..............................DLB-39

Swinburne, A. C. 1837-1909.......................DLB-35, 57

Swinnerton, Frank 1884-1982..........................DLB-34

Swisshelm, Jane Grey 1815-1884......................DLB-43

Swope, Herbert Bayard 1882-1958...................DLB-25

Swords, T. and J., and Company.......................DLB-49

Swords, Thomas 1763-1843 and
    Swords, James ?-1844.................................DLB-73

Symonds, John Addington 1840-1893...............DLB-57

Symons, Arthur 1865-1945..........................DLB-19, 57

Symons, Julian 1912- DLB-87

Symons, Scott 1933- DLB-53

Synge, John Millington 1871-1909..............DLB-10, 19

T

Tafolla, Carmen 1951- DLB-82

Taggard, Genevieve 1894-1948........................DLB-45

Tait, J. Selwin, and Sons.................................DLB-49

Talvj or Talvi (see Robinson, Therese)

Taradash, Daniel 1913- DLB-44

Tarbell, Ida M. 1857-1944..............................DLB-47

Tarkington, Booth 1869-1946..........................DLB-9

Tashlin, Frank 1913-1972...............................DLB-44

Tate, Allen 1899-1979..........................DLB-4, 45, 63

Tate, James 1943- DLB-5

Tate, Nahum circa 1652-1715.........................DLB-80

Taylor, Bayard 1825-1878...............................DLB-3

Taylor, Bert Leston 1866-1921.........................DLB-25

Taylor, Charles H. 1846-1921..........................DLB-25

Taylor, Edward circa 1642-1729.......................DLB-24

Taylor, Henry 1942- DLB-5

Taylor, Sir Henry 1800-1886...........................DLB-32

Taylor, Mildred D. ?- DLB-52

Taylor, Peter 1917- Y-81

Taylor, William, and Company.........................DLB-49

Taylor-Made Shakespeare? Or Is
    "Shall I Die?" the Long-Lost Text
    of Bottom's Dream?.....................................Y-85

Teasdale, Sara 1884-1933...............................DLB-45

The Tea-Table (1725), by Eliza Haywood
    [excerpt]..DLB-39

Tenn, William 1919- DLB-8

Tennant, Emma 1937- DLB-14

Tenney, Tabitha Gilman 1762-1837...................DLB-37

Tennyson, Alfred 1809-1892............................DLB-32

Tennyson, Frederick 1807-1898........................DLB-32

Terhune, Albert Payson 1872-1942...................DLB-9

Terry, Megan 1932- DLB-7

Terson, Peter 1932- DLB-13

Tesich, Steve 1943- Y-83

Tey, Josephine 1896?-1952.............................DLB-77

Thacher, James 1754-1844..............................DLB-37

Thackeray, William Makepeace
    1811-1863..DLB-21, 55

Thanet, Octave (see French, Alice)

The Theater in Shakespeare's Time...................DLB-62

The Theatre Guild..DLB-7

Theriault, Yves 1915-1983..............................DLB-88

Thério, Adrien 1925- DLB-53

Theroux, Paul 1941- DLB-2

Thibaudeau, Colleen 1925- DLB-88

Thoma, Ludwig 1867-1921..............................DLB-66

Thoma, Richard 1902- DLB-4

Thomas, Audrey 1935- DLB-60

Thomas, D. M. 1935- DLB-40

Thomas, Dylan 1914-1953.........................DLB-13, 20

Thomas, Edward 1878-1917............................DLB-19

Thomas, Gwyn 1913-1981 ....DLB-15

Thomas, Isaiah 1750-1831...........................DLB-43, 73

Thomas, Isaiah [publishing house]....................DLB-49

Thomas, John 1900-1932................................DLB-4

Thomas, Joyce Carol 1938- DLB-33

Thomas, Lorenzo 1944- DLB-41

Thomas, R. S. 1915- DLB-27

Thompson, Dorothy 1893-1961.......................DLB-29

Thompson, Francis 1859-1907 ....DLB-19

Thompson, George Selden (see Selden, George)

Thompson, John 1938-1976 ....DLB-60

Thompson, John R. 1823-1873 ....DLB-3, 73

Thompson, Maurice 1844-1901..................DLB-71, 74

Thompson, Ruth Plumly 1891-1976 ....DLB-22

Thompson, William Tappan 1812-1882 ....DLB-3, 11

Thomson, Edward William
    1849-1924 ....DLB-92

Thomson, James 1834-1882.............................DLB-35

Thomson, Mortimer 1831-1875.......................DLB-11

Thoreau, Henry David 1817-1862 ....DLB-1

Thorpe, Thomas Bangs 1815-1878...............DLB-3, 11

Thoughts on Poetry and Its Varieties (1833),
    by John Stuart Mill.....................................DLB-32

Thurber, James 1894-1961.....................DLB-4, 11, 22

Thurman, Wallace 1902-1934...........................DLB-51

Thwaite, Anthony 1930- DLB-40

Thwaites, Reuben Gold 1853-1913 ....DLB-47

Ticknor, George 1791-1871...........................DLB-1, 59

Ticknor and Fields DLB-49

Tieck, Ludwig 1773-1853..................................DLB-90

Ticknor and Fields (revived)............................DLB-46

Tietjens, Eunice 1884-1944...............................DLB-54

Tilton, J. E., and Company................................DLB-49

Time and Western Man (1927), by Wyndham
    Lewis [excerpts] DLB-36

Time-Life Books...DLB-46

Times Books DLB-46

Timothy, Peter circa 1725-1782 ....DLB-43

Timrod, Henry 1828-1867................................DLB-3

Tiptree, James, Jr. 1915- DLB-8

Titus, Edward William 1870-1952.......................DLB-4

Toklas, Alice B. 1877-1967 ....DLB-4

Tolkien, J. R. R. 1892-1973 ....DLB-15

Tolson, Melvin B. 1898-1966......................DLB-48, 76

Tom Jones (1749), by Henry
    Fielding [excerpt] DLB-39

Tomlinson, Charles 1927- DLB-40

Tomlinson, Henry Major 1873-1958 ....DLB-36

Tompkins, Abel [publishing house]...................DLB-49

Tompson, Benjamin 1642-1714........................DLB-24

Tonks, Rosemary 1932- DLB-14

Toole, John Kennedy 1937-1969 ....Y-81

Toomer, Jean 1894-1967..............................DLB-45, 51

Tor Books DLB-46

Torberg, Friedrich 1908-1979 ....DLB-85

Torrence, Ridgely 1874-1950...........................DLB-54

Toth, Susan Allen 1940- Y-86

Tough-Guy Literature DLB-9

Touré, Askia Muhammad 1938- DLB-41

Tourgée, Albion W. 1838-1905........................DLB-79

Tourneur, Cyril circa 1580-1626 ....DLB-58

Tournier, Michel 1924- DLB-83

Tousey, Frank [publishing house]......................DLB-49

Tower Publications..DLB-46

Towne, Benjamin circa 1740-1793....................DLB-43

Towne, Robert 1936- DLB-44

Tracy, Honor 1913- DLB-15

Train, Arthur 1875-1945...................................DLB-86

The Transatlantic Publishing Company DLB-49

Transcendentalists, American DS-5

Traven, B. 1882? or 1890?-1969?...................DLB-9, 56

Travers, Ben 1886-1980 ....DLB-10

Tremain, Rose 1943- DLB-14

Tremblay, Michel 1942- DLB-60

Trends in Twentieth-Century
   Mass Market Publishing DLB-46

Trent, William P. 1862-1939.............................DLB-47

Trescot, William Henry 1822-1898....................DLB-30

Trevor, William 1928- DLB-14

Trilling, Lionel 1905-1975 ....DLB-28, 63

Triolet, Elsa 1896-1970.....................................DLB-72

Tripp, John 1927- DLB-40

Trocchi, Alexander 1925- DLB-15

Trollope, Anthony 1815-1882 ....DLB-21, 57

Trollope, Frances 1779-1863 ....DLB-21

Troop, Elizabeth 1931- DLB-14

Trotter, Catharine 1679-1749 ....DLB-84

Trotti, Lamar 1898-1952 ....DLB-44

Trottier, Pierre 1925- DLB-60

Troupe, Quincy Thomas, Jr. 1943- DLB-41

Trow, John F., and Company DLB-49

Trumbo, Dalton 1905-1976................................DLB-26

Trumbull, Benjamin 1735-1820........................DLB-30

Trumbull, John 1750-1831................................DLB-31

T. S. Eliot Centennial Y-88

Tucholsky, Kurt 1890-1935................................DLB-56

Tucker, George 1775-1861 ....DLB-3, 30

Tucker, Nathaniel Beverley 1784-1851 ....DLB-3

Tucker, St. George 1752-1827 ....DLB-37

Tuckerman, Henry Theodore 1813-1871 ....DLB-64

Tunis, John R. 1889-1975 ....DLB-22

Tuohy, Frank 1925- DLB-14

Tupper, Martin F. 1810-1889 ....DLB-32

Turbyfill, Mark 1896- DLB-45

Turco, Lewis 1934- Y-84

Turnbull, Gael 1928- DLB-40

Turner, Charles (Tennyson) 1808-1879 ....DLB-32

Turner, Frederick 1943- DLB-40

Turner, Frederick Jackson 1861-1932................DLB-17

Turner, Joseph Addison 1826-1868 ....DLB-79

Turpin, Waters Edward 1910-1968 ....DLB-51

Twain, Mark (see Clemens, Samuel Langhorne)

The 'Twenties and Berlin,
   by Alex Natan..DLB-66

Tyler, Anne 1941- DLB-6; Y-82

Tyler, Moses Coit 1835-1900 ....DLB-47, 64

Tyler, Royall 1757-1826 ....DLB-37

Tylor, Edward Burnett 1832-1917......................DLB-57

U

Udall, Nicholas 1504-1556.................................DLB-62

Uhland, Ludwig 1787-1862 ....DLB-90

Uhse, Bodo 1904-1963.......................................DLB-69

Ulibarrí, Sabine R. 1919- DLB-82

Ulica, Jorge 1870-1926......................................DLB-82

Under the Microscope (1872), by A. C.
   Swinburne...DLB-35

United States Book Company DLB-49

Universal Publishing and Distributing
   Corporation DLB-46

The University of Iowa Writers'
   Workshop Golden Jubilee Y-86

"The Unknown Public" (1858), by
   Wilkie Collins [excerpt]................................DLB-57

Unruh, Fritz von 1885-1970 ....DLB-56

Upchurch, Boyd B. (see Boyd, John)

Updike, John 1932- DLB-2, 5; Y-80, 82; DS-3

Upton, Charles 1948- DLB-16

Upward, Allen 1863-1926 ....DLB-36

Urista, Alberto Baltazar (see Alurista)

Urzidil, Johannes 1896-1976.............................DLB-85

Ustinov, Peter 1921- DLB-13

V

Vac, Bertrand 1914- DLB-88

Vail, Laurence 1891-1968 ....DLB-4

Vailland, Roger 1907-1965..................................DLB-83

Vajda, Ernest 1887-1954 ....DLB-44

Valgardson, W. D. 1939- DLB-60

Van Allsburg, Chris 1949- DLB-61

Van Anda, Carr 1864-1945 ....DLB-25

Vanbrugh, Sir John 1664-1726 ....DLB-80

Vance, Jack 1916?- DLB-8

Van Doren, Mark 1894-1972 ....DLB-45

van Druten, John 1901-1957 ....DLB-10

Van Duyn, Mona 1921- DLB-5

Van Dyke, Henry 1852-1933...................DLB-71

Van Dyke, Henry 1928- DLB-33

Vane, Sutton 1888-1963 ....DLB-10

Vanguard Press...............................DLB-46

van Itallie, Jean-Claude 1936- DLB-7

Vann, Robert L. 1879-1940...................DLB-29

Van Rensselaer, Mariana Griswold
    1851-1934 ....DLB-47

Van Rensselaer, Mrs. Schuyler (see Van
    Rensselaer, Mariana Griswold)

Van Vechten, Carl 1880-1964 ....DLB-4, 9

van Vogt, A. E. 1912- DLB-8

Varley, John 1947- Y-81

Varnhagen von Ense, Karl August
    1785-1858 ....DLB-90

Varnhagen von Ense, Rahel
    1771-1833 ....DLB-90

Vassa, Gustavus (see Equiano, Olaudah)

Vega, Janine Pommy 1942- DLB-16

Veiller, Anthony 1903-1965 ....DLB-44

Venegas, Daniel ?-? DLB-82

Verplanck, Gulian C. 1786-1870 ....DLB-59

Very, Jones 1813-1880.......................DLB-1

Vian, Boris 1920-1959.......................DLB-72

Vickers, Roy 1888?-1965 ....DLB-77

Victoria 1819-1901 ....DLB-55

Vidal, Gore 1925- DLB-6

Viebig, Clara 1860-1952.....................DLB-66

Viereck, George Sylvester 1884-1962 ....DLB-54

Viereck, Peter 1916- DLB-5

Viewpoint: Politics and Performance, by David
    Edgar...................................DLB-13

Vigneault, Gilles 1928- DLB-60

The Viking Press............................DLB-46

Villanueva, Tino 1941- DLB-82

Villard, Henry 1835-1900 ....DLB-23

Villard, Oswald Garrison 1872-1949.......DLB-25, 91

Villarreal, José Antonio 1924- DLB-82

Villemaire, Yolande 1949- DLB-60

Villiers, George, Second Duke
    of Buckingham 1628-1687.................DLB-80

Viorst, Judith ?- DLB-52

Voaden, Herman 1903- DLB-88

Volkoff, Vladimir 1932- DLB-83

Volland, P. F., Company DLB-46

von der Grün, Max 1926- DLB-75

Vonnegut, Kurt 1922- DLB-2, 8; Y-80; DS-3

Voß, Johann Heinrich 1751-1826 ....DLB-90

Vroman, Mary Elizabeth circa 1924-1967 .....DLB-33

W

Wackenroder, Wilhelm Heinrich
    1773-1798 ....DLB-90

Waddington, Miriam 1917- DLB-68

Wade, Henry 1887-1969 ....DLB-77

Wagoner, David 1926- DLB-5

Wah, Fred 1939- DLB-60

Waiblinger, Wilhelm 1804-1830...............DLB-90

Wain, John 1925- DLB-15, 27

Wainwright, Jeffrey 1944- DLB-40

Waite, Peirce and Company DLB-49

Wakoski, Diane 1937- DLB-5

Walck, Henry Z..............................DLB-46

Walcott, Derek 1930- Y-81

Waldman, Anne 1945- DLB-16

Walker, Alice 1944- DLB-6, 33

Walker, George F. 1947- DLB-60

Walker, Joseph A. 1935- DLB-38

Walker, Margaret 1915- DLB-76

Walker, Ted 1934- DLB-40

Walker and Company..........................DLB-49

Walker, Evans and Cogswell Company DLB-49

Walker, John Brisben 1847-1931 ....DLB-79

Wallace, Edgar 1875-1932....................DLB-70

Wallant, Edward Lewis 1926-1962 ....DLB-2, 28

Walpole, Horace 1717-1797...................DLB-39

Walpole, Hugh 1884-1941 ....DLB-34

Walrond, Eric 1898-1966 ....DLB-51

Walser, Martin 1927- DLB-75

Walser, Robert 1878-1956....................DLB-66

Walsh, Ernest 1895-1926.................DLB-4, 45

Walsh, Robert 1784-1859 ....DLB-59

Wambaugh, Joseph 1937- DLB-6; Y-83

Ward, Artemus (see Browne, Charles Farrar)

Ward, Arthur Henry Sarsfield
   (see Rohmer, Sax)

Ward, Douglas Turner 1930- DLB-7, 38

Ward, Lynd 1905-1985.....................................DLB-22

Ward, Mrs. Humphry 1851-1920 ....DLB-18

Ward, Nathaniel circa 1578-1652 ....DLB-24

Ward, Theodore 1902-1983.............................DLB-76

Ware, William 1797-1852.................................DLB-1

Warne, Frederick, and Company......................DLB-49

Warner, Charles Dudley 1829-1900 ....DLB-64

Warner, Rex 1905- DLB-15

Warner, Susan Bogert 1819-1885..................DLB-3, 42

Warner, Sylvia Townsend 1893-1978 ....DLB-34

Warner Books DLB-46

Warr, Bertram 1917-1943 ....DLB-88

Warren, John Byrne Leicester (see De Tabley, Lord)

Warren, Lella 1899-1982......................................Y-83

Warren, Mercy Otis 1728-1814..........................DLB-31

Warren, Robert Penn 1905-1989..........DLB-2, 48; Y-80

Washington, George 1732-1799.........................DLB-31

Wassermann, Jakob 1873-1934 ....DLB-66

Wasson, David Atwood 1823-1887 ....DLB-1

Waterhouse, Keith 1929- DLB-13, 15

Waterman, Andrew 1940- DLB-40

Waters, Frank 1902- Y-86

Watkins, Tobias 1780-1855 ....DLB-73

Watkins, Vernon 1906-1967 ....DLB-20

Watmough, David 1926- DLB-53

Watson, James Wreford (see Wreford, James)

Watson, Sheila 1909- DLB-60

Watson, Wilfred 1911- DLB-60

Watt, W. J., and Company DLB-46

Watterson, Henry 1840-1921 ....DLB-25

Watts, Alan 1915-1973 ....DLB-16

Watts, Franklin [publishing house].....................DLB-46

Waugh, Auberon 1939- DLB-14

Waugh, Evelyn 1903-1966.................................DLB-15

Way and Williams DLB-49

Wayman, Tom 1945- DLB-53

Weatherly, Tom 1942- DLB-41

Weaver, Robert 1921- DLB-88

Webb, Frank J. ?-? DLB-50

Webb, James Watson 1802-1884 ....DLB-43

Webb, Mary 1881-1927.....................................DLB-34

Webb, Phyllis 1927- DLB-53

Webb, Walter Prescott 1888-1963 ....DLB-17

Webster, Augusta 1837-1894 ....DLB-35

Webster, Charles L., and Company DLB-49

Webster, John 1579 or 1580-1634?.....................DLB-58

Webster, Noah 1758-1843 ....DLB-1, 37, 42, 43, 73

Weems, Mason Locke 1759-1825............DLB-30, 37, 42

Weidman, Jerome 1913- DLB-28

Weinbaum, Stanley Grauman 1902-1935 ....DLB-8

Weisenborn, Günther 1902-1969.......................DLB-69

Weiß, Ernst 1882-1940 ....DLB-81

Weiss, John 1818-1879 ....DLB-1

Weiss, Peter 1916-1982 ....DLB-69

Weiss, Theodore 1916- DLB-5

Welch, Lew 1926-1971?....................................DLB-16

Weldon, Fay 1931- DLB-14

Wellek, René 1903- DLB-63

Wells, Carolyn 1862-1942.................................DLB-11

Wells, Charles Jeremiah circa 1800-1879 ....DLB-32

Wells, H. G. 1866-1946 ....DLB-34, 70

Wells, Robert 1947- DLB-40

Wells-Barnett, Ida B. 1862-1931........................DLB-23

Welty, Eudora 1909- DLB-2; Y-87

Wendell, Barrett 1855-1921 ....DLB-71

Wentworth, Patricia 1878-1961 ....DLB-77

Werfel, Franz 1890-1945 ....DLB-81

The Werner Company.......................................DLB-49

Wersba, Barbara 1932- DLB-52

Wescott, Glenway 1901- DLB-4, 9

Wesker, Arnold 1932- DLB-13

Wesley, Richard 1945- DLB-38

Wessels, A., and Company DLB-46

West, Anthony 1914-1988 ....DLB-15

West, Dorothy 1907- DLB-76

West, Jessamyn 1902-1984 ....DLB-6; Y-84

West, Mae 1892-1980...DLB-44

West, Nathanael 1903-1940 ....DLB-4, 9, 28

West, Paul 1930- DLB-14

West, Rebecca 1892-1983 ....DLB-36; Y-83

West and Johnson DLB-49

Western Publishing Company DLB-46

Wetherell, Elizabeth (see Warner, Susan Bogert)

Wetzel, Friedrich Gottlob 1779-1819.................DLB-90

Whalen, Philip 1923- DLB-16

Whalley, George 1915-1983...............................DLB-88

Wharton, Edith 1862-1937..................DLB-4, 9, 12, 78

Wharton, William 1920s?- Y-80

What's Really Wrong With Bestseller Lists Y-84

Wheatley, Dennis Yates 1897-1977.....................DLB-77

Wheatley, Phillis circa 1754-1784.................DLB-31, 50

Wheeler, Charles Stearns 1816-1843....................DLB-1

Wheeler, Monroe 1900-1988   ....DLB-4

Wheelock, John Hall 1886-1978.........................DLB-45

Wheelwright, John circa 1592-1679 ....DLB-24

Wheelwright, J. B. 1897-1940............................DLB-45

Whetstone, Colonel Pete (see Noland, C. F. M.)

Whipple, Edwin Percy 1819-1886 ....DLB-1, 64

Whitaker, Alexander 1585-1617 ....DLB-24

Whitaker, Daniel K. 1801-1881 ....DLB-73

Whitcher, Frances Miriam 1814-1852 ....DLB-11

White, Andrew 1579-1656 ....DLB-24

White, Andrew Dickson 1832-1918....................DLB-47

White, E. B. 1899-1985.............................DLB-11, 22

White, Edgar B. 1947- DLB-38

White, Ethel Lina 1887-1944 ....DLB-77

White, Horace 1834-1916 ....DLB-23

White, Phyllis Dorothy James
    (see James, P. D.)

White, Richard Grant 1821-1885.......................DLB-64

White, Walter 1893-1955..................................DLB-51

White, William, and Company...........................DLB-49

White, William Allen 1868-1944 ....DLB-9, 25

White, William Anthony Parker
    (see Boucher, Anthony)

White, William Hale (see Rutherford, Mark)

Whitechurch, Victor L. 1868-1933 ....DLB-70

Whitehead, James 1936- Y-81

Whitehead, William 1715-1785.........................DLB-84

Whitfield, James Monroe 1822-1871.................DLB-50

Whiting, John 1917-1963 ....DLB-13

Whiting, Samuel 1597-1679..............................DLB-24

Whitlock, Brand 1869-1934 ....DLB-12

Whitman, Albert, and Company DLB-46

Whitman, Albery Allson 1851-1901 ....DLB-50

Whitman, Sarah Helen (Power) 1803-1878.........DLB-1

Whitman, Walt 1819-1892 ....DLB-3, 64

Whitman Publishing Company DLB-46

Whittemore, Reed 1919- DLB-5

Whittier, John Greenleaf 1807-1892 ....DLB-1

Whittlesey House...DLB-46

Wideman, John Edgar 1941- DLB-33

Wiebe, Rudy 1934- DLB-60

Wiechert, Ernst 1887-1950...............................DLB-56

Wied, Martina 1882-1957.................................DLB-85

Wieners, John 1934- DLB-16

Wier, Ester 1910- DLB-52

Wiesel, Elie 1928- DLB-83; Y-87

Wiggin, Kate Douglas 1856-1923 ....DLB-42

Wigglesworth, Michael 1631-1705 ....DLB-24

Wilbur, Richard 1921- DLB-5

Wild, Peter 1940- DLB-5

Wilde, Oscar 1854-1900 ....DLB-10, 19, 34, 57

Wilde, Richard Henry 1789-1847 ....DLB-3, 59

Wilde, W. A., Company DLB-49

Wilder, Billy 1906- DLB-26

Wilder, Laura Ingalls 1867-1957......................DLB-22

Wilder, Thornton 1897-1975 ....DLB-4, 7, 9

Wiley, Bell Irvin 1906-1980..............................DLB-17

Wiley, John, and Sons DLB-49

Wilhelm, Kate 1928- DLB-8

Wilkes, George 1817-1885 ....DLB-79

Wilkinson, Anne 1910-1961..............................DLB-88

Wilkinson, Sylvia 1940- Y-86

Wilkinson, William Cleaver 1833-1920 ....DLB-71

Willard, L. [publishing house] DLB-49

Willard, Nancy 1936- DLB-5, 52

Willard, Samuel 1640-1707...............................DLB-24

Williams, A., and Company DLB-49

Williams, C. K. 1936- DLB-5

Williams, Chancellor 1905- DLB-76

Williams, Emlyn 1905- DLB-10, 77

Williams, Garth 1912- DLB-22

Williams, George Washington 1849-1891 ....DLB-47

Williams, Heathcote 1941- DLB-13

Williams, Hugo 1942- DLB-40

Williams, Isaac 1802-1865...............................DLB-32

Williams, Joan 1928- DLB-6

Williams, John A. 1925- DLB-2, 33

Williams, John E. 1922- DLB-6

Williams, Jonathan 1929- DLB-5

Williams, Raymond 1921- DLB-14

Williams, Roger circa 1603-1683 ....DLB-24

Williams, Samm-Art 1946- DLB-38

Williams, Sherley Anne 1944- DLB-41

Williams, T. Harry 1909-1979...........................DLB-17

Williams, Tennessee 1911-1983........DLB-7; Y-83; DS-4

Williams, Valentine 1883-1946..........................DLB-77

Williams, William Appleman 1921- DLB-17

Williams, William Carlos 1883-1963
....DLB-4, 16, 54, 86

Williams, Wirt 1921- DLB-6

Williams Brothers DLB-49

Williamson, Jack 1908- DLB-8

Willingham, Calder Baynard, Jr. 1922- DLB-2, 44

Willis, Nathaniel Parker 1806-1867 ...DLB-3, 59, 73, 74

Wilmer, Clive 1945- DLB-40

Wilson, A. N. 1950- DLB-14

Wilson, Angus 1913- DLB-15

Wilson, Arthur 1595-1652 ....DLB-58

Wilson, Augusta Jane Evans 1835-1909.............DLB-42

Wilson, Colin 1931- DLB-14

Wilson, Edmund 1895-1972 ....DLB-63

Wilson, Ethel 1888-1980 ....DLB-68

Wilson, Harriet E. Adams 1828?-1863? DLB-50

Wilson, Harry Leon 1867-1939 ....DLB-9

Wilson, John 1588-1667 ....DLB-24

Wilson, Lanford 1937- DLB-7

Wilson, Margaret 1882-1973.............................DLB-9

Wilson, Michael 1914-1978 ....DLB-44

Wilson, Woodrow 1856-1924 ....DLB-47

Wimsatt, William K., Jr. 1907-1975...................DLB-63

Winchell, Walter 1897-1972.............................DLB-29

Winchester, J. [publishing house].....................DLB-49

Windham, Donald 1920- DLB-6

Winsor, Justin 1831-1897..................................DLB-47

John C. Winston Company DLB-49

Winters, Yvor 1900-1968 ....DLB-48

Winthrop, John 1588-1649 ....DLB-24, 30

Winthrop, John, Jr. 1606-1676.........................DLB-24

Wirt, William 1772-1834..................................DLB-37

Wise, John 1652-1725 ....DLB-24

Wiseman, Adele 1928- DLB-88

Wisner, George 1812-1849...............................DLB-43

Wister, Owen 1860-1938..............................DLB-9, 78

Witherspoon, John 1723-1794..........................DLB-31

Wittig, Monique 1935- DLB-83

Wodehouse, P. G. 1881-1975 ....DLB-34

Wohmann, Gabriele 1932- DLB-75

Woiwode, Larry 1941- DLB-6

Wolcott, Roger 1679-1767 ....DLB-24

Wolf, Christa 1929- DLB-75

Wolfe, Gene 1931- DLB-8

Wolfe, Thomas 1900-1938................DLB-9; DS-2; Y-85

Wollstonecraft, Mary 1759-1797......................DLB-39

Wondratschek, Wolf 1943- DLB-75

Wood, Benjamin 1820-1900.............................DLB-23

Wood, Charles 1932- DLB-13

Wood, Mrs. Henry 1814-1887 ....DLB-18

Wood, Joanna E. 1867-1927.............................DLB-92

Wood, Samuel [publishing house] DLB-49

Wood, William ?-?...DLB-24

Woodberry, George Edward 1855-1930.............DLB-71

Woodbridge, Benjamin 1622-1684 ....DLB-24

Woodcock, George 1912- DLB-88

Woodhull, Victoria C. 1838-1927 ....DLB-79

Woodmason, Charles circa 1720-? DLB-31

Woodson, Carter G. 1875-1950 ....DLB-17

Woodward, C. Vann 1908- DLB-17

Woolf, David (see Maddow, Ben)

Woolf, Virginia 1882-1941 ....DLB-36

Woollcott, Alexander 1887-1943........................DLB-29

Woolman, John 1720-1772...............................DLB-31

Woolner, Thomas 1825-1892............................DLB-35

Woolsey, Sarah Chauncy 1835-1905..................DLB-42

Woolson, Constance Fenimore 1840-1894....DLB-12, 74

Worcester, Joseph Emerson 1784-1865 ....DLB-1

The Works of the Rev. John Witherspoon
    (1800-1801) [excerpts]...............................DLB-31

A World Chronology of Important Science
    Fiction Works (1818-1979) DLB-8

World Publishing Company DLB-46

Worthington, R., and Company........................DLB-49

Wouk, Herman 1915- Y-82

Wreford, James 1915- DLB-88

Wright, Charles 1935- Y-82

Wright, Charles Stevenson 1932- DLB-33

Wright, Frances 1795-1852 ....DLB-73

Wright, Harold Bell 1872-1944 ....DLB-9

Wright, James 1927-1980..................................DLB-5

Wright, Jay 1935- DLB-41

Wright, Louis B. 1899-1984..............................DLB-17

Wright, Richard 1908-1960 ....DS-2, DLB-76

Wright, Richard B. 1937- DLB-53

Wright, Sarah Elizabeth 1928- DLB-33

Writers and Politics: 1871-1918,
    by Ronald Gray...DLB-66

Writers' Forum..Y-85

Writing for the Theatre, by Harold Pinter........DLB-13

Wycherley, William 1641-1715 ....DLB-80

Wylie, Elinor 1885-1928.............................DLB-9, 45

Wylie, Philip 1902-1971 ....DLB-9

Y

Yates, Dornford 1885-1960...............................DLB-77

Yates, J. Michael 1938- DLB-60

Yates, Richard 1926- DLB-2; Y-81

Yeats, William Butler 1865-1939 ....DLB-10, 19

Yep, Laurence 1948- DLB-52

Yerby, Frank 1916- DLB-76

Yezierska, Anzia 1885-1970.............................DLB-28

Yolen, Jane 1939- DLB-52

Yonge, Charlotte Mary 1823-1901.....................DLB-18

A Yorkshire Tragedy.....................................DLB-58

Yoseloff, Thomas [publishing house] DLB-46

Young, Al 1939- DLB-33

Young, Stark 1881-1963....................................DLB-9

Young, Waldeman 1880-1938 ....DLB-26

Young, William [publishing house]....................DLB-49

Yourcenar, Marguerite 1903-1987............DLB-72; Y-88

"You've Never Had It So Good," Gusted by
    "Winds of Change": British Fiction in the
    1950s, 1960s, and After DLB-14

Z

Zamora, Bernice 1938- DLB-82

Zand, Herbert 1923-1970 ....DLB-85

Zangwill, Israel 1864-1926...............................DLB-10

Zebra Books..DLB-46

Zebrowski, George 1945- DLB-8

Zech, Paul 1881-1946......................................DLB-56

Zelazny, Roger 1937- DLB-8

Zenger, John Peter 1697-1746.....................DLB-24, 43

Zieber, G. B., and Company DLB-49

Zieroth, Dale 1946- DLB-60

Zimmer, Paul 1934- DLB-5

Zindel, Paul 1936- DLB-7, 52

Zolotow, Charlotte 1915- DLB-52

Zubly, John Joachim 1724-1781........................DLB-31

Zu-Bolton II, Ahmos 1936- DLB-41

Zuckmayer, Carl 1896-1977 ....DLB-56

Zukofsky, Louis 1904-1978 ....DLB-5

zur Mühlen, Hermynia 1883-1951 ....DLB-56

Zweig, Arnold 1887-1968..................................DLB-66

Zweig, Stefan 1881-1942 ....DLB-81

(Continued from front endsheets)

71: *American Literary Critics and Scholars, 1880-1900,* edited by John W. Rathbun and Monica M. Grecu (1988)

72: *French Novelists, 1930-1960,* edited by Catharine Savage Brosman (1988)

73: *American Magazine Journalists, 1741-1850,* edited by Sam G. Riley (1988)

74: *American Short-Story Writers Before 1880,* edited by Bobby Ellen Kimbel, with the assistance of William E. Grant (1988)

75: *Contemporary German Fiction Writers,* Second Series, edited by Wolfgang D. Elfe and James Hardin (1988)

76: *Afro-American Writers, 1940-1955,* edited by Trudier Harris (1988)

77: *British Mystery Writers, 1920-1939,* edited by Bernard Benstock and Thomas F. Staley (1988)

78: *American Short-Story Writers, 1880-1910,* edited by Bobby Ellen Kimbel, with the assistance of William E. Grant (1988)

79: *American Magazine Journalists, 1850-1900,* edited by Sam G. Riley (1988)

80: *Restoration and Eighteenth-Century Dramatists,* First Series, edited by Paula R. Backscheider (1989)

81: *Austrian Fiction Writers, 1875-1913,* edited by James Hardin and Donald G. Daviau (1989)

82: *Chicano Writers,* First Series, edited by Francisco A. Lomelí and Carl R. Shirley (1989)

83: *French Novelists Since 1960,* edited by Catharine Savage Brosman (1989)

84: *Restoration and Eighteenth-Century Dramatists,* Second Series, edited by Paula R. Backscheider (1989)

85: *Austrian Fiction Writers After 1914,* edited by James Hardin and Donald G. Daviau (1989)

86: *American Short-Story Writers, 1910-1945,* First Series, edited by Bobby Ellen Kimbel (1989)

87: *British Mystery and Thriller Writers Since 1940,* First Series, edited by Bernard Benstock and Thomas F. Staley (1989)

88: *Canadian Writers, 1920-1959,* Second Series, edited by W. H. New (1989)

89: *Restoration and Eighteenth-Century Dramatists,* Third Series, edited by Paula R. Backscheider (1989)

90: *German Writers in the Age of Goethe, 1789-1832,* edited by James Hardin and Christoph E. Schweitzer (1989)

91: *American Magazine Journalists, 1900-1960,* First Series, edited by Sam G. Riley (1990)

92: *Canadian Writers, 1890-1920,* edited by W. H. New (1990)

Documentary Series

1: *Sherwood Anderson, Willa Cather, John Dos Passos, Theodore Dreiser, F. Scott Fitzgerald, Ernest Hemingway, Sinclair Lewis,* edited by Margaret A. Van Antwerp (1982)

2: *James Gould Cozzens, James T. Farrell, William Faulkner, John O'Hara, John Steinbeck, Thomas Wolfe, Richard Wright,* edited by Margaret A. Van Antwerp (1982)

3: *Saul Bellow, Jack Kerouac, Norman Mailer, Vladimir Nabokov, John Updike, Kurt Vonnegut,* edited by Mary Bruccoli (1983)

4: *Tennessee Williams,* edited by Margaret A. Van Antwerp and Sally Johns (1984)

5: *American Transcendentalists,* edited by Joel Myerson (1988)

6: *Hardboiled Mystery Writers,* edited by Matthew J. Bruccoli and Richard Layman (1989)

7: *Modern American Poets,* edited by Karen L. Rood (1989)